THE

GEORGIA COAST

WATERWAYS & ISLANDS

THE

GEORGIA COAST

WATERWAYS & ISLANDS

Nancy Schwalbe Zydler
& Tom Zydler

SEAWORTHY PUBLICATIONS, INC.
Port Washington, WI

Photography by Tom Zydler
Charts and illustrations by Nancy Schwalbe Zydler
Design and composition by John Reinhardt Book Design

Published in the USA by:

Seaworthy Publications, Inc.
207 S. Park St.
Port Washington, WI 53074
Phone 262-268-9250
Fax 262-268-9208
e-mail: publisher@seaworthy.com
Web http://www.seaworthy.com

CAUTION: The charts in this publication are intended as supplements for NOAA, DMA, or British Admiralty charts and no warranties are either expressed or implied as to the usability of the information contained herein. The author and publisher take no responsibility for their misuse.

Library of Congress Cataloging in Publication Data

The Georgia Coast
    p. cm.
    ISBN 1-892399-07-5 (alk. paper)
    1. Pilot guides--Georgia. 2. Boats and boating--Georgia--Handbooks, manuals, etc. 3. Atlantic Coast (Ga.)--Guidebooks. 4. Outdoor recreation--Georgia--Handbooks, manuals, etc.

VK948.G4 G46 2001
623.89'29758--dc21

00-053793

We would like to dedicate this book
with sincere appreciation to the following people:

Frances Bentley Cantey
for sharing her wisdom and love of history

Herman Louis Schwalbe, III
who untiringly kept us digitally afloat

Bryant Whitfield "Mike" Cantey, Jr.
for his gracious generosity

Eleonora Zydler
for filling Tom's parental void

ACKNOWLEDGMENTS

VJ "Jack" Bryant of St. Marys

Joe Aldridge of Joe's Bait in St. Marys

Martha and Maurice Mixson—*Driftwood,* Darien

Rabbit Brigdon—Sunbury

The late Carolyn Hodges—Open Gates Bed and Breakfast, Darien

Joe Jurskis—Blackbeard School of Sailing and Navigation

Constance Riggins—Darien Welcome Center

Margaret Loutrell Poole—Darien Welcome Center Director

Jay Childers—St. Simons Boating & Fishing Club

Bill Hansen—Fine Line Printing, St. Simons

Carol Ruckdeschel of Cumberland Island

Mitty Ferguson of Greyfield Inn, Cumberland Island

Harold Hicks and Virginia Hobson Hicks—The Bookshop, Brunswick

Yvonne Grovnor—Sapelo Island

Peter Grange—Wassaw Island

Jimmy Wallace—crabber on South Newport River

Jim Odum—Savannah River

Bernie Dukes—US Coast Guard Marine Information specialist

Greg Teagle, BMC—United States Coast Guard

Tom Phillips—A1A Yachts, St. Augustine, FL

CONTENTS

THE

GEORGIA COAST

WATERWAYS & ISLANDS

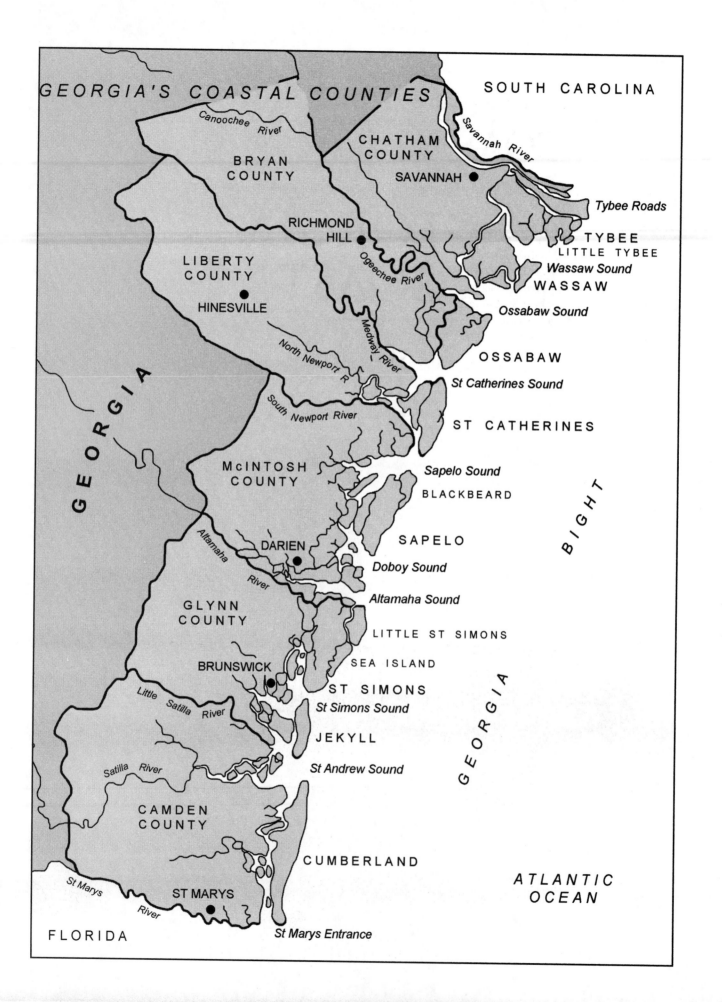

THE UNIQUE COASTAL TERRITORY

THE ISLANDS

We have good news for water-borne escapists. Right in the middle of the East Coast of the United States we can still find 100 miles of shoreline which looks like the coast the first Europeans saw in the sixteenth century. Well, almost. Out of eight large barrier island groups in Georgia, Tybee, Wassaw, Ossabaw, St. Catherines, Sapelo, St. Simons, Jekyll and Cumberland only three, Jekyll, St. Simons and Tybee are connected to the mainland by bridges and consequently developed. The remaining islands are protected as state, federal or private lands. Beaches stretch along the Atlantic coast crowded mostly with shore birds. Forests, often quite dense, cover these islands and offer shelter to several species of songbirds and raptors. The presence of both tidal creeks and fresh-water bogs and ponds promotes great biological diversity with alligators at the top of the food chain and wading birds and waterfowl somewhere in the middle. Large mammals common on the mainland, white-tail deer and feral hogs, run wild here, too. In addition some islands have populations of feral donkeys and horses. The actions of the National Park Service, the Nature Conservancy and the Georgia Conservancy combined with the good will (and a need for tax relief) of the island owners and a few far-sighted Georgia politicians have created a virtual environmental treasure coast. Its riches consist of varied ecological communities which in the other parts

Bordered by salt marsh, a tidal creek flows along a forested "neck" of the mainland.

The long beaches of St. Catherines Island begin at the mouth of Walburg Creek.

Shore bird and human foot prints cross on a Georgia beach.

of the east coast are fast disappearing under layers of concrete and lawns. This unique coast of Georgia nearly became a United Nations Biosphere Reserve, an honorable distinction vehemently and successfully fought off by Georgia politicians suspicious of the unwanted attentions of the outside world.

Fortunately for citizens weary of commuting, networking and clock punching, all of these coastal islands, private, state or federal, provide a vital escape venue - Georgia beaches are, by law, open to everybody up to the high-tide line. The Shore Protection Act of 1979 ensures that all motorized vehicles are banned from Georgia beaches except for the holders of special permits issued to park wardens, researchers and property owners on some islands. Such a lack of traffic bodes well for future generations of loggerheads, the sea turtles that make Georgia beaches their prime nesting area. And, unbelievably so, the sandy shores facing the Atlantic carry hardly a human foot-print. The remoteness of the coast from the mainland is a factor - one needs a boat to get to the best spots which makes it a perfect destination for pleasure boat owners, small boat fishermen, kayakers and canoeists. The low population density in the coastal Georgia counties is another reason for the lack of crowds.

THE MARSHLANDS

Although conspicuous and attractive, and important as a rampart against the Atlantic, the barrier islands form just one feature of the Georgia coast. Wide sounds combining deep channels and numerous sandbars divide the islands from each other. Along the west sides of the outer islands flow miles and miles of navigable tidal rivers (some included in the Intracoastal Waterway) and streams winding through vast marshlands. In areas subject to regular flooding by sea water the marshes are composed of smooth cordgrass—(*Spartina alterniflora*). Black needle rush (*Juncus roemerianus*) takes over on less frequently inundated higher levels, but only succulents like glasswort and saltwort can survive in the dry salty soil of even higher elevations where flooding water rises to less than a foot during the highest tides. Nothing but algae covers the salt pans in the middle of marshes that experience water few times in a season.

The marshes parallel the coast in a belt up to 6 miles wide and wedge into the mainland even farther along tidewater rivers. The huge marsh islands, veined with tidal streams and rivulets, are broken here and there by lumps of higher ground called hammocks. Most hammocks are remains of old

Black needle rush marshlands often border the pine uplands of the mainland.

eroded islands but some formed fairly recently over heaps of ballast stones dumped by sailing ships before loading cargo. For millennia the ancient hammocks served as Indian camps and quite often hammock shores reveal middens filled with oyster shells, the most durable remains of seafood meals. In a tangled riot of vegetation, trees, vines, shrubs and grasses compete for footholds on these precious chunks of solid land surrounded by watery marshes. Mammals such as raccoons, minks, otters, marsh rabbits and rice rats, which forage among *spartina* grasses and on mud banks at low tide, retreat to hammocks when high tide floods the marshes. Many species of birds roost, shelter and breed there, too. Lizards and snakes and many species of insects add to the species congestion on hammocks.

Salt marshes may look tidily trimmed but actually they shelter many species of wild animals which go about their business totally unseen by humans.

Salt marshes constitute the most important geographical feature of coastal Georgia. If you like numbers consider that, according to the *Final Environmental Impact Statement* by NOAA, the Georgia marshes and tidal rivers cover 701,000 acres while all the barrier islands add up to 76,300 acres. One-third of all the marshes remaining on the US Atlantic coast are in Georgia. The marshes contribute immensely to the biological health and productivity of this part of the coast. Growing marsh plants collect minerals and nutrients suspended in the muddy waters flowing from inland rivers. Dead marsh grasses add huge quantities of organic matter which supports basic forms of life; bacteria, fungi and other simple organisms so that marshes essentially fuel the cycle which feeds ever larger animals including alligators and dolphins. Some bird species spend their entire lives in the marshes. The penetrating mad laughter calls of clapper rails, commonly known as marsh hens, let you know they have colonized every bit of Georgia marsh. Small and comparatively quiet marsh wren males weave *spartina* leaves together into complex basket nests. Marshes also act as nurseries for fish, mollusks and crustaceans, nourishing generation after generation of shrimp, blue crab, oysters, clams, whelks and fish to mention just a few species that attract both recreational and commercial fishermen. In 1995, shrimp trawlers unloaded 7 million pounds of catch and commercial crabbers working from small boats caught 9 million pounds. Weekend warriors also harvest crab and shrimp during open seasons and anglers chase several fish species as they become legally available. Common sea mammals of coastal Georgia - bottlenosed dolphins - partake of the bounty of these waters, often chasing mullet many miles inland from the ocean. Entering on rising tides dolphins penetrate far into the coastal plain exploring tidewater creeks flowing past long fingers of the main-

land protruding into the wetlands. Some of these "necks" of hard soil, are beginning to cover with homes as retiring populations from other states move to the warmer

Spartina grasses hold together the muddy shores of Georgia tidal creeks.

climate and nearer the coast. Still, the wide buffer zone of wetlands keeps the development from spreading farther east by its very nature - an unstable mud base. In addition, since 1970, the *Coastal Marshlands Protection Act* protects Georgia wetlands from development.

THE TIDES

The biological wealth of coastal Georgia results in part from its location in the Georgia Bight, the westernmost part of the South Atlantic Bight, a gentle inland sweep in the Atlantic seaboard. This shape produces more intense tidal movement than in the neighboring states. The tidal range - the difference between low tide and high tide levels - may go up to 11 feet during exceptionally high spring tides caused by the proximity of the full or new moon and its alignment with the sun. Strong tidal currents reverse direction about every six hours mixing nutrients produced in the inland waters with ocean plankton, transporting eggs, larvae and the young of many species to new locations and even reshaping the marsh landscape itself. While performing beneficial services for some, the tides also make life harder for many animals and plants which must adapt to living in an environment that is alternately dry and hot in summer, dry and cold in winter, flooded with highly saline water or submerged in fresh rain water from occasional tropical storms. The *spartina* marshes have developed biological means to survive inundation by sea water which is why they dominate the landscape of coastal Georgia.

THE RIVERS

Tides of Georgia penetrate quite far inland from the coast and determine water levels of tidal rivers like Medway, Sapelo, Crooked and several others. As tides travel farther and farther from the ocean, the volume of water they carry gradually diminishes by the time it fills the maze of distant inland streams. Despite this gradual reduction the flood tide pushes rising waters as far as 40 miles up the major freshwater rivers. Five large rivers cut through the lowlands of Georgia on the way to the Atlantic. The Savannah River begins in the Blue Ridge mountains, the Ogeechee, the Altamaha and the Satilla carry water from the foothills, and the St. Marys drains the grand Okefenokee Swamp. Uniquely for a country where most rivers are dammed, the Ogeechee, the Satilla and the St. Marys flow freely and can be explored upstream from the coast in a large vessel as long as it does not need much vertical clearance, highway bridges being the main obstacle to navigation. The Savannah is dam-free for over 180 miles up to Augusta and only the upper tributaries of the Altamaha are

In a marshland anchorage.

crossed by dams. However, even a sailboat can navigate up the Satilla, the Ogeechee and the Altamaha to the point where the water turns fresh, where flooded forests of tupelos and bald cypress dominate and plant life explodes into semi-tropical profusion during spring and summer. The water may taste fresh in these swamps but the river levels go up and down every six hours as the tides push the heavier sea water under the fresh water of the river and then retreat.

THE FORESTS

When the first Europeans arrived on this coast from their de-forested homelands they probably could not believe their good fortune - a great diversity of trees densely covered the region. Axes began to fly early on and by 1900 the great forests were gone. Today only a few spots on the lower Altamaha still have virgin stands of riparian forests of buttressed tupelos, cypresses, water oaks, sweet bays and others. Everywhere else in coastal Georgia the forests have returned either as secondary growth or as managed forests replanted with fast growing pines suitable for the pulp and paper industries. Still, from the water the trees look virginal, green and ubiquitous - they cover 71% of total land surface in the coastal counties of Georgia. The forests vary in appearance. On the banks of the rivers which flow by the mainland "necks" you will see a narrow zone of mixed species although behind may stretch hundreds of acres of orderly planted pines. In the tidal freshwater rivers you can take a small boat into swamps of flooded forests of tupelos and cypresses. Barrier islands have small parcels of all types of forests: wild stands of pines, planted forests of pines, oak and magnolia groves, stands of tupelo and cypress in freshwater bogs, plus extensive tracts of the mature (climax) maritime forest—mainly live oaks mixed with cabbage (*Sabal*) palmettos all growing out from an almost impenetrable understory of saw palmetto.

WILD RICE MARSHES

In the 1700s the forests in the estuaries began to fall to make room for rice plantations and only the low tides that bare the remains of giant trees provide clues of how the estuarine lowlands looked in the past. Near the mouths of the Savannah, the Ogeechee, the Altamaha and the Satilla, where freshwater flows on top of the tidal seawater, the swamp forests were replaced by networks of man-made dikes, canals and flood gates. This scheme allowed planters to let only freshwater onto the fields

(Top) Severe erosion undermining forested shores affects many of the northern ends of Georgia's barrier islands.

(Bottom) Spartina marshes and forests create a wood stork rookery and refuge on Colonels Island.

while locking out the brackish mixture which would have killed the rice plants. The Civil War and the emancipation of slaves ended the plantation rice business. By the early 1900s cultivated rice was gone and freshwater marshes began reverting to wilderness. Some of the old plantation fields are managed by the US Fish and Wildlife Service and the gates are still used to flood marshes for the sake of shore and water birds in the Savannah Wildlife Refuge and the Altamaha River Waterfowl Management Area near Darien. However, huge plots of old rice fields in the Altamaha estuary and up the Satilla and the Ogeechee have gone wild without further human interference. Native plants have taken over and, in a small boat, one can explore miles of tight narrow channels bordered by tall grasses: wild rice, giant cordgrass, giant beard grass and bulrush. Where allowed, riparian trees returned to the higher banks of the rice canals along with colonies of brilliantly flowering smaller plants like spider-lily, blue flag iris, swamp rose, cardinal flower and many others.

ACCESSIBLE TO ALL

So there you are, free to explore a variety of ecological habitats in waters accessible to all kinds of vessels, from deeper draft sailboats to shallow draft cruisers, johnboats and especially small boats like canoes and kayaks. Some patient employees of the DNR and NOAA added all the mileage of tidal shores in Georgia and have come up with an astounding 2,344 miles. You do not even have to own a boat to get afloat on this waterlogged coast - several outfitters and charter boats (listed in this guide) serve the public from bases on the mainland and islands.

(Above) Where allowed the native Georgia pines grow to impressive heights.

(Left) A mixed forest of saw palmettos, oaks and other hardwoods covers many of the upland "necks" that meet tidal creeks and rivers.

RECREATIONAL ACTIVITIES

FISHING

Sport fishing from small boats certainly seems the most popular water activity among citizens of Georgia. The reason - the coastal waters containing a mixture of mineral laden freshwater rivers, tidal estuarine mud wigling with nutritious simple organisms plus phyto and zoo planktons from the Atlantic. Throughout the year resident as well as migrating fish find an endless supply of food close to the coast and in the lowland rivers. From mid-November till March anglers with even the smallest boats can easily find spotted sea trout in all waters, from inland brackish streams to creeks near the sounds. This sea trout moves out into the open waters of the sounds, inlets and along barrier island beaches in the spring and stays there through summer. As soon as the weather warms up in April medium-sized drums, croakers and spots become available in the estuaries. In the spring large numbers of sheepshead, excellent food fish, begin to spawn over sandy bottoms and afterwards move in near pilings, docks and oyster bars where they turn fiddler crabs dangling from your hook into a serious part of their diet. Larger fighting fish like black drum become available in March and April as they gather to spawn, but of course you can get them until October.

Whiting turn up in the coastal waters at the end of February and stay through the summer months. They spawn in spring when you can easily take them in great numbers.

The beaches of the barrier islands are good for surf casting for whiting. Surf casting also works for large red drum, a species which hangs, when younger and smaller, over mudflats near marsh islands. The brackish estuaries of the Ogeechee, the Savannah and the Altamaha are good for striped bass throughout the winter. Large tarpon savor the Altamaha estuary but also occur in offshore waters near tidal creeks spewing into the Atlantic from the east shores of barrier islands.

Fishermen who own boats with offshore capability can reach the 17 artificial reefs to tangle with larger specimens of black sea bass, grouper, red snapper, cobia, kingfish, bluefish and even sharks. The offshore trolling season begins in mid-April when schools of king mackerel, Spanish mackerel, cobia and bluefish chase northwards after smaller fish - their food. At the end of summer and during the autumn you can stay offshore bottom fishing for sea bass, vermillion snapper, red snapper, groupers, triggerfish and porgies. Gray's Reef, the only natural reef rising from the sandy expanse of Georgia's huge continental shelf, lies 17

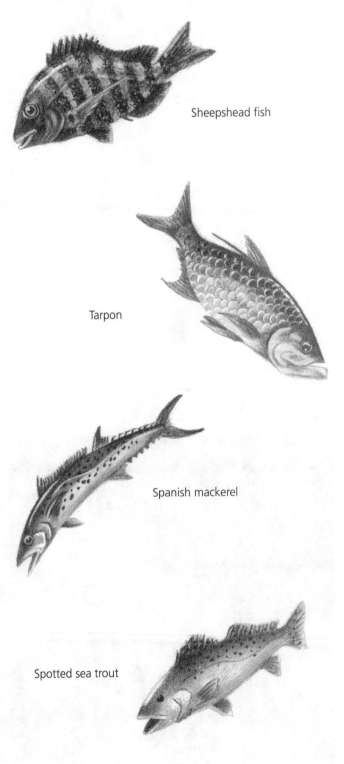

Sheepshead fish

Tarpon

Spanish mackerel

Spotted sea trout

9

Kemp's Ridley sea turtle

Wood storks

nautical miles offshore from Sapelo Island and apart from all resident fish species also attracts some tropical exotics. Although declared a Natural Marine Sanctuary with the additional status of International Biosphere Reserve bestowed by UNESCO, 17 square miles of waters over Gray's Reef are open to anglers. This may change due to new more protective measures now in the works. Any fishing activities that may alter the bottom (60 feet below the surface) are already strictly banned.

Most recreational fishermen appreciate other seafoods, too. Cast netting for shrimp, crabbing, that is catching blue crab in traps or by hand-held lines armed with chicken body parts, gathering oysters and clamming are all popular in their seasons. Every year the DNR establishes the open seasons for various species. All people engaged in any type of fishery, including shellfish harvesting and freshwater or saltwater angling, must have licenses which can be purchased in many marinas, tackle shops and even on-line. To learn how to obtain a license see the Appendix under Fishing Regulations.

SCUBA DIVING

You do not just jump into Georgia waters with a mask and snorkel and go looking at pretty fish. The fish, the colorful sponges, even soft corals are all there but you will not see them; all the nutritional elements that make coastal Georgia a Serengeti of aquatic life also block underwater visibility. Nevertheless, there are quite a few scuba divers in the state who grope through night-black tidal rivers in search of Revolutionary wrecks and artifacts. The clarity of water improves offshore and wreck diving attracts growing numbers of scuba divers. Gray's Reef with its concentration of species definitely makes the most exciting destination. During the cold winter months divers at Gray's Reef may encounter northern right whales, the world's most endangered sea mammal, which come south between November and March to give birth to their young. Several other species of whales and dolphins also occur here. Sea turtles, leatherback, loggerhead, hawksbill, Kemp's Ridley and green visit the area seasonally. Divers are also bound to see large predatory fish species and can, on the craggy limestone bottom, admire a variety of marine life absent from the sandy continental

This snowy egret fishes from the dry perch on our anchor line.

shelf surrounding the Reef. Scuba divers will find dive shops and technical support listed in the Appendix.

CRUISING

You would think, quite rightly too, that having a boat as a base will make exploring the Georgia islands and rivers much easier and exciting. If you anchor off the barrier islands you will have 68 miles of uninhabited beaches to comb and untold miles of hiking paths in the forests with hardly a soul to see except a few hikers on Cumberland Island. Anchoring in the tidal rivers will bring you close to shore birds and marsh birds with side shows of minks and alligators or an otter taking an evening bath at the edge of the marsh. During the spring and fall migratory birds will forage right outside your portholes. In Georgia a deep draft sailboat can venture into freshwater rivers (the Altamaha and the Ogeechee) and anchor with bald cypress and tupelo-gum trees in the background. A motor yacht with a vertical clearance under 30 feet can steam several miles farther up the Altamaha River Bioreserve and anchor in an environment resembling a tropical mainland river. If you enjoy visiting monuments to wealth anchor off the mansions of Cumberland Island or tie up in Jekyll Island right under its "millionaires' row". Old forts as a rule overlook traditional anchorages; Fort Frederica on St. Simons, Fort McAllister on the Ogeechee River, Fort Morris on the Medway to mention a few. Lighthouse freaks can dinghy over to climb the steps up the lighthouses on Tybee, Sapelo and St. Simons.

It does not matter whether yours is a motor yacht or a sailboat. All you need for comfortable cruising are accommodations to cook and sleep and a tender that can cope with strong tidal currents. For winter cruising the boat should have a good heating system. To keep cool in summer shade your boat with an awning when anchored and install a bimini top to protect the cockpit from the sun when moving. Each cabin and bunk should have a quiet electric fan, and, an air-conditioner certainly would help if you have a generator to power it. All opening hatches should have screens against tiny biting gnats, alias *"noseeums,"* which appear during the spring and fall months as soon as the breeze dies.

HIKING

You can hike on all barrier island beaches. As far as forest trails on barrier islands are concerned you will not be able to hike on St. Catherines. On Ossabaw Island you will need to apply for a hiking and camping permit - see the Parks and Wildlife Refuges appendix for the contact. On other islands you will walk on old dirt roads shaded by trees. Little other traffic will disturb you except white-tailed deer or feral hogs scampering away and rmadillos rustling through the underbrush. You will find locations of roads and hiking trails on the individual is-

A young brown pelican shows off his almost adult coloring.

land maps in this guide. For more information on hiking read the description of each island in the text which also covers state parks and river shores.

BIRD WATCHING

For watching birds from a boat you will have to use 7X50 binoculars which have a wider field coverage and produce less image vibration when the boat bounces around on water. To get a small boat close to where birds congregate you should switch from a loud internal combustion engine to an electric motor, a paddle or oars. Check the Appendix for a Birds of Coastal Georgia list and the Colonial Coast Birding Trail.

KAYAKING, CANOEING AND CAMPING

It takes little time to notice that tidal phenomena control all water explorations in coastal Georgia. Obviously, strong currents caused by flooding and ebbing tides have a major say when and where boats powered by hand can go. Canoes being slower than kayaks are really limited in their range to always going with the current whether up or down river. Winds, also affect the higher hulls of canoes much more. Consequently, canoeists should explore rivers sheltered by forests and plan their stops before the current turns to run against them. Several stretches on the upper parts of the tidal river sections of the Altamaha, the Ogeechee, the Satilla, the St. Marys, and the Savannah offer perfect canoeing and the chartlets in this guide show the details of depths and shore characteristics. All outfitters (listed in the Appendix) who offer canoe trips know their territories very well and will plan trips accordingly.

Kayakers tend to be more adventurous relying on the superior speed of their craft. Assuming their skippers have the training and experience, several of the sea kayak models can cope with rough water and make extensive trips across coastal waters and over to the barrier islands. The easiest way to explore in a kayak is to drive your boat to Tybee Island, Jekyll Island or St. Simons Island and use comfortable land bases for forays on the water. To experience other barrier islands will require tent camping and long hours of paddling. Kayakers will have to start from points on the mainland where they can leave their automobiles, launch kayaks and head seaward through creeks and marsh islands devoid of any solid land. The only places to set up camp are on the barrier island destinations miles ahead. One such island, Cumberland, has good camp sites with drinking water. However, the official ferry boat from St. Marys will not take kayaks. Kayakers typically put in at Crooked River State Park and then paddle over 10 nautical miles (12 statute miles) through tidal waters to the Brickhill River camp on Cumberland. There are ways around this difficulty if you work with the outfitters in St. Marys. Read more about kayaking to and around Cumberland Island in Chapter IX, *St. Andrew Sound to St. Marys River*.

Exploring tidal creeks in a silent kayak will bring you closer to nature.

PRECAUTIONS TO TAKE
ON LAND AND WATER

MANY OUTDOOR PEOPLE combine small boat cruising through protected river waters with camping on the river shores or even sandbars. Our river chartlets and descriptions point out dry ground areas.

Whether you explore on land or rivers you must carry drinking water. Cold weather while preventing sweating delays dehydration, but it still may occur. In the hot summer weather dehydration can abruptly end sweating which cools the body — hallucinations and collapse may follow. Most canned "sodas" contain caffeine which accelerates dehydration. Beverages containing alcohol have the same effect. Protection from the sun is equally important in cold and hot weather so wear a wide brimmed hat, apply sun block lotions to exposed skin and protect your eyes with sun glasses. Wear appropriate clothing for the time of the year. When playing with boats in cold weather you must overdress and have protection for the head and hands. Even a mild 40°F will chill you to the bone as soon as the wind picks up, or you make the apparent wind stronger by speeding up your boat. You can always take off excess clothing, but you cannot add what you do not have.

When about to go boating remember to check that you have enough fuel and some drinking water. Then load a compass, a spotlight or a strong flashlight, an oar or two to maneuver the boat when the engine quits, an anchor with a good length of line, a bailer (could be a small bucket) and the life jackets required by law. Carry a VHF radio, handheld or permanently mounted. Many people these days rely on cellular phones to call for help. They do not work very well in Georgia waters after you increase your distance from a town or a popular highway, whereas nearly all fish camps and marinas maintain radio watch on VHF Channel 16.

Except in winter and hot summer weather you will need insect repellent whenever you venture on water or land. The biting tiny gnats do come out as soon as the wind drops to a calm and they are at their worst during the nicest spring and fall temperatures. In calm weather gnats are everywhere, rivers, beaches and the edges of forests. During summer weather mosquitoes and biting flies will rule in mainland forests and on river banks especially near populated areas. You should always check your body, especially in nooks and crannies, for ticks. They are numerous and some carry Rocky Mountain spotted fever—a horrible disease. The tick-transmitted Lyme disease, although still rare in Georgia, is becoming a threat in places. Remove a tick after you have applied

alcohol over it for a few minutes—it will loosen its grip. Use tweezers to pull the tick off and do not squeeze its body as this will propel contaminated blood into you. Wearing long pants and long sleeve shirts helps to keep ticks off especially if you spray the fabric generously with repellent. Fire ants are named so for a good reason. Whenever stopping for a long while, check that your feet are not on top of a circle of granulated fine soil with some tiny ants running around. Larvae of chiggers (red bugs) climb on people to suck blood. Terrible persistent itching continues until the larvae drop off, well-fed, to mature. Use available medication to treat the red bite spots. Or better, do not sit down on rotten logs and loose leaves and twigs. People have a common fear of snakes and of course a venomous snake can really hurt you. Usually though, warned off by your foot steps, snakes take off before you can see them. However, look where you step if you walk through paths or grassy areas very early in the day. Cold-blooded snakes are sluggish then, not quite awake enough to vanish quickly. If you step on a snake, it will hit at your leg. When hiking through undergrowth you should wear knee high boots for protection. You will see many alligators in all of coastal Georgia both in the very saline waters near the ocean and far up the rivers. They avoid humans but a quiet paddler may get too close to them—a female will turn aggressive when guarding a nest or her young.

When swimming off the ocean beaches during a strong on-shore wind you may get caught in a riptide current or undertow. Onshore winds pile up water against the shore. This excess water changes into a longshore current flowing parallel to the beach. On meeting an obstruction like a sandbar this flowing water changes into a narrow river flowing seaward at considerable speed. When caught in such a current swim calmly across it until you get back into the regular onshore waves. Swimming even on a calm day you can have the misfortune of rubbing against a stinging jelly fish—one of those trailing long thin tentacles. Look before you jump in—they often come in armadas. Apply your own urine over the stings to relieve pain.

You may get some unexpected jolts when walking through shallow water—blue crabs will pinch your toes painfully and may draw blood. A stingray when stepped on will lash back with a barbed tail—very painful. You should slide your feet along the bottom when walking through water—it will give enough warning to all these creatures, except oysters which can't move once they settle down. The sharp edge of an oyster shell can cut your toe—a minor problem when compared to what an oyster shell can do to a "rubber" boat. Be extra careful messing about in inflatable dinghies. There is also another hazard coming from fellow humans. A few times in the fall of each year hunters appear in the mainland forests and on the barrier islands to cull the excessive numbers of deer and hogs. Wear an orange vest and be particularly noisy if your hiking coincides with the hunting days.

TIDEWATER NAVIGATION

Tides rule the seas in Georgia and you should always carry the tide tables with you. All the marinas, fish camps and even hardware stores carry give-away tables with corrections for various points along the rivers. The tables list times and heights for the Savannah River entrance as a reference point but the complex character of the coast delays the arrival of the flood tide and beginning of the ebb sometimes by over two hours in rivers reaching far inland. Tidal phenomena are also affected by barometric pressure—extremely high pressure will reduce the tabulated high tide and low pressure will increase it. Heavy precipitation over the mainland also changes the predicted values. All depths on the chartlets in this volume represent the low tide levels at springs to help readers avoid getting unexpectedly stranded. The depths on NOAA charts of the coast refer to Mean Low Water and consequently several times each month the actual depths drop below the charted values sometimes by as much as 3.5 feet. For some locations this discrepancy is printed on NOAA charts in a small table near the title of the chart.

The tidal level variations between flood and ebb produce strong currents which may reach three knots on some dates and in some locations. To make it even more complicated, on most rivers which continue far inland, the surface current usually keeps running out while the actual water level is already rising. The opposite is also true; the current continues to flow upriver while the water level is dropping. Both these phenomena matter a lot for a deep draft vessel trying to go over shallow bars on the rising tide.

You should take advantage of the rising tides to get into attractive and deep anchorages which are blocked by shallow bars. Navigating with a fair tide will also benefit boats with weak engines and kayakers who simply must work the currents to their advantage. This is not quite so straightforward in tidal rivers which parallel the outer islands between the sounds leading to the ocean. The incoming tide enters through the sounds at the ends of an island, begins to fill the river from opposite directions and somewhere the two flood tides have to meet. A skipper on a southbound yacht happily charging down Cumberland River with the current will, about half way down, discover that the boat is bucking a contrary current that is flooding via St. Marys Entrance. The meeting point of the opposing currents in the so-called "dividings"

shifts somewhat depending on the range of the tide and strong wind affecting the area.

ANCHORING HINTS

Basically the tidal rivers have a mud bottom where currents are weak. Where currents of moderate velocity predominate there will be a firmer mixture of sand and mud. Wherever currents flow swiftly, firm sediments with small shells will cover the bottom. Most types of anchors hold very well in these bottoms if given a generous "scope", i.e. the ratio of anchor rode to the depth. The minimum should be 5:1 if the rode is all chain and 7:1 when using a combination of chain and nylon. Allow for the increased depth at high tide. Seventy feet of anchor rode may suffice in ten feet at low tide, but at high tide the depth may increase to, say, eighteen feet so you need to add almost fifty feet for the anchor to stay nicely on the bottom. Look up the tides for the day in the tables. Also be aware that the tidal current will reverse and as the boat aligns with the new current the anchor rode can foul (wrap around) the anchor and drag it out of the bottom. A fouled Danforth type of anchor may not be able to dig back in while a wishbone, a CQR or other claw or plow-shaped anchors (without protruding elements) will grab the bottom again.

GETTING LOST IN THE MARSHES

Yachtsmen on large boats equipped with charts, compasses and electronic navigation equipment probably would never consider that possibility. However, put yourself in a small boat to explore some creeks and after your anchored mother ship swings peacefully out of sight your view of the world may change. At low tide all you see around you will be marshes crisscrossed by a maze of baffling winding creeks. You will very soon lose count of how many creeks you planed by and in what direction you steered. To avoid all that confusion, take time, before exploring in a small boat, to look at the chartlets in this guide, form a plan of action, then mark the first turn and which creek you will take from there. Your small boat should have a compass and these days you can add a small waterproof GPS unit. Take this guide with you and you will be able to refer to the chartlet of the area you are exploring. Notice the tide stage and the direction of the current. If desperately lost remember that the ebbing tide is flowing from your creek to the next larger one and eventually it must join a major tidal river or a sound. If the tide is flooding, i.e. rising, go against the current to find wider waters. Plan especially carefully if you start on a dropping tide—the entrances to many creeks have drying bars and you do not want to get stuck in the mud for a few hours waiting for the water to return and let you out. Oysters may cover these bars—very challenging even if your boat is light enough to drag over. Navigating through marshes on top of high tide is easy—you will see major features like familiar islands, marsh hammocks or beacons or even your own yacht at anchor. All these things look like being next door as the crow flies but it may take many miles of a winding river to get to them.

COURTEOUS BOATING

Customarily motor yachts slow down when passing slower craft, sailboats, fishermen angling from small boats and kayakers or canoeists. It does not always produce desirable results. Some designs of motor yachts may actually cause lower waves at high speed than at medium slow speed which will only increase the height of the wake. A semi-planing Hatteras type or trawler type yacht always drags a big wave behind and has to slow down considerably to smooth out its wake. But then, the sailboat that the motor yacht is trying to pass becomes too fast. In the end the motor yacht will speed up in order to overtake and the wake will roll the sailboat like a tsunami wave. To make things easier for all concerned the slower boat should cut down the speed, too. Both boats should use a VHF radio and agree on a procedure. However, when passing small open boats, both powered and paddled, motor yachts should take particular care. An excessive wake may swamp the smaller craft. Advice for power boaters when passing others—look back honestly at your wake! Few motor yacht skippers realize that their craft also pushes a wave ahead. In a narrow channel such a wave may set the slower boat aside and put it aground! A motor yacht should slow down a couple of its hull lengths from its, possibly, victim. An open slow boat like a kayak or canoe should head into the wave of an excessive wake. Some water may get inside over the bow but this is better than getting capsized.

PLANTS AND ANIMALS
OF THE BARRIER ISLANDS

THE PLANTS AND ANIMALS which have adapted to living conditions in various parts of coastal Georgia form, together with the geographical features of their environments, recognizable ecosystems. The recreational explorer of the Georgia coast will most likely come into intimate contact with some of the ecosystems—the Atlantic shores, barrier islands, estuarine wetlands, tidal freshwater rivers and swamps and upland, i.e. mainland forests. In order to facilitate the discussion of plant and animal relationships ecologists divide each of these environments into even smaller ecosystems but in fact most of them overlap or exist side by side. Georgia's barrier islands are the best example of such coexistence since they incorporate several ecosystems. Beaches, dunes, maritime forests, lowland swamps, upland forest and salt marshes come into close contact by virtue of being marooned on a small chunk of land surrounded by water. For many animals this water frontier meant isolation from other members of their species—serious enough to cause sub-speciation. Until recently Cumberland Island had unique pocket gophers (now extinct) and

Anastasia Island cotton mice (possibly extinct), St. Simons hosts a subspecies of raccoon and Blackbeard Island a particularly small white-tailed deer.

Some of the major Georgia barrier islands have developed around a core of old sandstone, others are all sand dunes reinforced by vegetation. However, each major island typically has a sandy beach and dunes facing the Atlantic on the eastern border, forests and swamps in the middle and another forest and marshland looking westward to the mainland. This western shore is relatively stable by comparison to the continuously changing sandy perimeters at the north, east and south borders. Tidal currents and wave action keep eroding soft sands at some part of an island and adding (accreting) them to the other. Natural and man-altered channels which run through the sounds dividing the islands influence the patterns of erosion and accretion—we describe what is happening to each island in the text. A well-established barrier island presents an easy opportunity to get acquainted with the natural world of coastal Georgia—all ecosystems meet within a small territory.

ON THE BEACH

The great difference between low and high tide levels in Georgia makes life very hard for animals and plants. For casual visitors like us humans a low tide uncovers the most interesting aspect of the ocean shore. While some islands may at extreme low tide suddenly join extensive sandy shoals to the east most often only one offshore sandbar comes above the surface a fraction of a mile off. A trench of shallow water divides the sandbar from the edge of the narrow intertidal beach which in turn may be separated from the upper beach, the berm, by a damp

Black skimmer

Sanderling

Royal tern

16

runnel. High tide, on the other hand, leaves only a narrow bit of soft sand combined with sandy lumps where the toughest salt, drought and sand resistant plants manage to maintain hold: the succulent and edible sea rocket (*Cakile harperi*), creeping vines like morning glories (*Ipomoea spp*) with beautiful large white flowers, poisonous creeping dune spurge (*Euphorbia polygonifolia*), along with Russian thistle (*Salsola kali*) and sandbur (*Cenchrus tribuloides*), both producing prickly burrs that are hell on bare feet.

As the tide recedes exposing more and more of the beach the birds begin to arrive. You will see some very conspicuous resident birds on a Georgia beach. A shrill call will announce a pair of oyster catchers (*Haematopus palliatus*), large, long-legged birds with white bellies, black backs and black heads and 5-inch long bright red beaks. On the beaches they probe for mussels and clams, but also wade chest deep to snatch shrimp or small crabs. Black skimmers (*Rynchops niger*), almost as large as oyster catchers have short stubby legs, white bellies with black caps and backs and large, long beaks–red with black tips. Their lower longer mandibles slice through the water and scoop small fish and shrimp as the birds fly low just above the surface. These nocturnal birds become most active at sunset. Wilson's plovers (*Charadrius wilsonia*), their large eyes also adapted to night foraging hunt at low tides both night and day. Willets (*Catoptrophorus semipalmatus*), greyish brown birds slimmer than oyster catchers, wade in the receding surf alone or in pairs to stab fish or probe the sands for coquina clams, crabs or worms. They are striking in flight with long white stripes on both sides of their wings. Laughing gulls (*Larus atricilla*), easily recognizable for their "cackling" exchanges and black hooded heads, visit low tide beaches to rest and add variety to their basic diet of fish. Royal terns (*Sterna maxima*) and the smaller sandwich terns (*Sterna sandvicensis*), named for a yellow "mustard" spot at the end of their beaks, rest on the sands exposed by low tides but they feed a little offshore by plunging in after small fish. The brown pelican (*Pelecanus occidentalis*) is the largest bird seen resting on low tide beaches; it feeds offshore by diving, from considerable heights, beak first. When lucky, this technique fills its bill pouch with small fish and water. After straining the water out the pelican will

Lettered olive

Quick as a fleeting image, a nocturnal ghost crab, stalks the ocean beaches of the barrier islands.

Steady erosion along the north tip of St. Catherines Island sends border trees crashing into the surf.

Horseshoe crabs, which occupy waters between just off the beach to about 75-foot depths, often wash out on Georgia beaches.

jerk his beak skyward and swallow the catch. A sideways wiggle of the tail confirms a satisfactory catch.

With autumn the barrier island beaches fill with crowds of shore birds migrating south from as far as the Arctic tundra in some cases. Several species spend the cold months in Georgia, others stay long enough to feed in the rich coastal waters and then carry on perhaps as far as Argentina. The fat ring billed gulls (*Larus delawarensis*) and herring gulls (*Larus argentatus*) rub shoulders with caspian terns (*Sterna caspia*), common terns (*Sterna hirundo*) and Forster's terns (*Sterna forsteri*). Piping plovers (*Charadrius melodus*), their future uncertain in parts of our continent, hop around on their orange-hued legs in search of prey. Small flocks of sanderlings (*Calidris alba*) forage along the surf edge often "limping" on one leg only and still successfully dodging the wave wash. Minute as they seem in their 7-inch bodies sanderlings migrate some 8,000 miles between breeding grounds above the Arctic Circle and Greenland to Chile in South America. Semipalmated sandpipers (*Calidris pusilla*) also work the sandy wet edge, colorful ruddy turnstones (*Arenaria interpres*) look for small prey by overturning shells, twigs and other loose objects that may hide something to eat. The largest of plovers, black-bellied plovers (*Pluvialis squatarola*), explore the drying sandbanks and beaches.

Seeing so many birds pecking and probing the intertidal zone makes you realize that some edible creatures must hide in these apparently empty sands. The smallest of sandpipers feed on sand amphipods (*Haustorius arenarius*) and mole crabs (*Emerita talpoida*) perfectly formed for a life under a beach surface. Their legs and feeding arms fold neatly along the body leaving powerful tails to propel them through wet sand. Rarely encountered by beach strolling humans, they coexist within wet loose sand with algae and are collectively known as *psammon*. Some of the algae, *euglena*, give the intertidal

Cannon ball jellyfish

sands an olive green tinge very early in the day before the sun becomes intense and the algae withdraw. Out of sight under a layer of sand lives the tiny coquina clam (*Donax variabilis*). Their rainbow-colored shells exhibit slightly different patterns for each individual. They utilize tidal movements to follow the swash of waves where they feed. You will notice raised tunnels in the intertidal sands. Looking as if made by small moles they are actually bulldozed by lettered olives (*Oliva sayana*) pursuing coquina clams. In the shallowest water just outside the low tide beach feed jacknife clams (*Ensis directus*) shaped like an old fashioned razor and the fastest diggers of them all.

Usually you will see all these mollusks in the open only after their empty shells, still adorned with spectacular colors and designs, wash out on the beach. Midway between the tide limits live two species of ghost shrimp (*Callianassa sp*) which dig in deep to wait through the dry time of the low tide—a sprinkle of tubular fecal pellets surround the openings to their burrows. Segmented worms sometimes over a foot long build tubes as homes, their locations betrayed by an accumulation of fecal pellets, too. In the wet wrack of washed-up seaweeds, broken *spartina* stems and soft coral fragments resides the wharf crab (*Sesarma cinereum*), a small skillful dodger with a square brown carapace. You may also spot the much larger stalk-eyed nocturnal ghost crab (*Ocypode quadrata*); pale, skittish and fast, it will vanish when you blink.

Except during powerful storms, Georgia beaches receive moderate wave action. A shallow band of depths under two fathoms (12 feet) runs into the ocean in places as far as 6 miles offshore. Out there large destructive waves arriving from the Atlantic rise steeply and turn into roaring surf losing much of their power by the time they roll onto the beaches. Still, onshore winds and waves bring a variety of strange flotsam to the beaches.

Carapaces of horseshoe crabs (*Limilus polyphemus*) range from a couple of inches to two feet. With origins some 400 million years back and family ties to trilobites they look prehistoric for a good reason. In early May horseshoe crabs come ashore in large numbers to mate and often get stranded when the tide recedes. Half-buried in wet sand most of them survive until the sea returns. Another strange sight on a low tide beach is sea pork (*Aplidium stellatum*)—pinkish or gray gobs of fleshy rubbery matter up to a foot long. This is actually a colony of tunicates, torn by rough weather from their usual habitat on wrecks or pilings. You will often come across an egg case of the clearnose skate (*Raja eglanteria*); usually about 2 inches long, it looks like a black toboggan with a tough leathery middle. The moon snail (*Polinices*

Shark's eye

Knobbed whelk, the official state seashell of Georgia

Channeled whelk

duplicatus) encloses its eggs in a case shaped like a doll's standing collar, a common sight, too. Both the channeled whelk (*Busycon canaliculatum*) and knobbed whelk (*Busycon carica*) string their eggs along with long necklaces of papery disks which often end up on the beaches. The empty shells of these and related mollusks stick out of the sand along with large lightning whelks (*Busycon contrarium*), some up to 15 inches long, being the most spectacular. Other large shells caught in the sand are pen shells of the genus *Atrina*, fan-shaped bi-valves up to 11 inches long with paper thin edges and iridescent nacre interiors. Smaller, equally spectacular shells like the shark's eye (*Neverita duplicata*) pop up here and there as well as angel wings (*Cyrtopleura costata*). Besides the empty shells of mollusks, shells taken over by hermit crabs, the remains of crabs and the ubiquitous sand dollars, a beach walker will soon pass stranded jellyfish. When a low sun hits their translucent fresh, damp bodies, they look like exquisite pieces of Venetian glass. The colors vary from the pale of the heavy bodied, deep bell-shaped and non-stinging cannon ball jellyfish to the blue and purple rosette of a flat domed moon jelly. Beware of all jellyfish that trail long thin tentacles—as a rule they sting even after death.

Besides humans many other outsiders visit low tide beaches. If you look at the most conspicuous tracks imprinted in the sand you will see that raccoons, hogs and deer regularly leave their forest homes to see what morsels the sea delivered overnight. Turkey vultures and black vultures enjoy a regular fare of dead fish and sometimes even a stranded dolphin or a sea turtle. Although other sea turtle species occasionally land or wash up dead on the coast, only the loggerhead turtle comes ashore in Georgia in order to lay eggs. Beginning in May you may find the bulldozer-size tracks a female loggerhead leaves after coming ashore to nest. As a rule she does a good

Yaupon holly

Sea oats

A great blue heron takes a nap after hard fishing at low tide.

job of covering about ten dozen eggs she lays but raccoons and hogs quite often raid the nests. Loggerhead hatchlings break out after two months of incubation and run for the ocean, prey to birds and ghost crabs while on land and to fish after they reach the sea.

THE DUNES

The primary dune begins above the level of the highest tides. Tall sea oat (*Uniola paniculata*) grasses send out subsurface rhizomes which stabilize dune soils and are possibly the most important plant protecting barrier islands from complete erosion by the ocean. At one point coastal inhabitants and visitors became so enamored of their beauty that the sea oats nearly vanished from the beaches and into living rooms. The plant is now protected from collectors by law. However, the native white-tailed deer will eat their young shoots; on Cumberland Island feral horses cause serious damage to this important dune plant while the northeast beach of Ossabaw has no sea oats left due to depredations by donkeys and deer. Other animals, sparrows, cardinals, doves, marsh rabbits and insects venture into the dunes to eat the sea oat seeds. The sea oats form the first line of defense against storms which would otherwise blow loose sands inland. Sea oats help hold soil for other plants such as salt meadow grass (*Spartina patens*), panic grass (*Panicum amarum*) and the low lying pennywort (*Hydrocotyle bonariensis*) with its round leaves refreshingly green in this tough dry environment. Sea purslane (*Sesuvium portulacastrum*) has fleshy edible leaves and blooms from late spring through fall with small purple and pink flowers. The exposure to wind driven salt and unmitigated sunshine makes the dunes a harsh environment but these few colonists thrive due to a lack of competition from more delicate plants. Surprisingly, mushrooms which we associate with wet ecosystems occur on dunes, both puffball fungi and mushrooms with gilled caps.

The vegetation becomes more varied after the primary dune dips lower forming a wide trench called a swale or interdune meadow. When walking through swales and especially through dunes always use a designated or well-established path in order to protect the important sand-stabilizing plants—they withstand desert living conditions but are very fragile to human impact. In the interdune meadows you will want to use the proper paths to protect your feet from prickly plants. The long-needled pads of devil-joint (*Opuntia pussila*), often scattered out of sight under other plants, break off with a slight touch and the long barbed needles easily penetrate rubber shoe soles. The needle sharp points at the end of the long outward pointing leaves of spanish bayonets (*Yucca aloifolia*) have, for good measure, sharp serrated edges. Spanish bayonet usually grows as a low shrub but may soar into 10 foot high trees. As a consolation for skin piercing leaves, Spanish bayonet blossoms in summer with snowy white round cup-shaped flowers. A specialized moth fertilizes these plants and its caterpillars feed on yucca fruit, which is also a favorite of deer, other insects and is quite edible for humans, too. Other plants in this area also produce conspicuous and spectacular flowers. Thistles wake up from winter hibernation and by April their flowers, white, yellow or purple, rise from rosettes of spiny leaves. In the spring colonies of gaillardia begin to brighten up with aster-shaped red and yellow blossoms as do two species of evening primrose with striking yellow flowers. Come summer, the buds on the edges of the unfriendly spiny pads of prickly pears (*Opuntia compressa*) open into 3-inch wide bowls of golden petals. Taking advantage of the plentiful sunshine many more flowering plants add color to the interdune meadows all through the summer. On a few islands the wider area behind the primary dunes may be home to extensive clumps of sweet grass (*Muhlenberghia filipes*) which turns reddish pink with the arrival of cold weather. Using the coil method, descendents of plantation slaves still weave this grass and related plants into handsome tightly woven baskets. Examples are often for sale at Hog Hammock on Sapelo Island.

Several other substantial plants also help stabilize the sandy soils. Tall wax myrtle (*Myrica cerifera*) shrubs are often the most common and their berries provide important nourishment for scores of birds. Sabal palmettos which grow scattered in the interdune swales become more numerous farther inland on the edge of higher ground. There they rise conspicuously above the yaupon holly (*Ilex vomitoria*) shrub, a small tree which produces red, possibly poisonous, berries in winter. Yaupon holly leaves were brewed by indigenous tribes into a strong purging potion, a sort of soul cleansing tonic. Huge amounts of this "tea" made from the dried and roasted yaupon leaves drunk during tribal ceremonies made the Indians vomit forcefully – a cleaning of their bodies as they saw it. The Spanish, appalled at the sight, called the drink "Black Tea" while the Indians thought of it as a "White Drink." Although prepared for the worst, we suffered no ill effects from drinking "yaupon tea" which tasted a bit like the *herba maté* of Argentina. The saw palmetto (*Serenoa repens*) named for the teeth on the stem of the fronds grows in dense colonies. It stays low on upland edges exposed to onshore winds but rises to 5 and 6 feet in the maritime forest. This plant sends powerful rhizome roots through the soil and contributes much to holding the land in place. The fruit of both the sabal palmetto and the saw palmetto feeds raccoons, squirrels, mocking birds, robins and crows. Dune greenbriar (*Smilax sp*) is

(Top) Spanish bayonet plants burst into flower in early summer.

(Bottom) Saw palmettos dominate the understory of the maritime forests.

an important and wide spread vine whose extensive root networks also tie together loose sands.

Various insects roam the area of the dunes. Most visible are seaside grasshoppers (*Trimerotropis maritima*) which frequently whir off from under a walker's feet. In the late fall orange fritillary butterflies move *en masse* through the sea oats; when they fold their wings to rest, silvery spots come into prominence. Harder to see is a small sand wasp (*Bembix americana spinolae*), mostly conspicuous for its convict-striped body and flying sand as it feverishly digs burrows, most never to be used. A hairy insect with bright red shoulders and back contrasting with a black stripe scurries around. This *Dasymutilla occidentalis* is variously known as a velvet ant or a cow killer for its bite, a painful wound but not really capable of killing even small mammals. Out in the washed-up *spartina* heaps wanders a tiny flower beetle (*Collops nigriceps*) distinct in an orange life jacket on its thorax. The slightly larger beautiful tiger beetle (*Cicindela formosa*) hunts other insects under plants within the meadow and only a bold dark shield design standing out against the yellow background of its wings will catch your eye. The wolf spider (*Geolycosa pikei*), less than an inch long, is the hardest to spot as it usually waits for passing victims within the opening of its burrow. Although these burrows have reinforced walls and may run to a depth of a few feet, the sand scattered during the construction is more conspicuous than their builders. Here and there in the sand you will see funnel-shaped pits in loose sand—clever insect traps with a voracious antlion larvae lurking at the bottom. When a small insect starts sliding down towards death an antlion will flick loose sand at it to make sure it will never get enough grip to climb out. By contrast, some short-lived adults in this order *Neoroptera* may lack mouths—their main function being a session of intense breeding.

Insects attract predators from the nearby forest. Obvious tunnels under the sand indicate the long subterranean travels moles make, but surface sand may be too loose to show the tracks of the green anole (*Anolis carolinensis*) lizards or even mice, marsh rabbits or raccoons. Mole skinks (*Eumeces egregius*), striped snake-like lizards with tiny legs, prefer digging and tunneling under the sand in search of juicy spiders. Snakes may venture in this territory, also. Feel privileged when you spot a rare and harmless coachwhip (*Masticophis flagellum*). The slender body may be up to 6 feet long and in a mature adult is black around the head part, the color gradually turning into brown and becoming paler towards the tail. The coachwhip has uncommonly large eyes and it feeds on lizards, smaller snakes and small mammals. Eastern diamond rattlesnakes (*Crotalus adamanteus*) like to hang around under the palmetto frond litter hunting squirrels, rabbits and rats. Only a young one will venture onto the dunes in search of small prey. Rattlesnakes, although very poisonous,

Live oaks growing along the seaward edge of the maritime forest tend to lean westward as a result of exposure to Atlantic winds.

are quite passive—back away from it and you will both be better off.

MARITIME FOREST

The forest begins where the ground rises from the back dune but, depending on the island, the transition may be gradual or abrupt. Saw palmettos and shrubs become a thick understory under a canopy of trees. Scattered loblolly pines appear here mixed with oaks and magnolia trees. Sabal palmettos have established a firm presence in this zone with slender trees like american holly (*Ilex opaca*), yaupon holly (*Ilex vomitoria*) and the spiky hercules'- club (*Zanthoxylum clavaherculis*). However, the most conspicuous and numerous are the evergreen live oaks (*Cuercus virginiana*). Live oaks have a complex structure of twisting contorted branches which combine with a wide and equally complex system of roots to anchor the trees against the ravages of wind and the maritime climate. Live oaks grow relatively low with the largest on record being 84 feet high and the average perhaps 40 to 50 feet. They make up for that by growing sideways with powerful branches snaking far outward. The branches of the largest live oak recorded in Georgia reach out 143 feet and its trunk is 10 feet in diameter. The oaks in the maritime forests on the barrier islands are much smaller and a lot younger since in the past colonists cut the live oak forests for use in ship building. Colonial shipwrights from New England quickly discovered how strong and how resistant to rot and even to ship-worm live oak timber is and how the compound curves in the tree structure could be sawed to match various curved components of a ship structure. Live oaking became a serious enterprise on the coast between Virginia and Alabama where the trees were thinned quite quickly. Fortunately, live oaks grow fast and when you walk through a thick forest under the interlocking canopies of live oaks you would never guess that the large ones are only 100 to 200 years old.

The shape of a live oak's crown depends a lot on its environment. On the Atlantic edges of barrier islands rows of slender live oaks lean over like wind blown smoking torches—a result of exposure to the salt laden onshore wind. Within a well-developed climax forest live oaks spread out evenly forming their own windbreaks and shade from the merciless sun. The trees help retain moisture under layers of fallen leaves—although the live oak is an evergreen generations of leaves change seasonally. The layers of old copper-colored leaves make it hard to spot a similarly hued terrestrial orchid, the coral root (*Collarorhiza sp*) which rises from among the oak roots. Depending on the species these orchids bloom in spring or fall. The deeply fissured oak bark holds moisture and nutrients for other plants and the long oak branches support colonies of resurrection fern (*Polypodium polypodioides*), named for its ability to change from papery brown curls caused by drought into lively green leaves

Live oak

The armadillo, a relatively recent arrival from Texas via Florida, thrives in the forests of Cumberland Island.

Come autumn, mushrooms such as this boletus pop out from the forest floor both on the barrier islands and the mainland.

after it rains. The epiphytic Spanish moss (*Tillandsia usneoides*) hangs down from live oaks in long curly tresses in which birds shelter and seminole bats roost. Soft filaments of Spanish moss are in great demand as nesting material by warblers and painted buntings. Another, less conspicuous epiphyte, (*Tillandsia recurvata*), grows on the oaks in self-contained round colonies of interwoven stems.

A complex tree like the live oak creates its own ecosphere. Vines proliferate within a mature forest using the oaks for support. Some of the vines grow thick and woody and loop over the oak branches to the ground. Many produce spectacular blooms, the lavender flowers of the poisonous wisteria vine (*Wisteria frutescens*) explode in spring and the poisonous yellow jessamine (*Gelsemium sempervirens*) may begin flowering as early as February during mild winters. Muscadine vine (*Vitus rotundifolia*) grapes are worth a grab when they turn dark purple, plump and sweet. People should avoid touching the poison ivy vine (*Rhus radicans*) with its give-away clusters of three pointed leaves, but during the winter some woodpeckers, cat birds, thrushes and deer relish the white berries it produces. Patchy lichens, pink, red or green and white, colo-

nize the smoother stretches of the trunk while bracket mushrooms wedge themselves into comfortable notches in the oak bark. Insects and ruby-throated hummingbirds feed on the flowers all these vines produce while the fruits nourish other birds and mammals.

Live oak acorns provide long term food supplies for squirrels, deer, raccoons, wild turkey, doves, woodpeckers, brown thrashers to mention just a few animals. A climax maritime forest of live oaks is hard to penetrate by humans—a fortunate circumstance for snakes, frogs, raccoons, opossums and armadillos.

Armadillos reached Georgia from Texas in 1970 and are now well-established on the barrier islands. When you hear a loud rustling in the oak leaf litter it is most likely a busy armadillo pushing its nose through the humus looking for grubs, worms, insects and even wolf spiders and scorpions. Now and then you will blunder into spider webs strung between trees and hard to see. The large golden-silk (*Nephila clavipes*) females, 4 inches across including the legs, weave nets over 6 feet in diameter anchoring them between trees sometimes ten to fifteen feet apart. The webs often stretch over paths at a height adequate for deer to go under so bend down, mate, and you will clear it, too. The females share the webs with tiny males and even smaller plump neighbors which scavenge the remains of caught insects. The 2-inch female of the silver argiope (*Argiope aurantia*) spins extensive webs between the lower shrubs and marks them with bands of heavier silky tufts along threads radiating from the center. The females of both these species are highly colorful and easy to spot. The much less conspicuous crablike spiny orb weaver (*Gasteracantha elipsoides*) is superbly colorful but only a half-inch across its spiny body. The female spins a new web every night decorating it with conspicuous tufts on some threads. All these spiders are quite harmless although may bite when handled roughly. Leave them be—they do eat the insects that sting us!

FRESHWATER PONDS, BOGS AND SLOUGHS

On all older barrier islands in Georgia, inland of the first ridge covered by maritime forest, you will come across ponds or sloughs in a variety of sizes and shapes. A few receive water from artesian wells, others depend on refills by precipitation while several have occasional connections to the sea and become brackish. In all of them the water level depends mainly on seasonal rains. During the dry months the water may evaporate completely and only stands of slender tupelo trees, red maples, myrtle dahoon (a holly with tiny leaves), pond cypress, the shrubby fetterbush and button bush indicate that there must be fresh water underground. In sloughs without the shade of a forest canopy the whole slough may turn into a meadow of tall sedges and grasses interspersed with patches of cracked dry mud. However, where fresh water persists as in the larger ponds or deeper sloughs the aquatic plants like duckweeds, duckmeat and bog mat survive and cover extensive areas. From the spring until fall the permanent ponds bloom. You will see yellow flowers on thin stalks growing from the base of floating bladderwort (*Utricularia radiata*), the yellow ball-shaped flowers of spatter dock or cow lily (*Nuphar luteum*) rising over big green leaves and wide-open white flowers resting on the plate-sized leaves of the fragrant water lily (*Nymphaea odorata*). Blue flag iris (*Iris virginica*) prefers at least the partial shade of nearby shrubs while pickerelweed (*Pontederia cordata*) will tolerate sunshine as long as it gets plenty of water.

These sloughs are the only source of drinking water for mammals, some of which may end up as food for alligators. Judging by the maze of footprints on the banks of the sloughs of Cumberland Island deer, opossums and raccoons are the most numerous visitors. Amphibians and reptiles also hang around the precious sloughs on the otherwise dry barrier islands. The deeper swamps on Sapelo Island, Blackbeard and Wassaw as well as Cumberland's Lake Whitney host aquatic salamanders that grow to two feet long and will bite if handled. The leopard frog, with its unmistakable yellow stripes, and cricket frogs make their homes in the bogs as does the big pig bullfrog. Green tree frogs congregate close to freshwater at breeding time, their odd barks resounding through the trees. Most frogs are easier to hear than to see, especially the grass frog with its nearly transparent body. In order to voice the desire for

White ibis feed by probing mud banks exposed by the receding tides.

mates these tiny creatures, relatives of the tree frogs, climb onto the tips of grass blades—a fitting substitute for trees considering the grass frog's size. On all barrier islands, when the water levels are high in the shaded sloughs surrounded by forest, you will see small diamondback terrapins (*Malaclemys terrapin*) warming up on fallen trees. The much larger snapping turtle (*Chelydra serpentina*) is harder to spot as it prefers to lie buried in mud. It has a

An alligator catches some warming rays in a creek at Blackbeard Island Wildlife Refuge.

Trumpet vine

Sabal palmetto

Finished with feeding, a wood stork takes off.

nasty temperament, powerful jaws and vicious claws which all come into action if you try to pick up the animal while it ventures on its rare trip across dry land.

It is difficult to define how a slough (pronounced "slew") differs from swamps, bogs and ponds. The main difference is in the amount of available water and open surface. Mature sloughs will slowly lose water at times of little precipitation, turn into bogs and in time will change into meadows which may eventually become emergent woods. Ponds, while always retaining some level of water, change character with the seasons; surface vegetation increases during the wet summers and contracts in the dry winter months opening more useable surface for migrating ducks. In ponds which get inundated by sea water the surface remains clear of vegetation and the pond will host large quantities of small fish—sheepshead minnow, sailfin molly, striped mullet—which feed on organic matter decaying on the bottom. The fish breed profusely and larger animals follow, from alligators and turtles to herons, egrets, ibis, wood storks and anhingas. Migrating mallards, hooded mergansers, black ducks, ringed-neck ducks, red-heads, pintails, teals, gallinules all stop to feed in the ponds. Ospreys survey the waters from the tops of high dead trees and recently bald eagles have again joined this busy scene. In early spring the ponds which are most remote from human interference become breeding grounds for wading birds. Great egrets (*Ardea alba*), snowy egrets (*Egretta thula*), little blue herons (*Egretta caerulea*), tricolored herons (*Egretta tricolor*), green herons (*Butorides virescens*) are joined by anhingas (*Anhinga anhinga*) and huge colonies of white ibis (*Eudocimus albus*). Most of their nests sit loosely on low trees and shrubs near the water. Purple gallinules (*Porphyrula martinica*) and common moorhens (*Gallinula chloropus*) weave nests somewhat lower but still in the vicinity of herons, while great blue herons (*Ardea herodias*) set their big platforms of sticks on high

Turkey oak, Live oak, Water oak

trees and often far from other birds. Wood storks (*Mycteria Americana*) build nests at various high levels on one tree which may, in the end, host a whole colony of birds. Red-winged blackbirds (*Agelaius phoeniceus*) and boat-tailed grackles (*Quiscalus major*) also nest in the vicinity. Such huge numbers of birds attract the predators of eggs and hatchlings. Alligators eat what falls into the water but raccoons, crows and some blackbirds will rob unprotected nests. Only about forty-five percent of laid eggs become hatchlings and then only forty-five percent of young birds live to maturity. As can be expected the most aggressive of all hatchlings, the young of the black-crowned night heron (*Nycticorax nictycorax*), have the best rate of survival. The young, even though still quite weak, vomit or defecate forcefully at intruders and then try to beak them as discovered by Mildred and John Teal when studying a nesting area on Sapelo Island. Add the strong smell associated with large bird nurseries and you will agree the best way to observe nesting birds is through binoculars.

WESTWARD THROUGH THE INTERIOR FOREST

Apart from interruptions here and there by sloughs and ponds the maritime forest should theoretically cover the whole of a well-developed barrier island. Due to man's activities, though, the barrier island forests vary from place to place. Pine forests have taken over where land was once cleared for pasture or crops and today you will encounter large stands of longleaf, slash and loblolly pines where oaks prevailed in the past. It is easy to walk under pines since the thick carpet of fallen needles keeps the understory plants in check. Pine trunks with their thick loose bark-pads are resistant to occasional wild fires which kill other plants competing for nutrients and sunshine. Such fires are a common threat in nature and other trees have also developed some protective measures. Cabbage (*Sabal*) palmettos will live through minor fires as long as their crowns survive. Live oak forests spread a thick carpet of non-flammable old leaves on the ground—an effective barrier to forest fires of modest intensity.

On parts of Cumberland Island and in particular on Wassaw Island, which did not experience severe logging and farming, the interior forests remain a dense mixture of hardwoods and palmettos. The trees stand over thick understories of saw palmettos with scattered open patches

of reindeer moss (*Cladonia evansii*), whitish bushy lichens growing in low round clumps over sandy soil. Other species of oaks join the scene and live oaks, now free from the pressures of wind, spread their curvy boughs equally in all directions. Quite often you will come across a ring of several oak trunks rising from a central area. They probably grew out of an old stump now long gone. In the interior forest woody vines grow thicker, wrapping themselves around the trees in great loops. Many oaks display odd lumps on the trunks called galls, where the tree has responded to an insect intrusion by building an isolation chamber for the unwanted guests. Pignut hickory (*Carya glabra*) rise straight up and the lucky climbing vines, cross vine (*Bignonia capreolata*) and trumpet vine

Pileated woodpecker

(*Campsis radicans*), which happen to settle on them follow the light upwards. These vines bloom with similarly shaped orangish reddish trumpet flowers, the cross vine in early spring and the trumpet vine throughout the summer. Other oaks occur here, water oak (*Quercus nigra*) with its leaves much wider at the tips and laurel oak (*Quercus hemisphaerica*) with leaves resembling live oak's but ending with a bristle tip. The small deeply furrowed turkey oak (*Quercus laevis*) is named after its turkey-foot shaped leaves. Many smaller trees struggle in the understory. Red bay (*Persea borbonia*) has shiny leaves and if you crush one and smell it you will see why they are sold as "bay leaves" for flavoring. Some people put these leaves into bags of rice to discourage weevils. Stag-

Sea ox-eye colonizes the western edges of the islands just before the uplands meet the salt marsh.

gerbush (*Lyonia ferruginea*) grows in skinny twisted trunks—its leaves having rusty scales on the undersides. Sparkleberry (*Vaccinium arboreum*), though small, produces black berries important as food for turkeys and raccoons. They are also edible for humans but you will find only a little pulp over the seeds. The southern magnolia (*Magnolia grandiflora*) grows to imposing heights and from March through May it blooms with large white flowers whose lemony sweet scent wafts through the forest. As you near the western edges of the barrier islands, not far from where the salt marshes begin, you will see southern red cedars (*Juniperus silicicola*), an evergreen whose reddish, often peeling, trunks assume strange twists when the trees have struggled up an eroding shoreline. Red cedars can grow straight but the perfect trees were heavily cut in the past to make pencils and furniture. Hackberry (*Celtis laevigata*) also occurs here and the tree is conspicuous for its trunk studded with pointed warts.

These dense interior forests provide perfect habitat for great numbers of animals, both in terms of food and shelter. The hiding opportunities in the tree crowns, in the trunks, under the roots and behind impenetrable shrubs are so good that it requires a person to wait patiently and quietly in order to see the forest denizens. On most of the barrier islands you will easily see deer

bouncing away in great leaps and hogs trotting away, the naïve piglets lagging behind. Eastern black swallowtail (*Papilio polyxenes asterius*), and on some islands zebra swallowtail butterflies (*Graphium marcellus*), will flit by unafraid of predators because of their chemical weaponry. Mocking birds (*Mimus polyglottos*) and mourning doves (*Zenaida macroura*) also explore the forest floor and are easy to spot. The majority of other animals prefer to hide or simply go about their business of living out of sight. To spot many of the forest songbirds you have to use binoculars.

The forest is also a source of all kinds of food throughout the year. That famously omnivorous raccoon feeds on small animals on the ground and, being a good climber, it also preys on eggs and young birds. In the fall raccoons eat acorns and the fruit of saw palmettos and sabal palmettos as well as the berries of American holly, sparkleberry and muscadine grapes. Even the small, mainly carnivorous, grey fox which climbs trees to reach nesting birds and lizards, supplements its summer diet with muscadine grapes, blackberries and the fruit of the common persimmon (*Diospyros virginiana*), also well-worth eating by us humans when ripe. Squirrels feed on acorns but also eat mushrooms, fungi and berries. Deer browse on twigs, leaves, as well as acorns. A truly rich food, the acorns also attract wild turkeys. Deer, turkeys and, on

At low tide the smooth cordgrass marsh plants stand tall creating an illusion of a forest

Cumberland Island feral horses, eat Spanish moss keeping this plant pruned at levels those browsers can reach.

Birds which during the "buggy" warm months chase insects will switch to a vegetarian diet when the weather becomes colder. Mocking birds eat fruit and berries when the numbers of beetles, bees and grasshoppers dwindle. In the fall migrating cedar waxwings (*Bombycilla cedrorum*) relish the little blue berries of red cedars while on the way north in the spring they chase flying insects. American holly berries provide food for thrushes, mockingbirds, robins, catbirds, bluebirds and thrashers and turkeys and rodents go after the berries that fall on the ground. Since many of the mainland mixed oak forests have been cut and replaced by the monocultures of farmed pines, the maritime forests on the islands have become increasingly important for songbirds. Now, as the human population on the coastal mainland is increasing and some farm pine forests are giving way to housing, even more bird species must come to the islands or face extinction. Sixty-seven species of birds visit or live in maritime forests—and that is a conservative count that includes frequent sightings only.

BETWEEN THE MARITIME FOREST AND THE MARSH

The forests end abruptly at the western margins of the barrier islands to be replaced by vast marshlands. Where undermined by a tidal river the island shore will step suddenly into a flooded margin of smooth cordgrass (*Spartina alterniflora*) but in many cases the upland slopes gently with the plant populations changing in response to the increasing salinity of the soil. Such shores may contain large amounts of shell material from old oyster beds or from shell middens left by the indigenous inhabitants of the coast. Sabal palmettos love the extra calcium produced by these shells. Southern red cedar (*Juniperus silicicola*) also likes the calcareous substratum and will persevere even as the solid land slowly erodes. The bushy sea myrtle (*Baccharis halimifolia*) stands in thick colonies along all types of shorelines and tufts of its white flowers fill the air in strong autumnal winds. Marsh-elder (*Iva frutescens*), a bushy shrub, thrives in that transitional zone and begins to bloom in August. At the same time of the year seaside goldenrod (*Solidago sempervirens*) thrusts up flags of small yellow flowers growing along multiple floral branches. The ubiquitous rhizomatous marsh-edge plant sea ox-eye (*Borrichia frutescens*) begins blooming at the end of May with round yellow flowers shaped like small sunflowers.

SALT MARSH

We once took an Englishman who lives in Hong Kong for a car ride on a highway cutting along the Georgia marsh savanna. He had never seen such natural, unpopulated marsh landscape and he assumed he was looking at a vast cropland. To some extent he was right, he was seeing the second most productive ecosystem in America surpassed only by cultivated sugar cane fields in Florida. These successful plants of the marsh deserve our admiration for they exist in an extremely harsh environment. The tidal marshland regularly undergoes amazing swings of temperature and humidity. The living conditions are at their most stable when the marsh is flooded by seawater at high tide. As soon as the ebb drops the water level, the plants exposed to air begin to dry under a film of concentrated salt and eventually, when the water runs out, the exposed mudflats begin to heat up in the sun. The dark mud may reach 80°F in winter and well over 120°F in summer only to start cooling rapidly when washed over by the first waves of the returning tide. Add the effect of a strong breeze causing fast evaporation and the same mud may bottom out at 30°F during cool weather. Many animals burrow to avoid such drastic environmental swings but plants have no choice but to adapt to them. Changing seasons add even a harder edge to the life in the marsh—summers often raise temperatures to either side of 90°F in the shade and each winter outdoorsmen in Georgia shiver for a few 28°F days. None of the environmental elements is one hundred percent reliable. Even those seemingly dependable semi-diurnal tidal cycles get disrupted by strong winds—an onshore wind will delay and weaken a low tide while an offshore gale may hold back the flood. Atmospheric pressure also affects the tides—high pressure lowers high tides and low pressure causes excessive flooding. Life in the marsh is no picnic and only a few plants and animals can survive it.

Smooth cordgrass (*Spartina alterniflora*) is the most important and the most visible plant in the marshlands regularly inundated by highly saline sea water. The new growth of smooth cordgrass begins turning the marsh edges green in the spring and by mid-summer green salt marshes stretch westward for many miles. In the fall the grasses gradually turn brown and yellow, or vividly golden in the warm rays of a rising or setting sun. In the depth of winter the grasses look drab until the first green shoots appear in late February. Except for the higher plants (up to 7 feet) on the bank edges of tidal creeks, the tops of *spartina* grasses maintain the same level although the plants vary in height—they grow shorter on higher mud levels close to the shore and longer as the mud dips down further away. When seen from a distance the plants look like a level field. The thick, dense, mud base excludes oxygen and marsh grasses, smooth cordgrass, saltmeadow grass (*Spartina patens*) and needle rush (*Juncus spp*), utilize a system of tubes to deliver vital oxygen to the roots. These plants can also excrete excess salt—an important ability for smooth cordgrass which sometimes disappears under extremely high tides.

The mud may seem a hostile environment, an impression reinforced when, after digging into it, you smell hydrogen sulfide, the product of anaerobic bacteria de-

Wharf crab

Sand fiddler crab

composing bits of matter trapped in the compressed sediments. Yet mud is also a source of nutrients waiting to be released by tides which remove waste products while delivering food to the plants. Some percentage of the live plants feeds insects but most of the grasses die intact and end up in the mud to be eventually broken up into ever smaller particles of organic detritus. The pulverized detritus mixes with the upper layers of mud, the home of one-celled algae so small that we learn of their existence only when they paint green or olive patches on the low tide mud. The moving tidal waters distribute these nutritious algae to animals which may feed by filtering like oysters and mussels or by collection like tiny fiddler crabs. The algae and decomposing plant and animal detritus enrich the basic food supply for small animals on whom, in turn, feed larger creatures. The rapid and changing currents stir up and deliver this bouillabaisse to unimaginable numbers of several species, many of which—shrimp, fish, oysters, clams and blue crabs—are harvested by fishermen.

Despite the deceptive uniformity at first sight, the plants of the salt marsh vary. Smooth cordgrass prevails in the areas of deepest flooding. On higher levels where the flood rises to only a foot or less the short *spartina*

grasses mix with sea lavender (*Limmonium carolinianum*), a small herb with salt expelling glands which blooms at the end of summer with shy tiny purple flowers. The less salt tolerant saltmarsh aster (*Aster tenuifolius*) blooms at about the same time—its white flower petals surrounding a yellow center. In some high, rarely flooded areas of the marsh the salinity exceeds even the capabilities of the tough salt meadow cordgrass (*Spartina patens*). Only halophytes, plants that can cope with very high salinity, grow on the edges of these salt pans. Perennial glassworts (*Salicornia virginica*) congregate in mats of erect fleshy plump succulent green stems ending in red tips. The larger and more scattered saltwort (*Batis maritima*), a low plant with woody stems and succulent leaves, takes up the same habitat. Needle rush (*Juncus roemerianus*) often takes over high marsh areas especially where water may easily become brackish as in the upper reaches of tidal rivers. Needle rush has unmistakable pointed stiff stems, five feet tall and sharp enough to puncture skin.

The salt marshes support several creatures but at high tide when the marsh is reduced to a few scattered clumps of grass tips you will see only the ones that have to escape being submerged. Tiny half-inch long saltmarsh snails (*Melampus bidentatus*), lung breathing and lacking operculums to close their shell homes, often swing at the very top of *spartina* tips awaiting the water to drop, for they can survive only one hour under water. Dark brown, usually hard to see, grasshoppers also retire above high water although they can live through a short term submersion. As the tide rises you may even notice ants running back to their nests in the thickest stems of *spartina*. At high tide it is also easier to spot spiders near the tops of the grasses—the rising water will destroy webs but spiders themselves can survive submersion. The wharf crabs (*Sesarma cinereum*) retire up the tallest *spartina* on the very edge of creeks. Marsh hens, or clapper rails (*Rallus longirostris*), who live and breed in the marshes but generally stay out of sight also move up with the tide and so become more visible. They become quiet, too, a very different behavior from their usual loud cackling resounding through the marshes. At high tide look for long-billed marsh wrens (*Cistothorus palustris*) and their nests in the highest specimens of smooth cordgrass which grow on the very margins of tidal creeks. The males of these small camouflaged birds weave together *spartina* leaves to form several rough nest baskets. It falls to a committed female wren to turn one of these sloppy structures into a decent home for the young. Sharp-tailed sparrows (*Ammodramus caudacutus*) and seaside sparrows (*Ammodramus maritimus*) live exclusively in the marshes and feed at ground level. Their camouflaging coloring makes them very hard to spot except at high tide when they flit at the top of the marshes. The highly visible red-winged blackbird (*Agelaius phoeniceus*), itself a marsh resident, at high tide takes advantage of the suddenly exposed insects. Other birds, swallows and even gulls, terns and songbirds, too, sweep the marsh for easy victims. In the creeks winding through the marsh clandestine feeding goes on at a high pace. You can often spot foraging blue crabs (*Callinectes sapidus*) when they come close to the surface but squid, although plentiful, are rarely seen in the dark muddy water. Several fish invade on high tide and in the fall and winter large numbers of spotted seatrout, Georgia fishermen's favorite catch, feed in the marsh creeks, their foot and half long bodies swirling the surface.

Ospreys (*Pandion haliaetus*) which patrol for available fish on the wing are eminently adapted for the job. Their pigmented eyes can cut through water glare like a polarized filter, their talons equipped with barbed hooks grip fish instantly and their angled wings help them rise off the water with large fish. Ospreys work hard for their food, dropping onto the fish feet first and often disappearing under water. Yet, even as large a bird as an osprey may become a victim. Bald eagles (*Haliaeetus leucocephalus*) have made a comeback in Georgia, their great funereal black and white silhouettes often surveying the marsh from high points on dead trees. Bald eagles, less perfectly endowed for fishing, often resort to aerial harassing of an osprey burdened with a fish until the honest fisherman drops its catch which the eagle will snatch in mid-air. The roles change then and the birds may chase each other even after the fish drops down in the mud, forgotten. Human watchers may also experience a thrill when bottlenosed dolphins, singly or in groups, take advantage of the high tide to explore remote very narrow marsh streams—their dorsal fins cutting at high speed after unseen quarry.

Low tide in the marshes reveals a different world. The *spartina* marshes rise above narrow creeks like dense forests. Muddy banks appear beaded as millions of mud snails (*Ilynassa obsoleta*) search for food—minute particles of dead fish suit this one-inch snail. Marsh periwinkles (*Littorina irrorata*), a 19th century import from Europe, eke a living on *spartina* plants going up and down with changing water levels even though it is equipped with an operculum and can seal itself inside. Two species of fiddler crabs, named after the males which sport one huge claw and look as if they are part of the violin section of an orchestra, feed steadily on exposed mud flats. Mud fiddlers (*Uca pugnax*) occur in astonishing numbers, some million crabs per acre. At low tide they chew little particles of mud leaving behind waste pellets. The sand fiddlers (*Uca pugilator*) have a similar omnivorous food habit yet these two species keep apart by digging burrows in different types of bottom. Up to two hours before and two hours after low tide is a good time to rig a chicken neck on a string and fish for blue crabs. They will hold on tenaciously to the bait while being pulled smoothly into a dip net. A license is needed, see the Appendix for more information on crabbing. Blue crabs (*Callinectes sapidus*) grow large; a mature male, easily recognizable by the blue claw tips and an elongated thin flap on the abdomen, can reach 9 inches across the carapace. Red tipped on the claws, adult females have a wide U-shaped flap on the abdomen, which in summer, will support a large cluster of orange eggs. Fishermen may keep crabs over 5 inches wide, others, including females with eggs must be released.

Low tide exposes large "reefs" of eastern oysters (*Crassostrea virginica*) which live in a narrow band between the tides. The exposure to air helps oysters rid themselves temporarily of their predators, starfishes and true fishes like drum, sheepshead and rays as well as oyster drills (*Urosalpinx cinerea*) which do not like becoming dry. This, roughly one-inch long, whelk-shaped snail uses a radula equipped mouth to abrade through an oyster shell and then sucks the victim out slowly, reportedly over a period of three weeks. In optimum conditions an oyster will grow about one-inch each year and live up to ten years. However, the once widely spread beds of huge Georgia oysters are diminished considerably today due to three decades of uncontrolled harvesting between the 1880s and 1910. Low tides also uncover small colonies of ribbed mussels (*Geukensia demissa*) making homes in the roots of smooth cordgrass. Although highly edible there are not enough of the mussels around to collect for eating. Oysters, however, are still there in moderate numbers and free for the taking. Make sure, though, you can see the signs approving the beds for public consumption and are in a designated public oyster harvesting area. See the Appendix for more information on oyster fishing. Mudflats in marsh creeks are the habitat of southern quohogs (*Mercenaria campechiensis*), big clams, up to 6 inches round, good to eat if you do not mind searching for them by shoving your feet through the mud. Carolina marsh clams (*Polymesoda caroliniana*) live in the mud, too, and though much smaller make good eating. Talking about eating, one must not forget white shrimp (*Penaeus setiferus*). During summertime low tides shrimp thrash in the shallows and you can catch the legal limit with a few throws of a cast net. A license is needed for this so see the Appendix for more information on shrimping.

As the water departs from marsh creeks the marine life crowds the available pools and streams of shallow water. They become visible to people, both harmless naturalists and predatory fishermen, and to various animals interested in finding an easy meal. Mammals which spend high tides on hammock islands scattered throughout the marshes slink down muddy trails prowling between grasses and on stream banks. Raccoons, after looking for nests with eggs or hatchlings, work the mud banks to dig for burrowed crabs, clams and mud worms one of which (*Lineus socialis*) grows to 8 inches long, a good size prey. Good swimmers, raccoons may even catch a blue crab or two. Red coated minks dive well and probably feed on fish just as much as on crabs. Killfish, the most numerous fish of the marsh creeks, feed on tiny marsh amphipods (*Gammarus palustris*) and in turn make easy prey for diamond-back terrapins which also dine on periwinkles, crabs and insects. Diamond back terrapins can become numerous in undisturbed places and at one tiny rivulet, at Plantation Creek near Brunswick, we saw a couple of dozen of them feeding. Alligators are the largest resident predator of the marsh creeks and you will see them stretched out on mud banks on cool spring and fall mornings in order to warm up their bodies. Their metabolism is very slow and alligators need about 1 pound of food per week but, when hungry, can launch lightning strikes after large fish, snakes, turtles, birds, raccoons and even white-tailed deer.

Great numbers of birds congregate along marsh creeks at low tide. Oyster catchers and boat-tailed grackles probe through uncovered oyster beds. Solitary great blue herons patiently stalk the very edge of the water. Green-backed herons (*Butorides striatus*) also like to fish alone and stealthily from a branch or oyster outcropping overhanging the water while other herons work in small groups. Great tribes of white ibis probe into the mud and wood storks work the shallow water by swinging their beaks sideways like spoonbills. In the marsh creeks flowing by shore bluffs you will see belted kingfishers (*Ceryle alcyon*) hovering and then plunging in after minnow-size fish. It would take pages to list all shore birds flocking to low tide flats and the species vary somewhat according to seasons. See the bird list in the Appendix. For the winter ibis and woodstorks fly south to Florida while white pelicans show up on the border of Georgia and Florida. Ducks crowd the marsh creeks and avocets (*Recurvirostra americana*), unmistakable in their striking coloring, sweep their upturned beaks through soft mud in a spoonbill manner. One sight that does not seem to excite birds so much but astounds us is when bottlenosed dolphins suddenly drive themselves right onto the mud or wiggle wildly in water less than their body girth, fins swaying and tails slapping. We have never established what prey they chase.

Evenings on a low tide marsh add an extra dimension. Nocturnal animals appear before all daylight goes out. An otter will play on a sloping mud bank and alligators are less wary while catching the last warmth of the air. After an all day absence, black skimmers suddenly swoop down to plow their lower beaks through schools of minnows, marsh hens (clapper rails) boldly stride in full view to take a bath and the red-eyed black crowned night herons (*Nycticorax nycticorax*) begin patrolling the shallows as the dark falls—they will make you jump with a horrific screech if you stir suddenly. During summer nights a dolphin swimming up a creek will trail a shiny sparkling wake of bioluminescence coming from schools of one-celled dinoflagellates. Other creatures, including squid, can also flash a shower of light through the muddy waters.

Although we enjoyed exploring Georgia's coastal waters through all the months of the year, the spring is the most memorable season. Apart from the first shy bursts of new leaves, one unmistakable sign of spring is the changing coloring of the common loon (*Gavia immer*), a regular visitor around the Savannah River. As the weather warms up they begin to dive in pairs calling in soft wails to maintain contact when on the surface. This large water bird suddenly transforms from a somewhat splotchy bundle of feathers into a striking creature with a soot-black head with glowing red eyes. Its neck gains a white collar and the upper wings acquire a black and white checkerboard pattern. Another sign of spring in the marsh creeks is the return of dolphins whose dorsal fins and audible breaths now appear in the midst of flocks of bufflehead (*Bucephala albeola*) ducks and scattered red-breasted mergansers. On really warm days and in sheltered mud bays alligators will crawl out of their winter hibernating lairs to warm up in the sun. At the end of March and beginning of April double-crested cormorants (*Phalacrocorax auritus*) gather in flocks. They fly north with the southerly winds in V-formations high in the sky but hug the marshes when northeasterlies blow hard from the Atlantic. On warm evenings about the middle of April the mud banks heated by afternoon sun look like a distant aerobics class. The fiddler crab males crawl out of their hibernating burrows and wave their large claws as if sawing on the strings of invisible and silent fiddles.

American avocet

South Altamaha River

THE WEATHER

Barbara Parks finds safe sailing conditions within the protected tidal creeks of Georgia.

WINTER

As far as winter temperatures are concerned Georgia definitely benefits from lying between the latitudes of 30°40'N and 32°05'N. Winters begin some time in December and by the end of February the smell of spring is in the air. In this period temperatures may fall into the mid twenties Fahrenheit and in March an occasional cold front may bring cold air to around thirty degrees. Generally, however, the temperature stays between 40° and 70°F. Consequently, boating season should never stop as long as your cruising boat has a heater or, when exploring in an open boat, you are bundled up in warm clothing. Camping continues in popular destinations like Cumberland Island. Because of the proximity to the ocean whose waters stay around 50°F in winter the barrier islands are always a few degrees warmer than uplands to the west. The wind will make low temperatures feel much worse and may lead to hypothermia—winter cruising on breezy days requires heavier protective clothing than the predicted weather would indicate.

WINTER BOATING

Sailing Georgia waterways in winter is delightful. As the depressions sweep though the area the wind switches predictably. It begins to blow from the southeast as a low approaches, then gradually veers, i.e. changes to south, southwest, or west. It usually hits hardest from the northwest as the cold front passes and may continue to blow from the northerly semicircle for a few days slowly moderating. Reef your sails and take off. The marshes which surround the rivers prevent a build-up of waves—you will sail fast in smooth water.

Small open boats, outboard powered or paddled need to watch the winter weather carefully. A strong wind will build up choppy waves that may easily swamp an open boat. A wind blowing against the current makes the waves particularly steep and breaking even in a river surrounded by marsh. When forced to move in such conditions make sure to choose a route and timing that will let you go with a following wind and fair current. While the contrary current flows, stop in the shelter of the marshes to wait for a change of direction.

SUMMER

Summers are a very different story. At the height of the hot season, say July and August, temperatures often soar to above 90°F and 100°F inland. Again, proximity to the ocean moderates the discomfort further relieved by day breezes which, on normal sunny days, begin to blow onshore at about noon close to the ocean and in the early afternoon farther inland. In the late afternoon and evening thunderstorms may roll eastward from the heated uplands and the associated squalls can hit hard although they do not last long. After the thundery weather expect a cooler night breeze from the west.

SUMMER BOATING

The prevailing summer winds come from the southwest and in the passage over the mainland lose much of their strength. A sailboat will need the largest and lightest sails to move especially when the current runs contrary to the course. Land and sea breezes occur regularly. The cooling of the mainland at night causes colder air to descend and eventually move seaward pulled by the warm ocean. This land breeze reaches the coastal areas well after midnight or even in the early morning so it does not help much in cruising unmarked rivers. On the other hand, the sea breeze caused by heated air of the day rising over the mainland and drawing in the cooler ocean air will give a sailboat a few afternoon hours of freedom from motoring.

In this gentle season thunderstorms, born as hot moist air rises and then cools rapidly, are the weather threat to watch out for. The first warning comes when a cumulonimbus, a billowing thunderhead over the uplands to the west, begins lightning and rumbling as it moves eastward. The main blast of wind comes when the horizontal dark underbelly rolls over the boat. A sailboat should douse the sails before it hits. The squall can raise ugly seas very quickly so small open boats should head for marsh creeks or even the marsh itself to avoid being swamped. These squalls usually pass as fast as they arrive.

SPRING, FALL AND THE BERMUDA HIGH

The high pressure area called the Bermuda High really determines the duration of good balmy weather on the Georgia coast. Before it forms we go through the spring months with comfortable temperatures but variable weather often interrupted by very strong stormy winds associated with intense lows. The formation of the Ber-

muda High buffers Georgia against such low pressure systems and begins the summer weather. Weakening of the high ushers in the summer's end and beginning of the Fall. From September till December the heat gradually subsides and the weather patterns moderate until the first cold front arrives, a harbinger of winter.

THE EXTREME WEATHER

Nor'easters

Northeast winds bring bad news to the Georgia coast. They blow the ocean waters onto the shore causing high water levels which aggravate damage from pounding ocean surf. These winds occur most often during winter and spring pummeling the coast for days. When a nor'easter arrives on top of a particularly high tide the barrier islands lose much of their beaches, maritime forests suffer and freshwater sloughs turn saline when the seas breach the primary dunes. Small, new islands may vanish. Storm surge combined with persistent rains and low barometric pressure may double the usual high tide levels on the whole coast. When the waters begin to subside the concentrated pollutants from inland farms and developed areas may overcome the cleansing powers of the wetlands leading to the closing of shellfish and crustacean fisheries. Small recreational boats stay on solid land in this kind of weather, but yachts in some marinas and private docks should consider leaving and anchoring off in order to avoid damage from collapsing pilings and torn docks.

A boat heading up the Medway River lowers its sails before a storm hits.

Hurricanes

Officially the hurricane season lasts from June through October, but during the last decade the season has lengthened through November. Georgia has been hit only a few times since 1898 when in August a severe hurricane landed in Savannah followed in October by another which caused a great loss of life and property around Brunswick and Darien. In August, 1940 a hurricane killed 34 people on Tybee Island. Due to an improved hurricane prediction system only one person died in the October 1947 hurricane. In 1964 the coast suffered damage from hurricanes in August and September. The next major threat came in October 1989 when *Hugo* headed for Georgia only to swerve off-shore when the evacuation of the Georgia coast began. *Hugo* caused devastation on the coast of South Carolina near Charleston. Another real scare came in 1999 when *Floyd* took a course for Tybee Island near Savannah. It, too, veered offshore at the eleventh hour and went north. Time and time again Georgia was saved by the fact that Atlantic hurricanes tend to scoot north in the warm waters of the Gulf Stream which follows the edge of the continental shelf some 80 miles from its coast. This fortunate geographical location will not help when a hurricane makes a landfall in the Gulf of Mexico and then crosses the US mainland on the way to the Atlantic. Or, when a storm gets pushed westward by a high pressure developing to the north—a likely situation during fall months. Due to the global coverage available from weather satellites the early hurricane warning system has never worked better. When boating in Georgia during the hurricane season listen diligently to the weather warnings available from several sources, the VHF radio, FM radio, TV stations and the Internet.

What To Do with Your Boat?

Hurricane arrival means torrential rains, high winds over 75 mph, tornadoes and water level surge. Several factors cause this hurricane surge. Storm force winds blowing onto the coast may pile up the water against the shore, stop the ebb tide and then combine with flood tide. When the extremely low pressure near the eye arrives the water under it will bulge upwards sometimes for several feet over the mean high water mark. It all depends on the combination of these factors. *Cleo* in 1964 caused a 14-foot surge even though the storm brought only gale force winds. The hurricane in August, 1881 caused a 16-foot surge and killed 335 people in Savannah with

Large freighters use the port of Brunswick facilities on a daily basis.

wind of only 80 mph. In August, 1893 a storm with winds of 72 mph caused a 17 to 20-foot surge, wiped out the houses on Tybee Island and went on to kill perhaps 2,000 people in South Carolina. With such dim statistics it seems wise to get away as far from the water as possible and that is what all authorities advise and eventually enforce.

Small boats will be safest hauled on the highest available ground. Larger boats should leave their docks to minimize damage but often boat owners have to follow the instructions of their insurers and take their boats to a recommended shelter. In extremely bad conditions no port is safe enough. However, transient boats may have no choice but to anchor in the best shelter nearby. In the marsh country of the Georgia coast bear in mind that the hurricane surge will rise several feet over the marsh and expose the boat to a long fetch and high waves even far inland. It is best to get as far away from the ocean coast as possible and, because of the highway bridges, motor cruisers have a big advantage here over sailboats. Avoid major large rivers which may flash-flood due to rains. Find an anchorage away from floating docks which may tear loose or float off over the tops of the pilings and ram your vessel. Try to find a place with high wooded land in the predicted direction of the strongest wind. The weather forecast will give you the idea of the wind direction. You can also assume that if a hurricane located to the south begins to move northward and parallel to the coast of Georgia while remaining offshore, the strongest winds will blow from the northeast. This northeast wind will change to north after the hurricane center passes the latitude of your location. When a hurricane makes landfall in Georgia the winds vary between northwest and northeast. If it crosses the coastline north of your location you will typically experience northwest wind diminishing in strength as the system goes away. When the system crosses the coast to the south, you will experience northeast winds which will intensify since most storms tend to drift northwards even when generally heading east. The closer the storm comes to you the worst the conditions become. Storms which cross the mainland from the Gulf of Mexico often lose much of their intensity but the rainfall, hurricane surge and tornadoes remain a strong possibility.

A vessel trying to weather a hurricane at anchor should use heavy nylon anchor rodes with generous lengths of chain next to the anchor. Chafe protection is absolutely necessary where the rope passes through the chocks. Some people swear by PVC hose but old T-shirts soaked in oil and tied in place with light cord will work, also. Allow a very generous ratio of line to depth, 10:1 being minimum.

It is reassuring to use at least two anchors but you must remember that the tidal currents in most Georgia anchorages reverse. The boat may then spin around and tangle the anchor rodes which will chafe through quickly in choppy waters caused by stormy winds. Should you moor the boat with two bow anchors in a "vee" bridle and two anchors from the stern similarly laid out, make sure to fix the rudder in a central position, otherwise the current may impose terrific strain on it. You should set up such a mooring system with a lot of scope for the anchor rodes to allow for storm surge, use a lot of chafe protection and then leave for high ground shelter. Whatever you do, always remove the sails from the spars and stow below deck roller-furled genoas, as well as all canvas dodgers. Otherwise, hurricane winds will tear them loose from all lashings and cause more damage than you thought possible. Leaving your boat anchored all alone may work well in the Georgia wetlands—after all, if she breaks free, the landing will be soft, cushioned by mud and marshes.

LOCAL WEATHER REPORTS

Twenty-four hour weather forecasts come to boaters via 10 channels included in modern VHF radios. By choosing the weather channel (marked WX on the radio) with the best reception, you can hear the general weather situation as well as the latest warnings about thunderstorms, floods, tornadoes and other severe weather. The Georgia county maps allow you to locate these threatening weather phenomena and relate their movements to your location.

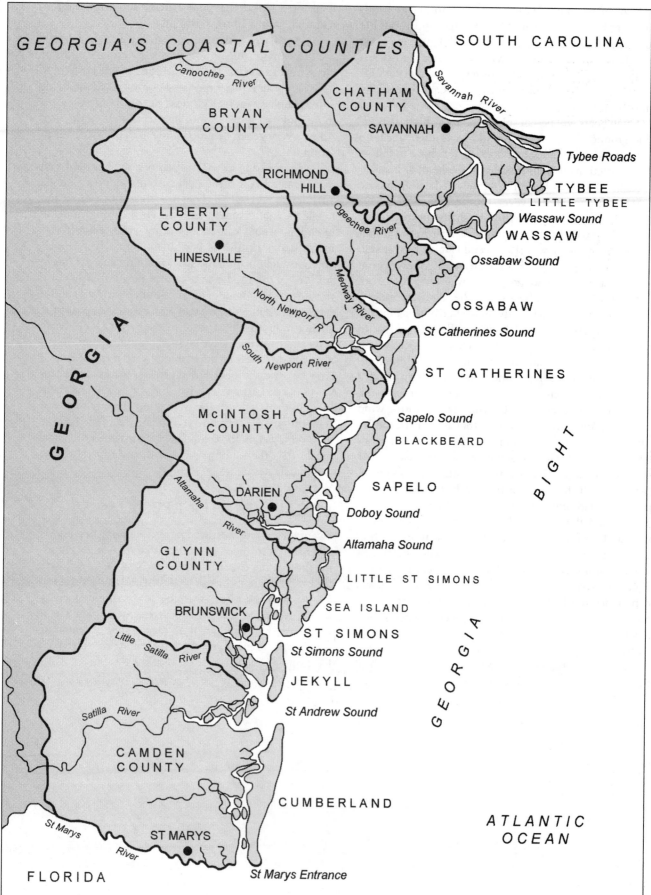

GEORGIA'S COASTAL COUNTIES

SOUTH CAROLINA

Canoochee River

CHATHAM COUNTY

BRYAN COUNTY

SAVANNAH

Savannah River

Tybee Roads

TYBEE

LITTLE TYBEE

RICHMOND HILL

Wassaw Sound

WASSAW

LIBERTY COUNTY

Ogeechee River

HINESVILLE

Ossabaw Sound

Medway River

OSSABAW

North Newport R.

St Catherines Sound

South Newport River

ST CATHERINES

McINTOSH COUNTY

Sapelo Sound

BLACKBEARD

B I G H T

Altamaha River

DARIEN

SAPELO

Doboy Sound

Altamaha Sound

GEORGIA

GLYNN COUNTY

LITTLE ST SIMONS

SEA ISLAND

BRUNSWICK

ST SIMONS

St Simons Sound

G E O R G I A

Little Satilla River

JEKYLL

St Andrew Sound

Satilla River

CAMDEN COUNTY

CUMBERLAND

A T L A N T I C
O C E A N

St Marys River

ST MARYS

St Marys Entrance

FLORIDA

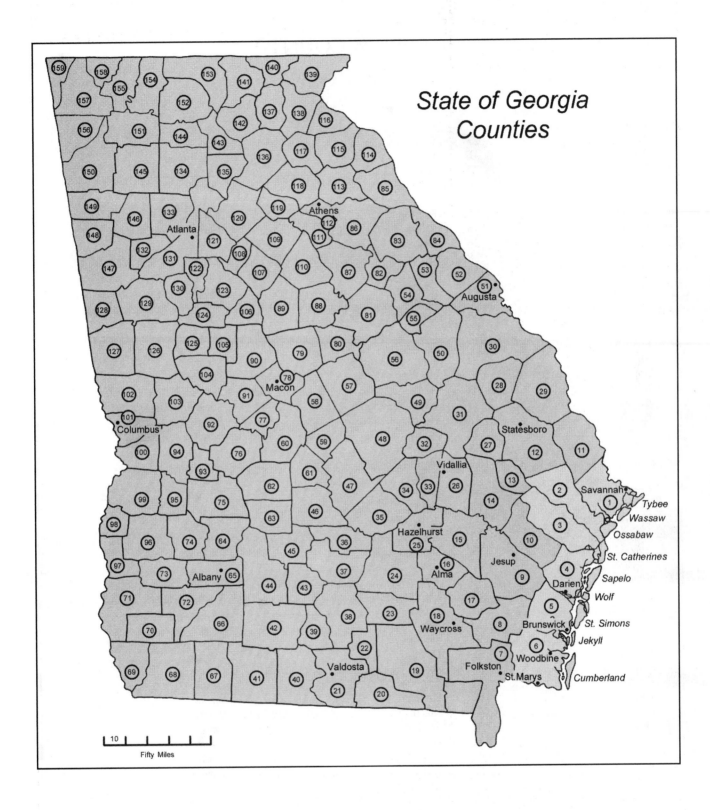

State of Georgia Counties

GEORGIA COUNTIES

Alphabetically

Appling 15	Evans 13	Newton 107
Atkinson 23	Fannin 153	Oconee 111
Bacon 16	Farly 71	Oglethorpe 86
Baker 72	Fayette 130	Paulding 146
Baldwin 80	Floyd 150	Peach 77
Banks 117	Forsyth 135	Pickens 144
Barrow 119	Franklin 115	Pierce 17
Bartow 145	Fulton 131	Pike 125
Ben Hill 36	Glascock 55	Polk 149
Berrien 38	Glynn 5	Pulaski 61
Bibb 78	Gordon 151	Putnam 88
Bleckley 59	Grady 67	Quitman 98
Brantley 8	Greene 87	Rabun 139
Brooke 40	Gwinnett 120	Randolph 96
Bryan 2	Habersham 138	Richmond 51
Bulloch 12	Hall 136	Rockdale 108
Burke 30	Hancock 81	Schley 93
Butts 106	Haralson 148	Screven 29
Calhoun 73	Harris 102	Seminole 69
Camden 6	Hart 114	Spalding 124
Candler 27	Heard 128	Stephens 116
Carroll 147	Henry 123	Stewart 99
Catoosa 158	Houston 60	Sumter 75
Charlton 7	Irwin 37	Talbot 103
Chatham 1	Jackson 118	Taliaferro 82
Chattahoochee 100	Jasper 89	Tattnall 14
Chattoga 156	Jeff Davis 25	Taylor 92
Cherokee 134	Jefferson 50	Telfair 35
Clarke 112	Jenkins 28	Terrell 74
Clay 97	Johnson 49	Thomas 41
Clayton 122	Jones 79	Tift 43
Clinch 19	Lamar 105	Toombs 26
Cobb 133	Lanier 22	Towns 140
Colquitt 42	Laurens 48	Treutlen 32
Columbia 52	Lee 64	Troup 127
Cook 39	Liberty 3	Turner 45
Coweta 129	Lincoln 84	Twiggs 58
Crawford 91	Long 10	Union 141
Crisp 63	Lowndes 21	Upson 104
Dade 159	Lumpkin 142	Walker 157
Dawson 143	Macon 76	Walton 109
Decatur 68	Madison 113	Ware 18
DeKalb 121	Marion 94	Warren 54
Dodge 47	McDuffie 53	Washington 56
Dooly 62	McIntosh 4	Wayne 9
Dougherty 65	Meriwether 126	Webster 95
Douglas 132	Miller 70	Wheeler 34
Douglas 24	Mitchell 66	White 137
Echols 20	Monroe 90	Whitfield 155
Effingham 11	Montgomery 33	Wilcox 46
Elbert 85	Morgan 110	Wilkes 83
Ellijay 152	Murray 154	Wilkinson 57
Emanuel 31	Muscogee 101	Worth 44

GEORGIA COUNTIES
Numerically

1	Chatham
2	Bryan
3	Liberty
4	McIntosh
5	Glynn
6	Camden
7	Charlton
8	Brantley
9	Wayne
10	Long
11	Effingham
12	Bulloch
13	Evans
14	Tattnall
15	Appling
16	Bacon
17	Pierce
18	Ware
19	Clinch
20	Echols
21	Lowndes
22	Lanier
23	Atkinson
24	Douglas
25	Jeff Davis
26	Toombs
27	Candler
28	Jenkins
29	Screven
30	Burke
31	Emanuel
32	Treutlen
33	Montgomery
34	Wheeler
35	Telfair
36	Ben Hill
37	Irwin
38	Berrien
39	Cook
40	Brooke
41	Thomas
42	Colquitt
43	Tift
44	Worth
45	Turner
46	Wilcox
47	Dodge
48	Laurens
49	Johnson
50	Jefferson
51	Richmond
52	Columbia
53	McDuffie
54	Warren
55	Glascock
56	Washington
57	Wilkinson
58	Twiggs
59	Bleckley
60	Houston
61	Pulaski
62	Dooly
63	Crisp
64	Lee
65	Dougherty
66	Mitchell
67	Grady
68	Decatur
69	Seminole
70	Miller
71	Farly
72	Baker
73	Calhoun
74	Terrell
75	Sumter
76	Macon
77	Peach
78	Bibb
79	Jones
80	Baldwin
81	Hancock
82	Taliaferro
83	Wilkes
84	Lincoln
85	Elbert
86	Oglethorpe
87	Greene
88	Putnam
89	Jasper
90	Monroe
91	Crawford
92	Taylor
93	Schley
94	Marion
95	Webster
96	Randolph
97	Clay
98	Quitman
99	Stewart
100	Chattahoochee
101	Muscogee
102	Harris
103	Talbot
104	Upson
105	Lamar
106	Butts
107	Newton
108	Rockdale
109	Walton
110	Morgan
111	Oconee
112	Clarke
113	Madison
114	Hart
115	Franklin
116	Stephens
117	Banks
118	Jackson
119	Barrow
120	Gwinnett
121	DeKalb
122	Clayton
123	Henry
124	Spalding
125	Pike
126	Meriwether
127	Troup
128	Heard
129	Coweta
130	Fayette
131	Fulton
132	Douglas
133	Cobb
134	Cherokee
135	Forsyth
136	Hall
137	White
138	Habersham
139	Rabun
140	Towns
141	Union
142	Lumpkin
143	Dawson
144	Pickens
145	Bartow
146	Paulding
147	Carroll
148	Haralson
149	Polk
150	Floyd
151	Gordon
152	Ellijay
153	Fannin
154	Murray
155	Whitfield
156	Chattoga
157	Walker
158	Catoosa
159	Dade

THE PAST, THE PRESENT AND THE FUTURE

ALONG THE BARRIER ISLANDS' shores twice each day low tides expose extensive sand bars running far seaward into the Atlantic. It is hard to believe that a drop of only 8 feet between the average high and low tides can add so much land to the state of Georgia. Now, imagine what a difference a drop of 350 feet would make as it did at the height of the last Ice Age. About 30,000 to 18,000 years ago (in the late Pleistocene Epoch) today's submerged continental shelf extended eastward as a vast forested plain until it plunged into the depths of the Atlantic. Approximately (an essential qualification) 18,000 years to 15,000 years ago (the beginning of Holocene Epoch in which we still are) the global ice cover began melting and sea levels began rising. Depending on the oscillations of global temperatures the ice cover expanded or contracted, yet generally the oceans kept on rising. Now and then the temperatures and sea level stabilized for a time leaving conspicuous landmarks on the coastal plain, among others the precursors of our familiar barrier islands.

Naturally, the formation of the main geographical features of the coastal plain as we know it today began a lot earlier—millions of years earlier. The sea levels changed drastically, although on a scale of time measured by millennia. At some point over 20 million years ago, when the earth must have been a hot place indeed, the ocean lapped the very edge of the Georgia piedmont along a line called the "fall line" leaving remains of marine animals imbedded in cliffs now hundreds of feet above the present sea level. Until the most recent Ice Age the temperature pendulum caused the borders of the ancient mainland to migrate back and forth and today geologists can recognize several shorelines which at some point of their histories met the Atlantic. When the sea periodically stopped receding these shorelines solidified into distinct vast bluffs but when the sea returned some of the less established mainland borders eroded into dunes and barrier islands.

The oldest parts of today's barrier islands, Cumberland, St. Catherines, St. Simons, Sapelo and Ossabaw, formed between 50,000 and 30,000 years ago. These ancient high remnants of old islands are today known as Pleistocene cores while the newer accreted land additions have been dubbed Holocene. Many of the barrier islands in Georgia today are a combination of the two, the result of the sea depositing and shaping a new supply of sand around the solid obstacles of the existing Pleistocene outcroppings. The Holocene islands date between 6,000 and 3,500 years

ago when the rate of the rising sea level slowed down. However, about 50 years ago the sea level began rising faster, in part at least, due to the increase of man-made atmospheric pollution and the resulting "greenhouse effect." Tentative estimates assume about 12 inches rise per century if the present rate remains constant. Conservative calculations indicate that the shoreline in Georgia will regress inland over 200 feet in a century.

As far as we know the first colonizers of North America crossed over from Asia spreading southward along the western borders of the continent. It is generally assumed that their descendants, described as Paleo-Indians, reached our shores sometime between 11,000 and 12,000 years ago. The coastal plain now called Georgia stretched much farther seaward since the sea level was 250 feet lower, although already rising at about 3 feet per century. What is known about the earliest indigenous groups comes from scarce archeological digs and dating spearpoints. Pottery remains, shell middens and shell rings from later coastal settlers pinpointed indigenous villages on Sapelo to about 4,500 years ago. The early inhabitants of the coast were definitely hunter gatherers and they probably developed pottery sometime between 5,000 and 3,000 years before present. Curious structures, shell rings, appeared on the coast around that time. The one on Sapelo Island measures 300 feet in diameter, is 12 feet high and took an estimated half a million bushels of oyster shells to create. Bows and arrows first appeared between 1500 and 1100 years ago. Cultivated corn, squash and beans from Mexico turned up in the southeast of North America around 1,000 B.P. Even though these cultivated crops led to the development of large permanent indigenous towns, not much evidence of that era remains. Being biodegradable all these cultural traces disappeared beyond recovery and what we really know about the indigenous peoples comes from the records kept by the first Europeans on the coast of Georgia—the Spanish explorers and missionaries. From these earliest written reports it appears that two linguistically distinct chiefdoms existed. Guale people who lived on and to the west of Ossabaw, St. Catherines and Sapelo spoke Muskogean. The Mocama spoke Timucuan and inhabited St. Simons, Jekyll, Cumberland, the nearby mainland and the territory to the south. To the north Yamasee were indigenous to the area around the Savannah River estuary and southern South Carolina. Later, several other groups moved to the coastal regions under pressures from European invaders. Westo arrived from the west settling in the present site of Augusta. Savannah River, which of course runs through Augusta, was for a time known as the Westoe. These people were replaced in 1681 by a band of Shawnee named Savana and so the longest river in Georgia owes its latest name to them.

In 1520, the first Spanish reached the barrier islands of Georgia—relatively inconsequential intrusions. However, in 1540 Hernando de Soto entered the western coastal plain on his way from the west coast of Florida into the North American interior. This extensive expedition brought to the indigenous populations the first experience of early European "values," greed for gold and senseless cruelty towards native people whose simple weapons were no match for 570 armored soldiers bearing steel weapons and riding 220 horses—frightening beasts unknown in America at the time. The excesses of Hernando de Soto who killed for pleasure—throwing bound victims to the hungry hounds being his favorite pastime—upset even contemporary Spanish chroniclers hardened by witnessing years of bloody violence during the other *conquistas* in the Americas. However, the most tragic outcome of his four year sojourn was the unwitting introduction of the viruses of smallpox, bubonic plague and others to which the natives of America had no immunity. The epidemics of these new diseases, reinforced by other European intrusions, eventually killed 90% of the indigenous population in Georgia and the southeast. Due to social disruptions caused by the wide-spread sudden and mysterious dying of thousands of people, the ancient, highly developed complex cultures led by hereditary chiefs began disintegrating into looser tribal groups.

In 1565, the Spanish established a fortified base in St. Augustine (Florida) from which missionaries spread north to Georgia. The missionaries usually infiltrated large indigenous communities and worked towards converting their inhabitants to Christianity and allegiance to the Spanish crown. Attractive items like iron tools, colorful European cloths, new crops like peaches and citrus fruit, domesticated hogs, all served to draw in converts. In return chiefs supplied young capable men as laborers and promoted Catholic canon in daily tribal living. Between 1595 and 1684 about 16 Franciscan missions were active on the barrier islands and the nearby mainland. Eventually, due to Indian uprisings, English sponsored slave raids and declining populations, the missionaries retreated to the barrier islands; the missions on St. Simons, St. Catherines and Cumberland lasting as late as 1683—1684 when they were destroyed by Indian raiders sponsored by the English in Carolina.

When the English settled in James Town in Virginia in 1607 the neighboring Carolina region (Georgia did not exist as a separate entity yet) became an outlaw country.

Equipped with fire arms and paid by the English the Indians chased and captured other Indians for the West Indian slave markets. Many of the indigenous tribes moved to seek safety around the Spanish missions in Georgia but English expansion continued. In 1670, Charles Town (Charleston today) became the center of the English in Carolina and by 1683 The Lords Proprietors managing the Carolina colony allowed only the captives from Indian wars to be sold into slavery. The high profits from this trade soon encouraged the new English colonists to develop an industry of slave raiding—after all nobody was checking how the captives were acquired. Charles Town became a major slave outlet for sale to the West Indies. The remote territory of what became Georgia, then "the debatable land" between Spanish and Eng-

Tabby ruins mark the old Chocolate plantation site on Sapelo Island

lish possessions, became increasingly dangerous for the Spanish and resident Indians with continuing attacks mostly by Westo and Chichimeco Indians financed by the English. Things turned ugly easily. At some point the English allied with the Savana Shawnees to destroy their previous Westo employees who had become too well-armed and aggressive for comfort. Georgia (then still theoretically Spanish) must have been the most lawless part of the southeast for all concerned with large slaving parties chasing un-allied victims down the Florida peninsula and the English traversing the area to attack the Spanish base in St. Augustine.

Despite drawing profits from the turmoil the Carolina colonists felt threatened, also. In 1700, the French established themselves along the lower Mississippi and the Gulf coast and as a countermove the Spanish took control of the Pensacola area and developed plans for taking Georgia territory and the lands west of Carolina. The French had a grand plan for uniting Indian populations all the way from Canada to Mississippi and so pushing the English off the coast. The Yamasee War in 1715-16, a big uprising in Carolina, combined with French traders getting a firmer foothold in the debatable land close to the Carolina colony shook the English into action. In 1721, on the grounds of a burned down Spanish mission overlooking a tributary of the Altamaha River, they built a settlement and Fort King George (today in Darien, Georgia) to guard against expected French and Spanish raids. Vociferous diplomatic protests by the Spanish and harsh living conditions led to abandoning the fort six years later but the Altamaha River became the actual if not official border between Spanish and English held territories.

The Carolina colonists continued pressing in England for establishing a buffer zone to the south and they were heard. Sir Robert Mountgomery, a Scottish baronet, proposed a region to be called Margravate of Azilia where soldier-farmers would protect the English possessions south of Carolina. The Lords Proprietors of Carolina granted him the lands between the Savannah River and the Altamaha River but due to a lack of investment money Mountgomery's plans came to naught. It was not until 1733 and the arrival of James Edward Oglethorpe on the good ship *Anne* with 120 settlers that the Carolinians began to have some expectations of future stability along their southern borders.

Oglethorpe's foremost job was to secure the territory of the new colony of Georgia as a buffer zone for the protection of South Carolina. After securing rights to a settlement on the Savannah River from the Yamacraw Chief Tomochichi, Oglethorpe brought his colonists from Charles Town to start a carefully planned town on a high bluff overlooking the river. The place where reputedly Oglethorpe shook Tomochichi's hand over the deal has a small memorial bench now overshadowed by the Hyatt Regency hotel. Oglethorpe, himself from a privileged background, was disappointed by his protegés. They did not much fancy his 1735 rules for the Colony of Georgia which banned hard liquor, slavery, unlicensed trading with Indians and the presence of lawyers. They were not inclined to work hard—"idle" was the word used in contemporary reports—and did not make good soldiers either. The Trustees for the Colony of Georgia in England then decided that Scottish Highlanders, born as farmers in poor lands and trained for armed combat from wee childhood, would do a lot better in the frontier situation. The Highlanders also agreed spiritually with Oglethorpe's high principles.

Though now he may seem an idealistic visionary, there was nothing wrong with his powers of planning and organizing the defenses of the colony named after King George II. In 1736, General Oglethorpe's Higlanders fortified a settlement named Darien on the Altamaha River where the first Fort King George had failed and, very soon after, Fort St. Andrew and Fort William were built on Cumberland Island to guard against Spanish invasion by sea. On St. Simons Island Oglethorpe's troops secured the land, built and manned Fort Frederica. The Spanish were losing what they considered their land in Georgia and may have welcomed the war that Britain declared in 1739 over poor Jenkins' ear. After Oglethorpe's foray against the Spanish in St. Augustine failed with heavy losses, the Spanish organized a huge retaliatory expedition. Fifty-two Spanish ships and 1,950 troops sailed in 1742 to St. Simons only to be ambushed and defeated during the Battle of the Bloody Marsh by Oglethorpe's forces of Englishmen, Highlanders and hard fighting Indian allies. Although the War of Jenkins' Ear did not end until 1748, Georgia became to all practical purposes a British possession challenged by the Spanish only in the remote backwoods.

When Oglethorpe appeared on the scene the indigenous peoples had already been in decline for several decades. The Indians last ditch attempt to retain some of their lands was the failed Yamassee and Creek rebellion of 1715 to 1716. In the following years the indigenous tribes felt defeated. No wonder that Oglethorpe, who presented a friendly attitude to the Indians in the area, and even guaranteed them the ownership of some barrier islands in exchange for the mainland around Savannah, got everything he wanted from Tomochichi. After General Oglethorpe returned to England in 1743 the increasingly numerous and powerful colonists continued to acquire more indigenous land in Georgia through treaties or purchases. Indians, despite official land grants, were gradually pushed south, first towards the Altamaha and then, in 1763 from the Altamaha to the St. Marys. And westward after that. In 1776 the new United States guaranteed that Cherokee and Creek nations would own their lands in Georgia in perpetuity. By 1802 Thomas Jefferson quietly promised to remove all Indians from Georgia if this state gave up its claims in Alabama and Mississippi. In 1827 new treaties and threats forced the Creeks to move again. In the 1830s, gold was discovered in north Georgia and the Cherokee lands were illegally distributed to whites in a lottery. In 1838 federal troops forced the Cherokees to march to new Indian territories on the infamous Trail of Tears killing 25% of the dispossessed.

Georgia was now ready for development as a prosperous white colony on the lines of South Carolina where black slave labor already enriched many of the land holders. A prominent group of the first Georgians, the Highlanders from Darien, strongly opposed slavery with the full support of Oglethorpe. However, the good general was recalled to England in 1743, never to return. Meanwhile, planters from South Carolina arrived with their slaves even though their claims for territory south of the Altamaha (where Georgia's border lay at that time) were rejected in England. The prosperity of these planters undermined the Scots' anti-slave convictions. In 1750, the Georgia Trustees approved slave labor and soon the clearing of trees for plantations of rice and indigo commenced. Forests of pines produced naval stores of tar, pitch and turpentine. In order to build ships the famous southern long leaf yellow pines were sliced into planks to use over the framing cut from the contorted limbs of Georgia live oaks.

The Revolutionary War of 1776 disrupted the growing economy of Georgia for a short time only. By 1786 the seeds of long staple cotton, also known as "sea island cotton," arrived from the Caribbean island of Anguilla. The planters on the large barrier islands, whose climate suited this cotton perfectly, were on their way to enormous wealth. When Eli Whitney adapted the old cotton gin to successfully process short staple cotton the planters expanded the cultivation of this previously less desirable cotton to the mainland. Savannah soon became the main cotton exchange in trade with Liverpool, England, a country which also needed rice. In response, rice plantations sprang up along the main rivers in Georgia. Both cultivations, very labor intensive, depended on an adequate supply of slave labor. The great plantations suffered a temporary set-back when the US Congress declared war against England in 1812 and the British promptly promised to free all slaves who chose to join their ships. Hundreds did and were taken to Bermuda and Canada only to be pursued by the planters or their agents trying to persuade them to return. Almost none agreed, to the great surprise of their ex-masters.

Although somewhat shaken, the plantations soon flourished again turning out cotton, rice, sugar cane and indigo. Shipping interests in Savannah prospered, too. In 1819, a local merchant group led by William

Scarborough sent from Savannah the first ever powered vessel to cross the Atlantic to England. The 98-foot 6-inch long *Savannah* had a 90HP steam engine to turn auxiliary paddle wheels and reached England in 20 days, a very good time for such a small vessel. Savannah contributed another maritime "first" in 1834 when the town launched the first American iron ship, the 100-foot *John Randalph*. The owner Gazaway B. Lamar had the pieces of the ship built in Birkenhead, Scotland before shipping them over to Savannah. The ship was assembled locally and did a profitable duty in river trading. The Ships of the Sea Museum in Savannah displays excellent models of these vessels.

At about the same time Georgia turned to manufacturing cloth from its cotton. The first mill appeared in

You should never miss an invitation to a low country boil, a feast of local seafoods, like this one prepared by the Mixson family.

1829 employing poor whites and some slaves. By 1860, four out of nine inhabitants of Georgia were slaves owned by the richest citizens—one tenth of Georgians holding nine tenths of the state's wealth. In demographic terms Georgia was very unbalanced with half of the free citizens owning no land in one of the ten richest states in the Union.

In 1861, Georgia joined the Confederacy against the Union. Initially, except for the blockade of the coast, the war had little effect on the average citizen's life. This changed tragically when Gen. Sherman entered the state on his March to the Sea. Of all the major Georgia cities built on the proceeds from cotton only Savannah escaped burning, a Christmas gift from Sherman to President Lincoln. The Confederate states surrendered in 1865 and all except Tennessee were placed under military rule. It took until 1870 for Georgia to be re-admitted to the Union as one of the poorest states in the nation.

Now with the slavery system gone the plantations broke up into smaller units based on tenant farming and sharecropping. Rice production slowed down but curiously the cotton output actually increased. Savannah grew as the main cotton exporting center with an imposing Cotton Exchange building completed in 1887. Warehouses along the Savannah River supplied bales of the fluffy gold to a steady stream of shipping. Timbering again became an important part of economy. Darien, in the 1820s a busy port exporting cotton, rice, timber and naval stores went through hard times only to boom again in the 1870s. The Altamaha River made a convenient route to Darien to float down huge rafts of big old growth trees from the forests growing on its banks. On any day during the height of the timber boom there could be 70 to 80 large schooners, under all flags, anchored in the deeper waters outside Darien River waiting to load logs for England and South America. The last decades of the 19th century saw similar activity at the mills of St. Simons Island, Brunswick and St. Marys. Marsh hammocks emerged on piles of ballast left by these sailing ships.

Even with all those activities few Georgians could boast any wealth. The timber trade was financed by northern industrialists so most of the profits flowed out of the state. In the cotton trade the middlemen creamed the profits until cotton farming exhausted soils and, combined with the boll weevil, reduced croplands to red dust. Eventually falling cotton prices forced smaller farmers to sell and become sharecroppers. Despite the beginning of agricultural diversification to peaches and pecans around the 1890s, the rural people stayed poor. In the 1880s industrialists from the northern states began buying the abandoned plantations on the large barrier islands turning them into vacation and hunting preserves. Virgin timber was gone by the early 1900s to be replaced by pine plantations supplying fast growing wood for the pulp and paper mills operating along the coast. Until World War II there were only two cash earning opportunities for the unprivileged: the textile mills, which proliferated in the South and employed mostly women, or hiring out as farm hands. In coastal Georgia low key fisheries, with oysters as the most important harvest, and producing naval stores based on the pine forests kept people going. World War II brightened the prospects for the local economy. Suddenly, ship yards in Savannah and Brunswick expanded dramatically. Ninety-nine Liberty ships were launched in Brunswick alone in just two years of operation. Because of WW II the Eighth Army Air Force was formed in the Savannah area and this military presence continues in Georgia. Fort Stewart Army Base in Hinesville, Hunter Army Air Field in Savannah and Kings Bay Naval Submarine Base in St. Marys all employ many citizens.

Today economical conditions on the coast have improved greatly; livestock and crop farming, several active wood processing plants in coastal Georgia, large commercial ports in Savannah and Brunswick, commercial fishing (shrimp and blue crab) and services for recreational fishermen all add to the well-being of coastal Georgians. Growing recreation and tourism industries have become a substantial economic factor in Georgia pointing to the need for continuing protection of natural areas from industrial influences— an increase of 23% in the coastal population was predicted after the 1990 census. Considering the current economic expansion in the US this figure may be low.

THE COASTAL WATERS
IN DETAIL

INSTRUCTIONS FOR THE USE OF THIS GUIDE

Each of the navigational chapters has a section of text and photos followed by the chartlets that pertain to that chapter. The size of the chartlets and lack of magnetic variation information make them unsuitable for plotting. For plotting courses and positions through offshore waters and within major sounds navigators must use NOAA charts for Georgia: 11502, 11503, 11504, 11506, 11508, 11509, 11510, 11511, and 11512. All distances are in **nautical miles** with a nautical mile marked on each chartlet. The Savannah River maps refer to statue miles although each Savannah River chartlet also has a nautical mile drawn on it.

The description of the coast progresses from north to south. Within each chapter we begin with the Atlantic coast—in this case always a major barrier island. The information about the anchorages and attractions around the islands follows. All the rivers running inland are treated in the sections entitled *Waters West of The Intracoastal Waterway*. The Intracoastal Waterway has its own chapter—Chapter I.

The qualifier "springs" that we use in describing tidal phenomena refers to the maximum high tide and low tide values. The opposite term is "neaps" and describes the minimum tidal differences. For instance, on some dates at the same exact geographical point the difference between sea level at low water and high water (called the range of the tide) may reach 11 feet while on other days it will be 6 feet. On these extreme days the actual depth of water at low tide will be less than the officially charted depth (in the US chart depths refer to Mean Low Water) and such *spring* tides are prefixed in the tide tables by (-). A skipper navigating by the NOAA charts without consulting the tide tables for the day can run aground in places charted as having deeper water. Since this discrepancy may reach as much as 3 feet we attempted to reduce the soundings on our chartlets to low water springs which should forewarn mariners navigating without the current tide tables aboard.

The piloting information below should be used in conjunction with the chartlets illustrating the area under discussion. The chartlets are oriented with true north at the top of the map. The soundings are reduced to Low Water Springs and only rarely will the astronomical tides drop below these values.

KEY TO ABBREVIATIONS AND SYMBOLS

⚓	anchorage	AWMA .... Altamaha Wildfowl Management Area	N .... nun buoy
■	green daybeacon	Bn .... beacon	obstn .... obstruction
▲	red daybeacon	C .... can buoy	ODAS .... ocean data acquisition
◆	caution daybeacon	c .... underwater cable crossing	PA .... position approximate
◊	buoy	cl. .... clearance	Q .... quick
◉	spherical buoy	Co Rd, CR .... county road	R ....red
◉	multiple colors buoy	DNR .... Department of Natural Resources	RR .... railroad
▢	range		s .... seconds
!	lighted beacon	Fl .... flashing	SNWR .... Savannah National Wildlife Refuge
⚓	wreck	G .... green	SP .... spherical
⊞	submerged wreck	HW .... high water	SR .... state road
⊶	overhead cable	ICW .... intracoastal waterway	St M .... statute mile
c	underwater cable	Iso .... isophase (duration of light and darkness equal)	subm dol .... submerged dolphin
○	pile	Lt .... light	UGA .... University of Georgia
⑬	circled numbers refer to shore descriptions in text	LW .... low water	vert. cl. .... vertical clearance
		MHW .... mean high water	W .... white
		Mo .... morse code	WHIS .... whistle
			Y .... yellow

CHAPTER ONE

A QUICK GUIDE TO THE INTRACOASTAL WATERWAY

NEWCOMERS to the Intracoastal Waterway in Georgia, and in fact in all the coastal states of the Eastern seaboard, expect to encounter 12-foot deep channels at mean low water, which, as the charts say is "the project depth". This ideal, but almost impossible to maintain, depth was approved by the River and Harbor Act of 1938 under pressure from local business interests which promised a great increase in the commercial use of the waterway should the 12-foot depth be achieved. These deeper channels dredged by 1943 served well during World War II when barges could move vital materials over safe inland waters. In the earlier days, before highways were built to reach all inhabited points in coastal Georgia, the Waterway was important for transporting local products such as cotton, naval stores, timber, rice and oysters between communities and to major ports in Savannah, Brunswick, St. Marys and Fernandina, Florida. People traveled by boat in those days with over 150,000 passengers shipped between Beaufort, South Carolina and St. Johns, Florida in the peak years of 1921 and 1923. Interestingly, the first government dredging in order to improve the inland waterways between Savannah and Fernandina began in 1883. Since then the choice of rivers and creeks which combine to make the Intracoastal Waterway has been changed a few times, though some of the old routes are still out there, such as the Alternate Waterway. The changes followed a need to find channels which, once dredged, would stay deep for a time without constant work. In the final version of the Waterway there are still several places where meeting tides cause faster silting than the Corps of Engineers can cope with. Anyway, the importance of the Intracoastal Waterway for Georgia diminished gradually until now mostly pleasure craft, shrimp trawlers and occasionally fuel barges use it. The expanding network of roads in the state and in particular the completion of I 95 through coastal Georgia made commercial transport by land more dependable, faster and less expensive. The dredging to maintain reasonable depths in the waterway often lags behind natural silting processes. Consequently, vessels may encounter less than 6 feet at spring low tides—skippers should watch their depthsounders even in the middle of marked chan-

nels. Below we indicate several places where shoaling habitually occurs.

SAVANNAH RIVER TO ISLE OF HOPE

A southbound vessel leaving South Carolina and heading for Georgia will encounter the first shallow spot in Field's Cut, just before it joins Savannah River. In the span of three months during the winter of 1999/2000 depths of 20 feet suddenly shoaled to 4 feet as indicated on chartlet ICW #001. Calibougue Sound offers an alternate way to Savannah River and the Intracoastal Waterway southward. See Chapter III, the section *Waters East of the Intracoastal Waterway*, chartlet #03. Another point to consider at this junction is that some very large ships steam through the Savannah River and by law they have the right of way. It seems commonsense that a small pleasure craft would stay out of the way of a 500-foot freighter drawing 40 feet in a narrow channel 42 feet deep. Yet, we once heard a 33-foot sailboat discussing right of way for crossing the Savannah River with the pilot on the bridge of just such a ship. It is worth adding that even in open waters a sailboat only has the right of way over motor vessels when she is actually sailing. Switching to auxiliary power makes that sailboat just another motor vessel. And a boat that is being propelled by sail only, still has to give way to tugboats, fishing boats engaged in fishing and several other vessels as listed in the International Regulations for Preventing Collisions at Sea, often referred to as Colregs. A copy of these, issued by the US Coast Guard as Navigation Rules, must be on board all US vessels.

Once across the Savannah River the Waterway passes St. Augustine Creek, a deep river where yachts up to 45 feet LOA can anchor and enjoy the marsh views. A southbound boat navigating between the Waterway markers will find a minimum of 11-foot depths until Causton Bluff Bridge. Use VHF channel 16 or 13 to communicate with the bridge tender or, if their radio is down, call 912-897-2511. The vertical clearance when closed is 21 feet at high tide. Monday through Friday the bridge does not between 6:30 A.M. and 9:00 A.M. However, if you are already there and waiting it will open at 7:00 A.M. and at 8:00 A.M. After that it opens on demand until a prolonged closing for rush hour traffic between 4:30 P.M. and 6:30 P.M. Again, the bridge will open at 5:30 P.M. for any boat already waiting. During holidays and weekends the bridge opens on demand.

About two miles south of the Causton Bluff Bridge you enter Thunderbolt, the location of major boat facilities in the Savannah area. On the west shore just before the fixed 65-foot clearance HWY 80 bridge sits Hinckley Marine Services offering transient dockage as well as repair services with a 35-ton travel lift. They monitor VHF 16/68, tel. 912-629-2400. See the Services Section for more details. Across the channel on the east shore is Savannah Bend Marina with transient dockage and fuel sales. They monitor VHF 16/68, tel. 912-897-3625. More details are in the Services Section. South of the HWY 80 bridge on the west shore you can find dockage at Bahia Bleu, VHF 16/68, tel. 912-354-2283, open 7 days. See the Services Section. Half a mile down river you can dock or haul out at Thunderbolt Marine, Inc. To arrange dockage or fuel call VHF 16, tel. 912-352-4931, and see the Services Section for more.

Less than a mile farther down you will see the entrance to Herb River, a deservedly popular stop-over anchorage for Waterway voyagers. You can leave your boat at anchor there and zoom over in the dinghy to Thunderbolt from where you could take a city bus (call 912-233-5767 for a schedule) or a cab to visit Savannah. Make sure to get permission to leave the dinghy at one of the marinas—you will find Bahia Bleu more accommodating. Continuing southward you pass the Savannah Yacht Club (members only). They will accept reciprocal yacht club guests only after your yacht club's dockmaster makes arrangements with

their dockmaster. Past the yacht club you have to take a sharp turn south at marker "40" to enter Skidaway River and stay in the Waterway. Often yachts misled by the conspicuous green marker "29" ahead make the error of carrying on southeast into Wilmington River. This marker is part of the system of aids which leads vessels navigating Wilmington River from the ocean. If you went that far you will see, right across from marker "29", the entrance to Turners Creek, also a big part of Savannah's sailing scene. Inside, in this river, you can find transient dockage at Sail Harbor Marina and Boat Yard, VHF 16, tel. 912-897-2896 or Hogan's Marina, VHF 16/9, tel. 912-897-3474. A small haul-out facility at Sail Harbor Marina and Boat Yard can handle motor yachts and sailboats up to 40 feet LOA for short term maintenance work including do-it-yourself, call 912-897-1914. See the Services Section for more details. Some yachts, up to 40 feet LOA, anchor occasionally a little farther up Turners Creek just past Sasser Seafood and Boatworks docks. Fishing boat traffic from up river forces yachts to anchor close to the east shore and limits swinging room in changing tides and winds. Larger yachts which would like to use the town's facilities like a large Publix grocery next to the river or the Post Office, a 15-minute walk away, may prefer to anchor out in Wilmington River. The best place to drop hook lies roughly between the Idle Speed sign south of Bradley Creek and the row of private docks fronting Turners Rock (as indicated on chartlet ICW #02).

The Waterway follows Skidaway River to Isle of Hope where transients can leave their boats safely and visit Savannah. Isle of Hope Marina offers transient dockage with the usual amenities and fuels. Contact them on VHF 16/68, or tel. 912-354-8187. See the Services Section for more details. Right past the marina you will see several local boats on moor-

Large yachts flock to Thunderbolt Marina in Thunderbolt.

ings. Sometimes transients anchor among them but be aware that you must leave the deep channel of the Waterway open for traffic which includes tugboats pushing large barges. Off the channel the water shoals rapidly towards the shore sparing little room to anchor.

SKIDAWAY NARROWS TO DELEGAL CREEK

Stay in the middle of the marked channel going south towards Skidaway Narrows as the deep channel is quite narrow. Skidaway Narrows Bridge, the second and the last opening bridge on Georgia's Intracoastal Waterway works on demand and monitors VHF 13, tel. 912-352-2733. A mile farther south you will reach Moon River, so named after Savannah native Johnny Mercer produced the famous song. It was simply Back River before. Traditionally a handy anchorage to transient yachts, Moon River is silting up. We found reasonable space for a couple of yachts just north of Marsh Island while the area south of Marsh Island has become very constricted and the approach extremely narrow and shallow. A much better overnight anchorage can be found farther on, about a quarter mile northwest of marker "76". Consult chartlet ICW #03.

As you travel on through the wide waters of Burnside River, Vernon River and into Green Island Sound you will find several easy to enter and spacious anchorages. You can drop the hook on the west side of Possum Point in Vernon River which opens up about west from marker "79". The Little Ogeechee offers several spots to anchor. Strong currents flow here and, when strong winds blow, it is wise to anchor near a marshy shore to windward in order to avoid the chop produced by the current running against the wind. Refer to chartlets #012 and #013 in Chapter III, *Savannah River to Ossabaw Sound* when you would like to navigate farther up the Little Ogeechee River to Coffee Bluff Marina (See the Service Section). In strong winds from an easterly direction an anchorage off Green Island south of marker "83" offers the best protection. See chartlet ICW #03 for depths and locations of all these anchorages.

The same chartlet ICW #03 shows the entrance to Delegal Creek where you can stay at anchor in perfect protection or tie up in the full-service Delegal Creek Marina located in particularly attractive surroundings with beautiful views of marsh and hammocks. Steamboat Cut, the approach to Delegal Creek, lies a quarter mile east-northeast of marker "86". All but very shallow draft yachts will need a rising tide to get over the 3-foot bar which crosses the marked channel. When in doubt about the entrance or to reserve a slip call on VHF 16

(working channel 68) or tel. 912-598-0023. For more details see the Services Section.

HELL GATE TO KILKENNY CREEK

A short jog through the dredged Hell Gate channel (chartlet ICW #04) demands extra attention because the strong cross current in the section between markers "87" and "89" tends to push your boat out of the channel and into the shallows. After Hell Gate an easy course through deep water marked by beacons leads towards the Ogeechee River until the turn into Florida Passage after marker "98". On the way you pass a good anchorage in northerly winds off the entrance to Charles Creek. To reach it from Hell Gate go around marker "92" and steer parallel to the marshy shore on Harveys Island. When approaching from the southwest you should pass close to marker "96" on Harveys Island and parallel the marshy shore. Other anchorages await farther south in the side creeks of Florida Passage. You can enter Redbird Creek at any state of tide. The mouth of Skipper

Isle of Hope Marina allows the opportunity to visit an old Savannah community and the city of Savannah itself.

Narrows carries only 6 feet at spring low tides and then gets deeper inside. Boats drawing over 3 feet will need a rising tide to enter the very attractive anchorage off Bear Island in Queen Bess Creek. A little farther south you can anchor in Cane Patch Creek which you enter by going east after passing marker "102". You will find deep water and attractive surroundings less than a mile in from the entrance. Chartlet ICW #04 illustrates this section of the Waterway.

The stretch of the Waterway on Bear River runs deep within the well marked channel. Easy to enter anchorages surrounded by extensive marshes await in Little Tom Creek and Big Tom Creek. Then comes Kilkenny Creek with Kilkenny Marina 1.5 miles from the entrance. The marina offers tie-ups along a floating dock of modest length so call VHF 16, or tel. 912-727-2215 to get a reservation well in advance if the season is in full swing. Kilkenny Marina is an important re-fueling stop for motor yachts. Lincoln Creek, a branch of Kilkenny Creek offers a good protected anchorage away from Kilkenny Creek which has a lot of shrimp boat traffic at all hours. Consult chartlet ICW #05 for detailed depth information.

FROM KILKENNY CREEK TO WAHOO RIVER

Next, the Waterway runs into the wide open St. Catherines Sound and then makes a jog to the south-west into North Newport River. You will pass Newell Creek, to the east, tricky to enter and quite narrow, as can be deduced from chartlet ICW #06. Wallburg Creek, ahead on St. Catherines Island provides a good anchorage. When heading for it from the north make sure to go far enough east in order to clear Middle Ground shoals. You can approach the north shore of St. Catherines very close and follow it south into the anchorage. You can leave and enter through the south arm of Walburg Creek if you steer around the shoals as illustrated on chartlet ICW #07. As far as anchorages along the north side of North Newport River are concerned skip Cedar Creek unless your boat draws very little water. Although it looks straightforward on the chart the entrance channel is difficult to follow since the currents tend to set the boat sideways. Less than a mile south, though, it is easy to enter Vandyke Creek by steering close to its northern side. Consult ICW #07 for this area.

As you can see on chartlet ICW #07 it is also easy to enter and anchor in Timmons River by following close to its southern side. Then, almost across from North Newport River lies the southern entrance/exit from Walburg Creek. ICW #07 illustrates the situation of the channel with a least depth of 9 feet. North Newport River is not only easy to enter along its northern shores but also leads to Halfmoon Marina where diesel powered vessels can re-fuel and spend the night at a dock. Privately maintained and designed markers lead to the marina as shown on chartlet #031 in Chapter V, *St. Catherines Sound*

Delegal Creek Marina, a full-service marina, lies in a particularly attractive area.

to Altamaha Sound. The marina monitors VHF 16 (working 68), their tel. 912-884-5819.

The short stretch of the Waterway in Johnson Creek from marker "125" to past marker "130" is well-marked, but the deep channel is rather narrow and it is easy to stray into shallower water. Right after marker "127" to the east you can enter a popular anchorage in Cattle Pen Creek—chartlet ICW #08. Then, after you leave Johnson Creek and marker "132" you could swing to the north, pass east of marker "1" and then anchor anywhere along the marshy shore to the east. It is a rather exposed anchorage except in easterly winds so sometimes you may have to continue farther south to marker "135", then turn west for the opposite shore—chartlet ICW #09. When close to the shore, turn north along that shore and head into Wahoo River where you anchor in perfect protection off Wahoo Island.

SAPELO SOUND TO DOBOY SOUND

Next comes a long stretch of the Waterway, first through the often rolly Sapelo Sound—chartlet ICW #09, then straight west towards Sapelo River until at marker "145" (chartlet ICW #10) the course bends to southwest and eventually, at marker "151" goes south into Front River—chartlet ICW #11. Tides meet in this section making Front River and Creighton Narrows prone to silting. Despite frequent dredging the least depth here at spring low tides can be as low as 7 feet. The proper course twists and turns where Crescent River and Mud River meet but the range there helps skippers negotiate the sharp curve into Old Teakettle Creek. Well-marked and deep, Old Teakettle Creek continues south into Doboy Sound (chartlet ICW #12) passing first by New Teakettle Creek which has plenty of room to anchor. Then just before the Waterway turns west by marker "178" you will see astern, to the northeast, the entrance to Duplin River with its wharf for the ferry which brings visitors to tour Sapelo Island. After dropping anchor a little past the docks in this protected river, yachtsmen are welcome to join the day trips. You can find depth information to the area on ICW #12. The details of the tours and Sapelo Island natural attractions are described in Chapter V, *St. Catherines Island to Sapelo Sound*.

FROM SAPELO ISLAND TO SOUTH ALTAMAHA RIVER

From marker "180" the Waterway runs south passing several side rivers each offering an opportunity to anchor. ICW #12 illustrates the entrance to Back River flowing east by Doboy Island. ICW #13 gives entrance details to Rockdedundy River going west and inland. If you are interested in entering North River or Darien River also on the west side see chartlet #045. The details for South River located between Queens and Wolf Island are on ICW #13. Show a bright anchor light when anchored in any of these rivers as shrimp boats from the port of Darien (described in Chapter VI, *Sapelo Sound to Altamaha Sound*) pass through these waters even at night.

Little Mud River which runs by the west side of Wolf Island tends to silt up and, despite frequent dredging, may have as little as 4 feet of water at extreme spring low tides. The depths improve when the Waterway runs southeast into Altamaha Sound and then back west towards the north shore of Little St. Simons. There is a protected anchorage near the southwest shore of Dolbow Island and it is best approached by going south from marker "206" and then paralleling the Little St. Simons shore eastward into the anchorage. ICW #13 shows the distribution of shoals and deep water channels in this area.

The Waterway continues along the shore of Little St. Simons until marker "209" when it takes a jog first to the northwest and then westward into Buttermilk Sound—chartlet ICW #13. Deep water runs close to the northern side of Buttermilk Sound passing by Altamaha River. Taking the deep entrance into that river will bring you to a protected anchorage off Fridaycap Creek. A marked channel with minimum depths of 6 feet leads up South Altamaha River to a full-service marina 4 miles from the river entrance. Two Way Fish Camp is a modern facility equipped to take large yachts. They monitor VHF 16, tel. 912-265-0410. Next door is Two Way Boat Yard with a 40-ton travel lift. Their telephone is 912-265-6944. For more details see the Services Section and chartlet #048 for the approach soundings. ICW #14 shows Buttermilk Sound and the South Altamaha River entrance. Chapter VII, *Altamaha Sound to St. Simons Sound* has chartlets of the western reaches of South Altamaha River. When navigating anywhere between Doboy Island and South Altamaha do not get alarmed on seeing large motor yachts manned by men armed with automatic weapons. They are students and instructors from the Federal Law Enforcement Training Center located near Brunswick playing cops and robbers and learning how to protect us all. The Center keeps their yachts in the Two Way Fish Camp marina where men in training may be hiding behind the trees.

FROM SOUTH ALTAMAHA TO ST. SIMONS SOUND, INCLUDING ST. SIMONS ISLAND

Right after passing the South Altamaha entrance you should steer by the range "B" behind you to keep in the deep channel as extensive shoals lie to either side of the Waterway. South of marker "221" you should steer by the range "A" ahead. The deep water widens off the entrance to Hampton River. When in need of dockage or fuel you can turn into Hampton River, passing north of marker "27". A marked channel leads to Hampton River Club Marina 3 miles down this river. Deeper draft vessels will need a rising tide as a few spots along the course have only 5 feet of water at spring low tides. ICW #14 shows the depths for the entrance and the western half of the Hampton River which has the shallow spots. The chartlet in Chapter VII, *Altamaha Sound to St. Simons Sound* shows soundings for the whole length of the Hampton River. To reserve a slip or ask for piloting instructions call Hampton River Club Marina on channel 16, or tel. 912-638-1210. See the Services Section.

Farther south on the waterway yachts can find protected anchorages in several places in Frederica River. Most prefer to stop off Fort Frederica National Park where a dinghy dock makes it easy to visit this interesting site. For a history of the place turn to Chapter VII, *Altamaha Sound to St. Simons Sound*. Frederica River was once part of the Waterway between Savannah and Fernandina but dredging here was abandoned in 1938 in favor of the deeper Mackay River. When entering Frederica River from the north keep well clear of marker "229"—a shoal is building northward from it. The river itself is deep until its southern exit—see ICW #15 for soundings in Frederica River. A few hundred yards further on the Waterway, south of marker "229", you can enter into Wallys Leg with its well-protected anchorage shown on ICW #15.

The Waterway in Mackay River is quite deep and well marked. To reach Troupe Creek Marina in Troup Creek favor the north side of the entrance—they have floating docks for transients but sell only gasoline, bait and ice—see the Services Section. The only shallow places in the

Waterway lie on the east side of the river near marker "237" and a quarter mile south, close to the mouth of Jove Creek. Farther south in Manhead Sound when you see marker "241" ahead you could decide to run along the northeast side of Lanier Island towards St. Simons Island. You can anchor in this part of the river or tie up in St. Simons Boating and Fishing Club which keeps docks open to transients. They do not monitor the VHF but you can call them at 912-638-9146. They sell only gasoline, bait and ice and there is always a dockmaster on duty there. A low bridge crosses the way south along this section of Frederica River which was once the site of lumber mills and wharves and busy with schooners from all over the world. To rejoin the Waterway you have to return to Mackay River then go under the 65-foot clearance fixed bridge. The Waterway parallels the west shores of Lanier Island and then enters St. Simons Sound. If you would like to anchor or tie up before heading into the Sound swing south of marker "249" and then turn north again. Pass between markers "2" and "3" and follow the range ahead, it will lead you through the channel to the marina docks. Golden Isles Marina is a modern and large facility with all marina services including a courtesy car to do shopping. They monitor VHF 16 so do not hesitate to call the dockmaster when in navigational doubt about the approach. See the Services Section. ICW #15 illustrates soundings and nav aids along the west side of St. Simons Island.

ST. SIMONS SOUND TO ST. ANDREW SOUND, INCLUDING JEKYLL ISLAND

On the way south from St. Simons the Waterway crosses the wide open waters of St. Simons Sound and for a while, until buoy "22", joins the main shipping channel into the port of Brunswick. Brunswick, by the way, has a full-service marina and a boat yard nearby. To go there you continue in the shipping channel towards a large bridge to the west. Just northwest of the bridge you will see the East River with several ships along the wharves. Brunswick Landing Marina which monitors VHF 16 (working 68), tel. 912-262-9264, lies at the end of East River just past the last shrimp boat docks. They sell fuels and keep several large slips open for transient yachts. Brunswick Landing Boatyard, a full-service and do-it-yourself facility, operates a 50-ton travel lift at the end of the canal past the marina. Use the marina VHF and telephone number to contact them. See the Services Section. ICW #16 shows the approaches to Brunswick and the marina.

Sailboats and motor yachts of all sizes find shelter and services in the Golden Isles Marina on St. Simons Island.

If, however, after passing marker "22", you plan to continue south on the Waterway, keep steering southwest aided by a green range ahead until you reach marker "2". Do not stray off the course to the west—a submerged jetty lies just outside the channel. Follow the red range ahead and pass west of beacons "1", "5" and "9" and turn south into the well marked channel of Jekyll Creek. ICW #17 illustrates this approach. Jekyll Creek has always been prone to silting, a nuisance to the wealthy industrialists who owned huge yachts unable to enter the creek and who made Jekyll Club their winter hang-out from the late 1880s until the 1930s. Silting worsened after 1947 when the state of Georgia acquired Jekyll Island and had a causeway constructed through the marshes separating it from the mainland. After the most recent dredging you will find a minimum of 8 feet of water in the traditionally most silted area between markers "19" and "20". Silting occurs very fast in Jekyll Creek so if you are bringing a deep draft boat through here at low tide call one of the marinas for information on the latest depths.

Jekyll Wharf Marina usually has openings for transients along the outer dock, use VHF 16, or tel. 912-635-3152 for contact. This place has the advantage of placing you at the very entrance to old Mansion Row, an architecturally interesting area with a museum. A dinner restaurant, Latitude 31, sits right at the marina and the Jekyll Club Hotel, a step away, offers formal and informal meals at all times. Less than half a mile ahead, on the south side of the fixed 65-foot clearance bridge, you will find another marina. Jekyll Harbor Marina dispenses all fuels, keeps dockage space open for transients and has a restaurant, Sea Jay's Waterfront Café and Pub, right at the marina. They monitor VHF 16, tel. 912-635-3137. You will find more information about both facilities in the Services Section.

Soon after leaving Jekyll Creek at marker "25", the waters of the Waterway deepen as they follow parallel to the south shores of Jekyll Island, past Jekyll Point and marker "29" and then turn southeast into St. Andrew Sound, wide and open to the ocean swell on windy days. This part of the Waterway (chartlet ICW #18) makes navigators of smaller craft uneasy and should not be used in bad visibility or darkness. Unpleasant conditions may persevere until the vessel turns around marker "32" and heads southwest towards the waters sheltered from swell by Little Cumberland Island. At marker "33" you enter the wide and deep Cumberland River which is also part of the Intracoastal Waterway.

ALTERNATE INTRACOASTAL WATERWAY

JEKYLL SOUND TO CUMBERLAND RIVER

However, skippers of moderate size vessels who are willing to play the tides in a few shallow spots can go south without sticking their bows into choppy waters. Sometime in 1937 local watermen demanded and received the dredging services for a protected route between Little Satilla River and Satilla River avoiding St. Andrew Sound. The route is marked with signs prefixed by "A". Consult chartlet ICW #17A to see how to reach the entry marker "A2" in Jekyll Sound at the beginning of this Alternate Waterway. From the Waterway marker "25" (by Jekyll Island) steer about west. Consider carefully what the tidal current is doing—an incoming tide will set you towards the shoal to the north of the course. Pass south of marker "A2" and head south into Little Satilla River steering between markers "A3" and "A4". Round marker "A5" and head into Umbrella Cut next passing east of marker

Transient yachts are welcome at the docks of the Jekyll Harbor Marina which is well-equipped with all facilities.

"A6". After recent dredging the bar here carries 6 feet of water at low spring tides. Depths get better as you wind your way south through marked but quite narrow creeks with a minimum of 6 feet until you reach the Satilla River. Some of the creeks are so narrow that at low tide a 45-footer, 20 feet wide, may be the maximum size vessel to go through. Chartlet ICW #17A shows the soundings and the run of Umbrella and Dover Creeks to Satilla River. By the way, chartlet ICW #17A also shows the approach into Satilla River and the Alternate Waterway from St. Andrew Sound.

Next the Alternate Waterway takes you southeast into the Satilla River until you pass east of marker "A20" and head south into the Floyd Cut opening by marker "A21". Go over the 7-foot bar and follow the markers down Floyd Cut and into Floyd Creek which eventually joins Cumberland River by marker "A34"—all shown on ICW #19. From "A34" steer southeast for a quarter of a mile to pass north of Waterway marker "40". You are now back in the Intracoastal Waterway.

BACK IN THE INTRACOASTAL WATERWAY

CUMBERLAND RIVER TO AMELIA RIVER, INCLUDING CUMBERLAND ISLAND

As you can see from chartlet ICW #19 boats traversing this section will find good anchorages in Floyd Creek on the west shore, off marker "40", Brickhill River on the east side off Cumberland Island and then, farther southwest, in Shellbine Creek, off marker "43". Of these both Floyd Creek and Shellbine Creek are surrounded by salt marshes while Brickhill River has a forested shore along its east shores. Cumberland Island is a National Park—read about the island, its history, attractions, regulations and fees (low) in Chapter IX, *St. Andrew Sound to St. Marys River*.

On the way south (chartlet ICW #20) pay attention to the markers since south of marker "45A" several shoals pop up right in the middle of these wide rivers. Just south of marker "50" you will see nice marina docks—these are private. They belong to Cabin Bluff Lodge owned by the Sea Island Company. The Lodge, which specializes in hosting corporate guests, offers recreation like clay pigeon shooting, horseback riding, fishing and hunting on the thousands of wooded acres they own on the mainland. See the Services Section. Cumberland Dividings is where the incoming tide from St. Andrew Sound meets the tide coming from St. Marys Entrance causing a build-up of large shoals in the middle of the Waterway—follow the markers diligently. Delaroche Creek whose mouth opens

just south of marker "57" offers an opportunity to anchor but is fairly narrow until you go farther in. About a mile south Brickhill River joins the Waterway. Yachts often enter here to anchor off Plum Orchard, one of the mansions the Carnegies built for their family. A little farther on you can anchor in the north arm of Crooked River to the west. The southern, wider, arm of Crooked River opens up about two miles later after you pass marker "70". Before turning into that river to anchor, continue south until you are almost at marker "71", then turn west to cross to the opposite shore and then head roughly northwest into Crooked River. ICW #20 and ICW #21 illustrate the situation on this stretch of the Waterway.

From marker "71" first follow the west shore of Stafford Island to stay in deep water, then cut over to pass close east of marker "74" and next steer from marker to marker to stay in the channel. After you get to marker "79" expect a sudden change in nav aid appearance. You are now entering the shipping channel from St. Marys Entrance into King's Bay Naval Base and so you will steer between red even-numbered aids to the east and green odd-numbered aids to the west. For the Waterway users heading south the shipping channel begins at marker "50". Quite likely you will see a huge but low-lying whale-shaped nuclear submarine slipping along this route. You may be asked by a patrol boat to turn around or go off the channel to open the deep water for one of these ships. Otherwise this channel presents no complications all the way to marker "38" on the Cumberland Island side. If you would like to anchor off Cumberland Island turn north earlier at marker "40" and follow the shore of the island until you pass the docks at Sea Camp with its Park Headquarters and ferry boat landing. Anchor anywhere north of there—consult ICW #21 for soundings. Land at Sea Camp dock to sample the Cumberland Island trails. For information on the island read Chapter IX, *St. Andrew Sound to St. Marys River.*

To continue on the Waterway keep going in the ship channel after marker "38". You will see ahead a profusion of buoys and beacons. Some of them belong to the St. Marys River ship channel ranges and others mark the entrance into St. Marys River and St. Marys town. To go there turn west towards marker "2", pass south of it and steer southwest to pass south of the front beacons of two ranges, then steer west into St. Marys River which is marked farther in. ICW #22 illustrates the initial approach. Lang's Marina in St. Marys operates two yacht basins, one equipped with diesel and gasoline pumps. For reservations call VHF 16, tel. 912-882-4452. For marina details check our Services Section and for the river soundings see the chartlets in Chapter IX, *St. Andrew Sound to St. Marys River.* To stay on the Waterway after marker "38" steer parallel to the shores of Cumberland Island and within the ship channel buoys until marker "29". From "29" turn southwest to pick up marker "1" leading into Amelia River and the town of Fernandina Beach, Florida.

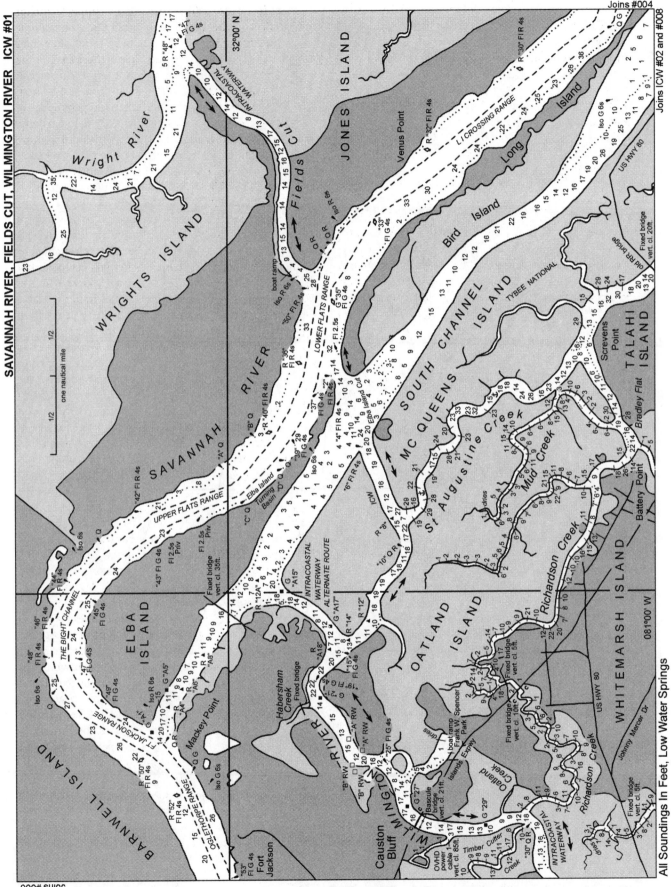

SAVANNAH RIVER, FIELDS CUT, WILMINGTON RIVER   ICW #01

Joins #004

Joins ICW #02 and #008

Joins #006

All Soundings In Feet, Low Water Springs

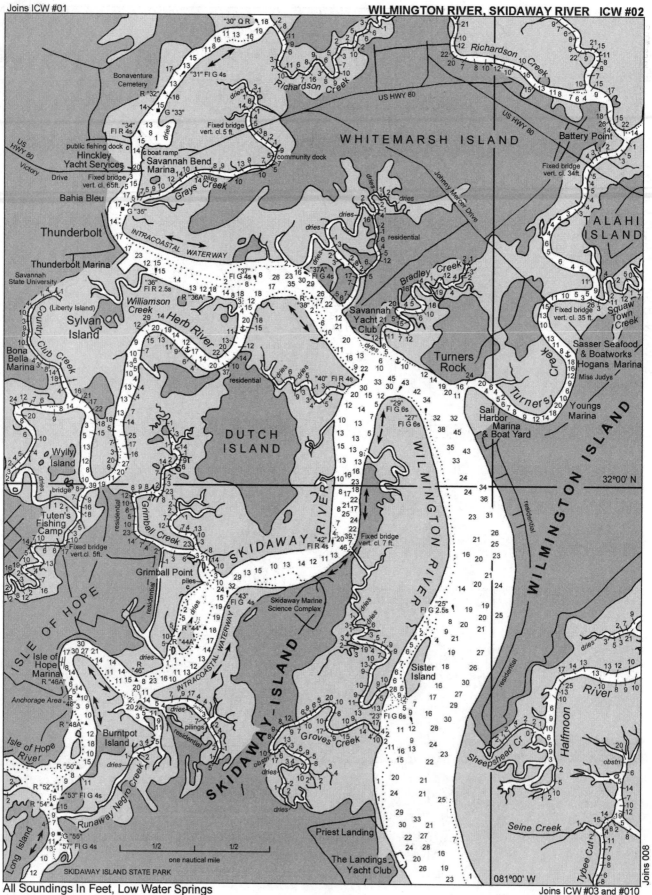

SKIDAWAY NARROWS, BURNSIDE RIVER, VERNON RIVER, DELEGAL CREEK ICW #03

Joins #007 and ICW #02

Joins #013

Joins #016

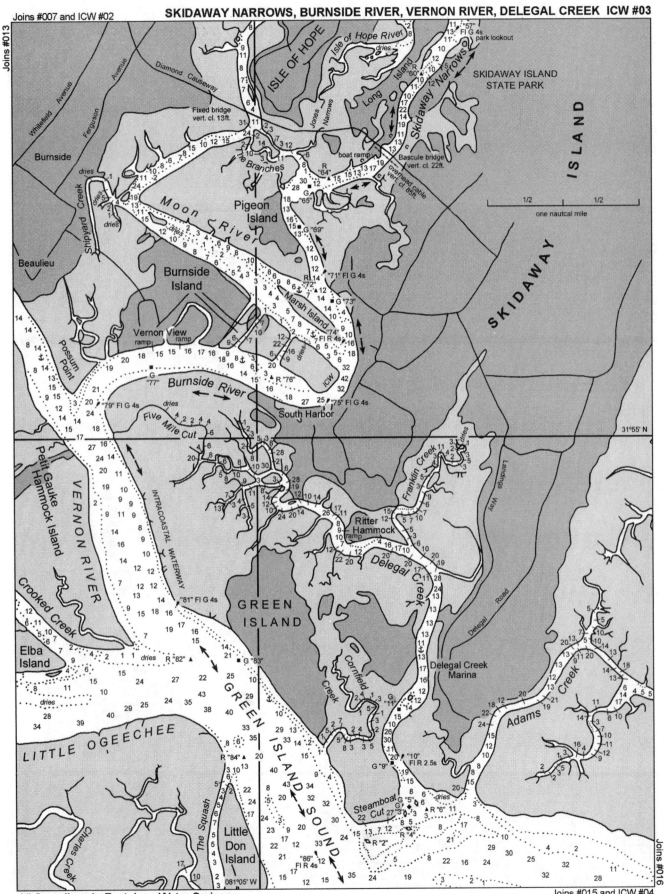

ISLE OF HOPE

Isle of Hope River

dries

"57" Fl G 4s
park lookout

SKIDAWAY ISLAND
STATE PARK

S K I D A W A Y

I S L A N D

Whitefield Avenue

Ferguson Avenue

Diamond Causeway

Long Island

Jones Narrows

Skidaway Narrows

R "60"

Burnside

Fixed bridge
vert. cl. 13ft.

The Branches

boat ramp

Bascule bridge
vert. cl. 22ft.
overhead cable
vert. cl 85ft.

R "64"

G "65"

Pigeon Island

G "69"

Shipyard Creek

dries

Moon River

dries

Beaulieu

Burnside Island

Marsh Island

R "72"

"71" Fl G 4s

G "73"

"74"
Fl R 4s

ICW

R "76"

Possum Point

Vernon View
ramp

Vernon View
ramp

G "77"

Burnside River

"79" Fl G 4s

Five Mile Cut

dries

South Harbor

"75" Fl G 4s

1/2   1/2
one nautcal mile

31°55' N

Petit Gauke Hammock Island

VERNON RIVER

INTRACOASTAL WATERWAY

Franklin Creek

Ritter Hammock
ramp

Delegal Creek

Landings Way

Crooked Creek

Elba Island

"81" Fl G 4s

GREEN
ISLAND

R "82"

G "83"

Delegal Road

Delegal Creek
Marina

Adams Creek

Cornfield Creek

LITTLE OGEECHEE

R "84"

GREEN ISLAND SOUND

The Squash

Charles Creek

Little Don Island

Steamboat
Cut

G "9"

"11"
R "10"
Fl R 2.5s

R "6"

G "5"

R "2"

"86"
Fl R 4s

081°05' W

All Soundings In Feet, Low Water Springs

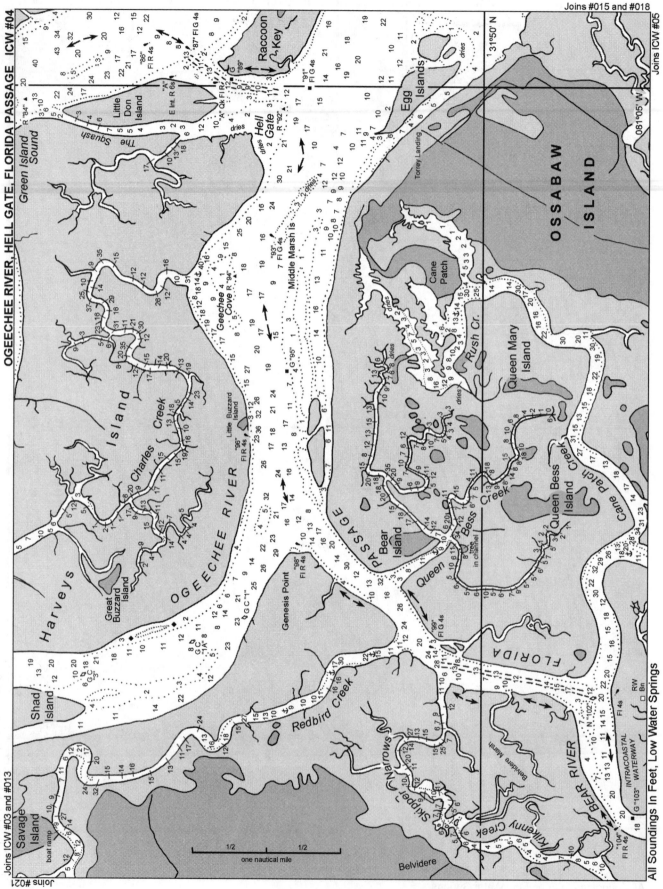

Joins #015 and #018

Joins ICW #05

Joins ICW #03 and #013

Joins #021

1/2   1/2

one nautical mile

All Soundings In Feet, Low Water Springs

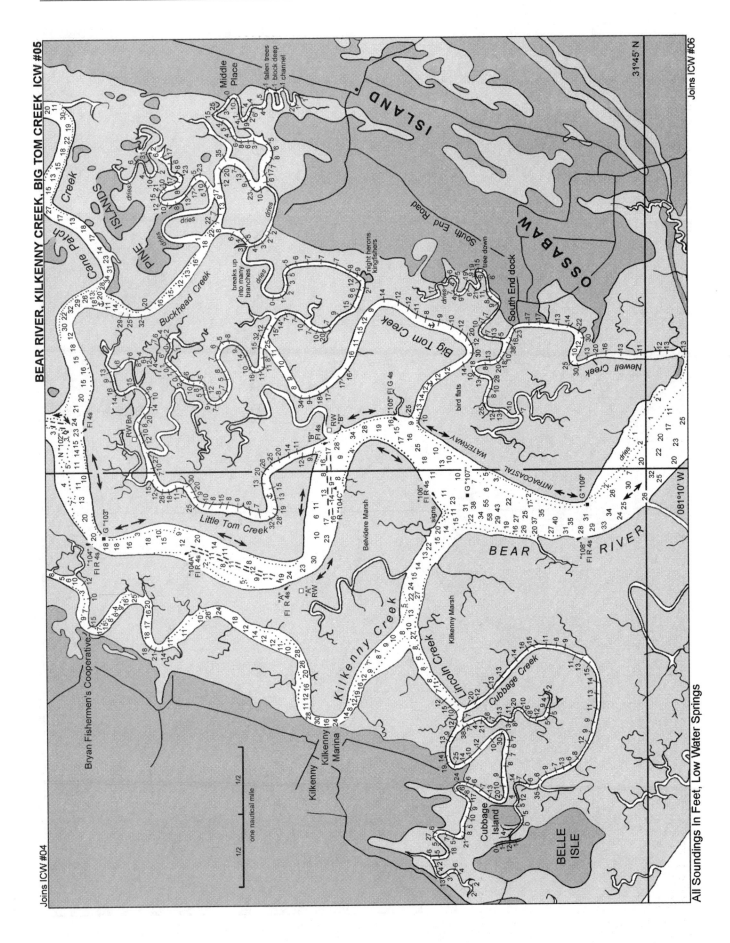

BEAR RIVER, KILKENNY CREEK, BIG TOM CREEK ICW #05

Joins ICW #05

Joins ICW #06

Joins ICW #04

All Soundings In Feet, Low Water Springs

one nautical mile

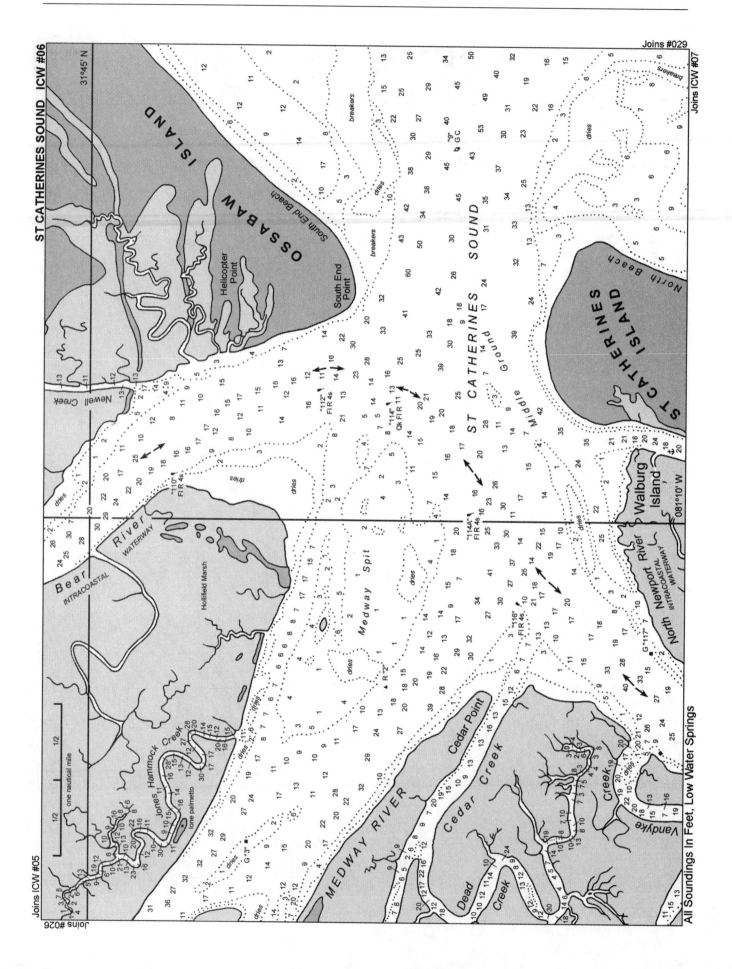

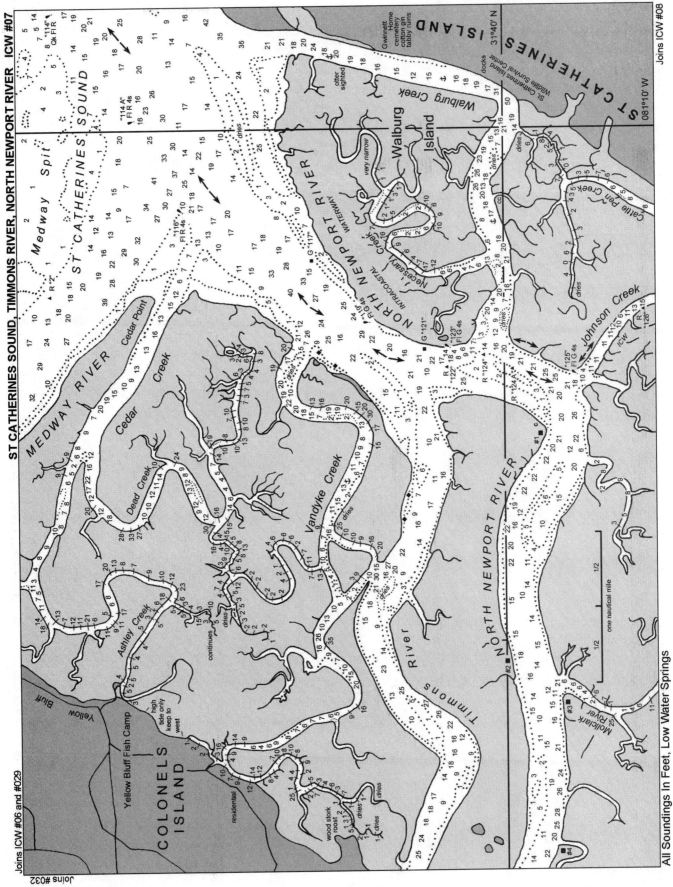

ST CATHERINES SOUND, TIMMONS RIVER, NORTH NEWPORT RIVER   ICW #07

ST CATHERINES ISLAND

Joins ICW #08

Joins ICW #06 and #029

Joins #032

All Soundings In Feet, Low Water Springs

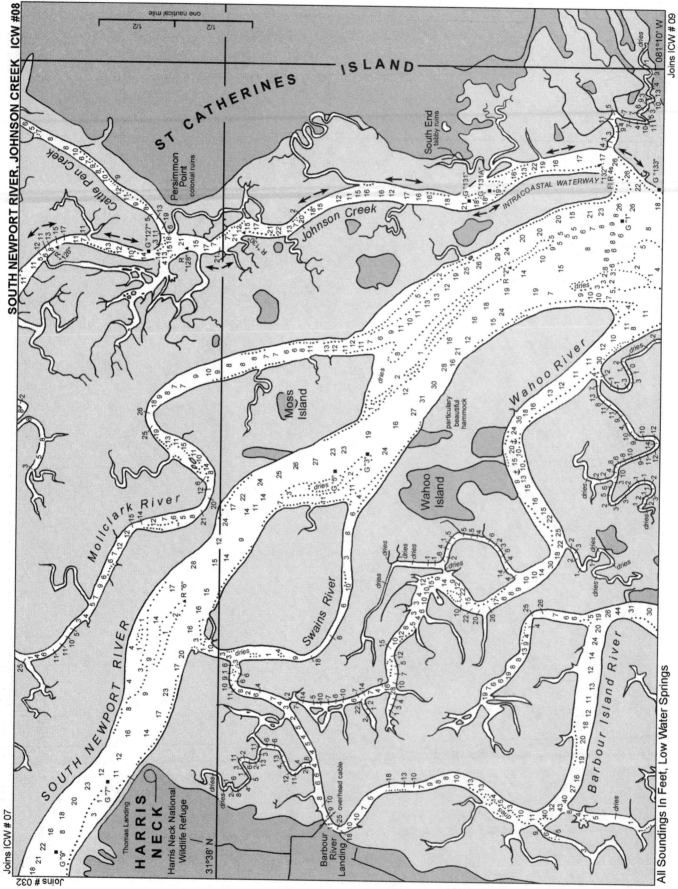

ST CATHERINES ISLAND

Joins ICW #09

081°10' W

Joins ICW # 07

Joins # 032

Cattle Pen Creek

Persimmon Point
colonial ruins

Johnson Creek

South End
tabby ruins

INTRACOASTAL WATERWAY

Moss Island

Wahoo River

Mollclark River

particularly
beautiful
hammock

Wahoo Island

SOUTH NEWPORT RIVER

Swains River

Barbour Island River

HARRIS NECK

Thomas Landing

Harris Neck National
Wildlife Refuge

31°38' N

Barbour
River
Landing

overhead cable

All Soundings In Feet, Low Water Springs

one nautical mile

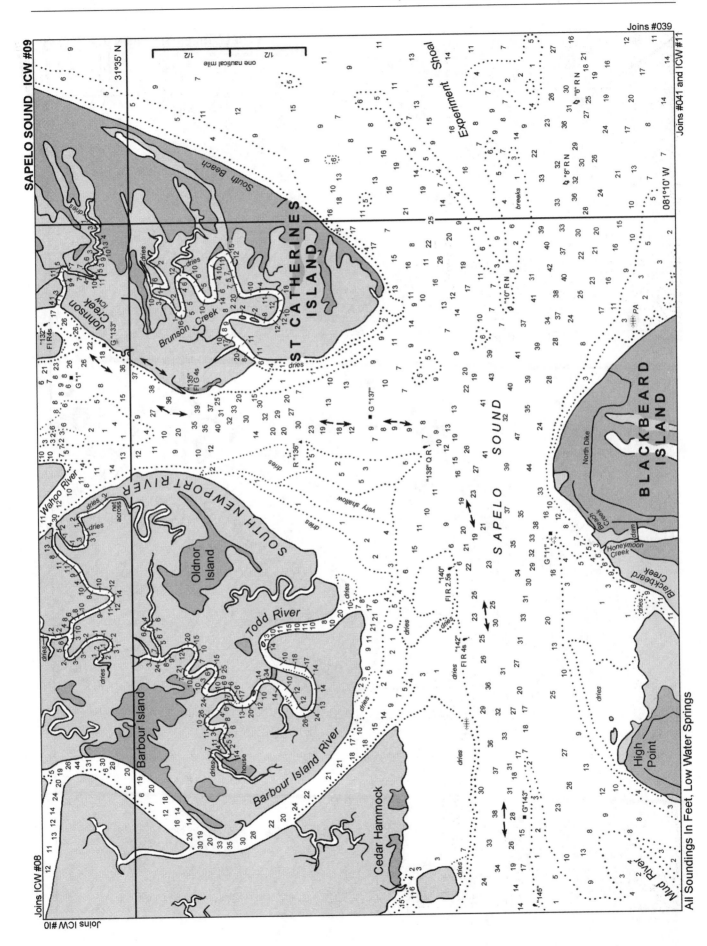

Joins #039

Joins #041 and ICW #11

31°35' N

081°10' W

one nautical mile

1/2   1/2

Experiment   Shoal

South Beach

ST CATHERINES ISLAND

Johnson Creek ICW

"132" Fl R 4s
G "133"
"135" Fl G 4s

Brunson Creek

G "1"

G "137"

R "136"

SAPELO SOUND

"138" Q R

"10" R N
"8" R N
"6" R N
PA

Wahoo River

SOUTH NEWPORT RIVER

Oldnor Island

Todd River

Barbour Island

Barbour Island River

Cedar Hammock

"140"
Fl R 2.5s

"142"
Fl R 4s

G "11"

North Dike

Beach Creek

Honeymoon Creek

BLACKBEARD ISLAND

dam

Blackbeard Creek

High Point

G "143"

"145"

Mud River

All Soundings In Feet, Low Water Springs

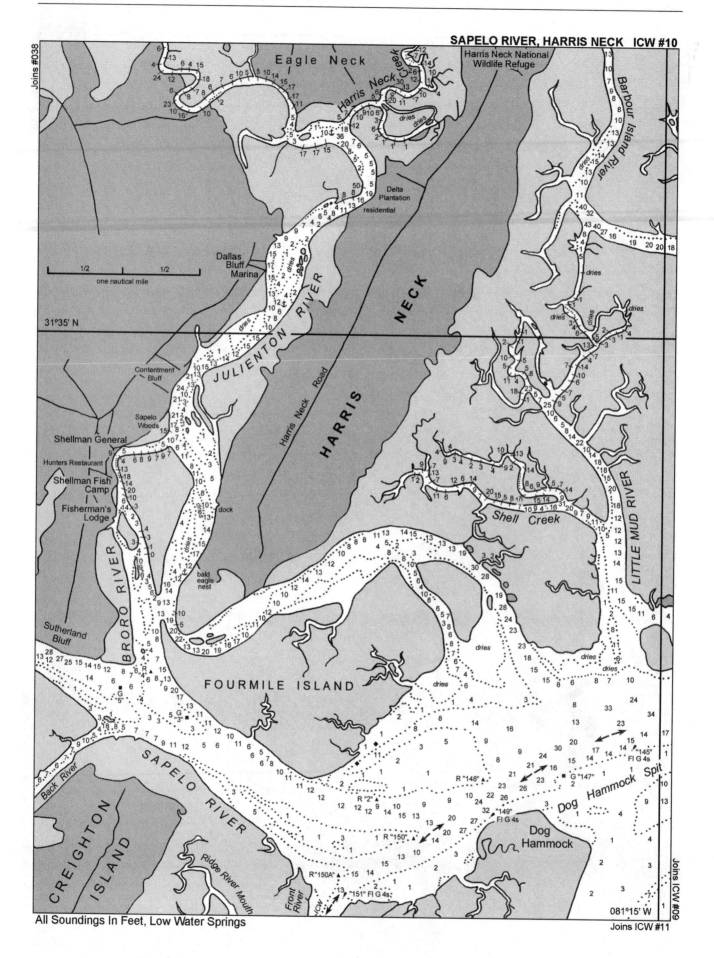

All Soundings In Feet, Low Water Springs

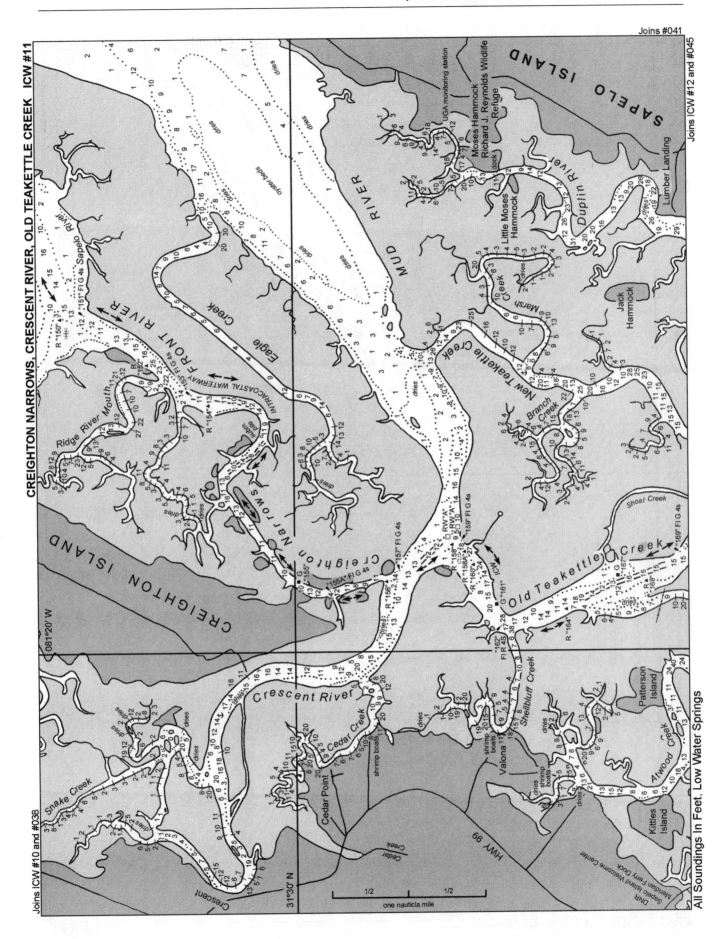

CREIGHTON NARROWS, CRESCENT RIVER, OLD TEAKETTLE CREEK ICW #11

Joins #041

Joins ICW #12 and #045

Joins ICW #10 and #038

All Soundings In Feet, Low Water Springs

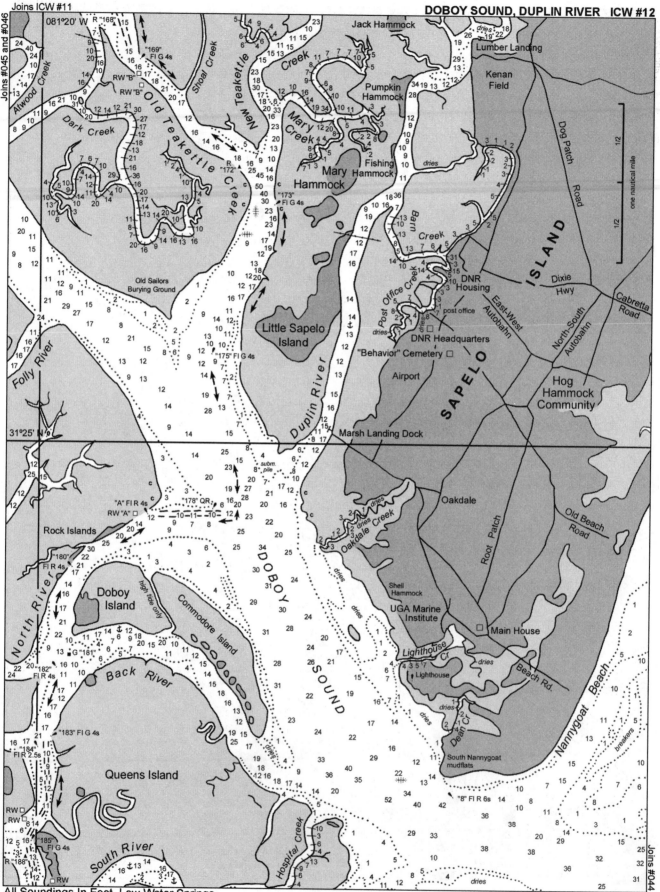

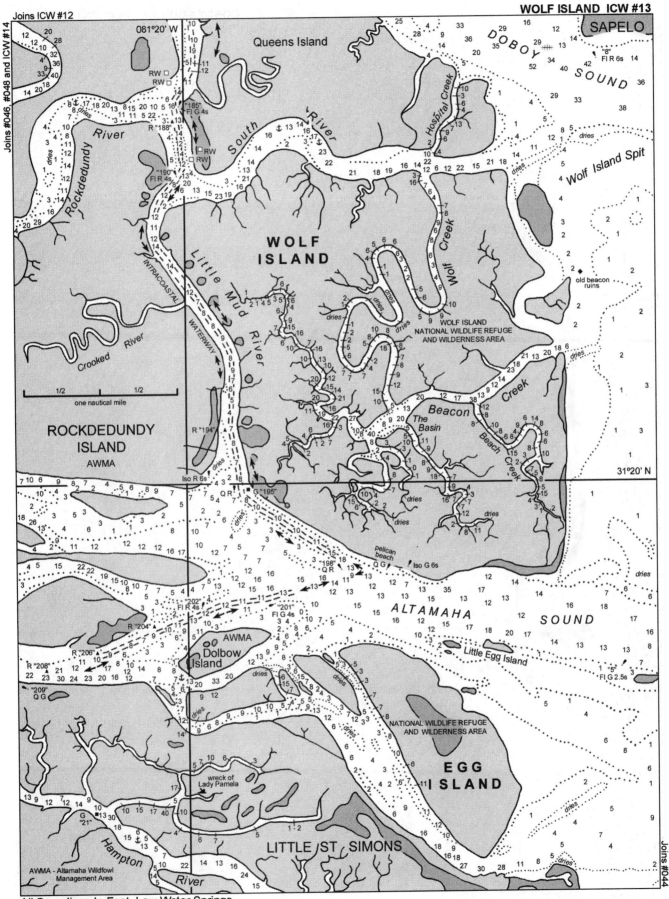

All Soundings In Feet, Low Water Springs

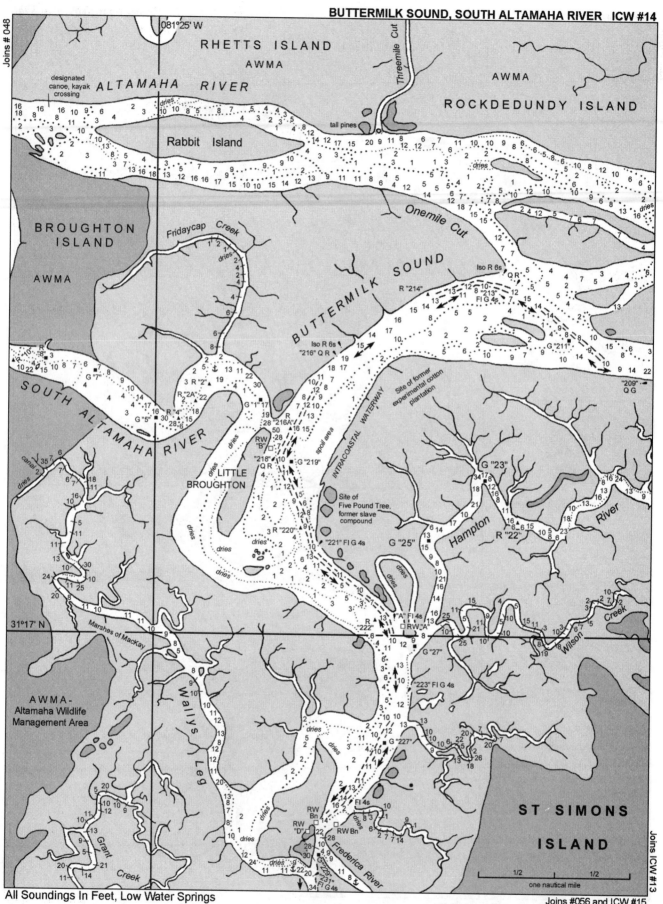

All Soundings In Feet, Low Water Springs

Joins #056 and ICW #15

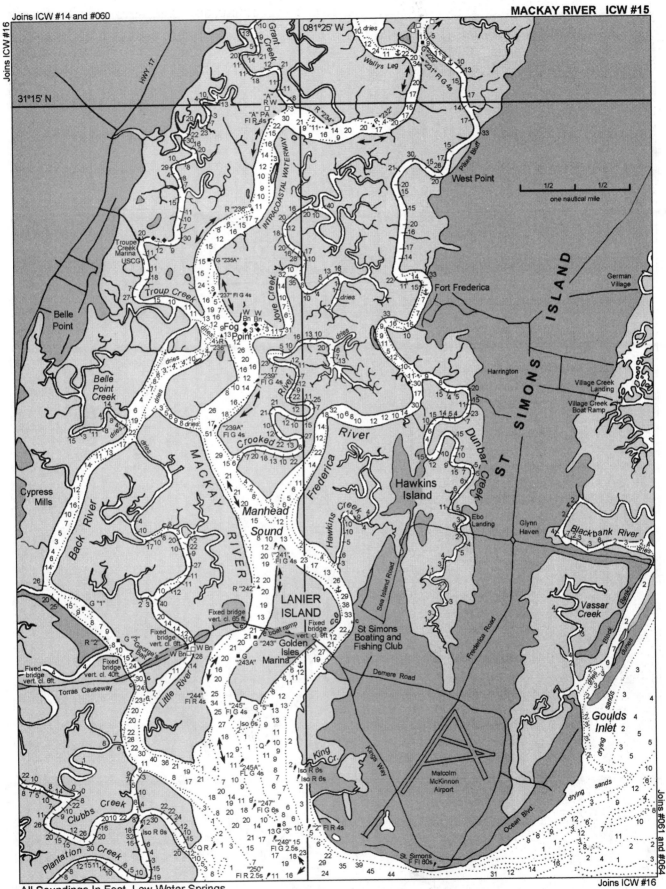

Joins ICW #14 and #060

Joins ICW #16

31°15' N

081°25' W

one nautical mile

All Soundings In Feet, Low Water Springs

Joins ICW #16

Joins #061 and #064

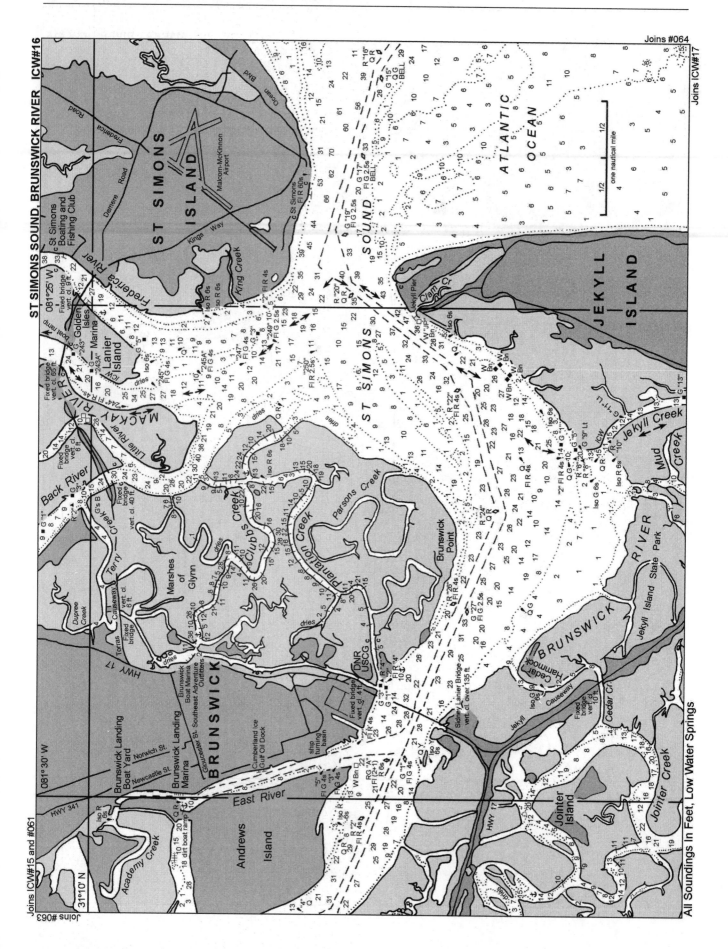

Joins #064

Joins ICW#17

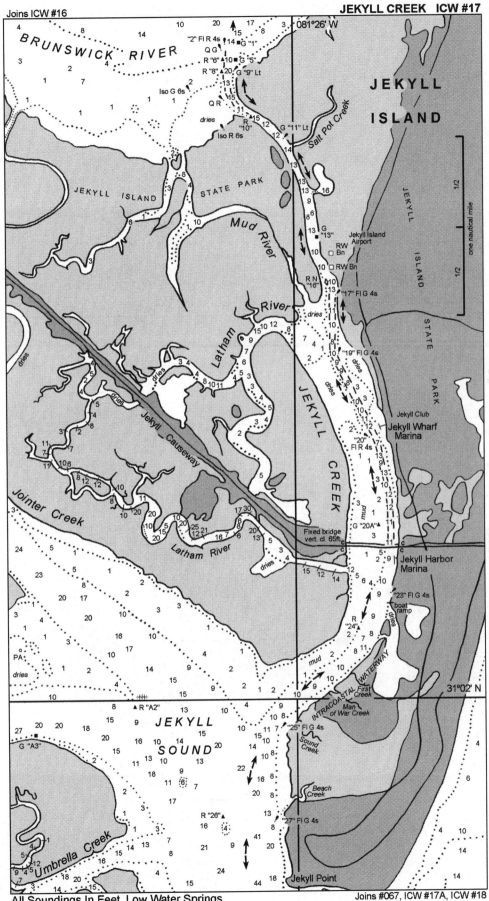

Joins ICW #16

JEKYLL CREEK   ICW #17

BRUNSWICK RIVER

JEKYLL ISLAND

JEKYLL ISLAND STATE PARK

Mud River

Latham River

Salt Pot Creek

081°26' W

Jekyll Island Airport

JEKYLL CREEK

Jekyll Club

Jekyll Wharf Marina

Jekyll Harbor Marina

boat ramp

Fixed bridge vert. cl. 65ft.

Jointer Creek

Jekyll Causeway

Latham River

INTRACOASTAL WATERWAY

Man of War Creek

First Creek

31°02' N

JEKYLL SOUND

Sound Creek

Beach Creek

Umbrella Creek

Jekyll Point

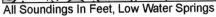

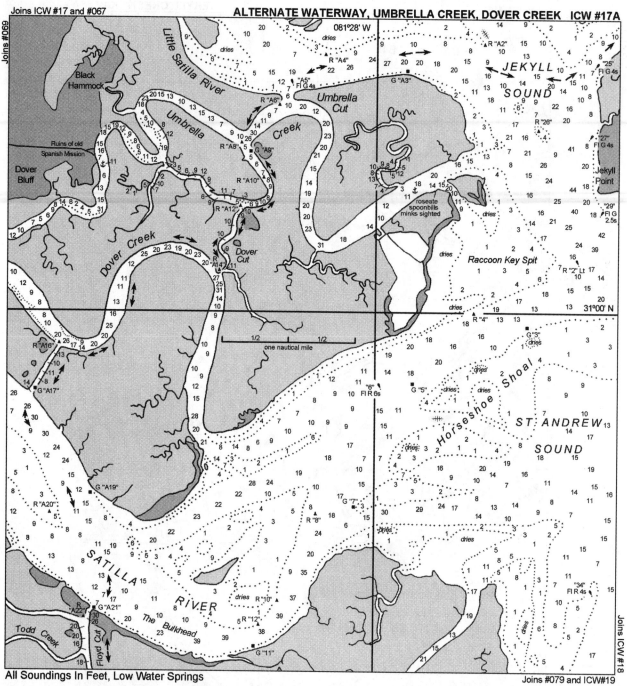

Joins ICW #17 and #067

Joins #069

Joins ICW #18

Joins #079 and ICW#19

All Soundings In Feet, Low Water Springs

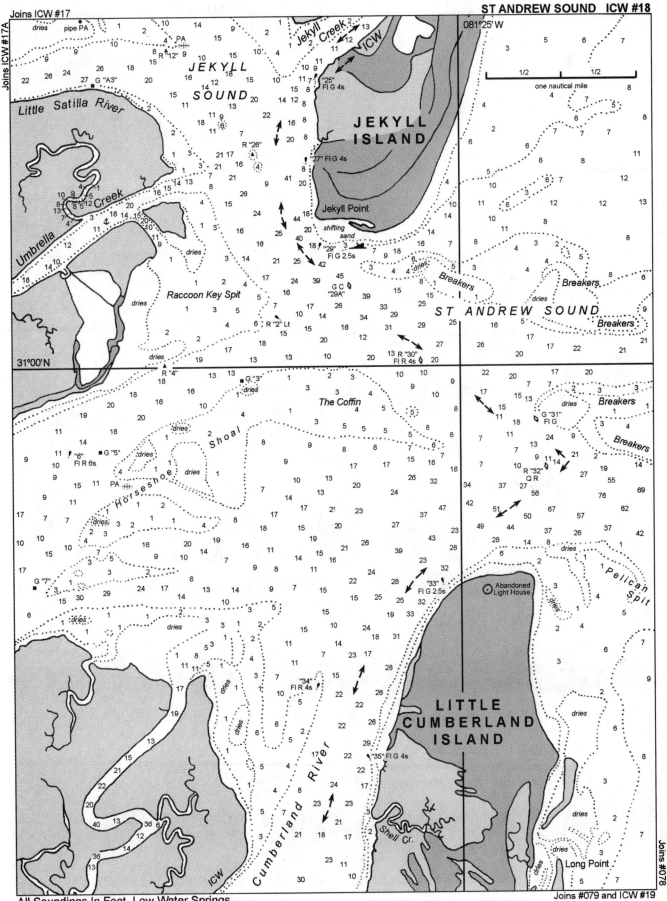

Joins ICW #17

Joins ICW #17A

081°25' W

one nautical mile

1/2   1/2

JEKYLL SOUND

Little Satilla River

Umbrella Creek

"25" Fl G 4s

JEKYLL ISLAND

"27" Fl G 4s

Jekyll Point

shifting sand

R "28"

"29" Fl G 2.5s

Raccoon Key Spit

G C "29A"

R "2" Lt

Breakers

Breakers

ST ANDREW SOUND

Breakers

31°00'N

R "4"

G "3"

R "30" Fl R 4s

The Coffin

G "31" Fl G

Breakers

Horseshoe Shoal

"6" Fl R 6s

G "5"

R "32" Q R

G "7"

"33" Fl G 2.5s

Abandoned Light House

Pelican Spit

"34" Fl R 4s

Cumberland River

LITTLE CUMBERLAND ISLAND

dries

"35" Fl G 4s

Shell Cr.

ICW

Long Point

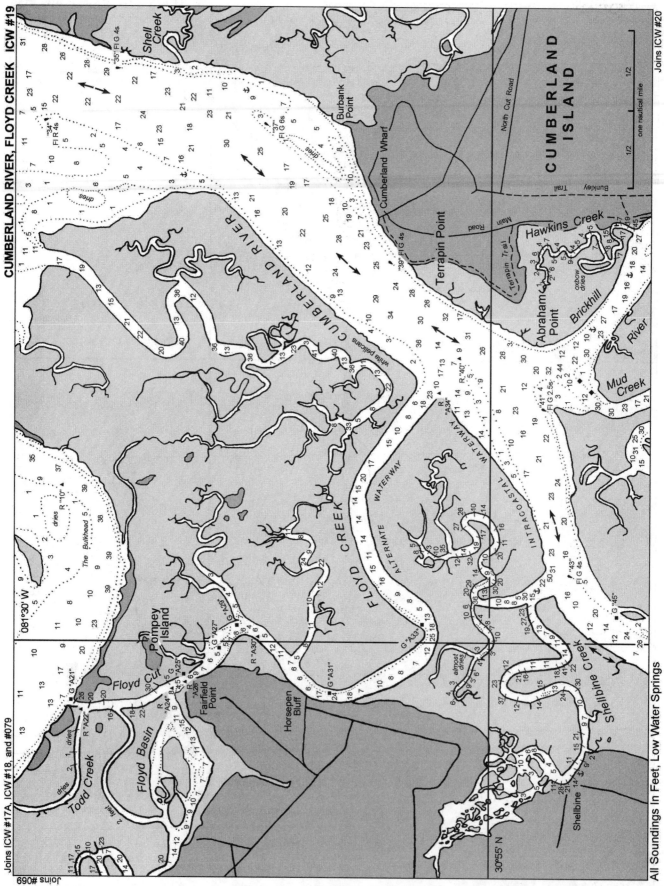

Joins ICW #17A, ICW #18, and #079

690# snioJ

All Soundings In Feet, Low Water Springs

Joins ICW #20

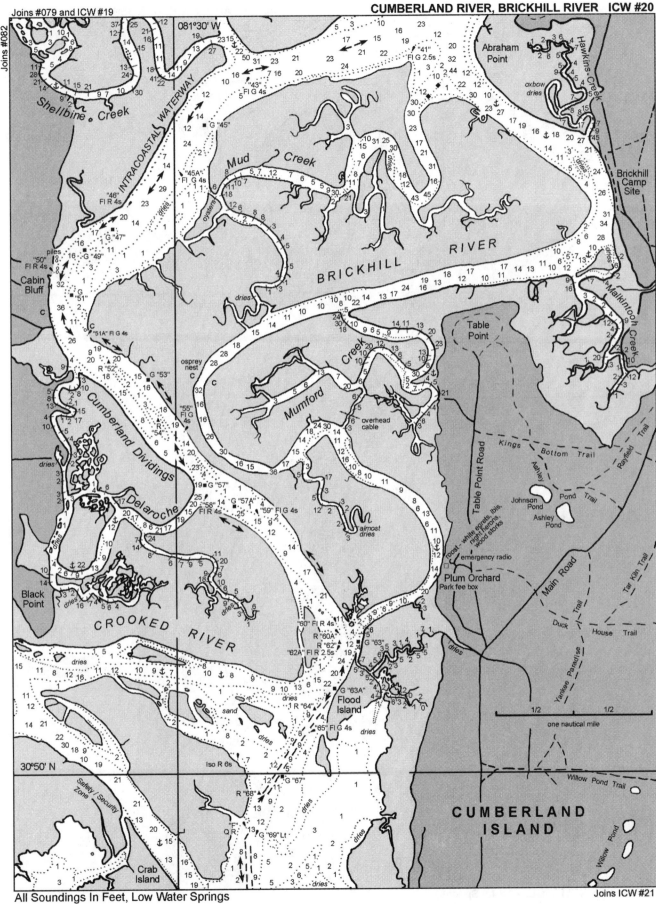

Joins #079 and ICW #19

Joins #082

081°30' W

Shellbine Creek

INTRACOASTAL WATERWAY

Mud   Creek

"43" Fl G 4s

"45A" Fl G 4s

"G 45"

"46" Fl R 4s

"G 47"

piles

"50" Fl R 4s

Cabin Bluff

"G 49"

"G 51"

"51A" Fl G 4s

osprey nest

R "52"

"G 53"

Cumberland Dividings

"55" Fl G 4s

"54"

Delaroche

"G 57"

"58" Fl R 4s

"57A"

"59" Fl G 4s

Black Point

CROOKED   RIVER

dries

BRICKHILL   RIVER

Table Point

Mumford   Creek

overhead cable

almost dries

Abraham Point

oxbow dries

Hawkins Creek

"41" Fl G 2.5s

Brickhill Camp Site

Malkintoch Creek

Table Point Road

Kings   Bottom   Trail

Ashley

Johnson Pond

Ashley Pond

Pond   Trail

Rayfield   Trail

roost - white egrets, ibis, night herons, wood storks

emergency radio

Plum Orchard

Park fee box

Main Road

Duck   House   Trail

Yankee Paradise

Tar Kiln Trail

"60" Fl R 4s

R "60A"

R "62"

"62A" Fl R 2.5s

"G 63"

"G 63A"

Flood Island

1 R "64"

sand

"65" Fl G 4s

dries

"G 67"

R "68"

"F"
Q R

"G 69" Lt

Iso R 6s

30°50' N

Safety / Security Zone

Crab Island

1/2   1/2

one nautical mile

CUMBERLAND ISLAND

Willow Pond Trail

Willow Pond

All Soundings In Feet, Low Water Springs

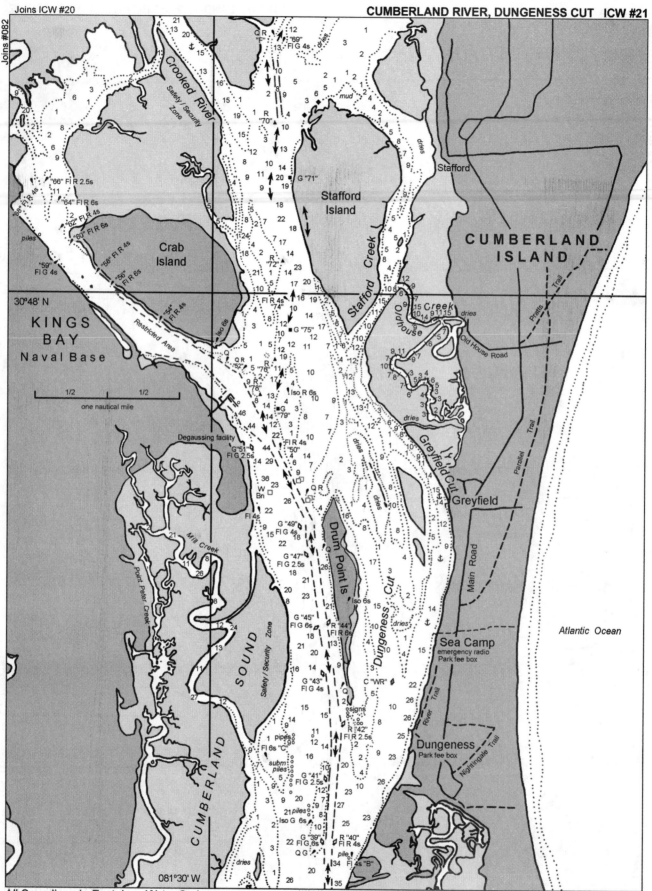

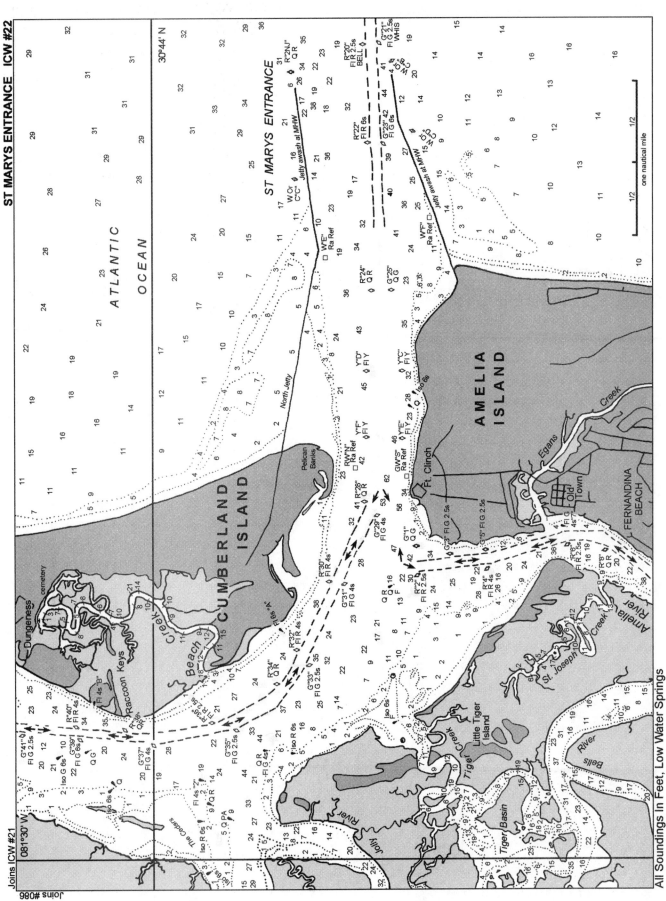

ATLANTIC OCEAN

ST MARYS ENTRANCE

CUMBERLAND ISLAND

AMELIA ISLAND

30°44' N

081°30' W

FERNANDINA BEACH

Joins ICW #21

Joins #086

All Soundings In Feet, Low Water Springs

CHAPTER TWO

SAVANNAH RIVER
FROM NEW SAVANNAH LOCK & DAM
TO PORT WENTWORTH

THE 187 STATUTE MILES of Savannah River from New Savannah Bluff Dam to the city of Savannah were a pleasant surprise to us. The river flows through forested shores with a very rare glimpse of industrial activities or residential development. The river is definitely deep enough for vessels drawing up to 6 feet to start in Savannah and reach the waterfront in Augusta through the lock flanking New Savannah Bluff Dam. The Lock operators require 24 hours notice and the lock opens Monday–Friday from 8:00 A.M. to 4:30 P.M. Boats awaiting transit can tie up along the wall below the lock. Near Savannah there are two low bridges which open. The Houlihan with a closed vertical clearance of 8 feet requires 3 hours (tel. 912-651-2144) notice to open and the CSX Railroad near I 95 requires 24 hour notice. The CSX has a closed vertical clearance of 7 feet. Further up river the lowest fixed bridge is the state road 119 crossing at Tuckasee King with a vertical clearance of 27 feet. However, most river users are kayakers, canoeists and small motor boat owners who begin below Augusta and get a boost from the current as they head downstream. There are enough ramps to launch boats ranging in size from outboard powered launches to canoes or kayaks. We list all public launching sites and describe how to reach them in the Savannah River Boat Ramps section. Paddlers who would like to take extensive trips and camp at night will find adequate sites on sandbars although at high river levels the distances between them might be rather long. However, the river will run faster when it is at a high level so manually propelled boats will easily cover longer distances. We took the soundings on the chartlets of the Savannah at a low level described officially as 2 feet. Tides begin to affect the river level around Ebenezer, slightly at first, but tidal influence becomes gradually more pronounced as you descend closer to the ocean. The depths that we indicate on our Savannah River chartlets all refer to a river level of 2 feet. Below Ebenezer the depths are reduced to the river level at low water springs which is below the Datum used on NOAA charts. In other words in the tidal areas we tried to show the lowest depths you can commonly encounter.

As you push off from below New Savannah Bluff Landing you soon vanish in a forested river, pleasant in winter when you can look far into the woods and spectacular in spring when everything turns green and birds break into song. Here are some highlights to expect down river. After you first swing by a river curve called the Head of Stingy Venus and then emerge from the Lower End (!) of Venus plan to slow down. With statute mile 175 astern (chartlet Savannah River #02) you will see on the South Carolina shore a streak of whitish silvery cliff which, as it rises even higher, changes colors to red and yellow—an evening sun really intensifies these hues. Named appropriately Silver Bluff, this shore is also a National Audubon Society Wildlife Preserve. In the corner of the north shore just before the cliff begins you will find a boat ramp—see Savannah River Boat Ramps for access.

The next great treat comes on the Georgia side after statute mile 150 (chartlet Savannah River #04) and after

Stinkhorn mushrooms add color and a strong odor to the coastal forests. The smell attracts pollinating flies.

the Georgia Power plant. Huge cliffs, over a hundred feet high, rise right out of the river between markers "70" and "69". The highest shore then recedes inland dropping gradually down to the river with a gentler forested slope. This area deserves planning your trip so that you can drift by in the morning to have the sunlight illuminating the cliff face. The cliff descends upon the river again around statute mile 147 in equally spectacular fashion. You may not land on the South Carolina shore soon after you pass mile 158, pretty and inviting though it is. The Savannah River Site (US Department of Energy) has closed the South Carolina shore from about mile 158 down stream to about Steel Creek Landing, half a mile short of statute mile 141. Another stretch of South Carolina shore closed for security reasons begins at statute mile 130 and continues downstream to about across from Little Randall Point, less than half a mile from statute mile 128. Apart from the unseen humming of top secret machinery, the 310 square-mile Savannah River Site also hosts and preserves extraordinary habitats with unparalleled diversity of plant and animal species. When, decades ago the site was nominated as a National Environmental Research Park, the government probably just wanted to learn about the impact of industrial development on a natural environment. What they found was groundwater contaminated by radioactive tritium, solvents leaking from dump pits as well as some radioactive fish and game. Due to the increase in envi-

ronmental awareness the cleanup work continues. Meanwhile, researchers discovered more thriving species of reptiles and amphibians at the Savannah River Site than even in the Everglades. Predatory mammals like foxes and bobcats, disappearing from other parts of Georgia, thrive here. Despite the logging of 25 million board-feet annually from the forests which cover 90% of the site, even threatened species like the gopher tortoise and red-cockaded woodpeckers have enough old growth longleaf pine to survive.

You will see more high forested cliffs on the Georgia side of the river around statute mile 147. Unfortunately, the best places to land for a closer look are marked with no trespassing signs. Just before statute mile 100 you will see the entrance to Miller Lake (chartlet Savannah River #09A). Enter this side channel and around the first curve you will begin passing bald cypresses which at the mouth of a small creek at the top of the oxbow grow up from huge buttressed bases. The dark interior of the creek entices a visitor to explore farther but at low water levels fallen trees block passage. A public ramp on the lake makes it possible to put in a boat right there and camp— see Savannah River Boat Ramps section. After statute mile 98, on the Georgia side, you will come upon the entrance to Brier Creek which begins far to the west in McDuffie and Warren counties and runs through Georgia for well over 100 miles before joining the Savannah River. A row of houses tops the high bluff along the south

The low level of the Savannah River allows a close look at the complex shapes of the riparian forest trees in Miller Lake.

side of the entrance. Past the houses a beautiful river forest begins, some of it marked as private, and then fallen trees bar any farther progress. Possibly at high river stages shallow boats could explore the upper run of Brier Creek from the Savannah—reputedly very beautiful.

Much farther down river after statute mile 58 keep a sharp lookout on the Georgia shore for the hidden entrance to Kennedy Lake (chartlet Savannah River #13) which may vanish behind before you know it. A 25-foot high bluff over the west side of the entrance gradually slopes down to the shore as you float between splendid bald cypresses ranging along both sides of the lake. Ahead just after statute mile 45 lies another treat—Ebenezer Creek (chartlet Savannah River #14). After entering this creek, past a bluff with some houses, the trees begin crowding together, growing so thick that you half expect trolls to peek out from behind the twisted bulbous bases of tupelos and bald cypress trees. Bald cypresses grow uncommonly slender trunks out of unusually fat buttresses and the bulbous bases of tupelos have this weird counterclockwise twist—a troll country, indeed. Aquatic plants like bog mat, duckweed, parrot feather, pennywort, the carnivorous bladderwort and mosquito fern cover the water surface in several places, their leaves shaped like the finest lace of complex design. Plant species vary according to the season but in late winter you may distinguish the mosquito fern when its tiny leaves turn the swamp surface into a saturated wine-red. At low water levels you will have no problem following the main stream and returning to it after taking side jogs in this maze of watery forest. However, local boatmen advise that at high water levels you may all of a sudden find yourself surrounded by trees on all sides without a clear way out. Water movement can be imperceptible. At such times carry a small portable GPS unit and jot down positions. A compass will help, too—the Savannah River always lies in a general easterly direction. The most amazing part of this forest grows between the bluff with houses and a boat ramp further up the creek. Easy access allows visitors to spend some quality time on Ebenezer Creek and, at low river level, you can land and have lunch ashore. If you do eat ashore please take your empty containers and wrappers back with you—unfortunately many boatmen on the Savannah River seem to expect some cleaning crew to follow their activities.

Back on the main river you may like to land on the Georgia side right outside of Ebenezer Creek. A privately owned boat ramp and landing operate on an honor system—leave payments in the box by the house nearby if launching. From the landing walk up the road to visit the site of New Ebenezer founded by a group of German speaking Salzburgers who arrived in Georgia in 1734 during the time of Gen. Oglethorpe's colonizing expansion. Their first settlement further up Ebenezer Creek failed and in two years they moved to the Savannah River site. The 1769 Jerusalem Lutheran Church, which stands there now, was built with bricks made by the Salzburgers

themselves. The settlement thrived on, among other endeavors, the production of silk. The British burned the town during the Revolutionary War and held it until 1782 when the Patriots booted them out. Unfortunately, most of the inhabitants had already settled in other places and only the church, a cemetery, some statues and a museum in the one remaining old home commemorate this important early town on the Savannah River. The museum opens between 3:00 P.M. and 5:00 P.M. on Wednesdays, Saturdays and Sundays.

Tides around Ebenezer may vary the river level by as much as a foot and a half and they affect the velocity of the current. Eventually, as you come closer to the sea the surface current of the river will reverse at the change of tide. By Abercorn Creek, statute mile 29, the tide range may reach 75% of the range on the coast although the high tide arrives there a good hour and half later. Until then you probably will not notice much of the tide until you drop down river and pass an industrial complex just after statute mile 43 and across from Little Kiffer Point (chartlet Savannah River #14). Keep away from the Georgia shore near this industry—a huge pipeline shoots out a powerful stream of hot water into the river. After that the river returns to a more natural appearance and at Coleman Run on the South Carolina shore, across from Hickory Bend on the Georgia side and a little north of statute mile 40, it again becomes spectacular. Coleman Run (chartlet Savannah River #14) goes inland in a deep wide channel, first by a pine forest and then, in its easterly arm, winds through another of those spectacular riverine forests of bald cypress, tupelos, red maples and other trees. Otters and raccoons feed on a plentiful supply of freshwater river clams. Back out on the Savannah River it does not take long to drop farther to another great place. Forks Lake, on the South Carolina shore, halfway between statute mile 40 and 39 (chartlet Savannah River #15), is smaller than Coleman Run but nearly as pretty and forested.

From Coleman Run down river the Georgia shore lies within the boundary of the Savannah National Wildlife Refuge. Just before you get to Purysburg at statute mile 35 you will find nice exploring in Meyer Lake on the South Carolina side (chartlet Savannah River #15). The entrance opens by the wreck of a wooden barge sprouting some interesting vegetation. Although the shores are less wild than the best places up river, Meyer Lake is a densely forested pond especially at the end of the wider water before fallen trees block the mouth to a small stream. Purysburg, a developed residential area on a 20-foot bluff on the South Carolina shore, has several docks along the river with some pretty large yachts tied up to them. After statute mile 34 and Mill Stone Boat Ramp the South Carolina shore of the river also becomes part of the Savannah River National Wildlife Refuge.

From now on the river shores assume a totally different character with forests on both sides composed mostly of slender riparian trees which can tolerate frequent flooding by tidal brackish waters. You will see relatively solid ground only at low tides. High tide turns the river edges into flooded swamps except around high bluffs covered mostly with pines and oaks. Soon after you drop statute mile 32 astern (chartlet Savannah River #15) look out on the Georgia shore for the entrance to Moody's Cut, a wide oxbow branch flowing around a large island. After the initial entry, in a boat deeper than a few inches, you should follow close to the north shore of the island to avoid running aground at low tide. After you pass the west tip of the island head south for the mainland shore. Just before that shore turns south, cut across to the west shore of the island before exiting into the Savannah. However, you may bump into some dead heads that tend to get caught in the south exit from Moody's Cut. A trip through Moody's Cut takes you past shores of grassy marsh alternating with willowy trees. After Moody's Cut several other exciting side trips await ahead down river.

On the Georgia side after statute mile 30 (chartlet Savannah River #16) you will see the entrance to Big Collis Creek—an extremely peaceful place with birds for companions and swamp forests on both sides. You will not care that the west side is privately owned and the east side lies in the national wildlife refuge—no places for camping exist here anyway. Next, at statute mile 29, Abercorn Creek joins the Savannah (chartlet Savannah River #16). After flowing by densely forested shores the creek hits a bit of upland on its west side which has an industrial complex with a barge dock, some houses then a boat ramp—see the Savannah River Boat Ramps section. After that nature returns and the narrow creek with minimum depths of 6 feet winds through swamp forest all the way to a small bridge (chartlet Savannah River #15). The wildlife refuge side of the creek is marked by the US Fish and Wildlife Service as closed to entry by people to protect wildlife—and you would have to be a dedicated poacher in a needle-thin boat to squeeze into that area. Earlier, about a mile south of the little bridge on Abercorn Creek you pass a fork into Raccoon Creek. Up to that fork, Abercorn Creek, though narrow, has impressive depths with a minimum of 6 feet and deep holes of 15 feet and 18 feet. Raccoon Creek itself forks into Mill Creek heading generally west through a swampy forest. Raccoon Creek, by the way, flows through the national wildlife refuge territory with the side swamps closed to human penetration but very beautiful to observe from a boat in the main stream. Raccoon Creek, about a mile from its connection with Abercorn Creek, passes under a small bridge—part of the road or trail that crosses over Abercorn Creek a half mile to the east.

A bit south of statute mile 28 the Savannah becomes very wide and flows under the 55 foot high I 95 bridge and then under the 7-foot vertical clearance of the CSX Railroad bridge which will open given 24 notice—call CSX at 904-381-4061. Very soon after the bridges the river heads almost directly south and its waters turn very choppy on days of strong southerly winds. After statute mile 27 the east shore by McCoys Cut suddenly rises in a 10 to 20 foot high wooded bluff which continues on both sides of the Cut and along Middle River until it turns into Union Creek. Union Creek, deep and winding, goes through wild forested shores and by grassy wetlands cut through with irrigation canals left over from the rice plantation days. This is the best of the Savannah National Wildlife Refuge which spreads east into South Carolina, in places bordering US HWY 17 and then extending south past US HWY 17. We describe boating in the Savannah National Wildlife Refuge in the next paragraph. After statute mile 26 the main body of the Savannah River runs south through Drakie's Cut to Port Wentworth and continues to the port of Savannah with its wharves and industrial development along the west shores. Powerful tidal currents, choppy waters in breezy weather and huge wakes thrown by tugboats make it an unfriendly, even hazardous place for small boats. The Houlihan Bridge boat ramp at Port Wentworth on the south

The stained trunks of tupelo gums in Ebenezer Creek reveal the variations in the river levels

side of the US HWY 17 bridge should be the end of the run for such boats. Yachts cruising up or down the river can have the US HWY 17 bridge, also called the Houlihan Bridge (vertical clearance 8 feet), open on work days on 3 hour notice by calling 912-651-2144.

SAVANNAH NATIONAL WILDLIFE REFUGE

The sheltered waters within the wildlife refuge are perfect for exploring in small boats whether fishing, bird watching or simply enjoying these wild habitats. Today you will see here a territory very different from what it looked like in pre-colonial times. According to archeological finds, scarce as they are, indigenous populations used the local natural resources through hunting and fishing at least 7,000 years ago. The Native Americans also settled in villages here, since there is evidence of cultivated corn which was introduced to North America from Mexico about 1,000 years ago. Still the thousands of acres of wetlands around the mouth of the Savannah must have been very forested for it took an inhumane amount of labor to open the grounds for plantations. When the English colonists decided to grow rice as a profitable commercial crop they used slaves and Irish laborers to clear the land, afterwards dividing it into orderly patterns of diked fields surrounded by canals which provided a supply of water regulated by tidal gates. By the early 1800s thirteen plantations operated within the limits of today's Savannah River National Wildlife Refuge. After the collapse of the plantation economy the area slowly reverted to a semi-wild state until the purchase by the federal government and the creation of a wildlife refuge in 1927. In 1976, the Nature Conservancy guaranteed the purchase of 12,500 acres of Argent Swamp from the Union Camp Corporation and soon after the US Fish and Wildlife Service acquired it increasing the Savannah National Wildlife Refuge to the present total of 26,350 acres. Argent Swamp, straddling the Savannah, added a spectacular area richer in flooded forest trees and virgin freshwater swamp than the rest of the refuge. When boating in these phenomenal side creeks of the Savannah River north of Argyle Island thank the Nature Conservancy for their foresight and good work.

The whole area of the Savannah National Wildlife Refuge now represents a variety of habitats, including tidal freshwater marshes, freshwater ponds, salt marshes, marsh hammocks, flooded cypress/tupelo forests and some upland areas. All animals typical of coastal Georgia can find refuge here and birds, both resident and migrant, come by the thousands either to feed during cold months or to breed. About 3,000 acres of former rice fields are still managed to maintain the best feeding conditions for some waterfowl. Visitors can access this part of the refuge from US HWY 17 and even take a 4 mile car trip on Laurel Hill Wildlife Drive which begins a few

miles east from the Savannah River. In addition, several embankments along the route allow walking or biking for better viewing. In all you will have a choice of nearly 40 miles of dike trails. Tupelo Swamp Trail, two miles north from the eastern end of Laurel Hill Wildlife Drive, leads to the observation tower near Vernezobre Creek where the swamp looks more like virgin nature than the old rice fields.

Nothing, however, beats getting to see the refuge in your own little boat. Use the boat ramp near the Houlihan Bridge as the base and work your way north (chartlet Savannah River #17) to Hog Marsh Island. Follow its southern shores, especially at low tide, to Middle River. If you are in a kayak or low powered boat you should assess the tidal current situation by the time you reach Houstown Cut. With the tide flooding in you should head north either on Middle River or take that narrow cut to Little Black River and then head north, in both cases with a fair tide helping you along. Use chartlets Savannnah River #16 and #17 to choose the course of action. Two creeks deserve consideration for their natural beauty and wildness. Union Creek, which begins north of the junction of Middle River with Little Back River, is a must and paddlers should time their return

The unusually bulky bases of the tupelo gums in Ebenezer Creek off the Savannah River have an added twist for unexplained reasons.

down this river with the ebbing tide. On Little Back River you should definitely go into Vernezobre Creek—from here paddlers must also time their way back according to the tide—the currents run very swiftly. Arm yourself with a bird book focusing on the southeastern US—songbirds, wading birds, raptors and waterfowl are always here and species vary according to seasons. Fishermen using high powered skiffs depend less on tides except when locating their fishing holes and they usually range up and down Little Back River as far south as Hog Island (chartlet #006 in Chapter III, *Savannah River to Ossabaw Sound*) and even to the tide gate by Hutchinson Island. By the way, a wire strung on buoys across the river closes the prohibited passage through the Tide Gate. People who boat solely for the appreciation of scenery will find that Little Back River widens and loses its charms south of Hog Island. Middle River ends about a mile and a half south of Houstown Cut and the US HWY 17 bridge by joining Front River, the main industrial part of the Savannah—see chartlet Savannah River #17.

SAVANNAH RIVER BOAT RAMPS

Savannah River Statute Mile 187—NEW SAVANNAH BLUFF LANDING, near Augusta Municipal Airport on the south side of Augusta. Chartlet Savannah River #01

From Interstate 520 use exit 8. Turn south onto spur 56. Drive about 1.3 miles to Lock and Dam Road. Turn left and drive approximately 2 miles to the end of the road. Turn left for the single lane ramp above the lock, turn right for the J. "Bob" Baurle ramp below the lock. There are garbage cans and water is available. The Baurle ramp is a wide single lane paved ramp with a floating dock. The Lock & Dam Tackle Shop, tel. 706-793-8053, is about .5 mile up the road.

Savannah River Statute Mile 174—SILVER BLUFF BOAT RAMP, west of Jackson, South Carolina. Chartlet Savannah River #02

On SC 125 north of Jackson drive to the junction with SC 302. Turn west (this is to the left coming from Jackson, to the right from Augusta) onto Silver Bluff Road. Silver Bluff Road is directly across the highway from SC 302. Drive about 5 miles. The road eventually becomes dirt and passes through Silver Bluff Plantation Nature Preserve, a project of the National Audubon Society. The dirt boat ramp is rough. This is a popular camping and fishing site in an unpopulated area.

Savannah River Statute Mile 170—AIKEN COUNTY BOAT RAMP, also called JACKSON LANDING, southwest of Jackson, South Carolina. Chartlet Savannah River #02

From SC 125 in Jackson turn west across from the BP gas station towards the center of Jackson. SR 62 is directly across the highway from this road. Proceed about .5 mile to a stop sign, turn right (north) on SR 5. Drive through

Jackson another .5 mile looking to the left for the boat ramp sign near the municipal buildings. Turn left at the sign (southwest). Drive about 2 miles, the road will become dirt, bear left at the fork in the road and continue to the railroad track. Cross the track carefully then bear to the left and proceed about 4 miles to the boat ramp. This is an unpopulated area and there are no nearby services. There is a good parking lot. The double lane ramp is concrete and has a floating dock to the side. The dock is located in an eddy, usually out of the main current.

Savannah River Statute Mile 162—SHELL BLUFF, east of Waynesboro, Georgia. Chartlet Savannah River #03

Use GA 80 from Shell Bluff, travel about 7 miles northeast to the end of the road, also called CR 477, at a residential area on a steep bluff. There is a fee to use the ramp.

Savannah River Statute Mile 152—HANCOCK LANDING, east of Waynesboro, Georgia. Chartlet Savannah River #04

From Shell Bluff (at the intersection of GA 80 and GA 23) travel south on GA 23 for about .8 mile to Claxton Lively Road (CR 98) turn to the left (east). Continue about 3 miles to Rouse Store Road, turn to the left and continue to the end of the dirt road. There is a single lane paved ramp.

Savannah River Statute Mile 149—GEORGIA POWER LANDING, north of Girard, Georgia. Chartlet Savannah River #04

From Girard go northwest on GA 23 for approximately .5 mile to the BP station. Turn right onto Brigham Landing Road, drive 3.7 miles to River Road, a good dirt road. Turn left (west) onto River Road and travel 4.7 miles to the Georgia Power Public Boat Ramp sign. Turn right and drive to the large paved parking lot in this uninhabited area. There is a double lane paved ramp. The area borders a tupelo swamp. It is a clean parking lot with garbage cans. There are no nearby facilities.

Savannah River Statute Mile 147—GRIFFIN LANDING, north of Girard, Georgia. Chartlet Savannah River #04

From Girard use GA 23, drive northwest 1.4 miles to Bethany United Methodist Church. Turn right (north) onto Griffin Landing Road. Travel 3.8 miles on this dirt road to a sign that reads "Rough Road, Travel at Own Risk." At 4 miles a sign reads "Road Closed". This ramp is not recommended.

Savannah River Statute Mile 144—BRIGHAM LANDING, north of Girard, Georgia. Chartlet Savannah River #05

From Girard go northwest on GA 23 for about .5 mile to the BP station. Turn right onto Brigham Landing Road (CR 79), drive approximately 5.3 miles on this mostly dirt road to two ramps. This landing is located in the Yuchi Wildlife Management area and is part of the Federal Aid in Sport Fish Restoration Project. There are two paved ramps, the ramp to the left is steep but still paved into the water and the ramp to the right has a gentle slope but drops off abruptly at the end. There are no nearby services.

Savannah River Statute Mile 142—STEEL CREEK LANDING, northwest of Allendale, South Carolina, the first boat ramp south of the Savannah River Site on the South Carolina side of the river. Chartlet Savannah River #05

Use SC 125. Just east of the Savannah River Site entrance turn south from SC 125 onto Steel Creek Road. Follow the edge of the quarter horse farm, Creek Plantation, until the pavement ends. Proceed on the dirt road to the river. There is a single lane paved ramp with a moderate slope. There are no nearby facilities.

Savannah River Statute Mile 135—LITTLE HELL LANDING, west of Allendale, South Carolina. Chartlet Savannah River #05

From the east: From SC 125 turn south (to the left) at Mill Pond Store. This is Furse Mill Road. Follow the road through a ninety degree turn to the right. Proceed 1.7 miles to the Little Hell Landing sign. Turn left, follow the road past the horse pastures and continue for nearly 2 miles to the river.

From the west: From SC 125 turn south (to the right) at Millet Road. Turn right onto Little Hell Road at the Little Hell Landing sign. Follow the road past the horse pastures and continue for nearly 2 miles to the river. There is a paved single lane ramp. This is an uninhabited area without any services. An artesian well pipe runs near the ramp and there is a large area for camping supplied with one garbage can.

Savannah River Statute Mile 132—STONY BLUFF, north of US 301 on the Georgia side of the river. Chartlet Savannah River #06

From US 301 turn north on Oglethorpe Trail, also called Wade Plantation Road. When the road begins to make a broad curve to the left, continue straight ahead onto the red clay River Road. At the stop sign turn right onto Stony Bluff Landing Road. Or, continue on Oglethorpe Trail around the curve to the left and turn right onto Stony Bluff Landing Road. (Oglethorpe Trail changes names on the big curve to Stony Bluff Road.) Drive 2.1 miles on Stony Bluff Landing Road past a few mobile homes to the landing. There are picnic tables and camping is possible. There are two paved ramps. The one on the left is very steep with an abrupt rocky drop off. The ramp on the right has a better grade and blends into a sandy bottom. There are no nearby facilities.

Savannah River Statute Mile 124—JOHNSON LANDING, west of Allendale, South Carolina. Chartlet Savannah River #07

From the north: From SC 125 at Martin turn south onto Chert Quarry Road (Martin Road) and drive approximately 4.8 miles to Johnson Landing Road. There is an access sign. Turn right (west) onto Johnson Landing Road and drive about .5 mile to the river.

From the south: From US 301 turn north onto 291, also called SR 102 and Chert Quarry Road. This road is about 1 mile west of the South Carolina welcome center. Drive approximately 3.6 miles to Johnson Landing Road. Turn left (west) and go about .5 mile to the river.

There is a good parking area and garbage cans. The double lane ramp is paved. The floating dock breaks some of the current but it can still flow at a strong rate by the ramp. This is an unpopulated area without any facilities nearby.

Savannah River Statute Mile 119—BURTON'S FERRY, at US 301 on the Georgia side of the Savannah River. Chartlet Savannah River #08

On US 301 travel to the Georgia (west) side of the river. Turn south onto a paved road and drive towards the river. The paved ramp is next to an open railroad bridge. A river level gauge is fixed to the bridge. Camping is possible under the railroad bridge next to US 301 but the area needs cleaning. There are no nearby facilities.

Savannah River Statute Mile 104—COHEN'S BLUFF, south of Allendale, South Carolina. Chartlet Savannah River #09

From US 301 turn south onto SC 3 (River Road). Travel about 9 miles to Cohen's Bluff Road, SR 41. There is a sign for the landing. Turn to the right, southwest, and drive 1.3 miles to the river. There is a good paved parking lot with a garbage can and room in the woods for camping. The camping area needs to be cleaned. There is a single lane paved ramp with a good non-skid surface. There are no nearby facilities.

Savannah River Statute Mile 100—MILLER LAKE—POSSUM EDDY, east of Sylvania, Georgia, part of the Tuckahoe Wildlife Management Area. Chartlet Savannah River #09A

From US 301 north of Sylvania turn southeast onto GA 24. Travel about 5 miles to Brannens Bridge Road. (This road will be Brannen's Bridge Road on the left and Ogeechee Street on right.) Turn left (northeast) and drive about 5 miles. Cross Brier Creek and go .10 mile to a Tuckahoe Wildlife Management Area sign on a dirt road. Turn to the right onto this road which will become River Road. During rainy periods this road can be slick and soft. Stay on the main road until Miller Lake Road. Turn right and continue to the ramp. The distance from the Tuckahoe sign to Miller Lake is about 4 miles. There are two paved ramps. The ramp to the left has a moderate slope and the ramp to the right is steeper. Also, the ramp to the right falls away into gravel. There are no nearby services.

Possum Eddy—we did not drive to the Possum Eddy ramp because the roads were too soft on our visits. At the River Road, Miller Road junction bear to the left and continue to the Possum Eddy Boat Ramp.

Savannah River Statute Mile 87—POOR ROBIN LANDING, east of Sylvania, Georgia. Chartlet Savannah River #09B

From GA 24, also called Newington Highway, turn east on Poor Robin Road. This dirt road, which may be hard to see, is just north of mile marker 18 close to Bettys Hair Corner. Coming from the north look for the sign "Poor Robin Road" on the west side of GA 24. Turn east onto Poor Robin Road, a dirt road, and drive 3.7 miles to the boat ramp. This landing is part of the Department of Natural Resources Wildlife Division's Federal Aid in Sport Fish Restoration Project. There is a wide paved ramp with a gentle slope in a very clean area with garbage cans. There are no nearby services.

Savannah River Statute Mile 78—BLUE SPRING, east of Sylvania, Georgia. Chartlet Savannah River #10

From GA 24, also called Newington Highway, turn east at mile marker 13 (at Blue Springs United Methodist Church) and drive about 1.8 miles to High Bluff Road. Turn to the right and drive .5 mile to the landing. There is a good dirt parking area. The steep ramp is paved and has an easy transition from concrete to sand. The current is slack at the ramp. The landing is near a residential area but there are no nearby services.

Savannah River Statute Mile 64—STOKES BLUFF, south of Garnett, South Carolina. Chartlet Savannah River #12

From SC 119 turn west just north of where SC 119 crosses the Savannah River. There is a sign for the Stokes Bluff Landing. Drive about 1.2 miles to the ramp. There is a big parking area. The current running by the ramp is slight. This is in a residential area without any nearby services.

Savannah River Statute Mile 62—TUCKASEE KING, north of Clyo, Georgia. Chartlet Savannah River #12

From GA 119, just south of the Savannah River bridge turn west onto Tuckasee King Road (CR 84). Drive .7 mile to the junction of Tuckasee King Road and Morgan Cemetery Road. The large new ramp is cut into the bank.

Savannah River Statute Mile 58—B&C LANDING, west of Ridgeland, South Carolina. Chartlet Savannah River #13

From US 321 at Tillman turn west on SR 119, Sand Hill Road. Drive more or less 6 miles to J. Lamar Brantley Road on the left. Turn to the left, southwest, and drive 1.7 miles to the landing. There is a paved parking lot and the ramp is paved. There are no nearby services.

Savannah River Statute Mile 45—EBENEZER LANDING, east of Springfield, Georgia. Chartlet Savannah River #14

From GA 21 between Rincon and Springfield turn east onto GA 275. Drive approximately 5 miles to the end of the road passing through the historic Ebenezer Cemetery and Church areas. At the end of the road turn to the left and drive down into a parking lot beside the ramps. There are two ramps, one paved and the other gravel. Water is available. The ramps belong to H. E. Fail and there is a $5.00 charge. A fee box is located on the side of his building for payments on the honor system as there may not be anyone around to collect the money. There are no nearby facilities.

Up Ebenezer Creek—EBENEZER CREEK LANDING, east of Springfield, Georgia. Chartlet Savannah River #14

From GA 21 between Rincon and Springfield turn east onto GA 275. Drive 2.3 miles to Long Bridge Road, CR 307. Turn to the left, north, and go .7 mile to Wylly (CR 122). There is a small boat ramp symbol sign. Turn right, to the northeast, onto Wylly. Wylly will change names to High Bluff Road. Proceed 1.8 miles to Tommy Long Road, a dirt road on the left. Turn left and drive .3 mile to the landing. This is a public Department of Natural Resources ramp. There is a gravel parking area and a single lane paved ramp with a gentle slope. This ramp is in the thick of the cypress—tupelo swamp of Ebenezer Creek. The Savannah River is 3.4 statute miles down the creek to the right. There are no nearby services.

Up Ebenezer Creek—LONG BRIDGE LANDING, east of Springfield, Georgia. Chartlet Savannah River #14

From GA 21 between Rincon and Springfield turn east onto GA 275. Drive 2.3 miles to Long Bridge Road, CR 307. Turn to the left, north, and go 1 mile to the bridge. Before the bridge turn to the left (west) and drive into the parking area. The ramp is very rough and broken up, it is not suitable for boats on trailers. Canoes and kayaks may utilize this ramp. The parking area needs cleaning. There are no nearby services.

Savannah River Statute Mile 39—PURYSBURG LANDING BOAT RAMP, northwest of Hardeeville, South Carolina. Chartlet Savannah River #15

From the junction of SC 46 and US 321 in Hardeeville drive north 2.9 miles to SR 521-170. Turn left (west) onto 170 and drive 2.2 miles to the landing. The pavement will end and a good dirt road runs the rest of the way to the river. There is a large parking lot. The double lane ramp is paved and there is a floating dock. A bulkhead protects the dock and ramp from the current.

Savannah River Statute Mile 33—MILL STONE LANDING, west of Hardeeville, South Carolina. Chartlet Savannah River #15

From US 321 in Hardeeville near the junction with SC 46 turn northwest onto Church Road (SR 31) at the Savannah River Access sign. Drive 2.1 miles to the Mill Stone Landing sign. Turn left (south) and go .5 mile. Turn right into the Marine Rescue Squadron parking area. Drive to the ramp by the river. There is a large parking lot. The wide ramp has a medium slope and a good corrugated concrete surface. The floating dock and ramp are out of the current. There is a river level gauge on one of the pilings.

Savannah River Statute Mile 29—ABERCORN LANDING, south of Rincon, Georgia. Chartlet Savannah River #16

From GA 21 between Rincon and I 95 turn to the east at CR 3. CR 3 is located at the historical marker commemorating the village of Abercorn. Quickly turn to the left (north). The small concrete road soon becomes dirt. Travel 2.3 miles to Abercorn Landing Road. Or, from GA 21 between Rincon and I 95 turn east at Moore Drive. At the nearby fork in the road bear left to almost make a U-turn. Drive 1.9 miles to Abercorn Landing Road. Once at Abercorn Landing Road turn to the right (east), bear left at the fork and drive .6 mile to the landing. There is a dirt parking lot. The steep ramp is paved and the current is slight. The cans and bottles need to be cleared from the area. There are no nearby facilities.

Savannah River Statute Mile 21—PORT WENTWORTH, HOULIHAN BRIDGE, north of Savannah. Chartlet Savannah River #17

From GA 25 in Port Wentworth drive north towards the Savannah River. Just before Houlihan Bridge turn to the right (south) into the Port Wentworth Marine Squadron parking area. There are picnic tables and garbage cans. The two double lane ramps are out of the current. The ramps can be very slippery at low tide. There is a floating dock.

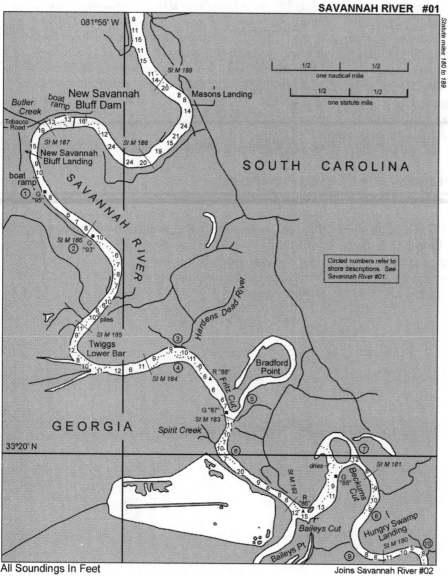

SAVANNAH RIVER #01

Statute miles 180 to 189

All Soundings In Feet

Joins Savannah River #02

Shore Descriptions for Savannah River Chart #01

1 .... Emergency sign: If you hear the emergency siren turn on FM radio channels 104.3, 99.5, 93.5 or TV channels 6, 12 or 26
2 .... Pilings extending out to channel
3 .... Pilings extending out to channel
4 .... Island
5 .... Side channel shoal
6 .... Bar, dries
7 .... Side channel shoal
8 .... Bluff, oak forest
9 .... Twenty foot bluff
10 .... Bluffs

Shore Descriptions for Savannah River Chart #02

1 .... Forested
2 .... Bluff, low shore on opposite bank
3 .... Bluffs
4 .... Ten foot bluff
5 .... Twenty foot bluff
6 .... Bluffs
7 .... Low shore
8 .... Bluffs
9 .... Bluff, forested
10 .... Low shore, bluff on opposite bank
11 .... Bluff, forested
12 .... Bluff, forested
13 .... Creek with a shallow bar
14 .... Rickety cabins
15 .... Very shallow
16 .... Cabins
17 .... River bank alternates with low shores and bluffs, there are many possibilities to land
18 .... Bluffs
19 .... General landing, no ramp
20 .... Floating house
21 .... Low bluff
22 .... Snags
23 .... Forest
24 .... Bluff
25 .... Dry bank
26 .... Low shore, bluff on opposite bank
27 .... Low bluff
28 .... Low shore, bluffs on opposite bank
29 .... Bluff
30 .... Low shore
31 .... Bluff
32 .... Low shore
33 .... Lower bluff
34 .... Low bluff
35 .... Low shore

Joins Savannah River #01

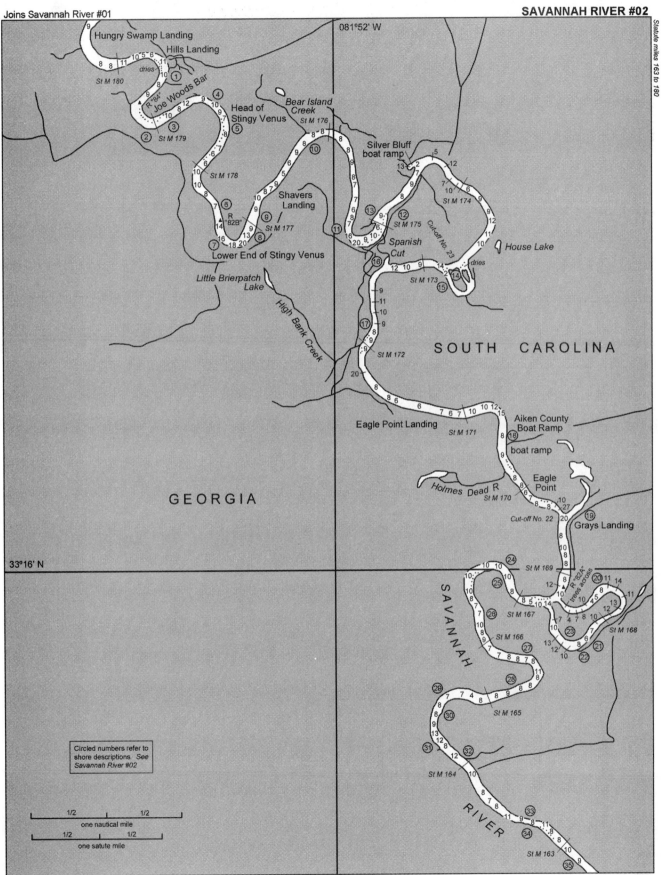

Statute miles 163 to 180

Hungry Swamp Landing

Hills Landing

dries

St M 180

R "84"

Joe Woods Bar

St M 179

Head of
Stingy Venus

Bear Island
Creek

St M 176

081°52' W

Silver Bluff
boat ramp

St M 174

St M 178

Shavers
Landing

R
"82B"

St M 177

Lower End of Stingy Venus

St M 175

House Lake

Little Brierpatch
Lake

Spanish
Cut

Cut-off No. 23

dries

St M 173

High Bank Creek

St M 172

SOUTH CAROLINA

GEORGIA

Eagle Point Landing

St M 171

Aiken County
Boat Ramp

boat ramp

Eagle
Point

Holmes Dead R

St M 170

Cut-off No. 22

Grays Landing

SAVANNAH

R "82A"
trees across

St M 169

St M 167

St M 168

St M 166

33°16' N

St M 165

St M 164

RIVER

St M 163

Circled numbers refer to
shore descriptions. *See
Savannah River #02*

| 1/2 | | 1/2 |
one nautical mile
| 1/2 | | 1/2 |
one satute mile

All Soundings In Feet

Joins Savannah River #03

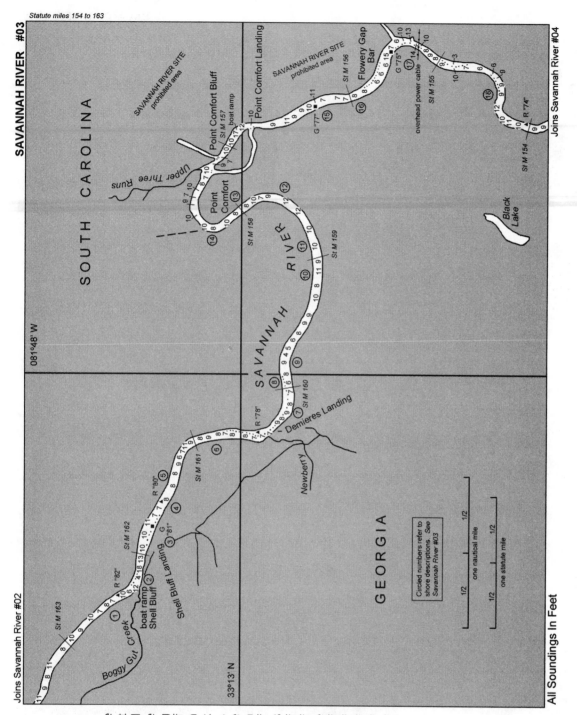

SAVANNAH RIVER #03

Statute miles 154 to 163

Joins Savannah River #02

Joins Savannah River #04

SOUTH CAROLINA

GEORGIA

SAVANNAH RIVER

081°48' W

33°13' N

Point Comfort Landing

SAVANNAH RIVER SITE
prohibited area

Point Comfort Bluff

Upper Three Runs

Point Comfort

Flowery Gap Bar

overhead power cable

Black Lake

Demieres Landing

Newberry

Shell Bluff Landing

boat ramp

Boggy Gut Creek

Shore Descriptions for Savannah River Chart #03

1 .... Low shore
2 .... Fifty foot bluff, steep cut to the road, residential
3 .... Private
4 .... Ramp, building
5 .... Low bluff
6 .... Low shore, bluff on opposite bank
7 .... Fifteen foot bluff, rough, steep shore
8 .... Statute mile 160 sign
9 .... Lower bluff
10 .... Bluffs on both banks
11 .... Lower bluff
12 .... Twelve foot bluff
13 .... Low shore
14 .... Bluff
15 .... Lower bluff
16 .... Ten foot bluff
17 .... Low bluff
18 .... Bluff

Circled numbers refer to shore descriptions. See Savannah River #03

one nautical mile

one statute mile

All Soundings In Feet

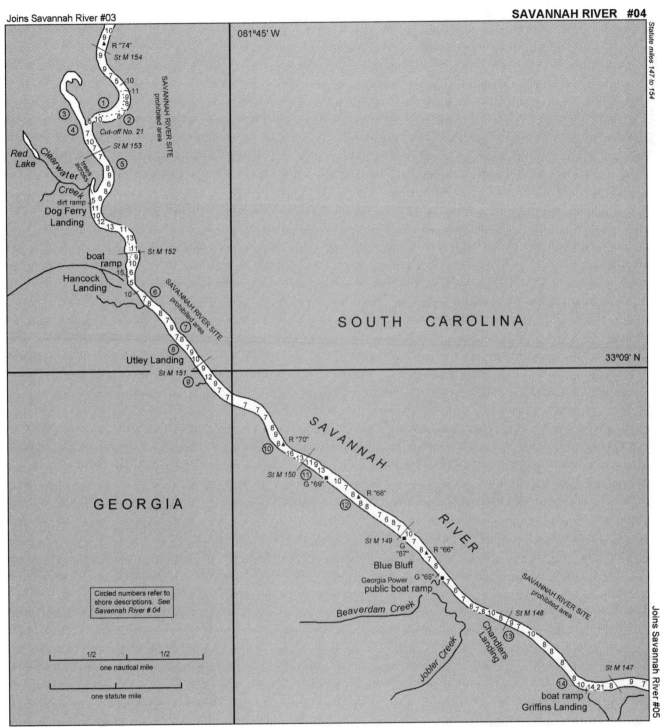

Joins Savannah River #03

SAVANNAH RIVER #04

081°45' W

Statute miles 147 to 154

SOUTH CAROLINA

33°09' N

GEORGIA

SAVANNAH

RIVER

Joins Savannah River #05

R "74"
St M 154

SAVANNAH RIVER SITE prohibited area

Cut-off No. 21
St M 153

Red Lake
Clearwater Creek
dirt ramp
Dog Ferry Landing

St M 152
boat ramp

Hancock Landing

SAVANNAH RIVER SITE prohibited area

Utley Landing
St M 151

R "70"
St M 150
G "69"

R "68"

St M 149
G "87"
R "66"
Blue Bluff
Georgia Power
public boat ramp
G "65"

Beaverdam Creek

SAVANNAH RIVER SITE prohibited area
St M 148

Chandlers Landing

Jobler Creek

St M 147

boat ramp
Griffins Landing

Circled numbers refer to shore descriptions. See *Savannah River # 04*

1/2   1/2
one nautical mile

one statute mile

All Soundings In Feet

Shore Descriptions for Savannah River Chart #04

1 .... Low bluffs	9 .... Big steel landing, power plant
2 .... Bluff	10 ..... Beautiful, steep 100 foot cliffs, shells embedded in soil
3 .... Houseboats	11 .... Steep forested hillside
4 .... Stranded trees	12 .... Low bluffs, forest
5 .... Low shore	13 .... Bluff
6 .... Low shore, bluffs on opposite bank	14 .... Single lane very rough ramp leading to dirt road
7 .... Low bluff	
8 .... Steel dock	

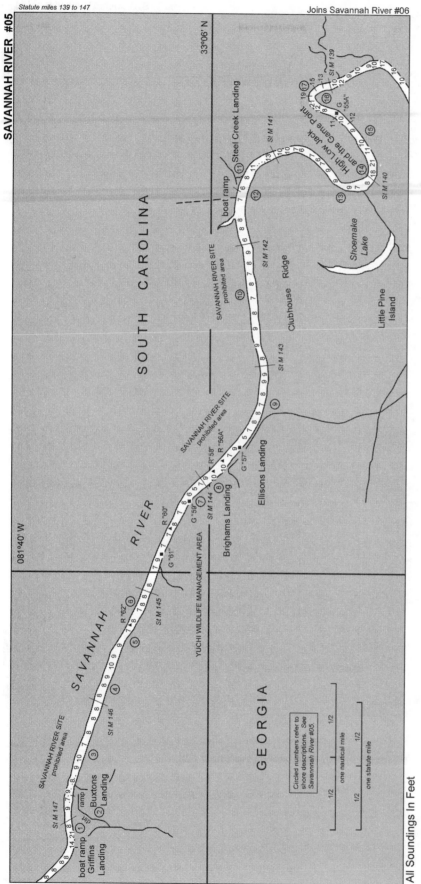

All Soundings In Feet

Shore Descriptions for Savannah River Chart #05

1 .... Steep high bluff
2 .... Single concrete ramp leading to dirt road
3 .... Low bluff
4 .... Low shore, bluff on opposite bank
5 .... Low thick forest
6 .... Low shore
7 .... Low shore

8 .... Sign: If you hear the emergency warning siren turn on your radio or T.V. WBBQ – FM 104.3, WBBQ – AM 1340, WBRO – AM 1310, WKXC – FM 99.5, WDCG – FM 93.5. TV channels WJBF – Ch 6, WRDW – Ch 12, WAGT – Ch 26.
9 .... Bluffs on both banks

10 .... Low bluff
11 .... Bluff
12 .... Low shore
13 .... Bluff
14 .... Statute mile 140 sign
15 .... Bluffs
16 .... Low beach
17 .... Steep bluff

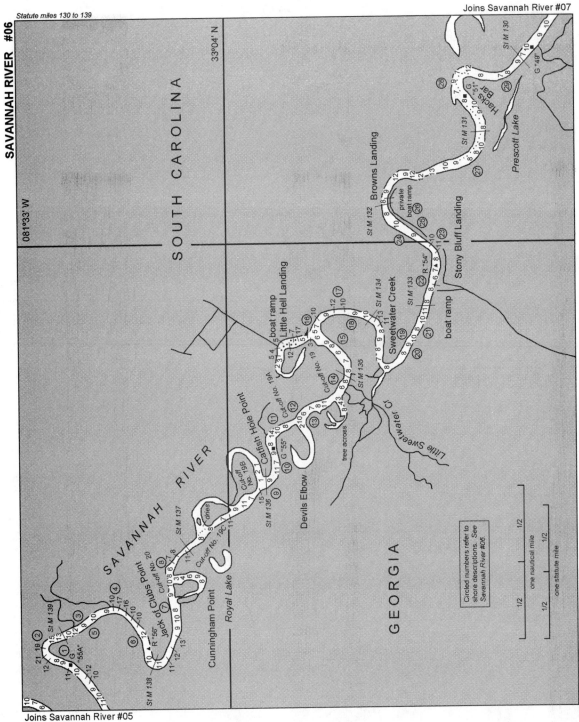

Joins Savannah River #05

All Soundings In Feet

Shore Descriptions for Savannah River Chart #06

1 .... Low beach
2 .... Steep bluff
3 .... Low bluff, easy gradient
4 .... Steep bluff
5 .... Steep bluff
6 .... Low shore
7 .... Low shore on both banks of the river
8 .... Bluffs on both banks of the river
9 .... Bluffs
10 .... Low shore
11 .... Steep bluff
12 .... Low shore
13 .... Low shore
14 .... Low shore
15 .... Bluffs
16 .... Barge wreck
17 .... Bluffs
18 .... Gentle bluff
19 .... Low shore
20 .... Bluff
21 .... Low bluff
22 .... Six to eight foot bluff
23 .... Cabins
24 .... Low shore
25 .... High wooded shore
26 .... Cabins
27 .... Steep shore
28 .... Six to eight foot steep bluffs
29 .... Low shore

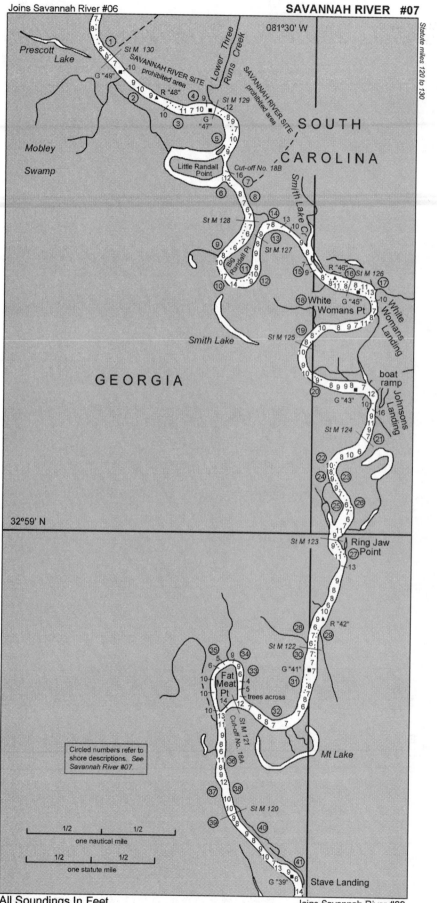

Joins Savannah River #06

SAVANNAH RIVER #07

081°30' W

Statute miles 120 to 130

All Soundings In Feet

Joins Savannah River #08

Circled numbers refer to shore descriptions. See Savannah River #07.

1/2   1/2
one nautical mile

1/2   1/2
one statute mile

Shore Descriptions for Savannah River Chart #07

1	Statute mile 130 sign
2	Bluffs on both banks
3	Bluff
4	Low shore
5	Sand bar
6	Very shallow bar
7	Low shore
8	Bluff
9	Low shore
10	Bluff
11	Gentle low bluff
12	Bluff
13	Low shore
14	Bluff
15	Low shore
16	Beach
17	Single lane concrete ramp
18	Low thick vegetation on White Womans Pt
19	Bluff
20	Bluff, low shore on opposite bank
21	Bluffs on both banks
22	Low shore
23	Low shore
24	Bluffs
25	Low sandy shore
26	Bluff
27	Ten foot bluff, both shores
28	Low shore, thick woods
29	Low shore
30	Bluffs, thick woods
31	Bluffs on both banks
32	Low shore
33	Bluff
34	Low shore
35	Bluffs
36	Bluffs
37	Bluffs
38	Low shore
39	Statute mile 120 sign
40	Bluff
41	Low shore on both banks

**Shore Descriptions for
Savannah River Chart #08**

1 .... Bluffs
2 .... Bluffs
3 .... Low shore
4 .... Low shore
5 .... Low shore
6 .... Bluffs
7 .... Bluffs
8 .... Low shore
9 .... Bluff
10 .... Low, sandy
11 .... Bluffs
12 .... Sandy spit
13 .... Bluffs
14 .... Low sandy point
15 .... Ten to twelve foot bluffs
16 .... Bluffs
17 .... Low scrub brush
18 .... Bluffs
19 .... Low shore
20 .... Low shore
21 .... Swift Creek dries
22 .... Bluffs
23 .... Low bluffs
24 .... Bluff
25 .... Low shore, scrub brush
26 .... Eight foot bluffs
27 .... Bluffs
28 .... Low shore
29 .... Bluffs on both banks
30 .... Bluff
31 .... Sandy split
32 .... Low Shore
33 .... Bluffs
34 .... Low sandy shore
35 .... Low sandy shore
36 .... Low sandy shore
37 .... Banks
38 .... Low shore, scrub brush
39 .... Bluffs on both banks
40 .... Six foot bluffs
41 .... Partly filled and dry basin
42 .... Bluffs on both banks
43 .... Low shore, scrub brush
44 .... Twenty foot bluff
45 .... Low shore, scrub brush

**Shore Descriptions for
Savannah River Chart #09A**

1 .... Twenty foot bluff
2 .... Low thick vegetation
3 .... Low scrub brush
4 .... Bluffs
5 .... Bluffs
6 .... Low sandy shore
7 .... Sandy spit
8 .... Fifteen foot bluff
9 .... Bluffs
10 .... Low bluffs
11 .... Bluffs
12 .... Grassy low shore
13 .... Bluffs
14 .... Low thick bush
15 .... Bluffs on both banks
16 .... Bluffs
17 .... Low sandy shore
18 .... Bluffs
19 .... Low shore
20 .... Bluffs, thick vegetation
21 .... Low shore, thick vegetation
22 .... Low shore, scrub brush
23 .... Bluffs
24 .... House
25 .... Low sandy shore
26 .... Bluffs
27 .... Sandy spit
28 .... Fifteen foot bluffs
29 .... Ten foot bluffs
30 .... Closed
31 .... Low bluffs on both banks
32 .... Ten foot bluffs, low bank on
opposite shore
33 ... Beautiful cypress trees, alligators
34 .... Statute mile 100 sign
35 .... Ten foot bluff
36 .... Bluff with low shore
on opposite bank
37 .... Steep ten to twelve foot bluff
38 .... Sandy spit
39 .... Bluff, low thick vegetation on
opposite bank
40 .... Rough concrete ramp
41 ...... Beautiful cypress trees, private
property at end of creek
42 ..... Twelve foot bluff, low opposite
shore with thick bush
43 ...... Low sandy shore with ten foot
bluffs on opposite shore
44 ...... Low bushy spot with bluffs on
both banks
45 .... Ten foot bluffs on both banks
46 .... Twelve foot bank with low
sandy shore on opposite bank

**Shore Descriptions for
Savannah River Chart #09B**

1 .... Bluffs on both banks
2 .... Oxbow blocked and dry
3 .... Ten foot bluffs, low banks on
opposite shore
4 .... Bluffs on both banks
5 .... Dry
6 .... Bluffs
7 .... Trees blocking creek
8 . Ten to twelve foot bluffs, low thick
vegetation on opposite bank
9 .... Low bluffs on both banks
10 .... Gentle slope, low bluff
on opposite bank
11 .... Six to eight foot bluffs
12 .... Low bluffs
13 .... Sandy spit
14 .... Six foot bluff, sandy spit on
opposite bank
15 .... Low bluff, sandy spit
on opposite bank
16 .... Six foot bluff, sandy spit
on opposite bank
17 ...... Very narrow, shallow entrance
18 .... Sandy spit, eight foot bluff
on opposite shore
19 .... Sloping bank alternating with
steep low bluffs
20 ... Six to eight foot bluff, low shore
on opposite bank
21 .... Sandy spit, cabin
on opposite bank
22 .... Very shallow entrance
23 .... Large flat sandy area
24 .... Six to eight foot bluffs
25 .... Low sloping shore
alternating with low bluffs
26 .... Low sandy shore, six foot
bluff on opposite shore
27 .... Low shore
28 .... Filled with floating plants
29 .... Very shallow
30 .... Bluff, sloping shore
on opposite bank
31 .... Sand bar, bluffs
on opposite shore
32 .... Eight foot bluffs
33 .... Stand of cypress trees

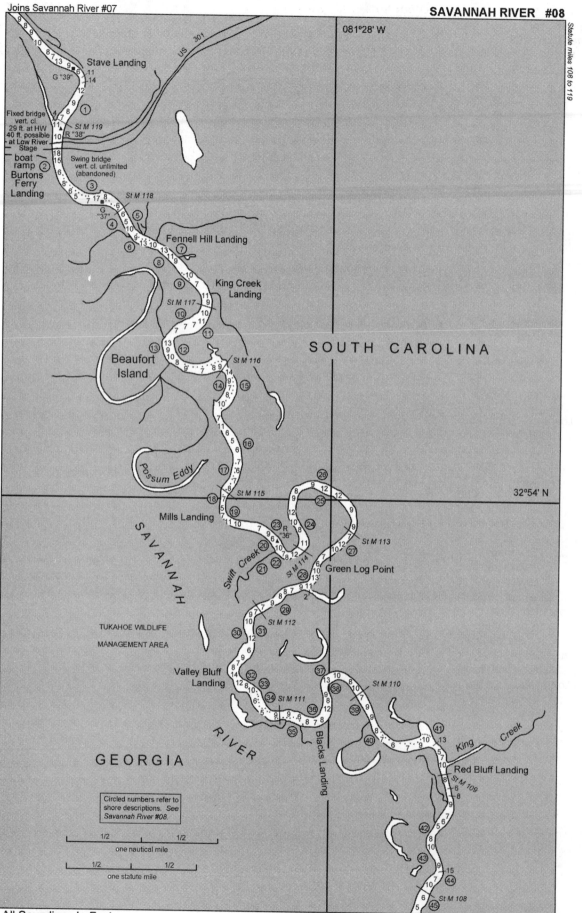

Joins Savannah River #07

SAVANNAH RIVER #08

Statute miles 108 to 119

081º28' W

Stave Landing

G "39"

Fixed bridge
vert. cl.
29 ft. at HW
40 ft. possible
at Low River
Stage

St M 119
R "38"

boat
ramp
Burtons
Ferry
Landing

Swing bridge
vert. cl. unlimited
(abandoned)

St M 118

G
"37"

Fennell Hill Landing

King Creek
Landing

St M 117

SOUTH CAROLINA

Beaufort
Island

St M 116

Possum Eddy

St M 115

32º54' N

Mills Landing

R
"36"

St M 113

Swift Creek

St M 114

Green Log Point

SAVANNAH

St M 112

TUKAHOE WILDLIFE

MANAGEMENT AREA

Valley Bluff
Landing

St M 111

RIVER

St M 110

King
Creek

Blacks Landing

GEORGIA

Red Bluff Landing

St M 109

Circled numbers refer to
shore descriptions. See
Savannah River #08.

1/2   1/2
one nautical mile

1/2   1/2
one statute mile

St M 108

All Soundings In Feet

Joins Savannah River #09A

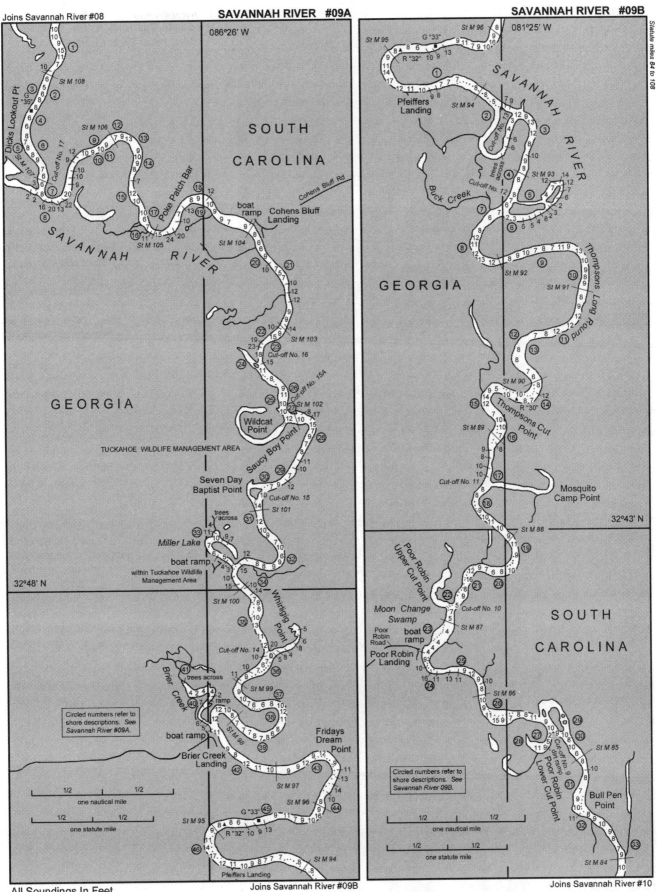

SAVANNAH RIVER #09A

086°26' W

Joins Savannah River #08

St M 108

Dicks Lookout Pt

G "35"

St M 107

St M 106

St M 105

Cut-off No. 17

Poke Patch Bar

St M 104

Cohens Bluff Rd

SOUTH CAROLINA

boat ramp

Cohens Bluff Landing

St M 103

Cut-off No. 16

GEORGIA

TUCKAHOE WILDLIFE MANAGEMENT AREA

Wildcat Point

Saucy Boy Point

Seven Day Baptist Point

Cut-off No. 15A

St M 102

Cut-off No. 15

St 101

trees across

Miller Lake

boat ramp

within Tuckahoe Wildlife Management Area

32°48' N

St M 100

Whirligig Point

Cut-off No. 14

Brier Creek

trees across

ramp

boat ramp

St M 98

St M 99

Fridays Dream Point

Brier Creek Landing

Circled numbers refer to shore descriptions. See Savannah River #09A.

St M 97

St M 96

G "33"

R "32"

St M 95

St M 94

Pfeiffers Landing

1/2   1/2
one nautical mile

1/2   1/2
one statute mile

All Soundings In Feet

Joins Savannah River #09B

SAVANNAH RIVER #09B

081°25' W

Statute miles 84 to 108

Joins Savannah River #09A

St M 96

St M 95

G "33"

R "32"

SAVANNAH RIVER

Pfeiffers Landing

St M 94

Cut-off No. 13

Buck Creek

Cut-off No. 12

St M 93

GEORGIA

St M 92

Thompsons Long Round

St M 91

St M 90

R "30"

Thompsons Cut Point

St M 89

15

Cut-off No. 11

Mosquito Camp Point

32°43' N

St M 88

Poor Robin Upper Cut Point

Moon Change Swamp

Poor Robin Road

boat ramp

Cut-off No. 10

St M 87

SOUTH CAROLINA

Poor Robin Landing

St M 86

St M 85

Cut-off No. 9

dirt ramp

Poor Robin Lower Cut Point

Bull Pen Point

Circled numbers refer to shore descriptions. See Savannah River 09B.

St M 84

1/2   1/2
one nautical mile

1/2   1/2
one statute mile

Joins Savannah River #10

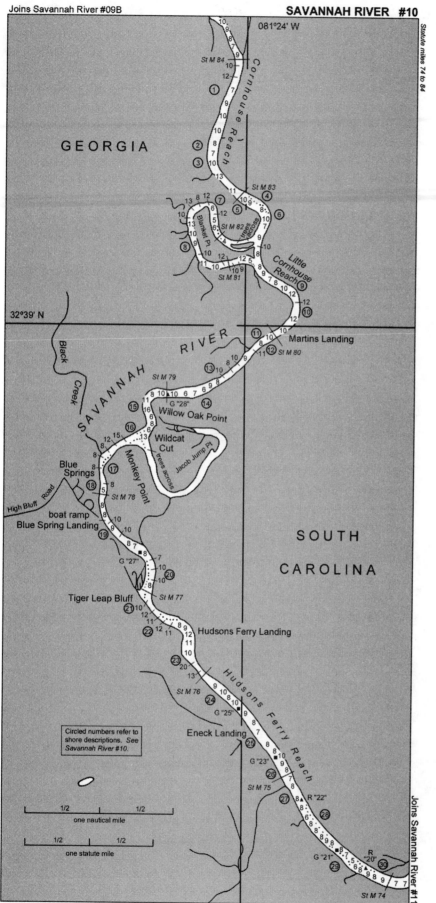

Joins Savannah River #09B

SAVANNAH RIVER #10

081°24' W

Statute miles 74 to 84

GEORGIA

32°39' N

Black Creek

SAVANNAH RIVER

Cornhouse Reach

Blanket Pt.

Little Cornhouse Reach

Martins Landing

Willow Oak Point

Wildcat Cut

Jacob Jump Pt.

Monkey Point

Blue Springs

High Bluff Road

boat ramp
Blue Spring Landing

Tiger Leap Bluff

Hudsons Ferry Landing

Hudsons Ferry Reach

SOUTH CAROLINA

Eneck Landing

Circled numbers refer to shore descriptions. *See Savannah River #10.*

1/2   1/2
one nautical mile

1/2   1/2
one statute mile

Joins Savannah River #11

All Soundings In Feet

Shore Descriptions for Savannah River Chart #10

1 .... Steep but low shore, thick vegetation, gentle slope on opposite shore
2 .... Bluffs on both banks
3 .... Steep bluffs, sloping bank on opposite shore
4 .... Sand bar
5 .... Steep bank
6 .... Six to eight foot bank
7 .... Steep shore
8 .... Houseboat on opposite bank
9 .... Steep shore
10 .... Six to eight foot bluffs
11 .... Low thick vegetation
12 .... Statute mile 80 sign
13 .... Bluffs, low slope on opposite bank
14 .... Steep, thick vegetation
15 .... Six foot bluffs, low shore on opposite bank
16 .... Low thick vegetation
17 .... Sloping shore
18 .... Steep, thick vegetation
19 .... Six foot bluff
20 .... Six to eight foot bluffs, low shore on opposite bank
21 .... High, steep forested shore
22 .... Residential, low thick vegetation on opposite bank
23 ...... High steep forested shore, low forest on opposite bank
24 .... Low foreshore, steep and high behind
25 .... Sandy shore, moderately steep on opposite bank
26 .... Sandy shore, six to eight foot bluffs on opposite bank
27 .... Low thick vegetation
28 .... Sandy shore, forest on opposite bank
29 .... Low shore on both banks
30 .... Gentle bank

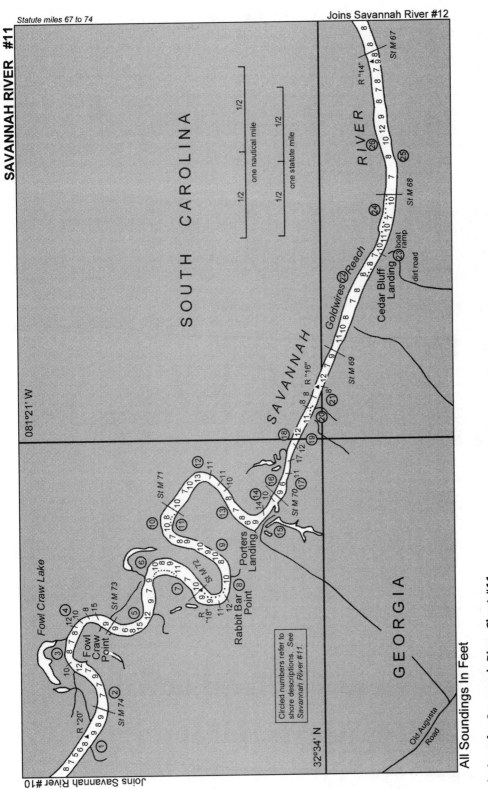

Statute miles 67 to 74

Joins Savannah River #12

1/2

1/2

one nautical mile

1/2

1/2

one statute mile

SOUTH CAROLINA

081°21' W

SAVANNAH

RIVER

GEORGIA

Fowl Craw Lake

Fowl Craw Point

St M 74

St M 73

R "18"

St M 72

Rabbit Bar Point

Porters Landing

St M 71

St M 70

St M 69

R "16"

Goldwires Reach

Cedar Bluff Landing

boat ramp

dirt road

St M 68

St M 67

R "14"

Old Augusta Road

Circled numbers refer to shore descriptions. See *Savannah River #11.*

32°34' N

Joins Savannah River #10

All Soundings In Feet

Shore Descriptions for Savannah River Chart #11

1 .... Undercut low bank
2 .... Bluff, low thick vegetation on opposite bank
3 .. Bluff, sandy shore on opposite bank
4 .... Six to eight foot bluff
5 .... Low thick vegetation on both banks
6 .... Eight foot bluff, sand bar on opposite shore

7 .... Low vegetation, bluff on opposite bank
8 .... Cabin on stilts, houseboat
9 .... Six to eight foot bluff, low vegetation on opposite shore
10 .... Five to seven foot bluffs
11 .... Six foot bluff with sand bar on the river
12 .... Six to eight foot bluff

13 .... Low thick bush
14 .. Gentle bluff, high wooded shore on opposite bank
15 .... Private landing
16 .... Statute mile 70 sign
17 .... Forty foot bluff, very pretty wooded cliffs
18 .... Wooded, gentle bluffs
19 .... Low foreshore, hills beyond

20 .... House
21 ...... Low shore at low water levels, high land behind forest
22 .... Bluffs
23 .... Low sandy shore
24 .... Bluffs on both banks
25 .... Six to eight foot bluffs
26 .... Sandy shore

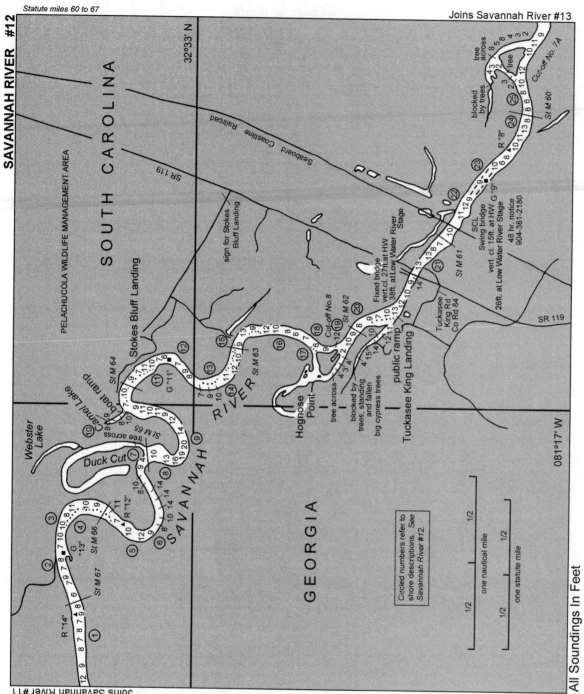

Statute miles 60 to 67

Joins Savannah River #13

SAVANNAH RIVER #12

Joins Savannah River #11

All Soundings In Feet

Shore Descriptions for Savannah River Chart # 12

1 .... Six to eight foot bluffs
2 .... Low shore
3 .... Six to eight foot bluffs
4 .... Sandy shore, bluffs on opposite bank
5 .... Bluffs, low bank on opposite shore
6 .... Six to eight foot bluffs, low shore with thick bush on opposite bank
7 .... Bluff
8 .... Sandy shore
9 .... Ten foot bluff, low sandy bank on opposite shore
10 .... Cypress forest
11 .... Sandy shore
12 .... Bluff, low shore with thick bush on opposite bank
13 .... Sandy foreshore, low bush behind
14 .... Six to eight foot bluffs
15 .... House
16 .... Low bluffs, six to eight foot bluffs on opposite bank
17 .... Almost dry, trees across
18 .... Bluffs
19 .... Low sandy shore
20 .... Bluffs, low shore on opposite bank
21 .... Low thick vegetation on both banks
22 .... Low shore on both banks
23 .... Six to eight foot bluffs, sandy shore on opposite bank
24 ... Low shore with thick vegetation
25 .... Statute mile 60 sign

SAVANNAH RIVER #13

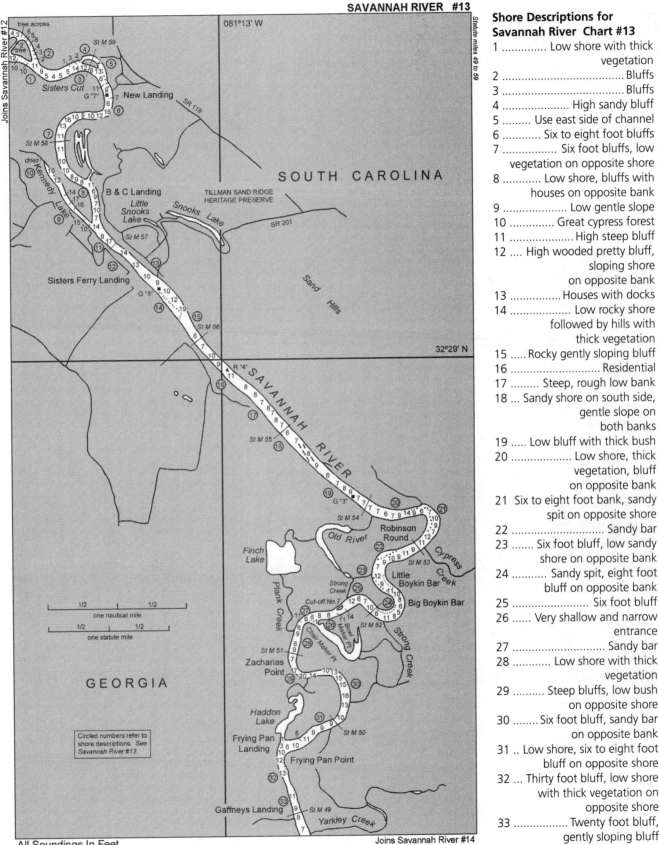

081°13' W

Joins Savannah River #12

tree across

St M 59

Sisters Cut

New Landing

G "7"

SR 119

St M 58

dries

Kennedy Lake

B & C Landing

Little Snooks Lake

Snooks Lake

SOUTH CAROLINA

TILLMAN SAND RIDGE HERITAGE PRESERVE

SR 201

St M 57

Sisters Ferry Landing

G "5"

St M 56

Sand Hills

32°29' N

R "4"

SAVANNAH RIVER

St M 55

St M 54

G "3"

Robinson Round

Cypress Creek

Finch Lake

Old River

St M 53

Little Boykin Bar

Plank Creek

Strong Creek

Cut-off No. 7

Big Boykin Bar

St M 52

Boat Marker Pt.

Strong Creek

St M 51

Zacharias Point

Haddon Lake

St M 50

Frying Pan Landing

Frying Pan Point

Gaffneys Landing

St M 49

Yarkley Creek

Statute miles 49 to 59

1/2   1/2
one nautical mile

1/2   1/2
one statute mile

Circled numbers refer to shore descriptions. See Savannah River #13.

GEORGIA

All Soundings In Feet

Joins Savannah River #14

Shore Descriptions for Savannah River Chart #13

1 .... Low shore with thick vegetation
2 .... Bluffs
3 .... Bluffs
4 .... High sandy bluff
5 .... Use east side of channel
6 .... Six to eight foot bluffs
7 .... Six foot bluffs, low vegetation on opposite shore
8 .... Low shore, bluffs with houses on opposite bank
9 .... Low gentle slope
10 .... Great cypress forest
11 .... High steep bluff
12 .... High wooded pretty bluff, sloping shore on opposite bank
13 .... Houses with docks
14 .... Low rocky shore followed by hills with thick vegetation
15 ..... Rocky gently sloping bluff
16 .... Residential
17 .... Steep, rough low bank
18 ... Sandy shore on south side, gentle slope on both banks
19 ..... Low bluff with thick bush
20 .... Low shore, thick vegetation, bluff on opposite bank
21 Six to eight foot bank, sandy spit on opposite shore
22 .... Sandy bar
23 .... Six foot bluff, low sandy shore on opposite bank
24 .... Sandy spit, eight foot bluff on opposite bank
25 .... Six foot bluff
26 ...... Very shallow and narrow entrance
27 .... Sandy bar
28 .... Low shore with thick vegetation
29 .... Steep bluffs, low bush on opposite shore
30 .... Six foot bluff, sandy bar on opposite bank
31 .. Low shore, six to eight foot bluff on opposite shore
32 ... Thirty foot bluff, low shore with thick vegetation on opposite shore
33 .... Twenty foot bluff, gently sloping bluff on opposite shore

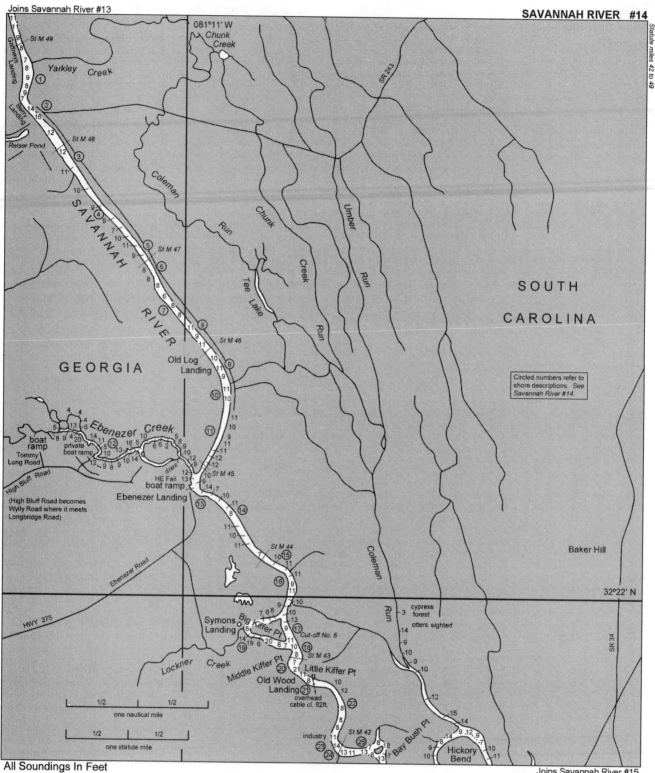

Shore Descriptions for Savannah River Chart #14

1 .... Bluffs, low shore with house on opposite shore
2 .... Low bluffs, fifty to thirty foot bluffs on opposite shore
3 .... Six foot bluffs on both shores
4 .... Ramp, houses, high bluff. Low bluff on opposite shore
5 .... Gentle bluff, rough landing on opposite shore
6 Five foot bluffs, low shore with houses on opposite bank
7 ....Low bluffs, residential
8 .... Low shore
9 .... Five foot bluffs, four foot bluffs on opposite shore
10 .... Low tangled bush
11 .... Four foot bluff, tangled vegetation on both banks
12 .... Beautiful cypress and tupelo forest, see *Ebenezer Creek*
13 .... Thirty foot bluff, Ebenezer Church and retreat
14 .... Wooded bluff, six foot bluff on opposite shore
15 .... Six to eight foot bluff
16 .... Low thick vegetation
17 .... Bluff, twenty foot bluff on opposite shore
18 .... Sandy beach
19 .... Cabin
20 .... Single lane ramp
21 .. Factory, industrial waste outlet, beware of hot water
22 .... Six foot bluff, low thick bush on opposite shore
23 .... Industrial bulkhead
24 .... Low bluff with thick vegetation on both banks
25 .... Low shore

Shore Descriptions for Savannah River Chart #15

1 .... Six to eight foot bluffs
2 ..... Low shore with thick vegetation
3 .... Six to eight foot bluffs
4 .... Six to eight foot bluffs, low bluffs on opposite shore
5 .... Six foot bluffs, low shore with thick vegetation on opposite bank
6 .... Low grassy bar
7 ....Low thick vegetation
8 .... Low shore
9 ...... Cypress—tupelo riverine forest, twenty foot bluffs, beautiful area
10 ....Dredging materials, canal
11 .... Low bluff on both banks
12 .... Low bluff
13 .... Sandy point, six foot bluff on opposite shore
14 .... Sandy bank, tangled vegetation on opposite shore
15 .... Low grasses, five to ten foot bluffs on opposite shore
16 .... Low thick bush, tangled vegetation on four to five foot bluffs on opposite shore
17 .... Sandy shore
18 .... Five foot bluff, six foot bluff on opposite shore
19 .... Steep bluff
20 .... Low shore
21 .... Wooden barge
22 .... Rocky ramp
23 .... Cypress forest, trees across two creeks, path
24 .... Low tangled vegetation, residential area on opposite shore
25 .... Twenty foot bluff
26 .... Residential area with docks
27 .... Low tangled vegetation
28 .... Mobile homes
29 .... Low tangled vegetation
30 .... Low tangled vegetation
31 .... Forest
32 .... Thick forest on both shores
33 .... Grassy
34 .... Low grasses
35 .... Wreck, deep water along opposite shore
36 ....Flooded forest on opposite shore
37 .... Thick forest
38 .... Thick forest which floods at times of high water
39 .... Flooded forest all the way to the Houlihan Bridge on Savannah River map #17
40 .... The depths range between 6 and 12 feet in this unmarked stretch

Shore Descriptions for Savannah River Chart #16

1 .... Flooded forests and marshes on both sides
2 ....Flooded forest
3 .... High bluff with pines
4 .... Flooded marshes and forest
5 .... Low wooded bluff
6 .... Marshes
7 .... Marshes
8 .... Marshes
9 .... High bluff with pines
10 .... Flooded forests
11 ....Trees along the river, marshes behind the trees
12 .... Abandoned rice fields and canals
13 .... Marshes
14 .... Marshes
15 .... Beautiful area, marsh with scattered trees
16 .. Abandoned rice fields and canals

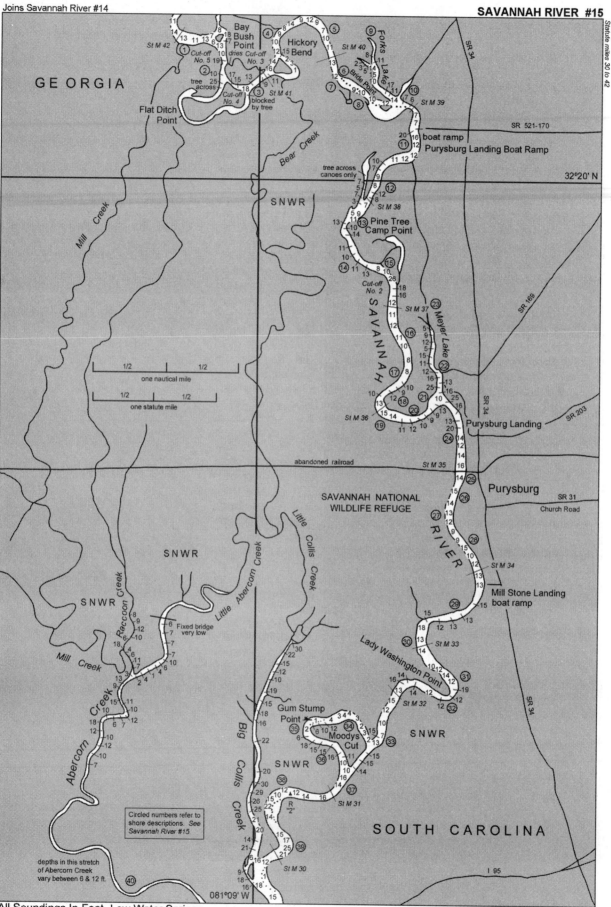

Statute miles 30 to 42

GEORGIA

Flat Ditch Point

Bay Bush Point

Hickory Bend

Forks Lake

Bride Point

St M 42
St M 41
St M 40
St M 39

Cut-off No. 5
Cut-off No. 4
Cut-off No. 3
tree across
blocked by tree

Bear Creek

Mill Creek

SNWR

boat ramp
Purysburg Landing Boat Ramp

SR 521-170

SR 34

32°20' N

tree across canoes only

Pine Tree Camp Point
St M 38

SAVANNAH RIVER

Meyer Lake

St M 37

Cut-off No. 2

SR 169

Purysburg Landing

St M 36

SR 203

SR 34

one nautical mile
one statute mile

abandoned railroad
St M 35

SAVANNAH NATIONAL WILDLIFE REFUGE

Purysburg

SR 31
Church Road

SNWR
SNWR
SNWR

Raccoon Creek

Little Abercorn Creek

Little Collis Creek

Fixed bridge very low

Mill Creek

St M 34

Mill Stone Landing boat ramp

St M 33

Lady Washington Point

Abercorn Creek

Big Collis Creek

Gum Stump Point

Moodys Cut

St M 32

SNWR

SNWR

St M 31

SOUTH CAROLINA

I 95

SR 34

Circled numbers refer to shore descriptions. See Savannah River #15

depths in this stretch of Abercorn Creek vary between 6 & 12 ft.

St M 30

081°09' W

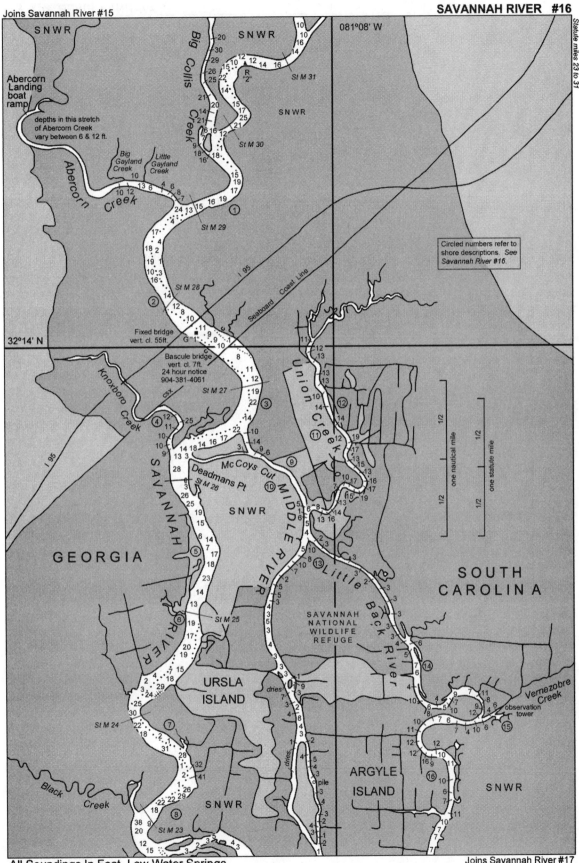

All Soundings In Feet, Low Water Springs

Joins Savannah River #17

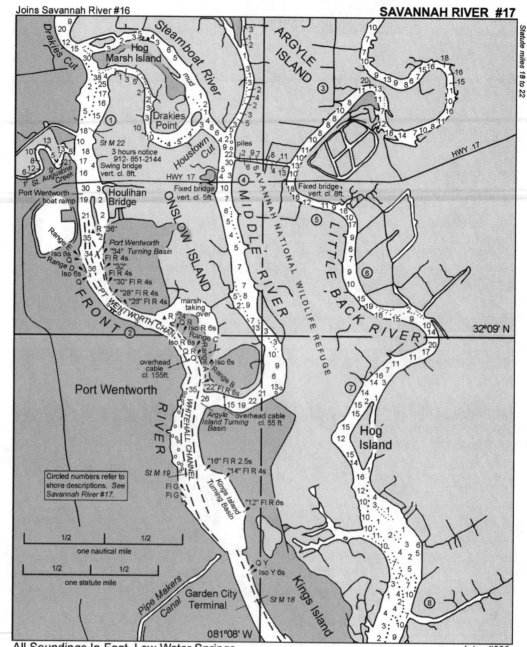

Joins Savannah River #16

SAVANNAH RIVER #17

Statute miles 18 to 22

32°09' N

All Soundings In Feet, Low Water Springs

081°08' W

Joins #006

Shore Descriptions for Savannah River Chart #17

1 .... Marshes
2 .... Industrial areas extend from here until east of the city of Savannah
3 .... Abandoned rice fields and canals
4 .... Marshes
5 .... Marshes
6 .... Abandoned rice fields and canals
7 .... Marshes
8 .... Abandoned rice fields and marshes

CHAPTER THREE

SAVANNAH RIVER TO OSSABAW SOUND

INCLUDING LITTLE OGEECHEE RIVER
CHATHAM COUNTY

THIS SECTION of the Georgia coast offers an unmatched variety of places to reach by water, from the old southern City of Savannah and the old beach resort island of Tybee to wildlife refuges on the outer barrier islands of Little Tybee, Williamson Island and Wassaw Island. People who chase ocean game fish for sport can charge out into the Atlantic through Wassaw or Ossabaw Sounds while kayakers will find enough miles of tidal creeks and marshes to spend a lifetime of vacations. Yachtsmen who cruise for the sheer pleasure of anchoring in quiet gunkholes away from crowds can find such places within a short distance from facilities that can service their boats.

THE CITY OF SAVANNAH

The approach up Savannah River from the Waterway and from offshore is illustrated on chartlets #004, #005 and #006. Two hotels offer well-equipped floating docks to yachts - Hyatt Regency, downtown on the south side of the river, and The Westin Savannah Harbor Resort on Hutchinson Island. Both are exposed to heavy wakes from passing tug boats. For reservations call the Hyatt at 912-238-1234 or the Westin Savannah Harbor Resort at 912-201-2000. The docks of Palmer Johnson Savannah, up the river, are for yachts undergoing work at the yard. A small public floating dock downtown lacks any amenities or security and is free for a three hour stay. For longer stays pay $.75 per foot at 100 Bryan Street garage.

The best way to visit the city when you travel by boat is to tie up in one of several marinas in Thunderbolt, a town that is virtually part of Savannah and overlooks the Intracoastal Waterway a few miles south from Savannah River. There you can always find a slip in Hinckley Yacht Services, VHF 16/68, tel. 912-629-2400; Savannah Bend Marina, VHF 16/68, tel. 912-897-3625; Thunderbolt Marina VHF 16, tel. 912-352-4931. Bahia Bleu, also on the same stretch of the Waterway in Thunderbolt, is closed on Mondays and their amenities are more modest, VHF 16/68, tel. 912-354-2283. Read the Services Section for details of any of these facilities.

To get to downtown Savannah from the marinas you can use a taxi cab or a city bus—for the schedule call 912-233-5767. Visiting old Savannah is well worth the effort, if only to see the largest historic district in the United States. The place was founded by James Edward Oglethorpe in 1733 after crossing the Atlantic with a shipload of families to establish the new colony of Georgia. Oglethorpe arranged the settlement according to a carefully thought-out plan dividing twenty-four square miles of land. The land was divided into wards, each with a public square. Despite the tremendous expansion of Savannah, twenty of the original squares still remain, surrounded by superbly preserved

US Coast Guard bark Eagle ties up at the Hyatt Regency Hotel waterfront dock in downtown Savannah.

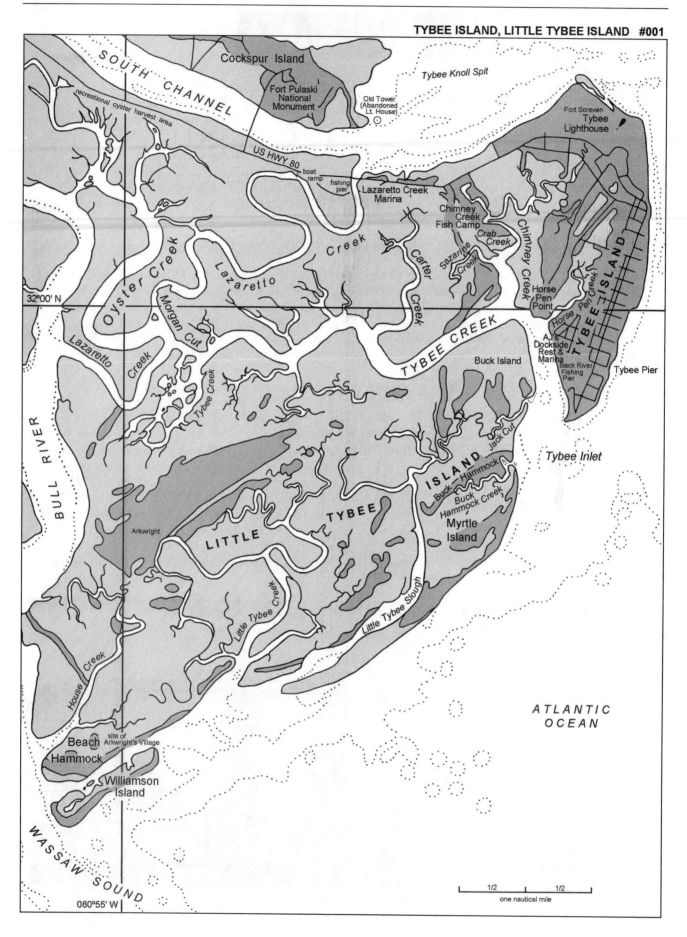

SOUTH CHANNEL

Cockspur Island

Fort Pulaski National Monument

recreational oyster harvest area

Tybee Knoll Spit

Old Tower (Abandoned Lt. House)

Fort Screven
Tybee Lighthouse

US HWY 80

boat ramp

fishing pier

Lazaretto Creek Marina

Chimney Creek Fish Camp

Crab Creek

Chimney Creek

Oyster Creek

Morgan Cut

Lazaretto   Creek

Carter   Creek

Sazarine Creek

Horse Pen Point

Horse Pen Creek

TYBEE ISLAND

32°00' N

Lazaretto Creek

Tybee Creek

TYBEE CREEK

Buck Island

AJ's Dockside Rest & Marina

Back River Fishing Pier

Tybee Pier

BULL RIVER

Jack Cut

Tybee Inlet

Buck Hammock

LITTLE   TYBEE   ISLAND

Buck Hammock Creek

Myrtle Island

Arkwright

ATLANTIC OCEAN

Little Tybee Creek

Little Tybee Slough

House   Creek

Beach Hammock

site of Arkwright's Village

Williamson Island

WASSAW   SOUND

080°55' W

1/2   1/2
one nautical mile

examples of various styles of American architecture. Live oaks draped with Spanish moss line the streets lending that deep-south touch to the place. In the Historic District the most interesting walking streets stretch through several blocks on the high land above the river. On the waterfront along River Street the old cotton warehouses have metamorphosed into art galleries, restaurants, bars and the like. From River Street short side streets paved with ship ballast stones join wrought iron staircases leading to the top of the bluff. Bay Street, lined with the old offices of shipping companies and agents, some of them still in the same business, runs parallel to the river. The Welcome Center with helpful brochures and information hides in the shade of the Hyatt Regency down on River Street. Savannah Visitors Center, another and larger service for visitors, occupies the old Railroad Station on Martin Luther King Jr. Blvd, a good walk away from the waterfront. It has a bookstore, a museum and a terminal for tours in a variety of vehicles. Whether you choose to ride or walk you will not go hungry—a good number of restaurants in the area cater to all tastes. Watercraft enthusiasts should make sure to visit the Ships of The Sea Museum located in the Scarbrough House also on Martin Luther King Jr. Blvd closer to Bay Street than Savannah Visitors Center.

TYBEE ISLAND

Due to its strategic position at the mouth of the most important river in Georgia, Tybee Island received plenty of attention in the very first days of the colony. Gen. Oglethorpe ordered the construction of a navigational beacon there in 1733. Finally finished in 1736, after Oglethorpe threatened to hang the chief carpenter, it lasted only until the winter storms of 1741. Three more lighthouses followed and today's 144-foot high Tybee Light stands on the 1773 foundations. By the Civil War the island already functioned as a beach retreat for the well-off. After a railroad connection was built with Savannah in 1887 Tybee became a major popular beach resort. US Hwy 80 supplanted the railroad in 1933 and Tybee Island (at various times in the past also named Ocean City and Savannah Beach) became even more thronged as the main beach playground for Savannahians and continues today as a popular family vacation destination.

For a boatowner Tybee Island makes a convenient base to pursue a variety of activities. The North Beach is included in the Colonial Coast Birding Trail. Sport fishermen can easily reach the offshore waters through Tybee Inlet as long as their boats draw little water and the weather is relatively calm. This shallow inlet gets very rough and dangerous in strong onshore winds blowing across the usual strong currents. Consult chartlet #004 *Savannah River, Lazaretto Creek, Tybee Creek*. However, there are plenty of protected marsh creeks nearby to keep anglers busy on stormy days. Kayakers, too, can enjoy exploring the creeks of the protected and undeveloped Little Tybee

Island across the water from the south shore of Tybee Island. Sea Kayak Georgia on Tybee Island will help with equipment and instruction—call 912-786-8732. The Tybee area is an island by virtue of being surrounded by Tybee Creek, Lazaretto Creek and the South Channel of Savannah River. Two smaller creeks, Carter Creek and Chimney Creek, cut far into the interior of Tybee Island.

MARINAS, FISH CAMPS AND BOAT RAMPS IN TYBEE ISLAND AREA

AJ's Marina is on Back River—the easternmost part of Tybee Creek. Basically a haul and launch facility, Marlin Marina also has a restaurant and floating docks for restaurant customers. Contact VHF 16, tel. 912-786-9533. See the Services Section.

Tybee Island Boat Ramp is a sloping beach landing on Chatham Avenue and Alley Way 3.

Chimney Creek Fish Camp on Chimney Creek outside the town is a haul/launch facility with gasoline and floating docks. There is a restaurant next door. Contact 912-786-9857. See the Services Section.

The 145-foot tall Tybee Island lighthouse rises from the 225-year old remains of previous lighthouses.

A long sandy shore faces Atlantic waves along the eastern perimeter of Little Tybee Island.

Lazaretto Creek Marina on Lazaretto Creek next to the US HWY 80 bridge has docks, gasoline, bait, tel. 912-786-5848. Dolphin watching and nature cruises leave from here. See the Services Section.

Lazaretto Creek Boat Ramp on Lazaretto Creek south of Lazaretto Creek Marina. A double ramp with a floating dock accessible from US HWY 80. See the Services Section for details.

Low tide uncovers a long sandbar extending into Jack Cut, a creek flowing into Little Tybee Island from Back River (Tybee Creek).

LITTLE TYBEE ISLAND

Tybee Creek on the north side, Bull River on the west and Wassaw Sound on the south side separate Little Tybee Island from other marshlands. It seems a miracle that this island still exists after all the plans to develop it, first by turning it into a giant recreational park, then a beachfront resort connected to Tybee Island by a causeway, and finally by mining for phosphates 40 feet deep under the marsh. The mining scheme caused enough public outcry for the Georgia legislature to pass the 1970 Coastal Marshlands Protection Act. Twenty years later the Nature Conservancy stepped in to arrange a satisfactory deal between the state and the island owners. Today the Georgia Department of Natural Resources watches over the Little Tybee Island Heritage Preserve which is a Holocene island of 6,780 acres of marshlands. A few hammocks with sandy soil rise less than 10 feet above the marsh, all together adding up to 600 acres. Now left in peace for the wildlife to roam, in the 1800s Little Tybee hosted a few homesteads. About three miles of long narrow beach serves as a buffer against the Atlantic. As a nesting area this whole island is essential for the survival of several species of shore birds. In the spring Tybee Creek has a good numbers of skimmers working the waters at dusk and even in the middle of the day building up reserves for breeding time.

Kayakers from Tybee Island, and any other small boat users, can explore Jack Cut and Buck Hammock Creek, two streams which face Tybee Island. Enter through the drying shoals on a rising tide only. Two substantial creeks, Little Tybee Slough and Little Tybee Creek, discharge through the island into the Atlantic. Using a rising tide small boats can go through Jack Cut all the way to Little Tybee Slough. The connection, a winding and very narrow stream, dries at low tide so explorers must plan accordingly. Bear in mind that it is easy to find the way through to Little Tybee Slough but much harder to decide which little creek to enter on the way back to Tybee Island. Here is a tip—enter the next creek south of the stream with a dead tree sticking out above surface. The GPS fix there at the mouth of the connecting creek, is 31°58'50"N and 080°52'15" W. After that the correct creek passes pretty close to the south end of a prominent long hammock and then winds in roughly an eastward direction. Going out into the ocean from Little Tybee Slough or entering it from offshore is tricky, too. Most of the time waves breaking on the shoals along the south shore of the island bar the entrances to these creeks. If you manage to get in from offshore on high tide during a calm summer day, make sure to leave before the tide drops too low to get out. Consult chartlet #004 to enter the creeks along the north side of Little Tybee Island. Both of them allow exciting exploration of the marshes passing near hammocks wooded with native trees. The westernmost part of Tybee Creek—its very beginning in the marshes of Little Tybee Island—calls for some attention to tides for the area dries completely. Chartlet #010 illustrates the entrance to House Creek, a stream which runs through the southwest part of Little Tybee and drains into Bull River.

Cruisers who plan to visit Tybee can anchor in the northeastern arm of Tybee Creek across from the mouth of Chimney Creek. The south arm of Tybee Creek traditionally called Back River has good anchoring depths but can get choppy and rolly when tidal current opposes the wind direction. Chartlet #004 shows the soundings here. Cruisers interested in other locations on Little Tybee will find smooth waters in Bull River, a little north from the westernmost point of the island opposite the entrance to Halfmoon River, or a little south of marker "6". Shallow draft boats may anchor off House Creek but deeper boats anchored further out may roll when a southerly swell arrives from Wassaw Sound.

WILLIAMSON ISLAND

At some time between 1957 and 1960 a sand spit off the south shore of Little Tybee Island grew into an island giving some hardy pioneering plants a chance to settle and hold the sands together. The island is still in transition and from consecutive surveys it appears to slide southwest. The Georgia Department of Natural Resources has taken charge of this island which has now become important for nesting loggerhead turtles as well as several species of birds nesting on the sandy grounds—least terns, Wilson's plovers, American oyster catchers among others. The DNR allows visitors to walk on the two mile long beach but the middle of the island is marked as off-limits in order to let these shore birds breed. A large prominent sign over the southwest tip of Williamson Island where you can find an easy landing plainly states visiting rules—no dogs! or other pets. The first time we visited the island we were appalled to see free running dogs while their owners stretched out in the sun under the sign. Most pet dogs probably will not actually attack birds but just the dogs' proximity, as much as ours, may startle the nesting birds into flying off the eggs or the hatchlings. It takes only a short time for the hot sun to cook unshaded eggs. Hatchlings are very vulnerable to predators like fish crows and gulls which always hover near the nesting areas in order to snatch the young the moment a parent flies off. I am sure that those loose dog owners enjoy the sight of soaring birds as much as the next citizen, yet . . . ? It is also worth remembering that domestic pets carry airborne viruses dangerous to wildlife which may have no immunity to them.

Williamson Island faces north towards Beach Hammock on Little Tybee Island.

An oyster shell bar marks the entrance to Cabbage Creek located west from Beach Hammock and Williamson Island.

WATERS EAST OF THE INTRACOASTAL WATERWAY

THE ATLANTIC APPROACH TO TYBEE ROADS AND SAVANNAH RIVER

To enter the Savannah River from offshore first locate the lighted buoy marked "T", also equipped with a whistle and topped with a red sphere. It lies at 30°57'53"N and 080°43'10"W. Soon afterwards you will see ahead, approximately northwest, lighted buoys "1" and "2", the first of several pairs of buoys marking the shipping channel to Savannah River. The position midway between these buoys "1" and "2", 31°58'18"N and 080°44'12"W, would also serve as a safe approach point for smaller vessels since these buoys lie in 30-foot-plus depths outside the 25-foot bank farther in.

CALIBOGUE SOUND

This sound, which joins the Intracoastal Waterway off Harbour Town on Hilton Head Island, South Carolina spills into the Savannah River estuary and the shipping channel by the front part of the Bloody Point Range. In order to enter Calibogue Sound steer north from buoy "13" of the shipping channel, pass either side of the front piling-dolphin marker of the Bloody Point Range and steer for lighted buoy "3". A red nun located northwest of the range dolphin also marks the entrance to Calibogue Sound but in this area of fierce currents it is better to consider buoys as unreliable aids of navigation. Soon after passing the piling-dolphin, you will go over the bar with a minimum of 8 feet—the shallowest part of this channel. Ahead, you will see red nun "4" on the east side of the channel and a lighted beacon "5" on the west side. You will now be in deepening water but you should take care not to stray too far eastward onto Barrett Shoals marked by a red day beacon "6". The Grenadier Shoal on the west side of this very deep channel is marked by green day beacon "7".

SAVANNAH RIVER— SOUTH CHANNEL

Chartlets #004 and #005 illustrate the South Channel of Savannah River from Elba Island Cut (Intracoastal Waterway) to the ship channel. This part of the river parallels the main Savannah River course and passes south of Bird Island and Cockspur Island. Apart from the indicated shoals the river has good depths and only the 10-

foot high bridge to Fort Pulaski on Cockspur Island limits this waterway to vessels with low superstructure. On the east end of Cockspur Island a small, now abandoned lighthouse used to mark the south entrance into South Channel, the main shipping channel in the old days. The last keeper of this light was George Washington Martus whose sister, Florence, waved at every passing ship for some fifty years—something to do with a missing sailor fiancee, some say. A 1971 bronze statue overlooking Savannah River from the east end of River Street immortalizes the indefatigable Florence, the waving girl. Marker "2" lying off the entrance to Lazaretto Creek, across from the old Cockspur Light, begins a marked channel leading seaward. The clearly marked channel with minimum 8-foot depths ends at marker "1". Seaward of marker "1", depths can be as little as 6 feet with shallower unmarked shoals. Leave marker "1" to the north. Even so, shrimp trawlers basing in Lazaretto Creek routinely use this route on the way to and from fishing grounds.

ST. AUGUSTINE CREEK

Chartlets #005 and #008 show the run of this narrow but deep creek, surrounded by wild marshes, from the ICW to Bull River at Screvens Point on Talahi Island. Boats which require less vertical clearance than 20 feet can continue eastward into Bull River and Wassaw Sound or to Tybee Creek. Just before Screvens Point, St. Augustine Creek forks south, passes Mud Creek and an unnamed creek which runs into undeveloped marsh, then at Battery Point on Whitemarsh Island it joins Richardson Creek and Turners Creek.

RICHARDSON CREEK

As shown on chartlet #005 from Battery Point this creek runs westward eventually joining Wilmington River and the Intracoastal Waterway. Two low bridges cross Richardson Creek which is also obstructed by several very shallow bars. On the Oatland Island side (north) the shores are mostly wild salt marshes. Homes and docks line up the Whitemarsh Island shores. By the way, Whitemarsh is pronounced Whitmarsh.

BULL RIVER

This large and important river connects St. Augustine Creek to Wassaw Sound. It also meets Lazaretto Creek and from there the South Channel of Savannah River and Tybee Creek. A large modern marina sits on the southeast side of the US HWY 80 bridge over Bull River. The attractively located Bull River Marina offers deep water slips for large (and small) vessels, sells fuels as well as ice and bait and operates a marine store. VHF 16/07, tel. 912-897-7300. See the Services Section.

Chartlet #008 shows how Bull River runs to Wassaw Sound passing by Shad River to the west and Lazaretto

Creek on the east side. Small creeks slash through the wild marshes on both sides of Bull River making this area very interesting for bird watchers and anglers. South of the narrow Pa Cooper Creek, Bull River meets Halfmoon River which runs west to the southern tip of Wilmington Island, a residential area with docks. The entrance to Halfmoon River passes on the north side of yellow beacon "BR". Across from that beacon you will see two pairs of danger signs marking an artificial fish haven. Along the shore of Little Tybee Island stands beacon "6", the last of the markers indicating the deep channel from Wassaw Sound. Shrimp boats use this channel on the way to Lazaretto Creek. They also often anchor in this area for the night. Yachts which stop there to have access to House Creek, Beach Hammock and Williamson Island should drop anchor just south of marker "6" to keep out of the way. To stay in the best channel between Bull River and Wassaw Sound pass east of beacon "1" and then steer about southwest to avoid the 3-foot shoal to the east—chartlet #010. We had a least depth of 6 feet on that heading. Pass west of buoy "14" by 300 feet or more. The incoming and outgoing currents set across this heading so you have to keep correcting the course.

LAZARETTO CREEK

Chartlet #004 illustrates the run of Lazaretto Creek and its connections to Tybee Creek and Oyster Creek. Lazaretto Creek, an important waterway for boats moving between Savannah River and Wassaw Sound suffers from extreme silting as shown on chartlet #004. Lazaretto Creek owes its name to a lazaretto (an Italian word for hospital) located at a quarantine station established in 1767 to process new arrivals into the Savannah area. It stood on the present site of the shrimp boat docks and the marina. African captives destined to be sold into slavery went through this station and those who died were buried somewhere around this area.

On US HWY 80, west of the bridge you will find a double launching ramp with a dock. Farther on along US HWY 80 just east the bridge you will find Lazaretto Creek Marina which sells gasoline, ice and dockage when available—tel. 912-786-5848, see the Services Section. Dolphin watching boats and fishing charter boats operate from Lazaretto Creek Marina which will make all the arrangements. The seafood store behind the marina is a good source of bait. Close to the marina you will find two restaurants overlooking the creek, Loggerhead's which has a dock for customers, tel. 912-786-9500 and Café Loco at 912-786-7810.

At Morgan Cut, about a mile after entering from Bull River, Lazaretto Creek forks into Tybee Creek, which goes east to Tybee Island. Oyster Creek runs off to the west eventually reaching a maze of side creeks which permit access to the public oyster beds marked as approved for consumption. Two short cuts demand your attention on

the depthsounder. The narrow short-cut to Lazaretto Creek has nasty oyster heaps at both ends. The wider short-cut to Bull River, a half mile farther north, also has hard oyster bars at both ends.

CABBAGE ISLAND

West of Beach Hammock on Little Tybee Island, across a vast shallow area, lies Cabbage Island, all marsh with a few tiny hammocks. Together with Little Tybee it makes the Little Tybee/Cabbage Island Natural Area. Cabbage Creek and another small creek exit on the east side of Cabbage Island—a popular fishing hole. You can locate it from a distance by a conspicuous heap of white oyster shells lying halfway between the creek outlets. Consult chartlet #010 for this area.

WILMINGTON RIVER

Chartlet #005 illustrates how Wilmington River begins where St. Augustine Creek takes off near Savannah River and Elba Island Cut. Soon after, Wilmington River, em-

Palmer Johnson yacht yard on the Savannah River is well-equipped to service very large yachts, both power and sail.

ployed as the Intracoastal Waterway, passes through the most populated, in a suburban way, parts of coastal Georgia. One bascule bridge at Causton Bluff interrupts the flow of boats higher than 21 feet with a complicated schedule. Monday through Friday it closes between 6:30 A.M. and 9:00 A.M. for the rush hour traffic. It will, however, open for waiting boats at 7:00 A.M. and 8:00 A.M. It again closes between 4:30 P.M. and 6:30 P.M. but will open at 5:30 P.M. if you are already waiting. During weekends and holidays the bridge opens on demand. See the Services Section.

About half a mile south of Causton Bluff bridge, on the east shore, you will see the entrance to Richardson Creek which connects to Bull River—chartlet #005. The entrance carries only 2 feet at low spring tides. Less than two miles south two yacht facilities claim opposite banks of Wilmington River just before you pass under a 65-foot clearance fixed bridge—chartlet #007. Hinckley Yacht Services, on the west shore is a boatyard with a marine store and transient docks, VHF 16/68, tel. 912-629-2400. Savannah Bend Marina, a modern facility on the east shore also monitors VHF 16/68, tel. 912-897-3625. Savannah Bend is owned by Sea Ray of Savannah next door where they can haul out boats weighing up to 8,000 pounds and always have technicians available. See the Services Section for more. Thunderbolt Boat Ramp, a public, single lane, launching ramp adjacent to the north side of Savannah Bend Marina, serves small boat owners. See the Services Section for access.

Thunderbolt, apparently named by Oglethorpe after a memorable lightning strike opened a spring of water here, is now virtually a suburb of Savannah. In the past serving mostly a busy fleet of shrimp boats, Thunderbolt's marine trades have now expanded to include yachts of all types. Boatowners will find here electronics repairmen, canvas makers, liferaft services, carpenters and engineers, the list goes on so check the Services Section. A regular bus line connects Thunderbolt with downtown Savannah and many transient yachts tie up here to visit the city. Bahia Bleu, the marina just south of the fixed bridge, has plenty of dock footage but it also caters to local sport fishermen operating a haul/launch hoist, selling bait, gasoline and offering dry storage. Contact, open 7 days a week, on VHF 16/68, tel. 912-354-2283. See the Services Section for details. Thunderbolt Marine owns a highly conspicuous yacht yard at the south edge of Thunderbolt. They also operate a large marina with all amenities, VHF 16/11, tel. 912-356-3875. See the Services Section.

Going southward after Thunderbolt Marine the river gradually widens, but do not stray outside the marked channel—mud banks extend far into the river from the shores. Herb River, joining Wilmington River south of marker "37", serves as a good protected anchorage for transient yachts. It also provides access to several communities farther inland. After taking a sharp curve a mile inland from the entrance, Herb River narrows and goes south. Tuten's Fishing Camp operates right under a bridge to Isle of Hope. They now only offer launch/haul service for boats up to 19 feet, dry storage and a floating dock. See the Services Section. After Tuten's the creek winds through marshes bordered by houses connected to the water by long docks. The creek which on the old maps joins Moon River has now diminished to a trickle. By returning all the way to the wide part of Herb River, where a fork called Country Club Creek takes off to the north, you can stay in good depths all the way to Bona Bella Marina, which has a haul/launch hoist, floating docks, bait and dry boat storage. VHF 16, tel. 912-355-9601. See the Services Section for details. Country Club Creek continues past Bona Bella, along a shore with houses and docks until the Savannah State University docks after which the stream becomes a trickle. On the way back to Herb River you pass a looped creek going around Wylly Island. Chartlet #007 shows that in its southern part this stream becomes dry at low tide.

After Herb River and the Savannah Yacht Club (members only) docks, Wilmington River turns into a wide and deep river. On the way south to Wassaw Sound it passes Turner's Creek, an important river with boat facilities. Deeper boats should enter on a rising tide to go over the shallow spots near the entrance—see chartlet #007. After the Sail Harbor docks the river deepens and stays deep until north of Johnny Mercer Drive bridge. It gets steadily shallower having only about 1 foot of water at low water springs where it joins St. Augustine Creek off Battery Point. All the boat fa-

Sail Harbor Marina in Turners Creek near Thunderbolt.

cilities of Turners Creek lie along the deep east shore. Closest to the Wilmington River entrance is Sail Harbor Marina and Boat Yardwhich offers dockage, a marine store and a small restaurant. VHF 16, tel. 912-897-2896. Next door they operate a small boat yard with a travel lift for boats up to 40 feet LOA, tel. 912-897-1914. Next up river, Young's Marina has docks, operates a haul/launch up to 4,000 pounds weight and offers wet and dry storage, tel. 912-897-6412. Continuing up river you will pass the docks of Miss Judy's Charters, a very popular and busy charter fishing and sightseeing operation, tel. 912-897-2478 and 912-897-4921. Just a bit farther, Hogan's Marina has transient docks as well all other services and amenities for sport fishermen, VHF 16/09, tel. 912-897-3474. Sasser Seafood and Boatworks ends the line-up of various marinas on the south side of Johnny Mercer Drive bridge. Sasser has a railway haul-out to accommodate one boat at a time and a wharf for shrimp boats. They also own the floating docks next door mostly used by resident boat owners, tel. 912-897-1154.

Back out on the Wilmington River you proceed south by a row of large homes with docks on the shores of Wilmington Island. You will see a wide belt of marshes on the west side of the river. Just south of Sister Island two narrow creeks join Wilmington River. The northern one, after going through marshes, shoals to become dry at low tides and connects to Skidaway River via a drying bridged canal. The other, Groves Creek, after a run through marsh swings by a wooded bluff—watch out for submerged tree stumps off this shore. You will find good fishing in this creek. After passing a large NOAA wharf on the way south you get to The Landings Yacht Club. Their marina offers docks, haul/launch up to 9,600 pounds, dry storage, a tackle shop and bait. The management has plans to dredge the depths of 3 feet to 4 feet (low tides at springs) in some parts of the basin. VHF 16/68, tel. 912-598-0023. Chartlet #007 shows the approach.

For the way south in Wilmington River switch to chartlet #010. The river joins Wassaw Sound between markers "20" and "19". Pole beacons mark the channel as you sail past the entrance to Romerly Marsh Creek and Romerly Marsh on the south side and the distant wide entrance to Bull River to the north. As you pass close to the north shore of Wassaw Island, south of beacon "16", the markers change to buoys.

WASSAW SOUND

When going seaward you will find that the depths within the buoyed channel hover around 20 feet-plus just past buoy "8". After that you should steer away from the red buoys planning to pass no less than a quarter of a mile west off buoy "4". There is only 7 to 8 feet if you pass close to buoy "4" and high swell may begin breaking in

this area. After rounding buoy "4" at the recommended distance head towards buoy "2W" passing about 300 yards west of it with never less than 13 feet. Sea buoy "2W" lies at 31°51'33"N, 080°53'00"W. It flashes red 4 seconds. Consult chartlet #011 for the soundings of Wassaw Sound. As in all channels in US waters you should leave the red aids to navigation to your right when steering towards a harbor—remember "red right returning"- and leave the green ones to your left. Wassaw Sound can get very rough when the ebbing, outgoing tide, is running against a high ocean swell. Use this channel only in smooth to moderate sea conditions and good visibility.

ROMERLY MARSH CREEK AND ROUTES TO WASSAW CREEK

As chartlets #010 and #016 show, Romerly Marsh Creek cuts westward towards Skidaway Island from the juncture of Wilmington River with Wassaw Sound. The mouth of Romerly Marsh Creek provides productive fishing grounds attracting local anglers. Farther in, the river runs through healthy salt marshes where birds find good fishing, too. The creeks radiating from the north shore of Romerly Marsh Creek eventually end as tiny drying rivulets far in the heart of the marsh. Two of them reach the residential areas on Skidaway Island before they expire. The very end of Romerly Marsh Creek comes to a maze of oyster bars which attract a large variety of birds from herons and oyster catchers to boat-tailed grackles. During early spring, fall and winter ducks always feed in the area. Habersham Creek, which is now silting and will probably be taken over by salt marsh in mid-length soon, used to join Wilmington River with Odingsell River and Adams Creek. In the 1800s Habersham Creek carried the busy traffic of small commercial boats which wanted to avoid the rough Wassaw Sound on the way southward from Savannah. In 1882, local interests persuaded Congress to approve dredging through the marshes to the east in order to open a new route which would connect Wilmington River to Wassaw Creek. The Georgia and Florida Steamship Company which carried passengers to the beaches on Wassaw Island was the most vociferous supporter of the project. Dredging began in 1883, ran into financial and topographical difficulties since the original survey delivered to the Corps of Engineers somehow failed to show a lot of solid land that had to be cut through. It took three years at the cost of $46,712 to complete the route which begins almost at the mouth of Romerly Marsh Creek, goes west of Dead Man Hammock and heads south through New Cut (once dubbed Parson's Cut after the owner of Wassaw Island). After passing through New Cut boats will need a rising tide to get over the drying parts of the creek before emerging into Wassaw Creek. This route, although requiring constant dredging, served as the Inner Waterway until 1905 when Congress ordered dredging a channel through Skidaway Narrows where the Intracoastal Waterway passes today.

SKIDAWAY RIVER

Chartlet #007 shows how at the Intracoastal Waterway marker "40" Skidaway River heads southward towards Isle of Hope. Isle of Hope Marina offers dockage, fuels, haul/launch for runabouts up to 26 feet long and a railway for shallow boats up to 55 feet LOA, a courtesy drive for grocery shopping, a marine store with several brands of outboard motors, kayaks, etc. VHF 16/68, tel. 912-354-8187. See the Services Section for details. Isle of Hope, an old community (and a National Historic District) overlooking the marina, has a great many interesting old homes to see on a street shaded by grand old oak trees and magnolias. A moderately long walk will take you to Wormsloe Plantation, a preserved estate from the times of Oglethorpe. Now Wormsloe Historic Site, it offers a forest walk, museum and that southern classic, a live oak lined avenue a mile and a half long. Isle of Hope also makes a good base for visiting Savannah, the city bus stops nearby and the marina will help with taxis and rental cars.

You will see several boats moored near shore south of the marina and sometimes transient yachts drop anchor among the local boats. However, the water is very shallow and the busy Waterway, which must be left open to heavy traffic, restricts the space—anchoring here is a bad idea with the exception of boats drawing 3 feet or less. Farther south the Waterway passes the entrance to Isle of Hope River which once carried small commercial boats on the way south from Savannah. This river has silted severely and Jones Narrows, once a drying creek is now solid salt marsh. In 1905 the Corps of Engineers dredged a channel through Skidaway Narrows (chartlet #012) which is still serving as part of the Intracoastal Waterway. The channel soon passes through the second and last opening bridge on the Intracoastal Waterway in Georgia. Skidaway Narrows bascule bridge opens on demand—use VHF channel 16 or 13. A public facility, Skidaway Narrows Boat Ramp, with two triple lane launching ramps sits on the west shore just south of the bridge. A small bait and snack shop serves the ramp users. See the Services Section. The Colonial Coast Birding Trail includes Skidaway Island State Park.

MOON RIVER AND BURNSIDE RIVER

Consult chartlet #012 for the way southward from Skidaway Narrows. Moon River, or Back River before its name was changed after Savannah native Johnny Mercer's successful hit song, has two entrances—both rather shallow. To anchor in the easier to enter northern arm, steer about northwest passing halfway between marker "72" and the north shore of Marsh Island. The southern arm has silted much more but shoal draft boats still use it. Consult the depths shown on chartlet #012.

Moon River cuts inland and then turns north through the marshes west of Isle of Hope. Chartlet #013 shows the whole run of Moon River which after the Diamond Causeway bridge enters attractive marshlands—a great wading bird habitat. Moon River eventually peters out in the marsh before joining Herb River up north. Boats which draw too much to anchor in Moon River will find more swinging room and depth in Burnside River, a short distance west from marker "76". A bit farther west, at Possum Point, Burnside River meets the Vernon River which takes over Intracoastal Waterway duties on the way south. You will find the comments on the northern part of Vernon River in *RIVERS WEST OF THE INTRACOASTAL WATERWAY* below.

Isle of Hope is an old riverside community on the fringes of Savannah.

VERNON RIVER TO HELL GATE

A mile and a half south from Possum Point Vernon River mixes waters with Little Ogeechee River and together they go into Green Island Sound eventually ebbing into Ossabaw Sound and the Atlantic. Meanwhile the Intra-coastal takes a side step into Hell Gate, a narrow passage along the west shore of Raccoon Cay which after the last dredging in 1999 carries a minimum of 9 feet but only 8 feet in the approach from the north—chartlet #015. Tidal currents set across the course into Hell Gate between markers "86" and "87", and south of "87", pushing the vessel off the deepest channel. Check by bearings if course corrections for the current set are necessary. The range "A" on the east side of Little Don Island facilitates navigation through the southern arm of Hell Gate channel.

DELEGAL CREEK

Chartlets #012 and #015 show how you can enter Steamboat Cut and Delegal Creek from Green Island Sound. Lying about east-northeast from Waterway marker "86" Steamboat Cut parallels the marsh along its north side. Red buoy "2" warns you to stay off the underwater shoal to the south (the island shown on NOAA charts no longer exists there). This channel gets shallow after you pass between buoys "3" and "4" having as little as 3 feet at low tide springs, so deeper boats need a rising tide to enter. Farther in depths improve and Delegal Creek Marina has nearly 20 feet at their outer docks. To book a slip or refuel call VHF 16/68, tel. 912-598-0023. Yachts which prefer to anchor off should do so a bit north of the marina docks. The marina charges a fee for tying up dinghies. See the Services Section. Attractive homes hide in the trees behind the marina where a walking trail winds northward along the marsh borders. Extensive marshes and uninhabited hammocks stretch along the west shores of Delegal Creek. Anglers often have good results in the upper reaches of this creek

OSSABAW SOUND

NORTH CHANNEL OF OSSABAW SOUND

Chartlet #015 illustrates the extensive shoals and the marked North Channel leading from Green Island Sound east to Wassaw Island. To continue past Wassaw Island and into offshore waters consult chartlet #017. Green can "7" off the southern tip of Wassaw Island is very small and hard to spot. You will find great depths near the south shore of Wassaw Island. Soon after you turn southward you will be able to see a large green can "5". Next ahead is a green/red nun "N". Pass to the east of it and, if you are heading off-shore, steer east of can "1". Pass north of "1" and head out to a tall lattice buoy with a light and a radar reflector painted red and white and marked "OS". Use this channel only in moderate ocean swell and good visibility. Sea buoy "OS" lies at 31°47'48"N, 080°56'10"W. A strong outgoing tide running against high swell will cause breaking waves especially in the vicinity of buoys "N" and "1" where you may encounter only 7 feet at low spring tides. In the offshore waters here you will commonly see northern gannets from the fall through the spring—the mature birds are white with black wing tips and their young are uniformly dark or mottled. Both ages feed by making spectacular bombing dives.

SOUTH CHANNEL OF OSSABAW SOUND

First locate buoy "OS" at 31°47'48"N, 080°56'10"W. To enter the South Channel from buoy "OS" steer west to pass north of buoy "1" and south of buoy "N". Next steer to pass south of buoy "4" and after that steer about midway between marker "5" on Ossabaw Island and the shoals in the middle of the sound. After "5" you can either continue northwestward towards the Waterway or swing into Bradley River to anchor. Consult chartlet #019. Read more about Bradley Creek in Chapter IV, *Ossabaw Sound to St. Catherines Sound*. The South Channel of Ossabaw Sound runs northwestward passing south of beacon "6"—see chartlet #019. Next northwestward, as shown on chartlet #020, will be the Intracoastal Waterway marker "91". If you are continuing west and south in the Waterway pass south of "91" and "92" and steer northwest between "93" and "96". After "96" you turn southwest into Florida Passage (The Intracoastal Waterway) passing east of marker"98".

WASSAW ISLAND

Wassaw Island National Wildlife Refuge is another example of the Nature Conservancy's contributions to the preservation of Georgia's barrier island coast.

Wassaw Island became private property in 1866 when George Parsons bought it as a holiday retreat. A little over a hundred years later, in 1969, the Parsons family sold the island to the Nature Conservancy, which later transferred the ownership, for $1, to the federal government. The island, except for some acreage still owned by the Parsons, thrives under US Fish and Wildlife Service patronage as an undeveloped refuge for animals and plants. Dense woods of native species cover the 2,500 acres of Holocene dunes which rise to 40 feet in the southern part of the island inland from the new accretionary beach. The relatively young sandy soils provide poor nourishment and trees, although growing thickly, lack the girth of the old growth possible on Pleistocene lands. Six miles of beach wrap around the Atlantic shores with hardly a human footprint—the stu-

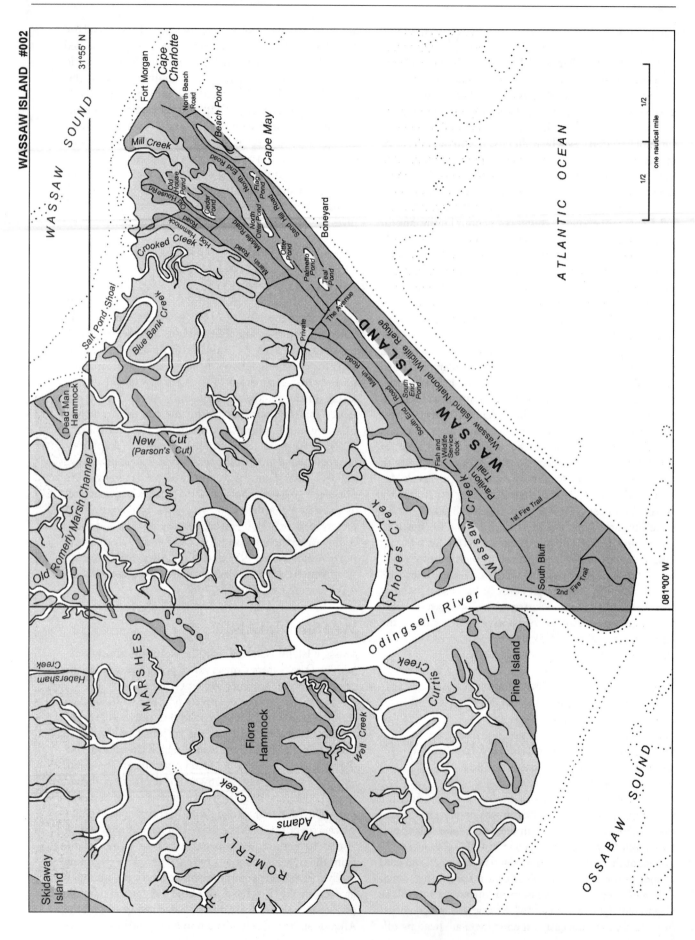

WASSAW ISLAND #002

31°55' N

WASSAW SOUND

Fort Morgan
Cape Charlotte
North Beach Road
Beach Pond
Mill Creek
Cape May
Old House Pond
Flag Pond
Old House Rd.
Cedar Pond
North End Road
North Otter Pond
Sand Hill Road
Boneyard
Hog Hammock Road
Crooked Creek
Marsh Road
Middle Road
Otter Pond
Palmetto Pond
Teal Pond
Salt Pond Shoal
The Avenue
Private
Blue Bank Creek
ISLAND
Dead Man Hammock
New Cut
(Parson's Cut)
Marsh Road
South End Pond
South End Road
Wassaw Island National Wildlife Refuge
WASSAW
Old Romerly Marsh Channel
Wassaw Creek
Fish and Wildlife Service dock
Pavilion Trail
Rhodes Creek
1st Fire Trail
South Bluff
2nd Fire Trail
081°00' W
Odingsell River
Curtis Creek
MARSHES
Habersham Creek
Flora Hammock
Well Creek
Pine Island
Skidaway Island
ROMERLY
Adams Creek
OSSABAW SOUND

ATLANTIC OCEAN

1/2   1/2
one nautical mile
1/2

dents of the programs provided by Skidaway Institute of Oceanography being almost the only visitors. Loggerhead turtles which nest on Georgia's barrier islands begin to land on Wassaw beaches in May. The eggs take about two months to hatch and on Wassaw Island volunteer observers rotate weekly to watch over and record the progress of each nest. Permanent and ephemeral ponds in the swales between the dune ridges support a healthy population of alligators and amphibians as well as provide popular breeding sites for resident birds and feeding sites for migrants. The infrequent human visitors who make it to the island on their boats have 20 miles of trails explore. The rules to this heaven include only daytime visits without pets and no camping. Take trash like snack wrappings and soda cans back with you. Another rule: the ranger's dock allows short tie-ups only to discharge and pick up visitors. Visitors from cruising boats should leave their dinghies along the bulkhead on the north side of the dock where no sharp oyster bank threatens inflatable boats and landing is easy on a sandy slope at low tide.

Ashore a large map of the area delineates the trails also shown on our chartlet #002. A long dirt road along the length of the island is called South End Road until it reaches the Avenue, a private road across the island, where it changes names to North End Road. The fastest way to reach the beach from the ranger's station is to walk south to the first trail to the east, Pavilion Trail. It enters the beach by a PVC pipe marked 60. South of it two bulldozed fire roads located at PVC pipes #64 and #68 can take you back into the shade of the forest and eventually to South End Road. To see the "boneyard" of trees felled by the sea eroding the northeast parts of the island, take a long walk northward on the beach and carry drinking water with you. If you would like to return in the shade of the forested main road, find PVC pipe marker #14 on the beach and walk inland until you get to North End Road (not marked by signs). Respect the areas marked as private. When you get to the Avenue do not turn west to the Parsons residence. You may, however, turn east to the beach—the Avenue exits onto the beach near marker #19. North End Road ends at the north tip of the island where you can see the remains of Fort Morgan built in 1898—a huge leaning lump of concrete-like mixture of tabby and granite gravel slowly sinking into the sands and half awash at high tide. Look at the sinking ruins as a good example of erosion by the sea which, in this area, can remove 33 feet of beach per year. The sea then transports the sand to the south where the island is growing at a good pace.

As you can see from chartlet #016 the most protected anchorage in the first arm of Wassaw Creek is completely sheltered by a wall of trees in winds from the northeast through east to the south. In gales from the northerly semicircle the marshes cut off all wave action so the water stays smooth. Another anchorage lies a little north of the dock. If you keep your boat's machinery off you will be able, from either anchorage, to see minks or alligators crossing the water, and in the evenings an otter may show up on the

banks. Ospreys who have a nest on a tall dead tree south of the dock regularly patrol the area.

Most yachts and cruisers navigate to Wassaw Creek from the west leaving Green Island Sound to join the marked channel through Ossabaw Sound. Chartlet #015 illustrates this approach. Bear in mind that the drying shoals south of Pine Island run far out from the beach. After passing can "7" head for the south shore of Wassaw Island—deep water runs close to the shore. Only very small runabouts can reach Wassaw Creek from Wilmington River through the Romerly Marshes and even they will need at least a part of the high tide to get over drying mud bars. Large yachts, for whom Wassaw Creek is too narrow, anchor in Odingsell River (chartlet #016) in depths between 17 and 23 feet. Odingsell River commemorates a black freeman, the slave owning planter Anthony Odingsell, who lived on Flora Hammock and Pine Island in the 1800s. From Odingsell River a small cruiser can reach Delegal Creek via Adams Creek using the rising tide to get over the shallow patches lying off the mouth of Adams Creek and towards Delegal Creek entrance (Chartlets #016, #012, #015).

Exceptionally tall healthy Spanish bayonets (yucca) overlook the beach at the Wassaw Island Wildlife Refuge.

RIVERS WEST OF THE INTRACOASTAL WATERWAY

Two substantial tidal rivers run inland from the Intracoastal Waterway: the six-mile long Vernon River and the Little Ogeechee River which continues into the interior for more than twelve miles plus several miles of side creeks.

VERNON RIVER

The Vernon River portrayed on chartlet #013 winds northward through marshes and heavily populated solid lands. Right after entering the river by Possum Point you will begin to see on the north shore large homes, some of them representing the antebellum era, an important phase of American architecture. A good anchorage lies half way between Possum Point and Beaulieu although there is plenty of room to anchor farther in. You can also find a secluded anchorage surrounded only by marshes after passing a shrimp boat dock on the west shore and Friday Creek on the east side. If you are in a sailboat anchor before those overhead power cables—they appear very tall but we could not ascertain the actual height. After that the river swings by the residential shores on Vernonburg, then splits into a deep channel to the east and a shallow stream along the west shore where, on a high tree right in front of some houses, a bald eagle couple has set up a big scraggly nest. From there all the way to Halcyon Bluff the river changes into a shallow creek with muddy banks only to get very narrow at Hahney's Creek.

LITTLE OGEECHEE RIVER

This large tidewater river took two chartlets, #013 and #014, to illustrate even without showing its end in Effingham County. As befits its impressive width the river holds good depths all the way to Coffee Bluff Marina, five miles from its junction with Green Island Sound. Besides haul/launch services, gasoline pumps and bait and tackle shop for the local sport fishermen, Coffee Bluff has deep water docks for transient and resident yachts.

The marina monitors VHF 16 on weekends, tel. 912-925-9030, closed Tuesdays. A city bus connects Coffee Bluff with Savannah. See the Services Section for details. Traffic on the Little Ogeechee is light and the stretch between Ella Island and Rose Dhu Island is good for anchoring except in strong northerly winds when you should move into the lee of Coffee Bluff with a particularly well-protected spot just west of the marina. Anchoring in the lower reaches, south of the marina, brings you close to interesting creeks. Crooked Creek is particularly scenic when it passes close to the east side of Rose Dhu Island with many resident shore and wading birds. The Girl Scouts utilize Rose Dhu Island for camping. Across the river from Ella Island, Harvey Creek and the connecting streams wind through pristine marshes providing good fishing.

West of Coffee Bluff (chartlet #014) Little Ogeechee splits into Grove River which runs through virgin salt marshes and connects to Rockfish Creek, all surrounded by wild marshlands. An arm of Rockfish Creek takes off southward through an abandoned rice canal and joins the Ogeechee River. Vegetation in this section changes to tall wild rice and bullrushes. Back at the junction with Grove River, the Little Ogeechee continues north as Forest River and has a side river leading towards residential areas. The Bells Landing area has a long stretch of private docks but there is also a public launching ramp and dock called Bell's Landing Boat Ramp—see the Services Section. Bell's Landing has a popular restaurant with a floating dock for customers. Back on Forest River and going north you pass through marshes which now begin to change to needlerush instead of smooth cordgrass. At the residential area called Windward you will see a creek taking off to the west. It goes to Grove Point Cove basin surrounded by homes. The basin dries at low tide except in the southwest corner. A (private) launching ramp with dock goes into the basin from the east shore. This river makes a loop southward through marshes and then along a row of substantial homes with docks eventually re-joining Grove River a few miles south. Back up at Windward where Forest River regains the title of Little Ogeechee, the river swings by Lotts Island fronted by docks and a hoist which belong to Hunter Air Force Base. The Salt Creek part of the river farther north winds through marshes and by forests—a great ambiance for contemplative angling.

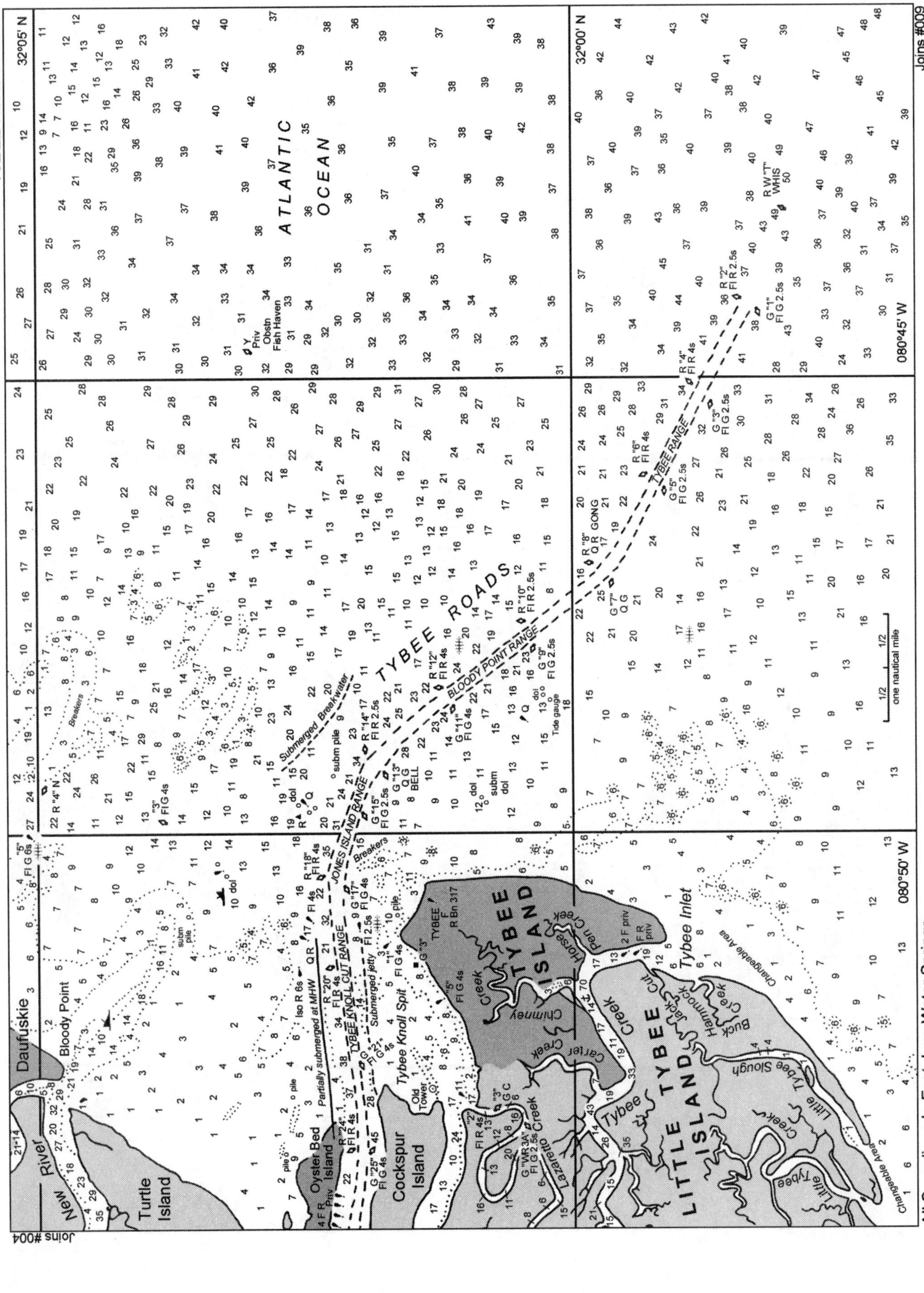

TYBEE ROADS   #003

32°05' N

32°00' N

ATLANTIC OCEAN

Y Priv Obstn Fish Haven

R W "T" WHIS

R "2" Fl R 2.5s

G "1" Fl G 2.5s

R "4" Fl R 4s

TYBEE RANGE

G "3" Fl G 2.5s

R "6" Fl R 4s

G "5" Fl G 2.5s

R "8" Q R GONG

G "7" Q G

TYBEE ROADS

BLOODY POINT RANGE

R "10" Fl R 2.5s

R "12" Fl R 4s

R "14" Fl R 2.5s

G "13" Q G BELL

G "11" Fl G 4s

G "15" Fl G 2.5s

JONES ISLAND RANGE

Submerged Breakwater

subm pile

dol

Q dol

Tide gauge

Breakers

R "8" Fl R 4s

Q R

Fl R 4s

G "17" Fl 2.5s

G "3"

TYBEE KNOLL CUT RANGE

Partially submerged at MHW

Iso R 6s

TYBEE F R Bn 317

Submerged Jetty

Fl 4s

TYBEE ISLAND

Chimney Creek

Horse Creek

2 F R priv

Tybee Inlet

TYBEE F priv

Carter Creek

Lazaretto Creek

G "WR3A" Fl G 2.5s

Fl R 4s

Buck Hammock Creek

LITTLE TYBEE ISLAND

Jack Cut

Tybee Creek

Little Tybee Slough

Little Tybee Creek

Changeable Area

Daufuskie

Bloody Point

New River

Turtle Island

Oyster Bed Priv

Cockspur Island

Old Tower

Tybee Knoll Spit

R "24" Fl R 4s

G "25" Fl G 4s

Breakers

subm pile

FlG 4s

1/2   1/2
one nautical mile

080°45' W

080°50' W

All Soundings In Feet, Low Water Springs

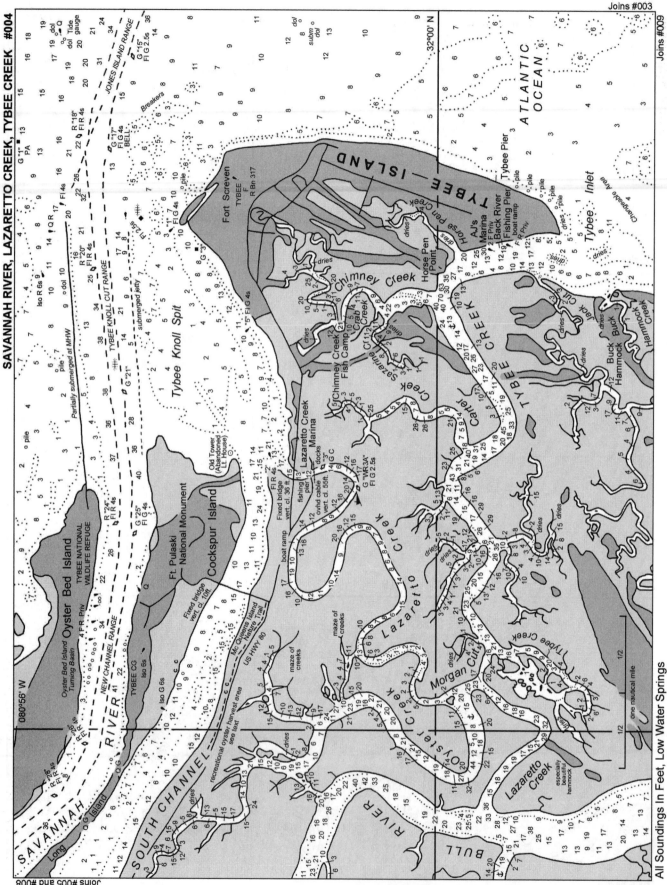

SAVANNAH RIVER, LAZARETTO CREEK, TYBEE CREEK #004

Joins #003

Joins #009

JONES ISLAND RANGE

TYBEE KNOLL CUT RANGE

Breakers

G "17" FIG 4s BELL

G "15" FIG 2.5s

R "18" FIR 4s

R "20" FIR 4s

Fort Screven

TYBEE F R Bn 317

TYBEE ISLAND

Horse Pen Point

AJ's Marina

Tybee Pier

ATLANTIC OCEAN

32°00' N

Tybee Inlet

Changeable Area

Fishing Pier Back River boat ramp

se Pen Creek

Chimney Creek

Crab Creek

Fish Camp

Sazarane Creek

Chimney Creek Fish Camp

Cattle Inlet

JACK CUT

TYBEE CREEK

Buck Hammock

Hammock Creek

Tybee Knoll Spit

submerged jetty

Old Tower (Abandoned Lt. House)

R "24" FIR 4s

G "25" FIG 4s

TYBEE National Wildlife Refuge

Oyster Bed Island Turning Basin

Oyster Bed Island

Ft. Pulaski National Monument

Cockspur Island

Lazaretto Creek Marina

fishing pier

ovhd cable vert. cl. 55ft.

G "WR3A" FIG 2.5s

Fixed bridge vert. cl. 36 ft.

boat ramp

Lazaretto Creek

maze of creeks

Mc Queens Island Nature Trail

US HWY 80

Fixed bridge vert. cl. 10ft

NEW CHANNEL RANGE

TYBEE CG Iso 6s

SAVANNAH RIVER

Long Island

SOUTH CHANNEL

recreational oyster harvest area see text

maze of creeks

Oyster Creek

Morgan Cut

Tybee Creek

BULL RIVER

Lazaretto Creek especially beautiful hammock

080°56' W

one nautical mile

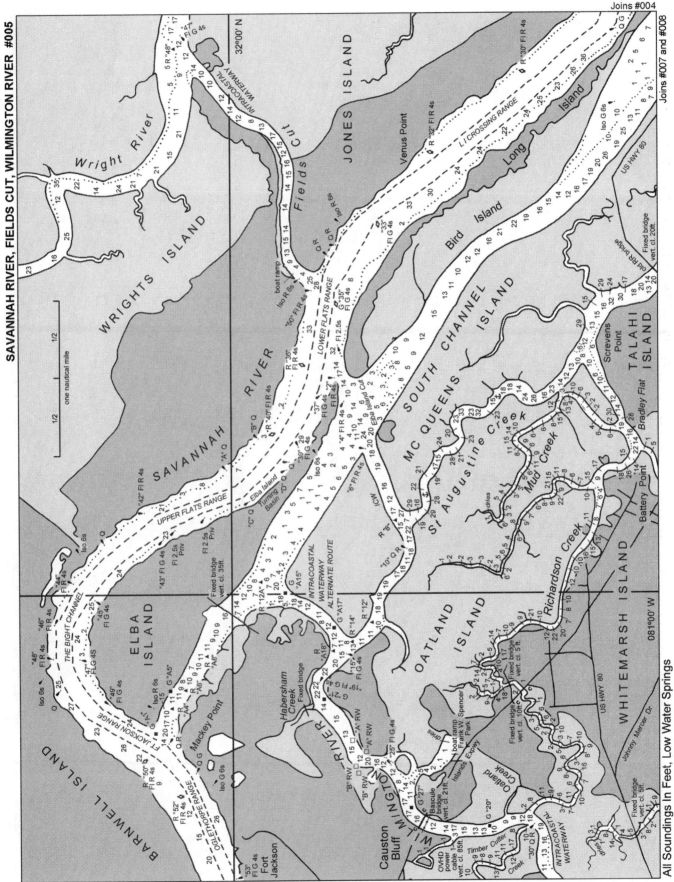

All Soundings In Feet, Low Water Springs

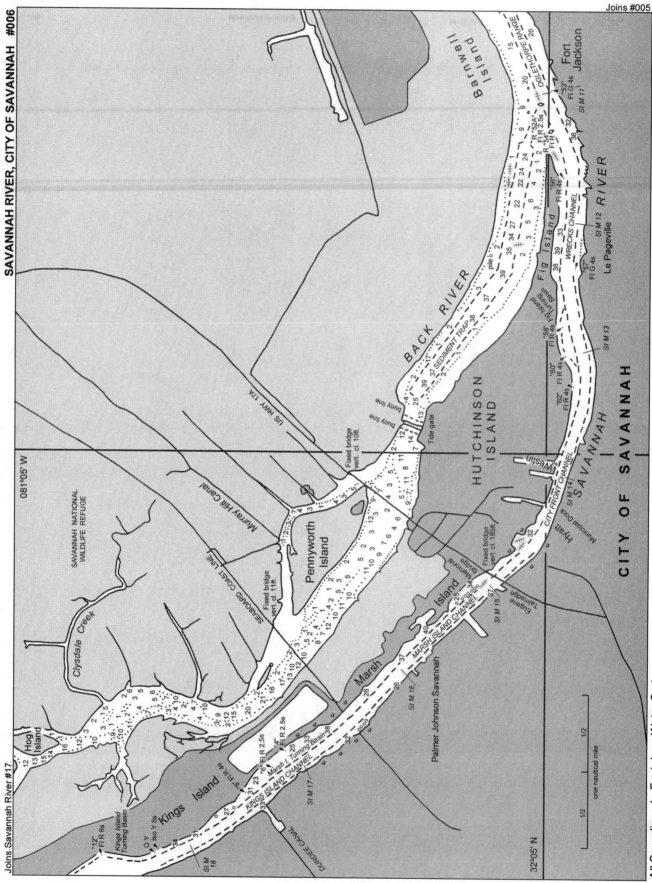

Joins #005

Joins Savannah River #17

081°05' W

SAVANNAH NATIONAL WILDLIFE REFUGE

Clysdale Creek

Hog Island

Murray Hill Canal

SEABOARD COAST LINE

Fixed bridge vert. cl. 11ft.

Pennyworth Island

Marsh Island

US HWY 17A

Fixed bridge vert. cl. 10ft.

BACK RIVER

Barnwell Island

Fig Island

HUTCHINSON ISLAND

SAVANNAH RIVER

Fort Jackson

OGLETHORPE RANGE

WRECKS CHANNEL

Le Pageville

CITY OF SAVANNAH

Palmer Johnson Savannah

MARSH ISLAND CHANNEL

KINGS ISLAND CHANNEL

Kings Island

DUNDEE CANAL

32°05' N

All Soundings In Feet, Low Water Springs

one nautical mile

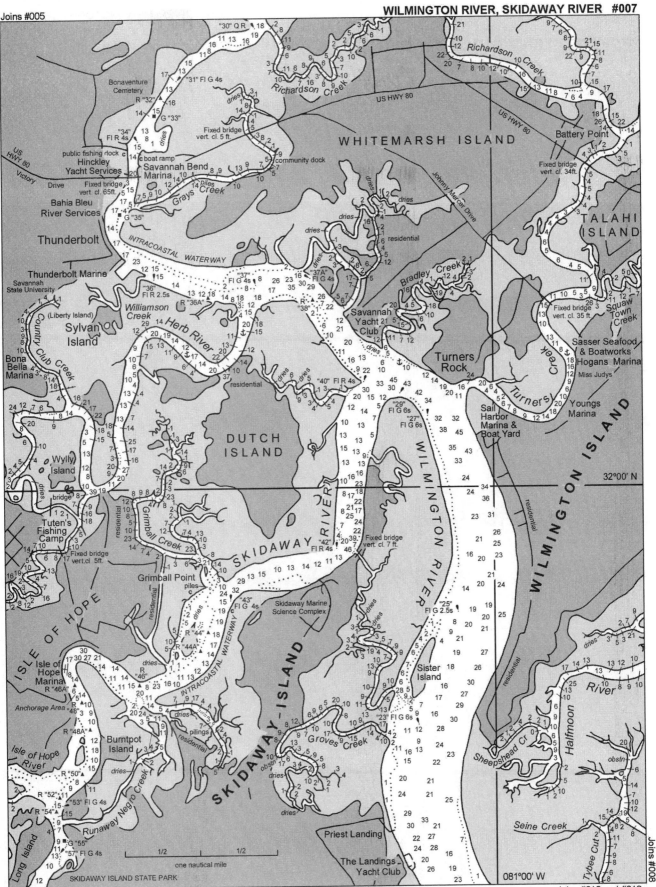

All Soundings In Feet, Low Water Springs

Joins #010 and #012

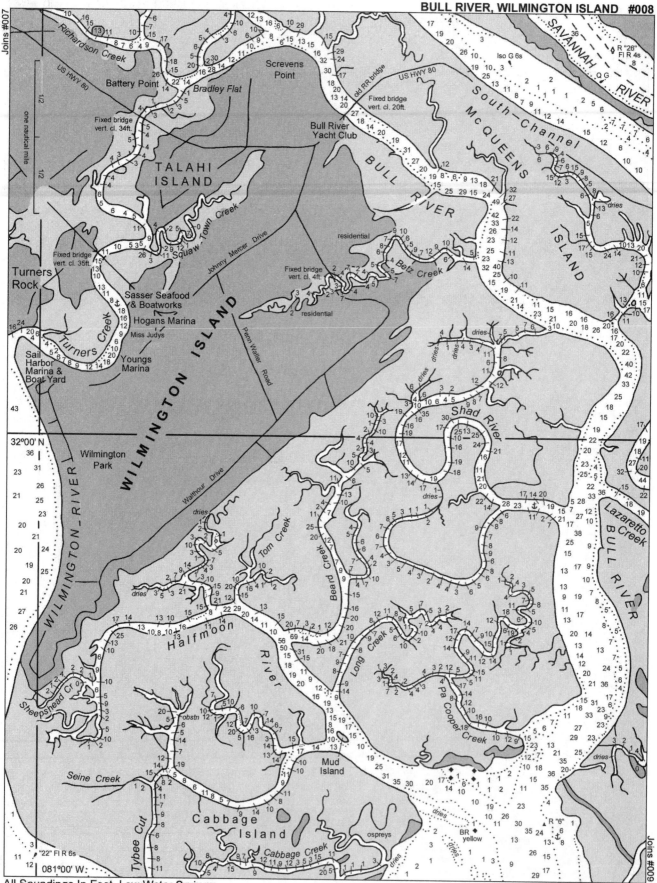

All Soundings In Feet, Low Water Springs

LITTLE TYBEE ISLAND, TYBEE ISLAND #009

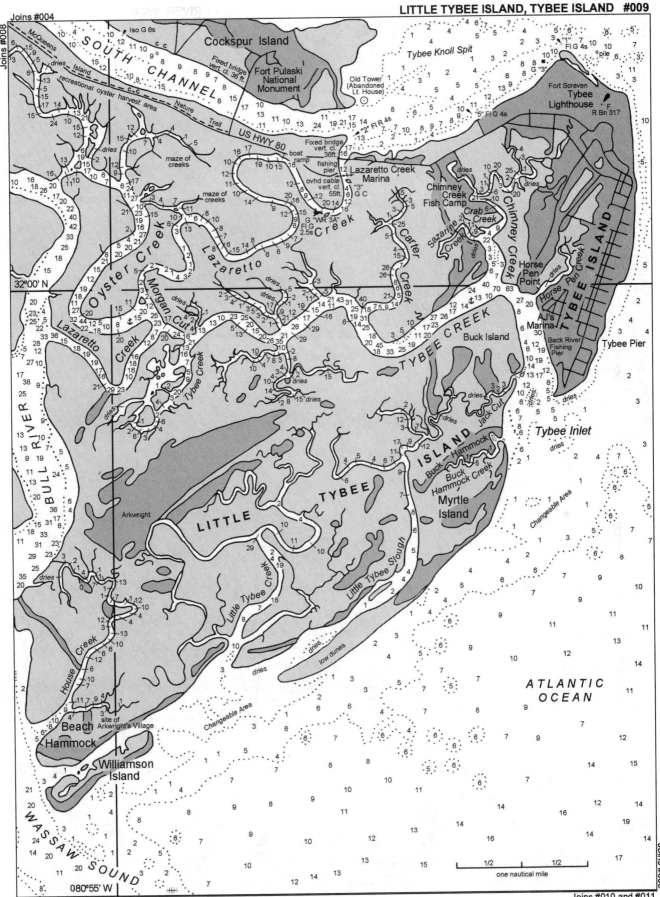

All Soundings In Feet, Low Water Springs

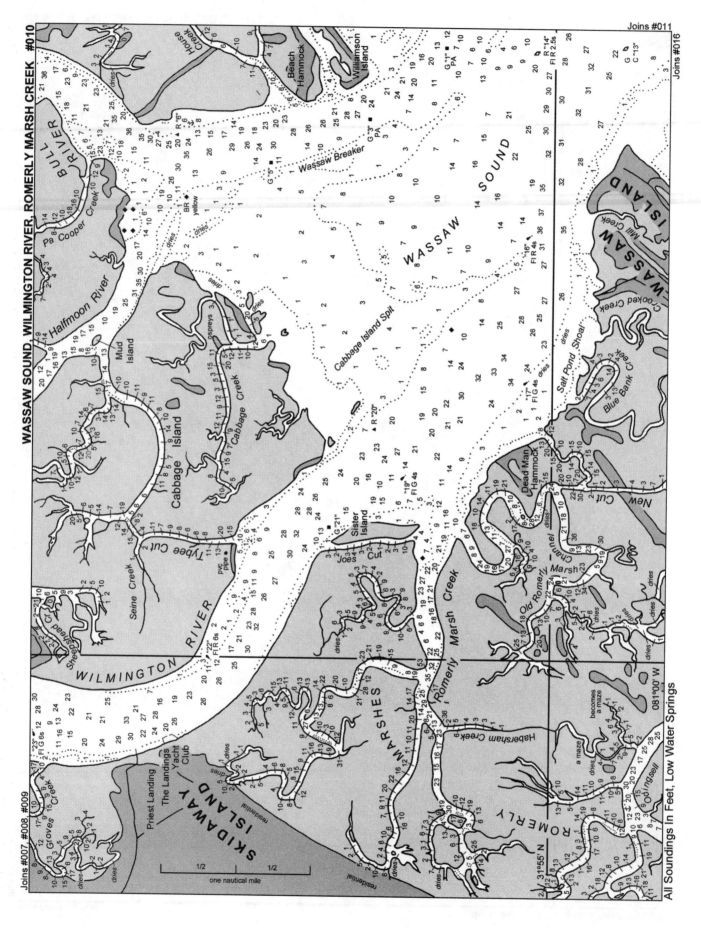

WASSAW SOUND, WILMINGTON RIVER, ROMERLY MARSH CREEK   #010

Joins #011

Joins #016

All Soundings In Feet, Low Water Springs

Joins #007 #008 #009

1/2   1/2
one nautical mile

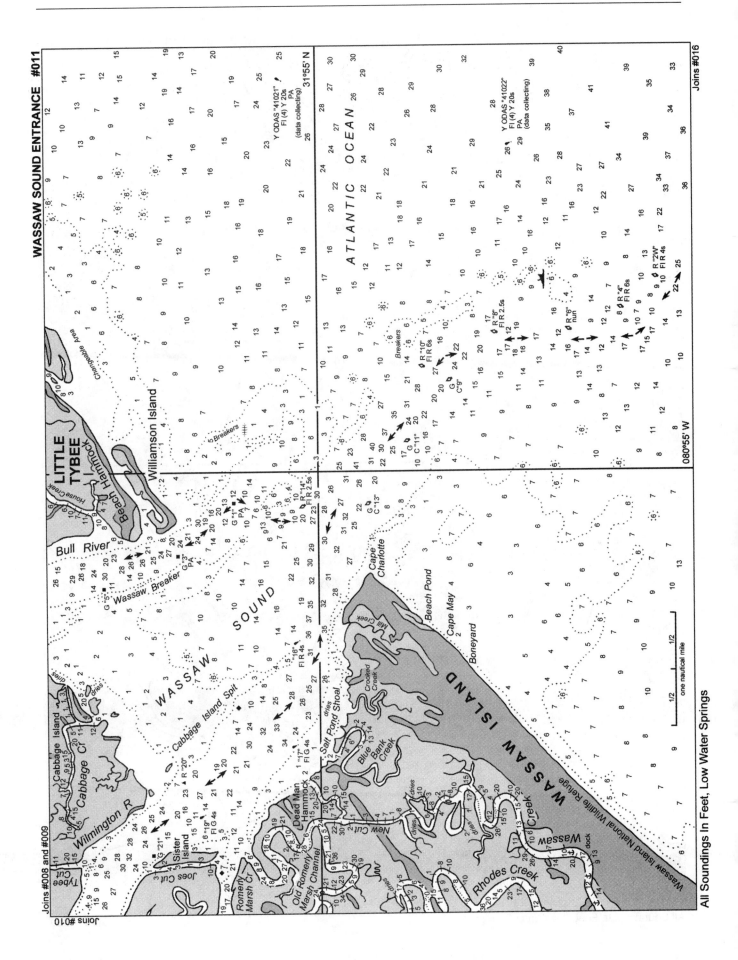

Joins #016

Joins #008 and #009

Joins #010

LITTLE TYBEE

Williamson Island

ATLANTIC OCEAN

Bull River

Wassaw Breaker

WASSAW SOUND

Cabbage Island

Cabbage Cr

Wilmington R.

Sister Island

Joes Cut

Tybee Cut

Romerly Marsh Cr

Dead Man Hammock

Old Romerly Marsh Channel

New Cut

Cape Charlotte

Beach Pond

Cape May

Boneyard

Mill Creek

Crooked Creek

Salt Pond Shoal

Blue Bank Creek

Rhodes Creek

Wassaw

WASSAW ISLAND

Wassaw Island National Wildlife Refuge

31°55' N

080°55' W

Y ODAS "41021" Fl (4) Y 20s PA (data collecting)

Y ODAS "41022" Fl (4) Y 20s PA (data collecting)

Breakers

Breakers

All Soundings In Feet, Low Water Springs

1/2   1/2   one nautical mile

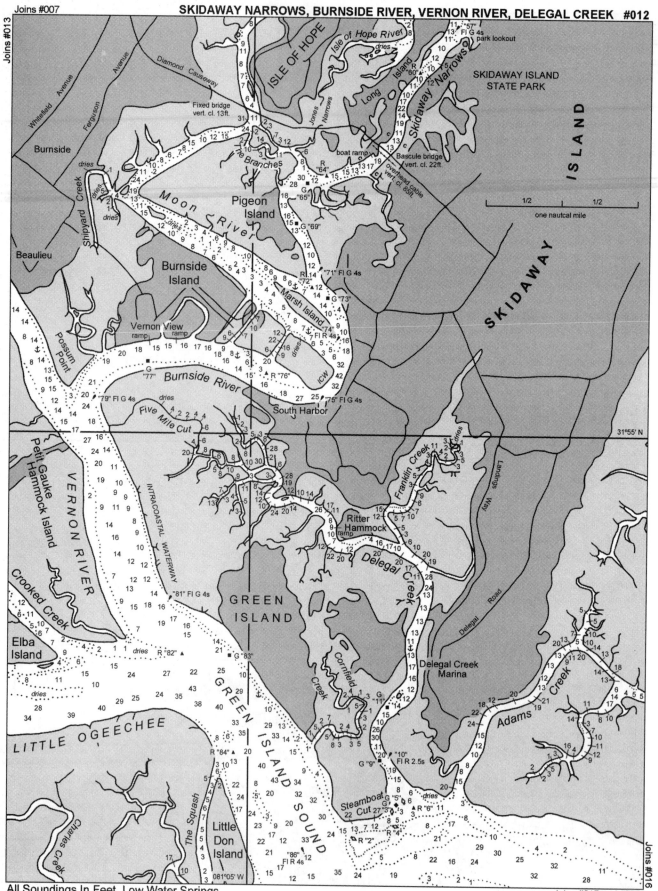

SKIDAWAY NARROWS, BURNSIDE RIVER, VERNON RIVER, DELEGAL CREEK   #012

All Soundings In Feet, Low Water Springs

VERNON RIVER, LITTLE OGEECHEE RIVER #013

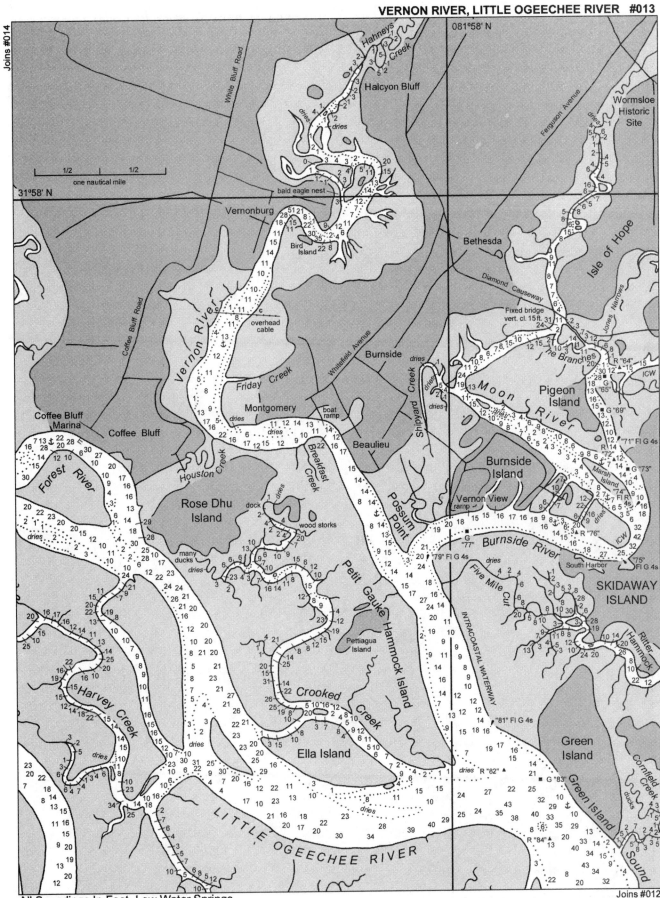

081°58' N

31°58' N

one nautical mile
1/2   1/2

Hahneys Creek
Halcyon Bluff
bald eagle nest
Vernonburg
Bird Island
Wormsloe Historic Site
Ferguson Avenue
White Bluff Road
Coffee Bluff Road
Vernon River
overhead cable
Friday Creek
Montgomery
Whitefield Avenue
Burnside
boat ramp
Beaulieu
Shipyard Creek
Bethesda
Diamond Causeway
Fixed bridge vert. cl. 15 ft.
The Branches
Moon River
Pigeon Island
Isle of Hope
Jones Narrows
R "64"
ICW
G "65"
G "69"
"71" Fl G 4s
"72"
G "73"
"74" Fl R
Marsh Island
Coffee Bluff Marina
Coffee Bluff
Houston Creek
Rose Dhu Island
dock
wood storks
many ducks
Breakfast Creek
Burnside Island
Vernon View ramp
Burnside River
South Harbor
"75" Fl G 4s
"76"
ICW
Forest River
Possum Point
Petit Gauke
Hammock Island
Pettiagua Island
Crooked Creek
Ella Island
INTRACOASTAL WATERWAY
Five Mile Cut
G "77"
"79" Fl G 4s
"81" Fl G 4s
SKIDAWAY ISLAND
Ritter Hammock
Green Island
Cornfield Creek
ducks
Harvey Creek
dries
R "82"
G "83"
R "84"
LITTLE OGEECHEE RIVER
Sound

FOREST RIVER, GROVE RIVER, COFFEE BLUFF #014

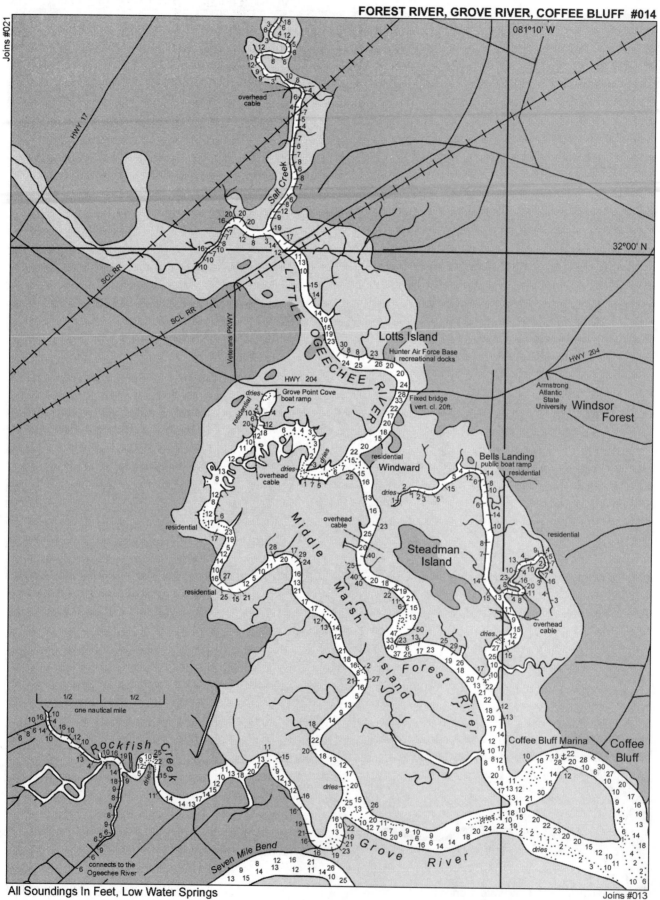

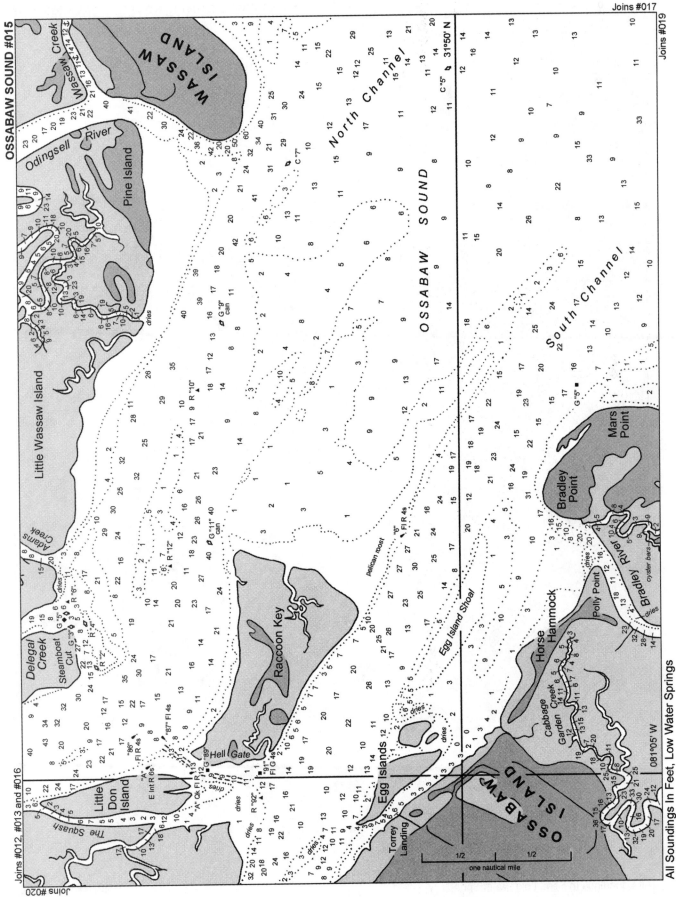

Joins #017

Joins #019

WASSAW ISLAND

Wassaw Creek

Odingsell River

Pine Island

Little Wassaw Island

Adams Creek

North Channel

OSSABAW SOUND

South Channel

Delegal Creek

Steamboat Cut

Raccoon Key

Hell Gate

Little Don Island

The Squash

Egg Islands

Egg Island Shoal

Pelican roost

Mars Point

Bradley Point

Horse Hammock

Polly Point

Bradley River

oyster bars

Cabbage Garden Creek

OSSABAW ISLAND

Torrey Landing

31°50' N

081°05' W

All Soundings In Feet, Low Water Springs

one nautical mile

1/2   1/2

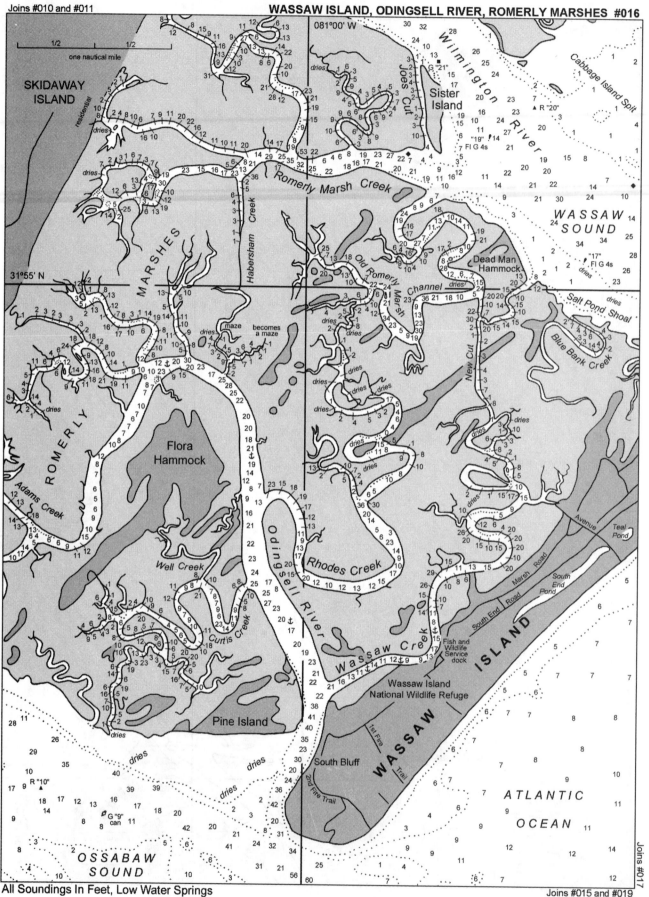

SKIDAWAY ISLAND

residential

dries

081°00' W

Joes Cut

Sister Island

Wilmington River

Cabbage Island Spit

G "21"

R "20"

"19" "14"

Fl G 4s

WASSAW SOUND

"17"
Fl G 4s

Romerly Marsh Creek

Habersham Creek

MARSHES

31°55' N

maze

becomes a maze

Old Romerly Marsh

Channel

Dead Man Hammock

dries

New Cut

Salt Pond Shoal

Blue Bank Creek

ROMERLY

Adams Creek

dries

Flora Hammock

Well Creek

Curtis Creek

Pine Island

Odingsell River

Rhodes Creek

Avenue

Teal Pond

South End Pond

Marsh Road

South End Road

Fish and Wildlife Service dock

Wassaw Creek

Wassaw Island National Wildlife Refuge

WASSAW ISLAND

1st Fire Trail

South Bluff

2nd Fire Trail

WASSAW

ATLANTIC OCEAN

R "10"

G "9" can

OSSABAW SOUND

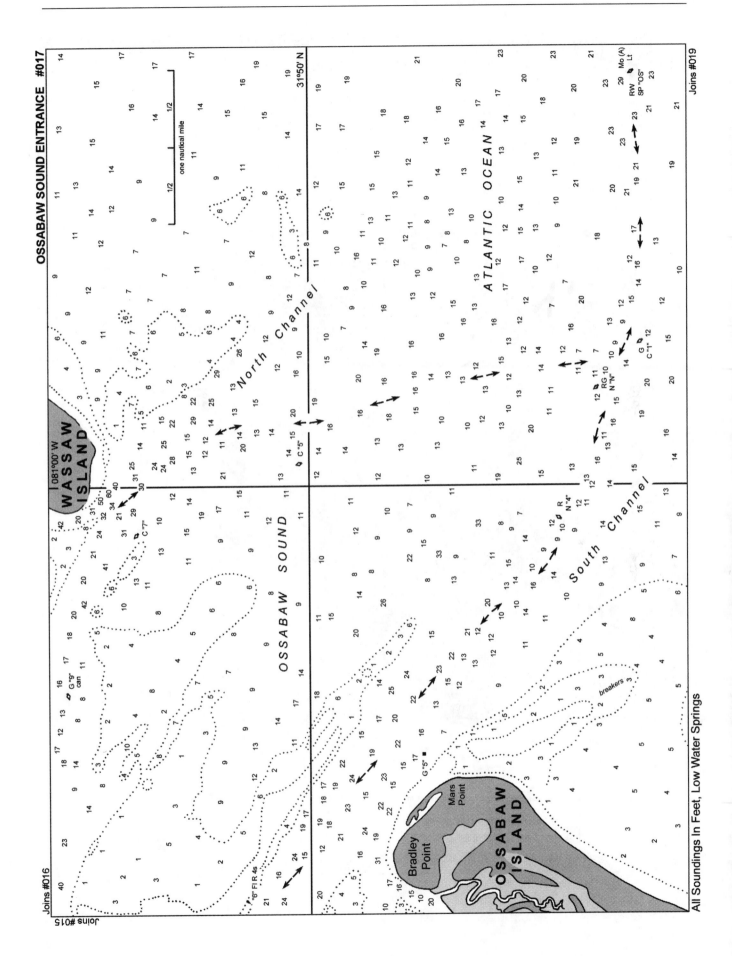

OSSABAW SOUND ENTRANCE   #017

Joins #019

Joins #016

Joins #015

All Soundings In Feet, Low Water Springs

WASSAW ISLAND

OSSABAW ISLAND

OSSABAW SOUND

North Channel

South Channel

ATLANTIC OCEAN

Bradley Point

Mars Point

breakers

31°50' N

081°00' W

one nautical mile

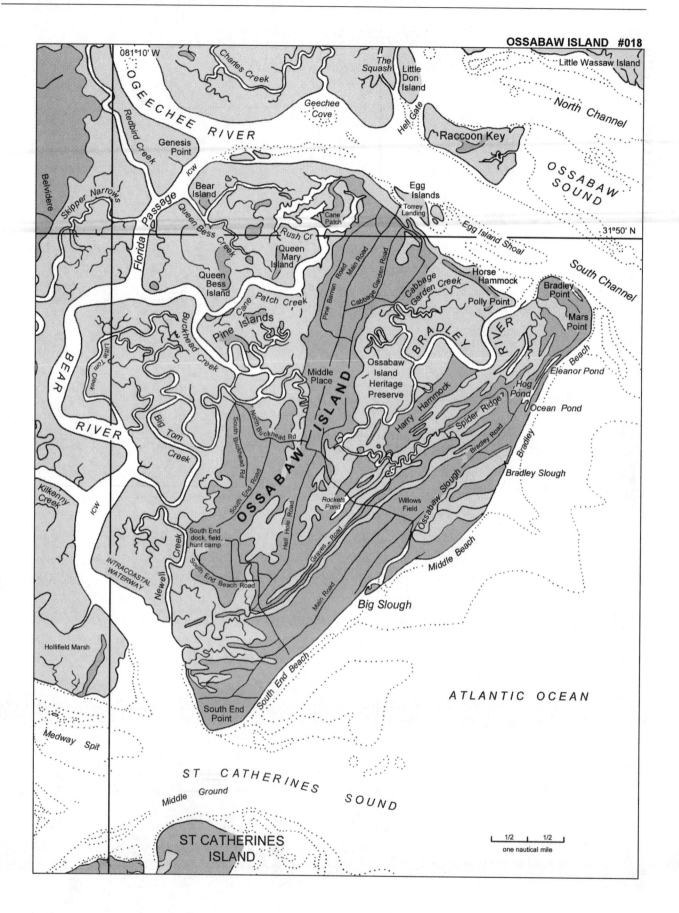

OSSABAW ISLAND #018

Little Wassaw Island

081°10' W

Charles Creek

The Squash

Little Don Island

Geechee Cove

North Channel

OGEECHEE RIVER

Redbird Creek

Genesis Point

ICW

Hell Gate

Raccoon Key

OSSABAW SOUND

Bear Island

Egg Islands

Belvidere

Skipper Narrows

Florida Passage

Queen Bess Creek

Cane Patch

Torrey Landing

31°50' N

Egg Island Shoal

Rush Cr

South Channel

Queen Mary Island

Queen Bess Island

Cane Patch Creek

Pine Islands

Horse Hammock

Cabbage Garden Creek

Bradley Point

Pine Barren Road

Main Road

Cabbage Garden Road

Polly Point

Mars Point

BEAR

Buckhead Creek

Little Tom Creek

Pine Islands

BRADLEY

RIVER

Beach

Eleanor Pond

RIVER

Middle Place

OSSABAW ISLAND

Ossabaw Island Heritage Preserve

Harry Hammock

Hog Pond

Ocean Pond

Big Tom Creek

North Buckhead Rd

South Buckhead Rd

Spider Ridge?

Bradley Road

Bradley

Bradley Slough

Kilkenny Creek

ICW

Hell Hole Road

Rockets Pond

Gravits Road

Willows Field

Ossabaw Slough

South End dock, field, hunt camp

Newell Creek

South End Road

South End Beach Road

INTRACOASTAL WATERWAY

Main Road

Middle Beach

Hollifield Marsh

South End Beach

Big Slough

ATLANTIC OCEAN

South End Point

Medway Spit

ST CATHERINES SOUND

Middle Ground

ST CATHERINES ISLAND

1/2   1/2

one nautical mile

CHAPTER FOUR

OSSABAW SOUND TO ST. CATHERINES SOUND

INCLUDING OGEECHEE RIVER AND MEDWAY RIVER
CHATHAM AND LIBERTY COUNTIES

THE AREA COVERED in this chapter includes Ossabaw Island with the surrounding waters, Ogeechee River, a major Georgia river which begins 245 miles from the coast and Medway, a substantial tidewater river. For a waterborne explorer Ossabaw Island alone provides enough exciting territory for a few weeks of cruising. In fact, to get there necessitates having a boat—the Ossabaw Island Heritage Preserve, the first island acquired under the Heritage Trust Fund of 1975, is closed to the general public except for participants in scientific projects and hunters who have won licenses through annual lottery draws. Not to worry, with a boat under your feet you will be legally and happily beach-walking or fishing or just plain gunkholing in an outstanding combination of marshlands and hammocks.

OSSABAW ISLAND

Boating to the portions of Ossabaw Island open to the public allows seeing the best side of the island: its remote beaches and marshlands. The island may look a lot more natural now than it was in the mid-1700s when the grounds began losing natural vegetation in order to make room for cattle and farming. Judging from the artifact rich results yielded by the 1890 excavations into the remains of an indigenous village, this large island, over 9 miles long and 5.5 miles wide, had seen about 4,000 years of human presence before the European arrival. In a 1733 land deal which secured the territory between the Savannah River and the Altamaha River for the colony of Georgia, General Oglethorpe guaranteed the Creeks the perpetual ownership of Ossabaw, St. Catherines Island and Sapelo. Soon afterwards the Creeks granted the islands to Mary Musgrove who had acted as an interpreter for Oglethorpe. Apparently, the half Creek woman was accepted as a tribal leader and enjoyed the great respect of the indigenous people. In 1750, slavery was approved in Georgia and Mary with her second husband, Thomas Bosomworth, were quick to begin moves towards turning the islands into plantations. Very soon the Bosomworths' claims to the islands

were challenged in the courts by the English trustees of the colony. In the end Ossabaw became state property. Sold to English planters, the island suffered through several owners until it was bought in 1924 by H. N. Torrey from Michigan. Removing thousands of cattle and feral hogs was the first improvement by the Torreys before changing the island into a private vacation and hunting retreat. It was not until the 1950s that Dr. Torrey's descendants returned to profitable logging and ranching. The Ossabaw Foundation, under the direction of Eleanor Torrey West, ran a variety of projects on the island from an artists' colony to a reputable commune for chosen college students. We owe the present undeveloped state of Ossabaw Island to the Nature Conservancy. In 1977, the organization negotiated the sale of Ossabaw for 8 million dollars, much under its estimated value of 15 million. Helped by a 4 million dollar donation by Robert W. Woodruff, Coca Cola's president at the time, and the acceptance of a lower price by the Torreys, the state of Georgia acquired the island in 1978. At present the Georgia Department of Natural Resources administrates the island while Ms. Torrey West retains her estate and influence over some of the environmental decisions. Only those participating in scientific projects may count on being invited to stay on the island. A few times a year hunters lucky enough to receive coveted licenses shoot on the island on dates posted by the DNR in late October, and in November, December, January and February.

Geologically very interesting, Ossabaw Island combines Pleistocene land up to 25 feet high with marshes to the west and Holocene beach ridges to the east. Due to the sediments carried by the Ogeechee River, Ossabaw Island is growing at its northeastern tip—since 1897 the shoreline has advanced over 3,400 feet adding more than 850 acres of land. However, what the sea gives in one place it takes away in another—just south of the accreting area erosion has removed over 1,500 feet of the beach in the same period. Similarly to other Georgia barriers islands, Ossabaw's southern tip is growing—at some periods by as much as 65 feet per year.

ANCHORAGES AT OSSABAW ISLAND

BRADLEY POINT

On weekends local pleasure boats come to the beach under the sandy cliff on the west side of Bradley Point. Deep water runs close to the edge of the sand and often as you walk along bottlenosed dolphins feed just a few yards away. Gently sloping, the nearly flat beach wraps around the northern tip of the island from Bradley Point to Mars Point. It continues south parallel to low dunes being slowly colonized by hardy pioneer plants backed by a thick wall of wax myrtles. Farther inland you will see the edge of a maritime forest. Damp low areas behind the primary dunes occasionally fill with rain water supporting low, yet rich plant life. Hog Pond, the permanent slough, is a boon for migrating and resident waterfowl. The dunes seaward of the pond would make a productive nesting area for ground nesting terns and oyster catchers were it not for the predatory feral hogs. It breaks one's heart to watch oyster catcher couples working on locating a nesting spot and knowing that their eggs will feed the hogs which scout the dunes every day. Neither nesting birds nor horseshoe crabs which come to spawn in the spring have a chance. Hogs easily overturn the shells, devour the crabs and root up the beach sand where the horseshoe crab eggs would mature. Loggerhead turtles come to nest on Ossabaw Island in record numbers—289 nests with eggs in 1999. During the turtle nesting season volunteers inspect the nest sites and protect them with hog wire fencing laid flat on the tops of the nests against predation by hogs and raccoons. Hogs, raccoons and ghost crabs will glean their share, anyhow, when the hatchlings break free and head for the sea.

After visiting the beaches at Wassaw Island you will be struck by the lack of sea oat colonies on Ossabaw— probably eaten by whitetailed deer whose hoof prints mark the sands. Donkeys, too, relish sea oats, and it does not take long to see small groups of them in the forest at the back of the dunes. Somehow you can not avoid wishing that the heirs and beneficiaries of Dr. H. N. Torrey would follow his example and eradicate or at least control the animals which do not belong in this environment. Some rough estimates quote 2,000 hogs and about 1,000 deer on the island. The two day hog hunt each February allows 100 hunters to take two hogs each. Not enough to diminish the hogs' foul presence on the island even when you assume that all hunters score hits.

BRADLEY RIVER

Cruisers who would like to spend more time in this wonderful area anchor in Bradley River where they find protection from the ocean swell. The anchorage close to the entrance gets choppy in strong winds from the north and northeast and you should then move farther into the river. Consult chartlet #019. This chartlet shows how Bradley River branches off into several streams with ample opportunities to fish or to see the marsh sights. Exploring the river branches to the north will bring you close to the higher forested Pleistocene upland. If you head south on Bradley River you will eventually enter the area south of Harry Hammock, an astounding maze of marshlands and numerous palmetto hammocks - a hangout for herons, ospreys and kingfishers. Traveling in a small low boat brings you close to the shores and shallow or dry banks but the area makes you wish you could soar to take in the whole of this amazing combination of wild land and water.

Anchored in the lower reaches of Bradley River we noticed how quiet the marshes were— missing were the usual mad cacklings of marsh hens (clapper rails) and we soon discovered the reason. As soon as the high tide receded large hogs foraged through the marsh, nosing through the *spartina* roots and the mud on the creek banks. Marsh hens nest low in *spartina* grasses with the egg sites of several birds scattered around one area—a single hog may easily wipe out a whole colony in one low tide.

A sandy bluff on the northwest side of Ossabaw Island descends into low dunes along the island's north shore.

QUEEN BESS ISLAND CREEK

Chartlet #020 illustrates this northernmost creek on the west side of Ossabaw Island. A shallow bar of 3 feet will force deeper boats to enter on a rising tide, but Bear Island makes it worth while. You can land on the island along its eastern bank but be prepared for some real wilderness. Tangled vegetation, spiders, snakes, bugs and startled rustlings in the bushes will slow your explorations. If you persevere, though, you may discover the brick remains of an old dwelling succumbing to nature under a soaring magnolia tree. The locals remember monkeys being marooned there for some arcane scientific project discontinued after boys from the mainland kept throwing foaming beer cans to the animals. The streams radiating from Bear Island between hammocks scattered through the marshes attract fishermen and crabbers and would challenge a painter's palette.

CANE PATCH CREEK

Chartlets #020 and #024 illustrate the intricacies of the convoluted connecting streams which, at high tide, join Cane Patch Creek to Little Tom and Big Tom Creek. Even large yachts will find spacious anchorages in Cane Patch Creek where it branches into Buckhead Creek. In its northern arm Cane Patch Creek changes into Rush Creek, a wide shallow body of water. During summer a small boat cruising here will send alligators sliding through the mud back into the safety of brown water. When startled fish begin churning the surface black skimmers suddenly appear to scoop up a treat. Wood storks swing their beaks through the thick water finding abundant food in the muddy flats of Rush Creek.

Chartlet #023 shows how Buckhead Creek passes by the oxbow which swings along the south shore of Pine Island. The oxbow dries but on a rising tide a small boat may potter along the low bluff shore overhung by palmettos, red cedars, wax myrtles and pines. A large osprey nest crowns an old dead tree, night herons nap in the lower branches and little green herons fish from small branches near the water. Across the water from the oxbow you will see a smaller stream which soon forks into a drying creek which joins Big Tom Creek a mile and a half farther. Another arm from the first fork goes east to a forested upland - low tide leaves sticky mud banks exactly where you would think of landing. Buckhead Creek eventually reaches Middle Place where a few small buildings mark the site.

BIG AND LITTLE TOM CREEKS

As illustrated by chartlet #024 both these creeks join the Intracoastal Waterway and are popular with transient yachts which move north or south with the seasons. Big Tom Creek is the somewhat wider of the two providing more swinging room for larger yachts. Both Tom Creeks invite small boat exploration through marshlands.

NEWELL CREEK

Chartlet #025 illustrates the entrance to this creek and #024 shows the depths to South End Hunt Camp. The floating dock serves hunters who tie up to unload their gear on the designated hunting dates. Past the dock the creek branches off and the easterly arm gets very narrow, in places too narrow for an alligator to swim past you and too shallow for him to dive under - during warm months slow for alligators here!

WATERS WEST OF THE INTRACOASTAL WATERWAY

Two important marinas and fuelling stops (including diesel) are located in the area. Kilkenny Creek hosts Kilkenny Marina and Ogeechee River has the Fort McAllister Marina. Ogeechee River and, further south, Medway River offer several interesting destinations for history buffs and nature lovers.

OGEECHEE RIVER

Ogeechee is Georgia's longest river flowing to the coast for 245 miles from its beginnings in Greene County, a good distance west from Augusta. The depths in its tidal section above a residential area called Fort Argyle restrict river use to very small, shallow draft boats. During our explorations we found a dry river bed about a mile up river from the Savannah and Ogeechee Canal entrance. Note that the high tide, much reduced in height, will arrive there about 4 hours later than the tabulated HW for the Savannah River entrance. Cruising boats can reach the Savannah and Ogeechee Canal as long as their superstructures are low enough to pass under three bridges down river—the lowest railroad bridge rises only 8 feet above mean high tide. Chartlets #020, #021, #022 and #023 provide the navigational data for the Ogeechee River from its outlet by the Intracoastal Waterway marker "98".

Entering the Ogeechee from the Intracoastal Waterway you will find no height restrictions for 21 nautical miles. Chartlet #020 shows the soundings and shoals at the river mouth. Above Shad Island, about five miles from the Waterway, privately maintained red markers mark a long shoal—pass south of the markers on the way to Ft. McAllister Marina—a full-service marina with deep water dockage, VHF 16/68, tel. 912-727-2632. See the Services Section. Just before the marina you will see a wooded area and a public launching ramp with a floating dock. This is Ft. McAllister State Historic Park which includes the park office, a small museum of the history of Fort McAllister and camping facilities, tel. 912-727-2339. See the Services Section. If you go ashore there note that on the way to the office you can turn right and reach the entrance to a 3.1 mile nature trail which loops through needle rush marshes, palmetto and other hardwood hammocks. The trail swings by a raised observation platform for viewing a vast open expanse of marshland and forests. The platform stands over a small tidal tributary of Redbird Creek and you can count on seeing there the resident belted kingfisher splashing in after minnows and then returning to his vigil on the contorted red cedars which line the stream bank. The park office (closed on Mondays unless a holiday) administers the camping and picnic site which overlooks the river near the fort. The same office manages a larger camping site on Savage Island which accepts trailers and tents, provides bathrooms with showers and canoe rental. The Savage Island Campground also has a launching ramp/dock complex on the bank of Redbird Creek. See the Services Section.

Attractive and peaceful nowadays, Fort McAllister saw a lot of action during the Civil War. For the Confederate States the Ogeechee River provided a vital link between the south and the outside world. Several routes passed through here - the river itself, the Savannah and Ogeechee Canal and two bridges carrying highway and railroad traffic. Fort McAllister, protecting these important supply lines, was an obvious obstacle to the Union forces.

A rare event—shelf fungi have managed to develop a hold on a sabal palmetto trunk growing in Fort McAllister State Park.

The river's defenses became the focus of the enemy's attention when a confederate blockade runner, a side-wheeler named *Nashville,* escaped up the Ogeechee and the pursuing Union ships could not get past the guns of Fort McAllister. *Nashville,* converted into an armed raider and renamed *Rattlesnake* was ready to leave the Ogeechee River when a Union fleet of gun ships led by the iron-clad *USS Montauk* arrived. The gun battle in February, 1863 destroyed the *Rattlesnake* but failed to subdue the fort. It took until 1864 before overwhelming forces led by General W. Tecumseh Sherman defeated the outnumbered confederate soldiers with a heavy loss of lives on both sides. Here on the Ogeechee, General Sherman reached the goal of his March to the Sea and soon afterwards the Confederate forces withdrew from Savannah. A leaflet available from the office guides visitors on a tour of the completely restored fortifications shaded by sprawling trees which have grown since the warring ended.

Henry Ford had the restoration work done at Fort McAllister when he owned tremendous tracts of land in the area. After the International Paper Company, the next owner of the fort, deeded it to the state, the Georgia Historic Commission brought the McAllister site to its present condition. In the 1970s the Nature Conservancy made a deal with the paper company and expanded the park area around the fort by 1,503 acres. Now, the fort participates in the Colonial Coast Birding Trail.

As you navigate up river through Seven Mile Bend you will find, at the top of the next S-curve, a canal through the abandoned rice fields—chartlet #021. A privately maintained sign "to Coffee Bluff" usually marks the entrance to this important connection between the Ogeechee River and Rockfish Creek which, in turn, takes you to the Little Ogeechee River. The position of this canal is 31°54'46"N and 081°14'22"W. Larger vessels utilizing the canal may prefer to travel on a rising tide which arrives here 2.5 hours after the Savannah River bar. Along the Ogeechee the tall grasses of the old rice fields cover the northern side of the river as far as the railroad bridge while the southern shores have a few residential areas up to the Ford Plantation. Along the river curve near Ford's you can look east at an island on which ospreys have built 5 huge nests on top of soaring dead tree trunks. Or you can look west at the old Ford mansion now all refurbished as the clubhouse for a residential development complete with a marina basin located on the west shore a half mile before the railroad bridge. Consult chartlet #022 for this part of the river.

When, in 1925, Henry Ford discovered the area, historically known as Ways Station, he started buying land and ended up owning 85,000 acres, which equals 110 square miles! Tremendous changes followed including the name change to Richmond Hill. The renowned moonshine industry vanished, a new clinic helped eradicate malaria, hookworm and other diseases common in the area, trade schools prepared local boys for work while girls received schooling appropriate for future house-wives. Ford's research laboratory here produced the first plastic thread, rayon, from the local black gum trees.

Sailing up river from the Ford Mansion keep along the east and north shores, pass to the east of an island covered with cypress trees and you will be able to drop anchor in a protected curve of the river as indicated on chartlet #022; the high tide, by the way, arrives here 3 hours later than at Ossabaw Sound. In the right time of the year a large nest on a conspicuous tree across the river may have the attentions of bald eagle parents. A little farther up you will see yachts in the marina basin which belongs to the Ford Plantation development and serves only the property owners. A couple of miles north on either side of the river by US HWY 17 bridge you have a choice of three facilities. Located on the west side of river, the Waterway RV Campground has a dock, a ramp, and a small bait and tackle shop which sells refreshments and cold drinks, tel. 912-756-2296. Across the water from them you can launch at Kings Ferry Community Park equipped with a boat ramp, fishing dock, picnic area, etc. See the Services Section. When you get hungry try Love's Seafood Restaurant on the east side of the river and on the north side of the US HWY 17 bridge. This full-service restaurant is open for dinner every evening except Monday, on Sundays they also serve lunch, tel. 912-925-3616.

After the I 95 bridge up river you will enter the most attractive parts of the lower Ogeechee-chartlet #022. Tides affect this part of the river and HW arrives here over 3 hours after the high tide in Ossabaw Sound. However, the root beer colored surface water is fresh, nourishing rich plant life along the undeveloped river banks. If you explore the burgundy colored waters of the Canoochee river (which branches off the Ogeechee just north of I 95 bridge) in summer you will encounter such a profusion of flowers, either rising from the water or dangling down from branches overhanging the water, that you may imagine yourself in some distant tropical destination. Large marsh pinks, eryngo, water primrose, pickerel weed, wapato and spider lily all bloom close to the water with flowers of the native wisteria and the trumpets of cross vine hanging down from above. The

Canoochee River flows through a military installation, though, so you must obtain permission to float through there from the Fort Stewart Military Reservation. Call 912-767-4794, it is well-worth a phone call to be able to vanish in this quiet world of flooded forests. This side of the river carried Fort Argyle in the 1730s—its construction ordered by General Oglethorpe to protect the new colony against the Spanish, French or Indian enemies. Reportedly, the site of the old fort teems with birds—call 912-767-4794 for permission to enter the military reservation.

The Ogeechee, though wider, easily matches the beauty of the Canoochee all the way up river to the Savannah and Ogeechee Canal entrance where you can land from a small boat (Chartlet #023). The canal, completed in 1830, carried barge traffic loaded with cotton, rice, lumber, naval stores and produce. Sherman's troops fought the Confederates over access to it and due to the resulting war damage canal operations stopped until 1866. During the next decade the enterprise did very well yielding nice dividends to investors. Eventually, as the local economy grew, the canal simply became too small and its maintenance ceased. Interest in its historical value led to the creation of the Savannah and Ogeechee Canal Society (912-748-8068) which organized the restoration work at the Ogeechee end of the old canal. Now you can see the brick remains of some of

An island of cypress trees and marsh on Ogeechee River.

the locks and walk the tow path enjoying a variety of native plants which took up residence within the silted canal—pretty clumps of obedient plant blooming in spring and summer and the spectacular flowers of marsh pink and swamp rose mallow adding color until September. In addition to four forest trails, there is the River Trail winding through the riperian forest of tupelo gums and other trees identified by tags. Ruby-throated hummingbirds and prothonotary warblers flit through the trees skillfully avoiding the huge webs of golden-silk spiders and argiope spiders some holding cicada remains - a great place to visit. The Savannah and Ogeechee Canal is part of the Colonial Coast Birding Trail. A small canal museum with nature displays stands at the entrance on HWY 204. The Nature Center has a good reptile section with live snakes and a pen to protect stray gopher-tortoises - a species facing extinction in Georgia. As it happens rattlesnakes tend to utilize gopher tortoise burrows as shelters. In rural Georgia, the sport of evicting rattlesnakes by pouring gasoline into these burrows not only kills tortoises but also pollutes forest soils. The Savannah and Ogeechee Canal Museum and Nature Center is free but they do not mind if you fill the donation box - it will be money well-spent to the benefit of all of us.

Up from the canal the river flows through a mixed growth forest until the Fort Argyle community of summer homes. As shown on chartlet #023, beyond them

A black and yellow argiope spider adds a zig-zag marker to warn birds of her web.

the river narrows and shoals considerably, its now tea-colored waters flowing over a sandy bottom through cypress forest - in this section even canoes will need portage or higher water levels than we experienced. People planning to sample the Ogeechee farther up will find a ramp on the west side of the HWY 204 bridge. Morgan's Bridge Public Boat Ramp has a paved surface. Nearby, at The Ogeechee Outpost you can buy bait and rent canoes.

REDBIRD CREEK

Chartlet #020 shows the soundings on this waterway all the way to the Savage Island campground. Redbird Creek continues past this facility for more than a mile - illustrated on chartlet #021. For yachts traveling the Waterway and looking for an anchorage to spend the night, Redbird Creek offers good protection by the surrounding marshes and an easy entrance. Otters and minks frequent the salt marshes of this creek. Farther up on Savage Island shore you will see a launching ramp and a floating dock - they are reserved for the campground customers and you can rent canoes here. For reservations call 1-800-864-7275.

KILKENNY CREEK

Chartlet #020 shows the northern portion of Kilkenny Creek where it joins Florida Passage and the Intracoastal Waterway. The section called Skipper Narrows suffers from severe shoaling and, apart from trailerable boats, only the local shrimp trawlers use this approach. To stay in the narrow deep channel requires abrupt course changes and even then you will encounter only 4-foot depths (at low water springs) in parts of this approach. Chartlet #024 illustrates the deep water soundings in Kilkenny Creek south of Bryan Fishermen's Cooperative docks. Kilkenny Marina, a full-service facility with fuels, transient docks as well as a haul/launch and tackle/bait shop for local fishermen receives pleasure boat traffic year round. The marina monitors VHF 16, tel. 912-727-2215. See the Services Section for details. Chartlet #024 illustrates the approach to the marina from Bear River near the marker "107".

Kilkenny Creek was once busy with ships which picked up cotton, rice and lumber from Kilkenny Plantation whose 1838 main house topped by a widow's walk still stands behind the marina office. The marina has a spectacular view, unbroken by any man-made structures, of a vast area of salt marshes stretching east to the dark margin of forest on Ossabaw Island. The road, shaded by grand live-oaks, leads inland and if you take the first turn to the right—Oyster House Road - and go straight to the wildlife management area gate you will find yourself on Duck Trail—a good place to stretch your legs after long hours of boating. Duck Trail continues through the forest on to the shrimp boat co-op but about half way along you will see a turn to the right—it leads to a dead end overlooking marshes.

During the busy transient season in the fall and spring the marina docks at Kilkenny fill quickly and yachts often anchor in Lincoln Creek. Show an anchor light at night here - local boats use the creek in the dark. When entering Lincoln Creek favor the south shore for a large shoal from the north shore extends far into Kilkenny Creek. The smaller creeks radiating from Lincoln Creek offer a great opportunity to explore in a small boat. The northern branch goes to a residential area but the southern arm, Cubbage Creek, swings through wild marshland and eventually touches the undeveloped shores on Cubbage Island and Belle Isle.

MEDWAY RIVER

Chartlet #025 shows where the wide mouth of Medway River meets St. Catherines Sound. To proceed up river you will have to pass north of the Waterway marker "116" and head northwest towards marker "2". Farther ahead you will spot marker "3" the second and the last of the aids to navigation in this river. Chartlet #026 provides soundings and the distribution of shoals all the way past the town of Sunbury. Jones Hammock Creek and Fancy Hall Creek which penetrate the marshland along the northern shores of Medway invite exploration in small boats whether to fish or simply to enjoy the solitude of open wild spaces. Only Fancy Hall Creek touches solid land with a couple of large homes in the trees - the area still remains superbly attractive.

The creeks on the south side of Medway also run mostly through marshlands with some exceptions. Sunbury Creek passes a residential spot on the northern tip of Colonels Island and Jones Creek swings by the relatively densely populated northwest shore of Colonels Island. If you explore Dickinson Creek you will at some point pass a small dock and the buildings at Palmyra. This is part of the Melon Bluff Nature and Heritage Preserve. The owners, Laura, Don and Meredith Devendorf, offer wildlife viewing on 3,000 acres of the preserve which stretches between Medway River and North Newport River to the south. You have a choice of several ways to explore 25 miles of nature trails, from biking, horseback riding to kayaking. A visit to their office located on HWY 84 is very informative, see chartlet #033. Kayaking is a big part of their repertoire with several scheduled events each year and participants can stay in their B&B style lodging in old plantation buildings. Bird watchers will find the preserve very satisfactory and well-prepared to receive them—Melon Bluff takes part in the annual Audubon bird count and is part of the Colonial Coast Birding Trail. Don Devendorf has spotted roseate spoonbills here! For information call 888-246-8188.

An old plantation house overlooks Kilkenny Creek and Kilkenny Marina.

Between voyages a shrimp trawler rests at Sunbury docks on Medway River.

After Dickinson Creek the river turns north and divides into Sunbury Channel and East Channel. Demeries Creek which goes inland from East Channel eventually reaches a DNR Law Enforcement base and Demeries Creek Boat Ramp and dock open to the general public. See the Services Section. Sunbury Channel, in 1770 a busy port hoping to extinguish Savannah as a shipping trade center, now hosts only shrimp boat docks, a small communal floating dock and Sunbury Boat Ramp, a public ramp with a floating dock and a fishing pier. See the Services Section. Visitors on cruising yachts should anchor north of the shrimper dock to keep out of their way. Unless you arrange to tie your tender at the private community dock, you should go the public dock at the Boat Ramp. A short walk up the road from there will bring you to a fork. Take a left and you will be on the way to Fort Morris State Historic Site - about half a mile. The site has a small museum and the earthworks offer a spectacular view of the river and the marshes. Fort Morris also participates in the Colonial Coast Birding Trail. If you turn to the right you will eventually reach a shaded old cemetery from the times when Sunbury played an important role in Georgia's political and cultural life.

Sunbury as a port followed the rise of the settlement of Midway founded by the descendants of a group of Puritans who first landed in Massachusetts in 1630. Hard to please as Puritans tended to be, some of the Massachusetts group migrated to South Carolina and then, in 1750 moved again.

This time they settled down in Georgia and soon developed a prosperous community based on a plantation economy in Midway, probably named after the English river Medway. The group strongly supported separation from England, not a popular cause in Georgia then, and of the three Georgia signers of the Declaration of Independence, Dr. Lyman Hall and Button Gwinnett came from this area. By the time of the War of Independence, Sunbury was an elegant port town with public squares, wealthy homes, wharves and its own customs house. A fort with a battery protected the river approaches and in 1776 Congress financed a larger fortification to oppose the expected British attacks. Fort Morris, named after Captain Thomas Morris, the first commander, was lucky until after the fall of Savannah in 1779 when the British took Midway and the fort. Sunbury recovered later as a smaller port and continued until the mid 1800s when better inland roads and railroads deprived the place of its importance. The burning of Sunbury and the neighboring plantations by Union forces during Gen. Sherman's March to the Sea finished the commercial standing of the town for good. Today you will find here a pleasant community with the 1700s cemetery the only reminder of the past. Take a look at the marker of Rev. Dr. William McWhirr, the founder (in 1793) and, for 30 years a principal of the Sunbury Academy, many of whose students later became prominent in American history. After listing the reverend's life achievements, the epitaph urges you "Reader! Go thou and do likewise!"

The northern opening of Sunbury Channel shoals to only 3 feet at low tide so deeper craft must use a rising tide to navigate that way. The high tide arrives off Sunbury 54 minutes after the standard reference time on the Savannah River bar. On the way inland Medway River changes first into Dutchman Bay and later splits into Jerico River and Laurel View River which, after branching off into small streams, flows west as Jones Creek. Chartlets #027 and #028 illustrate the meanderings of the rivers in this area. Note that Tivoli River and Belfast River begin at the same opening in the northern shores of Medway River. Tivoli River goes winding through marsh and by some residential shores which are just beginning to acquire large homes. The river narrows into a small stream after passing Tivoli River fishing dock and snakes north through pretty marshland (of needle rush mostly) backed by forested upland. Belfast River was once a site of a lumber mill and had some ship traffic. Only a pile of ballast stones commemorates those years and is a hazard to newcomers when it disappears under rising tides. The attractive homes along the bluff overlooking the river enjoy an undisturbed view of marshes with Sunbury barely visible in the distance. If you like anchoring in the middle of nowhere with marsh views all around you will like the area where the west end of Belfast Creek meets Jerico River. This place stays smooth when heavy northerly winds rattle palmetto fronds along the coast. About a mile north from this junction you will encounter a floating dock and a ramp which belong to the residential community in the area.

However, there is a public boat ramp half a mile farther up river. Dutchman Bay makes a nice anchorage but will get choppy when the ebbing tide runs against a strong breeze from the east. Jones Creek on the way west passes by Cross Creek, a short-cut for small boats traveling to Jerico River. Jeff's Crab and Bait House sits on the east side of Cross Creek just before a low bridge joining it to Isle of Wight. Jones Creek passes by a basin with Liberty County Recreational Park boat ramp and eventually joins a side creek which you can take to circumnavigate Isle of Wight, a heavily populated place with many docks. If you continue clockwise on this creek you will eventually join Jerico River which flows by Egypt Island and a man-made basin with a boat ramp. North of Limerick (St. George's) the creek runs through marshlands absolutely teeming with birds all the way to the low railroad bridge - see chartlet #028.

ST. CATHERINES SOUND

Medway River reaches the Atlantic through a wide and reasonably deep sound fringed by shallow banks off the southeast shores of Ossabaw Island and the northeast shores of St. Catherines Island. Chartlet #029 illustrates the channel marked by buoys which may be moved by

This oyster bank, raided by an unscrupulous harvester, will take decades to recover.

the Coast Guard to follow the changes in the configuration of the shoals. Only one channel buoy, green can "7", carries a light. The large red and white offshore buoy marked "STC" also carries a light. To stay in deep water all the way to 30-foot soundings offshore you must follow the rhumb line from green can "3" to the offshore buoy "STC". When entering, first locate buoy "STC" which lies at 30°40'13"N and 081°00'12"W, then steer for the green can "3". Since the important "3" does not have a light you should only use this channel in daylight with good visibility. We found 8-foot depths outside the recommended course to the northeast of green can "3" so high swell may begin breaking in this area—stay on course and use this approach only in good weather. Remember that ebbing, outgoing, tide running against ocean swell will cause breaking seas; flooding, incoming, tide will smooth the water surface to some degree. As in all entrance channels in the USA when steering towards a port you should leave red markers to your right and green to your left. When heading through St. Catherines Sound northwards into Bear River you will have deep water near the southwestern tip of Ossabaw Island. Heading west into Medway River and south into the Intracoastal Waterway avoid the unmarked shoals of Middle Ground—chartlets #029 and #025.

Joins #015 and #020

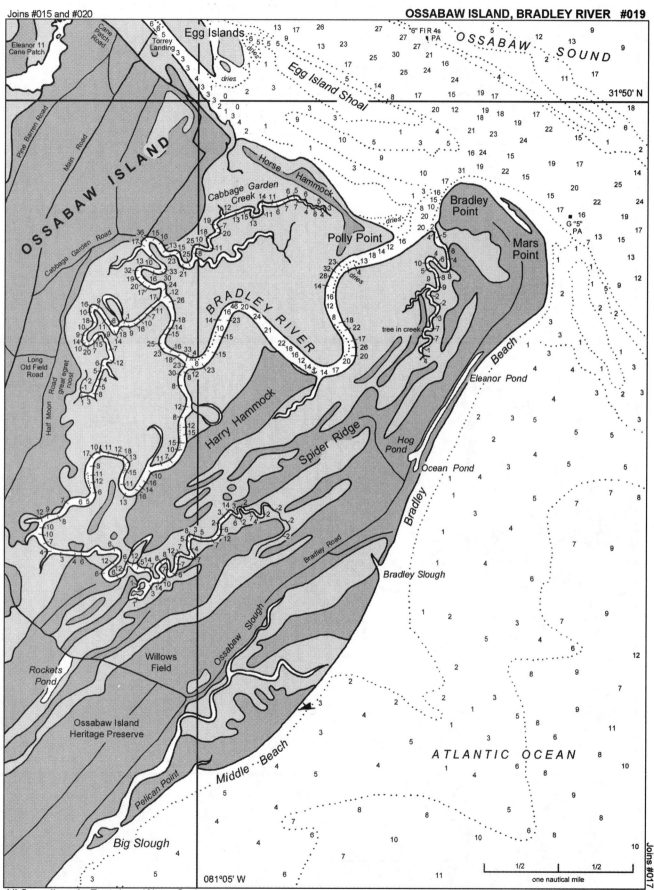

All Soundings In Feet, Low Water Springs

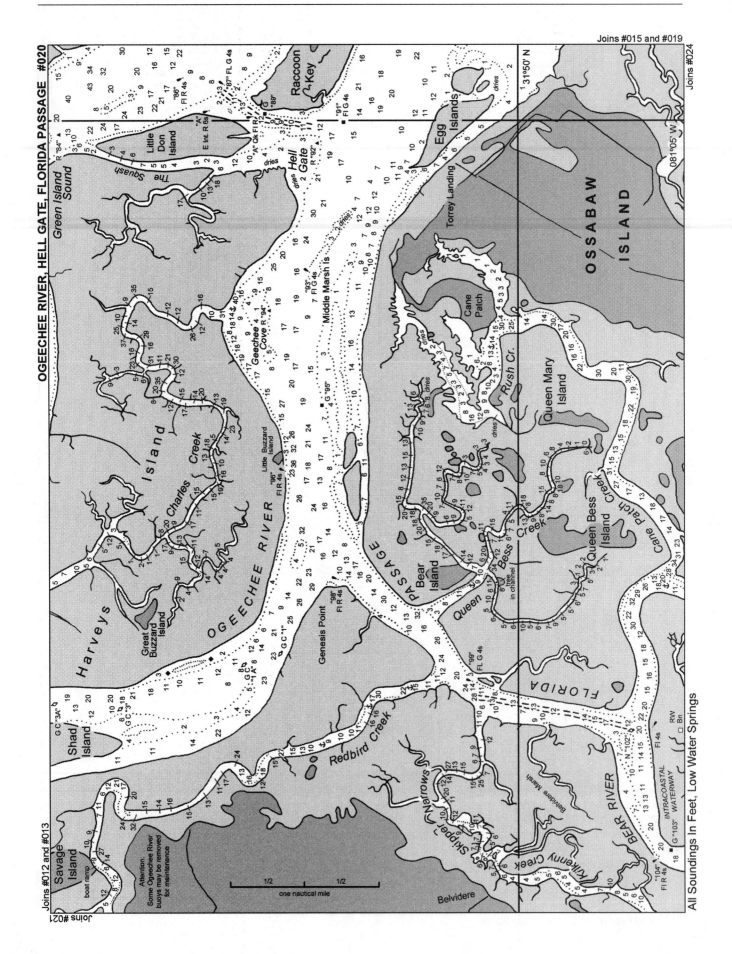

Joins #015 and #019

Joins #024

Joins #012 and #013

Joins #021

All Soundings In Feet, Low Water Springs

one nautical mile

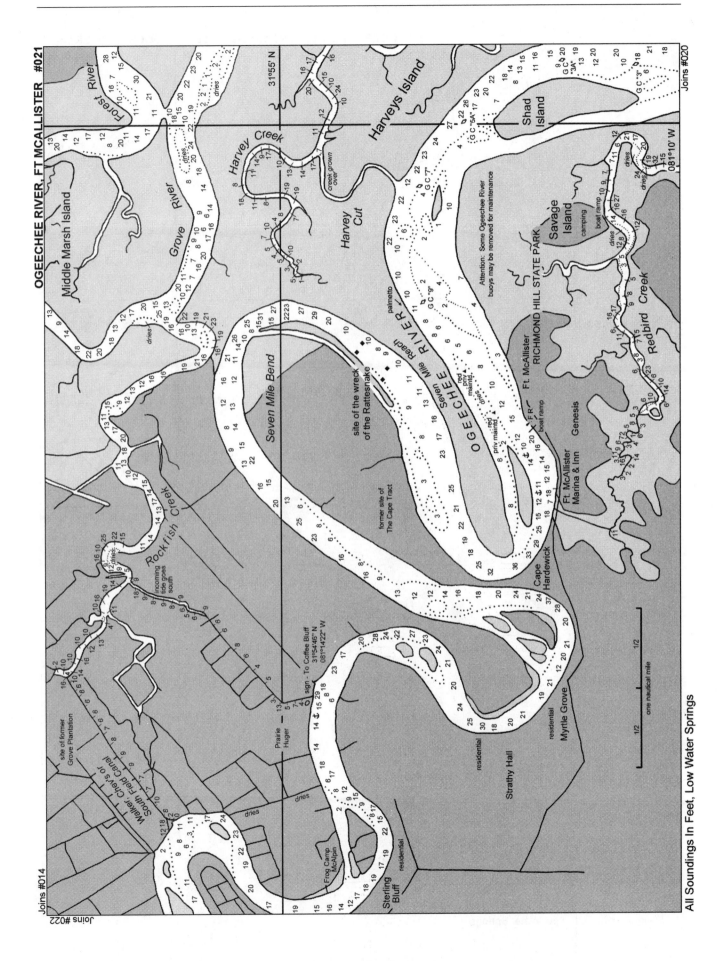

All Soundings In Feet, Low Water Springs

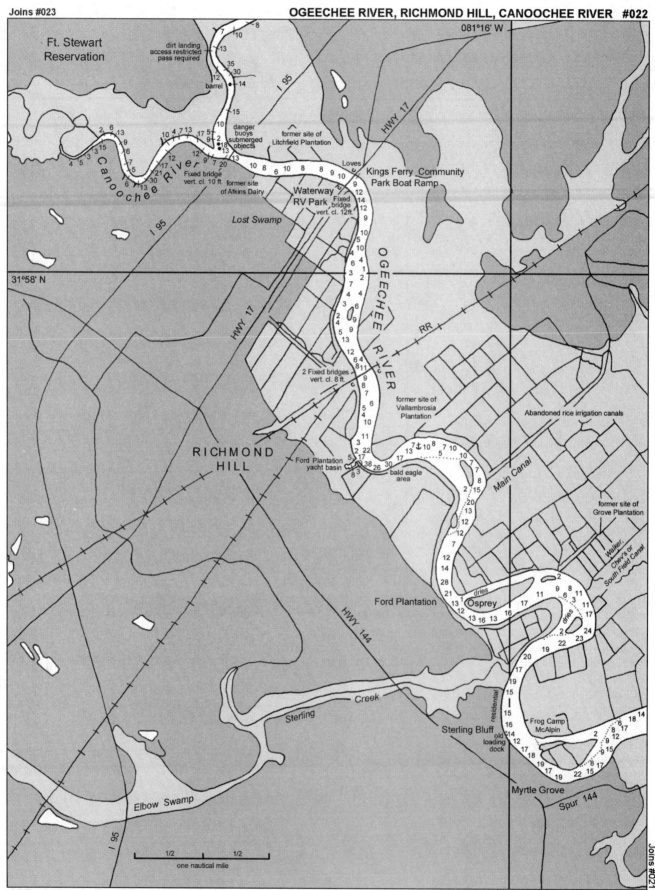

All Soundings In Feet, Low Water Springs

OGEECHEE RIVER, SAVANNAH AND OGEECHEE CANAL   #023

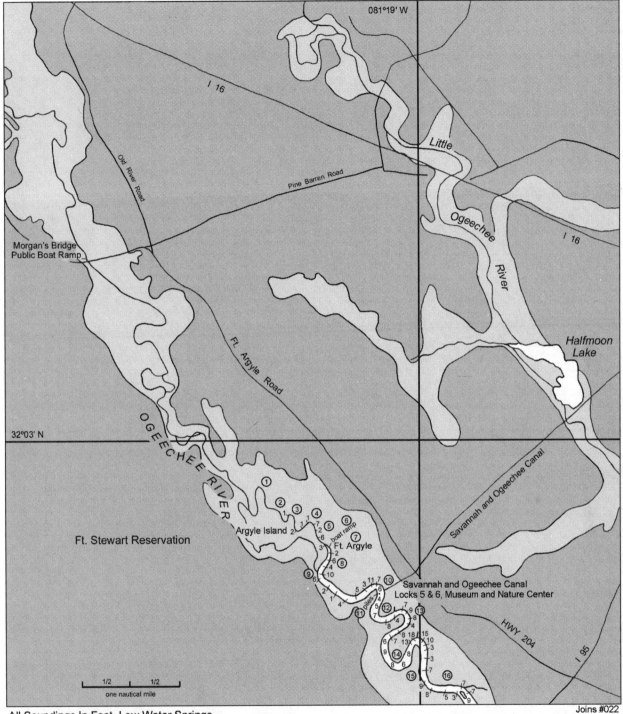

081°19' W

I 16

Little

Ogeechee River

I 16

Morgan's Bridge Public Boat Ramp

Halfmoon Lake

32°03' N

Pine Barren Road

Old River Road

Ft. Argyle Road

OGEECHEE RIVER

Ft. Stewart Reservation

Argyle Island

boat ramp

Ft. Argyle

Savannah and Ogeechee Canal

Savannah and Ogeechee Canal Locks 5 & 6, Museum and Nature Center

piles

HWY 204

I 95

1/2   1/2
one nautical mile

All Soundings In Feet, Low Water Springs

Joins #022

Shore Descriptions for Chart #023
OGEECHEE RIVER, SAVANNAH AND OGEECHEE CANAL

1 Many areas less than one foot deep

2 .. Landing possible, low sandy banks under thick forest

3 .... Narrow, many fallen trees

4 .. Landing possible, low sandy banks under thick forest

5 ... Thick forest, lots of cypress knees

6 .... Private concrete boat ramp

7 .... Small residential area

8 .... Thick undergrowth, grassy foreshore

9 .... Low, one foot bank, thick thin trunk forest

10 .... Ruins of brick canal lock

11 .... Pilings, remains of pre-civil war bridge

12 .. Grassy point, sandy sloping bank

13 .... Low mixed growth forest; pond cypress, bald cypress, gums, tupelo, hollies

14 .... Grassy point

15 .... Grassy bank

16 .... Thick, mixed growth forest

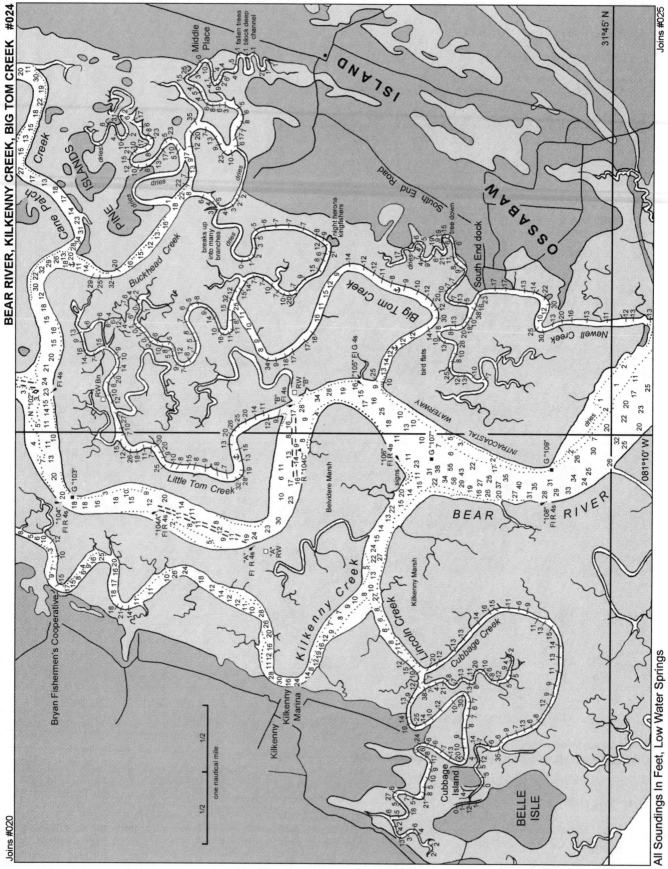

Middle Place

fallen trees
block deep
channel

PINE ISLANDS

Cane Patch Creek

dries

Buckhead Creek

breaks up
into many
branches

dries

ISLAND

OSSABAW

South End Road

tree down

South End dock

night herons
kingfishers

Big Tom Creek

Newell Creek

bird flats

"105" Fl G 4s

RW Bn

N "102"
Fl 4s

"B"
Fl 4s

RW
"B"

INTRACOASTAL WATERWAY

G "107"

G "109"

G "103"

Little Tom Creek

"106"
Fl R 4s

R "104C"

"104"
Fl R 4s

"104A"
Fl R 4s

"A"
Fl R 4s

RW
"A"

Belvidere Marsh

signs

BEAR   RIVER

"108"
Fl R 4s

Bryan Fishermen's Cooperative

Kilkenny

Kilkenny
Marina

Kilkenny Creek

Kilkenny Marsh

Lincoln Creek

Cubbage Creek

Cubbage
Island

BELLE
ISLE

1/2

1/2

one nautical mile

081°10' W

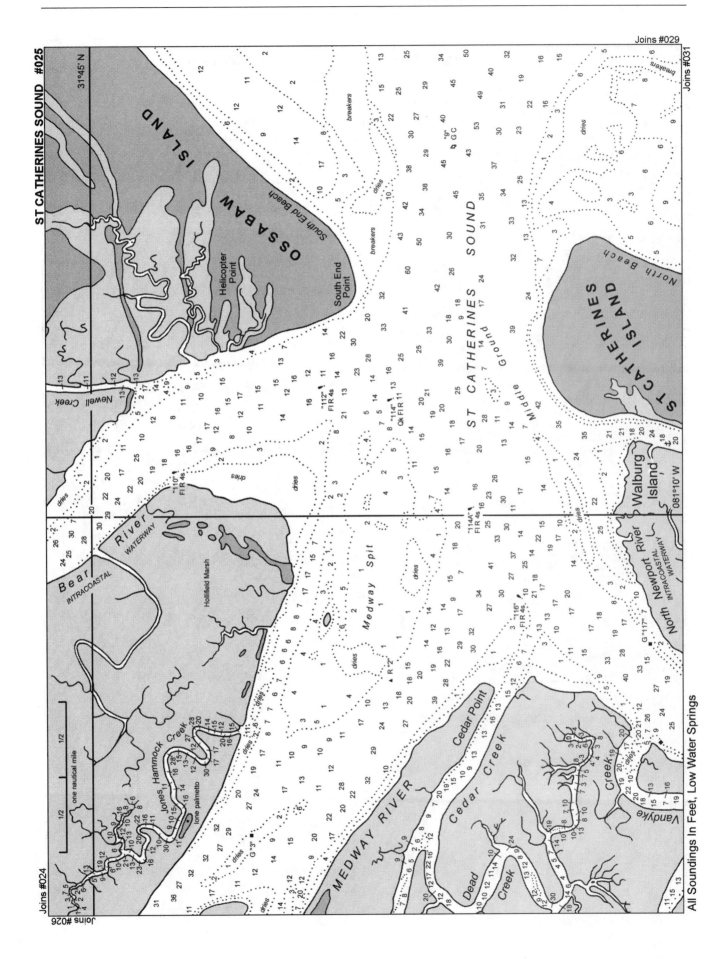

Joins #029

Joins #031

Joins #024

Joins #026

All Soundings In Feet, Low Water Springs

Joins #025

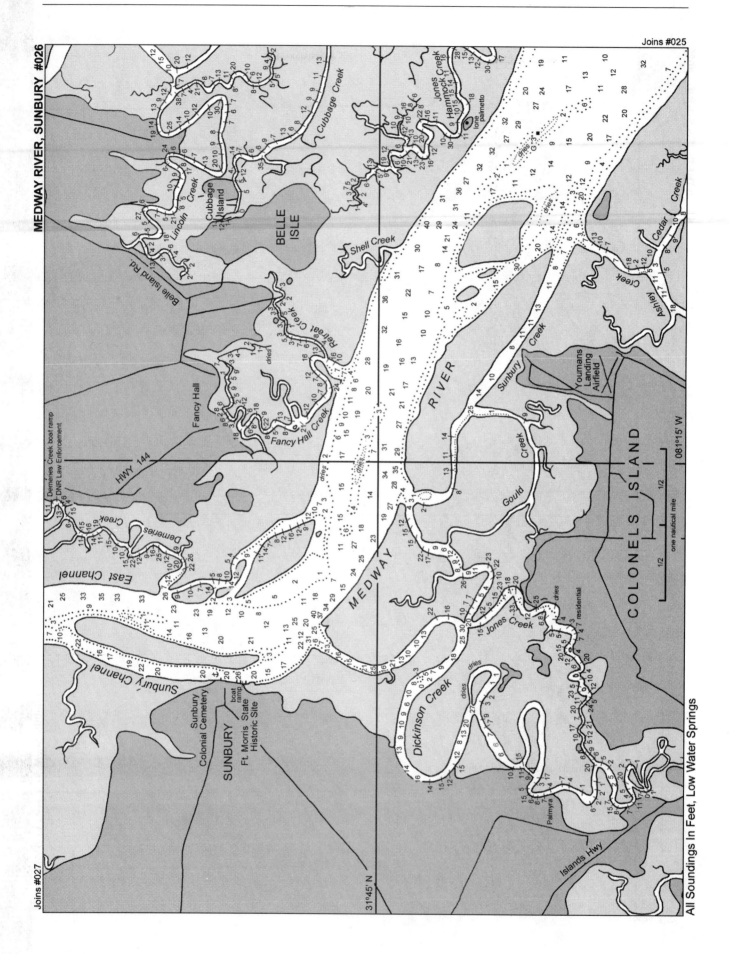

Joins #027

All Soundings In Feet, Low Water Springs

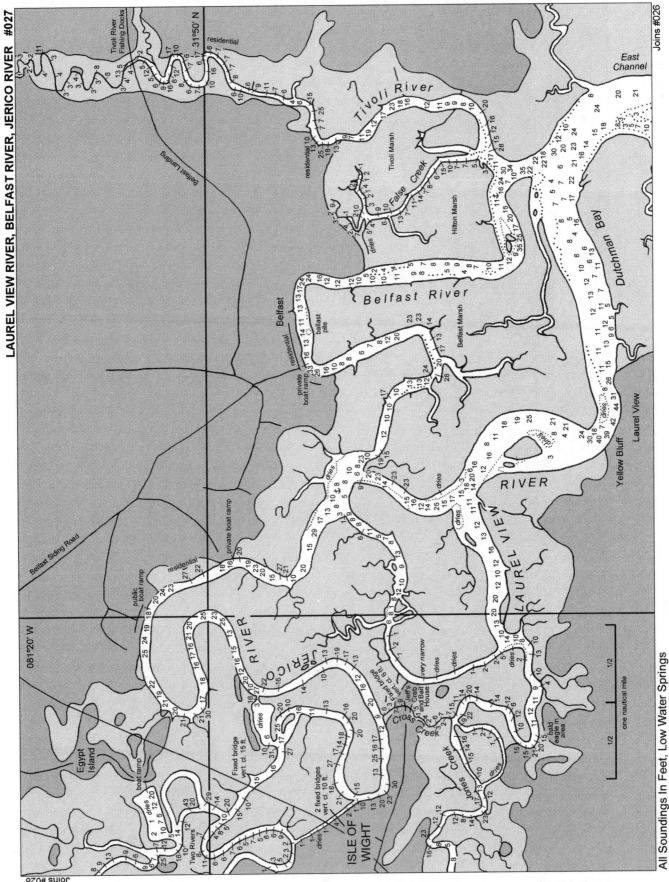

Joins #026

Joins #028

All Soundings In Feet, Low Water Springs

one nautical mile

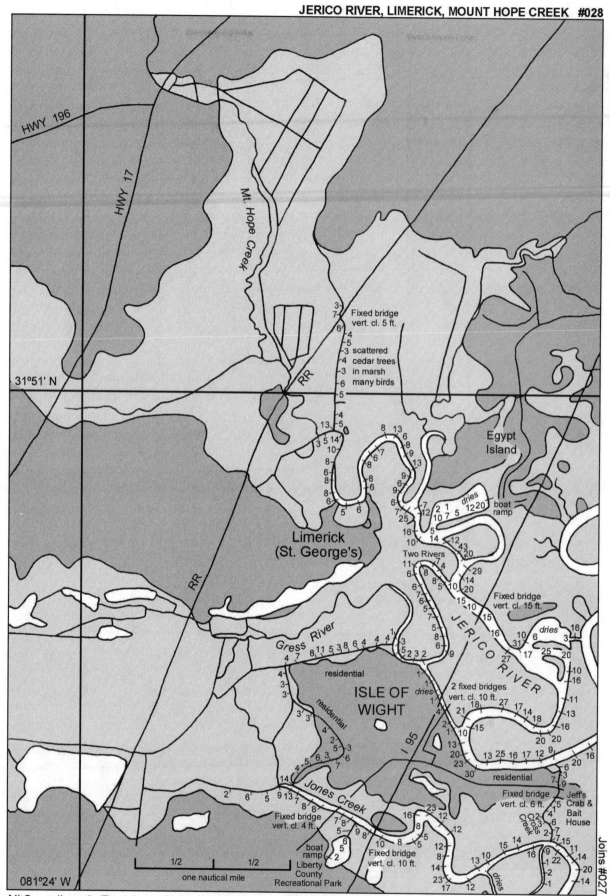

JERICO RIVER, LIMERICK, MOUNT HOPE CREEK #028

HWY 196

HWY 17

Mt. Hope Creek

RR

31°51' N

Fixed bridge
vert. cl. 5 ft.

scattered
cedar trees
in marsh
many birds

Egypt
Island

dries

boat
ramp

Limerick
(St. George's)

Two Rivers

Fixed bridge
vert. cl. 15 ft.

dries

JERICO RIVER

RR

Gress River

residential

ISLE OF
WIGHT

dries

2 fixed bridges
vert. cl. 10 ft.

residential

I-95

residential

Jones Creek

Cross Creek

Jeff's
Crab &
Bait
House

Fixed bridge
vert. cl. 6 ft.

Fixed bridge
vert. cl. 4 ft.

boat
ramp
Liberty
County
Recreational Park

Fixed bridge
vert. cl. 10 ft.

dries

Joins #027

1/2   1/2
one nautical mile

081°24' W

All Soundings In Feet, Low Water Springs

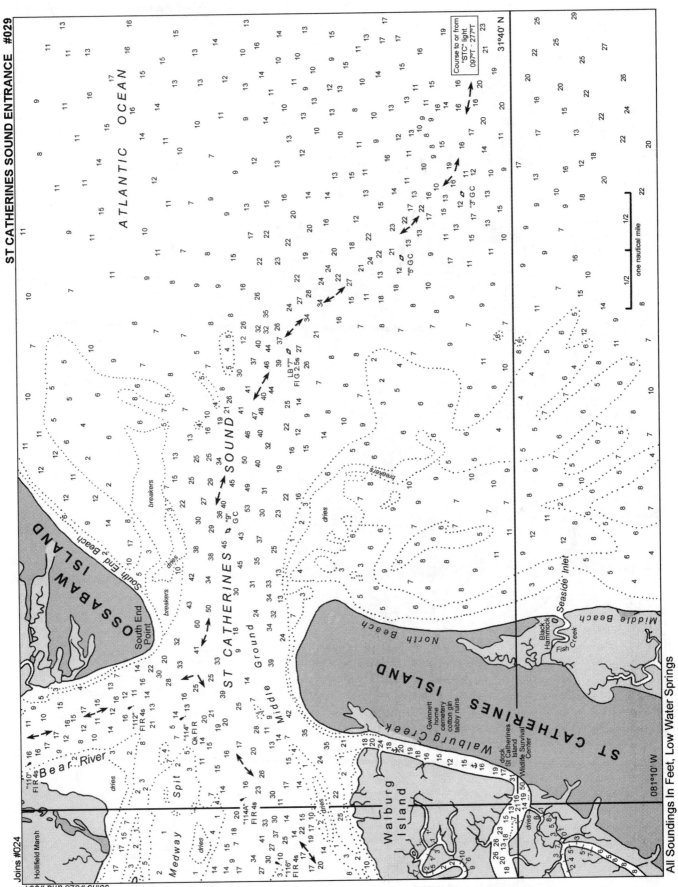

Joins #024

Hollifield Marsh

OSSABAW ISLAND

South End Beach

South End Point

breakers

dries

breakers

ATLANTIC OCEAN

ST CATHERINES SOUND

Middle Ground

St Catherines Ground

breakers

dries

breakers

dries

Bear River

"110" Fl R 4s

Medway Spit

dries

"116" Fl R 4s

"114A" Fl R 4s

"116" Fl R 4s

"112" Fl R 4s

"114" Qk Fl R

"gr" "b" GC

LB"7" Fl G 2.5s

"5" GC

"3" GC

Course to or from "STC" light
097°T – 277°T

31°40' N

081°10' W

ST CATHERINES ISLAND

North Beach

Walburg Creek

Gwinnett home
cemetery
cotton gin
tabby ruins
dock
St Catherines
Island
Wildlife Survival
Center

Walburg Island

dries

Seaside Inlet

Black Hammock

Fish Creek

Middle Beach

Low Water Springs

All Soundings In Feet, Low Water Springs

one nautical mile
1/2   1/2   1/2

Joins #025 and #031

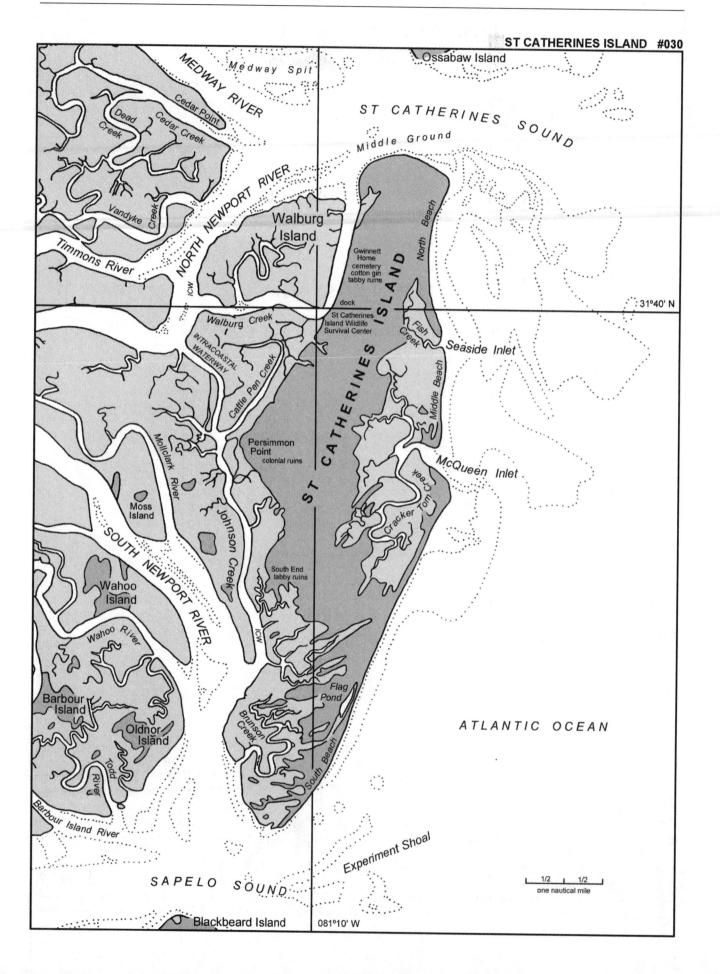

ST CATHERINES ISLAND #030

Ossabaw Island

ST CATHERINES SOUND

MEDWAY RIVER

Medway Spit

Middle Ground

Cedar Point

Dead Creek

Cedar Creek

North Beach

Vandyke Creek

NORTH NEWPORT RIVER

Walburg Island

Gwinnett Home cemetery cotton gin tabby ruins

Timmons River

ICW

31°40' N

dock

Walburg Creek

St Catherines Island Wildlife Survival Center

Fish Creek

INTRACOASTAL WATERWAY

Seaside Inlet

Cattle Pen Creek

Middle Beach

ST CATHERINES ISLAND

Persimmon Point
colonial ruins

McQueen Inlet

Mollclark River

Cracker Tom Creek

Moss Island

Johnson Creek

SOUTH NEWPORT RIVER

South End
tabby ruins

Wahoo Island

ICW

Wahoo River

Barbour Island

Flag Pond

ATLANTIC OCEAN

Oldnor Island

Brunson Creek

Todd River

Barbour Island River

South Beach

SAPELO SOUND

Experiment Shoal

1/2   1/2
one nautical mile

Blackbeard Island

081°10' W

CHAPTER FIVE

ST. CATHERINES SOUND TO SAPELO SOUND

INCLUDING NORTH NEWPORT RIVER, SOUTH NEWPORT RIVER AND SAPELO RIVER LIBERTY AND McINTOSH COUNTIES

FORESTED AND RINGED by white beaches, St. Catherines Island looms large in this chapter by virtue of its recovery from plantation days into an unusual combination of wilderness and biological laboratory for animals threatened with extinction. North Newport and South Newport Rivers, large tidal waterways navigable by deep draft vessels and practically uninhabited, offer exploration far into the mainland of coastal Georgia. Sapelo River, also a deep tidal river, provides great fishing sites within easy distance from small boat facilities located in quiet, low key, rural settlements. It also allows water access to Harris Neck, a National Wildlife Refuge important for bird watchers and nature lovers.

ST. CATHERINES ISLAND

Seen from the north St. Catherines Island's forests loom high, dark, majestic and full of secrets. And for the general public this private island remains a mystery except for its 11 miles of beaches. The 7,200 acres of St. Catherines are managed by the New York Zoological Society which, since 1974, has utilized the land for breeding and saving from extinction several very vulnerable species. A good example might be the St. Vincent parrot which thankfully still persists in the high forests of this Caribbean island. Ring-tailed lemurs, grevy's zebras, giant tortoises from the Aldabra archipelago in the Indian Ocean and Florida sandhill cranes, among others, have found shelter and safe breeding conditions on St. Catherines.

St. Catherines has a very large Pleistocene core with its edge meeting the Atlantic just south of the northeastern tip of the island. A cliff, 25 feet high in places, overlooks a beach which shows severe signs of erosion—apart from the tell-tale tree boneyard you can see densely compacted brown layers of ancient marsh peat. This is the only place on the Georgia coast where

the million year old Pleistocene shoreline has come to meet the ocean again. St. Catherines Island is eroding all along its shorelines except for an accretionary beach just north of the cliffs and the high dune and beach on the south side of McQueen Inlet. When you walk the beach along the northern end of the island you will see how the Holocene beach meets the border of the Pleistocene upland. At the southeastern end of the island you encounter another extensive tree boneyard - the result of intense erosion.

So it seems that the indigenous people on St. Catherines, even as recently as the European appearance here, lived along very different shores. All we know however, from written sources and archeological research by the American Museum of Natural History, is that there was probably a large Guale village on St. Catherines and that the Spanish managed to set up a large mission, Santa Catalina de Guale here in 1587. St. Catherines was also

The north tip of St. Catherines Island has a spectacular beach.

The northern tip of St. Catherines looks toward Ossabaw Island across the wide waters of St. Catherines Sound

one of the three barrier islands guaranteed in "perpetuity" to the Creeks by Gen. James E. Oglethorpe. After the tribe ceded the islands to the half-Creek Mary Musgrove and her preacher husband Thomas Bosomworth, the Royal Trustees of Georgia disputed the couple's ownership. Mary died before the courts decided to leave St. Catherines in Bosomworth's hands and give him the proceeds from a forced sale of the other islands. In 1765, the now re-mar-

Due to millions of years of steady erosion the ancient pleistocene land meets the ocean along the east shore of St. Catherines Island.

ried reverend sold the island to Button Gwinnett, an Englishman who became prominent in Georgia as a politician but somewhat infamous as a businessman. After Gwinnett died of an infection from a duel wound, the Bosomworths recovered most of St. Catherines as compensation for Gwinnett's debts. The island remained peaceful after that except for the fussilades of gun fire when various subsequent owners banged away at game animals. The great stir came after the Civil War when Gen. Sherman ordered the barrier islands between Charleston and Fernandina to become an independent state for freed slaves. These newly independent people elected Tunis Campbell as their leader and he chose St. Catherines as the capital and headquarters for an army of 275. This was too much for Congress, even though dominated by northerners. Sherman's orders were repealed and federal troops moved the black leader to McIntosh County. The island went through various ownerships by wealthy people until Edward J. Noble, a New Yorker, bought it in 1943 to raise cattle. After his death the ownership went to the Edward J. Noble Foundation and later to the St. Catherines Island Foundation beginning a more illustrious chapter in the island's history.

ANCHORAGES AT ST. CATHERINES ISLAND

WALBURG CREEK

This creek flows along the northwest side of St. Catherines and has enough room to anchor a fleet and in fact you may see a whole fleet of shrimp boats there when the conditions in the outer anchorage in the sound become rough. Walburg Creek has a straightforward entrance in its north end—you will find deep water right next to the beach. The western entrance which connects to the Waterway is a little more convoluted—consult chartlet #031 to see the soundings.

Anchoring in the northern arm of Walburg Creek brings you close to the sounds of the forest and sooner or later you will hear some exotic bird calls and, if you stay long enough, the squealing distress call of some unknown victim. We learned the identity of the departed the next day when, instead of the usual four, we saw only three little piglets feeding in the short grasses on the edge of the beach. A real treat was watching an otter feeding along the marsh bank on the west side of the creek, sometimes foraging through oyster banks and occasionally diving after some prey. With the morning light in his eyes and the wind from the mainland this usually secretive animal could not detect our presence. From that anchorage it takes only a few minutes in a dinghy to get to the north point where an endless beach will test your powers of endurance walking. Ocean erosion has brought down a great many trees that once stood inland and the fallen trunks of live-oaks have created a review of sculpted twisting shapes along much of the length of the north point. Two osprey couples keep busy propagating happily in the nests on top of dead pines overlooking the beach and a solitary bald eagle is the shy minority in this osprey world. Weekends bring a few speedboats from the mainland and then the north point of St. Catherines looks like a family hangout with beach chairs and beach umbrellas. More serious fishermen anchor their boats along the sandbanks in the Sound and try their luck with offshore fish.

On days of stiff northerly winds the chop builds up in the northern arm of the creek but you can always find an alternate anchorage in the west arm. Necessary Creek, a narrow tidal stream, attracts anglers who look for their own private fishing holes. On the south side of Walburg Creek one can take a small boat on the high tide and explore through the marshes all the way to Cattle Pen Creek. When your goal is to head south from Walburg Creek you can join the Waterway via the south exit. Consult chartlet #031 to see how you have to zigzag from the south shore to the north shore and then back to the south shore.

CATTLE PEN CREEK

Chartlet #035 shows the entrance to this creek popular among seasonal Waterway users as an overnight anchorage, narrow as it is for boats longer than 36 feet. The creek continues north and chartlet #031 shows the connection to Walburg Creek.

JOHNSON CREEK

As part of the Intracoastal Waterway Johnson Creek has plenty of aids to navigation shown on chartlets #031 and #035. Of the several streams branching off from Johnson Creek only Cattle Pen Creek is deep enough for migrating yachts to anchor. Smaller side streams which lead into the marshes to the east and west attract anglers in small boats. One arm of the unnamed creek which works its way eastward into St. Catherines Island across the Waterway from marker "132" makes a great destination for a trip in a small boat. Its main stream runs east to a shore with a very attractive and varied example of a maritime forest.

BRUNSON CREEK

Chartlet #036 shows the silting entrance to Brunson Creek and its soundings farther in.

Shallow draft boats which enter on the rising tide will pass by a spit formed from dead oyster shells—at times a popular resting station for oyster catchers which live around the mid-coast of Georgia. The creek winds through a healthy marshland and swings by upland hammocks.

WATERS WEST OF THE INTRACOASTAL WATERWAY

North Newport River, South Newport River and Sapelo River cut through this area branching into countless smaller, yet deep streams. Several gas and diesel fueling facilities can be found in this area.

CEDAR CREEK

Only shallow draft boats should attempt to enter this creek whose entrance you will see west of marker "116". You can see on chartlet #031 how shallow banks spread to either side of the deeper water. There are no landmarks to help steering in the centerline of the channel and the currents which run across this channel can set a vessel onto a shoal. Trailerable sport fishing boats use Cedar Creek to reach Yellow Bluff Fish Camp overlooking Ashley Creek from Colonels Island. Equipped with an electric hoist for boats up to 31 feet, docks, a basic tackle shop and all kinds of bait this fish-camp monitors VHF 16 and 68, tel. 912-884-5448. Yellow Bluff Fish

Looking like an old Pegleg's treasure chest, this strange flotsam, churned up and delivered by a nor'easter, ended upon the north shore of St. Catherines.

Camp is also home to The St. Catherines Sport Fishing Club, the Sea Tow boat and a couple of fishing charter boats—see the Services Section for details. Yellow Bluff is the oldest fish camp on the Georgia coast so generations of the same families rent their cabins in summer. The strange looking potbellied stove you see inside the store is an old US Army cannon ball heater. From Yellow Bluff Fish Camp bird watchers can easily reach, by long walk or a short car ride, Youman's Pond, a great place to see black-crowned and yellow-crowned night herons, all kinds of egrets, anhingas, common moorhens, wood storks, white ibis and sometimes purple gallinules. Small boats can have a great time exploring miles of creeks winding through the marshes fronting Colonels Island to the east. Using the tide one can, by navigating close the mainland shore, make it from Yellow Bluff all the way to Vandyke Creek. See chartlet #031 for details of all the creeks.

VANDYKE CREEK

Although a large drying shoal lies in the middle of the entrance this creek has an easy deep entry channel. Steer close to the north shore to stay in deep water—you will find the best anchorage for deeper draft boats when the creek begins to turn northwest. Consult chartlet #031 for soundings and connecting streams.

TIMMONS RIVER

This wide river has an easy entry along its south shore and chartlet #031 shows the locations of various drying banks in this stream which first winds through wild marshes and later joins North Newport River which will take you right to Halfmoon Marina. See the Services Section and North Newport River below.

NORTH NEWPORT RIVER

The entrance lies to the northwest of marker "125" and you should favor the north shore after entering the river. Pass close to the private marker "1" installed by Halfmoon Marina for its customers. The markers up river indicate the deeper side of the river and chartlets #031 and #032 will help you navigate to Halfmoon Marina which has deep water docks, gasoline and diesel fuels and can haul/launch boats up to 28 feet. They monitor 16/68, tel. 912-884-5819. See the Services Section.

Chartlets #032 and #033 show the upper reaches of North Newport River. On the way up river you will pass Cross Tide Creek connecting to South Newport River— to go through from North Newport River you should steer within kissing distance of the marshy east point at the north entrance to Cross Tide Creek. Should you want some help from a rising tide, bear in mind that high tides arrive here nearly two hours later than on the coast. Farther, on North Newport River, after you have left the residential shores of Colonels Island and the private docks

Jack's Island—one lucky man's refuge far up North Newport River.

on Carrs Neck Creek, you will see really wild undeveloped marshlands with very rare evidence of other humans. Payne Creek is a beautiful stream winding through healthy marshland and swinging by uninhabited hammocks—chartlet #033. Just north of Payne Creek, a fellow named Jack has erected a private holiday retreat on stilts in the middle of heavenly nowhere. About three miles on you will pass a dock which belongs to Melon Bluff Nature Preserve—see the Services Section for details. Somewhere under the muddy waters nearby lies the wreck of a confederate blockade runner the *Standard*, hence the name Standard Reach, and also the name of an annual kayak event Melon Bluff sponsors. After passing under I 95 bridge the river forks into Cay Creek which runs more or less parallel along beautiful undeveloped forested land winding on sharply enough to break a snake's back. Recently this area became a state park.

SOUTH NEWPORT RIVER

This huge tidal river heads inland from Johnson Creek and Waterway marker "132" and has privately maintained markers for the first section of the river up to the Belvedere residential area, the only development along this river. Chartlet #035 illustrates this approach. Right off marker "1" you might decide to go into Mollclark River—stay close to the east shore in order to keep in deep water. Mollclark River joins North Newport River and this junction is very narrow and shallow—use a rising tide if you navigate a boat that draws a few feet. The high tide arrives here about 1 hour later. Consult chartlet #031 for the depths at the northern end on Mollclark River.

South Newport River passes by Harris Neck National Wildlife Refuge but, at present, no landing is possible along that shore. Chartlet #032 shows how the river forks at the meeting point of Cross Tide Creek and South Hampton Creek. All these creeks flow through wild marshes teeming with birds during migrating times and also have a good representation of resident birds including ibis and wood storks. As shown on chartlet #034, South Newport River continues running west through undeveloped marshlands until a camping enterprise just before the US HWY 17 bridge. A public paved ramp located on the north side of the river by the US HWY 17 bridge can be accessed from I 95 by taking exit 67 and going east on HWY 17. See the Services Section.

WAHOO RIVER

For seasonal waterway users Wahoo River has been a popular overnight stop. Deeper draft vessels should head for the west shore from Waterway marker "135" and then follow that west shore until in the river. Despite some obvious logging there are enough tall trees on Wahoo Island to give good protection during northerly autumn gales. Consult chartlets #036 and #035 for Wahoo River details. After Wahoo Island the river runs through marshes eventually joining Barbour Island River and giving access to Barbour River Landing public launching ramp on Harris Neck—see the Services Section for details.

BARBOUR ISLAND RIVER

This large river has a surprisingly shallow mouth probably because of the outflow from Todd River and the sediment deposits from Sapelo River. Local fishing boats find this area very rewarding. After negotiating the tricky entrance, preferably on a rising tide, you will encounter deep water all the way to the residential shores on Barbour Island. Chartlet #036 shows this section of the river and chartlet #035 continues the run of Barbour Island River to Harris Neck shores and the public launching ramp—Barbour River Landing; see the Services Section for details and access. Just south of the public facility you will see the docks of a private boat club and to the north a DNR boat facility.

The Wahoo River anchorage often attracts yachts in search of good shelter.

SAPELO RIVER

Sapelo River hides away in the mainland haze and few Waterway travelers realize how important this waterway is to Georgia boatmen who are served by several facilities scattered in the area. Commercial fishermen have an important base on this river which provides convenient access to the coastal waters of the Atlantic.

Sapelo River joins Sapelo Sound and the Intracoastal Waterway at marker "150". To enter from the east steer north of Waterway marker "150" and head west steering south of marker "2" and then follow the south shore of Fourmile Island. Pass north of "3" and south of "4"—this is the shallowest part of the river and deep draft boats may choose to navigate here with a rising tide which arrives here about forty minutes later than on the coast. Chartlet #037 shows the soundings in the area. Depths improve by Sutherland Bluff, a residential area with docks extending into the river. On chartlet #038 you will see how the markers appear again when the channel narrows and shoals. Just after the last marker "10" you will come to the Belleville Point area with a haul-out railway for shrimp boats and a row of wharves for the commercial fishermen. These commercial facilities continue along the shore and into Roscoe's Canal. Both commercial and pleasure boats can fuel up with diesel at Philips Seafood docks—call Charlie Philips at 912-832-4423. The well-known Pelican Point Restaurant has a small dock for guests—it can accommodate only small boats. Larger vessels coming for dinner should anchor and use their dinghies. When eating there choose a table by the windows overlooking the river—you will likely see bottlenosed dolphins chasing *their* dinner which may be similar to yours—Pelican Point Restaurant offers a lot of seafood dishes. Another restaurant, Buccaneer Restaurant, also has a floating dock for guests' boats on the west side of Belleville Point. Gasoline powered pleasure craft usually fuel in Pine Harbor Marina located in the river curve north of Bellville Point. The marina has launch/haul hoist, gas sales and bait, tel. 912-832-5999. See the Services Section.

To keep out of the way of the shrimp boat traffic, cruising boats should anchor in the curve of the river just south of a private community dock on Shell Point. Tidal currents are light here and there are plenty of birds to watch in the marshes. To stretch your legs you should walk a block up the road behind Pine Harbor Marina to a three way intersection. Then go left through a pleasant residential community shaded by trees. At the intersection of Bell Hammock Road and Pine Harbor turn onto Pine Harbor and walk to some old oaks and a historical marker of the Mallow Plantation—the homestead of the McIntosh family, prominent as warriors and politicians throughout the history of Georgia. Back out, take Bell Hammock Road to the two markers describing a colonial cemetery.

As you can see on chartlet #038 south of Pine Harbor, the river shoals dramatically, the result of dredging Roscoe's Canal which redirected the flow of the Sapelo River. In the area called Fairhope you will notice two brick chimneys and the sign for the Sanctuary on the Sapelo (SOS) where for the last 18 years Emmy Minor has been taking care of and rehabilitating injured birds. You can see many of the shore birds of Georgia here as they recover from injuries. You should phone 912-832-5571 before visiting. And do not forget the donations box—the birds eat 500 pounds of fish a week!

Gradually becoming smaller, the river winds on towards the town of Eulonia eventually passing under the US HWY 17 bridge. During migrating seasons and in winter you will see many species of waterfowl in the marshes here.

On the way out from the anchorage off Shell Point you can simplify navigation by taking Savannah Cut—use a rising tide if your boat draws over 3 feet. There is another short-cut out of Sapelo River—useful when heading south to Crescent River. Snake Creek enters the marsh south of the shrimp haul-out ways and very close to a public boat ramp. You will definitely need help from the tide to go this way as there are places here having as little as 1 foot at low tide. Chartlets #038 and #042 show the run of Snake Creek.

WHITE CHIMNEY CREEK

Chartlet #038 illustrates the soundings on this creek which is home to Belle Bluff Marina, a large facility combining camping grounds with a launch/haul hoist, diesel, gasoline and propane sales, floating docks mostly for local boats, bait and snack shop, etc. They monitor VHF 16, tel. 912-832-5323. See the Services Section for more details. Just outside the entrance to White Chimney Creek you will see a smaller creek winding inland by Sutherland Bluff. The creek goes through a nice marsh and more or less parallel to a large golf course—Sapelo Hammock Golf Club located next door to Sutherland Bluff Plantation, a residential area built on the grounds of the old Brailsford Plantation and a sailing ship building site during the Revolutionary War.

BRORO RIVER

Use chartlet #037 to see the approach depths to several boat facilities lining the west shores of this short river. Extensive shoals occupy the middle of the river and you will find deeper depths along the marsh island to the east. A deep cut into Julienton River will serve deeper boats which want to reach the Broro River facilities at low tide. The southernmost marina on Broro is Fisherman's Lodge. They have the largest launch/haul hoist on the bluff (10,000 pounds capacity), gasoline pump, bait and snack store and plenty of dock space as well as dry storage on land. Fisherman's Lodge monitors

VHF 16, tel. 912-832-4671. See the Services Section for more details. Almost next door up river you will see Shellman Fishcamp which offers haul/launch for boats up to 26 feet, has docks and a gasoline pump as well as a bait and snack store. They monitor VHF 16, tel. 912-832-4331. See the Services Section for more details. The marinas sit on the east edge of Shellman Bluff, a small quiet community which has grown on the site of the antebellum Shellman Plantation. Hunter's Café and Mud Bar serves food and drinks within an easy stroll from either of the marinas—closed Mondays. Speed's Kitchen, where tasty seafood and relaxed service is the policy, lies a little farther inland and is open for dinner on Thursdays through Sunday.

JULIENTON RIVER

Julienton River combines the best of Georgia's natural environment with pockets of residential communities. At the south end, along the north shore of Fourmile Island you will have the wonderful feeling of being surrounded by wilderness with the forest on Harris Neck providing a backdrop for this pretty picture. Judging by the numbers of anglers in the area and outside by Julienton River's mouth, fishing is excellent here. As you swing around the southwest tip of Harris Neck keep close to the east shore to stay in deep water—large shoals have grown in the middle of the river. Heading north from the corner you will pass a large bald eagle nest with at least one of the birds in view. We found a pleasant and protected anchorage almost under the nest. Chartlet #037 shows how, off the private dock on Harris Neck, you should change the course for the western shores. A large dock complex ahead belongs to the residents of Sapelo Woods community but you can turn left into Broro River again if you need boat facilities or a restaurant. A little west of Sapelo Woods docks, on Broro River, you will see floating docks equipped with electricity and water. These docks which have nearly 9-foot depths alongside are open to transient yachts. For charges and availability call Shellman General at 912-832-5426 or walk to this general store to discuss the terms face to face.

Going north up the river you will pass Contentment Bluff Mobile Home Park with a dock for the residents. The river widens just south of Dallas Bluff forming an excellent anchorage. With luck you may find open dock space in Dallas Bluff Marina. Call 912-832-5116 well in advance—the place is very popular with sailboat owners from Savannah and has a waiting list for long term storage. Dallas Bluff Marina also has a one-ton capacity launch/haul hoist and an area to accommodate campers. See the Services Section for more details. Above Dallas Bluff Marina the river swings by the private docks for Delta Plantation residents and splits in two streams just before Eagle Neck. The west branch runs through marshes and some residential spots. Harris Neck Creek continues first by residential shores on the west side,

then becomes even narrower, goes under the low GA Rte. 131 bridge, passes a boat ramp, two fishing piers and winds through a marvelous wild marshland. Without any floating facilities for boats you have to land your boat on the mud bank near the boat ramp, secure it well with an anchor and then walk onto the main trail into this National Wildlife Refuge.

Taking up only 2,765 acres, the Refuge protects a small northern part of Harris Neck for wildlife. Harris Neck was once, like other upland areas in antebellum coastal Georgia, utilized as plantation land. Civil War and the end of slavery broke the backbone of the plantation economy and the former slaves bought much of Harris Neck to live and farm on a subsistence level. In 1942, the US Government, already involved in World War II, moved the farmers out in order to build a small air base which supported regular patrols against German U-boats along the East Coast. In 1962, the abandoned area was turned into a national wildlife refuge and now the paved landing strips reluctantly yield to native vegetation. Many visitors drive through the ref-

Spanish moss on a live oak tree and saw palmettos along a marsh creek combine to create a scene typical of coastal Georgia.

uge but people who arrive in their own boats can take interesting walks. We found the open view from the raised dike on the south side of Woody Pond particularly rewarding—you will see there many species of shore birds throughout the year as well as migrating wildfowl if the water level in the pond stays up. This freshwater swamp, offering many tree stumps as perches often hosts anhingas, ibis, wood storks and all species of egrets. Dense vegetation in the middle of the pond provides good shelter for smaller birds—bring binoculars. In May and June herons including tricolored herons, anhingas and wood storks nest here in numbers. Painted buntings and yellow-billed cuckoos also nest on Harris Neck in summer. Wood ducks, however, prefer nesting in February and March using nest boxes. Harris Neck is one of the stops on the Colonial Coast Birding Trail. In the recovering forest along the edges we found colonies of purple stinkhorn mushrooms and rare black pine-cone mushrooms. Bella moths or rattlebox moths flit over the open spaces flashing pink, rose and magenta colored wings. To get to the swamp from the landing on Harris Neck Creek walk to the left up the main dirt road, take the first major right turn and continue to the dike overlooking Woody Pond.

LITTLE MUD RIVER

You can see on chartlet #037 how this creek can take you to Barbour Island River and the Barbour River Land-ing on Harris Neck. Notice, however, that you will need a rising tide to enter Little Mud River from the south and then, depending on the draft of your boat, a few feet of tide to get over the drying shoals at the northern part.

SAPELO SOUND

Consult chartlet #039 to see how to enter from the Atlantic by steering first for the unlit red and white sea buoy marked "S" located at 31°31'12"N, 081°03'53"W. From there you have to navigate by the buoys which may be shifted around to suit the configuration of changing channels. The channel buoys are positioned by the rule "red right returning", i.e. you should keep the red markers to your right when heading to a port, and green ones to your left. At our latest passage the depths stayed above 12 feet until half way from buoy "3" to buoy "5" where we had 8 feet (low tide springs). After buoy "5" the depths improved and stayed deep while going west past beacon "11". Sapelo Sound should be used only in calm to moderate sea conditions with good visibility. Bear in mind that a strong outgoing tide running against a rough sea will cause breaking and dangerous seas. The flood tide coming in will smooth the sea surface.

Joins #031

Joins #035

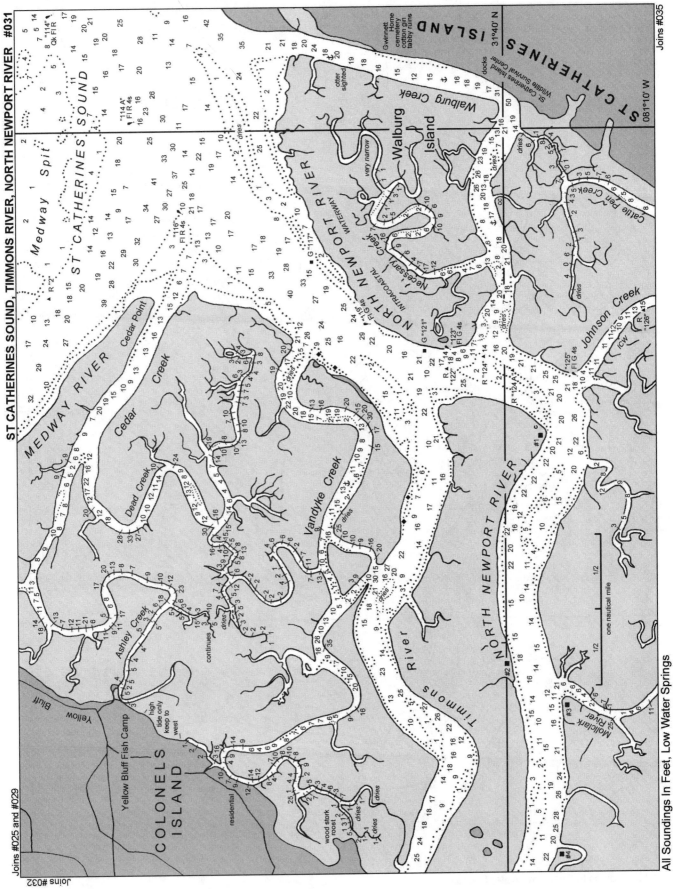

Joins #025 and #029

Joins #032

All Soundings In Feet, Low Water Springs

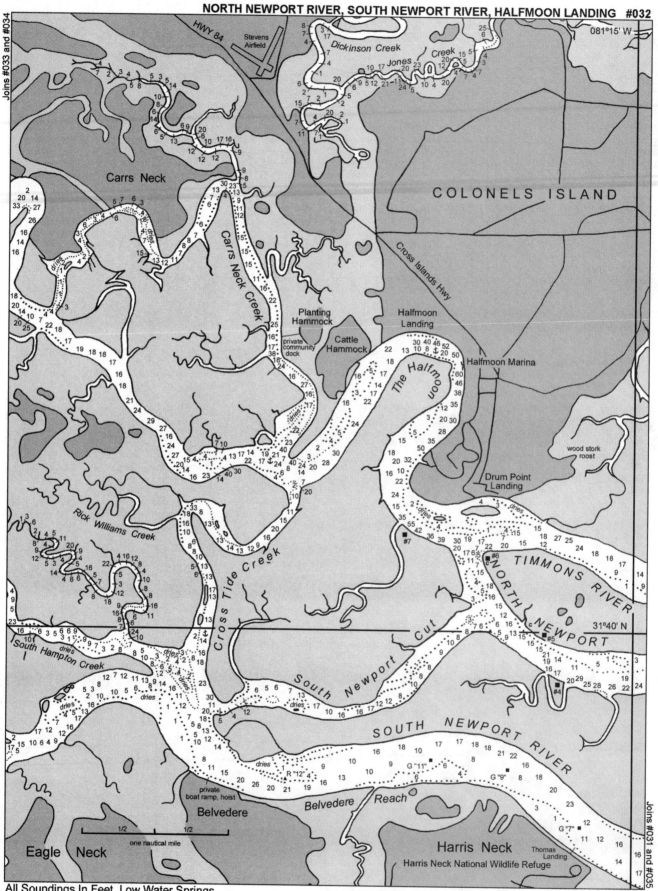

All Soundings In Feet, Low Water Springs

NORTH NEWPORT RIVER, PAYNE CREEK #033

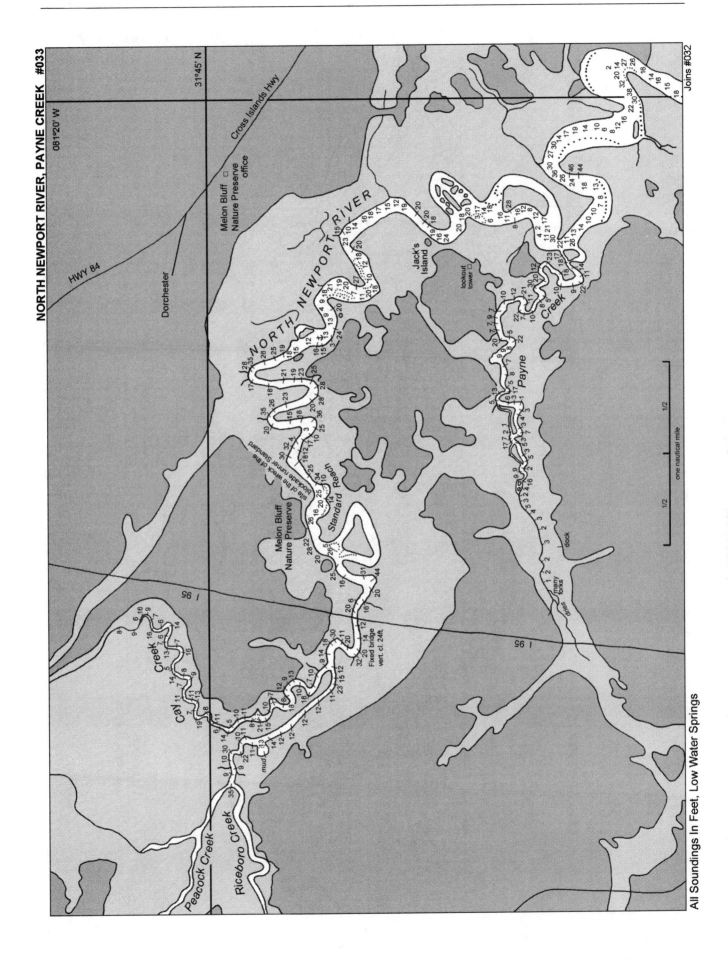

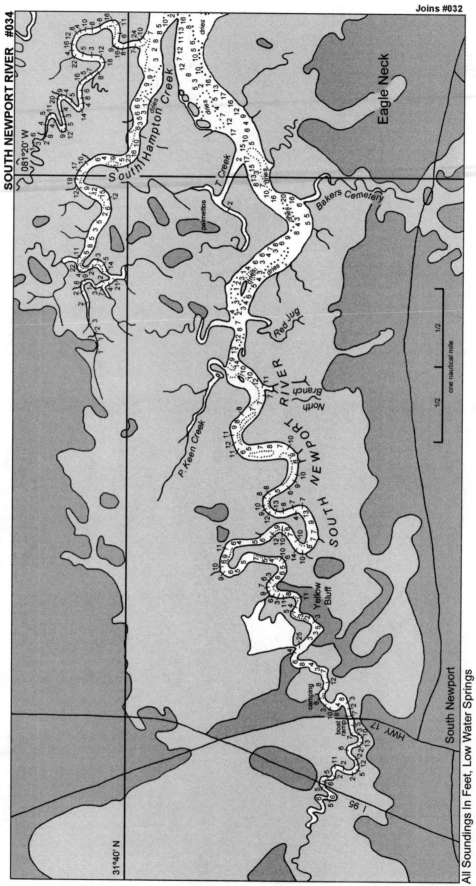

SOUTH NEWPORT RIVER #034

Joins #032

081°20' W

31°40' N

South Hampton Creek

T. Creek

palmettos

Bakers Cemetery

Eagle Neck

Red Jug

North Branch

P. Keen Creek

SOUTH NEWPORT RIVER

Yellow Bluff

camping

boat ramp

HWY 17

South Newport

I 95

one nautical mile

1/2   1/2   1/2

All Soundings In Feet, Low Water Springs

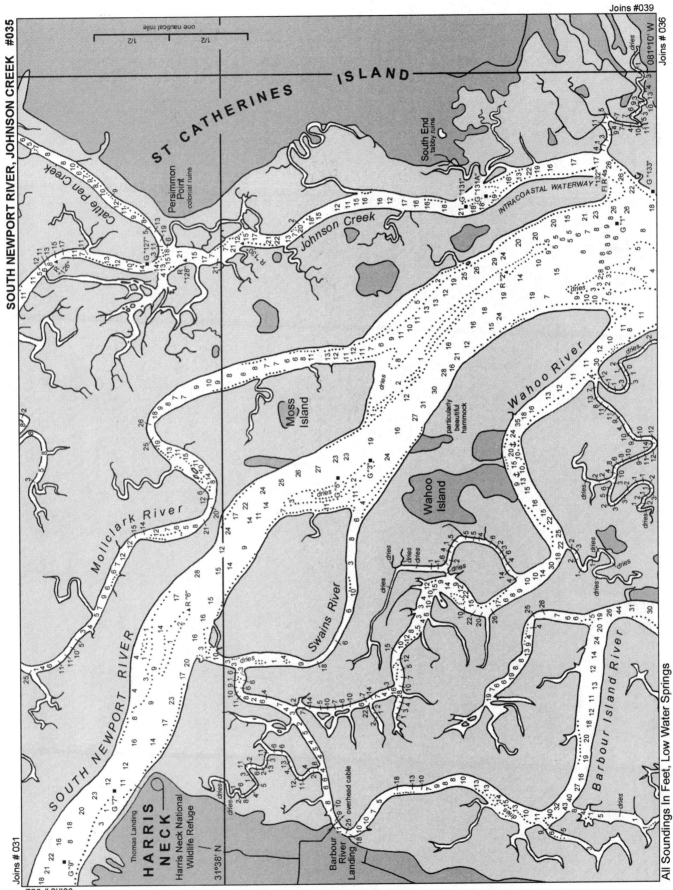

Joins #039

Joins # 036

081°10' W

Joins #031

Joins # 032

ST CATHERINES ISLAND

Persimmon Point
colonial ruins

Cattle Pen Creek

South End
tabby ruins

Johnson Creek

INTRACOASTAL WATERWAY

Mollclark River

Moss Island

Wahoo River

SOUTH NEWPORT RIVER

particularly beautiful hammock

Wahoo Island

Swains River

Barbour Island River

HARRIS NECK

Thomas Landing

Harris Neck National Wildlife Refuge

Barbour River Landing

overhead cable

31°38' N

one nautical mile

All Soundings In Feet, Low Water Springs

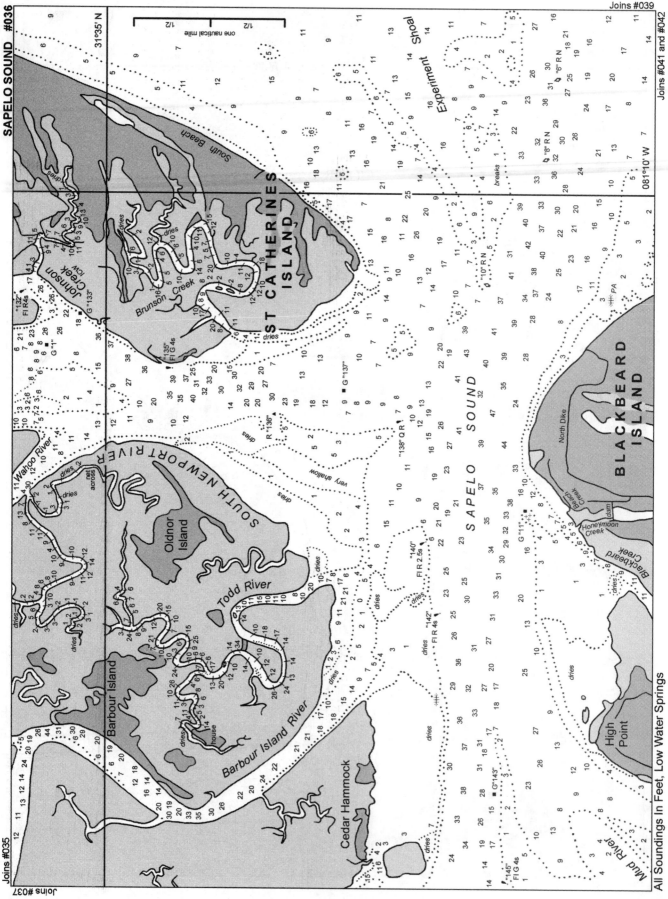

Joins #039

Joins #041 and #042

Joins #037

All Soundings In Feet, Low Water Springs

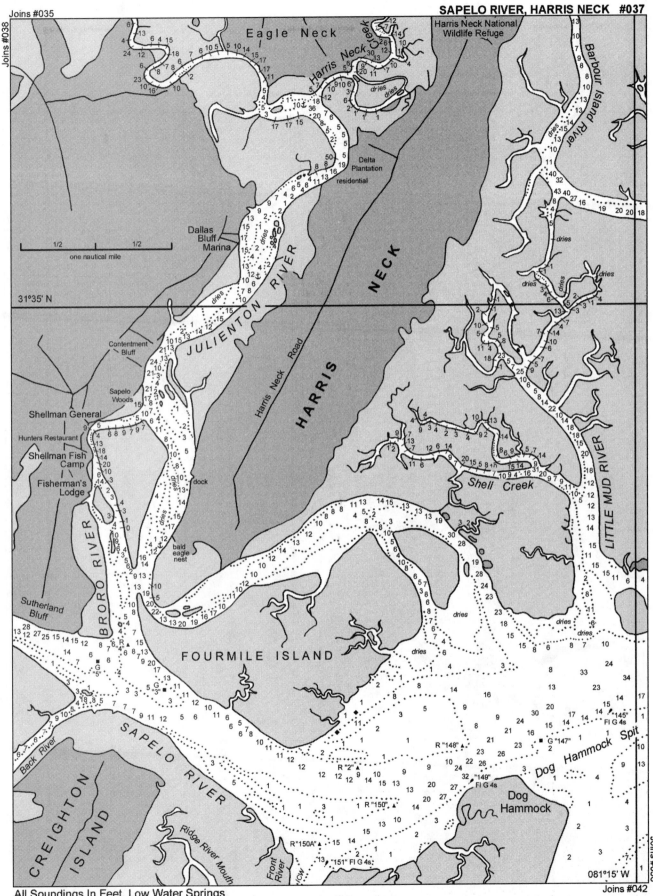

Joins #035

Joins #038

Eagle Neck

Harris Neck National
Wildlife Refuge

Barbour Island River

Harris Neck Creek

1/2   1/2

one nautical mile

31°35' N

Delta
Plantation
residential

Dallas
Bluff
Marina

dries

JULIENTON RIVER

HARRIS NECK

Harris Neck Road

Contentment
Bluff

Sapelo
Woods

Shellman General

HARRIS

dries

LITTLE MUD RIVER

Hunters Restaurant

Shellman Fish
Camp

Fisherman's
Lodge

BRORO RIVER

dock

Shell Creek

bald
eagle
nest

dries

Sutherland
Bluff

dries

dries

FOURMILE ISLAND

dries

dries

G
"5"

G
"3"

Back River

SAPELO RIVER

R "148"

Dog Hammock Spit

R "2"

G "147"

R "149"
Fl G 4s

R "150"

Dog
Hammock

"145"
Fl G 4s

CREIGHTON ISLAND

Ridge River Mouth

Front River

R "150A"

"151" Fl G 4s

ICW

Joins #036

081°15' W

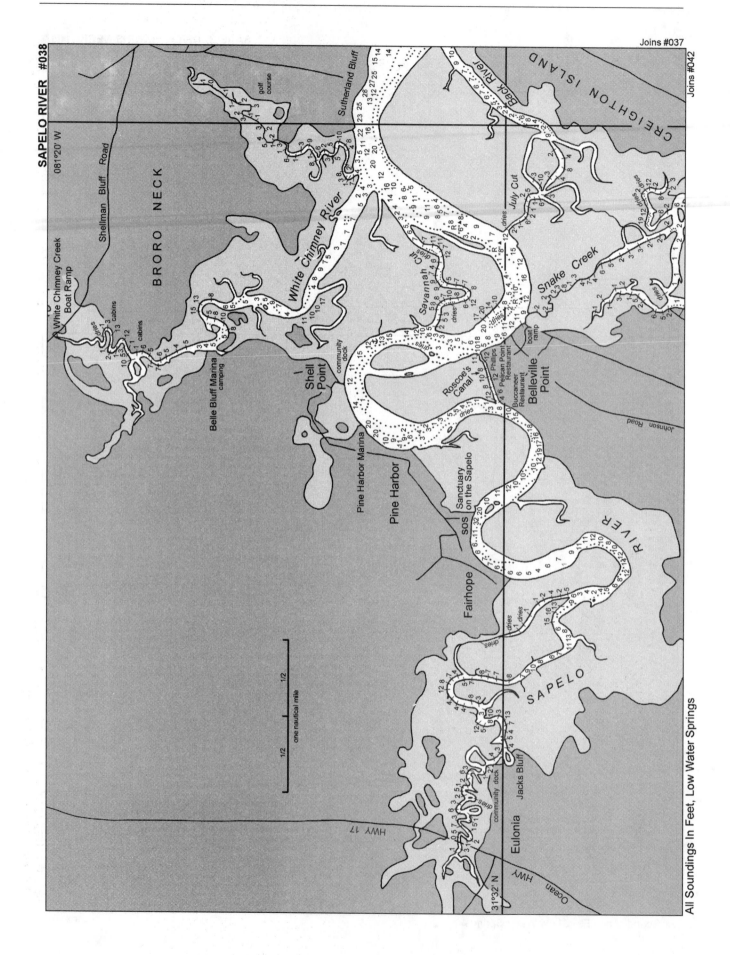

SAPELO RIVER #038

081°20' W

Joins #037

Joins #042

CREIGHTON ISLAND

BRORO NECK

Shellman Bluff Road

White Chimney Creek Boat Ramp

Belle Bluff Marina
camping

cabins
cabins

golf course

Sutherland Bluff

White Chimney River

Back River

Shell Point

community dock

Savannah Cut

Snake Creek

July Cut

dries

Roscoe's Canal

Phillips

Pelican Point Restaurant

Buccaneer Restaurant

boat ramp

Belleville Point

Johnson Road

Pine Harbor Marina

Pine Harbor

Sanctuary on the Sapelo

SOS

Fairhope

SAPELO
RIVER

one nautical mile
1/2
1/2

HWY 17

Eulonia

community dock

Jacks Bluff

Ocean HWY

31°32' N

All Soundings In Feet, Low Water Springs

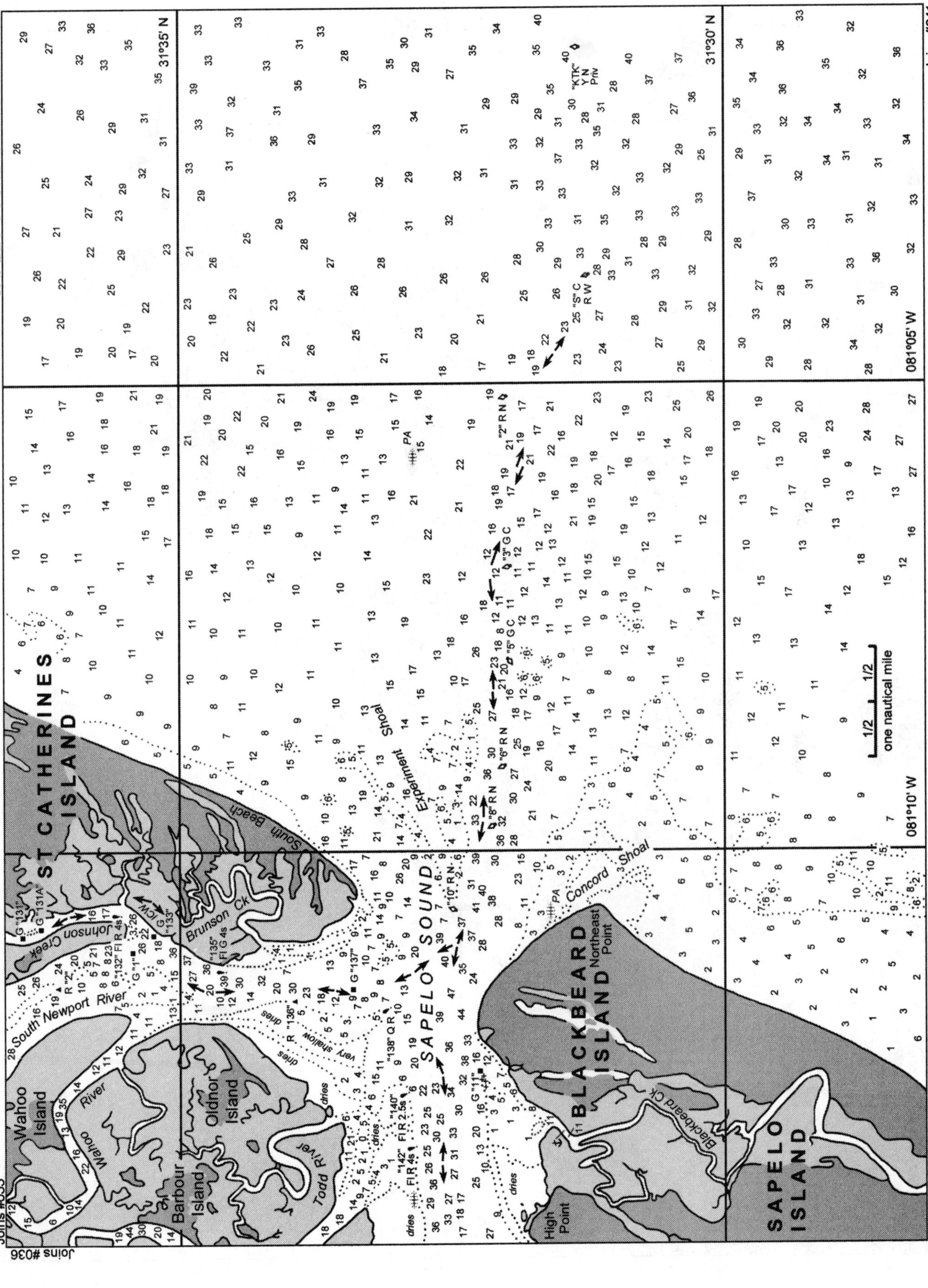

31°35' N

31°30' N

081°05' W

081°10' W

081°10' W

Joins #041

Joins #035

Joins #036

ST CATHERINES ISLAND

South Beach

Johnson Creek

ICW

Brunson Ck

SAPELO SOUND

Experiment Shoal

BLACKBEARD ISLAND

Northeast Point

Concord Shoal

SAPELO ISLAND

Blackbeard Ck

High Point

Wahoo Island

Wahoo River

South Newport River

Barbour Island

Oldnor Island

Todd River

very shallow

dries

dries

dries

dries

"KTK" Y N Priv

"S C" R W

"2" R N

"6" GC

"3" GC

"5" GC

"8" R N

"6" R N

"5"

"10" R N

"9" G

"11" G

"13" G

"137"

"136"

"138" Q R

"135" Fl G 4s

"142" Fl R 4s

"140"

"13A"

"131A"

"133"

"132" Fl R 4s

"1"

"R "2"

PA

PA

FlR 2.5s

one nautical mile

1/2   1/2

1/2   1/2

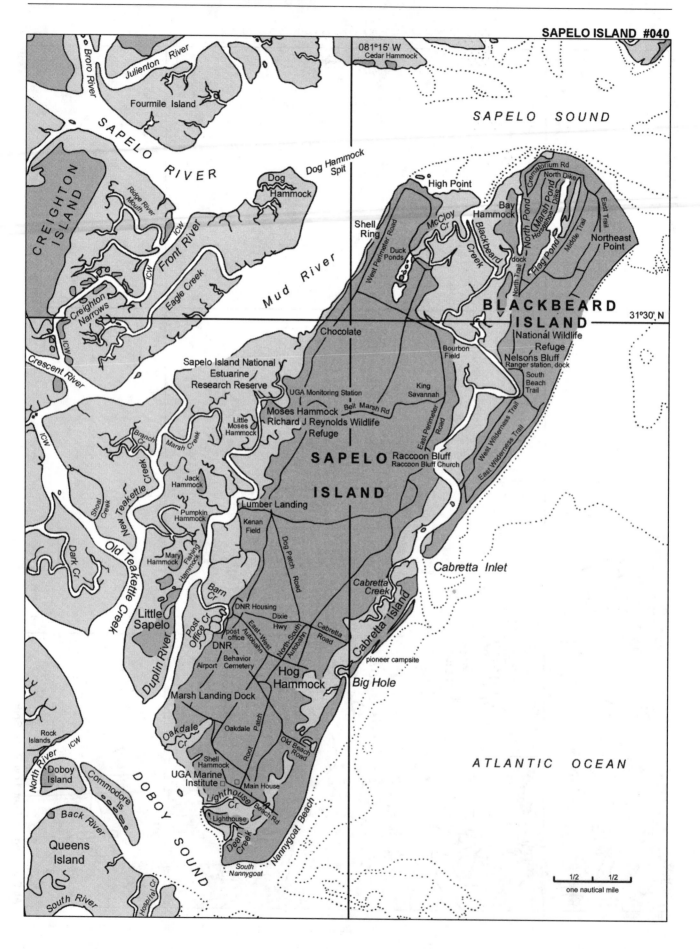

081°15' W
Cedar Hammock

SAPELO SOUND

Julienton River

Broro River

Fourmile Island

SAPELO RIVER

Ridge River Mouth

CREIGHTON ISLAND

ICW
Front River

Eagle Creek

Creighton Narrows

ICW

Crescent River

Dog Hammock Spit

Dog Hammock

Mud River

High Point

Shell Ring

Crematorium Rd
North Dike

McCloy Cr

Bay Hammock

Blackbeard Creek

North Pond
Marsh Pond
Horseshoe Dike
Flag Pond

East Trail

Middle Trail

Northeast Point

West Perimeter Road

Duck Ponds

dock

North Trail

31°30' N

BLACKBEARD ISLAND

Chocolate

Bourbon Field

National Wildlife Refuge

Sapelo Island National Estuarine Research Reserve

UGA Monitoring Station

King Savannah

Nelsons Bluff
Ranger station, dock

South Beach Trail

Moses Hammock

Belt Marsh Rd

Little Moses Hammock

Richard J Reynolds Wildlife Refuge

East Perimeter Road

West Wilderness Trail

East Wilderness Trail

Branch Cr

Marsh Creek

SAPELO

Raccoon Bluff
Raccoon Bluff Church

ICW

Teakettle Creek

Jack Hammock

ISLAND

Shoal Creek

New

Pumpkin Hammock

Lumber Landing

Dark Cr

Old Teakettle Creek

Mary Hammock

Fishing Hammock

Kenan Field

Dog Patch Road

Cabretta Creek

Cabretta Inlet

Duplin River

Barn Cr

DNR Housing

Little Sapelo

Post Office Cr

Dixie Hwy

post office

East-West Autobahn

North-South Autobahn

Cabretta Road

Cabretta Island

DNR

Airport

Behavior Cemetery

Hog Hammock

pioneer campsite

Big Hole

Rock Islands

ICW

Marsh Landing Dock

North River

Doboy Island

Commodore Is

Back River

DOBOY SOUND

Oakdale Cr

Oakdale

Root Patch

Old Beach Road

Shell Hammock

UGA Marine Institute

Main House

Lighthouse Cr

Beach Rd

Nannygoat Beach

ATLANTIC OCEAN

Queens Island

Lighthouse

Dean Creek

South Nannygoat

South River

Hospital Cr

1/2   1/2
one nautical mile

CHAPTER SIX

SAPELO SOUND
TO ALTAMAHA SOUND
INCLUDING DARIEN AND THE ALTAMAHA RIVER
McINTOSH COUNTY

SAPELO ISLAND takes much of the coast covered in this chapter and it deserves special attention. The surrounding estuarine waters are the subject of long term research by the University of Georgia and NOAA and the island itself hosts a wildlife refuge and a small African American village of descendants of the Gullah people who once worked on the Sapelo plantations. Add Sapelo's close consort, Blackbeard Island National Wildlife Refuge, and you have an outstanding chunk of undeveloped Georgia to explore. South of Sapelo lies Wolf Island, another national wildlife refuge. Several deep tidal rivers flow through large wild marsh islands which separate the Atlantic coast from the mainland and the historic port of Darien—in itself an interesting destination. Undammed and untamed the Altamaha River, by volume of its waters Georgia's largest river, has thousands of acres along its banks set aside as natural protected areas both up river and in its delta which includes large salt and freshwater marsh islands. The Altamaha River offers boat owners a unique opportunity to visit rare ecosystems typical of a tidal freshwater river.

BLACKBEARD ISLAND

The tidal Blackbeard Creek separates this 7 mile island from its bigger neighbor, Sapelo Island, in more ways than one; as a National Wildlife Refuge Blackbeard Island has been recovering nicely from excessive human activities and only the park ranger lives there full time. The US Fish and Wildlife Service keeps about 15 miles of trails open and annual archery hunts (3 days in October and November) reduce the deer population to manageable numbers—a necessary measure now that large mammal predators are gone. Otherwise the shore birds, wading birds, water fowl and song birds have the place to themselves as do raccoons, snakes and alligators. Blackbeard's

dunes make perfect nesting sites for terns and oyster catchers, the inland ponds provide protected roosts and nesting hideaways for several species of herons, wood ducks, purple gallinules and even anhingas. The maritime forest hosts breeding mocking birds, brown thrashers, wrens, warblers and bats, while in the marshes along the west side breed clapper rails (marsh hens), marsh wrens and willets. The Atlantic beach receives, in a good year, well over 200 nesting female loggerhead sea turtles. You cannot overemphasize the importance of places like Blackbeard Island for the future presence of our coastal animals.

Blackbeard Island has no ferry boat connection with the mainland and visitors need a boat to get there, which apparently is no obstacle for keen anglers or families in need of a beach. Scores of boats arrive off Blackbeard on weekends. A few anchor off the beach on the north point of the island but the majority of boats carry fishermen heading through Blackbeard Creek south to Cabretta Inlet separating the south end of Blackbeard from Cabretta Island. The wildlife refuge provides no camping areas and most visitors stay only a few hours. Only the annual hunters who moor their boats off the Rangers Station in the southern part of Blackbeard Creek may camp on the land around the National Park Service headquarters. When you come in your boat and plan to explore the island for a few days you should report your presence to the Refuge Office—a pleasant hike to the south on North Trail—see chartlet #041. Deeper boats will find an excellent anchorage in Blackbeard Creek near the entrance just before McCloy Creek—see chartlet #041. Bottlenosed dolphins forage in the creek and if you sleep on deck or in the cockpit you will hear them breathing next to you in the dark. Farther in you will have adequate depths but only boats up to 30-feet long will find enough room to swing with changing currents and winds. There is an excellent and pretty anchorage in the northern part of Buttermilk Channel under the forested bluff shore. However, to get there in a deeper draft boat will require negotiating a wind-

A boneyard of oaks lines the northern strand of Blackbeard Island.

Alligators often hunt at night - the beach reveals the evidence of their forays to the ocean.

ing shallow and narrow channel on a rising tide. Consult chartlet #041 and be warned that, although the creek may look wide at high tide the deeper trough in the center is quite narrow. If you anchor in the first recommended place, near McCloy Creek, you can take your dinghy to a dock located up the first creek to the south. From there you can walk to a shaded dirt road, North Trail, which leads south to the Refuge headquarters and from there to the other trails. On your way inland from the dock notice a worn-out trough across the trail—an alligators' crossing. During warm weather months you will encounter an active population of them in the creek waters. Just a bit farther on the dike along the south edge of North Pond you may see alligator crossings again and perhaps the reptiles themselves in the muddy rivulet under the brush.

The North Trail goes north, also, and it will take you to a brick oven-like structure. This crematorium served to reduce the victims of yellow fever to ashes and possibly was also used for cooking the vicious sulfur concoction with which ships arriving on this coast were fumigated against the plague. For thirty years beginning in 1880 a quarantine station on Blackbeard Island examined and fumigated all ships intending to trade between St. Augustine and Savannah. Apart from the brick crematorium nothing else on land remains of this large station which operated during the warm months of the year. The rocky shoal which rises above low tides by marker "11" at the mouth of Blackbeard Creek contains ballast rocks sailing ships dumped after arriving in the sheltered waters behind the island. Although much has been said about Blackbeard, the pirate, supposedly using this island in the early 1700s for quick raids against passing ships, there is no evidence of his presence here. The US Navy bought the island in 1800 as a source of live-oak timber for ship building. In 1940, Blackbeard Island became a national wildlife refuge after some short lived exchanges of custody between the US Government and private individuals.

People who visit on boats can make a rewarding and educational walking tour of the island by landing their dinghy on the calm western beach of the north point. Allow for the rise or fall of the tide when securing your boat. From there hike along the north face of the island and walk close to the water leaving the beach swale between the primary and secondary dune lines alone for nesting birds. In April/May several hundred black skimmers and as many or more royal and Forster's terns use the northern beach as a resting strip. During warm months you will see the tracks of alligators which explore the night beach from their daytime habitat—a little creek paralleling the beach swale. It takes only a short time to reach the western of two extensive tree boneyards—the evidence of continuing shore erosion typical of all barrier islands in Georgia. Farther east, having passed the second boneyard, you will suddenly come upon a high dune which ends just as abruptly as it starts. After Northeast Point, another birds' favorite stop-over (so stay close to the waters edge), you enter a wide beach area where the sea deposits a steady supply of new sand. With the sand arrive empty shells, knobbed whelks, channeled whelks, giant Atlantic cockles, disc dosinias, angel wings, coquinas, lettered olives—species typical for the coast. Following strong onshore winds you will encounter small sea cucumbers, many of them having shot out their intestines in reaction to rough treatment by the waves.

Continue south on the beach and after you have passed the end of a low forest of thick wax myrtles keep looking west towards the high secondary dunes for a cut through. If you find yourself at another tree boneyard you will have come too far south. Take the path across the dunes to the cut leading into the forest and, please, do not wander off this track into the dune swale for in some seasons you will crush bird eggs with your feet. In the shady forest you will at first head west until, at an obvious junction, you have reached East Trail. Turn to the right—northward, and you will be walking on top of a low ridge on a wide road covered with fallen live-oak leaves—a thick maritime forest on your right and a thinner forest and a wide grassy wet savannah to the left. In the cool of the morning you may come across snakes trying to warm themselves on the open road—the distinctly patterned orange corn snake is harmless although it grows to 4 feet. All snakes, even the big rattlers, take off as soon as they detect your presence—never try to touch them, even with a long stick! Now and then a short trail to the left allows you to reach the dike which parallels East Trail for a look over the mixture of wetland, grassy patches and hammocks there—toar savannah, technically speaking. If you continue to the north on East Trail you will eventually emerge from the forest onto the beach in the middle of the western boneyard and not far from the dinghy you left around the corner to the west. At an easy pace this hike takes about three hours so carry drinking water with you.

SAPELO ISLAND

You will not be able to do any of this self-guided Blackbeard-style touring on Sapelo Island. At 10,900 acres of forested uplands this island is almost three times the size of Blackbeard. Owned by the State of Georgia and divided into several areas managed by various organizations, Sapelo is simply too complex to allow free-ranging tourists. However, organized trips and autho-

Blackbeard Island has been protected as a wildlife refuge since 1926—long enough for the sign to become one with the tree.

rized stays are welcome and, as everywhere else in Georgia, boat owners can land from their craft and roam all of Sapelo's five miles of beach.

Except for the 435 acres of Hog Hammock village, populated by the descendants of plantation slaves from the 1800s, the grounds of the Reynolds Mansion and the Cabretta Island campsite, Sapelo Island is involved in some way or other in contributing to science or nature conservation. A large chunk of the island, over 8,200 acres, forms R. J. Reynolds Wildlife Refuge, sold to the state in 1969 by the tobacco magnate's wife. Georgia's DNR Wildlife Resources Division administers this area and they regulate the November and December hunting weekends which begin from a landing dock and station on the northern part of Duplin River. The DNR also controls the pine harvesting operations on the wildlife refuge—part of an effort to clear the pines which have grown on the old plantation fields and to encourage live oak trees to take over in future. The southern part of the island forms the Sapelo Island National Estuarine Research Reserve of 6,110 acres which includes 2,300 acres of upland (high ground), tidal marshlands and even the lighthouse tract at the very end of the island. The Reserve is managed by the Parks and Historic Sites Division of the Georgia DNR but the University of Georgia Marine Institute actually coordinates all research activities.

Prospective weekend guests at the Reynolds mansion will be happy to know that, although the hotel is managed by the North Georgia Mountain Authority, all they need to dial is 912-437-3224 at the Sapelo Island Visitors Center at Meridian on the coast or the Mansion direct at 912-485-2299. Use the Mansion number for campsite reservations. The Visitor's Center also coordinates reservations for the Reynolds Mansion as well as for the pioneer campsite on Cabretta Island. The Center will provide information on ferry departures and take reservations for scheduled day trips on the island. The most complete tours take place on the last Tuesday of each month March–October. School field trips and educational groups should get their reservations by calling the Sapelo Reserve at 912-485-2300. An interesting way to get to know Sapelo Island is to stay with Hog Hammock people. Cornelia Bailey, an author and story teller, has lodgings for guests and her phone is 912-485-2206. Maurice Bailey will take you around the island in a bus or mule drawn wagon—his telephone is 912-485-2170. Yvonne Grovenor, one of the guides for the DNR, will organize meals delivered to your boat. Yvonne also makes sweet grass baskets from materials gathered and cured on the island, her phone number is 912-485-2262. For general information on Sapelo contact:

SINERR
P.O. Box 15
Sapelo Island, GA 31327
TELEPHONE: 912-485-2251
FAX: 912-485-2141.
E-MAIL: buddy.sullivan@noaa.gov

Also, see the Services Section.

After the winter die-out, stalks of smooth cordgrass break away in large rafts which drift around slowly breaking down and releasing nutrients valuable to the salt marsh ecosystem.

Visitors by boat can often join the organized groups. Anchor north of the ferry wharf on Duplin River and use a dinghy to land temporarily at their usually crowded floating dock. If there is an opening there, ask a local person (there is always somebody around when the ferry arrives) to find out for how long you can leave your tender. You can also tie up to the barge on the north side of the pier. By all means take an extended island tour to sample the natural aspects of the island and gain an understanding of historical events that typically took place on the large barrier islands of Georgia. A mostly Pleistocene island, Sapelo has plenty of high forested ground which attracted human occupation. Extensive archeological diggings revealed enough material to date the large shell ring on the northwest shore back some 4,500 years. Three hundred feet in diameter and ten to twelve feet high, the ring was associated with a large indigenous village of long standing and all island tours go to this site. A 158-acre village occupied what is now called Kenan Field between 1,000 and 1,600 A.D. The Spanish set up a mission on the island in the late 1560s but due to English pressures were gone by 1687 when an English captain recorded the remains of some fortifications, a chapel and a house near an orchard of fruit trees.

Sapelo Island, to which Rev. Thomas Bosomworth and Mary Musgrove laid claims, was sold at public auction in 1760 and its new English owners used slave labor to begin plantation type cultivations. Around 1790 a few French gentlemen bought into the island but some of them turned out to be too excitable and amorous for the good of the little colony. In the end only one of them managed to persevere in a little plantation called Chocolate marked today by tabby ruins from later years. Tabby was an attractive and durable building material made by adding oyster shells, sand and water to a lime mixture, itself made by burning oyster shells. Many English colonial tabby ruins persist in coastal Georgia and especially on Sapelo where a prominent planter, Thomas Spalding, apparently brought this type of construction to perfection.

Spalding first moved to Sapelo in 1802 and eventually owned the whole island on which he cultivated "sea island cotton", a long staple cotton variety originally from the Caribbean island of Anguilla. He also ranched, fattening cattle on molasses from sugar cane grown on the plantation. Timber logging added to his wealth which he increased even further by planting rice after digging irrigating canals and ponds. Busy as a politician, too, he had great plans for Sapelo and the town of Darien located on the mainland some ten miles of sailing from his base on the island. To help shipping in the area he donated land for a lighthouse which was built in 1820 and still stands pretty after a 1998 renovation. His death in 1851 and later the Civil War brought an end to the island's busy agricultural use for a few decades. In the 1920s it was revived as a plantation by its new owner, Howard E. Coffin of Detroit. Coffin financed building new roads, bridging creeks and clearing land for his cattle. He went

Above: A cabbage palmetto hammock rises above the marsh of smooth cordgrass and provides an escape to dry land for many denizens of Georgia marshlands.

Below: Many coastal Georgians consider a day of fishing equal to a day in heaven.

In a natural process of erosion the sea undermines the forest along the north shore of Blackbeard Island.

The largest cockle of the East Coast, the Great Atlantic Cockle, often washes out on barrier island beaches.

A gnarly live oak.

Solitary oak trees stabilize dune mounds among the moving sands of Cumberland Island.

Nancy indulges in a bit of birdwatching in Pine Creek on Hampton River.

Sweet Grass.

The 1820 Sapelo lighthouse was recently restored.

Sabal palmettos on Cumberland Island.

A maritime forest spreads on Beach Hammock near Little Tybee.

Above: During the fall silver-winged fritillaries migrate through the sea oats along the beaches of Little St. Simons Island.

Below: The best of the riparian forests stretch along the banks of the Altamaha River near Lewis Island.

Above: The Roller Coaster Trail on Cumberland Island follows the ridge of an ancient sand dune seperated by rain water sloughs from the younger coastal dunes.

Below: During early summer, sweet bay trees burst into flower along the flooded shores of the Altamaha River.

A feral horse, or "marsh tacky" to the colonial planters, grazes along the dunes on the Atlantic shore of Cumberland Island.

TOM ZYDLER

190

into oyster farming scientifically and business-like, setting up a cannery for his oysters as well as for shrimp—another resource abundant around Sapelo. He brought to Sapelo Guatemalan *chachalaca* birds (still surviving in small numbers) and bred pheasants and wild turkeys as game birds. Lighthouse Creek at the south end of Sapelo had a boatyard to maintain a fleet of 27 boats and barges. He reorganized the descendants of Spalding's slaves who lived on the island scattered in several choice places and created the Hog Hammock community for them. In the 1920s the Coffins decided to live on the island themselves so they rebuilt Spalding's South End House in the antebellum style, using the original hurricane-proof tabby base and designing the interior to suit the aesthetics of the day. The storm of activities came to end with the 1929 stock market crash and the Great Depression—Coffin was forced to sell the island.

Sapelo's next owner, R.J. Reynolds of Winston-Salem, North Carolina continued maintaining the island on the lines of a profitable farming enterprise. From 1934 when he bought Sapelo until his death in 1964 Reynolds kept modernizing the South End House according to concurrent fashions ending with the definite "fifities" flavor preserved today. The mansion stands far inland from where it faced the Atlantic shore during Spalding's time—the island has been steadily growing at its south end.

Research activities focused on coastal ecology began on Sapelo in 1949 when R. J. Reynolds sponsored the first laboratory which later grew into the Marine Institute of the University of Georgia. In 1954, the Marine Institute moved into several buildings which originally housed a dairy complex and farm administration. At first supported by R. J. Reynolds and more recently by NOAA, the UGA Marine Institute employs full-time scientists and hosts visiting researchers. The traditional focus on barrier island, salt marsh ecology and maritime forest habitat has been expanding to microbial and biochemical profiling of estuarine waters as well as research into weather patterns. Meanwhile, the island habitats are recovering from intense exploitation—a boon for wild animals and feral scientists collecting data co-relating agricultural dike experimentation in the 1800s to current wetland status and the decline and recovery of oyster populations.

ANCHORAGES NEAR SAPELO ISLAND

DUPLIN RIVER

Chartlets #042 and #043 illustrate the run of Duplin River along the west side of Sapelo. Apart from a couple of extensive drying banks marked on the chartlets, Duplin River allows even deep draft boats to explore almost its whole length. Only sailboats with tall masts will be stopped by a power line crossing the river a little more than a mile north of the island wharf—we could not find out its vertical clearance. When anchoring anywhere south of Lumber Landing show a good anchor light as a tug/barge combo regularly steams this way. Barn Creek forks at Post Office Creek which heads south by the DNR complex and a real post office. The creek's north arm goes along a low bluff ashore with bird filled marshes on its west side. Duplin River above Lumber Landing passes through a very scenic combination of Pleistocene upland, hammocks and marshes. A large floating dock marks the landing for the annual hunts.

NEW TEAKETTLE CREEK

This waterway runs along the western side of the Sapelo Island marshes and, although farther from the island than Duplin, it has even more bird life. At its south end where the electricity poles pick up an underwater cable an osprey family prospers with two healthy year-2000 offspring looking down upon the water traffic. The creek itself feeds a good numbers of terns, least, royal and Forster's. At its northern end New Teakettle Creek has public shellfish beds approved for consumption. The creek joins Mud River, once part of the Intracoastal Waterway but officially abandoned because of its tendency to silt. Local shrimp boats run this river on the way to and from Sapelo Sound utilizing high tide. The trickiest part of this passage lies between the northeastern end of Mud River and High Point on Sapelo as its wide waters lack landmarks to refer to. See chartlets #041 and #042.

DOBOY SOUND

Doboy Sound (chartlet #044) has the advantage of running out into the Atlantic in a straight line. Unfortunately, only the sea buoy marked "D" has a light on it and the unlit intermediate aids lack radar reflectors. The wide bar which begins at can "3" stretches eastward almost to nun "2". With 7-foot depths at low water springs this area would break dangerously with a high swell opposing an ebbing current—use this passage only in good conditions and on a rising tide. The Sound is marked with red aids to the north of the channel and green to the south—"red right returning" as they say. The sea buoy "D" marking the seaward beginning of the channel lies at 31°21'14"N and 081°11'24"W.

DOBOY ISLAND

Today this small island with Back River on its south side serves as an anchorage for the Darien shrimp boats which work the coastal waters and for a handful of transient yachts. It is hard to believe that on some days in the 1880s three to four dozen large sailing ships anchored around here in order to load southern timber. The mill on Doboy

Island was important enough to have a direct telephone line from Darien. Nine small wooded hammocks along the south shores of Commodore Island, Doboy's neighbor, and the Rock Islands hammocks along North River, northwest of Doboy, all grew out of ballast heaps left by the ships before they loaded their cargoes. Seeds of the prevailing tree on these small islands, the salt-cedar, a tamarisk, arrived from Europe stuck to the ballast stones thrown into the marsh. The ballast stone weight in the ship bilges increased hull stability and the ship's ability to stand up to the press of canvas set high on the spars. The ships unloaded the ballast to make room for cargo whose weight in turn improved the righting moment.

The best anchorage off Doboy Island lies against the north shore in 12 to 15-foot depths. Chartlet #043 shows how to enter close to the north shore—you will have a minimum of 10 feet at the western point of the island. Keep a bright anchor light on at night as shrimp boats move through at all hours with their outrigger arms out—they need more clearance than the size of their hulls suggests. A deep channel leads from Back River to Doboy Sound hence its popularity with the shrimp boat fleet. Queens Island along the south side of Back River lacks good creeks for exploring in a dinghy except for Hospital Creek which flows to South River and Wolf Island.

WOLF ISLAND

This almost square, 3 by 2.7 miles, marsh island is now a National Wildlife Refuge, most of it contributed by the Nature Conservancy. When you cruise in a small boat through the island's creeks you will see vast numbers of shore birds and, during cool months, waterfowl—they like places without constant human interference. Not many people come here—all hunting is banned and summer beach-goers find the once sandy margins on the east and south borders too narrow to play on. Since 1857 the eastern shoreline has retreated 3,400 feet and at low tide you can see the remains of the 1868 lighthouse sticking above the water offshore. Only the northern margins seem to be accreting and building seaward in a narrow tongue of drying shoals—see chartlet #047. In the 1890s a few wealthy businessmen decided to have a hunting club building on 5 acres they bought on the south shore of Wolf Island. They got the completed building barged down from Savannah and erected, but the 1898 hurricane washed over the island killing the caretaker and destroying all structures including the lighthouse.

The first move to change the island into a wildlife sanctuary began in 1930 when the federal government set aside 538 acres. Through the efforts of Jane Hurt Yarn of Atlanta and the Nature Conservancy, Wolf Island together with Egg and Little Egg Islands in the mouth of the Altamaha River, became a National Wildlife Refuge in 1973. Nowadays you must not land on any of these islands but exploring by small boat will bring you plenty of pleasure particularly if you can move the boat silently (by paddle or electric motor). Here, especially at low tide, you can vanish in a world of tall marsh vegetation with birds, alligators, fiddler crabs and the occasional mink the only living creatures around. Chartlet #047 provides the latest situation of the waterways which tend to change with time, especially the run of Beacon Creek. A few small hammocks dot the fringes of Wolf Island—the ones along Little Mud River have grown over ballast rock deposits.

ANCHORAGES AT WOLF ISLAND

SOUTH RIVER

Enter South River from the Intracoastal Waterway giving wide berth to the bank extending from the north shore—see chartlet #047. You will find excellent holding in the curve under the north shore even in hard winds from the northerly semicircle. At high tide you will see the striped Sapelo lighthouse above the marsh and around dusk and dawn black skimmers work the waters along the edges of the marsh. Sometimes a Darien shrimp boat will pass through here in the dark—show a strong anchor light.

LITTLE MUD RIVER— INTRACOASTAL WATERWAY

This river tends to silt up in its south section by Wolf Island but a dredge was at work when we took the soundings on chartlet #047 so the depths may have improved.

WATERS WEST OF THE INTRACOASTAL WATERWAY

A very complex system of tidal rivers meanders through the marsh country which separates the outer barrier islands from the mainland. Due in part to a canal dug by 18th century planters one can take a fairly deep draft boat from the South Altamaha River all the way to Sapelo River with only a short side jog to join Old Teakettle Creek (and the Intracoastal Waterway). With our draft of 5.5 feet and judicious use of the tides we enjoyed this trip since it kept us from the bustle of the seasonal traffic on the Waterway. Sailing before a south wind we made little noise besides a murmuring bow wave and so passed close to unsuspecting animals, mostly alligators, minks and several species of herons.

CRESCENT RIVER

This tidal river goes inland from the south end of Creighton Narrows (the Intracoastal Waterway). Chartlet #042 illustrates the run of the creek. There is a good anchorage west of Creighton Island, a privately owned island, still very beautiful despite some logging and cattle ranching on the high ground in the middle. Two side creeks deserve attention. Cedar Creek despite an entrance complicated by drying shoals hosts several shrimp boats which enter along the south shore of the creek's mouth. The fishing boats tie up to private wharves and the narrow river allows only small boats to anchor—the place makes a pretty coastal scene, though. At its north end Crescent River joins Snake Creek named, we guessed, for the tortuous entrances. As you can see from chartlet #042 even shallow boats will need help from a rising tide to navigate from Crescent River to the straight part of Snake River. After entering from Crescent River you should follow and favor the north side, then at the east point of the marsh you should cut about northwestward along the west side of two islets. Snake Creek runs straight after that until the narrow winding part (shown on chartlet #038) which joins Sapelo River by Belleville Point.

SHELLBLUFF CREEK

This tidal river leads from the Waterway to Valona, a community with a good size shrimp boat fleet which has its own haul-out railway and wharves at Southern Seafoods—chartlet #042.

ATWOOD CREEK

Atwood Creek is one of the three creeks at the northwestern end of Doboy Sound (chartlets #042 and #045). It swings inland by the private and occupied Patterson Island (chartlet #045) and continues to the shrimp boat wharf of Gore Seafood Co. which also owns a haul-out railway. The creeks to the east of the area run through pristine marshes with only one house on a small hammock to the north of Patterson Island.

HUDSON CREEK

Hudson Creek (chartlet #045) leads to Meridian, the site of the Sapelo Island Visitor's Center and the Sapelo Island ferry boat. It continues about southwestward and ends in mud flats along the residential docks on the north shore of Pease Point.

CARNIGAN RIVER

Carnigan River (chartlet #045) makes a good anchorage surrounded by pristine marshes. We used it as a base to explore a maze of creeks which join Dead River and Folly River. A conspicuous hammock, Buzzard Roost, in combination with all the virgin marshes completes a miniature nature reserve. During the 1800s the heavy traffic of sailing ships in the area kept the creeks busy here. In 1847, a brig from Havana, Cuba arrived with yellow fever aboard. Thirteen of the crew died with "black vomit" and were buried on Buzzard Roost—all traces of the tragedy vanished long ago and access to the island disappeared, too, say the owners of the island.

NORTH RIVER

North River (chartlet #045), a wide tidal river which flows west from the Waterway passes by Hird Island Creek, a narrow stream used mostly by the inhabitants of Hird Island, surprisingly heavily populated for a place without a road connection. Farther west North River joins May Hall Creek and smaller streams flowing towards the populated mainland.

MAY HALL CREEK

This narrow waterway used to be very important for it connected the timber mill on Union Island to Darien. When Mr. Blue and Mr. Hall serviced two small steamships, S/S *Emmeline* and S/S *Hessie* from a dock across the water from Union Island the route must have been heavily used. Today it provides access to Blue n' Hall where you will find Blackbeard School of Sailing and Navigation—contact Joe Jurskis for schedules and curriculum at 912-437-4878. Next door you will see the ramp and dock of the McIntosh County Boat Ramp. A few yards south is the Hird Island private dock. Next south you will see the docks and launch/haul hoist belonging to the McIntosh County Rod and Gun Club. This facility also sells gasoline, bait, ice and refreshments. They monitor VHF 16, tel. 912-437-4677. See the Services Section.

Sailboats can move south through May Hall Creek as long as their masts make it under the power line with 51-foot clearance at mean high water. Chartlet #045 shows the soundings on the north part of May Hall Creek. We found good anchorages on either side of the point to the south of the marina where your boat will be out of the way of small boat traffic. Chartlet #046 illustrates the whole run of May Hall Creek to Darien River. At the Darien River junction and bar of May Hall Creek you will find 7 feet in a very narrow channel with about 4.5-foot depths to the sides. Black Island Creek which passes by the Black Island residential development joins May Hall Creek about half way south from Blue n' Hall near the conspicuous Pine Island. Farther south by Black Island the creek goes under a very low bridge and eventually swings by the site of Fort King George. Darien River used to run through the curve under the fort. However, a short cut created by planters changed this area into a shallow oxbow. Read about the fort in the historical sketch of Darien below.

DARIEN RIVER

Chartlet #046 illustrates the entrance into this deep river. Recently installed markers make the navigation here even easier with the only tricky place located where Rockdedundy River joins Darien River. In Darien, just before the US HWY 17 bridge, you will find the floating docks of the municipal marina. It does not cost anything to tie-up during the daytime but, if you want to spend the night, walk the wide staircase to the building on the bluff above the docks. There, in the Darien Welcome Center you will find the McIntosh County Chamber of Commerce where you can pay $.75 per foot for overnight dockage—tel. 912-437-6684. Along the wharves to the east of the marina you will find George's Boat Works, a haul-out railway used often by shrimp boats and, occasionally, by motor yachts. To schedule a haul-out call 912-437-4496. On the west side of the bridge by Skippers Seafood there is a public boat ramp and a small dock. Boats cruising the area will find groceries at the Piggly Wiggly on US HWY 17 about a mile from the marina.

DARIEN—THE TOWN

Judging by the archeological evidence, this river and the bluff shores were for a long time important to various peoples passing through the history of the region. Indigenous populations who lived simply off the land and the river, Spanish missionaries scheming a conversion of the Indians into docile workers and Anglo-Saxons, all realized the advantages of ruling this waterway between the mainland and the ocean. When England and France defied Spain over control of the southern regions of North America, The Darien River, navigable to substantial vessels and a convenient route to carry soldiers, became an important frontier. The English Carolina colony in 1721made an effort here at defending the approaches to the Carolina borders However, due mainly to disease, that first Fort King George lasted only six years. The territory between the Savannah River and St. Johns River remained "the debatable land" with the warring parties of whites and Indians allied with one of the European countries spilling blood and enslaving the losers.

The city owned marina docks welcome visiting boats to Darien.

After organizing the first stages of his Georgia colony, Gen. Oglethorpe realized he had to secure its southern borders. Disappointed with the first boatload of wimpy Englishmen he next turned to the hardy Scottish Highlanders who learned how to swing a sword and to wield a plow in early childhood. Factors like clan feuds, the conflict with the English and loss of land encouraged many Scots to sail for the new opportunity overseas. In 1736, Oglethorpe had his new colonists start the fortifications and a settlement named New Inverness about on the site of the first Fort King George. The Scots worked hard and soon cleared a road all the way to Savannah. New Inverness was renamed Darien to commemorate a 1698 failed Scottish colony on the Spanish Main, now in Panama and still called Puerto Escocés—the port of the Scots. Oglethorpe's principled Scots refused slave labor and fought and farmed by themselves until 1748 and the end of the war with Spain. When the British government cut off financial aid and South Carolina planters arrived in the territory with their slaves to start profitable plantations, the good intentions gave way—in 1750 slavery was approved in Georgia. By 1760, Darien began losing population as the settlers moved out to their plantations in the surrounding country. However, the town recovered in the early 1800s as a hub of commerce for shipping out cotton, rice and timber. Along the Darien River sprung up warehouses and brokerage offices. On some days over twenty ships would clear into the port. As other southern towns, Darien suffered badly in the Civil War burnt to the ground in 1863 by a Union colonel and his black troops.

It rebounded again as a timber port. The fabulous longleaf yellow pine and cypress forests of the Altamaha region fell to the ax and were rafted down river to Darien to be dressed in the lumber mills and then shipped out. In just one year in 1900, over one hundred million feet of timber left Darien aboard domestic and foreign ships. In 1905, the lumber mills had problems obtaining enough timber and in 1925 the mills were abandoned. The local people next turned to harvesting oysters in the same uncontrolled way—in twenty years the oysters were gone as a profitable resource and even today the oyster beds have not quite recovered. Shrimping was the next fishery in Darien and it boomed after an Italian boatbuilder in Fernandina Beach developed the prototype of the modern shrimp trawler. The pattern of unplanned exploitation continued—the shrimp catch has declined and fishermen blame it on turtle saving devices installed in their nets and on unfair foreign competition. Somehow no one will admit openly that uncontrolled fisheries do, in the end, kill the resource. Today subject to regulations,

Darien continues to act as a major base for shrimp boat companies.

shrimping remains the main industry of Darien and dozens of trawlers use the wharves along the Darien River.

The town authorities have, reluctantly at first, realized that tourism can actually be a profitable industry and the location and history of the place favors Darien as a destination. Despite plagues, accidental fires and

George's Boatyard in Darien specializes in fiberglassing and servicing shrimp trawlers.

burnings, the town has several historic buildings in the attractive Vernon Square, a short walk from the waterfront. Along the river and north of the US HWY 17 bridge you can see the tabby ruins of early 1800s warehouses. The shrimp boat wharves on the Darien River banks once hosted a busy fleet of trading schooners. The town has installed a small marina for visiting boats and while there is no water or electricity on the floating docks the water is deep enough for very large craft. A small building up the bluff a few steps from the marina houses The Darien Welcome Center where you can pay the fee for overnight stays—daytime tie-ups are free. A moderate length walk on Fort King George Drive which parallels the Darien River will take you to Fort King George, a faithfully restored replica of the 1721 fortification.

The greatest future of tourism in Darien lies in its proximity and water connections to the Altamaha River Bioreserve. The best of the vast reserve can be found along the north shore of Cambers Island and around Lewis Island, all less than 10 river miles distant from the town. Rhett's Island, Champney Island, Butler Island, Wrights and Cambers Islands, all large marsh islands between the Darien River and the Altamaha River proper, used to be rice plantations. Now the DNR maintains the area as the Altamaha River Waterfowl Area and Altamaha Wildlife Management where wildlife is left alone to feed

and propagate until the time comes for them to be shot at during the annual hunting days. These huge islands, once covered by riparian forests, were cleared in the mid 1700s to make room for rice planting. The planters utilized the steady supply of fresh water from the river and the rise and fall of the tides to flood or drain the cultivated fields. Man-made high banks protected the rice fields from uncontrolled floodings. Many of the dikes, dams and tidal gates are maintained by the DNR who, in a few places, also plant grains like millet to attract migrating birds. The original rice plants, a strain brought to South Carolina from Madagascar in 1685, did not survive long after the Civil War cut off slave labor and major hurricanes flooded the fields with sea water. Today, most of the vegetation on these islands are wild grasses like southern wild rice and giant beard grass and rushes—black needle rush or marsh bulrush with the species varying according to the salinity of the water or the ground. In places where the old rice fields were entirely left to themselves, like Hammersmith Creek on the South Altamaha, Rifle Cut on upper Darien River, the plantation creeks off Cathead Creek and especially along the west side of Potosi Island trees are returning in a combination of species adapted to growing in water. In order to explore this area, visitors without their own boats, can rent kayaks or canoes from the Altamaha Wilderness Outpost, 912-437-6010, or call one of the charter boats listed in the Services Section.

St. Andrews Episcopal Church, Darien.

EXPLORING TIDAL ALTAMAHA RIVER FROM DARIEN

Owners of shallow draft boats with low superstructures can do a lot of exploring up river by themselves. Chartlets #049 and #050 show Cathead Creek and the junction of Darien River to the Altamaha as well as the man-made channels Rifle Cut and Generals Cut. There are two boat ramps with floating docks in Darien—on the west side of the US HWY 17 bridge by Skippers Seafood docks and on the north side of Champney Island south of the US HWY 17 bridge. Kayakers and canoeists planning to explore Cathead Creek can put in at a small side stream off of Cathead Creek. From Darien go northwest on HWY 251 until a split in the road with a sign showing Townsend to the right. Turn left here and look for the first culvert along the road—it goes to the stream you need. You will find only a small space to park on the side of the road here.

CATHEAD CREEK

Chartlets #049 and #050 illustrate the whole run of this creek which retains deep water for several miles and in the past provided access to important rice plantations. Chartlet #050 shows how, in a small boat, you can explore the canals from Cathead Creek to a creek which joins Darien River at the west boundary of Potosi Island. The shore descriptions for chartlet #050 provide GPS points for the vital points along the route as the proliferation of canals may easily confuse new visitors. After the initial run along the populated high shores on the west perimeter of Darien, Cathead Creek flows through undeveloped lands, marshes with scattered cypress and tupelo trees. Farther up it passes the Nature Conservancy's Cathead Creek Preserve, 752 acres of a recovering bald cypress/tupelo forest, some uplands and abandoned rice fields. The Buffalo Swamp Natural Area, part of the Altamaha Wildfowl Management Area surrounds this hidden preserve. To explore the area you should contact the Nature Conservancy of Georgia, tel. 404-873-6946, or their office in Darien (downtown and near the marina), tel. 912-437-2161. A short distance past the preserve the navigable waters end and Cathead Creek spreads into a flooded forest, wild and beautiful but also easy to get lost in—keep track of the twists and turns in your course. Diamond back terrapins, alligators and flitting birds will distract your attention from navigation. Wading birds and, in winter, ducks prefer the marshy environment of the old rice fields leaving this flooded forest to the more secretive night herons which breed here during summer months.

RIFLE CUT

This 1830 man-made canal was supposed to straighten out the crooked flow of the Altamaha River—the timber business preferred a more direct connection to the ships in Darien. Today the canal has as little as 2 feet of water left at low tide but a slow trip through brings you into a shadowy world under trees locking branches over the stream. During spring and summer the canal banks glow with blooming spider lilies and blue flag irises.

GENERALS CUT

Excavated in 1808, the cut still serves the shrimp boat fleet navigating between Darien and the South Altamaha River. Chartlet #048 shows its surprisingly deep soundings (a minimum of 5 feet at low water springs) but does not adequately convey how narrow it will be if you encounter a shrimp trawler going the other way—and they do use this route.

ROCKDEDUNDY RIVER

Chartlet #046 shows that favoring the north side of the entrance you should find 6-foot depths. The main attraction here is the anchorage in the curve before the river turns south. At low tide a long sandbar emerges in that south reach, great fun to explore if you have kids on board. Keep an anchor light at night as a shrimp boat may swing by on its way to or from Darien. This river joins the marked channel in Darien River about a mile and a half from the entrance.

ALTAMAHA RIVER

Chartlets #047 and #048 illustrate the main outlet and the delta of the Altamaha River, which flows for 137 dam free miles from the confluence of the Oconee and Ocmulgee Rivers where it officially begins. The tides reach 22 nautical miles up the river where at Altamaha Park and the old Railroad Bridge the tidal range is so reduced that altering river levels often mask the tidal fluctuations. The muddy waters of the Altamaha hide a lot of marine life, including giant flathead catfish weighing up to 50 pounds. Huge shortnose sturgeon weighing up to 1,000 pounds come up river to spawn and, till the recent ban, were caught for their roe to be processed by a local company in Darien. To tell the truth, we were just as thrilled seeing a 4-foot garfish, exotic to our inexperienced eyes and somewhat like a sturgeon in appearance. West Indian manatees apparently visit the Altamaha and coastal waters of Georgia, but we failed to encounter them.

After suffering excessive exploitation the Altamaha River has returned to a state resembling natural wilderness in great part due to the efforts of the Nature Conservancy. Having first secured Wolf and Egg Islands in the mouth of the river, the organization next acquired Big Hammock Natural Area and Lewis Island, 5,633 acres of swamp and ancient cypress trees. A very important achievement in 1977 was the creation of the Altamaha River Natural Area on land running along the river shores donated by ITT-Rayonier. The Nature Conservancy successes in the protection of Altamaha's shores were crowned recently when they obtained the logging rights to even more acreage along the river.

UP ALTAMAHA RIVER FROM THE INTRACOASTAL WATERWAY

Again boat owners find themselves in the enviable situation of being able to spend some quality time in a unique area. Sailboats will be stopped by highway bridges but even they can get far enough up river to allow small boat forays to the best sites. Deep draft boats discouraged by the shoals of the Altamaha River delta may prefer to proceed up river via the South Altamaha River (chartlet

#048) where navigational aids assist with reaching a modern full-service marina, Two Way Fish Camp.

ALTAMAHA DELTA

The large area of shoals, sandbars and marsh islands between Altamaha Sound and Wood Cut dividing Broughton and Champney Islands (chartlets #047 and #048) is typical of a large river delta. The proliferation of shoals untouched by any aids to navigation discourages many larger yachts from entering this way although Darien shrimp boats use it routinely. And with the added assurance from a rising tide so could any other boats. Outboard motor powered, shoal draft boats, may still run aground in some places at low tide so our chartlets will help indicate deep channels. Anglers frequent this area in search of various species of fish, including large tarpon, which feed and breed in low salinity waters. Cruisers will find a convenient anchorage along the south shore of Rhetts Island (chartlet #047) where there is a canoe landing. It allows visitors to walk along the old rice field embankment and observe great numbers of birds and alligators making their homes in the shallow lagoon. The waterfowl numbers increase dramatically during the spring and autumn bird migrations while in summer white and glossy ibis and wood storks turn up in large flocks. The lagoon is home to breeding common moorhens—and here we observed them with their young swimming around like ducks, sometimes taking a ride on an adult's back. Alligators of all sizes drifted around

An old rice mill chimney marks the site of the plantation land owned by Major Butler.

motionlessly coexisting with the black skimmers plowing the water and terns plummeting after silvery sprats. Beauty berries and blackberries have almost taken over the top of the embankment where in several places we saw old terrapin nests with broken shards of the eggs. Canoeists or kayakers use this landing which was covered with sheets of plywood to facilitate dragging boats over to the lagoon.

BUTLER RIVER

This river joins Altamaha River to Darien River in two places including Generals Cut (chartlet #050) and continues westward in a winding shallow course until it connects to the Altamaha over a drying sandbar. It flows along the northern edge of Butler Island, the site of a plantation begun in 1784 by Major Pierce Butler, an English military man from minor Irish nobility. He succeeded in America financially and became prominent in political life at first through marrying into plantation money, and then by a mixture of ruthlessness and cleverness in business dealings. The history of Butler Island shows how a plantation was born. At first tupelo gums, cypresses and maple trees covered this 1,500 acres of swamp. After cutting the trees Butler's slaves built nine miles of embankment digging the soil out of the middle of the island. Next floodgates were installed in the protecting dike and the island was divided into a grid of cultivating fields surrounded by canals which served to deliver or drain water as necessary. Butler based his plan of action and design on the proven Dutch practices of protecting lowlands. Butler also understood the principles of crop rotation, which apart from getting the best from his soil, allowed him to grow what would sell, rice, cotton or sugar cane. As an extremely conservative politician and senator he fought the abolitionists and formed the Fugitive Slave Law criminalizing run-aways.

Butler Island Plantation became the subject of a great controversy long after Major Pierce Butler died in 1822. In 1838, his grandson Pierce Butler arrived to live on the island with his English wife, an actress and writer, Fanny Kemble Butler. The cultivation of rice, the harshest crop to work for the slaves, introduced Fanny Butler to the dark side of plantation life and economy. Her stay there eventually led to a divorce and the publication of her *Journal of a Residence on a Georgia Plantation in 1838-1839*. It came out in 1863, and might have contributed to the lack of British support for the Confederate States. The conspicuous chimney on Butler Island marks the site of a steam powered 1850 rice mill while the "plantation house" near it was built in 1927 by Col. T. L. Huston who grew and shipped iceberg lettuce from the island.

Today the island is part of the Altamaha Waterfowl Management Area and birds love it. Just on one day in May we counted there about 200 glossy ibis, dozens of white egrets, and relatively large flocks of stilts and godwits. A few ospreys and marsh hawks cruised above feeding well, we were sure, on cotton rats and marsh rabbits scooting through the underbrush on the drier ground.

CHAMPNEY RIVER

This river passes between Butler Island and Champney Island, another abandoned plantation and a bird management area (chartlet #050). The Ansley Hodges M.A.R.S.H. project on Champney Island is part of the Colonial Coast Birding Trail. Conveniently located right at the east side of the US HWY 17 bridge, lies a heavily used public boat ramp and a floating dock—the most neglected and trashed facility of the kind in coastal Georgia. A little farther west Champney River joins Altamaha River.

ALTAMAHA RIVER ABOVE CHAMPNEY ISLAND

The river changes as you leave Champney Island behind; its banks become densely-forested, its waters widen and become deep again as shown on chartlet #050. It passes by Carr's Island, an old plantation island, donated by the Jones family to the Georgia Conservancy in 1996. Next come Wrights and Cambers Islands, plantations once and now Altamaha Waterfowl Management Areas, divided by the pretty Minnow Creek. Past Pine Island and opposite Rifle Cut begins the best part of the river—its course to Valentine Creek illustrated on chartlet #051. Here the entrance to Rifle Cut lies at 31°22'35"N and 081°28'56"W. This is where sailboat owners will regret the inadequate 35-foot vertical clearances allowed by the bridge designers where US HWY 17 and I 95 cross the South Altamaha River effectively blocking taller boats from reaching the most scenic river areas. Along the north shore of Cambers Island pond cypress and bald cypress thrive with magnificent trunks and well-developed knees surrounding some of the trees—low tide makes viewing this area more exciting. The islands in the middle of the river bloom with great colonies of pickerelweed and wapato along the water edges while from the harder ground small trees of southern catalpa reach over the river with dense colonies of flowers showy enough to challenge orchids—they flower in spring and early summer.

LEWIS ISLAND

This island has the distinction of retaining some old growth tidewater cypress and tupelo gums—over 1,000 years old according to some sources. To visit the island you must have a boat and penetrating the interior may be challenging to inexperienced people—after all the ancient trees survived because even the tough loggers of the 19th century could not get their equipment to them. At the moment there are no naturalist trips or guides to the Lewis Island trees, but you should contact the Nature Conservancy office in Darien for the most up-to-date information tel. 912-437-2161.

Several creeks lead to the island or around it and Lewis Creek with its entrance at 31°22'41"N and 081°29'33"W will take you to a landing at a small cleared area just west of Fulton Creek. The clearing practically touches a wet tupelo swamp with dense patches of lizard's Tail blooming between May and July. Rattlesnakes keep to the drier ground here—keep your eyes and ears open when wandering off under the trees along the river bank. These snakes will silently slide away if you walk heavily enough to warn them of your approach. If you continue westward on Lewis Creek you will get to Big Buzzard Creek and by taking it on the way south you will come to another landing spot on Lewis Island. We marked it on chartlet #051 as it is quite inconspicuous—its GPS position 31°22'56"N and 081°33'36"W. Wear rubber boots when you walk from here in about a northward direction. There are no trails and this is not easy. Follow the raised higher ground, probably an embankment left from the logging days, through a thick growth of waist-high grasses, numerous slim river birches on your left where there is a tiny stream which dries at low tide and some big trees in a swampy area on your right. During spring and summer you will see the rare obedient plant (also called false dragon head) in bloom along the little stream and beneath a very large cypress; spider lilies and flag iris thrive in this wet environment, too. At the end of this stretch you will see some rusting sledded machinery the loggers left behind as well as thick steel cables they used to drag the trees out. Some of the cables draped

Powerful buttresses support riparian forest trees against river currents.

over the trees have now been swallowed and grown over by new branches. You are now in thick forest with very wet ground which may flood to some depth on rainy days. If you insist on walking farther use conspicuous tape to mark your return and pick it off the trees on the way back. Sloshing through the swamp, climbing over fallen trunks and around the big live trees will make you lose your direction even if using a compass—stop often to keep your tape markers in sight and perhaps note down GPS readings if you carry one of these useful devices. The damp forest makes you realize what man loses by clear cutting forests—the air here feels pure, smelling of flowers and leafage. The biting flies of the open marshes disappear leaving only an odd mosquito buzzing about, and a great soothing silence prevails until summer thunderstorms send echoing warnings that it is time to head back for shelter. Big Buzzard Creek goes on to the Altamaha, a route which can also be used to access the landing directly from the big river. The GPS position of Big Buzzard at its Altamaha end is 31°22'29"N and 081°31'16"W.

Even without landing on the island, the streams around here take you by forested shores with swamp roses and large marsh pinks glowing in the shadows. Sweetbay trees, relatives of magnolias, hang their flowers over the water and add to the bouquet of scents—just the smell of the air makes a visit special. Yellow-crowned night herons rest camouflaged in the foliage of the river trees. Anhingas, which lack the glands to exude protective oils for waterproofing their feathers and only dive in fresh water, commonly fly over Lewis Creek. Diamond back terrapins sun themselves on fallen logs which abound in these forested waters but unlike some of the larger alligators, turtles slide back in as soon as they see you coming. Even alligators can take only so

much human presence and eventually slither away through the mud into deeper water which sometimes, in narrow channels, means they will go right under your little boat. As in other waters, exploring by paddling or with an electric motor, without the engine noise, brings you much closer to the animals and you will see more of them, also. Past the junction with Dick Swift Creek, Lewis Creek flows by a flooded forest of tupelo and cypress trees with particularly spiky knees.

ALTAMAHA RIVER ABOVE LEWIS ISLAND

Important for paddlers, reversing tides still affect the river currents all the way to Altamaha Park. Chartlet #052 shows how the river runs almost straight now without any confusing side tributaries. The shores change from the wild subtropical vegetation around Lewis Island into more temperate straight walled forest. There are signs of people camping ashore in a few places with makeshift tables—a plank over 50-gallon drums, a plastic tarp roof. Apparently, a road near Clarks Bluff makes the river more accessible. At Alligator Congress a couple of speedboats may rest on the beach and you will see successful anglers barbecuing fish. The forest looks very young and thin there. After an S-turn a populated area comes in sight, weekend cabins, docks and Altamaha Park with its boat ramp and docks. The Country Store sells gasoline, bait, tackle and refreshments—see the Services Section for details. A campsite lies to the side.

SOUTH ALTAMAHA RIVER

This deeper and straightforward southern branch of the Altamaha River has several advantages for larger boats—a marked channel through the shallow areas and a full-service marina (Two Way Fish Camp) with deep water docks and a restaurant (Mudcat Charlie's). After tying up the big boat in the marina or anchoring nearby, the crew can use a tender to explore some of the best places on the Altamaha including Lewis Island, Hammersmith Creek, Honeygall and Minnow Creek. In addition you will not even need a boat to visit the perfectly maintained 1800s Hofwyl Broadfield Plantation Historic Site a mile away from the marina.

Chartlet #048 shows the deep entrance to South Altamaha River. From the south side of marker "216A" you should head for the river favoring the north side. Pass

Bald cypress line the shores of Altamaha River by Lewis Island.

north of the unlit marker "1" and you will soon see the red markers—pass east of them as the system follows the "red right returning" rule, returning to Two Way Fish Camp in this case. A good overnight anchorage lies off Fridaycap Creek. This narrow creek goes into a wild marsh and supports an amazing amount of life. During the spring plentiful black skimmers take advantage of the easily available young fish. In the summer, at low tide, shrimp trying to get away from your boat will jump into your lap; in the fall migrating waterfowl descend upon the place, so rich in food are the waters and the marshes. Somehow the muddy freshwater mixing with sea water delivers a rich soup of nutrients and the shallow flats south of the the South Altamaha entrance and around Little Broughton Island boil with fish attracting great numbers of fowl and alligators.

As you go farther into the South Altamaha River you will see several osprey nests along the south shores and by the time you swing into the view of Two Way Fish Camp you will be in a fresh water river bordered with lush vegetation along both shores. A good anchorage in the curve of the river just east of Wood Cut will bring you near the flowers and trees—the water is deep enough to swing close to shore. A large alligator, Albert, makes his home in these waters—he floats by slowly every day, his eyes rolling within the knobby turrets of his eyebrows over his light colored cheeks. Albert often dreams under the shadow of the trees along the shore, the ridges on his mud colored back outlined like saw teeth against the mirror-calm water surface. Calm and indifferent as he seemed, he kept us from jumping in the river to cool off even on the hottest summer days. We needed a few feet of rising tide to get into Wood Cut, the short connection flowing to Champney River, but anchoring in Wood Cut right in direct view of a bald eagle nest was worth the trouble. The eagle called in a high pitched voice both alike and different from the osprey call. Now and then he would take off swooping over the water his talons drawing a spraying wake. Was he cooling off his feet? we never saw him catch a fish this way. Keep a good light on at night here as the boat traffic, although light, goes on at all hours.

TWO WAY FISH CAMP AREA

If you plan to make exploratory trips in a small boat up the Altamaha you can tie up the mother ship in Two Way Fish Camp. Despite the name, this is a large marina with deep water docks and all amenities. They cater to local fishermen and have an electric hoist, sell gasoline, diesel, bait, ice and some tackle items. They monitor VHF 16, tel. 912-265-0410. See the Services Section for more information about their fishing charters and river trips. Next door to the marina is Mudcat Charlies, a popular restaurant which specializes in local seafood attracting customers from as far away as Brunswick. Owners of larger boats in need of hull repairs, propeller service or antifouling can use Two Way Boat Yard, also next door, which offers a 40-ton travel lift and all the essential technicians—912-265-6944—see the Services Section. The

The sand banks in the middle of the Altamaha River often develop into islands bordered with water plants and trees.

Two Way Fish Camp Marina is a modern full-service marina on the South Altamaha River.

One of the star attractions in the area, Hofwyl-Broadfield Plantation State Historic Site lies on US HWY 17 very close south of the marina. It would be a pleasant walk to get there but for a lack of a cleared side trail along the highway—find a ride if you want to visit the place. 1,268 acres of the old plantation became State of Georgia property in 1974 through the help of The Nature Conservancy which inherited the land in the will of Ophelia Troup Dent, the last owner. Visitors find a lot of interest here: the 1851 plantation house, the original farm buildings and pasture land shaded by great live oaks, 400 acres of old longleaf pine forest, a large parcel of typical maritime forest trees and a recovering freshwater marsh. Huge 100-year old magnolias, 300-year old live oaks as well as a particularly large American holly and sweet bay add to the attractions of the tour. Native Georgia animals abound—we thought we noticed a couple of escaped monkeys at our first sighting of the unusual southern fox squirrels, twice the size of the common gray squirrels. Hofwyl-Broadfield Plantation is also included on the Colonial Coast Birding Trail.

marina is a busy place serving boats of all sizes, running fishing tournaments for both ocean and fresh water fishermen—hence the name of Two Way—and hosting several boats, some quite large, belonging to the Federal Law Enforcement Training Center. Do not get spooked by seeing funny looking guys with weapons charging around in 50-footers—they do slow down politely near other boats to reduce their wake.

UP THE ALTAMAHA FROM TWO WAY FISH CAMP

Heading up river from Two Way Fish Camp you will pass, on the south shore, the entrance to a canal, now looking pretty wild, which once joined the Altamaha with Turtle River near Brunswick. Dug through in 1834, the canal served for moving plantation crops by barge to the ships moored in Brunswick. Close westward of I 95 bridge the South Altamaha makes a sharp S-curve passing Hammersmith Creek. This creek, popular with canoeists and kayakers, winds between old Hopeton Plantation owned in the 1700s by John Couper and James Hamilton of St. Simons Island and Carrs Island also the site of an old plantation—chartlet #050. The Carrs Island banks have plentiful flowers in the spring and early summer, blue flag irises, spider lilies, swamp roses and blooming sweet-bay trees. Tabby Creek, a small stream accessible at high tide, is favored as a safe nesting ground by yellow-crown night herons. After Hammersmith Creek, on the south shores of the South Altamaha you will see several osprey nests, all with hatchlings in spring time. Honeygall Creek, another small shallow creek runs off southward about a mile and a half west of Hammersmith. Thirty to forty feet wide at first, it narrows to twenty feet in places with many trees across—an ideal exploring creek for canoes which put in from more solid ground in a privately owned pineland. Ft. King George in Darien often sponsors canoe expeditions in these creeks, call 912-437-4770. The South Altamaha joins the Altamaha near Lewis Island after flowing though a shallow forested reach—chartlet #051.

A cruising motor yacht anchors off Woods Cut near Two Way Fish Camp on South Altamaha River.

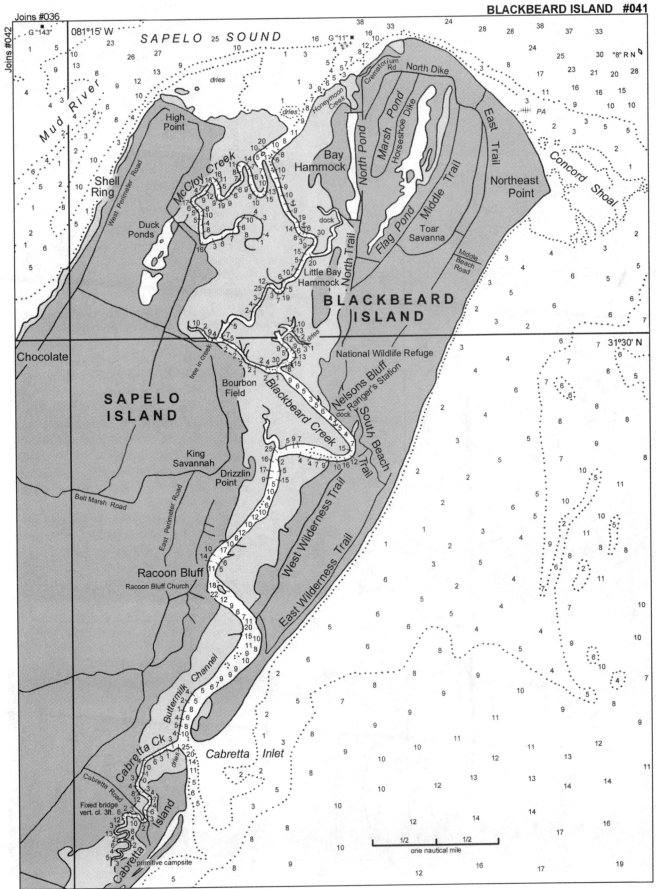

All Soundings In Feet, Low Water Springs

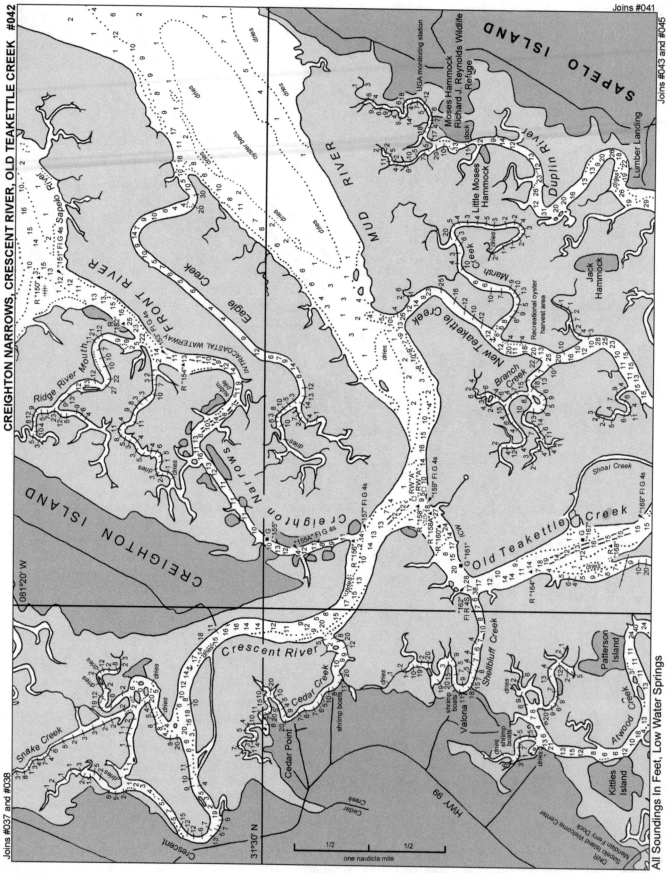

Joins #041

Joins #043 and #045

Joins #037 and #038

All Soundings in Feet, Low Water Springs

one nauticla mile

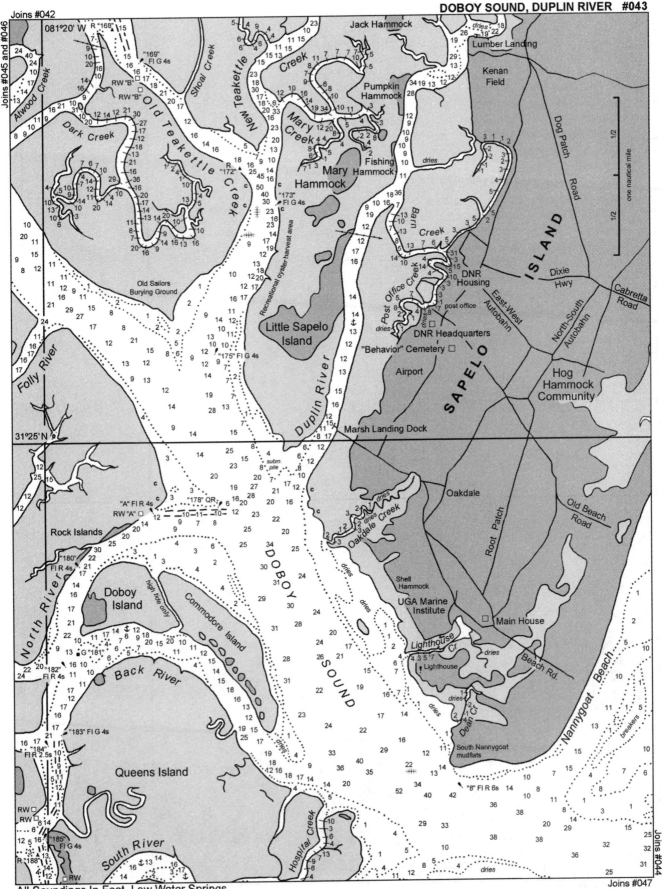

All Soundings In Feet, Low Water Springs

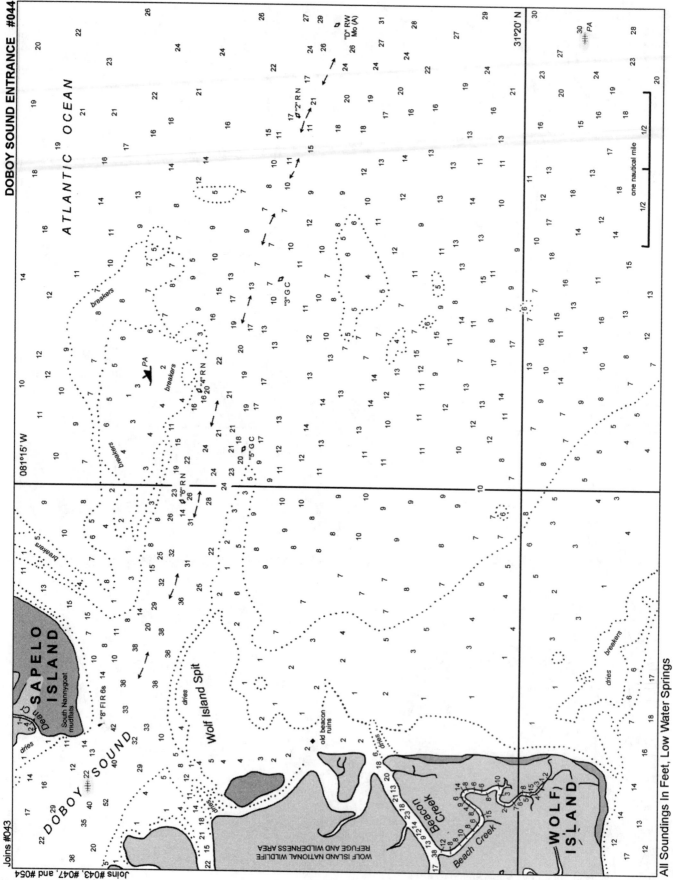

ATLANTIC OCEAN

081°15' W

31°20' N

one nautical mile

1/2   1/2

breakers

"D" RW
Mo (A)

"2" RN

"3" GC

"4" RN
breakers

PA

"6" RN

"5" GC

SAPELO ISLAND

Dean C.

dries

South Nannygoat
mudflats

"8" FlR 6s

DOBOY SOUND

breakers

Wolf Island Spit

dries

old beacon
ruins

WOLF ISLAND NATIONAL WILDLIFE
REFUGE AND WILDERNESS AREA

Beacon Creek

Beach Creek

WOLF ISLAND

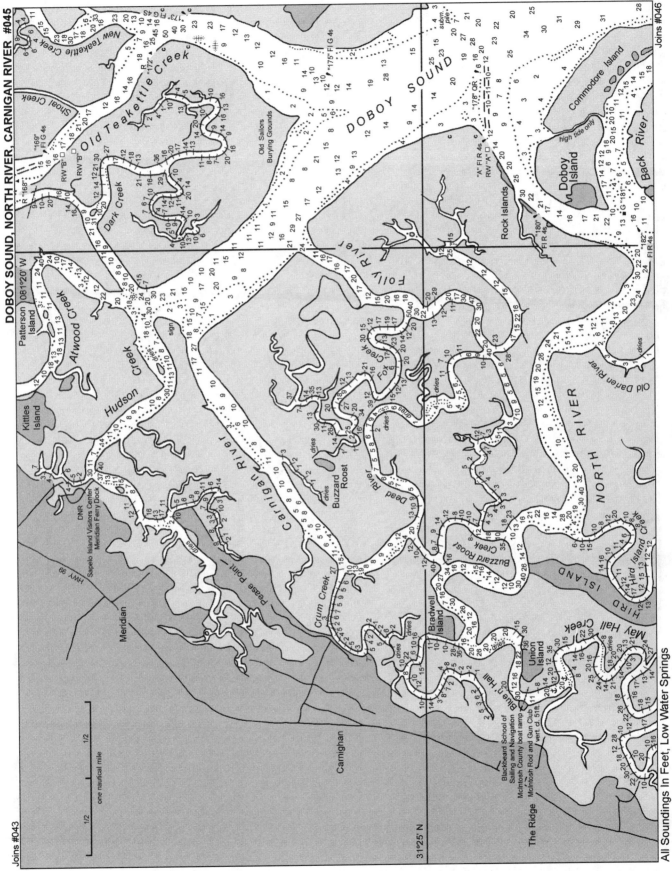

DOBOY SOUND, NORTH RIVER, CARNIGAN RIVER #045

DOBOY SOUND

Old Teakettle Creek

New Teakettle Creek

Shoal Creek

Dark Creek

Old Sailors Burying Grounds

Commodore Island

Doboy Island

Rock Islands

Back River

Folly River

Atwood Creek

Hudson Creek

Kittles Island

Patterson Island

Carnigan River

Fox Creek

Dead River

Buzzard Roost

Old Darien River

NORTH RIVER

Pease Point

Sapelo Island Visitors Center
Meridian Ferry Dock
DNR

Meridian

HWY 99

Carnighan

Crum Creek

Buzzard Roost Creek

Bradwell Island

Union Island

Blue n' Hall

HIRD ISLAND

Hird Island Creek

May Hall Creek

Blackbeard School of Sailing and Navigation
McIntosh County boat ramp
McIntosh Rod and Gun Club
vert. cl. 51ft.

The Ridge

Patterson 081°20' W

31°25' N

one nautical mile

1/2

All Soundings in Feet, Low Water Springs

Low Water Springs

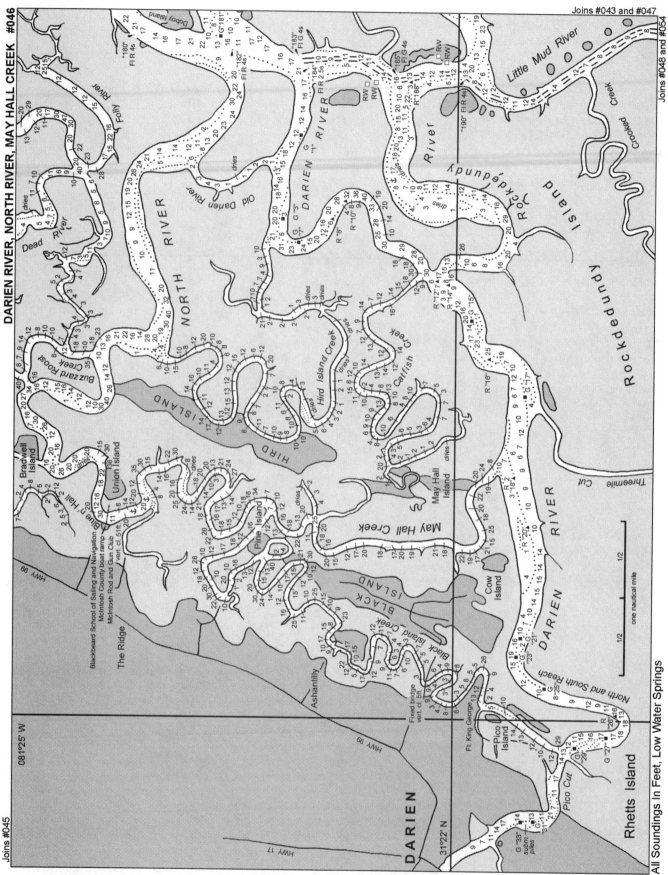

Joins #043 and #047

Joins #048 and #054

Joins #045

081°25'W

31°22'N

All Soundings In Feet, Low Water Springs

one nautical mile

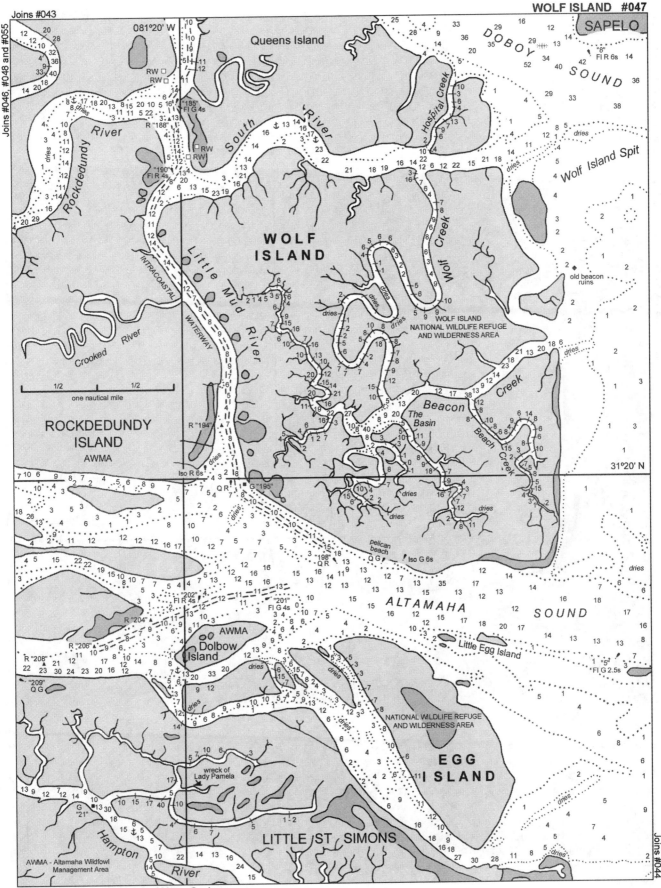

SAPELO

Joins #043

081°20' W

Queens Island

DOBOY SOUND

"8"
Fl R 6s

RW
RW

"185"
Fl G 4s

R "188"

RW
RW

"190"
Fl R 4s

South River

Hospital Creek

Wolf Island Spit

Rockdedundy River

Joins #046, #048 and #055

WOLF ISLAND

Wolf Creek

old beacon ruins

INTRACOASTAL WATERWAY

Little Mud River

Crooked River

WOLF ISLAND NATIONAL WILDLIFE REFUGE AND WILDERNESS AREA

dries

Beacon Creek

Beach Creek

1/2   1/2
one nautical mile

ROCKDEDUNDY ISLAND
AWMA

R "194"

The Basin

31°20' N

Iso R 6s

Q R   G "195"

pelican beach
Q G   Iso G 6s

ALTAMAHA   **SOUND**

"198"
Q R

"202"
Fl R 4s

"201"
Fl G 4s

R "204"

R "206"

AWMA
Dolbow Island

Little Egg Island

"5"
Fl G 2.5s

R "208"

"209"
Q G

NATIONAL WILDLIFE REFUGE AND WILDERNESS AREA

EGG ISLAND

wreck of
Lady Pamela

G "21"

Hampton River

LITTLE ST SIMONS

AWMA - Altamaha Wildfowl
Management Area

Joins #044

All Soundings In Feet, Low Water Springs

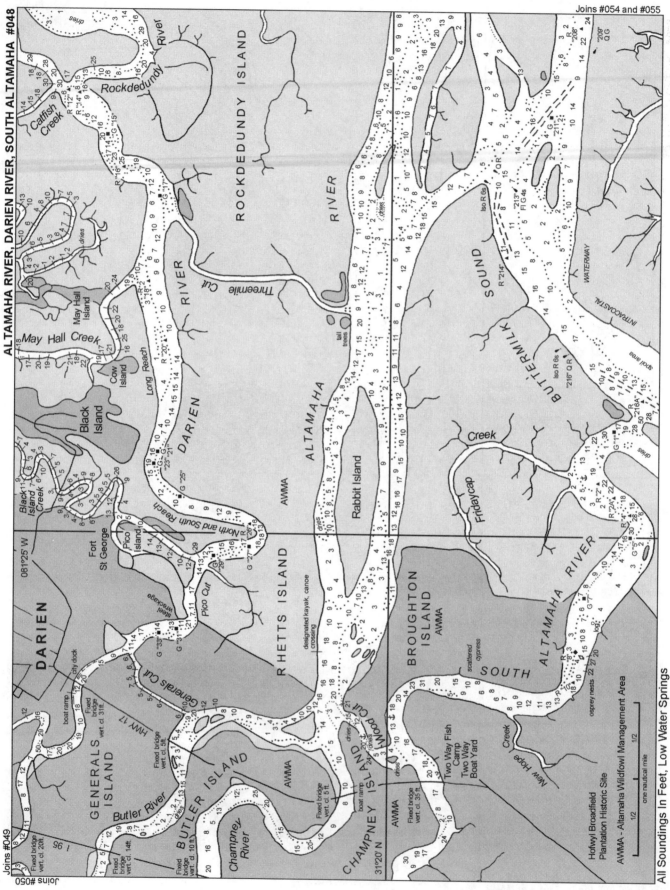

ALTAMAHA RIVER, DARIEN RIVER, SOUTH ALTAMAHA #048

All Soundings In Feet, Low Water Springs

Hofwyl Broadfield
Plantation Historic Site

AWMA - Altamaha Wildfowl Management Area

one nautical mile

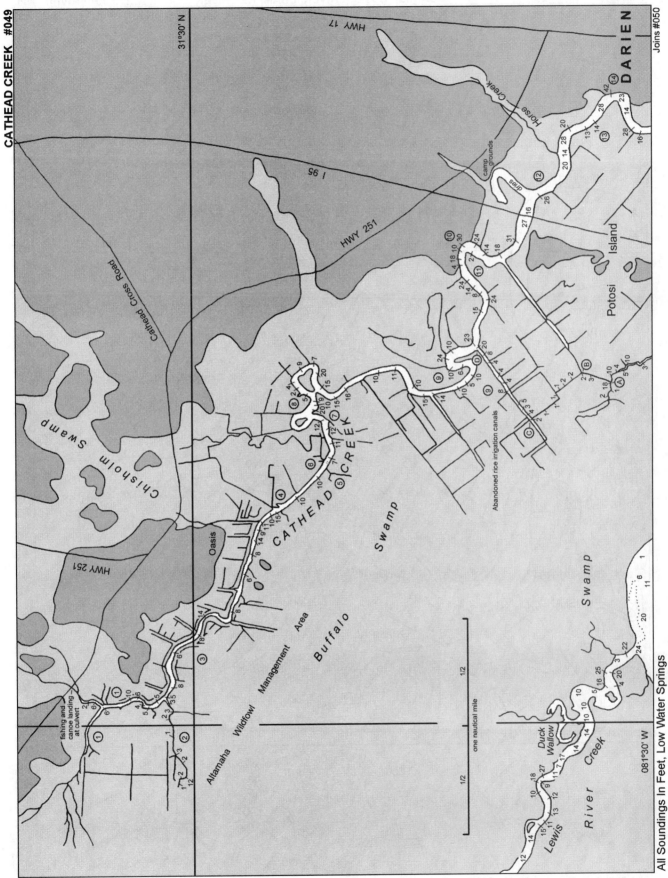

All Soundings In Feet, Low Water Springs

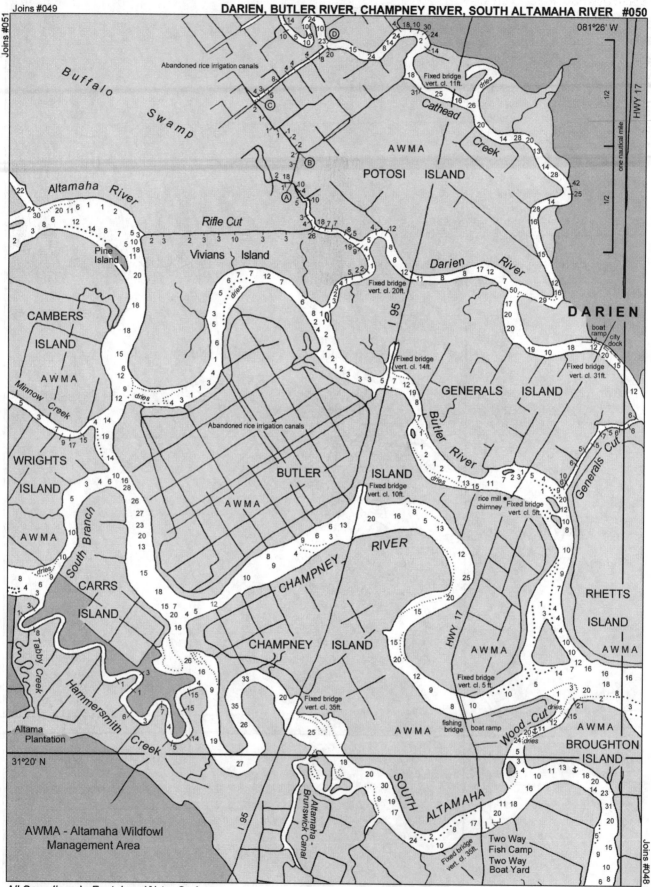

All Soundings In Feet, Low Water Springs

Shore Descriptions for Chart #049
CATHEAD CREEK

1 .... Flooded forest
2 .... Flooded forest—many birds
3 .... Abandoned rice canals
4 ...... Forest on edge of old rice fields
5 .... Many pilings—may be partially
submerged at high tide
6 .... Abandoned rice fields
7 .... Landing possible
8 .... Beautiful area, many side
channels, landing possible
in places, many hammocks
9 .... Marsh
10 .... Bluff with residential area
11 .... Big shoal on inside of curve
12 .... Marsh with scattered
cypress trees, osprey nests
13 .... Marsh
14 .... Bluff

A .... 31°22'49.0" N
081°27'58.9" W

B .... 31°22'57.9" N
081°27'55.4" W

C .... 31°23'16.9" N
081°28'14.4" W

D .... 31°23'31.5" N
081°27'48.0" W

Shore Descriptions for Chart #050
DARIEN, BUTLER RIVER,
CHAMPNEY RIVER, SOUTH
ALTAMAHA RIVER

A .... 31°22'49.0" N
081°27'58.9" W

B .... 31°22'57.9" N
081°27'55.4" W

C .... 31°23'16.9" N
081°28'14.4" W

D .... 31°23'31.5" N
081°27'48.0" W

East wind brings maritime cumulus clouds over South Altamaha River.

Shore Descriptions for Chart #051
ALTAMAHA RIVER, LEWIS CREEK, LEWIS ISLAND, SOUTH ALTAMAHA RIVER

1 .... Landing
2 .... Dirt ramp leading to a dirt road
3 .... Sand bars along bank
4 .... Shallow sand bank,
keep to north bank
5 .... Mixed forest with thick
undergrowth
6 .... Large drying sand bar
7 .... Small landing, shoal extending
into the river from the point,
keep to the outside of the bend
8 .... Muddy low foreshore,
thick tangled forest
9 .... Grassy marsh foreshore,
long sand bar on north bank
10 .... Sand bar on north side with
thick undergrowth
in mixed forest
11 .... Bushy foreshore
12 ...... Forest with thin trunked trees,
many yellow-crowned
night herons
13 .... Sand bar on north coast
of island
14 .... Thick bushy undergrowth
15 .... Low thick swampy woods
16 .... Both islands have long grassy
points on their NW points
17 ... Abandoned rice irrigation canals
18 .... Forest along shore with
abandoned rice fields
behind the trees
19 .... Lots of mistletoe in the trees
20 .... Beautiful cypress trees with
Spanish moss and
many bird boxes

21 .... Low thick forest, landing
possible if wearing boots
22 ..... Thick undergrowth, no landing
23 .... Drowned trees, deeper
on SW side of the river
24 .... Shallow on NE side
25 .... Thick undergrowth,
mixed growth forest
26 .... Grasses
27 .... Two foot bank with thick
undergrowth, mixed forest
28 .... Thick undergrowth
29 .... Landing possible
30 .... Undergrowth too thick
for landing
31 .... Two foot bank, thick forest
of slender trees
32 .... Good landing SE of a
12 foot high bluff
33 .... Low forest
34 .... Low forest
35 .... Easy landing possible
36 .... Low, thick forest
37 .... Three foot bank,
landing possible
38 .... Landing possible
39 ...... Landing possible, old Scagway
logging machinery, see text
40 .... Landing possible
41 .... Cross
42 .... Landing possible
on both sides of the river
43 .... Landing possible
44 .... Landing possible in ferns
45 .... Landing possible

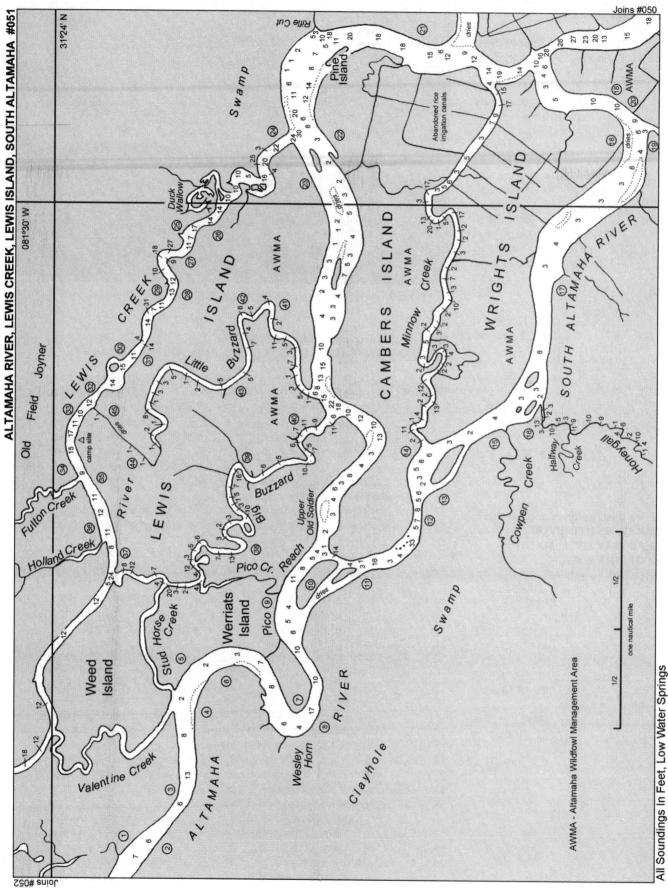

ALTAMAHA RIVER, LEWIS CREEK, LEWIS ISLAND, SOUTH ALTAMAHA #051

Joins #050

Joins #052

AWMA - Altamaha Wildfowl Management Area

All Soundings In Feet, Low Water Springs

one nautical mile

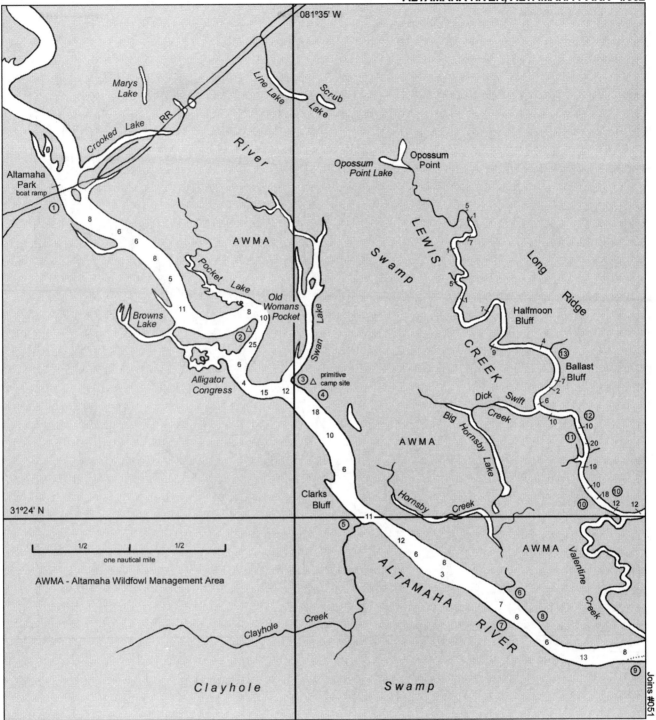

All Soundings In Feet, Low Water Springs

Shore Descriptions for Chart #052

1 .... Cabins	8 .... Sand bars along bank
2 .... Primitive camping	9 .... Shallow sand bar – keep to north bank
3 .... Primitive camping	10 .... Landing possible
4 .... Landing	11 .... Thick brush
5 .... Dirt ramp	12 .... Landing
6 .... Landing	13 .... Bluff with a landing
7 .... Dirt ramp, dirt road	

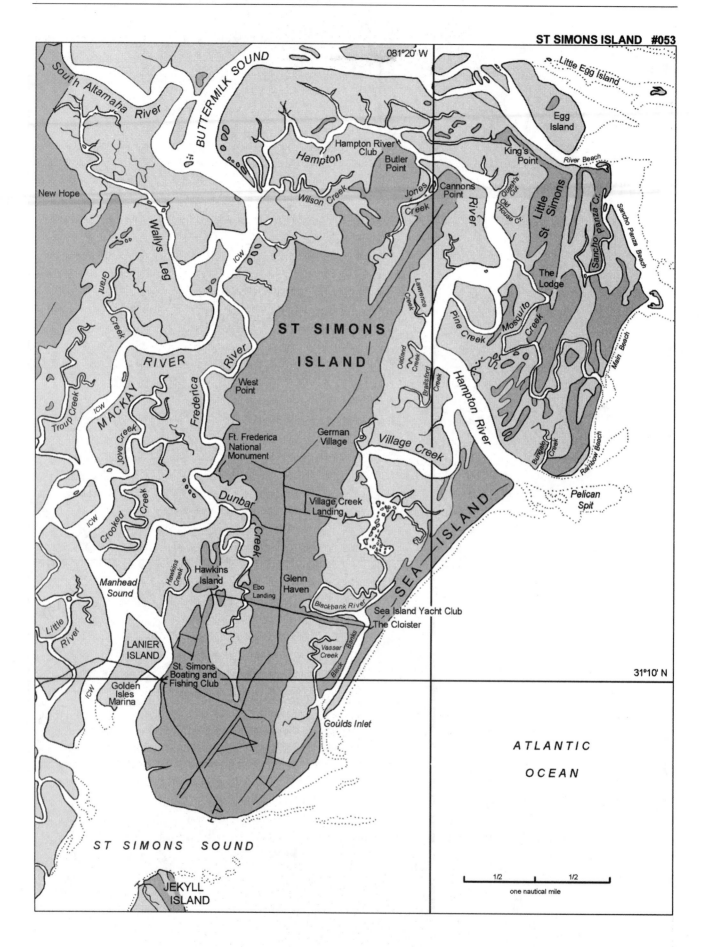

CHAPTER SEVEN

ALTAMAHA SOUND TO ST. SIMONS SOUND
INCLUDING ST. SIMONS ISLAND AND BRUNSWICK
GLYNN COUNTY

ONE OF GEORGIA'S developed barrier islands, St. Simons faces the Atlantic along this stretch of the coast. A major bridge and causeway link St. Simons to the mainland providing easy access for residents and visitors. People come to sample a variety of recreational facilities from beach hotels to golf courses and to tour well-preserved historical sites. Little St. Simons, a privately owned island adjacent to greater St. Simons, welcomes vacationers who enjoy an unspoiled barrier island on foot or on horseback. For boating people St. Simons offers three marina facilities, while the historical port and town of Brunswick eight miles away on the mainland also has a modern marina, a boatyard, as well as facilities to serve fishing enthusiasts.

ALTAMAHA SOUND AND EGG ISLANDS

Although marked by fixed and lighted aids to navigation Altamaha Sound would be very dangerous in heavy swell conditions especially with an outgoing current. The bar carries 4 to 5 feet of water at low water springs and since a wave begins to break in depths that equal its height, and even earlier with a strong contrary current, conditions can easily turn nasty here. Nevertheless, small sport fishing boats and shrimp boats use this entrance at the right stages of the tide and weather. The entrance marker "2" lies at 31°18'30"N and 081°13'45"W and the channel leads between red markers on the north and green markers on the south side. Farther in the shoals on the south side have grown from Little Egg Island eastward into long islets topped with mops of smooth cordgrass marsh. The much larger and substantial Egg Island has a forested hammock in the middle of thick marshes. All of the Egg Islands belong to the Wolf Island National Wildlife Refuge managed by the US Fish and Wildlife Service. While anglers may enjoy the fish-rich waters around the islands

no landing is allowed in order to let shore birds breed unmolested—they need such places badly and we need birds to fill the blanks in the sky. Cruisers will find a handy anchorage near the southwest side of Dolbow Island. Chartlet #054 illustrates the easy approach to the anchorage from the west along the shore of Little St. Simons. The holding ground is good in mud of which there is a constant supply available—Dolbow Island lies within the Altamaha delta with the muddiest and thickest waters on the coast. One can make great trips in a small boat by going east towards and then along the west side of Egg Island—only a few small shrimp boats come in from the ocean to spend the night at anchor between Little St. Simons and Egg Island. Low tide in this area bares many sand bars and birds congregate to feed in the intertidal zone.

BUTTERMILK SOUND

Several ranges and markers help navigating from Altamaha Sound into Buttermilk Sound and on to Mackay River—chartlets #047, #048 and #055. On the way south you will pass by the entrance to the South Altamaha River with its handy anchorage near the deep entrance (consult Chapter VI for more details). Little Broughton Island whose north tip borders the South Altamaha entrance is, at low tide, surrounded by shallow mud flats with a rivulet of water running through along the west side of the island. The nutritious mixture of salt and freshwater draws wading birds and waterfowl to this area. Black skimmers plow these waters regularly and during cold months ducks feed here. From late spring through late fall you will see at least a dozen alligators in the shallows on the east side of Little Broughton. Next, the Waterway swings southeastward and passes by the hammocks of Five Pound Tree where, during the times of Major Butler's plantation on Butler Point (1800s), the less malleable slaves were banished as punishment. Isolated from their own kind and treated even more harshly, they worked Experiment Plantation first growing cotton and later rice.

Low tide bares a sand bank on one of the Egg Islands just north of Little St. Simon.

Caught among the treacherous and uncharted shoals near the coast this tugboat ended up on the beach of Little St. Simons Island—a warning to careless navigators.

LITTLE ST. SIMONS ISLAND

A superficial look on the charts and maps gives the wrong impression that Little St. Simons is part of the much larger St. Simons Island. In fact, Hampton River, a deep tidal river, separates the two. The islands differ—the natural environment of Little St. Simons has been improving in recent years as opposed to steady residential and commercial development on its large neighbor. Although a rather low Holocene island, Little St. Simons has enough solid land to have done its duty as a plantation, most efficiently when it was planted, together with Hampton on the north end of greater St. Simons, by Major Butler in the 1800s. Civil War and the abolition of slavery finished the plantation days and the island, since the early 1900s owned by the Berolzheimer family, has been used as a vacation retreat, hunting lodge and in some degree as a cattle run. Still owned by the same family, Little St. Simons now hosts small groups of paying guests who come to immerse themselves in its rich natural beauty. Many of them participate in bird counts, enjoying sightings of large numbers of resident species, migratory visitors and some unusual visiting birds like a sandhill crane temporarily tired of migrating. Needless to say cattle are long gone and only a small controlled population of the deer introduced from Europe in the 1920s runs free in the woods. The dunes vegetation, especially sea oats, has expanded and the island can boast one of the most perfect beaches in Georgia. Fortunately for nesting loggerhead turtles, horseshoe crabs as well as beach nesting shorebirds—American oyster catchers, least terns, Wilson's plovers—the sandy shores are widening thanks to the accretionary contributions from the Altamaha estuary. Owned and managed by people who care about local ecology, Little St. Simons has a better success rate for hatchlings of all species, whether winged or carapaced, than some of the State owned barrier islands in Georgia. The only conspicuous sign of human influence on the beach is a small tugboat wreck slowly sinking deeper in the sand.

While guests of Little St. Simons (888-733-5774) have the privilege of exploring the interior of the island under the guidance of a naturalist, boat owners cruising Hampton River will have to be satisfied with walking miles of the Little St. Simons beach (up to the high tide line) and poking around in small boats through Mosquito Creek. At mid-tide a small boat can traverse the whole width of the island to the creek's ocean outlet having alligators, kingfishers and wading birds for company. As you can see on chartlet #057 at low tide your boat will get stuck aground and at high tide it may have difficulty squeezing under the little bridge—time your trip very carefully. Several places in Hampton River provide protected anchorages and in Pine Creek (chartlet #057) your cruising boat will lie within earshot of bird calls from the marsh and the forest.

HAMPTON RIVER

This tidal river flows between the Intracoastal Waterway and the ocean, passes by virgin salt marshes, a full-service marina, an upscale residential development and then flows again through a seemingly untouched landscape all the way to the Atlantic. Of course, there is plenty of residential development on the side of greater St. Simons Island but it is all tastefully hidden in a thick coastal forest. Hampton River also provides access to Village Creek which in turn leads to the Sea Island Yacht Club docks and other branching creeks joining St. Simons Island.

Boats entering Hampton River from the Waterway pass north of Hampton River marker "27" located about a quarter mile north of Waterway marker "223". A large sign listing all the attractions of staying in Hampton River Club Marina also marks this entrance conspicuously. Boats heading eastward must leave the green markers to starboard and red ones to port—the aids to navigation mark the channel for boats navigating from the ocean. Chartlet #056 indicates a few shallow spots along the way so new visitors on deeper draft boats may want to have a couple of feet of rising tide for assurance. In fact, once you know the river you can take 6 feet of draft through at low tide. Hampton River Club Marina sells gasoline and diesel and has all the amenities on their deep water docks as well as a laundromat and showers. They also launch trailerable sport fishing boats weighing up to 10,000 pounds and sell bait and ice—see the Services Section. They monitor VHF 16, tel. 912-638-1210. Transient boats sometimes anchor a little to the east of the marina and can tie-up their dinghies at the marina docks for a small charge. However, the grounds outside the marina are all private and residential. Without stores or restaurants in the area it is a long taxi haul to do shopping or to eat out on the island.

Hampton River Club development stands on the grounds of Hampton, a successful plantation started in 1790s and managed from afar by Major Butler, an absentee owner busy in Pennsylvania as a pro-slavery politician. Several quiet creeks cut into the wild marshes on Little St. Simons Island facing Hampton River Club. Abandoned in one of them, the wreck of the schooner *Pamela*, once starring in the Pipi Longstocking movie series, now makes a handy perch for white and glossy ibis and other coastal birds foraging in the marshes. A family of marsh hawks, easily identified by the white patch on the upper side of the base of the tail, patrol this area hunting rodents and sometimes waterfowl injured by autumn hunters. A tidal stream called

Strings of whelk egg capsules often end up on beaches after strong onshore winds.

Jones Creek flows between the Pleiostecene upland ridges of Hampton and Cannons Point. Several substantial homes rise between the trees along the west side of Jones Creek, sometimes their existence betrayed only by half-mile-long docks rising over the marsh on the way to the water. Cannons Point, a tract owned by the Jones family, remains undeveloped and beautifully forested. Navigating towards the ocean and about at marker "3" you will see, through the trees, the tabby ruins on Cannons Point, a plantation contemporary with Major Butler's Hampton but owned by John Couper, a Scot from Glasgow. Couper's hospitality and humane treatment of slaves presented many visitors from the continent with a prettified aspect of slavery.

Little St. Simons Island shore by Pine Creek.

Chartlet #057 illustrates the most beautiful parts of Hampton River with open views of the marshes and hammocks and bluish outlines of distant forests. Yachts of all drafts will find a multitude of places to anchor depending on the wind direction—the rule being to avoid long stretches of the river where a strong current can run against a strong wind and cause choppy water. If you anchor off Old House Creek you can go in your tender into the marsh and you will see flocks of ducks in the fall months. The creek next to the north of Old House Creek is a lot deeper; at the very end it swings by solid ground where you will see the remains of an old oven or fire place—a "no trespassing" sign here. You will find the most protected anchorage in Pine Creek and from there you can use the boat tender to explore Old House Creek, Mosquito Creek or even go across the river to visit Taylors Fish Camp up Lawrence Creek on St. Simons. This place launches small sport fishing boats and offers dry storage on the boat owners' trailers, 912-638-7690 and 912-638-5731, see the Services Section. Down the pretty road leading from the dock, under big live oaks with extraordinarily long arms, you will see a tiny old slave cabin made of tabby. This is Peggy Buchan's studio and gallery showing her paintings of local scenes—during weekends you will find her tending the boats at the fish camp.

Hampton River carries deep water a long way down towards the ocean and there was once a protected anchorage for deep boats by Pelican Spit, a small island with sea oats and a protected nesting area. The high swell brought by Hurricane Dennis in 1999 charging north along the coast washed away the island and now at low water only you will see a pristine sandbar running out eastward into the sea. In early May mature horseshoe crabs, their carapaces studded with barnacles, turn up here to mate and leave their tiny eggs in the sand—a great feeding opportunity for shore birds. Somehow a good many of the crabs end up upside down on the beach during low tide—we could never understand how it could happen. They cannot hurt you in any way, so carry them back into the sea and they will come alive swimming away gracefully for such oddly-shaped animals. Lately horseshoe crabs, which have been around some 400 million years, have come under threat since commercial interests have found that they make good bait for eels which in turn are sold to the Far East and European markets. During the mating season on some parts of the East Coast fishermen drive down the beaches to shovel their trucks full of horseshoe crabs. Will we ever learn? is the big question. At present, in order to explore Pelican Spit at low tide one should anchor the mother ship in Hampton River either off the north shore a little

Dawn lights up the sky over Hampton River by St. Simons Island.

west of Bungalo Creek or off the golf course and the beach on the Sea Island side. The wind direction decides which anchorage stays smoother. After anchoring use the tender to move round—to explore the beach on Little St. Simons you can beach or anchor the tender at the mouth of Bungalo Creek. Shallow draft boats often venture offshore through a deep trench between Pelican Spit and Little St. Simons. At low tide they can easily follow the north edge of the spit in deep water. Farther out when the spit begins to disappear under water they should stay close to the breaking shallows at its northeastern end where you can find 5 to 6 feet of water. This trench is very narrow and be aware that if you miss it you will be going through 2 to 3-foot depths—very dangerous in high swell coming in from the ocean. Offshore, to the east and northeast of Pelican Spit, you will encounter deeper channels intermixed with drying shoals—in calm weather local boats fish there successfully. Anglers love the waters along the north edge of Pelican Spit at low tide when the spit rises above the sea and cuts off the ocean waves. After the tide covers the protecting sands fishermen move to the north side of Sea Island to fish very close to the oyster bar along the marsh off the golf course.

It was not the first time that a hurricane driven swell wreaked havoc on this coast. In 1804, a hurricane hit Little St. Simons and Major Butler's slave "driver" Maurice had to use his whip to prevent more than one hundred slaves from trying to leave the island in the raging weather. He forced them into a strong building where they survived, unlike seventy slaves on Broughton Island Plantation in the Altamaha. Major Butler rewarded Maurice with an inscribed silver tankard. Maurice said no to the offer of freedom which came along with the tankard since Major Butler did not include his wife and children. Twenty years later, in 1824, a hurricane hit the same area and contemporary reports quote 100 sheep lost on Little St. Simons and extensive damage to the plantations on St. Simons and the Altamaha.

VILLAGE CREEK

To enter Village Creek you should approach from south of green beacon "11" on Hampton River—chartlets #057 and #058. Cruisers can anchor in several places after the creek deepens on its way northwest although we particularly liked the anchorage further south, at the mouth of a bunch of creeks pointing about southeast. A great number of small marshy islands with oysters along the edges attract numbers of birds from red-wing blackbirds, fish crows, boat-tailed grackles to American oyster catchers and cormorants. Brown pelicans plunge into the water here when small fish run and dolphins enter even the smaller streams when the tide rises. It is fishy here

In spring, horseshoe crabs come ashore to lay and fertilize eggs. Left high and dry by the receding tide they can survive till the next high water.

and an 83-pound state record Black Drum was caught in these waters some years ago. Just a bit farther south from this anchorage a side branch leads to Village Creek Landing. Anglers launch their boats from a public ramp. An old great blue heron hangs around there as do grackles and other marsh birds including clapper rails—marsh hens—which take shelter on the premises when the hunting season begins. Marsh rabbits feel at home there, minks regularly go through and otters spend nights on his dock. This creek dries out at low tides so check your timing carefully when planning to visit there.

Village Creek eventually runs by the west side of Sea Island and the Sea Island Yacht Club docks reserved for the island's residents. Two classic motor yachts, the 1923 *Zapala* and the 1929 *Belle,* which tie up here, too, take guests on trips through the creeks, marshes and out to Hampton River. They also charter out for dinner parties and *Belle* goes on extended coastal trips—see the Services Section under charters. Village Creek reaches the sea by a shallow lagoon running along the dunes on the south tip of Sea Island and then spills out into Goulds Inlet. Low tide leaves mud flats and long sandy spits bare, the best time for birds to feed. You may see here reddish egrets which frequent the area—you will immediately notice the reddish neck and bluish body so very different from the more commonly seen snowy egrets. Reddish egrets sometimes occur in a white feathered form but you can spot them by their feeding behavior—they hop around with open wings. Large flocks of brown pelicans, gulls and terns often line the sandy shores on Sea Island. You may also spot northern gannets in the sky to seaward—the mature birds have immaculately white bodies with black wing tips and yellow below their eyes, but the young ones stay dark for up to three years. They feed by bullet-like plummeting into the sea from considerable heights and if you sail offshore along the coast of Georgia in the colder months you will see many of them. The area around Gould's Inlet is part of the Colonial Coast Birding Trail.

ST. SIMONS ISLAND

Over 11 miles long with an area over 38 square miles, St. Simons is the second largest island on this coast. The Pleistocene uplands of the main island receive a lot of protection from the younger Holocene barriers—Little St. Simons and Sea Island. Indigenous people must have lived on the island for a few thousand years. During the construction of the McKinnon Airport on St. Simons, first the contractors and then the Smithsonian Institution's archeologists uncovered a large village and a burial ground used long before the 1500s when the first Spanish showed up on the coast. The Spanish established at least three missions on the island between 1605 and the 1680s when they retreated to St. Augustine. The first well-documented European presence here came with Gen. James E. Oglethorpe in 1736 when he built Fort St. Simons on the south tip of the island and a more substantial fortification and a village on Frederica River, a navigable river flowing along the west shores of St. Simons. By 1740, Frederica had 500 people living in a town neatly divided into squares, equipped with a battery and barracks, protected by a moat and backed by a designated farm land and a cemetery. Frederica maintained communication with Fort St. Simons via Military Road, part of the present Frederica Road. Oglethorpe prepared for war and went at it with a passion as soon as an excuse turned up. The first one was when the outrage over one ear of an English coastal smuggler named Jenkins brought England into a long-sought confrontation with the Spanish. After two of Oglethorpe's Highlander scouts on Amelia Island were killed by the Indians allied with the Spanish, the good general thought it was time to unite all the English forces in the area, including the Carolina colony, and subdue St. Augustine. His few initial forays against the minor Spanish forts in Florida went well. In 1740, Oglethorpe sent the Carolina Englishmen, Highlanders and allied Indians south for the final strike against the Spanish power base in St. Augustine. Serious disagreements between the English and the Scots, who would not take orders from the Brits and spoke only Gaelic, weakened the operations; a retaliatory dawn raid by the Spanish forces killed most of the Highlanders and the British withdrew.

It was now or never for the Spanish if they wanted to secure their borders. In 1742, an invasion fleet of 52 small ships, some from Havana, Cuba and others from St. Augustine, brought 1,950 soldiers to Georgia. Off the south tip of Cumberland Island the cannon fire from Fort William and a British armed schooner forced the Spanish to sail away and into St. Andrew Sound. After minor skirmishes, one involving Gen. Oglethorpe sailing in a open boat, the Spanish managed to land their forces on the south end of St. Simons and took over the little fortification there. After the first Spanish attack was repulsed short of Frederica, Oglethorpe prepared a clever ambush for the main bulk of Spanish troops. Even though the Spanish were trapped they fought effectively enough to send three British platoons running away leaving the remaining platoon to fight it alone. Rounded up from their retreat by Oglethorpe, the English returned only to find out that the Spanish had already left the battlefield. This skirmish, in which less than a dozen Spanish were killed, went down in later history as the Battle of Bloody Marsh. The war between England and Spain continued in other lands until 1748 but the

Two classic motor yachts, *Belle* and *Zapala*, dock at Sea Island Yacht Club.

landing on St. Simons was the last major Spanish attempt against the Georgia colony. Gen. Oglethorpe was recalled to England in 1743 never to return.

Various inhabitants of Frederica and participants of Oglethorpe's wars received land grants on St. Simons Island and at some point they or their descendants sold to wealthier investors and merchants who added to their fortunes by planting sea island cotton. John Couper owned Cannon's Point while Major Butler ruled the Hampton Plantation, both on the north end of the island. James Hamilton, a merchant from South Carolina owned a large chunk along Frederica River that was then and through the early 20th century used as the main port on St. Simons. Another South Carolinian, Major William Page acquired Retreat, a large acreage at the south end of the island, owned in the late 1700s by James Spalding, the first planter to grow sea island cotton on the barrier islands of Georgia. All through the mid-1800s some fourteen cotton plantations operated on the island's arable uplands. Due to soil exhausted by this demanding crop, a saturated English cotton market, a boll weevil infestation and eventually competition from short staple cotton grown on the mainland, planting cotton became less lucrative even before the abolition of slavery. The Civil War dealt the last blow and just a few years later wealthy northerners began buying cheap Georgia real estate. St. Simons became a resort destination with grand hotels entertaining guests from as far away as the mid-West. Passenger steamers puffed busily between the Brunswick railroad terminal and the wharves on Frederica River. Hamilton Plantation along Frederica River developed into a timber milling operation with shipping wharves until Georgia ran out of trees in the 1900s. And then in 1949 a large part of Hamilton Plantation became Epworth by the Sea—a Methodist Conference Center with youth programs and a hotel open to all visitors. Retreat Plantation, owned by the Sea Island Company since 1929, has developed into the famous Sea Island Golf course.

The creation of Sea Island itself is part of coastal Georgia history. Fired by St. Simons' success as a resort the State of Georgia embarked upon building a land connection between Brunswick and St. Simons and since 1924 a roadway over four miles long has run east over causeways and bridges. After a dozen years of developing Sapelo Island into a profitable modern-day plantation it did not take long for Howard Coffin to see the potential for a different kind of development on St. Simons, already an established destination. He focused on the 5 mile long and 2 mile wide barrier island off the east shore of St. Simons aptly named Long Island. Young and highly unstable because of its exposure to eroding ocean forces, Long Island served as a cattle run in colonial times and as a hunting retreat later. Coffin promptly renamed it Sea Island and hired an architect, already famous for his Palm Beach designs, to draw a hotel on similar Spanish-Mediterranean lines. After a causeway

over the marshes connected Sea Island to St. Simons and Coffin's own power plant worked reliably, the Cloister Resort opened in October, 1928. The stock market crashed a year later. Already financially overextended Coffin had to sell Sapelo Island to keep the Cloister going during the Great Depression. The strain imposed on the ailing man eventually led to his suicide. It was not until 1941 that the place, then run by Alfred W. Jones, Coffin's cousin, showed profits. Today, apart from the up-scale Cloister Beach Club and Resort, small condominiums and a residential community of large impressive homes hide in a manicured environment of live-oaks, pines and other trees introduced for their pleasing appearance. The Atlantic Ocean insists on taking away the expensive real estate and since the 1960s concrete seawalls of various shapes and beach re-nourishment efforts have had to protect the central ocean front. Sea Island is, however, growing steadily at its south end by Gould's Inlet where dunes and beaches attract naturalist-led excursions from the Cloister as well as large numbers of shore birds. Surprisingly, Sea Island receives more nesting loggerhead turtles than the pristine, uninhabited beaches of Little St. Simons.

FREDERICA RIVER

Chartlet #059 shows the whole length of this river once vital for the economy of St. Simons Island. Chartlets #060 and #061 illustrate the same river in greater detail. The northern entrance deserves some attention. Do not come close to the north or east side of marker "229" but favor the east side of the entrance where you will find only 5 feet at low tide. However, the beauty of the river makes it worthwhile to plan the visit around the tides. After the bar the river becomes quite a bit deeper (chartlet #060) and you will soon notice that Frederica River could be easily renamed after the alligators which always roam its waters except during the cold months when they tend to hibernate. You can anchor anywhere in the river when the view of the forest and the marsh pleases you. Many cruising boats prefer the anchorage off wonderful old trees at Fort Frederica where there is a small dock for dinghies and good access to this preserved 1736 historic site and a small museum and a gift shop with excellent books about the area. Read about the exciting history of Fort Frederica in *St. Simons Island* above.

At its southern part (chartlet #061) Frederica River spills into Manhead Sound over a 5-foot bar and then swings southeast towards St. Simons Island and Gascoigne Bluff. Gascoigne captained the British sloop-of-war *Hawk,* active in Oglethorpe's times. This shore, now covered by a relatively young live oak forest was once deforested—live oak timber from this area was used in the construction of the USS *Constitution* in 1794. Timber became an important commodity again in 1868 when some New Yorkers, G. P. Dodge among others, created the Georgia Land and Lumber Company, purchased Gascoigne Bluff and set up four mills with a capacity of 125,000 board feet a day to process logs floated in rafts from the Satilla River and the Altamaha. For thirty years up to nine schooners at a time lay at the wharves on Frederica River to load dressed wood for world and home destinations—southern wood built the Brooklyn Bridge in New York in 1878. In addition, the trade in naval stores—pine rosin, spirits of turpentine and pitch, was in the 1880s second only to the revived cotton industry.

Today, as you come towards St. Simons on this part of Frederica River (chartlet #061) you will first see the crosses at Epworth By The Sea Methodist Conference Center and then the docks of St. Simons Boating and Fishing Club. Farther south, unless you are on a boat lower that 9 feet, you will find your way barred by the bridge for the F. J. Torras Causeway. Transient boats may anchor in this stretch of river and many choose to drop anchor across from the docks of the fishing club. The northern docks of St. Simons Boating and Fishing Club often have enough room to accept short term visitors. The docks south of the launching well are reserved for members. They also have two boat hoists and sell gaso-

line, bait and ice, phone 912-638-9146. See the Services Section for more details. Ashore, behind the marina you will find a beautiful grove of live-oaks and southern red cedars planted about 150 years ago to replace the logged-out forest. If you walk towards Epworth make sure to see the two tabby slave cabins preserved from plantation days in a somewhat idealized condition. Just a bit to the north of them take a look at the certified largest southern red cedar in Georgia with a circumference of 15 feet and a crownspread of 74 feet. Three hammocks rise on the marshes across Frederica River from Epworth—a reminder of the great shipping era at St. Simons. These islands covered mostly with salt cedar, a tamarisk from Europe, grew over the heaps of ballast stones tossed into the marsh from sailing ships waiting to load timber at Gascoigne Bluff.

To reach Golden Isles Marina, the most important yacht facility on St. Simons, you have to stay on Mackay River (the Intracoastal Waterway) and go under the 65-foot fixed bridge (chartlets #061 and #059). You will see just south of the bridge on the west shore the Manhead Marina dock—the place is closed. Across from it, on the east shore by the bridge, you will see a public boat ramp accessible from the Causeway. Carry on south to marker "249" and, if you want to go to Golden Isles Marina, turn north, pass

Golden Isles Marina welcomes all sizes of yachts to St. Simons Island.

east of marker "3" and then steer by the range ahead. The range is difficult to follow at night because the lights on both markers are about the same height—when you are on the range you will see only one light instead of the customary two lights in a vertical alignment. Deep draft vessels should use a rising tide here—at low water springs they may find only 6 feet for a good stretch of the approach—see chartlet #062. Many transients anchor north of marker "5". If you continue to the marina docks, pass a floating breakwater and two sets of docks—they belong to the condominium visible ashore. Yachts at anchor must pay $7 to leave their dinghies in Golden Isles Marina. On the other hand yachts which tie-up in the marina receive, in addition to all the normal modern amenities, the use of a courtesy car for an hour to do shopping for groceries or other business in town. The marina sells all marine fuels and is large enough to have, almost always, an open slip. If you need advice on navigating the approach or want to reserve a slip call on VHF 16 or tel. 912-634-1128. See the Services Section.

In order to see the usual historic sites on the island and hear their history you should book a sightseeing trip with the St. Simons Transit Company located in the shopping and office complex by the marina docks—912-638-5678. In the same location you will find a marine store carrying boat hardware, equipment, boat clothing and cruising guides, ask for this one! A couple of restaurants offer their fare here, too. Check the Services Section for dive shops, kayak outfitters, etc.

ST. SIMONS SOUND

Serving large ships heading to the port of Brunswick, the St. Simons Sound channel carries an excellent array of aids to navigation maintained in good working order—chartlet #065. The lighted whistle buoy marked "STS" at 31°03'14"N and 081°15'09"W marks the outer limit of the channel which next leads between 8 paired lighted buoys to a lighted bell buoy "17" lying south of St. Simons Lighthouse and town pier. Aided by ranges, merchant ships follow the deep channel by buoys "19", "20", "22" and so on towards Brunswick.

Yachts entering from the ocean and intending to go to Golden Isles Marina should head from buoy "17" for the deep water along the south shore of St. Simons and turn northwards passing between lighted beacon "2" and a day beacon "3" after which they can follow the range to the marina—chartlet #062.

Yachts entering from the ocean and intending to continue northward on the Intracoastal Waterway should steer about northwest from buoy "17" until they pass south of lighted beacon "249"—chartlet #062.

Yachts entering from the ocean and intending to follow the Waterway south should steer to buoy "19" and then head southwest for the northwest shore of Jekyll Island. Deep water runs close to the Jekyll Fishing Pier so yachts can stay south of the ship channel steering parallel to the Jekyll shore until they locate the green range leading into Jekyll Creek. The red lighted beacon "2" and green day beacon "1" begin the channel leading through Jekyll Creek—chartlet #066. This part of the Waterway was recently dredged and chartlet #066 shows the latest depths. This creek tends to silt so deeper draft craft intending to go through at low tide should contact one of the marinas on Jekyll Island for an update on current depths.

WATERS WEST OF THE INTRACOASTAL WATERWAY

The port of Brunswick and a major coastal river, Brunswick River, dominate in this section. However, upstream from the industrial and urban development, on the uppper reaches, you will encounter attractive wild marshlands and wooded hammocks.

Crane cottage in Jekyll Island historic district.

WALLEYS LEG

Chartlet #055 illustrates the whole run of Wallys Leg from the Intracoastal Waterway to the creek's end. An anchorage popular with transient yachts lies off the large island with an inaccessible hammock at the mouth of the creek. Note the large shoal which extends from the southwest shore of the island into the anchorage area. Beyond the anchorage Wallys Leg meanders through totally undeveloped marshes—a temporary home to waterfowl during the cold months.

TROUP CREEK

South of marker "237" you see the entrance to Troup Creek. As suggested by chartlet #059 you should favor the north side of the entrance when entering Troup Creek. As you come around the curve you see, unexpectedly for this rather small river, a Coast Guard Station and its docks where the *Smilax,* a large buoy tender ties up. Just a little farther you come across the floating docks and a snack bar for Troupe Creek Marina. They welcome transient yachts although their main business comes from serving local sport fishermen who launch their boats here and buy gasoline and bait. Troupe Creek Marina monitors VHF 16, tel. 912-264-3862. See the Services Section for more information. After the homes

with docks near the marina the creek winds through undeveloped marshes to the east and an occasional dock to the west.

BACK RIVER

The northern entrance to Back River runs along the west shore of the island which has marker "238" at its northern tip. Chartlet #059 shows how the trough of deeper water in this part of the river runs between wide drying mudflats until Belle Point Creek. Back River widens after that and in its southwestern arm, where it flows by a row of residential docks, depths become quite respectable and two markers help with the navigation. Terry Creek on the river's west shore is an industrial canal to the factories in Brunswick—do not eat anything caught in its dangerously contaminated waters! Very close, to the south of Terry Creek you will see the Torras Causeway bridge with a 40-foot clearance at high tide, a boon to sailboats moored at the docks on Back River. On its way south after the bridge Back River passes Little River which is crossed by a very low bridge with 6 feet vertical clearance—chartlet #062. On the west shore, north of the bridge, lies the dock of George's Bait—customers are welcome 7 days a week from 6 A.M. until 4 P.M. See the Services section. After the bait place Little River winds northwards and branches off through very pretty undeveloped marshes. South of Little

City Hall, Brunswick.

In Brunswick's historic district.

River and on the south shore, just before Back River runs out into St. Simons Sound, you will see the entrance to Plantation Creek described below.

PLANTATION CREEK

This creek, cutting through the marshes southward to Brunswick River, was in the 1880s and through the early 1900s much in use by commercial craft carrying cargoes from the Altamaha area to Brunswick. These small, always overloaded, vessels considered St. Simons Sound, often rolling with ocean waves made even rougher by strong tidal currents, as a real threat. This narrow waterway, still open, has one very shallow area where Clubbs Creek meets it—chartlet #062. Clubbs Creek goes on towards the east side of Brunswick and Spanky's Restaurant which has a dock reserved for customers. See chartlet #062. Spanky's overlooks an expanse of marshes and bird watchers will love the place as avocets and ducks often feed around here. Right there you will also find Southeast Adventure Outfitters who organize kayaking expeditions throughout most of the southern Georgia coastal area—see the Services Section. Next to them Brunswick Boat Marina serves local sport fishing boats but access to their facility is very shallow at low tide. They launch trailerable boats and sell gasoline and bait—see the Services Section. After the junction with Clubbs Creek the depths improve in Plantation Creek— see chartlet #062. Still the creek remains very narrow with a few shallow places until it meets Brunswick River. At the south end of Plantation Creek, near the junction with the river, you will see a dock which belongs to the headquarters of the Georgia Department of Natural Resources, the Coastal Resources Division. Next to it is the dock and station of the US Coast Guard. Small boats may tie-up temporarily to the DNR dock in order to visit their Earth Day Nature Trail supplied with name tags for some plants. You will see more natural history displays inside the DNR building and they give away a lot of enlightening literature pertaining to various facets of coastal Georgia.

BRUNSWICK RIVER

This body of water connects St. Simons Sound with the port of Brunswick in East River and other commercial ship facilities up Turtle River. As a result, lighted aids to navigation lead mariners in day or night—chartlet #062.

A large fleet of shrimp trawlers is based in Brunswick.

The Sidney Lanier Bridge crosses the river. If for one reason or other, you need to anchor east of the bridge do so between the south entrance to Plantation Creek and a big hammock with a dock on its shore to the southeast. This position will keep you out of the way.

Brunswick Landing Marina provides first class services to resident and transient yachts.

One fleet of shrimp boats ties up to the wharf at Mary Ross Waterfront Park in Brunswick.

The inhabited hammock, you will notice, has grown on a huge pile of ballast rocks.

EAST RIVER

East River, between Andrews Island and Brunswick, creates a protected harbor for large ships, shrimp boats and yachts. Heading up the river you will navigate along many commercial docks to the east as the yacht facility lies north of the last group of shrimp boats. Brunswick Landing Marina has several sets of well-equipped floating docks big enough to receive very large yachts. They have a fuel dock by the dock master's office on the southernmost finger pier. Due to the 5 nautical mile distance from the Intracoastal Water-

way they receive only light traffic during most of the week. As a result, the dockmaster may be away from the marina and in their boat yard—call Brunswick Landing Marina on VHF 16 or tel. 912-262-9264. See the Services Section for more. Brunswick Landing has a great shower/bathroom complex together with a free laundry and a crew lounge; they also hold mail and receive packages. Brunswick Landing Boat Yard located at the end of a canal closing the East River operates a 50-ton travel lift. Apart from offering all services they also allow do-it-yourself work. See the Services Section for details. A large grocery store is only a short taxi ride away and a hardware store with some marine items lies within a short walk. Due to the shrimp boat fleet based in town you will find good mechanics here as well as machine shops familiar with the marine industry. A very short walk along the shore of East River will take you to the farmers market with local produce for sale on Saturdays, Tuesdays and Thursdays. This area, called Mary Ross Waterfront Park, borders a river wharf where shrimp boats dock every day and visiting tall ships tie up occasionally. The very good Brunswick Library is located only two blocks farther south. Within walking distance from the marina you can also see nice examples of late 1800 American architecture with many interesting homes located south of Gloucester Street and east of Newcastle Street.

A stay in Brunswick Marina has some unexpected benefits. You will see great assemblies of shorebirds on the sandy causeway across river from the docks, American avocets, black skimmers, yellow-crowned and black-crowned night herons. White ibis often sit on the wreck of the barge. Lately heavy earth moving equipment began converting Andrews Island into a ship terminal and it may affect bird activities in the area—so far the birds still come to the causeway beach. You will get to observe there another activity, rare in these modern days. Shrimpers routinely run their boats onto the sloping causeway beach at high tide. When the receding tide leaves the boats high and dry the men can do repairs to the propellers or caulk leaks in the bottom planking. The procedure, called careening, was a common maritime practice before the development of dry docks and travel lifts.

Brunswick, founded in the 1770s on property granted to one of Oglethorpe's officers, Captain Mark Carr, has an interesting maritime past. Old photographs show the East River packed with tall sailing ships loading timber. During World War I large wooden ships slid down the shipyard ways in Brunswick, their wooden hulls considered safe from German magnetic mines. During World War II, in 1943, J. A. Jones shipyard in Brunswick began building Liberty ships to help England in the war effort. The Liberty ship derived from a 1879 British Tramp de-

Shrimp boats routinely careen for repairs on a sandbar facing the port of Brunswick.

sign, a 447-foot steamer first launched in Newcastle-upon-Tyne. Powered by oil fired steam engines Liberty ships could carry nearly 10,000 tons of cargo with their fuel tanks full. Their production in the US began in 1941 and 2,700 hulls were launched by the end of the war. Brunswick shipyard contributed 99 ships and the speed of the production cycle defies imagination—in just one December of 1944 Brunswick launched 7 ships. With such feverish construction, Liberty ships suffered structural problems during storms in arctic waters but even today old patched-up Liberty ships carry cargoes in the tropical backwaters of Asia. You can see one of these ships yourself—a 23-foot accurate model of a Liberty Ship occupies the southeast corner of Mary Ross Waterfront Park.

SOUTH BRUNSWICK RIVER

South Brunswick River is also well-endowed with aids to navigation since it serves as a channel for the ships bringing automobiles to the terminal on Colonels Island. After the terminal, consult chartlet #063 for the depths leading up river. On the west shore of South Brunswick River you will see the entrance to Fancy Bluff Creek by which small boats and low boats (two bridges cross the creek) can reach the Little Satilla River—see chartlet #063. Farther up on the north shore of the South Brunswick River you will come to Blythe Island State Park. The park docks are open to visitors and the facility has a 6-ton hoist for trailerable boats and a launching ramp as well. They sell bait, ice, basic tackle items and refreshments, tel. 912-261-3805. See the Services Section. The park focuses on the camping public and it offers nice walking trails with paths overlooking the marshlands and a fishing pier for anglers without boats. Transient cruising boats may anchor in good protection just slightly to the west of the docks. Small boats can explore farther up past the two bridges crossing the river. Owners of trailerable boats will find a boat ramp on the southwest side of the HWY 303 bridge. On the way to Hillary Slough you will pass Ratcliff Creek and sand bars which at low tide turn into beaches. North of that area watch the banks of Hillary Slough at low tide for numerous stumps and roots of big trees which once grew on the solid parcels of the local lowlands. Later Hillary Slough narrows and the shores become wide mud flats at low tide—by Glynn Camp the creek almost dries out at low tide. However, if you get stuck there you will be able to watch a flock of wood storks and white ibis which occupy the tall trees of the hammock—here shrimp tend to jump into your boat and large trout swirl through the muddy thick water.

TURTLE RIVER

All the way to the HWY 303 and I 95 bridges Turtle River flows by industrial or ex-industrial areas to the east with the last complex just south of Cowpen Creek. Cowpen Creek, by the way, spreads into a complex maze of marsh islands very attractive to wading birds and water fowl. The next tributary of a considerable size, Buffalo River, on the north shore of Turtle River, passes a nice set of docks which belong to the residential development of Oak Grove Island and then flows through a spectacular area of marshlands till it splits in two narrow streams, both soon barred by very low bridges. Turtle River west of Buffalo River gradually narrows between very attractive shores—mostly marshland islands and lagoons—and then divides into two streams snaking into even more marshland. This far from the sea the marshes are mostly of black needle rush next to the water and mixed forests or pines beyond the marsh on the uplands. Many anglers frequent these waters fishing for sport and hopefully not consuming their catch. The waters and, particularly, bottom sediments have for years been polluted by the surrounding industrial plants and, due to the presence of PCBs and Mercury, people should not eat any shellfish—blue crabs, oysters, clams or mussels, and severely limit consumption of fish—for details consult DNR publications such as the *Georgia 2001-2002 Sport Fishing Regulations* and *Guidelines for Eating Fish from Georgia Waters*. This publication is produced yearly and is widely available in fish camps, marinas and marine stores.

Several wharves on the East River serve a large fleet of shrimp trawlers based in Brunswick.

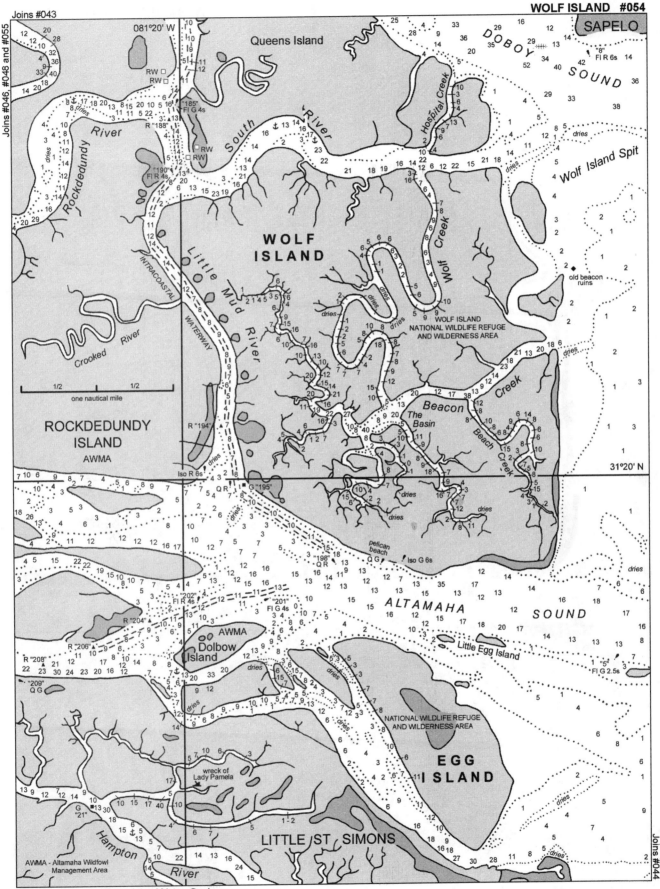

SAPELO

Joins #043

081°20' W

Joins #046, #048 and #055

Queens Island

DOBOY SOUND

Rockdedundy River

South River

Hospital Creek

Wolf Island Spit

WOLF ISLAND

Wolf Creek

old beacon ruins

INTRACOASTAL WATERWAY

Little Mud River

Crooked River

1/2   1/2

one nautical mile

R "194"

WOLF ISLAND NATIONAL WILDLIFE REFUGE AND WILDERNESS AREA

Beacon Creek

Beach Creek

Beacon Basin

The Basin

ROCKDEDUNDY ISLAND

AWMA

Iso R 6s

31°20' N

G "195"

pelican beach

Iso G 6s

"198" Q R

Q G

ALTAMAHA SOUND

Little Egg Island

"5" Fl G 2.5s

"202" Fl R 4s

"201" Fl G 4s

R "204"

AWMA

R "206"

Dolbow Island

R "208"

"209" Q G

NATIONAL WILDLIFE REFUGE AND WILDERNESS AREA

EGG ISLAND

wreck of Lady Pamela

G "21"

Hampton River

LITTLE ST SIMONS

Joins #044

AWMA - Altamaha Wildfowl Management Area

All Soundings In Feet, Low Water Springs

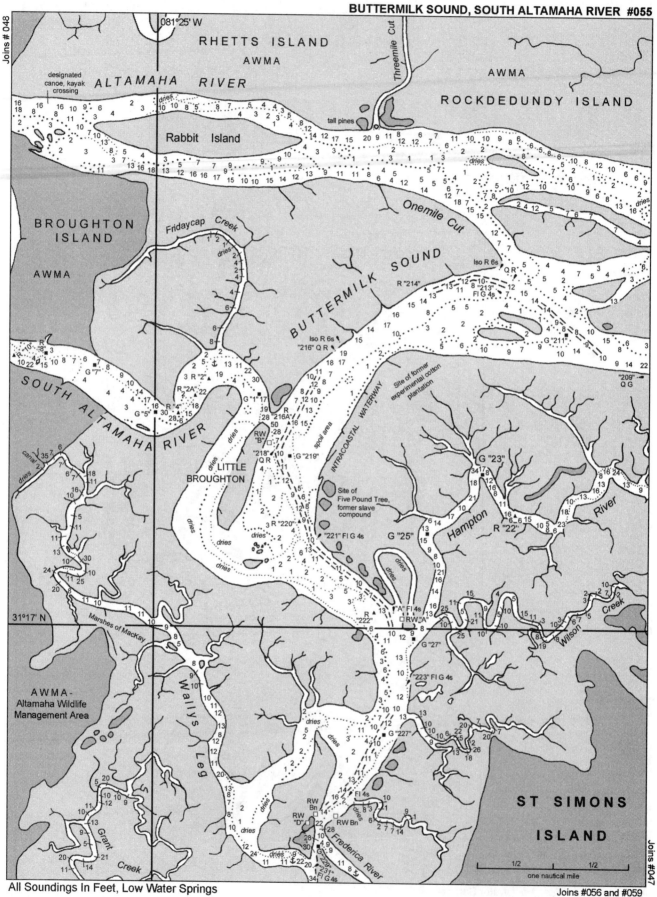

Joins # 048

081°25' W

RHETTS ISLAND

AWMA

Threemile Cut

AWMA

ROCKDEDUNDY ISLAND

designated
canoe, kayak
crossing

ALTAMAHA   RIVER

dries

tall pines

Rabbit   Island

Onemile Cut

BROUGHTON
ISLAND

AWMA

Fridaycap   Creek

dries

BUTTERMILK   SOUND

Iso R 6s
Q R

R "214"

Iso R 6s
"216" Q R

"213"
Fl 4s

G "211"

R
"8"

G "7"

R "2"

R "2A"

G "1"

R
"216A"

RW
"B"

"218"
Q R

G "219"

Site of former
experimental cotton
plantation

"209"
Q G

SOUTH   ALTAMAHA   RIVER

R "4"

G "5"

dries

LITTLE
BROUGHTON

spoil area

INTRACOASTAL   WATERWAY

G "23"

canal

dries

Site of
Five Pound Tree,
former slave
compound

Hampton

R "22"

River

3 R "220"

dries

"221" Fl G 4s

G "25"

31°17' N

Marshes of MacKay

dries

R
"222"

"A" Fl 4s
RW "A"

Wilson   Creek

G "27"

AWMA –
Altamaha Wildlife
Management Area

Wallys   Leg

"223" Fl G 4s

dries

G "227"

ST SIMONS

Fl 4s

RW
Bn

RW
"D"

RW Bn

ISLAND

Grant   Creek

dries

Frederica   River

"231"
Fl G 4s

1/2   1/2

one nautical mile

Joins #047

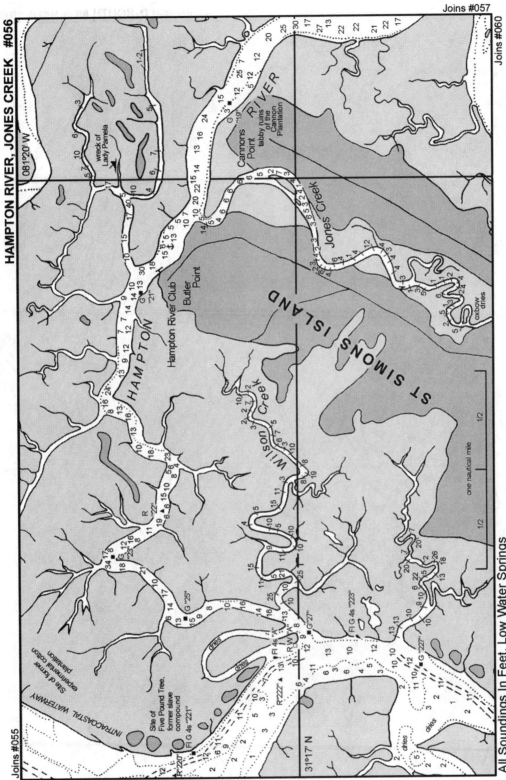

HAMPTON RIVER, JONES CREEK #056

081°20' W

Joins #057

Joins #060

Joins #055

wreck of
Lady Pamela

Cannons
Point

tabby ruins
of the
Cannon
Plantation

HAMPTON

RIVER

Jones Creek

Butler
Point

Hampton River Club

ST SIMONS ISLAND

Wilson Creek

oxbow
dries

Site of former
experimental cotton
plantation

Site of
Five Pound Tree,
former slave
compound

INTRACOASTAL WATERWAY

dries

dries

dries

31°17 N

one nautical mile

1/2

1/2

All Soundings In Feet, Low Water Springs

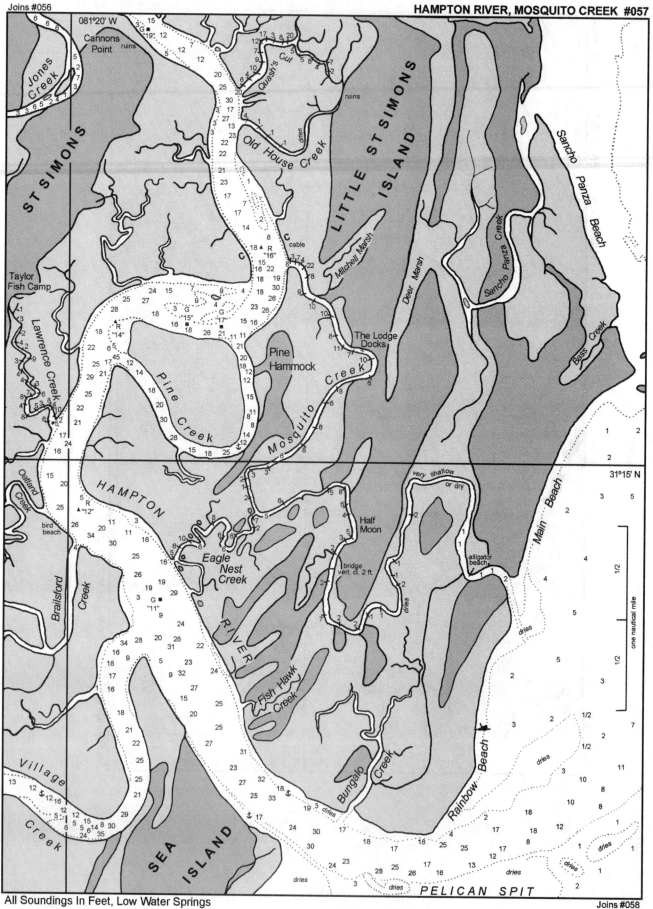

Joins #057

HAMPTON RIVER, VILLAGE CREEK #058

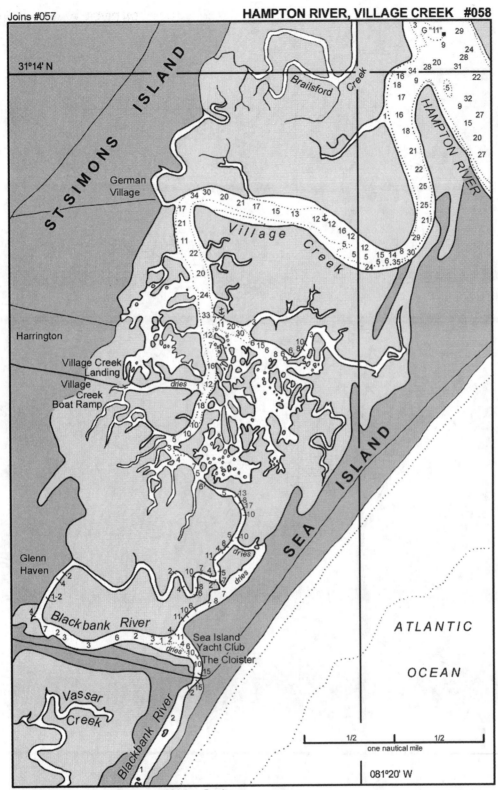

All Soundings In Feet, Low Water Springs

081°20' W

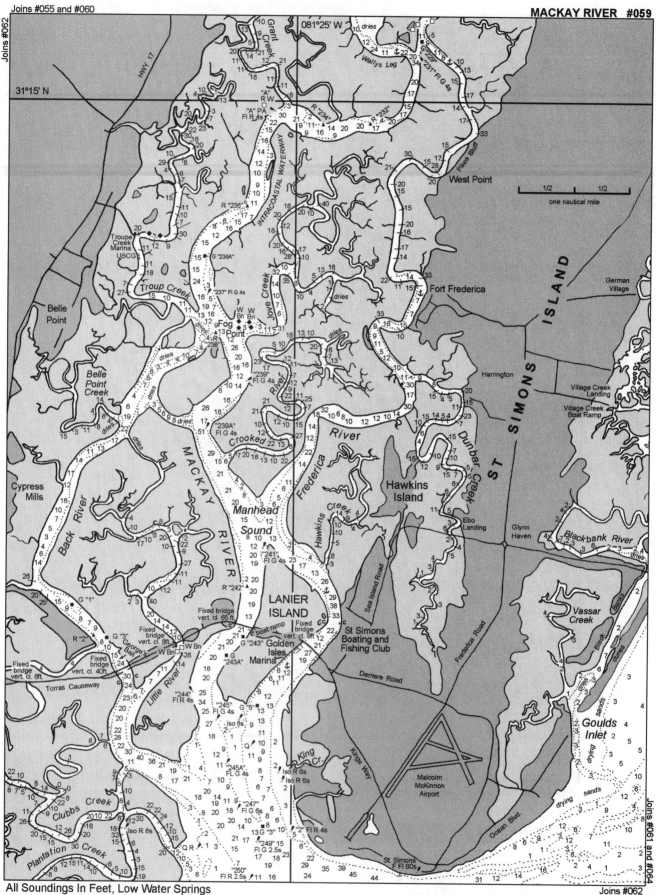

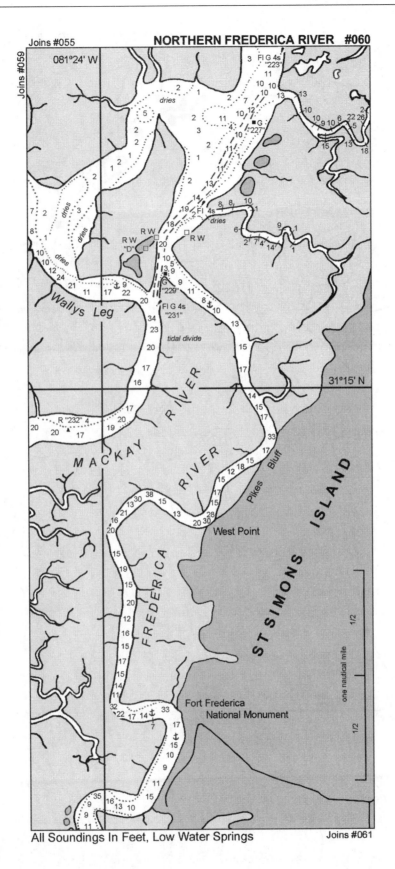

Joins #055

Joins #059

081°24' W

Fl G 4s "223"

G "227"

dries

Fl 4s

dries

R W

R W "D"

R W

G "229"

Fl G 4s "231"

tidal divide

Wallys Leg

MACKAY RIVER

RIVER

R "232"

31°15' N

FREDERICA

Pikes Bluff

West Point

ST SIMONS ISLAND

one nautical mile

1/2

1/2

Fort Frederica
National Monument

All Soundings In Feet, Low Water Springs

Joins #061

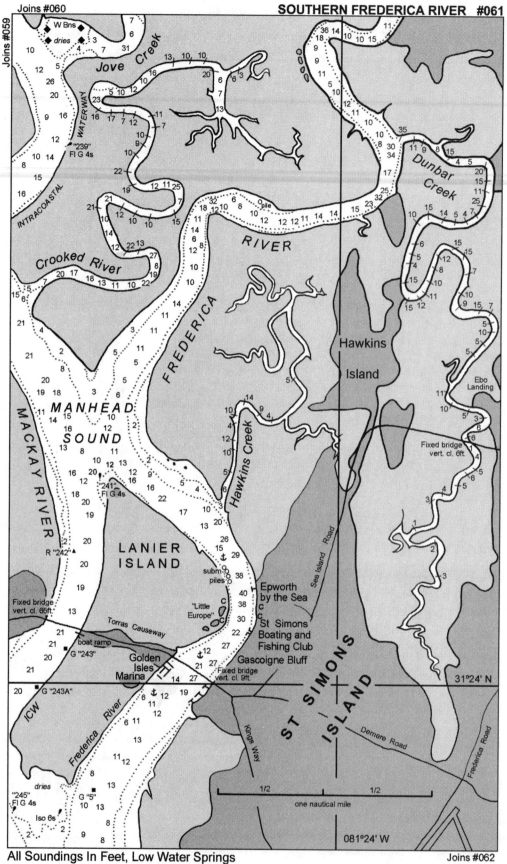

All Soundings In Feet, Low Water Springs

Joins #062

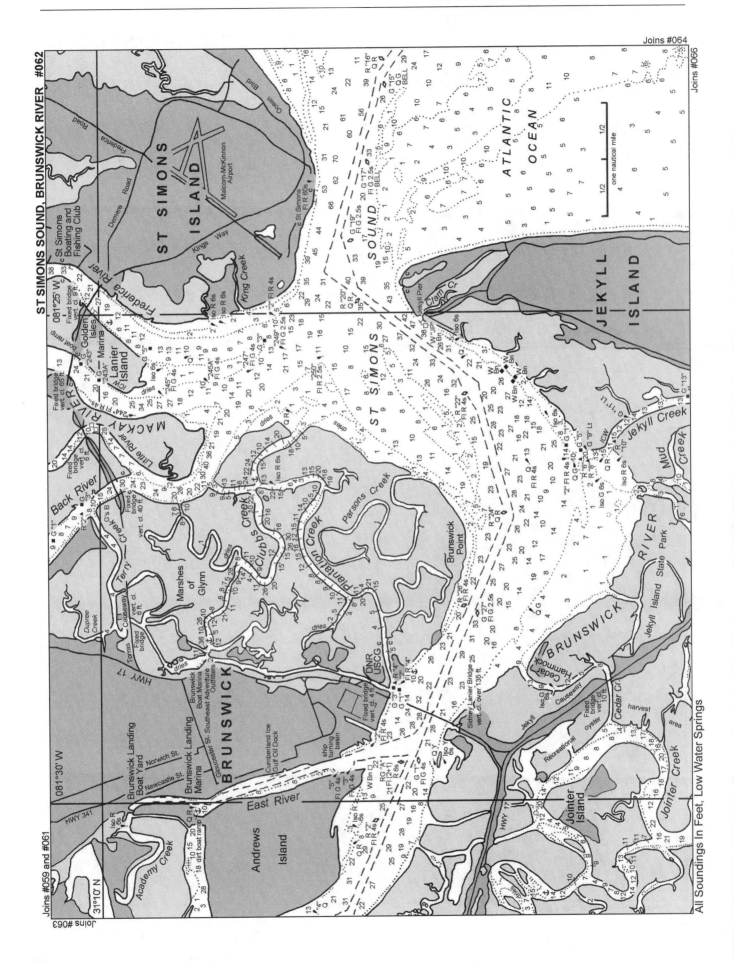

Joins #064

Joins #066

Joins #059 and #061

Joins #063

All Soundings In Feet, Low Water Springs

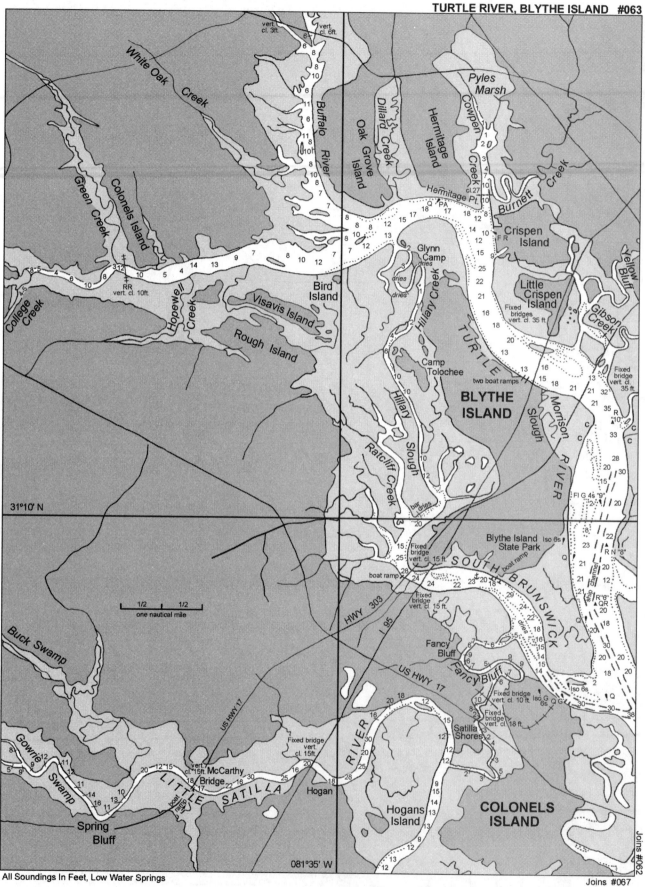

All Soundings In Feet, Low Water Springs

Joins #067

Joins #062

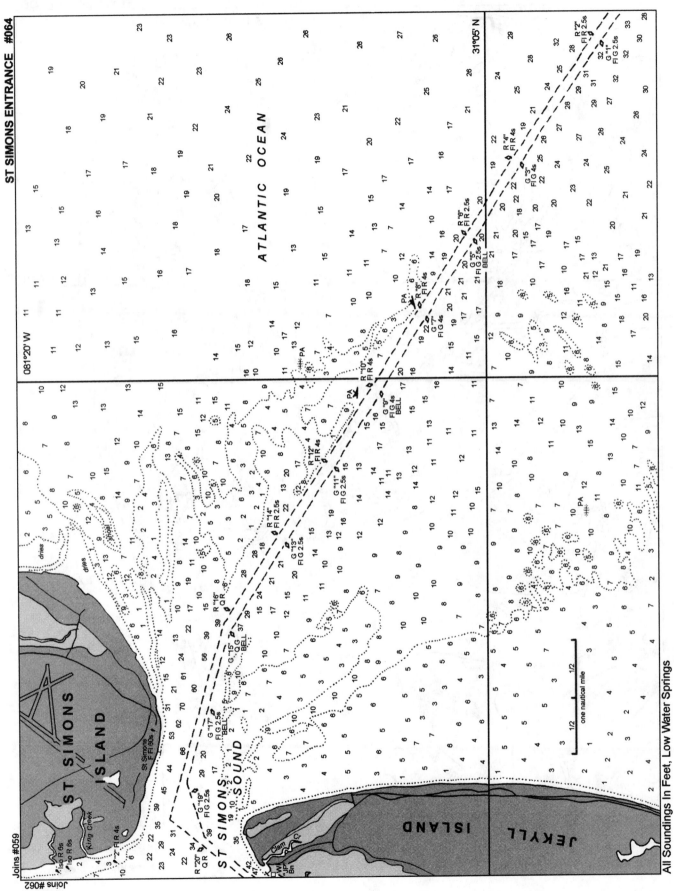

ATLANTIC OCEAN

ST SIMONS ISLAND

ST. SIMONS SOUND

JEKYLL ISLAND

31°05' N

081°20' W

All Soundings In Feet, Low Water Springs

one nautical mile

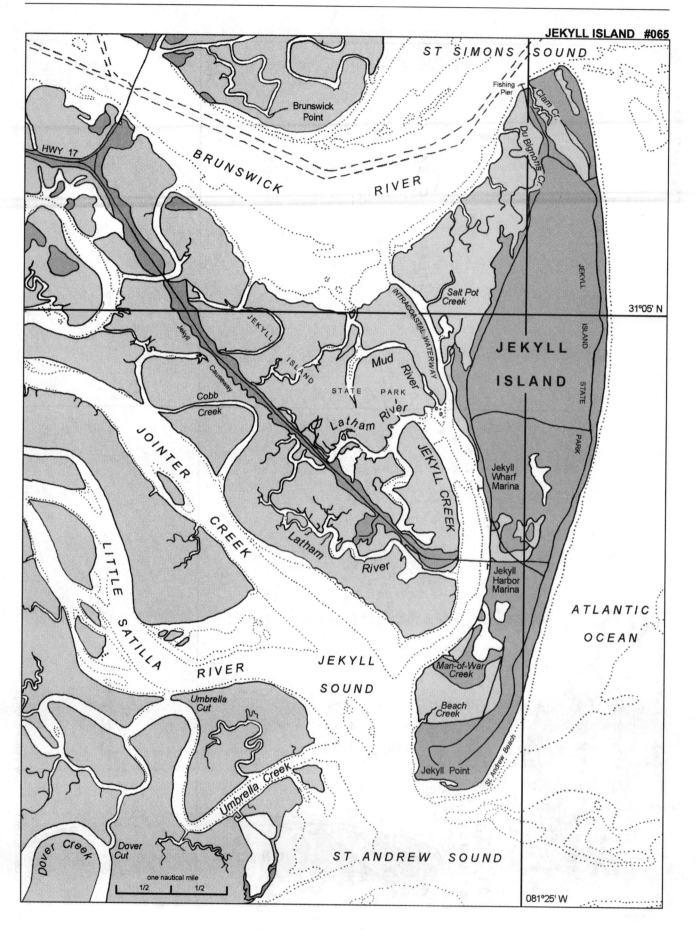

CHAPTER EIGHT

JEKYLL CREEK TO ST. ANDREW SOUND

INCLUDING JEKYLL ISLAND, LITTLE SATILLA RIVER AND SATILLA RIVER
GLYNN COUNTY

JEKYLL CREEK

The 1954 construction of a causeway over the marshes between Jekyll Island and the mainland seriously disturbed the flow of Latham Creek and other marsh streams. Jekyll Creek, never very deep to begin with, now tends to silt in record time requiring annual dredging in order to keep it open for Intracoastal Waterway traffic. The relatively deep trough is rather narrow and after a range astern takes you south by marker "17" you will see at low tide extensive mud flats coming down towards the channel. This is the time to scan these shoals for some uncommon shorebirds. During the time of bird migrations you may see here avocets, easily recognizable by their up-turned bills which they swing sideways through the water when feeding. In April their winter black and white coloring changes to their summer suit of russet neck and head. Scaups, in flocks of over two dozen birds, also feed by the mud flats of Jekyll Creek. Chartlet #066 shows the depths. Again, deeper draft vessels should call one of the marinas operating in Jekyll Creek for the latest information on depths. Two facilities serve yachts here. Jekyll Wharf Marina is first from the north and offers a row of floating docks attached to the 1886 Jekyll Island Club wharf which used to serve tenders from massive yachts, too deep to enter the Creek even when the waterway was naturally deeper. They sell dockage, fuels, ice, cold drinks, snacks and gifts. You can also rent bicycles from them to tour the islands best sites, both historic and natural. Jekyll Wharf Marina lies right in the middle of the historic district of old mansions and shares the dock with Latitude 31 Restaurant. The marina monitors VHF 16, tel. 912-635-3152. While Latitude 31 opens in the afternoons, you can get all meals including breakfast in the Jekyll Island Club Hotel across the road from the marina. Plantation Oak, the oldest and largest live oak on the island grows a little north of the Hotel. Despite some skeptics the tree looks like it has been around for 350 years as claimed by the local Chamber of Commerce historians. See the Services Section for more details about the marina.

Jekyll Island Club Hotel, a short walk from Jekyll Wharf Marina, houses a formal dining restaurant as well as casual lunch and breakfast establishments.

Jekyll Harbor Marina, a larger facility, lies south of the fixed bridge rising 65 feet over the Intracoastal Waterway. Here transient yachts can tie up at a floating dock adjacent to Sea Jay's Waterfront Café and Pub. The marina sells all fuels, ice, bait and also has a hoist/launch service for sport fishing boats up to 30 feet. A small store carries refreshments and local charts. They monitor VHF 16, tel. 912-635-2633. See the Services Section.

Down river from Jekyll Harbor Marina the river flows past a public ramp and picnic area and after that spills into the wide waters of Jekyll Sound, the meeting place for Jointer Creek and Little Satilla River, two large tidal rivers.

JEKYLL ISLAND

About 7 miles long and only 2.3 miles wide Jekyll is one of the smaller Georgia barrier islands formed around a Pleistocene upland core. Undoubtedly, for a few thousand years indigenous Americans visited or even lived on the island but today no real traces of their activities remain. We know for sure that in 1736 Gen. Oglethorpe sent Major William Horton to command the troops in a little fortification on the north tip of the island. Oglethorpe named the island for Sir Joseph Jekyll, an investor in the Georgia colony. Major Horton promptly applied himself to growing hops and brewing beer, a liquid as important for the 18th century English soldiers as it is for modern Americans. The Spanish retreating from the defeat at Bloody Marsh burnt Horton's house and brewery but the old brave soldier rebuilt them *pronto*. Sea Island cotton planting arrived on Jekyll in 1784 with a new owner, Richard Leake. Ten years later Poulain duBignon, a ship captain and merchant from Brittany, France, escaping the French Revolution, bought the island and his family stayed for nearly a century. You can see the tabby ruins of Major Horton's and later duBignons' house as well as the duBignons' family cemetery on the north part of the island. The family heirs sold the island to a group of northerners whose names, Morgan, Vanderbilt, Astor, Rockefeller, Macy, Pulitzer, Goodyear to mention just a few, ring a loud bell even in these days of software and dot com billionaires. From 1886, the first year of the Jekyll Island Club, the island served mainly as a winter retreat and a hunting preserve for this group of very privileged Americans who built cottages along the west shore overlooking the marshes. The size of these cottages, mansions really, matched their yachts, Astor's 263-foot *Nourmahal*, Pulitzer's 250-foot *Liberty*, or several *Corsairs* owned by J. P. Morgan from 181 feet to 304 feet. They were beautiful vessels. Although totally dependent on engines for high speeds, the hulls had sweeping clipper bows and curved overhanging sterns. Tall raked masts used mostly for decorative flags added to the seaworthy appearance. The aftermath of World War II and the gradual fading away of the founding members forced the Club managers to sell or face condemnation by the state for unpaid taxes. In 1947 the State of Georgia paid about $600,000 for Jekyll Island with plans to turn it into a state park open to the public. A road and a bridge from the mainland followed together with development schemes, some bordering on insane. As a result, shore restoration projects which involved shaping new dunes with bulldozers followed in the 1980s. These conservation efforts worked, especially after exposing the public to some basic ideas of environmental protection. Today the island, a popular summer resort for Georgians, presents the visitor with several options to pursue, all of them accessible to a boat visitor because of the popular bike rentals. Or for a change you can go through some designated nature trails on horse back—call 912-635-9500.

The Historic District is definitely worth a visit for its architectural value and the views of the marshes from under some really old trees. The limbs of the largest live oak, Plantation Oak, sweep down touching the earth in a circle 128 feet in diameter. Up at the north end of the island you can walk along a typical tidal marsh creek, through a maritime forest and then onto a beach through a boneyard of trees. The tree skeletons have been undercut by eroding sea action much accelerated by the dredging of St. Simons Sound for a shipping channel. The north and south ends of Jekyll Island, plus the Jekyll Causeway are part of the Colonial Coast Birding Trail. We found the south end of the island particularly exciting at low tide in the early mornings. Once several wood storks and herons stalked the southwest beach facing Jekyll Sound. They were feeding on small fish, baby flounders and incapacitated blue crabs, unwanted by-catch washed from the decks of the shrimp boats which had anchored in Jekyll Sound after scraping the offshore sea bottom all day in search of shrimp. On the south tip of that same beach over a hundred black skimmers were taking a rest after nocturnal feeding. On one spring morning several royal terns mixed among them performing their mating strut. In a pool of seawater left after the ocean retreated with the ebb we observed three red knot couples, three black bellied plovers, willets and dunlins in their distinct summer coloring. This south end of Jekyll Island is growing fast—the sands now swallowing a fishing boat wreck which a few years ago was lying offshore.

WATERS WEST OF THE INTRACOASTAL WATERWAY

The Satilla, a major Georgia river, flows to the Atlantic through the area covered in this section. The Satilla's shores have little population with only one small town, Woodbine, on its south shore. Little Satilla River has some residential development on its higher bluffs, otherwise it travels through wild marshes. Unknown to many boat owners outside of Georgia, the Alternate Waterway begins its marked and maintained run southward on Umbrella Creek, an arm of Little Satilla.

JOINTER CREEK

Chartlet #066 illustrates the entrance to this tidal river while chartlet #067 shows the whole length of Jointer Creek. Jointer Creek runs northwest inland from Jekyll Sound and flows through totally uninhabited marshes until, at the very end, it reaches Credle's Complete Marine. Marker "A2"—chartlet #067—makes it easy to enter the wide estuary of Jointer Creek. Chartlet #067 shows the route to take and also illustrates the advantage, for deeper draft boats, of going by the west side of Jointer Island—this twisting creek has deeper water than the route around the north tip of the island.

Uninhabited Jointer Island is great fun to explore, although vegetation has taken over all trails and the remains of cabins. Cruising boats can anchor in several places as marked. If you plan to go to Credle's in a deeper draft boat you may have to anchor a little further east as marked in order to wait for the rising tide to get you over the shallows ahead. Captain Credle operates a traveling lift of his own design capable of lifting boats, including sailboats, up to 40 feet LOA. He has a long term storage area and a work area for do-it-yourself boat owners, but the yard is not set up for living aboard out of the water. Although you have to approach the area at rising tide, the docks at the yard have 6 feet of water. The yard monitors VHF 16, phone 912-261-1935. See the Services Section.

LITTLE SATILLA RIVER

You will find entering Little Satilla River very easy by following the beacons marking the route into the Alternate Waterway via Umbrella Cut. Refer to chartlet #067 to see the soundings after you have passed south of marker "A4". For several miles the river runs through a seemingly totally uninhabited country of marshlands and distant forests. The first signs of civilization, homes on the northeast tip of Hazzards Neck, come in view when you head west from the river curve at the south tip of Colonels Island. This part of Colonels Islands invites anchoring nearby because you can land on the forested shore right at the beginning of a wide dirt road. The lack of any "no trespassing" signs encourages walks on the trails in this forested land. South of this wilderness, private homes and the large Georgia (Baptist) Conference Center hide up Honey Creek. Maiden Creek meets Little Satilla River almost at the same place as Honey Creek. Maiden Creek flows through pristine marshes which gave me an opportunity to learn what wetland mammals do when their territories flood up to the very tips of marsh grasses at extremely high tides. Powering up Maiden Creek in our dinghy I passed an almost red-colored mink curled up and napping on one of the rafts of dead marsh stalks

which drift around for months after the *spartina* die-out during the winter. Almost at the end of Maiden Creek you will come across the docks of Ocean Breeze Marina which can launch boats up to 23 feet, sells bait, ice, basic tackle items, snacks and cold drinks, tel. 912-262-0058. See the Services Section.

Above the anchorage off Colonels Island and Sams Creek, which offers great exploring in a small boat, the river flows past Hickory Bluff Marina with floating docks for transients, gasoline, ice, bait and tackle sales and an 8,000 pound electric hoist for trailerable sport fishing boats. They monitor VHF 16, tel. 912-262-0453. See the Services Section for additional information. A residential area has spread among the trees on the bluff shores near the marina but soon afterwards the river again flows through undeveloped marshes. Chartlet #063 shows how Little Satilla River next swings by high bluff shores and a residential area with docks down to the water. Just before this area, called Satilla Shores, you will see a creek disappearing into the marsh on the east shore—it runs all the way past the Fancy Bluff residential shores to South Brunswick River. Farther west, after running under two bridges and passing by Spring Bluff the river enters a very beautiful marshy landscape, with black needle rush on the lowlands and forests of oaks, pines, palmettos and other trees on the background uplands—small cabin cruisers and especially kayakers could explore any of the two final branches of Little Satilla River for many miles. Tidal currents still run here fairly strongly so plan to go in with the flood and out with the ebb.

ALTERNATE INTRACOASTAL WATERWAY

The Alternate Waterway has been maintained to allow less seaworthy vessels to continue on their way when St. Andrew Sound kicks up in anger. Just recently the aids to navigation—prefixed by "A"—in this Alternate route have been updated and the habitually silting Umbrella Cut received a bit of dredge work. Chartlet #068 illustrates the depths and you may expect that as time goes by Umbrella Cut will begin to fill again. While the approaches to Umbrella Cut from Little Satilla River are marked and easy to follow, deeper draft vessels may, in the case of Umbrella Cut silting, enter Umbrella Creek from its east outlet also shown on chartlet #068. Under the heading *Umbrella Creek* below, you will find advice on this entrance based on GPS readings.

The Alternate Waterway enters Dover Creek at marker "A14" and eventually joins the Satilla River, crosses it, and then resumes its run in Floyd Cut. You will find the complete description of the Alternate Waterway in Chapter II, *Intracoastal Waterway* and the description of Floyd Creek (chartlet #080) in Chapter IX, *St. Andrew Sound to St. Marys River*. Before entering the Alternate Waterway you should realize that several stretches of it are quite narrow and, while it is presumptuous to make such suggestions, 45-foot long vessels, 20 feet wide and drawing about 5 feet may be the maximum size for this passage at low tide.

UMBRELLA CREEK

The entrance to Umbrella Creek lies west from Jekyll Point on Jekyll Island. Before entering from the east you have to clear the shoal building southward from marker "26". By steering west along latitude 31°01'00"N you will clear that shallow area. Maintain this latitude until the depth diminishes from around 20 feet to 15 feet when you should change course to starboard until you reach 31°01'08"N. At this point head for the entrance which you should enter at 31°01'10"N. This approach should take you through a minimum of 8 feet at low tide, but make sure to allow for strong currents, ebbing or flooding across your course. On our last visit there, we were about to drop anchor when three roseate spoonbills swung across the sky flashing their intensely pink colors and landed on the mud flats along the south shore of the creek. We let the anchor down quietly and they kept swinging their wide bills at the edge of the water. Soon after a mink swam across, climbed over the bank near the spoonbills and slinked into the marsh. The tide was still falling uncovering more of the bank with all its edible creatures when a clapper rail—a marsh hen—emerged from the dense forest of *spartina* marsh to probe and pick up creatures too small for us to identify even through binoculars. Then, wonderfully, two black skimmers cruised by with their long lower bills skimming the water next to the spoonbills.

On Raccoon Key along the south side of the anchorage stands the building of the Marine and Experimental Farm—apparently an abandoned project. A large man-made pond in the marsh along the south side of this anchorage attracts wading birds which roost on the neighboring trees. Woodstorks are common. In the mornings and evenings you will witness flocks of commuting birds. During the winter hundreds of ducks like hooded mergansers and buffleheads feed in here as well as in Jointer and the Little Satilla Rivers. At the height of summer bottlenosed dolphins run themselves onto the mud banks here chasing some prey we never identified. Shrimp boats often come in to anchor in this part of Umbrella Creek—show a good anchor light at night.

Umbrella Creek runs southwest past a private landing and dock, makes a long S-turn past Umbrella Cut and then winds on towards Dover Bluff-chartlet #068. Consult chartlet #069 to see how, after paralleling the residential shores of Dover Bluff, the creek flows through marshes, sends side branches towards the forested upland on Hazzards Neck and joins Dover Creek and Noyes Cut. All together these western reaches of Umbrella Creek are a delight for anglers and bird watchers. A good anchorage for cruising boats lies between two abandoned docks on the north-south stretch of the creek, east of Dover Bluff. The land around here belongs to the Dover Bluff Club. Tabby ruins of two old buildings, a short walk from the river, used to house a Spanish mission, or so maintain reliable local sources. As historians have established lately the early Spanish missionaries built their houses with wattle and daub—walls of woven canes were filled with a mixture of sand and mud with some vegetable matter. Many tabby ruins in Georgia described as Spanish missions turned out to be sugar cane mills producing rum and molasses. And surely the inhabitants of Lampadosia, a settlement of loggers and turpentine makers which still stood here at the turn of century, would find use for these commodities.

SATILLA RIVER

For the practical purposes of this guide Satilla River *begins* in St. Andrew Sound, a somewhat absurd approach since the sound is really the *exit* for a volume of water so tremendous that it has scoured the deepest natural channel on the Georgia coast. The recently refurbished system of markers into the river begins with beacon "2" off Raccoon Key Spit half a mile south of Jekyll Island. Chartlet #068 illustrates this deep, and now easy, approach past the entrance to Floyd Creek (which continues the Alternate Waterway on the way south) and then goes northwest-

The anchorage off Long Bluff on Satilla River provides perfect shelter from winter storms.

ward past the exit of Dover Creek, also part of the Alternate Waterway. The Satilla River continues its deep run to Bailey's Cut. This narrow channel was once part of the inner waterway from Satilla River to Dover Creek via Noyes Cut, which is now slowly silting from the sides leaving only a narrow deep trench winding through. Chartlet #069 and #070 shows the continuing river run to Crow Harbor hammock, a good anchorage should a strong norther come through in winter.

WHITE OAK CREEK

Right after Crow Harbor hammock you will see the entrance to White Oak Creek. Similarly to Satilla River, this sizable creek runs through undeveloped marshes except for I 95 bridges popping into view now and then. About a mile and a half from the entrance to White Oak Creek a man-made canal cuts into the marsh on the west shore and leads to a basin with a hammock which has enough hard ground to camp on. Marsh has taken over all this area and, but for the noise of traffic on I 95 you could imagine yourself in total wilderness. Traveling on White Oak Creek you may miss the narrow creek into Horseshoe Harbor, a man-made area with a residential development overlooking marshes. The dredged basin inside is beginning to silt up badly. Chartlet #071 illustrates this part of White Oak Creek which flows west past Goat Island. This wild hammock, easy to land on and camp or just explore, has a thick cover of saw palmettos under tall oaks, magnolias and bay laurels. Going through marshes of *spartina* and black needle rushes

with sea myrtles and marsh elders on the drier ground, the creek continues to the east side of US HWY 17 bridge where you will find a boat ramp with a floating dock. The creek continues as a stream branching out into White Oak Swamp. Another arm of White Oak—Waverly Creek—branches to the northwest at Red Bluff. Once the site of a plantation and settlement, Red Bluff has changed into a residential area with docks. One of the docks supports Dick's Bait, live and dead, a help-yourself operation based on the honor system. West of Red Bluff, Waverly Creek again flows through pristine marshes with forests coming close.

BACK ON SATILLA RIVER

After White Oak Creek the Satilla cuts by a high bluff at Ceylon (chartlet #070), forested by mixed growth on the edges with planted pines behind. You will find an attractive anchorage under the high shore. Marshes mixed with shore trees make for an interesting dinghy trip in Lang Creek. The I 95 bridge has 44 feet of vertical clearance which allowed our sailboat to go through at low tide. Woodbine, the only town on the lower Satilla, lies a bit inland on the south shore at the US HWY 17 bridge. A boat ramp and a park equipped with a deep water floating dock welcomes transient boats. Again, at low tide we made a safe passage under this 43-foot bridge and through the decommissioned railroad bridge. We found a good anchorage just south of Hopewell where the pilings remaining from old wharves sprout exotic combinations of flowering plants and epiphytes; a few

Peaceful morning off Ceylon on Satilla River.

homes take up the higher ground on the north shore. See Chartlet #072. The lower Satilla used to support several large rice plantations here—hence the remains of the loading wharves along the banks. The old irrigation ditches still run between abandoned rice fields taken over by native marsh plants. The water runs fresh from now on—bald cypress trees grow along the densely forested shores. Up around Long Bluff you will see that the water has turned tea color—the reason for the Satilla to be classed as a blackwater river. The river begins to run over a sandy bottom and without muddy sediments the water remains relatively clear—it would be translucent but for the tannic acid content produced by decaying vegetation. The tides, much diminished and delayed, still affect the level of the river up to Magnolia Bluff and perhaps beyond but the currents are less swift. Several places can serve as excellent anchorages (marked on chartlet #073) and we found the anchorage on the curve of the river between Long Bluff and Riley Creek particularly attractive and superbly protected by river trees from strong winter winds. Wild azaleas bloom along the shores forested with trees typical for freshwater tidal rivers like red maples and hollies. An owl hooted every night and occasionally the resident bald eagle swooped over the water. The wild edges of the river support rich animal life—one day we met a biologist tracking a panther collared with a tiny transmitter. Behind this buffer zone of wilderness you will find many pine farms taking over the old plantation grounds. Nothing remains of the 1793 Burnt Fort which once housed soldiers fighting the Indians. Magnolia Bluff, a mile farther up river has very old magnolia trees growing close to cypresses and tupelos—reportedly a virgin forest.

The names of places on the Satilla go back to the days of rice plantations and especially logging. Bullhead was first a plantation which later changed to a lumber mill. In the 1890s the Suwanee Canal Co. built a railway on the edge of Okefenokee Swamp and delivered the logs to Bullhead Bluff where thousands of railway cross ties were loaded on ships coming up river from the ocean. Owens Ferry was also a busy mill owned by The Woodbine Timber Co. Long trains of rafts of trees also came to Baileys Mills. Many cypress logs rolled into the river and sank creating a side line business for "sunk log lighters" whose crews specialized in their recovery. Kids visiting the fishing cabins along the banks in the summer search for old ballast stones from the vessels that came up river to load timber.

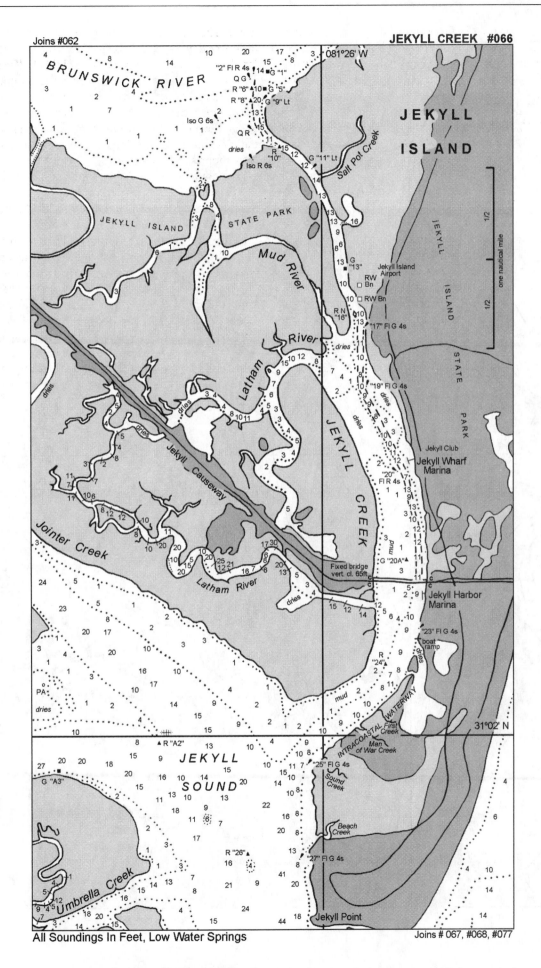

BRUNSWICK RIVER

JEKYLL CREEK #066

081°26' W

"2" Fl R 4s 14 ■ G "1"
Q G
R "6" ■ 10 ■ G "5"
R "8" ▲ 20 ▲ G "9" Lt

**JEKYLL
ISLAND**

Iso G 6s

Q R

R
"10"
Iso R 6s

G "11" Lt

Salt Pot Creek

dries

JEKYLL ISLAND   STATE PARK

Mud River

13 16

G
"13"
Jekyll Island
Airport
RW
Bn
RW Bn

one nautical mile

1/2

1/2

1/2

JEKYLL ISLAND STATE PARK

Latham   River

R N
"16"

"17" Fl G 4s

dries

"19" Fl G 4s

dries

Jekyll Club

Jekyll Wharf
Marina

Jekyll Causeway

JEKYLL CREEK

"20"
Fl R 4s

G "20A" ▲

mud

Fixed bridge
vert. cl. 65ft

Jekyll Harbor
Marina

Jointer Creek

Latham River

"23" Fl G 4s
boat
ramp

R
"24"

dries

mud

INTRACOASTAL   WATERWAY

First
Creek

31°02' N

PA
dries

R "A2"

JEKYLL

Man
of War Creek

"25" Fl G 4s

G "A3"

SOUND

Sound
Creek

Beach
Creek

R "26"

"27" Fl G 4s

Umbrella Creek

Jekyll Point

All Soundings In Feet, Low Water Springs

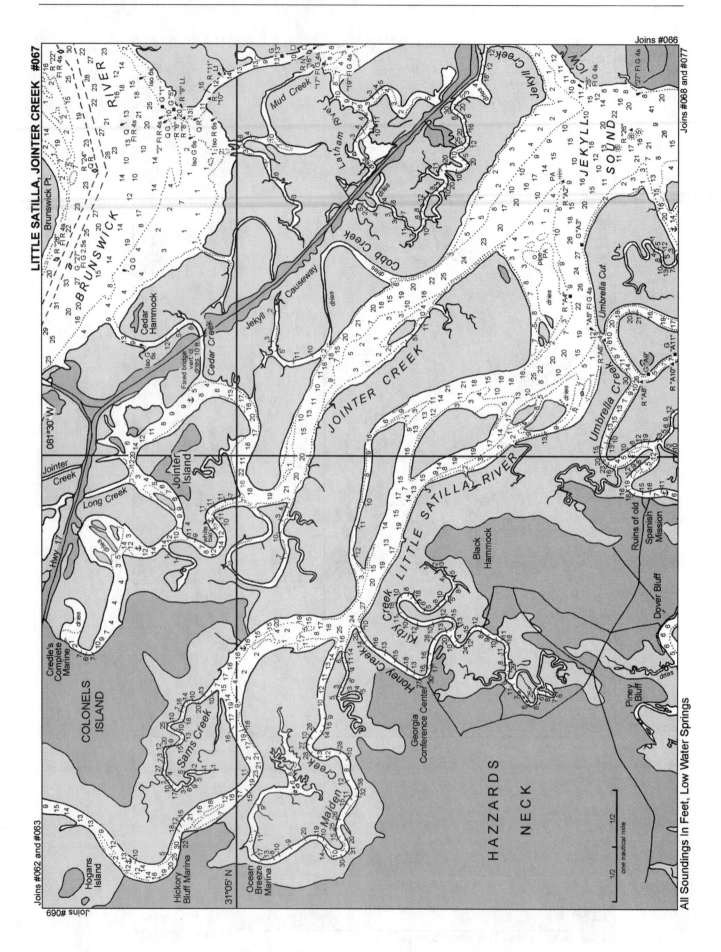

All Soundings In Feet, Low Water Springs

one nautical mile

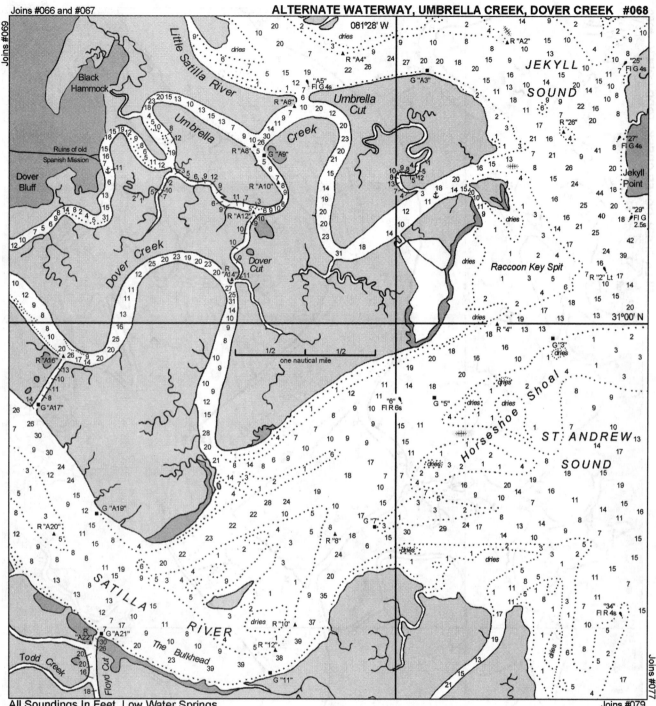

All Soundings In Feet, Low Water Springs

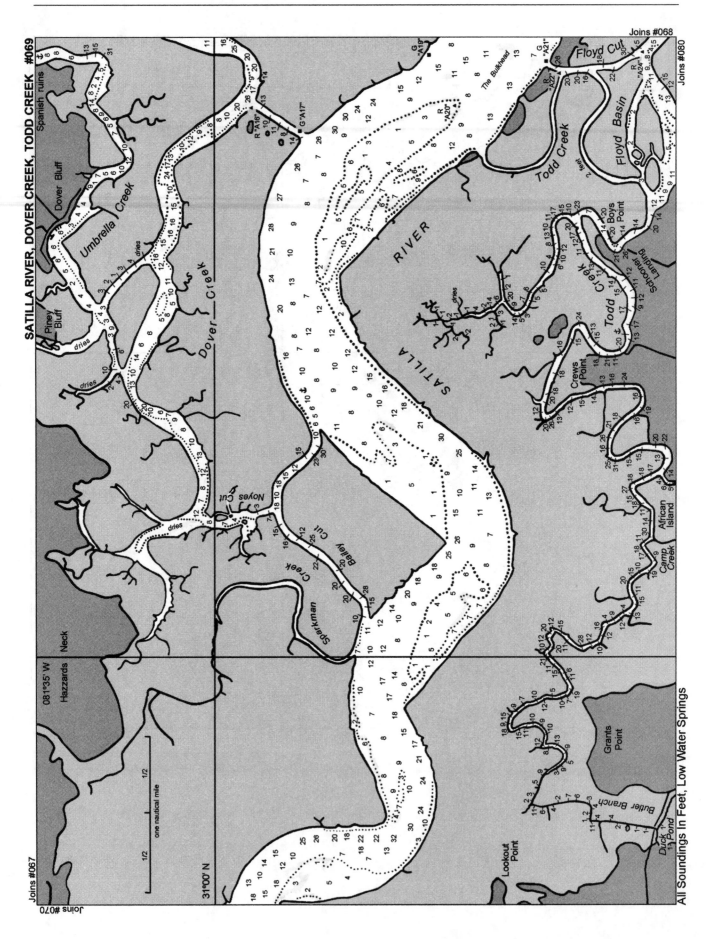

SATILLA RIVER, DOVER CREEK, TODD CREEK #069

All Soundings In Feet, Low Water Springs

Shore Descriptions for Chart #070
SATILLA RIVER, CROW HARBOR REACH TO WOODBINE

1 .... Marsh
2 .... Low muddy bank, pine forest
3 .... Low bluff, mud at low water, forest with thick understory
4 .... Marsh, muddy shore
5 ... Marsh, needle rush, muddy shore
6 .... Marsh, muddy shore
7 .... One dock, forested shore, high bluff
8 .... Muddy shore, pine farm
9 .... Marsh, mud, mixed forest behind
10 .... High bluff, muddy shore, mixed forest
11 .... Marsh and sea myrtle (groundsel)
12 .... Marsh mixed wtih sea myrtle and marsh elder
13 .... Forest with pines and cedars, landing possible at high water
14 .... Landing possible on small island, mostly pine forest, creek goes under I 95

Shore Descriptions for Chart #072
SATILLA RIVER, WOODBINE TO OWENS FERRY

1 .... Docks
2 ..... Thin strip of trees, marsh behind
3 .... Low bank, thick forest
4 ... Marsh, sign for Ivanhoe Plantation
5 .... Forested point
6 .... Historic crossing, see text
7 .... Many pilings
8 .... Low, new growth
9 .... Thin edge of trees, marsh behind
10 .... Crumbled pilings
11 .... Mobile homes
12 .... Low shore, swampy
13 .... Cattle farm, boat ramp
14 .... Marsh, little access to land
15 .... Cypress trees, low land
16 .... Scattered clumps of trees in the grasses
17 .... Marsh along shore, thin trunk forest behind
18 .... Marsh, old rice canals
19 .... Scattered trees along shore, marshy land
20 .... Beautiful point, moss draped trees, muddy bank
21 .... Many pilings
22 .... Homes with docks
23 .... Very muddy banks, marsh with scatterd trees
24 .... Marsh
25 .... Marsh
26 .... Residential area
27 .... Marsh

Shore Descriptions for Chart #073
SATILLA RIVER, CLARKS BLUFF TO BURNT FORT

1 .... Forest
2 .... Forested along the river, pine farm inland
3 .... 5 foot bluff, forest along the river, cleared inland
4 .... White sandy spit with grasses at either end, low mainland, easy access forest
5 .... Firm, low water beach
6 .... Beautiful grasses leading into creek, the creek is an old oxbow curve
7 .... Low, swampy
8 .... Low bank
9 .... Short sandy beach
10 .... Thick forest with thin trunk trees
11 .... 3 to 4 foot low bank
12 .... Low bank
13 .... About an 8 foot bluff, trees along the river, cleared behind
14 .... Low shore
15 .... 4 to 5 foot bluff, forested
16 .... 10 foot bluff, Mays Bluff
17 .... Low wetland thick with trees
18 ...... Low bank, marsh on the point
19 .... 3 to 4 foot low bank
20 .... 3 to 4 foot low bank
21 .... 4 foot low bank
22 .... 5 foot bluff
23 .... Marsh, thick forest with thin trunk trees
24 .... Sandy bluff with saw palmettos
25 .... Thick forest
26 .... Low thick forest
27 .... Channel close to northern shore, anchorage has good sandy mud
28 .... Heavily wooded point
29 .... 3 foot bank, forested
30 .... Ramp, dock (private)
31 .... Forested
32 .... Forested
33 .... 3 foot bank, marsh on point, thick forest
34 .... Residential area on south shore, forested to the north with marsh along the river

35 .... Thick thin trunk forest with grasses along the bank
36 .... 3 foot bank, thick forest comes to the shore
37 .... Good anchorage
38 .... 3 foot bank, thick forest on both shores
39 .... Marsh along the river, forest behind
40 .... 3 foot bank with thick undergrowth, cypress trees
41 .... Dead heads sticking out from both shores
42 .... Marsh along the river, forest behind
43 .... Forest, easy undergrowth
44 .... Old rice canal
45 .... Beautiful, mixed forest point
46 .... Thick forest, muddy shore at low water
47 .... Keep to north shore, forested point
48 .... Dock and ramp
49 .... Muddy shore, thin forest, mostly underbrush
50 .... 3 foot bank, mixed forest
51 .... 3 foot bank, good forest
52 .... Cabins
53 .... Thin trunk forest, low bank, ballast stone pile
54 .... Grasses
55 .... Excellent creek
56 .... Particularly beautiful stretch of the river
57 .... Thickly wooded
58 ...... Cabins, dock, light on at night
59 .... Forest
60 .... Marsh with forest behind
61 .... Forest along creek
62 .... Marsh
63 .... Thin strip of trees, marsh behind
64 .... Marsh edge, forest behind
65 .... Low bank, thick forest
66 .... Docks

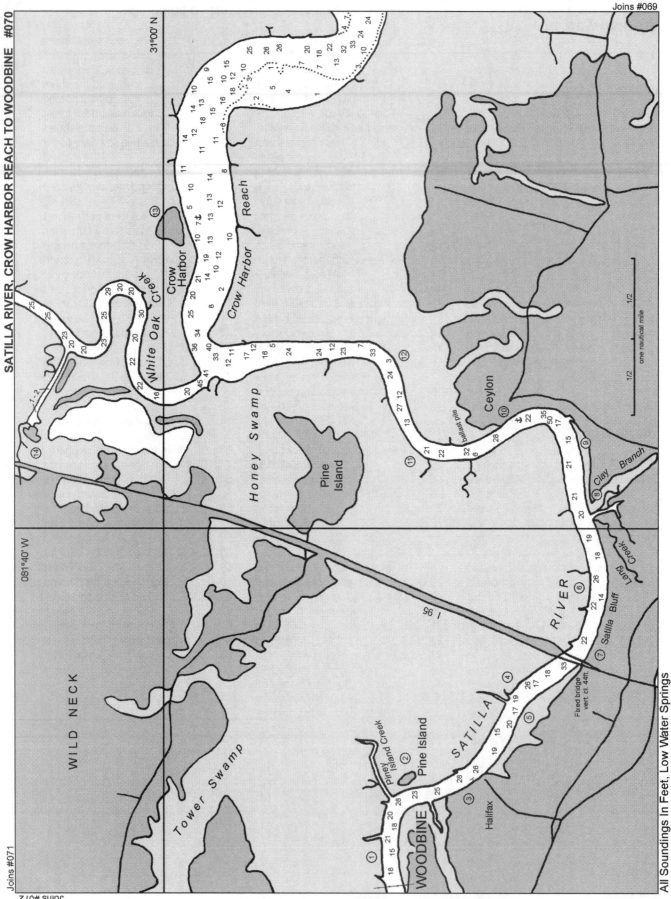

SATILLA RIVER, CROW HARBOR REACH TO WOODBINE #070

Joins #069

Joins #070

31°00' N

081°40' W

Joins #071

Joins #072

WILD NECK

White Oak Creek

Crow Harbor

Crow Harbor Reach

Honey Swamp

Pine Island

Ceylon

Tower Swamp

Pine Island

Piney Island Creek

SATILLA

RIVER

Satilla Bluff

Clay Branch

Lewis Creek

Fixed bridge
vert. cl. 44ft.

I 95

WOODBINE

Halifax

ballast pile

one nautical mile
1/2   1/2

All Soundings In Feet, Low Water Springs

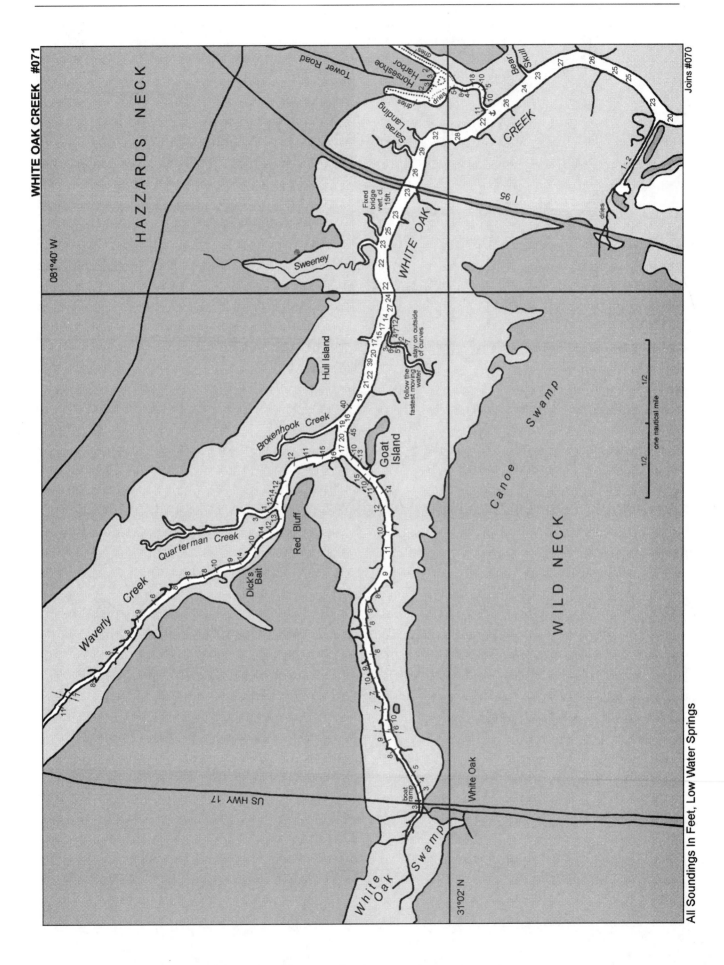

WHITE OAK CREEK #071

HAZZARDS NECK

081°40'W

Tower Road

Horseshoe Harbor

dries

Saras Landing

dries

Bear

Skull

CREEK

Joins #070

27

26

25

25

23

23

24

20

1-2

dries

I 95

Fixed bridge vert. cl. 15ft.

WHITE OAK

Sweeney

follow the fastest moving water stay on outside of curves

Hull Island

Brokenhook Creek

Goat Island

Canoe Swamp

WILD NECK

1/2   1/2
one nautical mile

Quarterman Creek

Dick's Bait

Red Bluff

Waverly Creek

boat ramp

White Oak

US HWY 17

31°02'N

White Oak Swamp

All Soundings In Feet, Low Water Springs

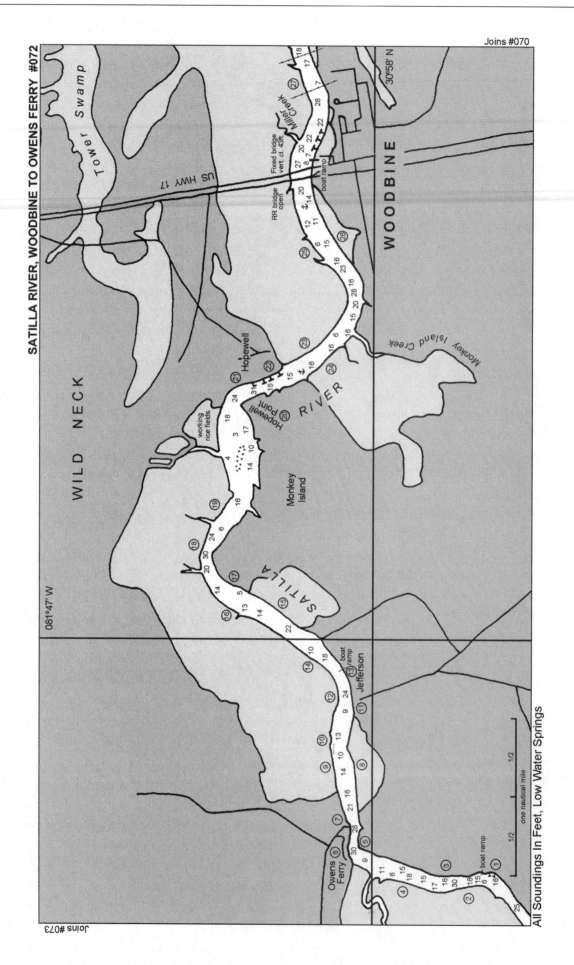

SATILLA RIVER, WOODBINE TO OWENS FERRY #072

Joins #070

WOODBINE

30°58' N

Tower Swamp

WILD NECK

081°47' W

Hopewell

Hopewell Point

working rice fields

Monkey Island

Miller Creek

Monkey Island Creek

RIVER

SATILLA

Jefferson

Owens Ferry

US Hwy 17

Fixed bridge vert. cl. 43ft

RR bridge open

boat ramp

boat ramp

boat ramp

All Soundings In Feet, Low Water Springs

one nautical mile

Joins #073

Joins #072

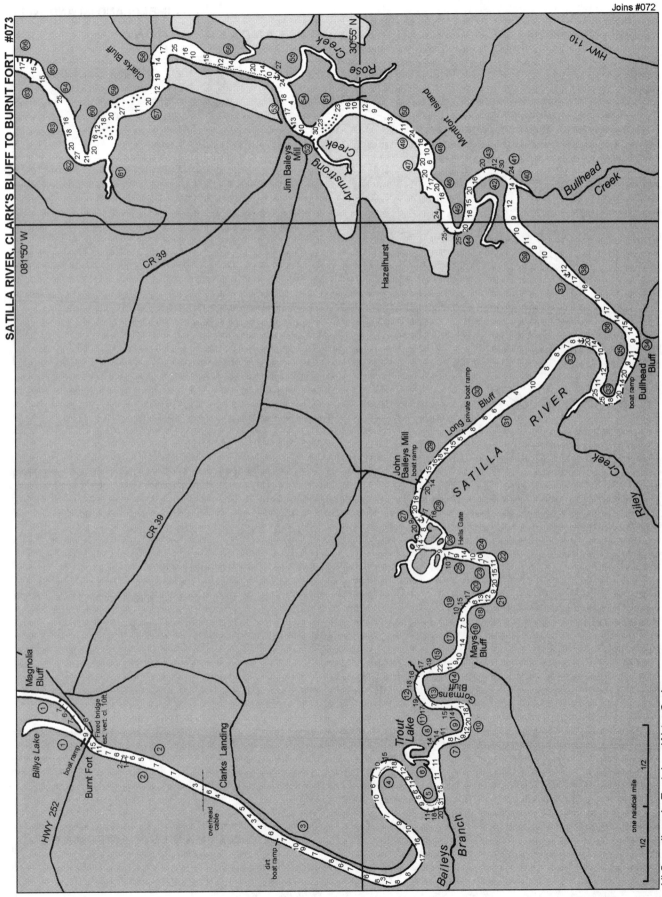

SATILLA RIVER, CLARK'S BLUFF TO BURNT FORT #073

All Soundings In Feet, Low Water Springs

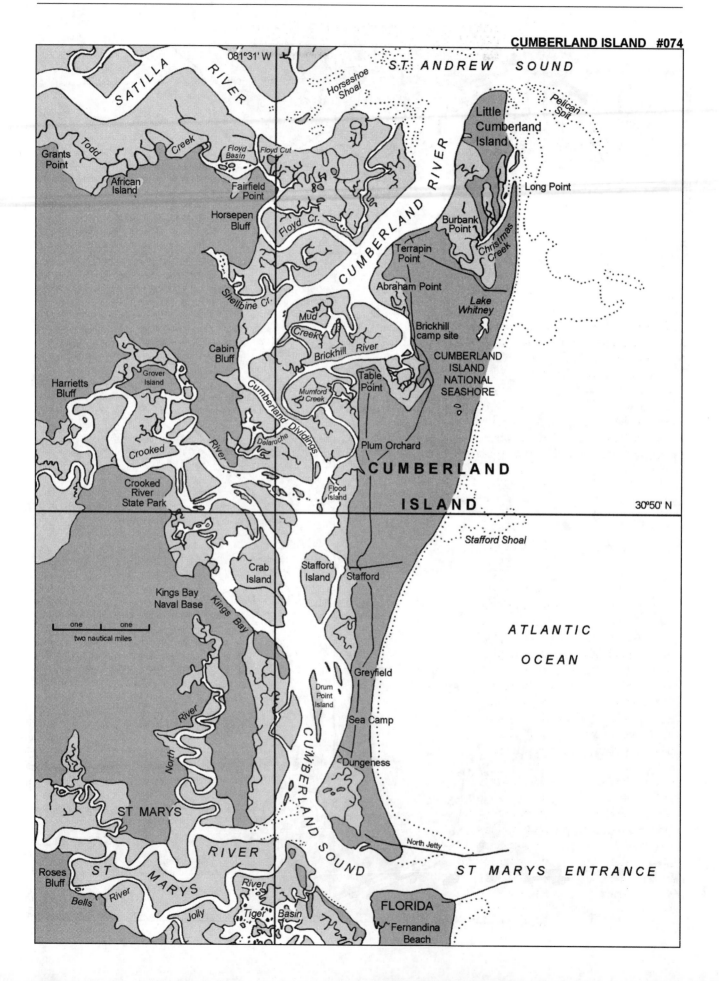

CHAPTER NINE

ST. ANDREW SOUND TO ST. MARYS RIVER

INCLUDING CUMBERLAND ISLAND, CROOKED RIVER AND ST. MARYS RIVER CAMDEN COUNTY

THIS CHAPTER DESCRIBES several natural treasures on Georgia's coast. Cumberland Island, protected as the Cumberland Island National Seashore, is a destination famous far outside of the State of Georgia. Crooked River, a large tidal river which serves as an important departure point for kayakers heading to Cumberland Island, is also worth cruising for its own attractions and wilderness. After exploring about 30 miles of St. Marys River from the ocean to Kings Ferry we wish we had gone all of its 125 miles to the Okefenokee Swamp and had spent days in the wild tributaries on the way.

ST. ANDREW SOUND

Due to the outflow from several rivers, the Satilla River in particular, currents run strongly in this Sound. Combine the effects of the currents with strong onshore winds and the waters here can become extremely choppy. However, in good weather, the marked channel through the sound into the Atlantic provides a reasonable route in and out of the ocean. See chartlets #077 and #078. Use the channel in daylight only as none of the buoys are lit. The sea buoy marked "STA", white and red, large but unlit, bobs on the swell at 30°55'35"N and 081°19'00"W. Relatively deep water over the bar—a minimum of 11 feet close to buoy "1"—allows passage at low tide in moderate sea conditions. The entrance channel is marked from the sea on the principle of "red right returning". Be sure to leave the red nun buoy "2" to starboard when entering from the ocean. A breaking shoal very close to the east of the buoy is not marked on NOAA chart 11504. Also remember that the buoys may get moved around by the Coast Guard to respond to shifting shoals. After buoy "9" the channel joins the Intracoastal Waterway and, in order to head north to Jekyll Island, you must navigate north of buoy "32" and south of buoy "31"—forget "red

right returning" at this point. Heading south from the St. Andrew Sound channel you will have to pass south of buoy "32" and west of beacon "33".

LITTLE CUMBERLAND ISLAND

You will notice from the giant size of the "Wildlife Refuge, Private Property, No Trespassing" boards along the shores of Little Cumberland how strongly the property owners on the island feel about protecting nature. A Holocene island 3 nautical miles long and about a mile wide, Little Cumberland rises high above sea level—up to 40 feet at the north end dunes. Christmas Creek flows from the Atlantic into a wide wedge of marshes separating the Little from the greater Cumberland Island. By design three quarters of Little Cumberland's 1,600 acres of solid earth are and will be left in the wilderness state and only a few dozen homes are scattered around, mostly out of sight for somebody passing by in a boat. Along the north shore you will see impressively massive dunes mixed with maritime forest. A de-activated lighthouse from 1838 pops its head above the trees overlooking the beach, which wraps around the headland from northwest to east, and more than doubles in size at low tide. Loggerhead females begin nesting on Little Cumberland in May and Little Cumberland Island Association protects the nests from foraging raccoons by covering them with hog wire fencing.

Little Cumberland Island Association manages this private island and you would need an invitation to explore the woods. However, you may land on their beaches and walk to your heart's desire up to the high water level—early morning and low tide are the best time. The beauty of the shores with the background of high dunes more than justifies the visit. While there take a look at the abandoned cottage sliding off the dune onto the beach—a result of ignoring natural forces at work on exposed coastlines. You obviously need a small boat to land here. At low tide you can enter an S-shaped trough of water which runs near the north shore, inland of the outer sand bank. Put the anchor on a dry sand spit leaving the tender floating. If you cruise in a larger boat you will have to anchor it either off the east or west shores of Cumberland River depending on the wind. See chartlet #079. A popular anchorage lies just south of Shell Creek which leads to the dock serving the property owners. Strong northerly winds would make it very uncomfortable to anchor anywhere near the west shore of Little Cumberland Island. In westerly winds you will find a smooth anchorage close to the marshes across the river from Shell Creek—deeper water lies close to the point.

CHRISTMAS CREEK

This creek which divides Little Cumberland from the greater Cumberland Island draws avid anglers who hope for Georgia record catches. Gary Altman caught a 4 pound 15 ounce Florida pompano right in the creek and the largest spotted trout at 9 pounds 7 ounces was hooked here by Tommy Hall, both state records. Outside the creek in the sound you have a good chance of tangling with big sharks and tarpon. The entrance to Christmas Creek is very unstable—it moved northward some 1,700 feet in just the eight years between 1974 and 1982. To enter the inner waters begin the approach well south of the wide opening to the creek. From a position near the sandy shores of Long Point on Cumberland Island steer north close to the beach hoping to stay in the deeper water west of the breaking shoal to seaward. The bar, located in a narrow passage between breaking waves on the shoal extending north from Long Point to the west and a line of offshore breakers to the east, has only 2 feet at low tide. It is wise to go in a couple of hours after the tide begins rising so, when you turn west, you can still see the edge of the beach to the north. The deeper water flows along that edge. Having said all that I must add that sand bank configurations change rapidly here after storms or periods of heavy precipitation. This entrance should be attempted only in the best weather and preferably with someone on board who has done it before. Inside, Christmas Creek deepens and branches off winding through marshes. Its westernmost branch flows past a bluff on Cumberland Island, all of which is private property.

CUMBERLAND ISLAND

Even excluding Little Cumberland Island, the greater Cumberland has the longest uninterrupted beach coast in Georgia—17 miles of it without any development except for a few picnic shelters erected by some of the private property owners who remain on this National Seashore Island. Landward of the low primary beach, 20 to 40-foot high dunes run almost the whole length of the island. They formed during colonial times when large numbers of livestock grazed on and destroyed the vegetation that previously stabilized the primary dunes. After the stabilizing plants disappeared onshore winds pushed the loose sands against the edge of the maritime forest and the dunes piled up high against the resisting trees. Following the Civil War livestock numbers diminished as the plantation owners took some cattle off the island and poachers gleaned the rest. The dune vegetation returned stabilizing the primary dunes until the livestock was brought back in the 1900s. Today in a good many sections of the island the primary dunes have returned with sea-oat colonies—the main stabilizing plant. However, other parts of the island lose the sand-stabilizing plants as soon as the young shoots grow out of the ground and get eaten by feral horses and deer.

The coast makes, of course, only an unstable fringe along the whole length of the island. Most of the territory is a Pleistocene core dating between 25,000 and 50,000 before present and here recovering forests thrive. The National Park Service runs this national treasure limiting visitors to 300 a day and allowing camping in several designated areas. Visiting on your own boat will put you in the privileged situation of being able to hike vari-

A recovering forest shades a trail at the north end of Cumberland Island.

ous trails from the most accessible points. Remember to pay the park fee of $4 per stay, which on the Cumberland Island campsites is limited to 7 days. You will find "honor boxes"—just slip the envelope with the money in the slot—at the Plum Orchard site on Brickhill River, at Sea Camp and at Dungeness Dock. We marked the locations on chartlets #075, #076, #081 and #083.

Although today you will rarely see another person on the 50 miles of trails winding through the forests, this large island with 15,100 acres of uplands obviously attracted human occupation in the past. Pottery shards from the nearby mainland indicate an indigenous presence 4,000 years before present. 1972 excavations on the southernmost parts of Cumberland Island in the vicinity of Dungeness uncovered a one mile long shell midden which suggested the past existence of a large village. The dig seemed to point to an occupation by the Tacatacoru group of the Timucuan people later displaced by Yamassee. This agrees with historical events—in the 1700s the English in Carolina defeated an uprising by Yamassee and the tribe escaped south. The Spanish missions probably stood in that general area, also. The buildings, made in wattle and daub and easily biodegradable, vanished during the activities of later colonists, but descendants of the hogs the Spanish brought with them still root through the forests of Cumberland.

That ubiquitous overachiever Gen. Oglethorpe gave the island its present name apparently at the request of chief Tomochichi's nephew who, after a visit to England and experiencing kind treatment by British Royalty and their kin, insisted on having the island renamed after the Duke of Cumberland. The name Missoe, meaning sassafras, was dropped. This new name, by the way, did not go very well with Oglethorpe's trusty Highlanders who had lost relatives during the English cruelties perpetrated against Scots. Expecting the Spanish to attack, Oglethorpe had Fort Andrew built on the high bluff at the north end of Cumberland Island and a village, Barriemackie, housing the soldiers' families, followed. Barriemackie vanished with the soldiers in the 1750s when the Spanish threat no longer loomed. The smaller Fort William stood on the south end of Cumberland facing Amelia Island across St. Marys River.

The English plantations on Cumberland began in earnest in the early 1800s on the lands originally owned by General Nathanael Greene and Thomas Lynch. The Stafford family, too, owned plantation land here contemporaneously with the Greenes. The plantations grew tropical fruits, edible field crops and, of course, sea island cotton, indigo, sugar cane and some rice. Live oaking figured as an industry in the 1800s when expanding American shipping interests invested heavily in the con-

Plum Orchard mansion on Cumberland Island recently received restoration funds.

A sabal palmetto, a lonely bastion against encroaching sands, manages to survive on the east shore of Cumberland Island.

struction of wooden ships. Feral horses were already around on Cumberland Island in the early and mid-1800s—Robert Stafford charged $5 for a "marsh tacky" which had to be lassoed by the customers themselves.

The Civil War wrecked the plantations relying on slave labor and some violent acts followed the Emancipation Proclamation. The great Dungeness mansion and estate begun by Gen. Greene and then enjoyed by his re-married wife, Catherine Miller, were burned in 1866, some sources claim by freed slaves. Robert Stafford, on the other hand, torched his slaves' shacks after they refused to work for him—the famous Chimneys, located on private land, still remain from that time. Some of the freed slaves, first removed by the

Union forces to Amelia Island, returned and lived in the Settlement on the north end of Cumberland. Their little 1893 First African Baptist Church was rebuilt in 1937, and all of a sudden sprang into national attention when John F. Kennedy, Jr. married Carolyn Bessette there in 1996.

After the plantation era, Cumberland became almost deserted with the exception of the High Point area at the north tip of the island where, at the turn of the century, the Hotel Cumberland operated with the help of a steamer connection with Brunswick. The competition from new resorts on St. Simons Island, located closer to Brunswick, ended that venture whose grounds are now private property. Meanwhile, in 1881 Thomas

The First African Baptist Church at the settlement on Cumberland Island became famous in 1996 when John F. Kennedy, Jr. married Carolyn Bessette there.

M. Carnegie of Pittsburgh acquired Dungeness and began turning his holdings into a family retreat. The Carnegies cut several roads to gain easier access to good hunting spots and most of the trails today were named by them. A new giant Dungeness mansion was built surrounded by scores of buildings and run by a staff numbering hundreds. After Thomas's death his widow, Lucy, acquired the rest of the available land on Cumberland eventually owning about 90% of the island. She financed several other buildings for the members of her family, Plum Orchard, Stafford and Greyfield—now the only inn on the island.

After Mrs. Carnegie died in 1916, all her holdings became a trust as a home for her children until their death. The arrangement prompted some moves towards making the island self-supporting or even turning it into a money making concern. One of the heirs challenged these plans in court and eventually the Superior Court stopped a proposed island lease to the Glidden Paint Company which planned mining rare minerals like ilmenite, luecozene, rutile and zirconium. After the Carnegie trust came to an end, the heirs, now the individual owners of demarcated lands, were in 1968 approached by Charles Fraser, the developer of Hilton Head Island. Offered a fistful of millions, three of the Carnegies did sell nearly a fifth of the island. However, rumbling bulldozers converting blue prints of lots and paved roads into reality, as well as the vision of a proposed giant ski lift bringing people from the mainland in cars swinging on steel cables rallied such opposition that eventually Fraser sold his holdings to the National

Park Foundation provided with money from the Andrew Mellon Foundation. The Cumberland Island National Seashore bill was signed by Richard Nixon in 1972. As you walk the trails or the beach on Cumberland ponder how close we came to losing this national treasure. You should also realize that this fight is not over yet. Schemes to allow more vehicular traffic on the island and more visitors are afoot. There is enough string pulling and tugging of the federal purse in the region to fill an environmental thriller.

Feral horses of Cumberland Island roam the dunes in search of green plants to graze on.

WILD HORSES OF CUMBERLAND

The first horses probably turned feral after the Spanish withdrew from Georgia in the late 17th century. The population was reinforced with 50 high-bred horses released on the island in 1916 in accordance with the will of Lucy Coleman Carnegie. Today about 200 feral horses (the 1998 census counted between 192 and 222) roam the island in about sixty packs. You will definitely come across them, even on a day trip, as they wander on the Atlantic beaches, in the forest and on the saltmarshes along the west shores. You should not attempt to touch them or the rare donkey or two that occasionally join the horse packs; although accustomed to human presence they are wild animals and kids approaching to pet them have been kicked or bitten. You will also see horses along Brickhill River, especially off Plum Orchard and either north or south of Hawkins Creek near the Brickhill Bluff Campsite as they graze on the marsh vegetation and young shoots of *spartina alterniflora*—the most common plant of the flooded lowlands. They are very common near the Dungeness area of the island—near the ruins or on the backside of the high dunes.

Historians and biologists agree that since early colonial times livestock has contributed to the reduction of interdune vegetation on Cumberland—the first line of defense the land has against stormy seas and winds. The grazing continues today and the National Park Service has proposed to reduce the herd to about 60 horses. Cute as the "ponies" are, watch them graze which they do throughout daylight hours every day. In the marshes young shoots of smooth cordgrass go first—you will not see this plant around South End at the tip of the island, feral horse territory. Mile-long stretches of the Atlantic beach along the wilderness area look odd—scattered cones of sand held together by tough plants like sabal palmettos or wax myrtles rise over eroded valleys of wind blown sand. The statistics explain the scenery—38% of horses forage mainly on *spartina* grasses and 30% on interdune and beach vegetation with 45% of the animals occupying the wilderness area north of Stafford. The results of interdune overgrazing are quite visible around the beach exits from Duck House Trail and South Cut Trail. Standing on the ocean shore there during a strong onshore wind at high tide when waves sweep unimpeded inland you cannot help thinking that perhaps feral horse management would ensure an abundance of sand-stabilizing plants and reduce damage when a serious hurricane strikes the coast of Georgia.

ANCHORAGES AT CUMBERLAND ISLAND NORTH PART

We follow the descriptions of the anchorages with information on the character of the trails. When hiking you must take a trail map with you—we provide trail routes and names used on trail markers on chartlets #075 and #076 which have more details than the map supplied by the Park Administration. Park Administration maps are available at Sea Camp. Always carry drinking water as you will probably hike longer than planned—such are the enticements of the area. All trails accessible from the anchorages on Brickhill River lie within the designated wilderness area—bicycling is out as an option of getting around. All garbage must leave the island with the visitor—no disposal sites exist.

BRICKHILL RIVER ANCHORAGES
Brickhill Campsite

You can anchor in several places in the northern arm of the river as shown on chartlet #081—we prefer to anchor in the lesser depths off Malkintooh Creek. In Hawkins Creek you will see a private dock—you need a resident's permission to leave your tender there. The semi-cleared area under the trees just south of Hawkins Creek is Brickhill Bluff Camp Site managed by the National Park Service. Be careful landing your dinghy on the river bank by the campsite—dead tree snags and oyster shell heaps obstruct some stretches. If you use an inflatable tender check the area at low tide for sharp oyster shells—they will slice through the fabric like a razor. You will find an old-fashioned well pump on the site—the Park recommends boiling the water before consumption. When landing here be aware that the campers here have hiked 10.6 miles with all of their gear to get to this spot.

A towering pine tree rises over the shore bared by low tide. The powerful deep roots reach to the underground freshwater and help the tree thrive despite daily inundations by tidal sea water traveling up Brickhill River.

Hiking Inland—Chartlet #075

The straightforward hike from Brickhill to the beach on the Atlantic coast takes about 45 minutes of medium-brisk walking. From the campsite, hardly noticeable under grand live oaks wrapped in impressive woody vines, head inland to the Main Road. Turn right and walk south on this sandy road shaded by trees. Pass by other trails on your left until you come to South Cut Trail across from a Private Property sign. Animals use trails, too, so watch out for white-tailed deer, feral horses or hogs. You will probably spot a raccoon as it makes its get-away up a tree. A noise low in the forest floor betrays an armadillo so focused on finding its food under rotting logs and in the leaf litter that it becomes oblivious of its own safety—armadillos tend to forage in the afternoons. South Cut Trail goes east crossing some low wet sloughs—likely places to see alligators lounging among the water lilies or, at least, their tracks after they crossed the trail. While picking blackberries (they begin ripening in late May) from the bushes along the trail take a good look at the sweeping alligator foot prints on each side of its tail groove—we saw some far exceeding the length of a large man's foot. Horses and deer come to the sloughs, too, to find water or at least some moisture during dry spells. Successionary forest has claimed the old pasture lands that you pass in a few places before crossing Roller Coaster Trail.

After another slough, filled with grasses, sedges and some willowy tupelos, you emerge in the open at the back side of high dunes inexorably encroaching onto the maritime forest of predominantly live-oaks and saw palmettos. Then the trail runs down and flattens out on the beach. On the north side of the beach trail a small pond behind a sandy berm has nourished a thick colony of grasses and flowering plants like the common marsh pink. Young alligators and horses frequent this pool. Look southward on the beach and, by comparison with other wild barrier islands, you will be struck by absence of the primary dune. Deprived in the past of stabilizing vegetation by grazing livestock, primary dunes contributed all their loose sand to building the high dunes. The virgin sands of the area faithfully record animal passages and you may be surprised how many visit the beaches, from omnivorous raccoons which can feed on any stranded creatures to vegetarian deer definitely out for a stroll along the wavelets of the low tide. Turkeys commonly venture into the back dunes and you may, in the right season, spot a male displaying on the higher points to an admiring hen. For bird watching carry a light scope or binoculars—turkeys spook easily when you try to get near them. In cold months hundreds of ducks bob in the waves along the beaches—mostly lesser scaups, black scoters, red-breasted mergansers and ruddy ducks. Again you will need some vision enhancing tool to see their details.

The round trip to the beach and back is about 5 miles long but you could make it a day and an exciting one too, by taking Roller Coaster Trail northward after you retreat inland from the beach. This narrow foot trail goes up and down less than the name suggests. After the bright beach it is a relief to walk in the shade of live oak branches dripping with Spanish moss and through a green tunnel bordered by saw palmettos, American hollies, sabal palmettos and other small native trees. You walk on top of an old dune ridge above the level of Sweetwater Lake slough on the east side and an impenetrable maritime forest in the swale on your west hand. Hopefully, when you have the wind in your face you will have the good luck to see one of the bobcats who patrol this area—bobcats were re-introduced to Cumberland in the 70s. The 40 acres of Lake Whitney attract numbers of nesting birds which generally keep to the west shores. You can step off the trail down to the lake muck and take a look at floating bladderwort plants whose small yellow flowers begin to appear in May and persist into fall. This insectivorous plant comes into bloom in large numbers when the conditions are right, but look out for alligators before you bring your nose near water level. You may see anhingas here, rare on the coast except near freshwater ponds on the barrier islands. In a good year the lake may have 3 to 4 feet of water and some of the property owners keep small boats on the shore in the northern part. There, dunes spill into the lake pushed westward by the onshore winds.

After Lake Whitney the trail trudges through soft sands between clumps of trees and eventually joins North Cut Road. Go on to the east and you will end up on the beach. Go to the west and you will walk first on a dry open sandy road. Further on the sides of the road become wetter and have freshwater ditches where animals come to drink and huckleberry bushes line the road—we saw another bobcat marching ahead of us here. On the north side stretches a swampy area with thick saw palmettos and sabal palmetto hammocks resembling Florida more than Georgia. Bunkley Trail takes off southward from North Cut Road and brings welcome shade if you do your walking early or late in the day as you should. At its northern section the trail goes between thick walls of young trees and scrub and later emerges into a pine and oak forest. This round loop via South Cut Trail, up Roller Coaster Trail and back on Bunkley is worth about 8 miles and you definitely need to carry water.

Another hike of about 6.5 miles will take you from Brickhill Camp to the north on Main Road until you sidetrack west to Terrapin Point Trail which goes through a tall mixed forest—oaks, American holly, magnolias, southern red cedar many wrapped in vines. The trail swings by Abraham Point and follows close to the marshes along the western borders of the island—you will look upon Cumberland River across a wide stretch of *spartina* marshes where feral horses, "marsh tackies", often graze. The trail dips into a stream then rises again to the high bluff overlooking

A swallowtail butterfly on Cumberland Island

CUMBERLAND ISLAND NATIONAL SEASHORE— TRAILS, THE NORTHERN PART

These numbers designate the sites of old fields used during the plantation era and later. Most of these fields have not been used since the turn of the century.

1. High Point Farm pond
2. Ray Field
3. Yankee Paradise
4. Savannah
5. Swamp Field drainage

CUMBERLAND ISLAND NATIONAL SEASHORE— TRAILS, THE SOUTHERN PART

Number 13, south end flats, is an area used by nesting birds and should not be visited during the summer months.

1. Baltimore Field
2. Benne Field
3. Old Swamp Field
4. New Swamp Field
5. Susanne Field
6. Hickory Hill Field
7. Sassafras Field
8. Beach Field
9. Little Old House Field
10. Gray Field
11. Little Gray Field
12. Beach Field
13. South end flats

See maps next page.

CUMBERLAND ISLAND NATIONAL SEASHORE - TRAILS, the NORTHERN PART #075

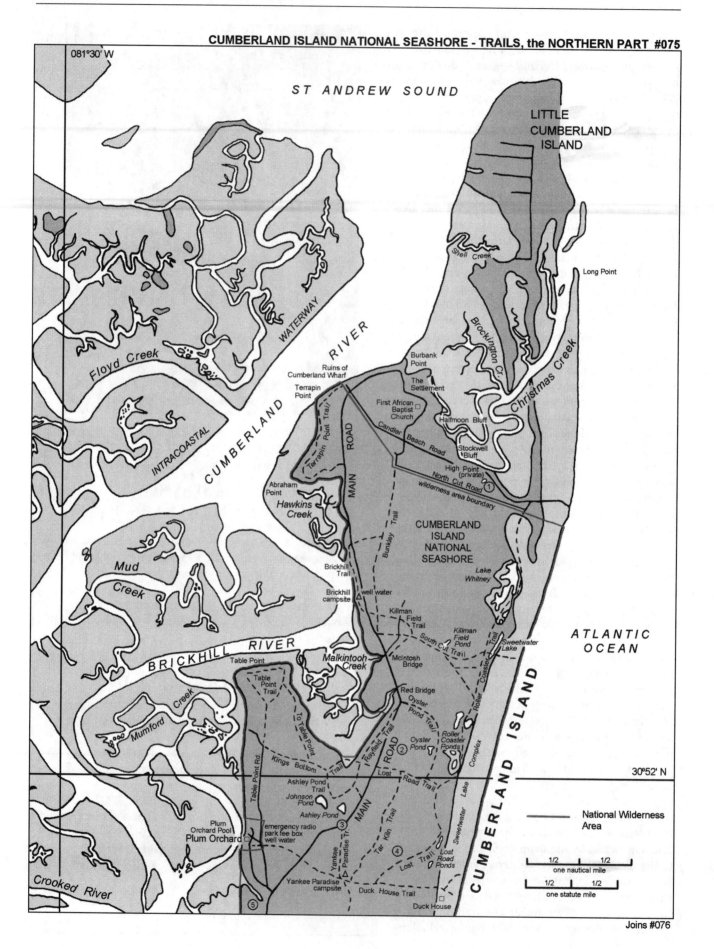

081°30' W

ST ANDREW SOUND

LITTLE CUMBERLAND ISLAND

Shell Creek

Long Point

Floyd Creek

INTRACOASTAL WATERWAY

CUMBERLAND RIVER

Brockington Cr.

Christmas Creek

Ruins of Cumberland Wharf

Terrapin Point

Burbank Point

The Settlement

First African Baptist Church

Halfmoon Bluff

Terrapin Point Trail

MAIN ROAD

Candler Beach Road

Stockwell Bluff

High Point (private)

North Cut Road

wilderness area boundary

Abraham Point

Hawkins Creek

Bunkley Trail

CUMBERLAND ISLAND NATIONAL SEASHORE

Lake Whitney

Mud Creek

Brickhill Trail

Brickhill campsite

well water

Killman Field Trail

Killman Field Pond

ATLANTIC OCEAN

Roller Coaster Trail

Sweetwater Lake

BRICKHILL RIVER

Table Point

South Cut Trail

McIntosh Bridge

Malkintooh Creek

Table Point Trail

Mumford Creek

To Table Point Trail

Kings Bottom

Rayfield Trail

MAIN ROAD

Red Bridge

Oyster Pond Trail

Oyster Pond

Roller Coaster Ponds

Complex

Sweetwater Lake

CUMBERLAND ISLAND

30°52' N

Lost Road Trail

Ashley Pond Trail

Johnson Pond

Ashley Pond

Plum Orchard Pool

Plum Orchard

emergency radio park fee box well water

Yankee Paradise Tr.

Tar Kiln Trail

Lost Trail

Lost Road Ponds

Sweetwater

Yankee Paradise campsite

Duck House Trail

Duck House

Crooked River

National Wilderness Area

1/2   1/2
one nautical mile

1/2   1/2
one statute mile

Joins #076

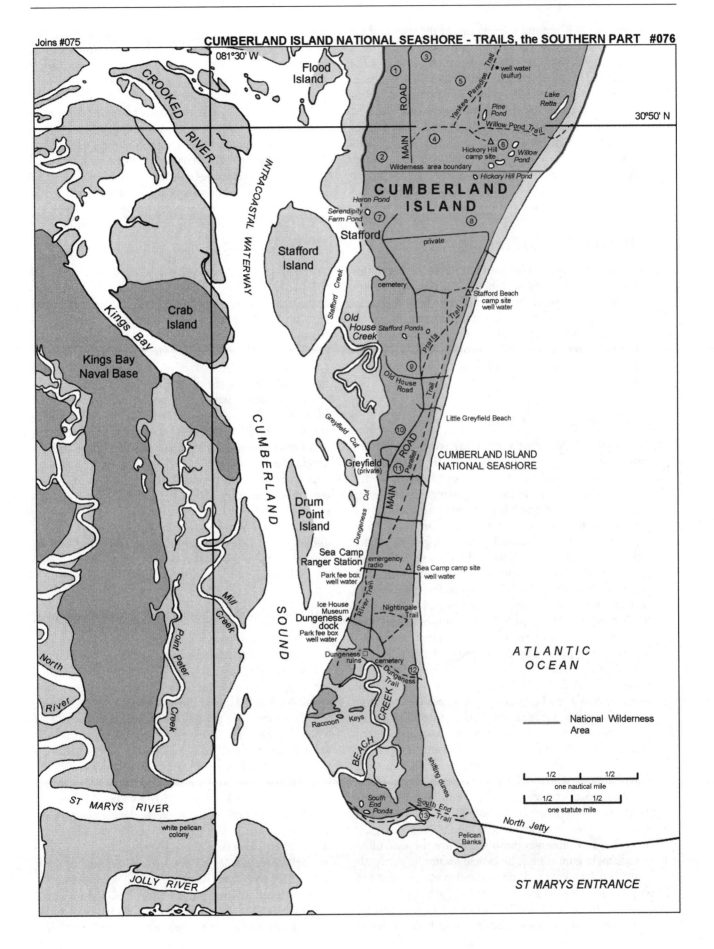

CUMBERLAND ISLAND NATIONAL SEASHORE - TRAILS, the SOUTHERN PART #076

081°30' W

Flood
Island

CROOKED RIVER

well water
(sulfur)

Yankee Paradise Trail

Lake
Retta

30°50' N

Pine
Pond

Willow Pond Trail

ROAD

MAIN

Hickory Hill
camp site

Willow
Pond

Wilderness area boundary

CUMBERLAND
ISLAND

Hickory Hill Pond

INTRACOASTAL WATERWAY

Heron Pond

Serendipity
Farm Pond

Stafford

private

Stafford
Island

Stafford Creek

cemetery

Stafford Beach
camp site
well water

Crab
Island

Old
House
Creek

Stafford Ponds

Pratts

Kings Bay

Trail

Kings Bay
Naval Base

Old House
Road

Trail

Little Greyfield Beach

Greyfield Cut

CUMBERLAND ISLAND
NATIONAL SEASHORE

Greyfield
(private)

ROAD

Parallel

Dungeness Cut

MAIN

Drum
Point
Island

CUMBERLAND SOUND

Sea Camp
Ranger Station

emergency
radio

Sea Camp camp site
well water

Park fee box
well water

River Trail

Mill Creek

Ice House
Museum

Nightingale
Trail

Dungeness
dock
Park fee box
well water

ATLANTIC
OCEAN

North
River

Point Peter Creek

Dungeness
ruins

cemetery

Dungeness Trail

National Wilderness
Area

BEACH CREEK

Raccoon   Keys

ST MARYS RIVER

shifting dunes

white pelican
colony

South
End Ponds

South End
Trail

1/2   1/2
one nautical mile

1/2   1/2
one statute mile

North Jetty

Pelican
Banks

JOLLY RIVER

ST MARYS ENTRANCE

Cumberland River and the remains of the wharf where the steamer bringing guests from Brunswick used to dock around the turn of the century. Between the end of the trail and Main Road you will walk under huge oak trees and red cedars—open and pretty. The Main Road eventually passes by a small airfield and continues to the now famous First African Baptist Church and some houses where the Settlement was until all of its black residents moved to the mainland. The Main Road then swings south, crosses Candler Beach Road leading to a private residence and rejoins North Cut Road where you can take Bunkley Trail back to the south.

MUMFORD CREEK

We anchored within Mumford Creek itself for it put us near a dinghy landing on Table Point. The creek is narrow and we moored the boat between bow and stern anchors so she would not swing with the changing winds and tides. However, the anchorage outside the mouth to Mumford Creek offers perfect protection, too. You can land a small boat on the bank near the western side of Table Point.

Hiking Inland—Chartlet #075

When cruising Mumford Creek you have to sleep aboard your boat as there are no campsites nearby. After securing your tender on the shore clear of the oyster shells, you can walk into the forest by a conspicuous magnolia tree. Look over the marsh before you disappear into the trees—marsh hawks are common here and you may see cooper's and sharp-shinned hawks. The ground ashore appears to be an old shell mound and in several places powerful tree roots have ripped out layers of oyster shells mixed with whelk shells. A very mixed forest grows here with numbers of southern red cedars and live oaks all connected by looping woody vines. You can walk from the north side of the point eastward and then south on a narrow path squeezed by encroaching saw palmettos and sparkleberry bushes. This part of Table Point Trail joins Kings Bottom Trail which will lead you to the edge of the marsh at a muddy area—slosh across it in order to pick up the trail again. Do not get distracted by a side trail taking off to the left before the wet marsh—used and worn out by animals it suddenly vanishes in thick growth. After the muddy crossing the trails split into Rayfield Trail, which offers good views of the marshes, and Lost Road Trail which crosses Main Road then leads to the east. Lost Road Trail passes Oyster Pond Trail to the north. Little used and rough, Oyster Pond Trail goes over a narrow causeway passing a freshwater pond filled with tupelo gum trees. The tupelo swamp is pretty although it may be dry during droughts when lizard tail plants thrive on the barely moist surface.

After the Oyster Pond Trail junction, Lost Road Trail continues east and then, after meeting Roller Coaster Trail, turns south. Roller Coaster Trail goes off to the north towards some ponds with wading birds. We consider the Roller Coaster Trail the most exciting trail in these parts. On the way back west on Lost Road Trail you can side track to Ashley Pond and Johnson Pond on Ashley Pond Trail—as usual ponds have a lot of bird life and you may see wood ducks and anhingas there. Horses come to the ponds to drink and the approach to the lakes leads through softish turf disturbed by hooves. Depending on your meandering in the area you will have walked as much as 8 miles or as little as 5 and will have seen a lot of varied forest scenery. Keep track of where you are since the trails in this part of the woods can become confusing.

PLUM ORCHARD ANCHORAGE

Anchor slightly north of the dock to leave room for the ferry boat which each Saturday and Sunday brings tourists to view the big house. These tours will cease during renovations to Plum Orchard. Meanwhile, right from the water you can watch dozens of ibis, wood storks and herons which have chosen to roost on a big tree slightly north of Plum Orchard mansion. Plenty of other animal life to watch here—alligators swim across the river here routinely, a pack of horses makes the area their home and a couple of armadillos may still keep home under a tangle of oak roots on the bluff. You will find the fee box near the dock and, except during Saturdays and Sundays when the ferry brings sightseers to the Plum Orchard mansion, you can tie your dinghy to the floating pontoon. East of the mansion and on the east side of Table Point Road you will find a small building with an emergency radio connection to Park headquarters—signs point the way.

Hiking Inland—Chartlets #075 And #076

Duck House Trail and a 50-minute hike will lead you from Plum Orchard across the island to the Atlantic beach. In order to find this trail walk east from the landing, pass the sign for the emergency radio, cross Table Point Road and follow the sign to Duck House Trail. Soon after crossing the Main Road the trail becomes a typical Cumberland maritime forest trail, a narrow tunnel winding through oaks and pines and bordered by head high saw palmettos. After the juncture with Yankee Paradise Trail, and a nice camping area on ground slightly above trail level, you will pass Tar Kiln Trail and a bit later—the Lost Trail. In several places you will pass fetter bush or maleberry both of which give off a nice smell when flowering during spring. The trail goes through three swales of low ground which in rainy weather fill with fresh water—you will see tupelo trees surrounded by other plants typical of a freshwater swamp. Next, the trail climbs over a sandy hill through pines and again dips down through a lowland and dense shrubby vegetation before hitting the sands and the open view of the ocean. Gentle dunes with scattered conical clumps of dune vegetation stretch north and south. If you decide to return to Plum Orchard on Duck House Trail you should at least take Lost Trail northwards for half an hour. This trail leads to a very different landscape. Soon after entering you will go through a lowland which will easily turn to swamp and even shallow ponds after heavy rains. In dry weather dense plant growth develops here drawing moisture from the saturated soil. After the second wooden deck over the swamp the trail climbs onto an old dune ridge and now you can look down on damp swales on both sides. Shoulder high, and higher, saw palmettos border the trail now shaded by oak branches. Look carefully at the curly long tresses of Spanish moss hanging down to your eye level. You will notice, next to the Spanish moss, another similar plant with finer, softer, straighter strands and bright olive green coloring. It rarely occurs in other parts of the island. Lost Trail in this area is similar to our favorite trail—Roller Coaster Trail—which also follows an old dune ridge through maritime forest of the same character. When you feel like a longer hike you can, after reaching the beach on Duck House Trail, go south along the coast to a junction with Willow Pond Trail marked, as all other beach trail exits, with tall black/white checkered posts. Willow Pond Trail will take you back west by

freshwater ponds thick with acquatic plants and a swale near the beach with roosting ibis, feeding ducks and often turkeys. From Willow Pond Trail you can return north on Yankee Paradise Trail or on the Main Road—see chartlet #076. This loop lengthens the hiking to about 8 miles. Staying aboard your boat at anchor offers splendid freedom to sample other trails from the Plum Orchard area. Table Point Road north and back is one interesting alternative which you can extend to a longer hike when you feel like it—check out chartlet #075.

CUMBERLAND RIVER

After St. Andrew Sound this river stays very wide and well marked calling for a navigator's concentration only after Intracoastal Waterway marker "43"—chartlet #081. Suddenly, extensive shoals take most of the mid-river leaving a relatively narrow channel for larger and deeper craft. Across from marker "43", on the west shore, lies the deep entrance to Shellbine Creek—a good anchorage. Don't jump up in panic when you hear shooting anywhere close to marker "50"—the sure-shot guests in The Cabin Bluff Lodge aim only at clay pigeons. The marina docks here also belong to The Cabin Bluff Lodge which in turn is owned by the Sea Island Company. The Cabin Bluff which began in the 20's as a hunting lodge

The upscale Greyfield Inn, is the only inn on Cumberland Island.

Vines slowly take over the crumbling ruins of Dungeness, once the Carnegie residence.

A sculptured Lucifer carries the burden of a fountain near the Dungeness ruins on Cumberland Island.

owns thousands of acres on the adjacent mainland and can accommodate 32 guests. They offer recreational activities like hunting, horseback riding, saltwater angling, etc. The Lodge caters to groups of corporate executives—see the Services Section for details. In the area called Cumberland Dividings (the incoming tides from St. Andrew Sound and St. Marys Entrance meet here and outgoing tides go in opposite directions), by marker "57" you can safely enter Delaroche Creek to anchor in good protection—read more about Delaroche Creek later in this chapter. After the south entrance to Brickhill River (which has only 5 feet of water on the bar) pay attention to the markers. Off the Crooked River entrance depths begin to diminish to 8 feet at low springs tides—chartlet #081. An additional complication arises when the aids to navigation change from the Intracoastal Waterway system to the system marking the ship channel from the ocean to the Kings Bay submarine base. After passing between markers "78" and "79" expect to see marker "50" to the east of your course. The aids will continue to be red to the east of the channel and will show diminishing numbers until you leave Cumberland Island behind at buoy "29" and head south into Amelia River and the Intracoastal Waterway whose entrance begins the Waterway buoy "2"—chartlet #084.

ANCHORAGES AT CUMBERLAND ISLAND— SOUTH PART

Unless you are running a very shallow draft boat or like playing the high tide, you will have to go all the way south of Drum Point Island and buoy "41" before turning towards Cumberland Island. Once around that point follow close to the shore of the island and enter the channel where most transient boats anchor in order to go ashore at the Sea Camp dock. Make sure to anchor north of the dock to leave the approach open for the ferry boat and to avoid their rolling wake. When you expect strong winds from westerly and northwesterly directions move even farther north to gain the shelter from the marsh islands off Greyfield. The only traffic through here are the boats which bring guests and supplies to Greyfield Inn—show an anchor light at night.

STAFFORD CREEK

You will find plenty of water to anchor in the southeast part of Stafford Creek south of Oldhouse Creek. However, boats deeper than typical outboard powered trailerables will have to enter at high tide—see chartlet #083. In fact, you do not have to go to all this trouble—anchor your big boat off Greyfield and explore Stafford

Creek, only about a mile away, in a shallow draft tender or a kayak for that matter. The bird life and fish life are both amazing here. Going through Stafford Creek we had around us two ospreys so focused on fish that they plunged into the water mere yards away from our dinghy. Just before we turned into Oldhouse Creek a pair of otters climbed up the mud bank and ran into the marsh. In the creek itself we counted a couple of hundred ibis preening on a dock running into the marsh. Farther in the creek, as we moved through muddy soup inches deep, panicked shrimp were jumping into our laps. At its southern end Oldhouse Creek dries at low tide exposing high heaps of live oysters—a hazardous area for an inflatable boat—a heavenly adventure for a kayak.

Hiking Inland—Chartlet #076

Before you start walking after tying your dinghy to the Sea Camp dock get your ticket from the fee box by the path to the office. Inform the rangers about leaving your little boat at their dock. The rangers have maps and bird lists available. Visitors planning to camp receive instructions from a park ranger in front of the office. To camp on Cumberland you must make reservations. The outstanding trails of Cumberland begin right behind the Sea Camp station. The very first trail is magnificent. Day trippers take the usual three quarter mile walk past the Sea Camp camping area to the beach—just enough to whet your appetite for more hikes through tunnels of live oaks locking branches overhead complete with Spanish moss hanging down in bunches and saw palmettos lined up along the sides. The walk on River Trail which runs south along the bluff to the Ice House Museum by the Dungeness Dock is about the same length and you will probably see raccoons in the trees and armadillos in the underbrush along this way. White-tailed deer and horses may put in an appearance, too. Horses and sometimes turkeys hang around the Dungeness Ruins ogling tourists. Not far away, just off Dungeness Trail, the first colonists' cemetery overlooks marshes and Beach Creek. A brand new decked trail begins a little east of the Greene/Miller cemetery and leads along the creek to the back slopes of dunes. It provides an excellent opportunity to view the marshes quite often filled with flocks of white ibis which probe the mud for fiddler crabs—and there may be as many as one million fiddler crabs per acre! Horses often hoof it across the dunes at the east end of the decked trail on their way to the succulent marsh grasses by Beach Creek. After a short trudge through a sandy area you can pick up another decked trail which leads to the Atlantic beach through wax myrtles and dune swale filled with typical dune vegetation.

You can of course choose to reach the Dungeness area and the decked trails by walking from Sea Camp on Main Road. In that case you will pass Nightingale Trail which loops through a maritime forest. Fifteen examples of various species of coastal trees and plants have been assigned numbers on this trail and with the aid of a reference leaflet from the box at the entrance you can identify them and learn a bit of their natural history. The markers begin at the south entrance.

Sea Camp station is the starting point for several guided tours to the places mentioned above and you will be able to learn more about the human and natural history of Cumberland from knowledgeable National Park Service employees and volunteers. On Fridays a vehicle takes a limited number of visitors to the north end of the island, to the Settlement, and the famous little church—sign up in advance. Also put your name in the Sea Camp office if you want to see Plum Orchard mansion—the ferry goes there on Saturdays and Sundays. These tours will cease when renovations begin.

Apart from these popular sites and trails you should really march up north from Sea Camp first on the Main Road and then take Parallel Trail north. The trail passes by five side trails to the Atlantic beach. After Parallel joins Pratts Trail it leads north to the Stafford Beach campsite and soon after changes into a path towards the beach, first dipping into a swale and then cutting through dense thickets of wax myrtles where more than 20 species of song birds feed or hide depending on the time of the year. It will give you an 8 mile round tour through a prime example of maritime forest which grows so thick overhead that you can hike in the middle of the day without getting fried by the sun—carry water, though. The water at Stafford Beach tastes great but a posted note advises you to boil it before drinking. The advantage of hiking on the Parallel Trail is that you can cut it short at any point and still love your surroundings on the way back.

An excellent 8 mile hike would take you from the Sea Camp ranger station east to the beach, then along the beach north to Stafford Beach. From May till July you have a good chance of coming across loggerhead turtle nests and the deep fresh tracks females make dragging themselves up the beach and beyond the reach of high water. There they laboriously dig a deep hole, deposit over a hundred eggs, cover the nest with sand, use their body weight to pummel the sand down and return to the sea. They come at night on high tides to make the job of dragging several hundred pounds of body and carapace weight through the sand easier. Over two hundred female loggerheads nest on Cumberland every year and their nests receive protective wire cagings by ranger patrols in the early mornings. This stops most raccoons and hogs from digging up the eggs. If the eggs survive, the next trial for the turtle hatchlings comes when they break free after about two months of incubation. On their run to the ocean many get intercepted by fleet-footed ghost crabs, hogs or raccoons and after they dive in they become prey to fish and sea birds. Researchers estimate that only one hatchling out of two thousand eggs lives to maturity.

This hike parallels a long sandy dune system with a healthy cover of sea oats and other dune plants in the interdune dip leading to the high dunes on the edge on the maritime forest. You can best observe the interdune vegetation from the raised deck of the wooden walkway at the Sea Camp Beach exit. At the Stafford Beach exit you will walk through the sandy trail and you should not venture onto the dunes on either side. I am sure that after the beach walk you will enjoy the shade of the forested trails on the way back south. The Stafford Beach camp site, which lies very close to the dunes, stretches along the edge of a live oak forest and looks upon a young pine forest growing over some old pasture land. Pratts Trail goes south from here—see chartlet #076—either to Parallel Trail or to Main Road.

BEACH CREEK

This narrow but deep creek has an extremely shallow bar at the entrance—see chartlet #085. However, we found it enticing enough to bring our 38-foot yawl in at high tide and stayed there several days moored between bow and stern anchors—not enough room to swing to a single anchor. Around us we constantly saw great numbers of white ibis, many woodstorks, willets and clapper rails while up on the marsh flats fed families of "marsh tackies"—feral horses. In fact they keep a lot of marsh vegetation cropped short all around this area and out on the dunes at South End. Beach Creek gave us access to the very little used and indistinct South End Trail which goes by South End Ponds, full of waterfowl in cold months. The trail continues by the dunes area passing close to tidal flats serving black skimmers, American oyster catchers, royal and least terns and whimbrels. On the beach facing the long rock jetty you will see dozens of brown pelicans, laughing gulls, ring-billed gulls and good numbers of sanderlings, dunlins and other sandpipers and plovers—species change with the seasons.

KAYAKING AT CUMBERLAND ISLAND

First of all, kayakers must make reservations for the camping grounds in advance by phone at 912-882-4335. Next, they must figure out how to get the kayak to the island since the regular ferry boats from St. Marys will not take kayaks or bicycles. Most kayakers plan to put in at Crooked River State Park and hopefully catch the ebbing tide to easily shoot the 11 nautical miles to Brickhill Campsite right on the river bank on Cumberland Island. You can shorten the trip to 5 nautical miles if you stop in Plum Orchard, leave the kayaks by the dock there and set up tents at Yankee Paradise Campsite—about 25 minutes of walking away. If you do not mind spending $65 for a round trip on a chartered boat from St. Marys (call Lang's

Seafood 912-882-1056) you will get yourself and your gear delivered to the Sea Camp area where you can set up your tent in the Sea Camp Site. You can then divide the pleasures of your stay between hiking and kayaking to the Stafford Creek area or to Beach Creek and South End—both of these destinations will make it a happy visit.

No matter how you get yourself and your gear to Cumberland Island you must first have the camping reservations and then pay $2 per day for a primitive campsite or $4 per day for the Sea Camp campsite where there are bathrooms and showers. The only other fee is $4 per stay of a maximum 7 days.

WATERS WEST OF THE INTRACOASTAL WATERWAY

The southern part of the Alternate Waterway flows through this area before joining the Intracoastal Waterway. The large tidal Crooked River runs past Crooked River State Park, the put-in place for kayaks heading to Cumberland Island. Upstream of the park the river spreads through lightly developed and wild marshlands.

St. Marys, the largest river in this section, offers facilities for all boats in St. Marys. Past the town, the river provides outstanding opportunities for exploration.

FLOYD CREEK—THE ALTERNATE WATERWAY

You can approach Floyd Creek from Dover Creek across the Satilla by following markers from "A17" and "A19" on the north shore of the Satilla and after "A20" steer south for marker "A21" at Floyd Cut—see chartlet #068, Chapter #VIII. You can also come straight in from lighted marker "2" in Jekyll Sound off the tip of Raccoon Key Spit. You will then see the rest of the markers leading into Floyd Creek, chartlet #068. You should find about 8 feet on the Floyd Creek bar and 20 feet or more in the channel. The markers will lead you through the tricky parts after which Floyd Creek (chartlet #080) becomes wider and deeper ending at Cumberland River with its own marker, "A34". To join the Intracoastal Waterway you must steer about east to pass north on the Waterway of marker "40".

TODD CREEK

Todd Creek was an unexpected treat after the confusing entrance through Floyd Basin. You should pass north of marker "A24", steer close to the point on the north side on the entrance and from there steer directly for the south shore—see chartlets #069 and #080. Boats deeper than 3 feet should enter on the rising tide as the deeper trough is very narrow. Once you come close to the south shore you will have better depths. We found a good anchorage in the southwestern corner of Floyd Basin—from there you can explore the creeks in a dinghy or watch birds which come to the marsh islands to the north. Another place to anchor is off the bluff at Crews Point where the swinging room was a little tight for our 38-footer—we moored with bow and stern anchors. The uplands here are all planted with pines and owned by the Brunswick Pulp Land Company. Cabin Bluff Lodge—you pass it going south on the Waterway—uses the woods to hunt turkeys and other game. You will not experience much boat traffic on this river but big alligators cruise freely up the creeks ahead. African Island, a name probably left over from the days when the Hermitage Plantation operated in this area, is connected to the mainland by a small bridge over a creek. Planted pines cover most of the island except for the edges where wild scrubby vegetation and smaller trees hold ground. The main creek continues through marshes until some old rice canals and small hammocks in Butler Branch where we saw a roost of at least two dozen night herons and our record big Georgia alligator.

SHELLBINE CREEK

On the west shore, across from marker "43" you will see the entrance to Shellbine Creek—chartlet #080. Easy to enter, it often hosts transient yachts stopping for the night after a day of navigating the Intracoastal Waterway. You can carry on farther up the creek towards the mainland but the deeper water ends soon after the forested curve in the river where you will find good holding. The planted forest supports a great number of resident birds, woodpeckers, sparrows, red-winged blackbirds, fish crows and boat-tailed grackles. A wide shallow area of marsh islands to the northwest faces a line of clay pigeon launchers on the edge of the forest—and they do practice here a lot. A factory overlooks the other shore of this area. The eastern branches of Shellbine invite dinghy explorations if you want to see, and not just hear, a marsh hen (clapper rail) or to surprise a mink.

DELAROCHE CREEK

You can swing into this deep creek right from marker "57"—chartlet #081. Boats longer than 35 feet will probably find the creek intimidatingly narrow—bow and stern anchors are the usual solution when we expect strong winds and much swinging. You will find a wider area farther in where the creek turns west. Black Point's shores, forested with yaupon holly, southern red cedar, bay trees and oaks overhanging the water make a great background for a dinghy trip along the mainland—all private property. A stream with the forest on the west side and marshes to the east goes north eventually entering the Waterway. The Delaroche area is totally unpopulated and frequented mostly by wading birds like ibis and woodstorks.

CROOKED RIVER

Crooked River joins the Intracoastal Waterway through two outlets. The northern channel, illustrated on chartlet #081, generally carries less depth and requires more attention when entering, but we found the combination of marsh island and sandbars very attractive. You will find navigating into the southern channel of Crooked River more straightforward—see chartlet #083—head about northwest from marker "71" and favor the western shores on the way in. You can anchor anywhere between the marsh islands bordering the entrance channel. However, the huge hangars in Kings Bay Submarine Base nearby intrude upon the otherwise unspoiled view of the marshes, birds and the sky. Do not despair though—just sail farther in and you will find plenty of wilderness left to enjoy. Black Point Creek is particularly attractive especially in the oxbow that swings by the forested Black Point. The creek itself runs inland and swings along the north shore of Grover Island. While

A crumbling boardwalk points towards an abandoned home on a marsh hammock by Crooked River.

A floating dock extends the hunting range for this great blue heron.

Black Point has plenty of No Trespassing signs and in winter months hunters probably make the place somewhat dangerous, Grover Island is yours to explore. You will find the best landing on its Crooked River side.

About a mile west of the entrance to Black Point Creek you will see a high bluff and some of the buildings of Crooked River State Park. This large Park offers visitors such luxuries as rental cottages, a swimming pool, a playground, miniature golf, hook-ups for RVs, as well as sites for tents. Call 912-882-5256 for information and 800-864-7275 for reservations which you should make well in advance—it is a popular park. A couple of nature trails help acquaint visitors with typical scenes of coastal ecology. The Sempervirens Trail provides an excellent example of a maritime forest, both wet and dry versions, meeting salt marshes, an environment which soon becomes familiar to people who explore coastal Georgia in boats. The Palmetto Trail combines a saw palmetto understory with succesionary pine forest—also a beautifully familiar scene in Georgia. Crooked River State Park is part of the Colonial Coast Birding Trail.

At the end of Crooked River Road, Spur 40 you will find a double boat ramp and floating docks. Kayakers planning to reach Cumberland Island on their own bottoms, so to speak, often park their vehicles in the state park and put in Crooked River. If they depart from Crooked River when the outgoing current begins they can count on fair current all the way down Crooked River and Brickhill River. When planning the trip, bear in mind that at Crooked River Park the ebb begins about one and three quarters hours after the standard reference time for the Savannah River bar. On some dates of the year the tidal ranges fluctuate so that you may lose the fair tide between the northern exit from Crooked River and the entrance to Brickhill River. However, the outgoing tide will flow with you again within Brickhill River all the way to the Brickhill campsite. To speed up the trip and make it more interesting use chartlet #081 to go through the short-cut via Mumford Creek—an overhead

powerline is the landmark for its south entrance. Between late November and April the weather in Georgia is affected by cold fronts which bring strong northerlies after the frontal passage and strong southerlies before the arrival of the front. Crooked River becomes very choppy in winds 20 mph and over—kayakers with limited experience or with children should instead explore the more sheltered and attractive waters in Black Point Creek.

For larger and deeper vessels several good anchorages farther inland on Crooked River offer great exploring opportunities in small tenders. Shallow draft cruisers will be even happier—they can easily explore almost to the I 95 bridge. Grover Island protects the anchorage off its south shore in strong winds from the north to northeast—in westerly to northwesterly winds the waters become so choppy on incoming tides that you should move to the lee of Harrietts Bluff where calm airs will prevail. Grover Island is a recovering wilderness with relatively open forest close to the river shores and then gradually becoming impenetrable. Woodstorks and ibis roost every evening, at least in winter, on the trees overhanging the river. Grover Creek will let a small boat meander into the marshes filled with wading birds and ducks during the cold months especially in the Deep Creek area.

Harrietts Bluff is a residential area but you can land at the public dock and ramp from where you can stretch your legs along the community roads. From Harrietts Bluff use chartlet #082 to go around drying shoals and stay in deep water all the way to Drizzel Bluff where you can anchor in a wide area off a small creek as marked on chartlet #082. For some reason this place attracts otters and minks which you may observe late in the day. Although most of the grounds ashore must be private property we landed on shore free of "posted" signs and had several walks through the woods alive with deer and feral pigs. Along the east borders of Sheffield Island spurs of wooded upland overlook Sadlers Creek. Sadlers Creek, by the way, has plenty of deep water after you sneak into it along the marsh shore west of the offlying marsh islets and shoals lying south of Harrietts Bluff. One long dock reaches the shores of Sadlers Creek at the beginning. Then the stream runs through pristine marshes, now mostly of black needle rush, until more residential development at the very end.

The small creek going southward off Drizzel Bluff eventually reaches Laurel Island and joins a maze of creeks and some old rice-canals all undeveloped and quite beautiful as well as filled with all species of coastal birds and flocks of ducks (in winter). A small creek next west (chartlet #082) goes south to the border of Laurel Island Links Golf course passing on the way a neglected marsh boardwalk to an abandoned home hiding in the midst of a perfect wooded hammock. Crooked River runs along Sheffield Island, continues past the two creeks just described, swings by another residential area and eventually sneaks under the I 95 bridge raised only 5 feet above water.

ST MARYS RIVER

The first entrance marker "2" to St. Marys River lies awkwardly far from where vessels approaching from the north should make their turn to the west. New visitors will find it easier to head directly west from ship channel buoy "35"—chartlet #084. On this course, and roughly off the mouth of Jolly River on the south side, you will pass south of the front range marker for the shipping channel. After that you can steer in mid stream although the river stays deep across its width, see chartlet #086. Point Peter, the wooded point on the north shore now occupied by a private house and a dock, was twice the site of forts, first in 1778 and then again in 1812. Point Peter Creek, a pleasant stream popular with local anglers runs at first along a wooded bluff where a large sunken tree can snag your propeller when the tide is high enough to cover it; at low tide fishermen tie their boats to its branches to do some casting for speckled trout and drums. Across St. Marys River on the south shore you will see a conspicuous white oyster shell bar which, during the cold months, serves as a rest stop for a flock of 50 to 60 White Pelicans, winter immigrants from inland lakes far in the northwest of the continent. Much larger than our resident brown pelicans, they feed in the dark hours while floating, instead of plunging from heights as the browns do.

You can see from chartlet #086 that St. Marys River runs quite deep on to North River. South of the mouth to North River the marked channel begins to be marked again with beacon "3". If you look carefully in the marsh across the water from number "3", you will see a ballast stone pile. So many ships once visited the port that the town designated disposal sites in 1763 and imposed fines of up to $2,000 for dumping ballast stones and other "rubbish, coal or ashes" in other parts of the river. The aids to navigation end with beacon "13" off the town of St. Marys. Two marina basins welcome yachts here. Lang's East has, in addition to fully-serviced floating docks, fuel pumps for gasoline and diesel. Lang's West has all the amenities of a marina minus fuel sales. But it can boast a popular restaurant, Lang's Marina Restaurant which specializes in serving shrimp caught by Lang's trawlers. They open for dinner on Thursdays, Fridays and Saturdays, tel. 912-882-4432. To contact the marinas for dockage or fuel sales call VHF 16 or tel. 912-882-4452. See the Services Section. If you choose to anchor, do it to the south of Lang's West Marina—see chartlet #086—and leave adequate room for their customers' boats to go in and out. Here you will have great protection in strong northerly winds but swift currents in this wide stretch of the river (1,200 feet wide off the town) make it choppy in strong southerly blows.

On the waterfront west of Langs East Marina are shrimp boat docks, then the dock for anglers and sightseers, and the dock for the ferry taking visitors to Cumberland Island. Next west you will see the public

White pelicans, winter immigrants from northern inland lakes, find safety and good weather along St. Marys River.

The west basin of Lang's Marina in St. Marys.

St. Marys began its official existence in 1787 and in 1801 was incorporated as a result of its importance as a trans-shipment port for timber and plantation products. The town especially prospered after the United States gained Florida in 1821. Shipbuilding was a vital business in St. Marys in the late 1700s and early 1800s. It began with the arrival of John Patterson, a master ship-builder from Philadelphia. His yard built several high quality sailing ships for merchants in Savannah and other ports on the southeastern coast. Although the yellow fever epidemic of 1801 struck down John Patterson and many in his family, the shipbuilding business continued. By the 1830s St. Marys shipyards produced more vessels than any other port along the coast. Boat racing also became a popular sport among the planters from the surrounding area. A shipwright named Zeb Rudulph built the best racing canoes out of solid cypress logs and finished them in mahogany with brass fittings. Divided into classes by size, the canoes were manned by crews of four to eight slaves—the planters, members of the St. Marys Boat Club, preferred to watch and bet money on them.

ramp with a floating dock and The Fishing Outpost. In the old days you would see a good amount of boat building along the waterfront. It is all gone now from the town but up North River, which you passed on the way to St. Marys, you will find North River Boat Yard equipped with a 37-ton travel lift and 200-ton haul-out ways for commercial vessels with a draft limited to 9 feet—you have to approach the haul-out at high tide. Their docks have 3 feet of water at low tide, tel. 912-882-8781 and 912-882-3932. See the Services Section.

Until the 1840s the town thrived on the trade of cotton, lumber, rice and naval stores. After the Civil War the town stagnated and the lack of nearby rail service contributed to a continuing decline. Employment opportunities improved when a large paper mill (still in business) moved to town in the forties. In the fifties, the opening of a new submarine base in nearby King's Bay farther improved the economy. Since the creation of the Cumberland Island National Seashore in 1972 a regular flow of tourists comes to town to board the ferry to the island. A short walk through the main street of this pleasant town will take you to well preserved examples of early 1800s architecture, Clark home, Orange Hall which houses the St. Marys Welcome Center and museum and the First Presbyterian Church. Make sure to visit the Oak Grove Cemetery where old Acadian tombs are still standing.

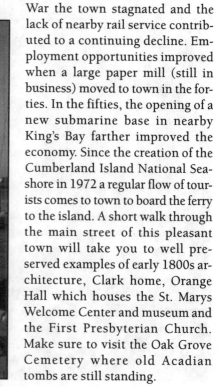

A cruise ship stops annually in Lang's Marina in St. Marys.

You should not miss a chance to explore farther up St. Marys River. Soon after Devil's Elbow you can enter the north end of Bells River and go to the anchorage off Roses Bluff—chartlet #086. The more than sixty-foot high sandy cliff topped with a mixed forest along the edge and pines inland creates a perfect background for the anchorage with a view of the marshes to the east. Across from Bells River on the St. Marys north shore you will see the entrance to Borrell Creek which is deep enough for shrimp boats to go as far as Julia Street— chartlet #086. Soon afterwards, Borrel Creek joins Dark Entry Creek. Borrel Creek on the way west parallels a residential area and then splits into a maze of smaller creeks where often the only clue as to where the exit might be is the direction of the tidal current. This area provides an example of how important it is to know the times of high and low tides for the day. Dark Entry Creek goes north from Borrell through many very shallow spots and eventually passes under a railroad trestle. Beware here of two sets of submerged old trestle pilings—if you spot one row of their tops it means the shorter ones are still lurking under the surface. A rough boat ramp goes into the water from the west shore almost under the HWY 40 bridge. Anglers come here for freshwater catfish at times of heavy precipitation. Otherwise, they catch saltwater fish in the same place!

You will find another special anchorage up St. Marys River off Reids Bluff—chartlets #086 and #087. A high cliff (over 60 feet) overlooks a long stretch of marshes over a 600-foot wide river. The high shore begins along the east side of the river and continues west to Crandall where some homes hide among the trees and a small dirt surfaced boat ramp goes into the water. St. Marys is a blackwater river with the color of dark tea becoming especially noticeable when you get up as far as the I 95 bridge. The vertical clearance of 33 feet will stop most sailboats from continuing their progress up this deep river. However, sailboats can anchor, as we did, before the bridge and then continue their explorations in a motorized tender. Despite the proximity of the noisy busy expressway the surrounding area is attractive. Even the little Casey Creek which flows through the marshes on the east shore of the river will take small boat explorers through saltmarsh creeks in which migrating ducks feed. A branch of Casey Creek goes to Osprey Cove, an upscale residential development with its own paved boat ramp and floating dock, and then winds through pristine marshland with forest in the background. Casey Creek itself joins St. Marys River a short distance north of Crandall—chartlet #087.

Past the I 95 bridge comes Scrubby Bluff with its residential area and after that St. Marys assumes a wilder look. Catfish Creek, which cuts into the north shore of the St. Marys is worth a visit—shortly before the HWY 17 bridge the stream changes into a primeval swamp with trees growing out of the water. A small dirt surfaced ramp, adequate for canoes and kayaks, reaches the water be-

The 1829 Orange Hall now houses a museum and a welcome center in St. Marys. Directly across the street you can see the 1808 Presbyterian Church.

tween the HWY 17 and railroad bridges. This picturesque territory stretches in all directions. Bald cypresses, tupelos, bay trees rise from the dark water and although the channel could barely accommodate our five foot wide tender it was deep, over 6 feet in places. This is a tidal freshwater river with salt water along the bottom and fresh on top—good for anglers who look for freshwater and saltwater species.

St. Marys River holds its deep soundings after Catfish Creek, the reason for its importance for the shipping business before the introduction of rail service. Both the HWY 17 and the railroad bridge across the river open after calling CSX Transportation at 904-381-4060/ 904-381-2746 and the DOT at 904-695-4000. These days probably only shrimp boats looking for shelter from a hurri-

The forest-topped sand cliff of Reid's Bluff rises over St. Marys River just a few miles upriver from the town of St. Marys.

cane or pile drivers going up river to build docks would request a bridge opening. Little St. Marys River cuts into the wetlands on the south shore soon after these bridges (chartlets #087 and #088) and, judging by its first half mile, it can take you through beautiful wilderness attractive to wading and marsh birds for several more miles. Before and after Little St. Marys the big river winds through flooded forests. Leafless trees during the winter reveal an abundance of nests so the place buzzes with

song birds in the spring and wild azaleas hold tight to the edge of the river. The river water, a dark burgundy color from the tannic acid content, was once appreciated as long lasting drinking water for sailing ships involved in transoceanic voyages.

After such a pristine river scene it is a surprise to come upon a groomed landscape edged with boat docks along the south side of the river, the grounds of White Oak Plantation, owned by the Gilman Paper Company of St. Marys—chartlet #088. President Clinton visited here during his second tenure. Before reaching the Temple boat ramp and landing you will pass Horsepen Creek, a forested wild stream on the north shore with fallen trees across the water blocking passage far inland at the time of our visit. Around the river curve and on the south shore is the tiny entrance to Cabbage Creek filled with flooded tupelos, red maples and some cypresses. Wax myrtles grow on the dry edges of the stream's banks which could accommodate campers. The St. Marys continues to flow inland maintaining considerable depth and a width of 125 feet all the way to Traders Hill, the end of navigation for vessels penetrating up river through the 19th century.

ST. MARYS RIVER OCEAN ENTRANCE

St. Marys River Entrance from the Atlantic begins at a large red and white buoy topped with a red sphere and marked with the letters "STM". This lighted buoy lies at 30°40'48"N and 081°11'47"W and after passing it on either side you will soon pick up the line of buoys leading inland and between two breakwaters which disappear at high tide. See chartlet #084. Beware of these submerged breakwaters. The entrance range, equipped with powerful white lights clearly visible even in bright daylight, further assists with navigation.

Sailing by Reid's Bluff on St. Marys River.

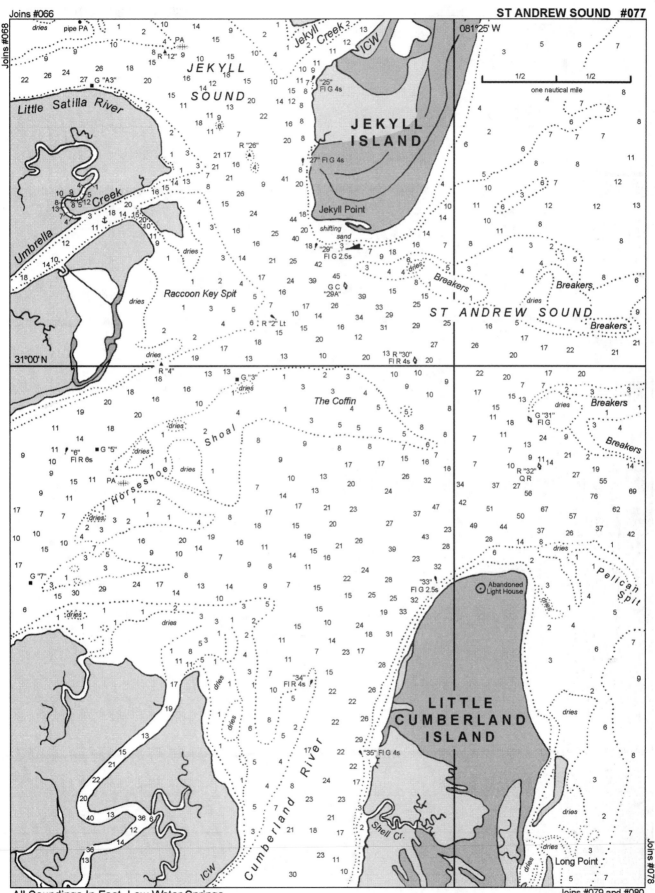

Joins #066

Joins #068

dries   pipe PA

Little Satilla River

J E K Y L L

S O U N D

R "12"

G "A3"

R "26"

Umbrella   Creek

JEKYLL

ISLAND

Jekyll Creek

ICW

"25"
Fl G 4s

"27" Fl G 4s

Jekyll Point

shifting
sand

"29"
Fl G 2.5s

G C
"29A"

R "2" Lt

Raccoon Key Spit

dries

dries

ST ANDREW SOUND

Breakers

Breakers

Breakers

081°25' W

1/2   1/2
one nautical mile

31°00' N

R "4"

G "3"

dries

The Coffin

Horseshoe   Shoal

dries

dries

"6"
Fl R 6s

G "5"

PA

G "7"

R "30"
Fl R 4s

R "31"
Fl G

R "32"
Q R

Breakers

Pelican Spit

"33"
Fl G 2.5s

Abandoned
Light House

LITTLE
CUMBERLAND
ISLAND

Cumberland River

dries

dries

"34"
Fl R 4s

dries

"35" Fl G 4s

Shell Cr.

dries

dries

Long Point

ICW

Joins #078

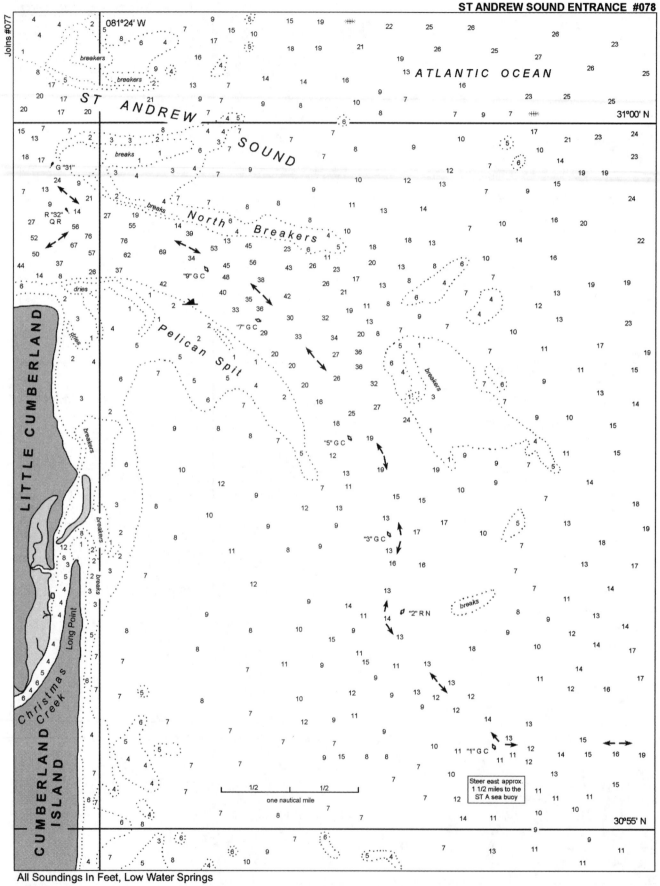

All Soundings In Feet, Low Water Springs

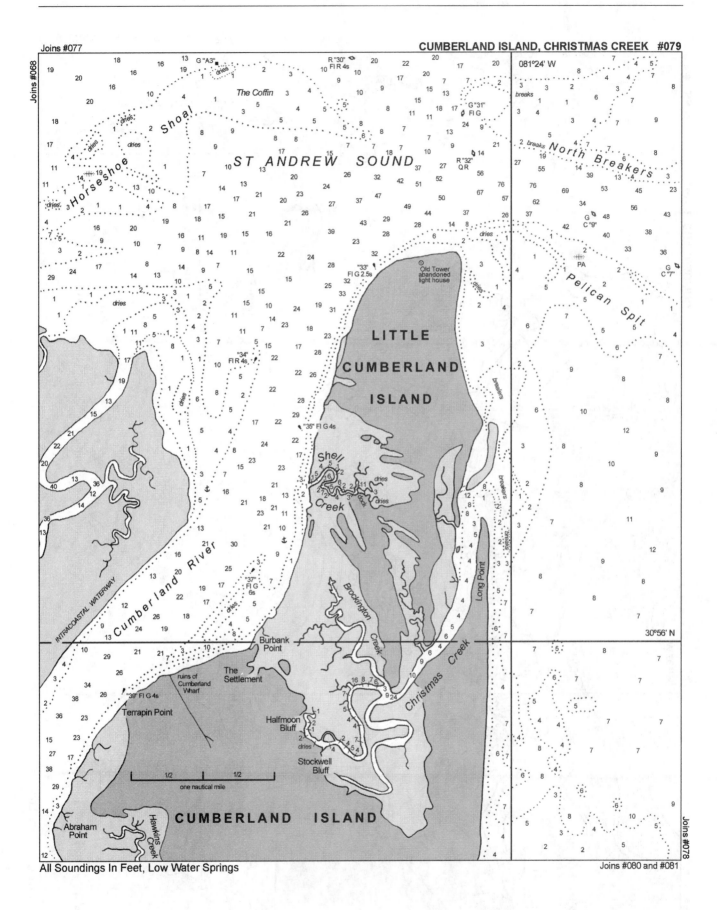

All Soundings In Feet, Low Water Springs

Joins #080 and #081

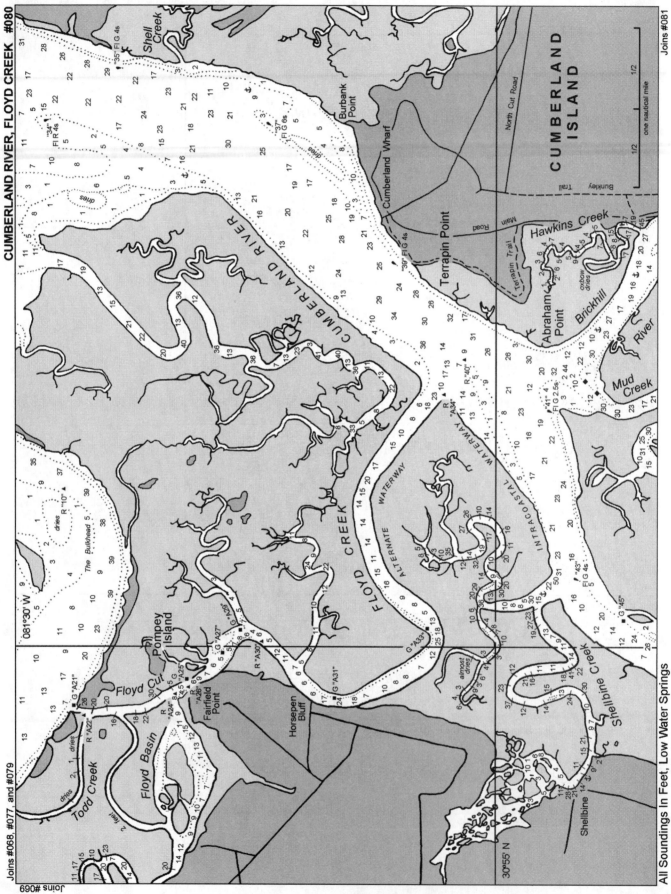

Joins #068, #077, and #079

Joins #069

Joins #081

All Soundings In Feet, Low Water Springs

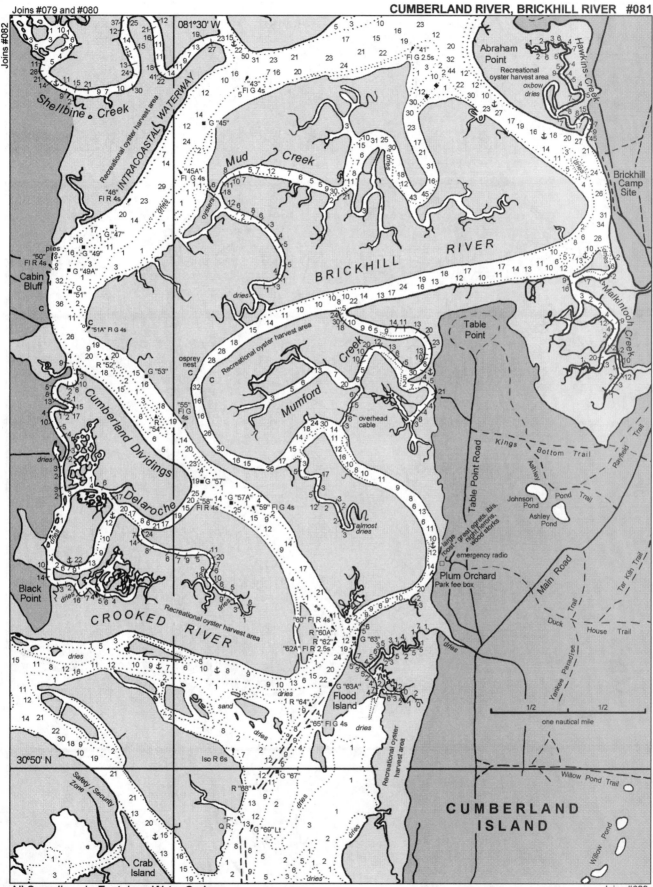

081°30' W

Joins #082

Shellbine Creek

INTRACOASTAL WATERWAY

Recreational oyster harvest area

"46" Fl R 4s

"43" Fl G 4s

G "45"

"45A" Fl G 4s

oysters

Mud Creek

Abraham Point

Recreational oyster harvest area

oxbow dries

Hawkins Creek

Brickhill Camp Site

"41" Fl G 2.5s

BRICKHILL RIVER

dries

Malkintooh Creek

piles

"50" Fl R 4s

Cabin Bluff

"47"

G "49"

G "49A"

G "51"

"51A" Fl G 4s

osprey nest

R "52"

G "53"

"55" Fl G 4s

R "54"

Recreational oyster harvest area

Mumford Creek

overhead cable

almost dries

Table Point

Kings Bottom Trail

Rayfield Trail

Ashley Pond

Johnson Pond

Ashley Pond

Table Point Road

Cumberland Dividings

Delaroche

G "57"

"58" Fl R 4s

G "57A"

"59" Fl G 4s

large roost - great egrets, ibis, night herons, wood storks

emergency radio

Plum Orchard
Park fee box

Main Road

Tar Kiln Trail

Black Point

CROOKED RIVER

Recreational oyster harvest area

dries

"60" Fl R 4s

R "60A"

R "62"

"62A" Fl R 2.5s

G "63"

Duck House Trail

Yankee Paradise Trail

30°50' N

dries

sand

dries

G "63A"

R "64"

Flood Island

Recreational oyster harvest area

**CUMBERLAND
ISLAND**

Safety/ Security Zone

Iso R 6s

"65" Fl G 4s

dries

Willow Pond Trail

R "88"

G "67"

"F" Q R

"69" Lt

Willow Pond

Crab Island

dries

1/2   1/2
one nautical mile

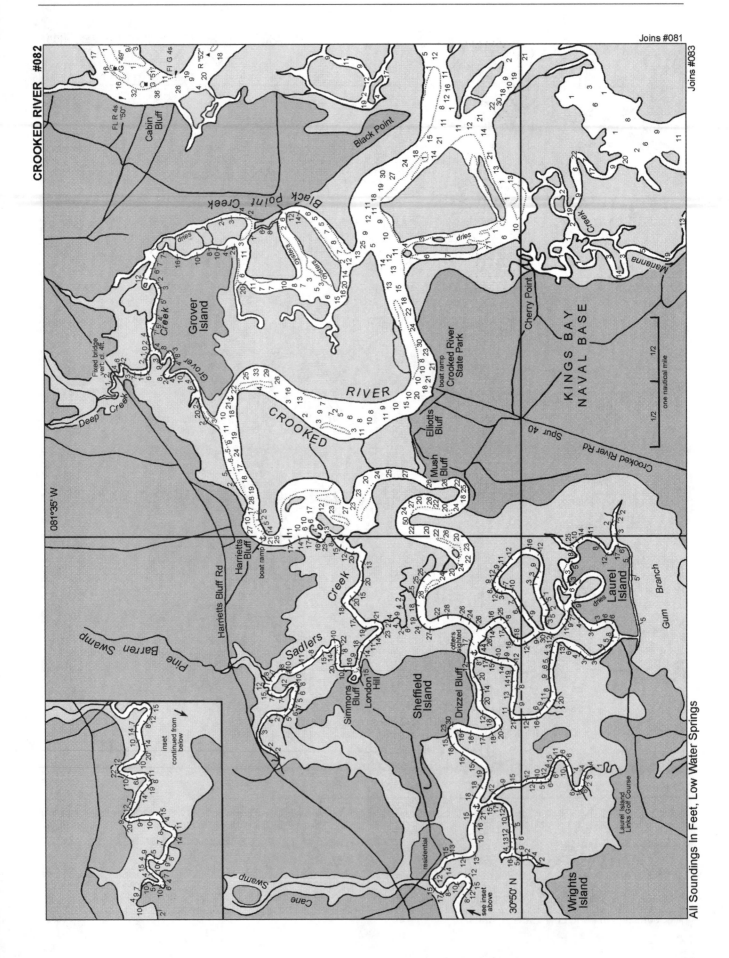

CROOKED RIVER #082

Joins #083

All Soundings In Feet, Low Water Springs

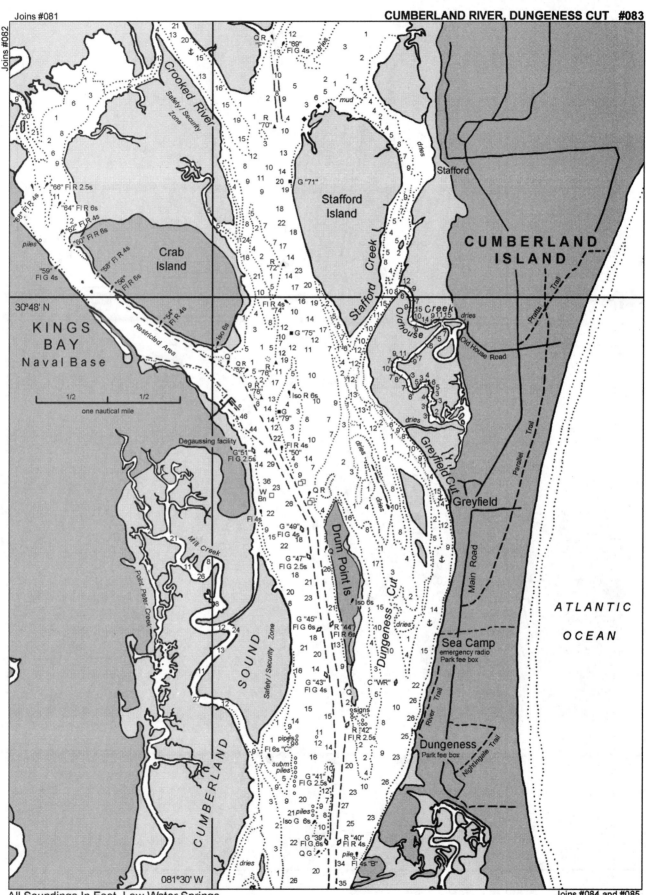

All Soundings In Feet, Low Water Springs

Joins #084 and #085

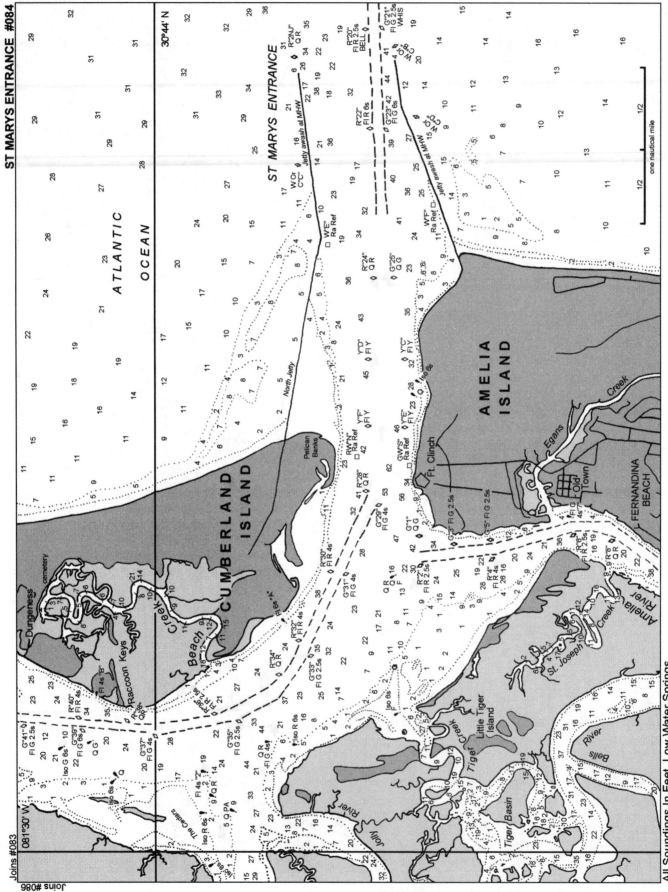

All Soundings In Feet, Low Water Springs

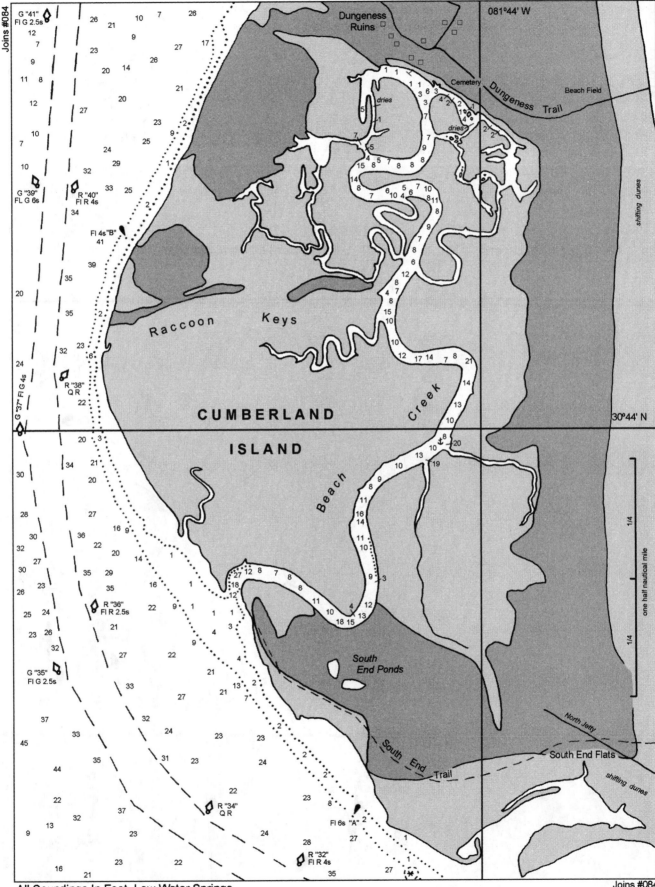

Joins #084

081°44' W

Dungeness
Ruins

Cemetery

Dungeness Trail

Beach Field

dries

dries

shifting dunes

Raccoon Keys

Fl 4s"B"
41

G "41"
Fl G 2.5s

G "39"
FL G 6s

R "40"
Fl R 4s

R "38"
Q R

G "37" Fl G 4s

CUMBERLAND

ISLAND

Beach Creek

30°44' N

1/4

one half nautical mile

1/4

R "36"
Fl R 2.5s

G "35"
Fl G 2.5s

South
End Ponds

North Jetty

South End Flats

South End Trail

shifting dunes

R "34"
Q R

Fl 6s "A"

R "32"
Fl R 4s

All Soundings In Feet, Low Water Springs

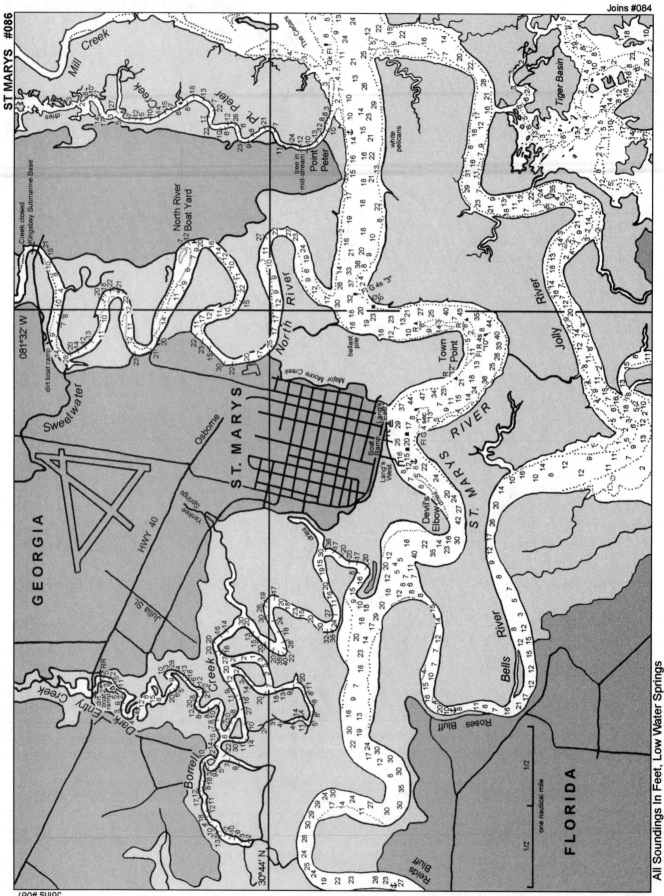

GEORGIA

FLORIDA

ST. MARYS

North River

St. Marys River

Bells River

Jolly River

Mill Creek

Pt. Peter Creek

Sweetwater

Entry Creek

Dark Creek

Borrell Creek

Point Peter

Town Point

Devils Elbow

Roses Bluff

Reids Bluff

Tiger Basin

Kingsbay Submarine Base

North River Boat Yard

Major Moore Creek

Osborne

Yankee Springs

Julia St.

HWY 40

081°32' W

30°44' N

dirt boat ramp

Creek closed

white pelicans

ballast pile

Boat Ramp

Lang's East

Lang's West

FIG 4 sec

All Soundings In Feet, Low Water Springs

one nautical mile

1/2   1/2   1/2

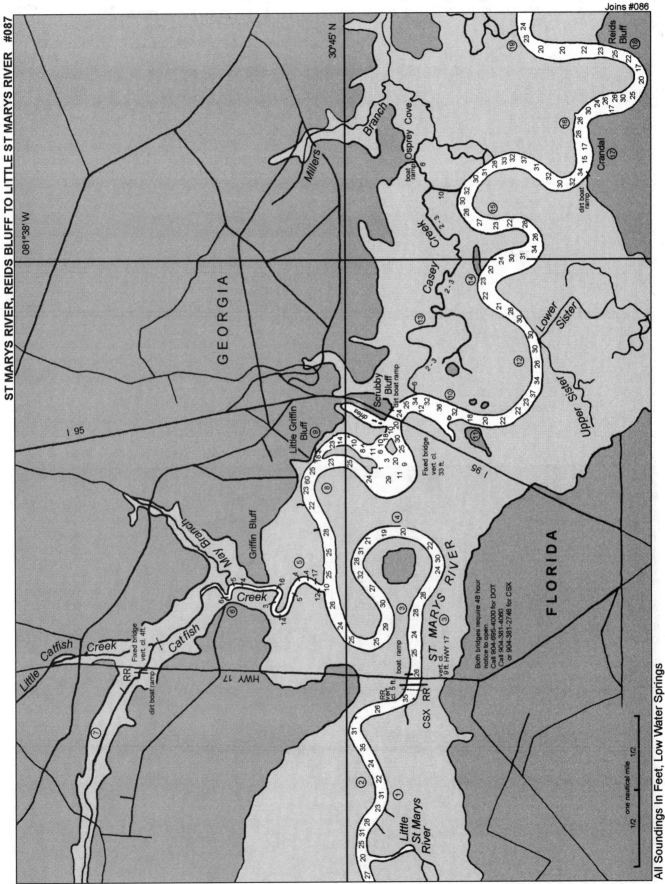

ST MARYS RIVER, REIDS BLUFF TO LITTLE ST MARYS RIVER #087

Joins #086

081°38' W

30°45' N

GEORGIA

I 95

Millers

Branch

Osprey Cove

boat ramp

Casey Creek

Scrubby Bluff

Little Griffin Bluff

Griffin Bluff

May Branch

Catfish Creek

Little Catfish Creek

Fixed bridge vert. cl. 4ft.

dirt boat ramp

RR

HWY 17

Creek

dirt boat ramp

Fixed bridge vert. cl. 33 ft.

I 95

Lower Sister

Upper Sister

Reids Bluff

Crandal

dirt boat ramp

Reids Bluff

ST MARYS RIVER

vert. cl. 9 ft. HWY 17

boat ramp

RR vert. cl. 35 ft.

CSX RR

Both bridges require 48 hour notice to open.
Call 904-695-4000 for DOT
Call 904-381-4060
or 904-381-2746 for CSX

FLORIDA

Little St Marys River

All Soundings In Feet, Low Water Springs

one nautical mile

1/2   1/2

Joins #088

Shore Descriptions for Chart #087
ST. MARYS RIVER, REIDS BLUFF TO
LITTLE ST. MARYS

1 .... The landscape from Little St. Marys to Scrubby Bluff continues as marsh with scattered trees
2 .... Marshy foreshore, drowned trees, pine forest
3 .... Marsh, scattered trees
4 .... Marsh, scattered dead trees
5 .... Marsh
6 .... Farm
7 .... Swamp, narrow channel through thick drowned froest
8 .... Marsh
9 .... Residential
10 .... Marsh
11 ...... Landing possible on hammock
12 .... Marsh
13 .... Marsh
14 .... Wild growth hammock, landing possible
15 .... Marsh
16 .... Marsh
17 .... House
18 .... High dune bluffs, mixed forest, pine forest further in
19 .... Marsh

Shore Descriptions for Chart #088
ST. MARYS RIVER, LITTLE ST. MARYS TO KINGS FERRY

1 .... Dry land, thick undergrowth
2 .... Low land, thick undergrowth
3 .... Both dry and flooded banks, landing possible
4 .... Dry, landing possible
5 .... Forested, medium thick undergrowth
6 .... Forest, thick undergrowth
7 .... Flooded forest
8 .... Houses
9 .... Flooded, occasional dry spots
10 .... 6 to 12 foot bluffs, mixed growth forest, landing possible
11 .... Flooded forest
12 .... 2 foot bluff, forest with thick undergrowth
13 ..... Thick forest of thin trunk trees
14 .... 4 to 6 foot bluff, forest, landing possible
15 .... 3 foot bank, pine forest
16 .... Drowned forest
17 .... House
18 .... Drowned forest
19 .... 1 foot bank, forest with thick undergrowth
20 ..... Thick forest of thin trunk trees
21 .... 1 foot bank, forest with thick undergrowth
22 .... Dry land, residential section
23 .... Houses with docks
24 .... Wet, low forest
25 .... Wet, thin trunk mixed forest, wild azaleas
26 .... Drowned forest
27 .... Wet forest
28 .... Low bank, forest with thin underbrush
29 ..... Thin trunk forest, hard to land
30 .... Marsh
31 ...... Marsh, scattered cypress trees

White pelicans along St. Marys River.

Joins #087

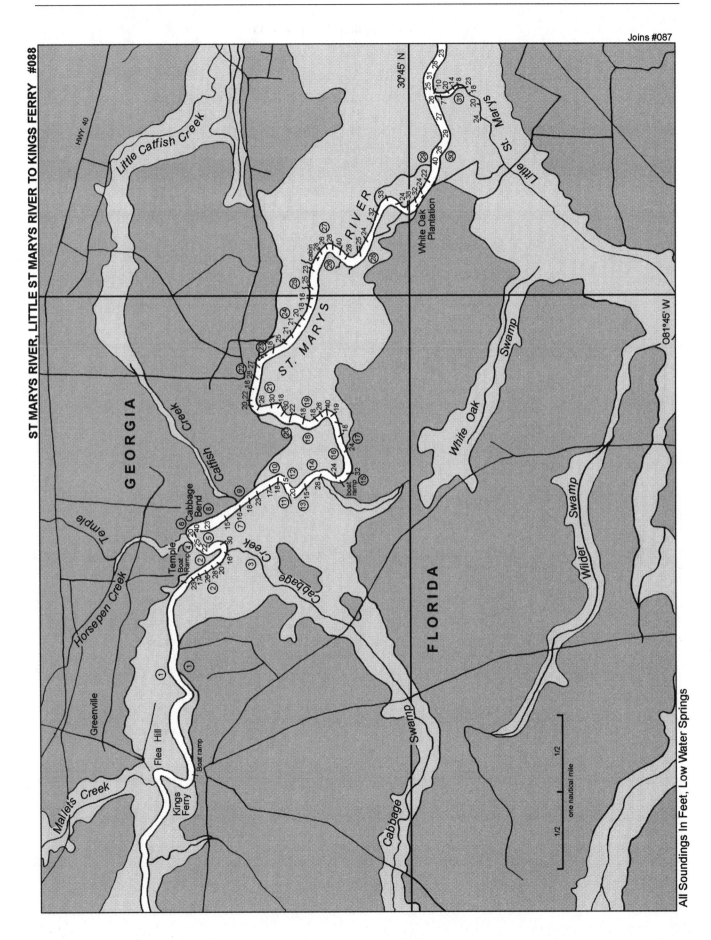

ST MARYS RIVER, LITTLE ST MARYS RIVER TO KINGS FERRY #088

30°45' N

081°45' W

All Soundings In Feet, Low Water Springs

one nautical mile

APPENDIX

IMPORTANT INFORMATION ABOUT THE LIST OF NAVIGATIONAL AIDS

The information in the light list has not been fully verified and is subject to change without notice. We do not intend to represent this information as accurate. Do not use this information for navigational purposes. This list serves to alert the navigator to the possible existence of navigational aids in the area.

Key to Light List abbreviations:

B ....buoy	LB .... lighted buoy	Q .... quick
DBN ....daybeacon	LT .... light	R .... red
F .... fixed	Mo .... Morse code	Racon .... radar responder beacon
Fl .... flashing	OC ...... occulting, the total duration of	RBN .... radio beacon
G .... green	light in each period is clearly longer	RF .... range front
Iso .... a rhythmic light in which all	than the total duration of darkness	RGE .... range
durations of light and	and in which the intervals of	RR .... range rear
darkness are equal	darkness are of equal duration	S .... seconds
Jty ....jetty	OR .... orange	W ....white

---

LIST OF NAVIGATIONAL AIDS

SAVANNAH RIVER TO PORT WENTWORTH

DESCRIPTION	LOCATION	APPROXIMATE LATITUDE			APPROXIMATE LONGITUDE		
		DEG.	MIN.	SEC.	DEG.	MIN.	SEC.
Mo (A) W	Tybee Sea Buoy	31°	57'	52.517"N	080°	43'	09.772"W
LBB 1 Fl G 2.5s	Tybee Ship Channel	31°	58'	17.471"N	080°	44'	12.016"W
LB 2 Fl R 2.5s	Tybee Ship Channel	31°	58'	24.462"N	080°	44'	07.657"W
LB 3 Fl G 4s	Tybee Ship Channel	31°	58'	43.420"N	080°	45'	09.359"W
LB 4 Fl R 4s	Tybee ship Channel	31°	58'	50.426"N	080°	45'	04.980"W
LB 5 Fl G 2.5s	Tybee ship Channel	31°	59'	09.587"N	080°	46'	06.921"W
LB 6 Fl R 2.5s	Tybee ship Channel	31°	59'	16.574"N	080°	46'	02.484"W
LB 7 Q G	Tybee ship Channel	31°	59'	39.733"N	080°	47'	07.021"W
LGB 8 Q R	Bloody Pt Rng	31°	59'	47.241"N	080°	46'	59.717"W
LB 9 Fl G 2.5s	Bloody Pt Rng	32°	00'	23.974"N	080°	47'	49.795"W
LB 10 Fl R 2.5s	Bloody Pt Rng	32°	00'	28.508"N	080°	47'	42.792"W
RFL Q Fl W	south of Tybee shipchannel	32°	00'	25.495"N	080°	48'	43.929"W
LB 11 Fl G 4s	Bloody Pt Rng	32°	01'	09.071"N	080°	48'	30.595"W

DESCRIPTION	LOCATION	APPROXIMATE LATITUDE			APPROXIMATE LONGITUDE		
		DEG.	MIN.	SEC.	DEG.	MIN.	SEC.
LB 12 Fl R 4s	Bloody Pt Rng	32°	01'	13.659"N	080°	48'	23.535"W
LBB 13 Q G	Bloody Pt Rng	32°	01'	48.996"N	080°	49'	14.395"W
LB 14 Fl R 2.5s	Bloody Pt Rng	32°	01'	58.381"N	080°	49'	06.509"W
RFL Q W	Jones Island Rng	32°	02'	31.746"N	080°	51'	10.057"W
RRL Iso W 6s	Jones Island Rng	32°	02'	37.459"N	080°	51'	29.841"W
LB 15 Fl G 2.5s	Jones Island Rng	32°	02'	01.963"N	080°	49'	49.016"W
LBB 17 Fl G 4s	Jones Island Rng	32°	02'	12.016"N	080°	50'	30.976"W
LB 18 Fl R 4s	Jones Island Rng	32°	02'	22.467"N	080°	50'	25.896"W
Jty LT Fl W 4s	Savannah Riv N Jty	32°	02'	29.587"N	080°	50'	57.196"W
Jty LT Fl W 2.5s	Savannah Riv S Jty	32°	02'	04.452"N	080°	51'	04.116"W
LT 1 Fl G 4s	S Ch	32°	01'	45.806"N	080°	51'	09.196"W
DBN 3 G	S Ch	32°	01'	35.817"N	080°	51'	17.405"W
LT 5 Fl G 4s	S Ch	32°	01'	14.870"N	080°	51'	53.498"W
LT 2 Fl R 4s	Lazaretto Cr	32°	01'	05.631"N	080°	52'	54.340"W
Obst B 3 G	Lazaretto Cr	32°	00'	34.500"N	080°	53'	2.000"W
LB WR 3A Fl G 2.5s	Lazaretto Cr	32°	00'	35.000"N	080°	53'	14.000"W
RFL Q R	North of Tybee shipchannel	32°	02'	31.746"N	080°	51'	10.057"W
RRL Iso R 6s	North of Tybee shipchannel	32°	02'	37.459"N	080°	51'	29.841"W
DBN 1 G	Calibogue Sound Ent	32°	02'	50.740"N	080°	50'	31.604"W
LT 3 Fl G 4s	Calibogue Sound Ent	32°	03'	49.900"N	080°	49'	49.616"W
LT 5 Fl G 6s	Calibogue Sound Ent	32°	05'	00.690"N	080°	50'	02.086"W
LT 6 Fl R 6s	Calibogue Sound Ent	32°	06'	22.190"N	080°	49'	41.688"W
LB 20 Fl R 4s	Tybee Knoll Cut Rng	32°	02'	16.867"N	080°	51'	26.397"W
LB 21 Fl G 4s	Tybee Knoll Cut Rng	32°	02'	05.567"N	080°	52'	23.398"W
LB 24 Fl R 4s	Tybee Knoll Cut Rng	32°	02'	07.967"N	080°	53'	24.999"W
LB 25 Fl G 4s	Tybee Knoll Cut Rng	32°	02'	02.027"N	080°	53'	29.728"W
RFL Q W	Tybee Knoll Cut Rng	32°	02'	00.035"N	080°	53'	54.430"W
RRL Iso W 6s	Tybee Knoll Cut Rng	32°	01'	57.099"N	080°	54'	25.770"W
RFL Q G	Long Island Crossing Lower	32°	02'	08.925"N	080°	55'	11.608"W
RRL Iso G 6s	Long Island Crossing Lower	32°	01'	48.622"N	080°	54'	50.864"W
LB 26 Fl R 4s	New Channel Rng	32°	02'	20.165"N	080°	55'	06.499"W
RFL Q G	New Channel Rng	32°	02'	21.478"N	080°	55'	37.241"W
RRL Iso G 6s	New Channel Rng	32°	02'	27.208"N	080°	56'	18.489"W
LB 28 Fl R 4s	Long Island Crossing	32°	02'	31.436"N	080°	55'	29.648"W
LB 30 Fl R 4s	Savannah River	32°	03'	02.244"N	080°	56'	00.835"W
LB 32 Fl R 4s	Savannah River	32°	03'	38.560"N	080°	56'	38.700"W
LB 33 Fl G 4s	Savannah River	32°	04'	00.158"N	080°	57'	10.100"W
RFL Q R	Lower Flats Rng	32°	04'	16.362"N	080°	57'	17.502"W
RRL Iso R 6s	Lower Flats Rng	32°	04'	15.027"N	080°	57'	08.083"W
RFL Q R	Long Island Crossing Up	32°	04'	20.806"N	080°	57'	26.487"W
RRL Iso R 6s	Long Island Crossing Up	32°	04'	31.814"N	080°	57'	37.672"W
LB 35 Fl G 4s	Lower Flats Rng	32°	04'	16.983"N	080°	57'	44.799"W
Jty LT Fl W 2.5s	Bird Is	32°	04'	18.000"N	080°	58'	06.000"W
LT 50 Fl R 4s	Fields Cut	32°	04'	27.457"N	080°	57'	42.155"W
LT 2 Fl R 4s	Elba Is	32°	04'	17.399"N	080°	58'	22.117"W
LB 36 Fl R 4s	Lower Flats Rng	32°	04'	29.552"N	080°	58'	18.606"W
LT 37 Fl G 4s	Elba Is	32°	04'	23.422"N	080°	58'	29.533"W
LT 39 Fl G 4s	Elba Is	32°	04'	32.955"N	080°	58'	55.237"W
LB 40 Fl R 4s	Elba Is	32°	04'	40.955"N	080°	58'	49.201"W
RFL Q W	Upper Flats Rng	32°	04'	35.036"N	080°	59'	01.736"W
RRL Iso W 6s	Upper Flats Rng	32°	04'	24.645"N	080°	58'	56.738"W
LT 42 Fl R 4s	Elba Is Training Wall	32°	05'	32.519"N	080°	59'	24.633"W
LT 43 Fl G 4s	The Bight Channel	32°	05'	25.939"N	080°	59'	37.390"W
RFL Q W	Elba Is Basin	32°	05'	49.050"N	080°	59'	38.791"W
RRL Iso W 6s	Elba Is Basin	32°	05'	58.610"N	080°	59'	43.531"W
Fl W 2.5s	LNG Term S Mooring	32°	05'	06.753"N	080°	59'	29.401"W
Fl W 2.5s	LNG Term S Mooring	32°	05'	20.452"N	080°	59'	32.801"W
LT 44 Fl R 4s	The Bight Channel	32°	06'	01.943"N	080°	59'	56.877"W
LT 45 Fl G 4s	The Bight Channel	32°	05'	52.626"N	081°	00'	05.505"W

DESCRIPTION	LOCATION	APPROXIMATE LATITUDE DEG.	MIN.	SEC.	APPROXIMATE LONGITUDE DEG.	MIN.	SEC.
LT 46 Fl R 4s	The Bight Channel	32°	06'	09.373"N	081°	00'	15.481"W
LT 47 Fl G 4s	The Bight Channel	32°	05'	58.588"N	081°	00'	32.090"W
LT 48 Fl R 4s	The Bight Channel	32°	06'	10.668"N	081°	00'	32.024"W
RFL Q W	Ft. Jackson Lower	32°	06'	07.636"N	081°	00'	45.404"W
RRL Iso W 6s	Ft. Jackson Lower	32°	06'	13.088"N	081°	00'	41.219"W
LT 49 Fl G 4s	Elba Is	32°	05'	46.926"N	081°	00'	52.942"W
LB 50 Fl R 4s	Barnwell Is Flats	32°	05'	31.938"N	081°	01'	17.425"W
DBN A 1	South Ch	32°	05'	28.996"N	081°	01'	05.714"W
RFL Q R	Oglethorpe	32°	05'	23.329"N	081°	01'	10.847"W
RRL Iso R 6s	Oglethorpe	32°	05'	29.307"N	081°	00'	54.432"W
RFL Q R	Ft. Jackson Up	32°	05'	12.424"N	081°	01'	27.864"W
RRL Iso R 6s	Ft. Jackson Up	32°	05'	06.748"N	081°	01'	32.256"W
LB 52 Fl R 4s	Barnwell Is Flats	32°	05'	17.990"N	081°	01'	34.701"W
LB 52 A Fl R 2.5s	Barnwell Is Flats	32°	05'	01.156"N	081°	02'	18.139"W
LT 53 Fl G 4s	Ft. Jackson	32°	04'	57.213"N	081°	02'	11.866"W
LB 54 Fl R 4s	Fig Is Jty	32°	04'	57.604"N	081°	02'	30.835"W
LT 56 Fl R 4s	Fig Is	32°	04'	53.162"N	081°	02'	53.334"W
LT 57 Fl G 4s	Fig Is	32°	04'	47.467"N	081°	03'	36.762"W
LT 58 Fl R 4s	ACL TB	32°	04'	54.200"N	081°	03'	59.700"W
LT 60 Fl R 4s	ACL TB	32°	04'	52.182"N	081°	04'	14.636"W
LT 62 Fl R 4s	City Front Channel	32°	04'	48.833"N	081°	04'	29.658"W
LT 4 Fl R 2.5s	Marsh Is TB	32°	06'	41.712"N	081°	07'	15.890"W
LT 6 Fl R 2.5s	Marsh Is TB	32°	06'	49.933"N	081°	07'	22.826"W
LT 8 Fl R 4s	Kings Is TB	32°	06'	59.603"N	081°	07'	37.882"W
RFL Q Y	Kings Is TB	32°	07'	34.567"N	081°	08'	03.467"W
RRL Iso Y 6s	Kings Is TB	32°	07'	33.154"N	081°	08'	02.215"W
LT 12 Fl R 6s	Kings Is TB	32°	07'	54.581"N	081°	08'	04.510"W
LT 14 Fl R 4s	Kings Is TB	32°	08'	07.924"N	081°	08'	14.144"W
LT 16 Fl R 2.5s	Kings Is	32°	08'	10.912"N	081°	08'	23.030"W
LT 22 Fl R 6s	Pt Wentworth Ch	32°	08'	41.881"N	081°	08'	25.010"W
RFL "B" Q W	Pt Wentworth Ch Rng	32°	08'	54.713"N	081°	08'	30.377"W
RRL "B" Iso W 6s	Pt Wentworth Ch Rng	32°	08'	53.891"N	081°	08'	29.251"W
RFL "A" Q R	Pt Wentworth Ch Rng	32°	08'	57.254"N	081°	08'	32.502"W
RRL "A" Iso R 6s	Pt Wentworth Ch Rng	32°	08'	58.755"N	081°	08'	32.829"W
RFL "C" Q R	Pt Wentworth Ch Rng	32°	09'	01.588"N	081°	08'	36.392"W
RRL "C" Iso R 6s	Pt Wentworth Ch Rng	32°	09'	01.187"N	081°	08'	34.697"W
DBN 24 R	Pt Wentworth Ch Rng	32°	09'	06.431"N	081°	08'	44.524"W
LT 26 Fl R 4s	Pt Wentworth Ch Rng	32°	09'	10.139"N	081°	08'	58.651"W
LT 28 Fl R 4s	Pt Wentworht Ch Rng	32°	09'	14.264"N	081°	09'	05.448"W
RFL "D" Q W	Pt Wentworth Ch Rng	32°	09'	17.131"N	081°	09'	16.699"W
RRL "D" Iso W 6s	Pt Wentworth Ch Rng	32°	09'	17.939"N	081°	09'	18.148"W
LT 30 Fl R 4s	Pt Wentworth Ch Rng	32°	09'	17.737"N	081°	09'	08.867"W
LT 32 Fl R 4s	Pt Wentworth Ch Rng	32°	09'	22.662"N	081°	09'	09.930"W
RFL "E" Q W	Pt Wentworth Ch Rng	32°	09'	25.877"N	081°	09'	20.357"W
RRL "E" Iso W 6s	Pt Wentworth Ch Rng	32°	09'	27.497"N	081°	09'	21.764"W
LT 34 Fl R 4s	Pt Wentworth Ch Rng	32°	09'	29.630"N	081°	09'	10.405"W

FIELDS CUT TO WASSAW SOUND

DESCRIPTION	LOCATION	APPROXIMATE LATITUDE DEG.	MIN.	SEC.	APPROXIMATE LONGITUDE DEG.	MIN.	SEC.
LT 47 Fl G 4s	Fields Cut	32°	05'	19.731"N	080°	55'	43.907"W
B 48 R nun	Fields Cut	32°	05'	20.740"N	080°	55'	47.681"W
LT 50 Fl R 4 s	Fields Cut	32°	04'	27.457"N	080°	57'	42.155"W
Jty LT Fl W 2.5 s	Savannah River	32°	04'	18.000"N	080°	58'	06.000"W
LT 2 Fl R 4s	Elba Is Cut	32°	04'	17.399"N	080°	58'	22.117"W
Jty LT Fl W 2.5 s	Elba Is Cut	32°	04'	17.947"N	080°	58'	06.964"W
LT 4 Fl R 4s	Elba Is Cut	32°	04'	13.727"N	080°	58'	31.932"W

DESCRIPTION	LOCATION	APPROXIMATE LATITUDE DEG. MIN. SEC.			APPROXIMATE LONGITUDE DEG. MIN. SEC.		
LT 6 Fl R 4s	Elba Is Cut	32°	04'	06.672"N	080°	58'	54.186"W
DBN 8 R	Elba Is Cut	32°	03'	55.227"N	080°	59'	27.068"W
LT 10 Fl Q R	Elba Is Cut	32°	03'	49.905"N	080°	59'	41.816"W
DBN 12 R	Elba Is Cut	32°	04'	03.970"N	081°	00'	13.465"W
DBN 14 R	Elba Is Cut	32°	04'	11.130"N	081°	00'	22.662"W
LT 15 Fl G 4s	Elba Is Cut	32°	04'	14.560"N	081°	00'	28.329"W

Alternate Route from Savannah

DESCRIPTION	LOCATION	DEG.	MIN.	SEC.	DEG.	MIN.	SEC.
DBN A1 G	S Ch from Savannah	32°	05'	28.996"N	081°	01'	05.714"W
DBN A4 R	S Ch from Savannah	32°	05'	22.147"N	081°	00'	54.321"W
DBN A5 G	S Ch from Savannah	32°	05'	22.221"N	081°	00'	45.744"W
DBN A6 R	S Ch from Savannah	32°	05'	17.337"N	081°	00'	45.076"W
DBN A8 R	S Ch from Savannah	32°	05'	09.486"N	081°	00'	29.475"W
DBN A12 R	S Ch from Savannah	32°	04'	47.238"N	080°	59'	55.408"W
DBN AI5 G	S Ch from Savannah	32°	04'	37.382"N	081°	00'	01.101"W
DBN A17 G	S Ch from Savannah	32°	04'	18.160"N	081°	00'	16.534"W
DBN A18 R	S Ch from Savannah	32°	04'	20.324"N	081°	00'	26.781"W
LT 19 Fl G 4s	Wilmington Riv	32°	04'	24.396"N	081°	00'	41.499"W
DBN 21 G	Wilmington Riv	32°	04'	23.608"N	081°	00'	50.633"W
RF DBN "A"	Wilmington Riv	32°	04'	10.265"N	081°	01'	08.472"W
RR DBN "A"	Wilmington Riv	32°	04'	05.525"N	081°	01'	14.152"W
RF DBN "B"	Wilmington Riv	32°	04'	09.355"N	081°	01'	20.062"W
RR DBN "B"	Wilmington Riv	32°	04'	08.285"N	081°	01'	23.532"W
LT 25 Fl G 4s	Wilmington Riv	32°	03'	56.595"N	081°	01'	19.704"W
DBN 27 G	Wilmington Riv	32°	03'	49.250"N	081°	01'	40.609"W
DBN 29 G	Wilmington Riv	32°	03'	17.982"N	081°	01'	47.644"W
LT 30 Q R	Wilmington Riv	32°	02'	59.595"N	081°	01'	47.074"W
LT 31 Fl G 4s	Wilmington Riv	32°	02'	39.207"N	081°	02'	26.507"W
DBN 32 R	Wilmington Riv	32°	02'	30.855"N	081°	02'	33.376"W
DBN 33 G	Wilmington Riv	32°	02'	24.547"N	081°	02'	35.946"W
LT 34 Fl R 4s	Wilmington Riv	32°	02'	13.827"N	081°	02'	46.195"W
DBN 35 G	Wilmington Riv	32°	01'	48.316"N	081°	02'	52.743"W
LT 36 Fl R 2.5s	Wilmington Riv	32°	01'	22.611"N	081°	02'	35.482"W
DBN 36A R	Wilmington Riv	32°	01'	14.379"N	081°	02'	12.742"W
LT 37 Fl G 4s	Wilmington Riv	32°	01'	20.022"N	081°	01'	49.187"W
LT 37A Fl G 4s	Wilmington Riv	32°	01'	20.923"N	081°	01'	21.826"W
DBN 38 R	Wilmington Riv	32°	01'	14.329"N	081°	01'	21.202"W
LT 40 Fl R 4s	Skidaway Riv	32°	00'	40.700"N	081°	00'	56.828"W

WASSAW SOUND

DESCRIPTION	LOCATION	APPROXIMATE LATITUDE DEG. MIN. SEC.			APPROXIMATE LONGITUDE DEG. MIN. SEC.		
LB "2W" Fl R 4s	Offshore	31°	51'	36"N	080°	53'	00"W
LB 4 Fl R 6s	Offshore	31°	52'	16"N	080°	53'	23"W
B 6 R nun	Offshore	31°	52'	43"N	080°	53'	30"W
LB 8 Fl R 2.5s	Wassaw Snd	31°	53'	24"N	080°	53'	30"W
B 9 G can	Wassaw Snd	31°	53'	49"N	080°	53'	59"W
LB 10 Fl R 6s	Wassaw Snd	31°	54'	03"N	080°	53'	52"W
B 11 G can	Wassaw Snd	31°	54'	11"N	080°	54'	38"W
B 13 G can	Wassaw Snd	31°	54'	32"N	080°	55'	17"W
LB 14 Fl R 2.5s	Wassaw Snd	31°	55'	06"N	080°	55'	19"W
DBN 1 G	Bull Riv	31°	55'	42"N	080°	55'	20"W
DBN 3 G	Bull Riv	31°	56'	14"N	080°	55'	53"W
DBN 5 G	Bull Riv	31°	56'	52"N	080°	56'	15"W
DBN 6 R	Bull Riv	31°	57'	31"N	080°	56'	03"W
DBN BR	Half Moon Riv	31°	57'	32"N	080°	56'	31"W
LT 16 Fl R 4s	Cabbage Is Spit	31°	55'	09"N	080°	56'	44"W

DESCRIPTION	LOCATION	APPROXIMATE LATITUDE DEG.	MIN.	SEC.	APPROXIMATE LONGITUDE DEG.	MIN.	SEC.
Shl Daybeacon	Cabbage Is Spit Shl	31°	55'	41"N	080°	57'	28"W
LT 17 Fl G 4s	Wassaw Is	31°	55'	11"N	080°	57'	51"W
LT 19 Fl G 4s	Romerly Marsh Cr.	31°	55'	58"N	080°	58'	35"W
DBN 21 G	Romerly Marsh	31°	56'	28"N	080°	59'	03"W
DBN 20 R	Cabbage Is	31°	56'	12"N	080°	58'	12"W
LT 22 Fl R 6s	Cabbage Is	31°	57'	15"N	081°	00'	03"W
LT 23 Fl G 6s	Wilmington Riv	31°	58'	27"N	081°	00'	36"W
LT 25 Fl G 2.5s	Wilmington Riv	31°	59'	13"N	081°	00'	17"W
LT 27 Fl G 4s	Wilmington Riv	32°	00'	25"N	081°	00'	24"W
LT 29 Fl G 6s	Wilmington Riv	32°	00'	34"N	081°	00'	36"W

INTRACOASTAL WATERWAY
SKIDAWAY RIVER TO GREEN ISLAND SOUND

DESCRIPTION	LOCATION	APPROXIMATE LATITUDE DEG.	MIN.	SEC.	APPROXIMATE LONGITUDE DEG.	MIN.	SEC.
LT 40 Fl R 4s	Skidaway Riv	32°	00'	40.709"N	081°	00'	56.828"W
LT 42 Fl R 4s	Skidaway Riv	31°	59'	35.749"N	081°	01'	13.832"W
DBN 44 R	Skidaway Riv	31°	59'	01.073"N	081°	02'	13.084"W
LT 43 Fl G 4s	Skidaway Riv	31°	59'	15.068"N	081°	02'	02.783"W
DBN 44A R	Skidaway Riv	31°	58'	55.673"N	081°	02'	18.138"W
DBN 46A R	Skidaway Riv	31°	58'	43.042"N	081°	03'	17.266"W
DBN 48 R	Skidaway Riv	31°	58'	35.592"N	081°	03'	13.446"W
DBN 48A R	Skidaway Riv	31°	58'	24.673"N	081°	03'	09.879"W
DBN 50 R	Skidaway Riv	31°	58'	06.872"N	081°	03'	12.974"W
DBN 52 R	Skidaway Riv	31°	57'	59.479"N	081°	03'	22.616"W
LT 53 Fl G 4s	Skidaway Riv	31°	57'	54.607"N	081°	03'	22.724"W
DBN 54 R	Skidaway Riv	31°	57'	50.929"N	081°	03'	26.666"W
DBN 55 G	Skidaway Narrows	31°	57'	39.103"N	081°	03'	24.440"W
LT 57 Fl G 4s	Skidaway Narrows	31°	57'	34.135"N	081°	03'	27.500"W
DBN 60 R	Skidaway Narrows	31°	57'	18.618"N	081°	03'	44.373"W
DBN 65 G	Skidaway Narrows	31°	56'	36.949"N	081°	04'	33.560"W
DBN 69 G	Skidaway Narrows	31°	56'	21.613"N	081°	04'	39.593"W
LT 71 Fl G 4s	Skidaway Narrows	31°	56'	02.758"N	081°	04'	28.088"W
DBN 72 R	Skidaway Narrows	31°	55'	57.386"N	081°	04'	29.982"W
DBN 73 G	Skidaway Narrows	31°	55'	52.520"N	081°	04'	24.168"W
LT 74 Fl R 4s	Skidaway Narrows	31°	55'	35.612"N	081°	04'	18.618"W
LT 75 Fl G 4s	Burnside Riv	31°	55'	11.991"N	081°	04'	29.030"W
DBN 76 R	Burnside Riv	31°	55'	22.024"N	081°	04'	52.353"W
DBN 77 G	Burnside Riv	31°	55'	25.649"N	081°	05'	47.388"W
LT 79 Fl G 4s	Burnside Riv	31°	55'	12.000"N	081°	06'	13.000"W
LT 81 Fl G 4s	Vernon Riv	31°	53'	58.826"N	081°	05'	40.338"W
DBN 82 R	Vernon Riv	31°	53'	36.758"N	081°	05'	44.694"W
DBN 83 G	Vernon Riv	31°	53'	31.745"N	081°	05'	08.934"W
DBN 84 R	Vernon Riv	31°	52'	56.273"N	081°	05'	09.000"W
LT 86 Fl R 4s	Green Is Snd	31°	52'	18.834"N	081°	04'	34.288"W

OSSABAW SOUND

DESCRIPTION	LOCATION	APPROXIMATE LATITUDE DEG. MIN. SEC.	APPROXIMATE LONGITUDE DEG. MIN. SEC.
LB R W "OS" Mo (A) W	Offshore	31° 47' 48"N	080° 56' 10"W
B 1 G can	Offshore	31° 47' 49"N	080° 58' 50"W
B "N" R G nun	Ossabaw Snd	31° 48' 05"N	080° 59' 11"W
B 5 G	Ossabaw Snd N Ch	31° 50' 06"N	080° 59' 38"W
B 7 G	Ossabaw Snd N Ch	31° 51' 06"N	081° 00' 14"W
B 9 G can	Ossabaw Snd N Ch	31° 51' 36"N	081° 01' 34"W
DBN 10 R	Ossabaw Snd N Ch	31° 51' 43"N	081° 02' 05"W
B 11 G can	Ossabaw Snd N Ch	31° 51' 41"N	081° 03' 14"W
DBN 12 R	Ossabaw Snd N Ch	31° 51' 55"N	081° 03' 25"W
B 4 R nun	Ossabaw Snd S Ch	31° 48' 20"N	080° 59' 59"W
DBN 5 G	Ossabaw Snd S Ch	31° 49' 15"N	081° 02' 02"W
LT 6 Fl R 4s	Ossabaw Snd S Ch	31° 50' 21"N	081° 03' 08"W

INTRACOASTAL WATERWAY
GREEN ISLAND SOUND TO ST. CATHERINES SOUND

DESCRIPTION	LOCATION	APPROXIMATE LATITUDE DEG. MIN. SEC.	APPROXIMATE LONGITUDE DEG. MIN. SEC.
LB 87 Fl G 4s	Raccoon Key	31° 51' 59.699"N	081° 04' 43.215"W
RFL Q W	Little Don Is	31° 51' 49.662"N	081° 04' 58.417"W
RRL Iso W 6s	Little Don Is	31° 52' 04.083"N	081° 04' 55.982"W
DBN 89 G	Hell Gate	31° 51' 41.095"N	081° 04' 57.902"W
LT 91 Fl G 4s	Hell Gate	31° 51' 25.341"N	081° 05' 01.184"W
LT 92 Q R	Hell Gate	31° 51' 21.348"N	081° 05' 06.529"W
LT 93 Fl G 4s	Middle Marsh	31° 51' 23.334"N	081° 06' 16.159"W
DBN 94 R	Middle Marsh	31° 51' 40.920"N	081° 06' 29.515"W
DBN 95 G	Ogeechee Riv	31° 51' 18.181"N	081° 07' 11.581"W
LT 96 Fl R 4s	Ogeechee Riv	31° 51' 34.051"N	081° 07' 39.572"W
B 1A G	Ft. McAllister Approach	31° 53' 45.770"N	081° 09' 59.387"W
B 3A G	Ft. McAllister Approach	31° 52' 58.773"N	081° 09' 29.385"W
B 5A G	Ft. McAllister Approach	31° 51' 57.776"N	081° 09' 18.383"W
LT 98 Fl R 4s	FL Passage	31° 51' 11.128"N	081° 08' 32.598"W
LT 99 Fl G 4s	FL Passage	31° 50' 17.354"N	081° 09' 17.575"W
B 102 R nun	FL Passage	31° 49' 14.763"N	081° 09' 41.097"W
RFL Fl W 4s	FL Passage	31° 49' 08.387"N	081° 09' 38.171"W
RR DBN R W	marsh	31° 48' 44.983"N	081° 09' 42.975"W
LT 104 Fl R 4s	Bear Riv	31 49' 03.529"N	081° 10' 38.192"W
DBN 103 G	Bear Riv	31° 48' 56.957"N	081° 10' 34.593"W
LT 104A Fl R 4s	Bear Riv	31° 48' 19.462"N	081° 10' 41.283"W
RFL "A" Fl R 4s	Bear Riv	31° 47' 35.687"N	081° 10' 58.024"W
RR DBN "A" R W	Bear Riv	31° 47' 31.742"N	081° 11' 02.485"W
DBN 104C R	Bear Riv	31° 47' 17.074"N	081° 10' 08.973"W
RFL "B" Fl W 4s	Bear Riv	31° 47' 19.809"N	081° 09' 43.324"W
RR DBN "B" R W	Bear Riv	31° 47' 19.887"N	081° 09' 36.671"W
LT 105 Fl G 4s	Bear Riv	31° 46' 48.055"N	081° 09' 33.234"W
LT 106 Fl R 4s	Bear Riv	31° 46' 34.151"N	081° 10' 13.049"W
DBN 107 G	Bear Riv	31° 46' 17.202"N	081° 10' 11.197"W
LT 108 Fl R 4s	Bear Riv	31° 45' 27.620"N	081° 10' 33.345"W
DBN 109 G	Bear Riv	31° 45' 26.219"N	081° 10' 17.487"W
LT 110 Fl R 4s	Bear Riv	31° 44' 25.965"N	081° 09' 38.467"W
LT 112 Fl R 4s	Bear Riv	31° 43' 28.378"N	081° 08' 58.736"W
LT 114 Q R	St Catherines Snd	31° 43' 01.209"N	081° 09' 05.610"W
LT 114A F1 R 4s	St Catherines Snd	31° 42' 34.671"N	081° 09' 42.418"W

ST. CATHERINES SOUND

DESCRIPTION	LOCATION	DEG.	MIN.	SEC.	DEG.	MIN.	SEC.
		APPROXIMATE LATITUDE			APPROXIMATE LONGITUDE		
LB R W "STC" Mo (A) W	Offshore	31°	40'	12"N	081°	00'	12"W
B 3 G can	Offshore	31°	40'	30"N	081°	03'	37"W
B 5 G can	Offshore	31°	41'	14"N	081°	04'	18"W
LB 7 Fl G 2.5s	St Catherines Snd	31°	42'	04"N	081°	05'	16"W
LT "C" Fl (2+1) G 6s	St Catherines Snd	31°	42'	37"N	081°	08'	08"W
B 9 G can	St Catherines Snd	31°	42'	35"N	081°	07'	08"W
LT 114 Q R	St Catherines Snd	31°	43'	01"N	081°	09'	06"W
LT 114 A Fl R 4s	St Catherines Snd	31°	42'	35"N	081°	09'	42"W
DBN 2 R	Medway Riv	31°	42'	57"N	081°	11'	16"W
DBN 3 G	Medway Riv	31°	43'	56"N	081°	12'	27"W

INTRACOASTAL WATERWAY
ST. CATHERINES SOUND TO SAPELO SOUND

DESCRIPTION	LOCATION	DEG.	MIN.	SEC.	DEG.	MIN.	SEC.
		APPROXIMATE LATITUDE			APPROXIMATE LONGITUDE		
LT 116 Fl R 4s	N Newport Riv	31°	42'	07.820"N	081°	10'	39.906"W
DBN 117 G	N Newport Riv	31°	41'	16.567"N	081°	11'	00.642"W
Caution DBN	Vandyke Reef N Obstr	31°	41'	10.000"N	081°	11'	45.000"W
Caution DBN	Vandyke Reef S Obstr	31°	41'	06.000"N	081°	11'	50.000"W
LT 119 Fl G 4s	N Newport Riv	31°	40'	52.851"N	081°	11'	31.535"W
Caution DBN	Timmons Reef E Obstr	31°	40'	38.000"N	081°	12'	50.000"W
Caution DBN	Timmons Reef W Obstr	31°	40'	39.000"N	081°	12'	56.000"W
DBN 121 G	N Newport Riv	31°	40'	32.956"N	081°	11'	40.269"W
LT 123 Fl G 4s	N Newport Riv	31°	40'	20.850"N	081°	11'	42.872"W
DBN 122 R	N Newport Riv	31°	40'	22.915"N	081°	11'	49.271"W
DBN 124 R	N Newport Riv	31°	40'	06.982"N	081°	11'	46.821"W
LT 125 Fl G 4s	Johnson Cr	31°	39'	32.944"N	081°	11'	53.973"W
DBN 126 R	Johnson Cr	31°	39'	07.785"N	081°	11'	22.943"W
DBN 128 R	Johnson Cr	31°	38'	15.196"N	081°	11'	23.381"W
DBN 130 R	Johnson Cr	31°	37'	55.059"N	081°	11'	18.467"W
DBN 131 G	Johnson Cr	31°	36'	23.010"N	081°	11'	00.478"W
DBN 131A G	Johnson Cr	31°	36'	12.766"N	081°	10'	56.543"W
LT 132 Fl R 4s	Johnson Cr	31°	35'	31.213"N	081°	10'	44.655"W
DBN 1 R	S Newport Riv	31°	35'	24.100"N	081°	11'	10.300"W
DBN 2 R	S Newport Riv	31°	36'	06.700"N	081°	11'	32.300"W
DBN 3 G	S Newport Riv	31°	37'	01.800"N	081°	12'	55.900"W
DBN 5 G	S Newport Riv	31°	37'	23.400"N	081°	12'	59.200"W
DBN 6 R	S Newport Riv	31°	38'	07.900"N	081°	13'	53.200"W
DBN 7 G	S Newport Riv	31°	38'	38.600"N	081°	15'	16.600"W
DBN 9 G	S Newport Riv	31°	39'	07.900"N	081°	15'	56.400"W
DBN 11 G	S Newport Riv	31°	39'	07.600"N	081°	16'	37.900"W
DBN 12 R	S Newport Riv	31°	38'	57.900"N	081°	17'	35.800"W
DBN 133 G	S Newport Riv	31°	35'	10.525"N	081°	10'	54.225"W
LT 135 Fl G 4s	S Newport Riv	31°	34'	36.699"N	081°	11'	18.743"W
DBN 136 R	S Newport Riv	31°	33'	53.959"N	081°	11'	41.201"W
LT 138 Q R	Sapelo Snd	31°	33'	03.054"N	081°	11'	43.946"W

SAPELO SOUND AND SAPELO RIVER

DESCRIPTION	LOCATION	APPROXIMATE LATITUDE DEG. MIN. SEC.	APPROXIMATE LONGITUDE DEG. MIN. SEC.
B "S" R W can	Offshore	31° 31' 12.846"N	081° 03' 53.548"W
B 2 R nun	Offshore	31° 31' 58.977"N	081° 05' 13.430"W
B 3 G can	Offshore	31° 31' 58.015"N	081° 06' 59.864"W
B 5 G can	Offshore	31° 32' 00.012"N	081° 07' 59.944"W
B 6 R nun	Offshore	31° 32' 00.930"N	081° 09' 08.321"W
B 8 R nun	Sapelo Snd	31° 32' 05.232"N	081° 09' 44.166"W
B 10 R nun	Sapelo Snd	31° 32' 28.804"N	081° 10' 42.343"W
DBN 11 G	Sapelo Snd	31° 32' 14.340"N	081° 12' 24.960"W
LT 138 Q R	Sapelo Snd	31° 33' 03.054"N	081° 11' 43.946"W
LT 140 Fl R 2.5s	Sapelo Snd	31° 32' 53.700"N	081° 12' 39.000"W
LT 142 Fl R 4s	Sapelo Snd	31° 32' 47.520"N	081° 13' 11.160"W
DBN 143 G	Sapelo Riv	31° 32' 25.288"N	081° 14' 32.633"W
LT 145 Fl G 4s	Sapelo Riv	31° 32' 21.300"N	081° 15' 13.560"W
DBN 147 G	Sapelo Riv	31° 32' 10.980"N	081° 15' 44.820"W
LT 149 Fl G 4s	Sapelo Riv	31° 31' 54.720"N	081° 16' 19.680"W
DBN 150 R	Sapelo Riv	31° 31' 47.941"N	081° 16' 45.484"W
DBN 2 R	Sapelo Riv	31° 32' 59.880"N	081° 17' 11.640"W
DBN 3 G	Sapelo Riv	31° 32' 30.757"N	081° 18' 40.790"W
DBN 4 R	Sapelo Riv	31° 32' 47.580"N	081° 18' 56.580"W
DBN 5 G	Sapelo Riv	31° 32' 41.940"N	081° 19' 11.880"W
DBN 6 R	Sapelo Riv	31° 32' 11.820"N	081° 20' 45.960"W
DBN 8 R	Sapelo Riv	31° 32' 01.620"N	081° 20' 51.000"W
DBN 10 R	Sapelo Riv	31° 31' 50.940"N	081° 21' 21.060"W

INTRACOASTAL WATERWAY
SAPELO SOUND TO DOBOY SOUND

DESCRIPTION	LOCATION	APPROXIMATE LATITUDE DEG. MIN. SEC.	APPROXIMATE LONGITUDE DEG. MIN. SEC.
LT 138 Q R	Sapelo Snd	31° 33' 03.054"N	081° 11' 43.946"W
LT 140 Fl R 2.5	Sapelo Snd	31° 32' 53.700"N	081° 12' 39.000"W
LT 142 Fl R 4s	Sapelo Snd	31° 32' 47.520"N	081° 13' 11.160"W
DBN 143 G	Sapelo Riv	31° 32' 25.288"N	081° 14' 32.633"W
LT 145 Fl G 4s	Sapelo Riv	31° 32' 21.300"N	081° 15' 13.560"W
DBN 147 G	Sapelo Riv	31° 32' 10.980"N	081° 15' 44.820"W
LT 149 Fl G 4s	Sapelo Riv	31° 31' 54.720"N	081° 16' 19.680"W
DBN 150 R	Sapelo Riv	31° 31' 47.941"N	081° 16' 45.484"W
LT 151 Fl G 4s	Front Riv	31° 31' 21.937"N	081° 17' 27.261"W
DBN 152 R	Front Riv	31° 30' 57.240"N	081° 17' 49.560"W
LT 153 Fl G 4s	Front Riv	31° 30' 39.960"N	081° 18' 02.340"W
DBN 154 R	Front Riv	31° 30' 29.646"N	081° 18' 10.010"W
DBN 155 G	Creighton Narrows	31° 29' 59.029"N	081° 19' 27.090"W
LT 155A Fl G 4s	Creighton Narrows	31° 29' 48.189"N	081° 19' 31.701"W
DBN 156 R	Creighton Narrows	31° 29' 22.189"N	081° 19' 25.870"W
LT 157 Fl G 4s	Creighton Narrows	31° 29' 17.665"N	081° 19' 21.806"W
RF DBN "A" R W	Old Teakettle Cr	31° 28' 59.705"N	081° 19' 06.718"W
RR DBN "A" R W	Old Teakettle Cr	31° 28' 55.080"N	081° 19' 01.980"W
DBN 158 R	Old Teakettle Cr	31° 28' 58.344"N	081° 19' 11.043"W
LT 159 Fl G 4s	Old Teakettle Cr	31° 28' 54.437"N	081° 19' 07.069"W
DBN 158A R	Old Teakettle Cr	31° 28' 52.457"N	081° 19' 12.321"W
DBN 160 R	Old Teakettle Cr	31° 28' 48.808"N	081° 19' 15.785"W
DBN 161 G	Old Teakettle Cr	31° 28' 40.600"N	081° 19' 37.337"W
LT 162 Fl R 4s	Old Teakettle Cr	31° 28' 39.287"N	081° 19' 47.350"W
DBN 164 R	Old Teakettle Cr	31° 28' 11.813"N	081° 19' 40.373"W
DBN 167 G	Old Teakettle Cr	31° 27' 52.111"N	081° 19' 25.784"W

DESCRIPTION	LOCATION	APPROXIMATE LATITUDE DEG.	MIN.	SEC.	APPROXIMATE LONGITUDE DEG.	MIN.	SEC.
DBN 168 R	Old Teakettle Cr	31°	27'	40.751"N	081°	19'	25.970"W
LT 169 Fl G 4s	Old Teakettle Cr	31°	27'	28.523"N	081°	19'	14.391"W
RF DBN "B" R W	Old Teakettle Cr	31°	27'	22.178"N	081°	19'	15.264"W
RR DBN "B" R W	Old Teakettle Cr	31°	27'	18.014"N	081°	19'	13.821"W
DBN 172 R	Old Teakettle Cr	31°	26'	46.203"N	081°	18'	29.158"W
LT 173 Fl G 4s	Old Teakettle Cr	31°	26'	32.388"N	081°	18'	11.051"W
LT 175 Fl G 4s	Old Teakettle Cr	31°	25'	34.077"N	081°	18'	40.416"W
LT 178 Q R	Doboy Snd	31°	24'	33.972"N	081°	18'	40.098"W

DOBOY SOUND

DESCRIPTION	LOCATION	APPROXIMATE LATITUDE DEG.	MIN.	SEC.	APPROXIMATE LONGITUDE DEG.	MIN.	SEC.
LB R W "D" Mo (A) W	Offshore	31°	21'	12"N	081°	11'	24"W
B 2 R nun	Offshore	31°	21'	27"N	081°	12'	10"W
B 3 G can	Offshore	31°	21'	30"N	081°	13'	27"W
B 4 R nun	Offshore	31°	22'	00"N	081°	14'	00"W
B 5 G can	Doboy Snd	31°	21'	51"N	081°	14'	38"W
B 6 R nun	Doboy Snd	31°	22'	14"N	081°	15'	12"W
LT 8 Fl R 6s	Doboy Snd	31°	22'	43"N	081°	16'	49"W

INTRACOASTAL WATERWAY
DOBOY SOUND TO ALTAMAHA SOUND

DESCRIPTION	LOCATION	APPROXIMATE LATITUDE DEG.	MIN.	SEC.	APPROXIMATE LONGITUDE DEG.	MIN.	SEC.
LT 178 Q R	Doboy Snd	31°	24'	33.972"N	081°	18'	40.098"W
RFL "A" Fl R 4s	N Riv	31°	24'	31.800"N	081°	19'	10.200"W
RR DBN "A" R W	N Riv	31°	24'	32.172"N	081°	19'	15.505"W
LT 180 Fl R 4s	N Riv	31°	24'	11.936"N	081°	19'	45.485"W
DBN 181 G	N Riv	31°	23'	37.490"N	081°	19'	45.390"W
LT 182 Fl R 4s	N Riv	31°	23'	32.180"N	081°	19'	51.906"W
LT 183 Fl G 4s	Rockdedundy Riv	31°	23'	05.319"N	081°	19'	53.041"W
LT 184 Fl R 2.5s	Rockdedundy Riv	31°	23'	00.813"N	081°	20'	00.350"W
RF DBN "A" R W	Rockdedundy Riv	31°	22'	33.900"N	081°	20'	06.060"W
RR DBN "A" R W	Rockdedundy Riv	31°	22'	37.449"N	081°	20'	07.050"W
LT 185 Fl G 4s	Rockdedundy Riv	31°	22'	25.723"N	081°	20'	02.259"W
DBN 188 R	Rockdedundy Riv	31°	22'	19.740"N	081°	20'	04.860"W
RF DBN "A" R W	Little Mud Riv	31°	22'	05.100"N	081°	19'	56.220"W
RR DBN "A" R W	Little Mud Riv	31°	22'	09.224"N	081°	19'	53.119"W
LT 190 Fl R 2.5s	Little Mud Riv	31°	21'	58.302"N	081°	20'	03.300"W
DBN 194 R	Little Mud Riv	31°	20'	19.293"N	081°	19'	41.628"W
LT 195 Fl G 2.5s	Little Mud Riv	31°	19'	56.220"N	081°	19'	31.140"W
RFL "B" Q R	Little Mud Riv	31°	19'	55.558"N	081°	19'	37.493"W
RRL "B" Iso R 6s	Little Mud Riv	31°	20'	02.218"N	081°	19'	49.896"W
LT 198 Q R	Altamaha Snd	31°	19'	25.325"N	081°	18'	48.533"W
RFL "A" Q G	Altamaha Snd	31°	19'	24.077"N	081°	18'	27.421"W
RRL "A" Iso G 6s	Altamaha Snd	31°	19'	25.833"N	081°	18'	17.219"W

DARIEN RIVER

DESCRIPTION	LOCATION	APPROXIMATE LATITUDE DEG. MIN. SEC.			APPROXIMATE LONGITUDE DEG. MIN. SEC.		
DBN 1 G	Darien River	31°	23'	05"N	081°	20'	31"W
DBN 3 G	Darien River	31°	23'	14"N	081°	21'	08"W
DBN 5 G	Darien River	31°	23'	14"N	081°	21'	18"W
DBN 7 G	Darien River	31°	23'	07"N	081°	21'	22"W
DBN 8 R	Darien River	31°	22'	52"N	081°	21'	08"W
DBN 10 R	Darien River	31°	22'	47"N	081°	21'	00"W
DBN 12 R	Darien River	31°	22'	09"N	081°	21'	31"W
DBN 14 R	Darien River	31°	22'	04"N	081°	21'	36"W
DBN 15 G	Darien River	31°	21'	55"N	081°	21'	53"W
DBN 16 R	Darien River	31°	21'	46"N	081°	22'	09"W
DBN 17 G	Darien River	31°	21'	33"N	081°	22'	27"W
DBN 18 R	Darien River	31°	21'	35"N	081°	23'	05"W
DBN 20 R	Darien River	31°	21'	26"N	081°	23'	47"W
DBN 21 G	Darien River	31°	21'	35"N	081°	24'	22"W
DBN 23 G	Darien River	31°	21'	35"N	081°	24'	30"W
DBN 25 G	Darien River	31°	21'	27"N	081°	24'	42"W
DBN 26 R	Darien River	31°	20'	54"N	081°	24'	54"W
DBN 27 G	Darien River	31°	20'	57"N	081°	25'	05"W
DBN 29 G	Darien River	31°	21'	08"N	081°	25'	08"W
DBN 31 G	Darien River	31°	21'	25"N	081°	25'	42"W
DBN 33 G	Darien River	31°	21'	32"N	081°	25'	44"W

ALTAMAHA SOUND

DESCRIPTION	LOCATION	APPROXIMATE LATITUDE DEG. MIN. SEC.			APPROXIMATE LONGITUDE DEG. MIN. SEC.		
LT 2 Fl R 4s	Offshore	31°	18'	30"N	081°	13'	49"W
LT 3 Fl G 4s	Altamaha Snd	31°	18'	39"N	081°	15'	22"W
LT 4 Fl R 6s	Altamaha Snd	31°	18'	52"N	081°	15'	20"W
LT 5 Fl G 2.5s	Altamaha Snd	31°	18'	48"N	081°	16'	37"W

INTRACOASTAL WATERWAY
ALTAMAHA SOUND TO ST. SIMONS SOUND

DESCRIPTION	LOCATION	APPROXIMATE LATITUDE DEG. MIN. SEC.			APPROXIMATE LONGITUDE DEG. MIN. SEC.		
LT 198 Q R	Altamaha Snd	31°	19'	25.325"N	081°	18'	48.533"W
RFL "A" Q G	Altamaha Snd	31°	19'	24.077"N	081°	18'	27.421"W
RRL "A" Iso G 6s	Altamaha Snd	31°	19'	25.833"N	081°	18'	17.219"W
LT 201 Fl G 4s	Altamaha Snd	31°	19'	12.368"N	081°	19'	19.069"W
LT 202 Fl R 4s	Altamaha Snd	31°	19'	09.530"N	081°	19'	52.912"W
DBN 204 R	Altamaha Snd	31°	19'	03.660"N	081°	20'	14.400"W
DBN 206 R	Altamaha Snd	31°	18'	53.340"N	081°	20'	40.740"W
DBN 208 R	Altamaha Snd	31°	18'	46.020"N	081°	21'	04.440"W
LT 209 Q G	Altamaha Snd	31°	18'	40.500"N	081°	21'	13.500"W
DBN 211 G	Altamaha Snd	31°	18'	57.780"N	081°	21'	45.600"W
RFL "C" Q R	Altamaha Snd	31°	19'	17.899"N	081°	22'	12.538"W
RRL "C" Iso R 6s	Altamaha Snd	31°	19'	21.519"N	081°	22'	17.653"W
LT 213 Fl G 2.5s	Buttermilk Snd	31°	19'	13.680"N	081°	22'	18.840"W
DBN 214 R	Buttermilk Snd	31°	19'	14.649"N	081°	22'	50.674"W
RFL "A" LT 216 Q R	Buttermilk Snd	31°	18'	47.580"N	081°	23'	34.740"W
RRL "A" Iso R 6s	Buttermilk Snd	31°	18'	54.819"N	081°	23'	30.356"W
DBN 216A R	Buttermilk Snd	31°	18'	20.040"N	081°	23'	55.680"W

DESCRIPTION	LOCATION	APPROXIMATE LATITUDE			APPROXIMATE LONGITUDE		
		DEG.	MIN.	SEC.	DEG.	MIN.	SEC.

South Altamaha River

DESCRIPTION	LOCATION	DEG.	MIN.	SEC.	DEG.	MIN.	SEC.
DBN 1 G	S Altamaha Riv	31°	18'	31.200"N	081°	24'	09.540"W
DBN 2 R	S Altamaha Riv	31°	18'	36.840"N	081°	24'	33.840"W
DBN 2A R	S Altamaha Riv	31°	18'	26.838"N	081°	24'	42.686"W
DBN 4 R	S Altamaha Riv	31°	18'	23.864"N	081°	24'	48.400"W
DBN 5 G	S Altamaha Riv	31°	18'	25.324"N	081°	24'	59.574"W
DBN 7 G	S Altamaha Riv	31°	18'	42.360"N	081°	25'	26.460"W
DBN 8 R	S Altamaha Riv	31°	18'	44.220"N	081°	25'	54.000"W
DBN 10 R	S Altamaha Riv	31°	18'	45.660"N	081°	26'	04.620"W
RFL "B" 218 Q R	Buttermilk Snd	31°	18'	08.820"N	081°	24'	02.700"W
RR DBN "B" R W	Buttermilk Snd	31°	18'	12.331"N	081°	24'	04.869"W
LT 219 Fl G 2.5s	Buttermilk Snd	31°	18'	06.620"N	081°	23'	55.373"W
DBN 220 R	Buttermilk Snd	31°	17'	40.711"N	081°	23'	50.724"W
LT 221 Fl G 4s	Frederica Riv	31°	17'	34.740"N	081°	23'	42.180"W
DBN 222 R	Frederica Riv	31°	17'	06.300"N	081°	23'	14.460"W
RFL "A" Fl W 2.5s	Frederica Riv Cut	31°	17'	05.580"N	081°	23'	05.700"W
RR DBN "A" R W	Frederica Riv Cut	31°	17'	02.223"N	081°	23'	00.793"W

Hampton River

DESCRIPTION	LOCATION	DEG.	MIN.	SEC.	DEG.	MIN.	SEC.
DBN 27 G	Hampton Riv	31°	16'	56.220"N	081°	22'	57.060"W
DBN 25 G	Hampton Riv	31°	17'	37.200"N	081°	22'	50.460"W
DBN 23 G	Hampton Riv	31°	18'	00.365"N	081°	22'	24.336"W
DBN 22 R	Hampton Riv	31°	17'	45.000"N	081°	22'	09.180"W
DBN 21 G	Hampton Riv	31°	17'	50.820"N	081°	20'	44.940"W
DBN 19 G	Hampton Riv	31°	17'	20.520"N	081°	19'	29.760"W
DBN 18 R	Hampton Riv	31°	16'	09.960"N	081°	18'	46.140"W
DBN 17 G	Hampton Riv	31°	15'	43.380"N	081°	19'	02.580"W
DBN 15 G	Hampton Riv	31°	15'	43.800"N	081°	19'	15.420"W
DBN 14 R	Hampton Riv	31°	15'	44.760"N	081°	19'	42.240"W
DBN 12 R	Hampton Riv	31°	14'	43.500"N	081°	19'	56.100"W
DBN 11 G	Hampton Riv	31°	14'	12.720"N	081°	19'	24.600"W
LT 223 Fl G 4s	Frederica Riv	31°	16'	37.560"N	081°	22'	59.340"W
DBN 227 G	Frederica Riv	31°	16'	17.612"N	081°	23'	09.308"W
RFL "C" Fl W 2.5s	Frederica Riv	31°	15'	52.740"N	081°	23'	27.540"W
RR DBN "C" R W	Frederica Riv Cut	31°	15'	45.360"N	081°	23'	32.220"W
RF DBN "D" R W	Frederica Riv	31°	15'	43.800"N	081°	23'	40.980"W
RR DBN "D" R W	Frederica Riv	31°	15'	40.302"N	081°	23'	45.149"W
LT 229 Fl G 2.5s	Mackay Riv	31°	15'	32.700"N	081°	23'	39.720"W
LT 231 Fl G 4s	Mackay Riv	31°	15'	24.720"N	081°	23'	41.820"W
DBN 232 R	Mackay Riv	31°	14'	48.300"N	081°	24'	12.060"W
DBN 234 R	Mackay Riv	31°	14'	48.720"N	081°	24'	42.120"W
RFL "A" Fl R 4s	Mackay Riv	31°	14'	54.940"N	081°	25'	13.306"W
RR DBN "A" R W	Mackay Riv	31°	14'	57.036"N	081°	25'	18.857"W
DBN 236 R	Mackay Riv	31°	14'	03.736"N	081°	25'	31.030"W
DBN 235A G	Mackay Riv	31°	13'	36.420"N	081°	25'	58.620"W
LT 237 Fl G 4s	Mackay Riv	31°	13'	15.600"N	081°	25'	57.420"W
DBN 238 R	Mackay Riv	31°	12'	54.900"N	081°	25'	51.600"W
LT 239 Fl G 4s	Mackay Riv	31°	12'	29.040"N	081°	25'	30.240"W
LT 239A Fl G 4s	Mackay Riv	31°	12'	02.880"N	081°	25'	55.440"W
LT 241 Fl G 4s	Mackay Riv	31°	10'	57.840"N	081°	25'	18.000"W
DBN 242 R	Mackay Riv	31°	10'	37.440"N	081°	25'	26.820"W
DBN 243 G	Mackay Riv	31°	10'	11.160"N	081°	25'	29.340"W
DBN 243A G	MacKay Riv	31°	10'	00.840"N	081°	25'	38.700"W
LT 244 Fl R 4s	Mackay Riv	31°	09'	40.440"N	081°	26'	02.700"W
LT 245 Fl G 4s	Mackay Riv	31°	09'	30.337"N	081°	25'	51.052"W
LT 245A Fl G 4s	Mackay Riv	31°	08'	59.700"N	081°	25'	41.280"W
LT 247 Fl G 6s	Mackay Riv	31°	08'	34.766"N	081°	25'	33.408"W

DESCRIPTION	LOCATION	APPROXIMATE LATITUDE DEG. MIN. SEC.	APPROXIMATE LONGITUDE DEG. MIN. SEC.
LT 249 Fl G 2.5	Mackay Riv	31° 08' 21.286"N	081° 25' 14.138"W
LT 250 Fl R 2.5	Mackay Riv	31° 07' 55.294"N	081° 25' 22.316"W

South Frederica River

DESCRIPTION	LOCATION	APPROXIMATE LATITUDE DEG. MIN. SEC.	APPROXIMATE LONGITUDE DEG. MIN. SEC.
LT 249 Fl G 2.5	Mackay Riv	31° 08' 21.286"N	081° 25' 14.138"W
LT 2 Fl R 4s	S Frederica Riv	31° 08' 24.120"N	081° 24' 59.340"W
RFL Q W	S Frederica Riv	31° 09' 07.682"N	081° 25' 24.302"W
RRL Iso W 6s	S Frederica Riv	31° 09' 26.174"N	081° 25' 33.828"W
DBN 5 G	S Frederica Riv	31° 09' 33.752"N	081° 25' 19.173"W

ST. SIMONS SOUND TO PORT OF BRUNSWICK

DESCRIPTION	LOCATION	APPROXIMATE LATITUDE DEG. MIN. SEC.	APPROXIMATE LONGITUDE DEG. MIN. SEC.
LB R W "STS" "Mo (A) W Racon B dash dot dot dot Whistle	Offshore	31° 03' 12.000"N	081° 15' 06.000"W
LB 1 Q G	Offshore	31° 03' 56.639"N	081° 16' 27.701"W
LB 2 Q R	Offshore	31° 04' 00.771"N	081° 16' 24.538"W
LBB 3 Fl G 2.5s	Offshore	31° 04' 40.170"N	081° 17' 44.466"W
LB 4 Fl R 2.5s	Offshore	31° 04' 44.301"N	081° 17' 41.303"W
LB 5 Fl G 4s	Offshore	31° 05' 06.630"N	081° 18' 31.136"W
LB 6 Fl R 4s	Offshore	31° 05' 10.762"N	081° 18' 27.973"W
LBB 7 Fl G 2.5s	Offshore	31° 05' 33.089"N	081° 19' 17.810"W
LB 8 Fl R 2.5s	Offshore	31° 05' 37.222"N	081° 19' 14.674"W
LB 9 Fl G 4s	Offshore	31° 05' 59.530"N	081° 20' 04.550"W
LB 10 Fl R 4s	Offshore	31° 06' 03.682"N	081° 20' 01.323"W
LBB 11 Fl G 4s	St Simons Snd	31° 06' 26.010"N	081° 20' 51.168"W
LB 12 Fl R 4s	St Simons Snd	31° 06' 30.142"N	081° 20' 48.004"W
LB 13 Fl G 2.5s	St Simons Snd	31° 06' 52.470"N	081° 21' 37.852"W
LB 14 Fl R 2.5s	St Simons Snd	31° 06' 57.222"N	081° 21' 34.213"W
LBB 15 Q G	St Simons Snd	31° 07' 23.791"N	081° 22' 33.145"W
LB 16 Q R	St Simons Snd	31° 07' 24.046"N	081° 22' 20.185"W
LBB 17 Fl G 2.5s	St Simons Snd	31° 07' 33.155"N	081° 23' 23.057"W
N Tower LT Iso R 6s	St Simons Is	31° 08' 55.197"N	081° 25' 06.379"W
S Tower LT Iso R 6s	St Simons Is	31° 08' 50.630"N	081° 25' 04.577"W
RFL Q R	Plantation Cr	31° 08' 13.920"N	081° 25' 59.580"W
RRL Iso R 6s	Plantation Cr	31° 08' 24.420"N	081° 26' 45.720"W
LB 19 Fl G 2.5s	St Simons Snd	31° 07' 40.644"N	081° 24' 12.568"W
LB 20 Q R	St Simons Snd	31° 07' 36.978"N	081° 24' 49.365"W
LT 2 Fl R 4s	Frederica Riv	31° 08' 24.120"N	081° 24' 59.340"W
DBN 3 G	Frederica Riv	31° 08' 27.335"N	081° 25' 10.036"W
RFL Q W	Frederica Riv	31° 09' 07.682"N	081° 25' 24.302"W
RRL Iso W 6s	Frederica Riv	31° 09' 26.174"N	081° 25' 33.828"W
DBN 5 G	Frederica Riv	31° 09' 33.752"N	081° 25' 19.173"W
RFL Q G	Jekyll Is	31° 05' 39.480"N	081° 26' 29.640"W
RRL Iso G 6s	Jekyll Is	31° 05' 25.325"N	081° 26' 42.182"W
LB 22 Fl R 4s	St Simons Snd	31° 06' 38.175"N	081° 25' 48.441"W
RFL Q G	Cedar Hammock	31° 06' 01.020"N	081° 28' 05.100"W
RRL Iso G 6s	Cedar Hammock	31° 05' 50.160"N	081° 28' 51.900"W
O/B RFL Q W	Cedar Hammock	31° 06' 37.500"N	081° 25' 24.065"W
O/B RRL Iso W 6s	Cedar Hammock	31° 06' 39.120"N	081° 25' 16.860"W
LB 24 Q R	Brunswick Riv	31° 06' 18.014"N	081° 27' 02.703"W
LB 26 Fl R 4s	Brunswick Pt Cut	31° 06' 37.528"N	081° 27' 59.737"W
LB 27 Fl G 2.5	Brunswick Pt Cut	31° 06' 32.039"N	081° 28' 02.500"W
RFL Q W	Brunswick Pt Cut	31° 05' 59.285"N	081° 26' 22.293"W

DESCRIPTION	LOCATION	APPROXIMATE LATITUDE DEG.	MIN.	SEC.	APPROXIMATE LONGITUDE DEG.	MIN.	SEC.
RFL Fl R 4s	Brunswick Pt Cut	31°	05'	59.285"N	081°	26'	22.293"W
RRL Iso W 6s	Brunswick Pt Cut	31°	05'	52.155"N	081°	26'	03.011"W
DBN 1 G	Plantation Cr	31°	07'	16.380"N	081°	28'	49.140"W
LT 2 Fl R 2.5s	Plantation Cr	31°	07'	15.360"N	081°	28'	47.520"W
DBN 3 G	Plantation Cr	31°	07'	18.000"N	081°	28'	46.380"W
DBN 4 R	Plantation Cr	31°	07'	17.460"N	081°	28'	45.120"W
LB "A" Fl (2+1) R 6s	Andrews Is Spit	31°	07'	13.113"N	081°	29'	37.935"W
LT 2 Fl R 4s	Brunswick Hbr Ch	31°	07'	29.160"N	081°	29'	25.380"W
Jty DBN	Andrews Is	31°	07'	31.140"N	081°	29'	39.660"W
TB LT 3 Fl G 4s	Brunswick Hbr TB	31°	07'	40.980"N	081°	29'	41.640"W
TB LT 5 Fl G 4s	Brunswick Hbr TB	31°	07'	49.200"N	081°	29'	43.920"W
RFL Q R	Brunswick Hbr	31°	09'	06.240"N	081°	30'	02.400"W
RRL Iso R 6s	Brunswick Hbr RRL	31°	09'	46.252"N	081°	30'	15.863"W
RFL Q Y	Andrews Is Spit	31°	06'	56.521"N	081°	29'	33.688"W
RRL Iso W 6s	Andrews Is Spit	31°	06'	52.500"N	081°	29'	33.720"W
LB 1 Fl G 4s	Turtle Riv	31°	07'	05.832"N	081°	29'	31.159"W
LB 2 Fl R 4s	Turtle Riv	31°	07'	27.451"N	081°	30'	12.892"W
O/B RFL Q R	Colonels Island	31°	07'	39.516"N	081°	30'	27.532"W
O/B RRL Iso R 6s	Colonels Island	31°	07'	38.367"N	081°	30'	19.007"W
RFL Q G	Colonels Island	31°	07'	52.629"N	081°	32'	08.466"W
RRL Iso G 6s	Colonels Island	31°	07'	53.729"N	081°	32'	16.666"W
RFL Q W	Turtle Riv Lower	31°	07'	55.025"N	081°	31'	40.896"W
RRL Iso W 6s	Turtle Riv Lower	31°	08'	01.020"N	081°	31'	57.180"W
LT 4 Q R	Turtle Riv	31°	08'	01.830"N	081°	31'	12.364"W
LB 6 Q R	Turtle Riv	31°	05'	58.981"N	081°	31'	43.288"W
RFL Q W	Blythe Is	31°	09'	23.202"N	081°	31'	58.090"W
RRL Iso W 6s	Blythe Is	31°	09'	43.018"N	081°	32'	07.542"W
RFL Q W	Turtle Riv Up	31°	08'	44.552"N	081°	31'	48.229"W
RRL Iso W 6s	Turtle Riv Up	31°	08'	01.020"N	081°	31'	57.180"W
B 8 R nun	Turtle Riv	31°	09'	33.828"N	081°	31'	36.167"W
LT 9 Fl G 4s	Turtle Riv	31°	10'	16.740"N	081°	31'	34.140"W
DBN 10 R	Turtle Riv	31°	10'	54.120"N	081°	31'	27.180"W

INTRACOASTAL WATERWAY
ST. SIMONS SOUND TO ST. ANDREW SOUND

DESCRIPTION	LOCATION	APPROXIMATE LATITUDE DEG.	MIN.	SEC.	APPROXIMATE LONGITUDE DEG.	MIN.	SEC.
LT 250 Fl R 2.5s	Mackay Riv	31°	07'	55.294"N	081°	25'	22.316"W
LT 20 Q R	St Simons Snd	31°	07'	36.978"N	081°	24'	49.365"W
LT 22 Fl R 4s	St Simons Snd	31°	06'	38.175"N	081°	25'	48.441"W
RFL Q G	Jekyll Is	31°	05'	39.480"N	081°	26'	29.640"W
RRL Iso G 6s	Jekyll Is	31°	05'	25.325"N	081°	26'	42.182"W
DBN 1 G	Jekyll Cr	31°	05'	41.820"N	081°	26	21.900"W
LT 2 Fl R 4s	Jekyll Cr	31°	05'	40.240"N	081°	26'	28.244"W
RFL Q R	Jekyll Cr Jty	31°	05'	21.280"N	081°	26'	27.747"W
RRL Iso R 6s	Jekyll Cr Jty	31°	05'	12.561"N	081°	26'	28.186"W
DBN 5	Jekyll Cr	31°	05'	34.898"N	081°	26'	24.886"W
DBN 6 R Jty warning	Jekyll Cr Jty	31°	05'	35.459"N	081°	26'	28.762"W
Jty warning DBN 8 R	Jekyll Cr Jty	31°	05'	30.366"N	081°	26'	28.685"W
LT 9 Q G	Jekyll Cr	31°	05'	27.729"N	081°	26'	25.845"W
DBN 10 R	Jekyll Cr	31°	05'	16.591"N	081°	26'	18.641"W
LT 11 Fl G 4s	Jekyll Cr	31°	05'	07.975"N	081°	26'	02.983"W
DBN 13 G	Jekyll Cr	31°	04'	35.925"N	081°	25'	50.327"W
RF DBN R W	Jekyll Cr	31°	04'	24.537"N	081°	25'	45.749"W
RR DBN R W	Jekyll Cr	31°	04'	31.119"N	081°	25'	45.659"W
B 16 R nun	Jekyll Cr	31°	04'	20.600"N	081°	25'	48.096"W

DESCRIPTION	LOCATION	APPROXIMATE LATITUDE			APPROXIMATE LONGITUDE		
		DEG.	MIN.	SEC.	DEG.	MIN.	SEC.
LT 17 Fl G 4s	Jekyll Cr	31°	04'	16.327"N	081°	25'	44.119"W
LT 19 Fl G 4s	Jekyll Cr	31°	03'	55.530"N	081°	25'	43.449"W
LT 20 Fl R 4s	Jekyll Cr	31°	03'	26.700"N	081°	25'	29.460"W
DBN 20A	Jekyll Cr	31°	03'	05.940"N	081°	25'	24.000"W
LT 23 Fl G 4s	Jekyll Cr	31°	02'	35.160"N	081°	25'	22.620"W
DBN 24 R	Jekyll Cr	31°	02'	24.462"N	081°	25'	32.963"W
LT 25 Fl G 4s	Jekyll Cr	31°	01'	51.060"N	081°	26'	07.080"W
DBN 26 R	Jekyll Cr	31°	01'	20.516"N	081°	26'	31.095"W
LT 27 Fl G 4s	Jekyll Cr	31°	01'	18.025"N	081°	26'	09.825"W
LT 29 Fl G 2.5	Jekyll Cr	31°	00'	45.180"N	081°	26'	04.020"W
B 29A G can	St Andrew Snd	31°	00'	29.486"N	081°	25'	50.560"W
LB 30 Fl R 4s	St Andrew Snd	31°	00'	00.984"N	081°	25'	17.395"W
LB 31 Fl G	St Andrew Snd	30°	59'	39.562"N	081°	24'	27.669"W
LB 32 Q R	St Andrew Snd	30°	59'	19.376"N	081°	24'	14.269"W

ST. ANDREW SOUND

DESCRIPTION	LOCATION	APPROXIMATE LATITUDE			APPROXIMATE LONGITUDE		
		DEG.	MIN.	SEC.	DEG.	MIN.	SEC.
B R W"STA"	Offshore	30°	55'	36"N	081°	19'	02"W
B 1 G can	Offshore	30°	55'	36"N	081°	20'	42"W
B 2 R nun	Offshore	30°	56'	24"N	081°	21'	15"W
B 3 G can	Offshore	30°	57'	06"N	081°	21'	24"W
B 5 G can	Offshore	30°	57'	47"N	081°	21'	46"W
B 7 G can	St Andrews Snd	30°	58'	36"N	081°	22'	37"W
B 9 G can	St Andrews Snd	30°	58'	55"N	081°	23'	05"W
LB 31 Fl G	St Andrews Snd	30°	57'	32"N	081°	29'	01"W
LB 32 Q R	St Andrews Snd	30°	59'	20"N	081°	24'	19"W
LT 33 Fl G 2.5	Cumberland Riv	30°	58'	35"N	081°	25'	06"W
LT 2 Fl R 2.5s	Raccoon Key Spit	31°	00'	21"N	081°	26'	14"W
DBN 3 G	Horseshoe Shl	30°	59'	55"N	081°	26'	40"W
LT 6 Fl R 6s	Satilla Riv	30°	59'	25"N	081°	27'	58"W
DBN 7 G	Satilla Riv	30°	58'	35"N	081°	28'	11"W
DBN 8 R	Satilla Riv	30°	58'	28"N	081°	28'	31"W
DBN 10 R	Satilla Riv	30°	57'	51"N	081°	28'	49"W
LT 11 Fl G 2.5s	Satilla Riv	30°	57'	32"N	081°	29'	01"W
DBN 12 R	Satilla Riv	30°	57'	43"N	081°	29'	03"W
DBN "A" 21 G	Satilla Riv	30°	57'	47"N	081°	30'	27"W
DBN "A" 19 G	Satilla Riv	30°	58'	36"N	081°	30'	24"W
DBN "A" 20 R	Satilla Riv	30°	58'	24"N	081°	30'	47"W
DBN "A" 17 G	Satilla Riv	30°	59'	26"N	081°	30'	58"W

ST. ANDREW SOUND TO SATILLA RIVER

DESCRIPTION	LOCATION	APPROXIMATE LATITUDE			APPROXIMATE LONGITUDE		
		DEG.	MIN.	SEC.	DEG.	MIN.	SEC.
B 1 G	St Andrew Snd	30°	55'	35.849"N	081°	20'	42.331"W
B 2 R	St Andrew Snd	30°	56'	23.848"N	081°	21'	15.333"W
B 3 G	St Andrew Snd	30°	57'	05.847"N	081°	21'	24.333"W
B 5 G	St Andrew Snd	30°	57'	46.846"N	081°	21'	46.335"W
B 7 G	St Andrew Snd	30°	58'	35.845"N	081°	22'	37.238"W
B 9 G	St Andrew Snd	30°	58'	54.945"N	081°	23'	05.239"W
LT 2 Fl R 2.5s	Raccoon Key Spit	31°	00'	20.707"N	081°	26'	13.707"W
DBN 3 G	Horseshoe Shl	30°	59'	54.792"N	081°	26'	40.177"W
LT 6 Fl R 6s	Satilla Riv	30°	59'	24.614"N	081°	27'	57.890"W

DESCRIPTION	LOCATION	APPROXIMATE LATITUDE			APPROXIMATE LONGITUDE		
		DEG.	MIN.	SEC.	DEG.	MIN.	SEC.
DBN 7 G	Satilla Riv	30°	58'	35.280"N	081°	28'	11.460"W
DBN 10 R	Satilla Riv	30°	57'	50.520"N	081°	28'	49.440"W

Alternate Route from Jekyll Sound to Cumberland River

DESCRIPTION	LOCATION	DEG.	MIN.	SEC.	DEG.	MIN.	SEC.
DBN "A" 2 R	Little Satilla Riv	31°	01'	55.900"N	081°	27'	05.300"W
DBN "A" 3 G	Little Satilla Riv	31°	01'	48.839"N	081°	27'	43.778"W
DBN "A" 4 R	Little Satilla Riv	31°	01'	53.700"N	081°	28'	18.780"W
LT "A" 5 Fl G 4s	Umbrella Cut	31°	01'	40.955"N	081°	28'	42.130"W
DBN "A" 6 R	Umbrella Cut	31°	01'	36.000"N	081°	28'	45.120"W
DBN "A" 8 R	Umbrella Cr	31°	01'	15.831"N	081°	29'	11.183"W
DBN "A" 9 G	Umbrella Cr	31°	01'	12.720"N	081°	29'	07.980"W
DBN "A" 12 R	Dover Cut	31°	00'	45.840"N	081°	29'	12.600"W
LT "A" l4 Fl R	Dover Cut	31°	00'	19.020"N	081°	29'	22.200"W
DBN "A" 16 R	Dover Cr	30°	59'	44.999"N	081°	30'	47.745"W
DBN "A" 17 G	Satilla Riv	30°	59'	26.040"N	081°	30'	58.320"W
DBN "A" 19	Satilla Riv	30°	58'	36.000"N	081°	30'	24.000"W
DBN "A" 20 R	Satilla Riv	30°	58'	24.180"N	081°	30'	46.920"W
DBN "A" 21 G	Floyd Cr Cut	30°	57'	46.200"N	081°	30'	25.500"W
DBN "A" 22 R	Floyd Cr Cut	30°	57'	40.200"N	081°	30'	33.000"W
DBN "A" 24 R	Floyd Cr Cut	30°	57'	13.300"N	081°	30'	24.200"W
DBN "A" 25 G	Floyd Cr Cut	30°	57'	02.520"N	081°	30'	13.800"W
DBN "A" 27 G	Floyd Cr	30°	56'	46.024"N	081°	30'	02.942"W
DBN "A" 29	Floyd Cr	30°	56'	38.880"N	081°	29'	54.420"W
DBN "A" 30	Floyd Cr	30°	56'	30.120"N	081°	29"	56.700"W
DBN "A" 31	Floyd Cr	30°	56'	01.500"N	081°	30"	26.100"W
DBN "A" 33	Floyd Cr	30°	55'	24.060"N	081°	29"	48.180"W
DBN "A" 34 R	Floyd Cr	30°	55'	20.812"N	081°	28'	05.545"W
DBN 40 R	Cumberland Riv	30°	55'	12.054"N	081°	27'	49.798"W

INTRACOASTAL WATERWAY
ST. ANDREW SOUND TO ST. MARYS RIVER

DESCRIPTION	LOCATION	APPROXIMATE LATITUDE			APPROXIMATE LONGITUDE		
		DEG.	MIN.	SEC.	DEG.	MIN.	SEC.
LB 32 Q R	St Andrew Snd	30°	59'	19.376"N	081°	24'	14.269"W
LT 33 Fl G 2.5	Cumberland Riv	30°	58'	35.429"N	081°	25'	06.780"W
DBN 33A G	Cumberland Riv	30°	58'	14.819"N	081°	25'	22.350"W
LT 34 Fl R 4s	Cumberland Riv	30°	57'	55.800"N	081°	26'	05.640"W
LT 35 Fl G 4s	Cumberland Riv	30°	57'	28.020"N	081°	25'	41.760"W
LT 37 Fl G 6s	Cumberland Riv	30°	56'	28.144"N	081°	26'	06.942"W
LT 39 Fl G 4s	Cumberland Riv	30°	55'	38.760"N	081°	27'	08.160"W
DBN 40 R	Cumberland Riv	30°	55'	12.054"N	081°	27'	49.798"W
DBN "A" 34 R	Floyd Creek	30°	55'	20.812"N	081°	28'	05.545"W
LT 41 Fl G 2.5s	Cumberland Riv	30°	54'	38.196"N	081°	28'	13.566"W
LT 43 Fl G 4s	Cumberland Riv	30°	54'	27.301"N	081°	29'	27.727"W
DBN 45 G	Cumberland Riv	30°	54'	09.900"N	081°	29'	46.260"W
LT 45A Fl G 4s	Cumberland Riv	30°	53'	53.396"N	081°	29'	57.105"W
LT 46 Fl R 4s	Cumberland Riv	30°	53'	38.933"N	081°	30'	23.782"W
DBN 47 G	Cumberland Riv	30°	53'	30.266"N	081°	30'	29.369"W
DBN 49 G	Cumberland Riv	30°	53'	21.960"N	081°	30'	42.180"W
DBN 49 A G	Cumberland Riv	30°	53'	11.171"N	081°	30'	48.637"W
LT 50 Fl R 4s	Cumberland Riv	30°	53'	14.040"N	081°	30'	55.440"W
DBN 51 G	Cumberland Riv	30°	53'	05.700"N	081°	30'	48.480"W
LT 5lA Fl G 4s	Cumberland Riv	30°	52'	50.100"N	081°	30'	40.920"W
DBN 52 R	Cumberland Riv	30°	52'	39.264"N	081°	30'	31.579"W
DBN 53 G	Cumberland Riv	30°	52'	32.520"N	081°	30'	12.840"W

DESCRIPTION	LOCATION	APPROXIMATE LATITUDE DEG. MIN. SEC.	APPROXIMATE LONGITUDE DEG. MIN. SEC.
DBN 54 R	Cumberland Riv	30° 52' 17.100"N	081° 30' 09.240"W
LT 55 Fl G 4s	Cumberland Riv	30° 52' 12.300"N	081° 29' 56.100"W
DBN 57 G	Cumberland Riv	30° 51' 51.816"N	081° 29' 47.314"W
LT 58 Fl R 4s	Cumberland Riv	30° 51' 45.540"N	081° 29' 46.260"W
DBN 57A G	Cumberland Riv	30° 51' 43.620"N	081° 29' 34.140"W
LT 59 Fl G 4s	Cumberland Riv	30° 51' 40.260"N	081° 29' 23.220"W
DBN 58A R	Cumberland Riv	30° 51' 10.014"N	081° 28' 55.747"W
DBN 59A G	Cumberland Riv	30° 51' 08.680"N	081° 28' 48.637"W
LT 60 Fl R 4s	Cumberland Riv	30° 50' 58.920"N	081° 28' 45.389"W
LT 60A R	Cumberland Riv	30° 50' 49.100"N	081° 28' 37.900"W
DBN 62 R	Cumberland Riv	30° 50' 53.607"N	081° 28' 42.590"W
LT 62A Fl R 2.5s	Cumberland Riv	30° 50' 51.305"N	081° 28' 45.658"W
DBN 63 G	Cumberland Riv	30° 50' 48.058"N	081° 28' 38.908"W
LT 63A Fl G 4s	Cumberland Dividings	30° 50' 33.487"N	081° 28' 49.063"W
DBN 64 R	Cumberland Dividings	30° 50' 25.320"N	081° 28' 58.260"W
LT 65 Fl G 4s	Cumberland Dividings	30° 50' 16.088"N	081° 29' 01.716"W
DBN 67 G	Cumberland Dividings	30° 49' 59.600"N	081° 29' 11.100"W
DBN 68 R	Cumberland Dividings	30° 49' 54.060"N	081° 29' 24.540"W
RFL Q R	Cumberland Snd	30° 49' 40.560"N	081° 29' 31.020"W
RRL Iso R 6s	Cumberland Snd	30° 50' 05.820"N	081° 29' 32.460"W
LT 69 Fl G 4s	Cumberland Snd	30° 49' 37.262"N	081° 29' 26.797"W
DBN 70 R	Cumberland Snd	30° 49' 06.720"N	081° 29' 31.440"W
DBN 71 G	Cumberland Snd	30° 48' 45.600"N	081° 29' 23.880"W
DBN 72 R	Cumberland Snd	30° 48' 12.780"N	081° 29' 28.500"W
LT 74 Fl R 4s	Cumberland Snd	30° 48' 00.110"N	081° 29' 25.065"W
DBN 75 G	Cumberland Snd	30° 47' 46.442"N	081° 29' 23.003"W
DBN 76 R	Cumberland Snd	30° 47' 36.480"N	081° 29' 31.440"W
DBN 78 R	Cumberland Snd	30° 47' 28.889"N	081° 29' 37.613"W
LT 52 Q R	Cumberland Snd	30° 47' 32.460"N	081° 29' 46.500"W
DBN 79 G	Cumberland Snd	30° 47' 21.172"N	081° 29' 35.729"W
RRL "D" Iso R 6s	Cumberland Snd	30° 47' 23.568"N	081° 29' 24.671"W
LB 51 Fl G 2.5s	Cumberland Snd	30° 47' 03.180"N	081° 29' 38.990"W
LT 50 Fl R 4s	Cumberland Snd	30° 47' 02.880"N	081° 29' 27.840"W
N Degaussing RF DBN Y	Cumberland Snd	30° 46' 53.118"N	081° 29' 21.624"W
R Sensor DBN DR	Cumberland Snd	30° 46' 48.960"N	081° 29' 17.123"W
N Degaussing RR DBN Y	Cumberland Snd	30° 46' 53.795"N	081° 29' 20.094"W
S Degaussing RF DBN Y	Cumberland Snd	30° 46' 43.308"N	081° 29' 15.641"W
S Degaussing RR DBN Y	Cumberland Snd	30° 46' 43.979"N	081° 29' 14.760"W
LT Fl W 4s	Cumberland Snd	30° 46' 35.400"N	081° 29' 35.100"W
RFL "D" Q R	Cumberland Snd	30° 46' 44.881"N	081° 29' 17.749"W
LB 49 Fl G 4s	Cumberland Snd	30° 46' 30.180"N	081° 29' 20.490"W
RFL "E" Q W	Cumberland Snd	30° 46' 23.452"N	081° 29' 09.015"W
RRL "E" Iso W 6s	Cumberland Snd	30° 46' 04.018"N	081° 28' 57.247"W
LB 47 Fl G 2.5s	Cumberland Snd	30° 46' 19.544"N	081° 29' 16.592"W
RRL "C" Iso W 6s	Drum Point Is	31° 46' 03.937"N	081° 28' 57.302"W
LB 44 Fl R 6s	Cumberland Snd	30° 45' 55.351"N	081° 29' 05.538"W
LB 45 Fl G 6s	Cumberland Snd	30° 45' 52.930"N	081° 29' 11.335"W
LB 43 Fl G 4s	Cumberland Snd	30° 45' 35.826"N	081° 29' 08.023"W
RFL "C" Q W	Cumberland Snd	30° 45' 30.646"N	081° 28' 59.997"W
Wreck Buoy "WR" can orange bands	Cumberland Is	30° 45' 30.616"N	081° 28' 35.466"W
LB 42 Fl R 2.5s	Cumberland Snd	30° 45' 14.664"N	081° 28' 58.568"W
LT C Fl W 6s	Cumberland Snd	30° 45' 03.960"N	081° 29' 33.480"W
LB 41 Fl G 2.5s	Cumberland Snd	30° 44' 51.847"N	081° 29' 05.928"W
RRL "B" Iso G 6s	Cumberland Snd	30° 44' 36.975"N	081° 29' 14.396"W
LB 39 Fl G 6s	Cumberland Snd	30° 44' 31.296"N	081° 29' 07.440"W
RFL "B" Q G	Cumberland Snd	30° 44' 26.074"N	081° 29' 12.112"W
LB 40 Fl R 4s	Cumberland Snd	30° 44' 30.852"N	081° 29' 01.636"W
LT "B" Fl W 4s	Cumberland Is	30° 44' 25.440"N	081° 28' 53.040"W

DESCRIPTION	LOCATION	APPROXIMATE LATITUDE DEG.	MIN.	SEC.	APPROXIMATE LONGITUDE DEG.	MIN.	SEC.
RRL "A-2" Iso W 6s	Cumberland Snd	30°	44'	16.198"N	081°	29'	28.504"W
RFL "A-2" Q W	Cumberland Snd	30°	44'	14.158"N	081°	29'	27.225"W
LB 38 Q R	Cumberland Snd	30°	44'	09.168"N	081°	29'	03.857"W
LB 37 Fl G 4s	Cumberland Snd	30°	44'	01.183"N	081°	29'	10.145"W
LB 36 Fl R 2.5s	Cumberland Snd	30°	43'	41.352"N	081°	28'	58.335"W
LT 2 Fl R 4s	Cumberland Snd	30°	43'	41.500"N	081°	29'	25.332"W
RRL "A-1" Iso R 6s	Cumberland Snd	30°	43'	41.293"N	081°	29'	40.756"W
RFL "A-1" Q R	Cumberland Snd	30°	43'	36.348"N	081°	29'	31.725"W
RRL "A" Iso W 6s	Cumberland Snd	30°	43'	39.869"N	081°	30'	05.238"W
RFL "A" Q W	Cumberland Snd	30°	43'	30.497"N	081°	29'	41.052"W
LB 35 Fl G 2.5s	Cumberland Snd	30°	43'	29.342"N	081°	29'	04.018"W
LB 34 Q R	Cumberland Snd	30°	43'	16.717"N	081°	28'	45.328"W
RRL "C" Iso R 6s	Cumberland Snd	30°	43'	03.456"N	081°	29'	12.153"W
LT "A" Fl W 6s	Cumberland Is	30°	43'	09.600"N	081°	28'	18.840"W
RFL "C" Q R / Fl G 4s	Cumberland Snd	30°	43'	17.161"N	081°	29'	11.029"W
RRL "C" Iso R 6s	Cumberland Snd	30°	43'	03.456"N	081°	29'	12.153"W
LT "A" Fl W 6s	Cumberland Snd	30°	43'	09.600"N	081°	28'	18.840"W
LB 32 Fl R 4s	Cumberland Snd	30°	43'	03.852"N	081°	28'	24.334"W
LB 33 Fl G 2.5s	Cumberland Snd	30°	43'	00.853"N	081°	28'	32.987"W
LB 31 Fl G 4s	Cumberland Snd	30°	42'	51.553"N	081°	27'	54.433"W
LB 30 Fl R 4s	Cumberland Snd	30°	42'	46.853"N	081°	27'	56.833"W
LB 28 Q R	Cumberland Snd	30°	42'	41.353"N	081°	27'	26.332"W
LB 29 Fl G 2.5s	Cumberland Snd	30°	42'	37.753"N	081°	27'	33.332"W
RFL "A" Q W	Cumberland Snd	30°	42'	19.758"N	081°	26'	39.701"W
RRL "A" Iso W 6s	Cumberland Snd	30°	42'	17.348"N	081°	26'	33.568"W

ST. MARYS APPROACH AND ENTRANCE

DESCRIPTION	LOCATION	APPROXIMATE LATITUDE DEG.	MIN.	SEC.	APPROXIMATE LONGITUDE DEG.	MIN.	SEC.
LB R W "STM" "Mo (A)	Offshore	30°	40'	48"N	081°	11'	42"W
LB 1 Fl G 2.5	Offshore	30°	41'	14"N	081°	13'	08"W
LB 2 Fl R 2.5	Offshore	30°	41'	18"N	081°	13'	06"W
LB 3 Fl G 4s	Offshore	30°	41'	37"N	081°	14'	15"W
LB 4 Fl R 4s	Offshore	30°	41'	42"N	081°	14'	13"W
LB 5 Fl G 6s	Offshore	30°	42'	01"N	081°	15'	21"W
LB 6 Fl R 6s	Offshore	30°	42'	05"N	081°	15'	15"W
LB 7 Fl G 2.5s	Offshore	30°	42'	24"N	081°	16'	28"W
LB 8 Fl R 2.5s	Offshore	30°	42'	28"N	081°	16'	26"W
LB 9 Q G	Offshore	30°	42'	39"N	081°	17'	13"W
LB 10 Q R	Offshore	30°	42'	53"N	081°	17'	33"W
RFL Q W "(4) Mo (U)	Offshore	30°	43'	00"N	081°	18'	04"W
RRL Oc W 4s"(2) Mo (U)	Offshore	30°	43'	33"N	081°	19'	41"W
LB 11 Q G	Offshore	30°	42'	46"N	081°	17'	56"W
LB 12 Fl R 2.5	Offshore	30°	42'	51"N	081°	18'	38"W
LB 13 Fl G 2.5	Offshore	30°	42'	45"N	081°	18'	37"W
LB 14 Fl R 4s	Offshore	30°	42'	48"N	081°	19'	59"W
LB 15 Fl G 4s	Offs hore	30°	42'	42"N	081°	20'	01"W
LB 14A Fl R 6s	Offshore	30°	42'	45"N	081°	20'	48"W
LB 15A Fl G 6s	Offshore	30°	42'	40"N	081°	20'	48"W
LB 16 Fl R 2.5s	Offshore	30°	42'	44"N	081°	21'	34"W
LB 17 Fl G 2.5s	Offshore	30°	42'	39"N	081°	21'	33"W
LB 16A Fl R 4s	Offshore	30°	42'	42"N	081°	22'	23"W
LB 17A Fl G 4s	Offshore	30°	42'	37"N	081°	22'	23"W
LB 18 Fl R 6s	Offshore	30°	42'	40"N	081°	23'	11"W
LB 19 Fl G 6s	Offshore	30°	42'	36"N	081°	23'	11"W
LB 20 Fl R 2.5s	Offshore	30°	42'	39"N	081°	23'	59"W
LWB 21 Fl G 2.5s	Offshore	30°	42'	33"N	081°	23'	59"W

DESCRIPTION	LOCATION	APPROXIMATE LATITUDE			APPROXIMATE LONGITUDE		
		DEG.	MIN.	SEC.	DEG.	MIN.	SEC.
Jty LB "2NJ" Q R	St Marys N Jty	30°	43'	07"N	081°	24'	10"W
Jty B "B" W can orange bands	St Marys S Jty	30°	42'	28"N	081°	24'	06"W
Jty B "D" W can orange bands	St Marys S Jty	30°	42'	18"N	081°	24'	37"W
LB 22 Fl R 6s	St Marys Ent	30°	42'	37"N	081°	24'	53"W
LB 23 Fl G 6s	St Marys Ent	30°	42'	32"N	081°	24'	53"W
RFL fixed W / Q W	Offshore	30°	42'	28"N	081°	27'	54"W
RRL fixed W / Iso W 6s	St Marys Ent	30°	42'	25"N	081°	28'	60"W
Jty B "C" W can orange bands	St Marys N Jty	30°	43'	07"N	081°	24'	58"W
Jty DBN "F" W	St Marys S Jty	30°	42'	14"N	081°	25'	15"W
Jty DBN "E" W	St Marys N Jty	30°	42'	54"N	081°	25'	33"W
LB 25 Q G	St Marys Ent	30°	42'	30"N	081°	25'	45"W
LB 24 Q R	St Marys Ent	30°	42'	35"N	081°	25'	45"W
TB LB "C" Fl Y 2.5s	St Marys Ent	30°	42'	26"N	081°	26'	19"W
TB LB "D" Fl Y 2.5s	St Marys Ent	30°	42'	39"N	081°	26'	19"W
TB LB "E" Fl Y 2.5s	St Marys Ent	30°	42'	25"N	081°	26'	52"W
TB LB "F" Fl Y 2.5s	St Marys Ent	30°	42'	37"N	081°	26'	51"W
RFL "A" Q W	Amelia Island	30°	42'	20"N	081°	26'	40"W
RRL "A" Iso W 6s	Amelia Island	30°	42'	17"N	081°	26'	34"W
DBN "N" R	St Marys Ent	30°	42'	43"N	081°	27'	11"W
DBN "S" G	St Marys Ent	30°	42'	23"N	081°	27'	07"W
LB 28 Q R	Cumberland Snd	30°	42'	41"N	081°	27'	26"W
LB 29 Fl G 2.5s	Cumberland Snd	30°	42'	38"N	081°	28'	33"W
LB 1 Q G	Amelia Riv	30°	42'	17"N	081°	27'	40"W
LB 2 Q R	Amelia Riv	30°	42'	15"N	081°	27'	51"W
LB 30 Fl R 4s	Cumberland Snd	30°	42'	47"N	081°	27'	57"W
LB 31 Fl G 4s	Cumberland Snd	30°	42'	52"N	081°	27'	54"W
LB 33 Fl G 2.5s	Cumberland Snd	30°	43'	01"N	081°	27'	33"W
LB 32 Fl R 4s	Cumberland Snd	30°	43'	04"N	081°	28'	24"W
LT "A" Fl W 6s	Cumberland Is	30°	43'	10"N	081°	28'	19"W
RRL "C" Iso R 6s	Cumberland Snd	30°	43'	03"N	081°	28'	19"W
RFL "C" Q R / Fl G 4s	Cumberland Snd	30°	43'	17"N	081°	29'	12"W
LB 34 Q R	Cumberland Snd	30°	43'	17"N	081°	28'	45"W
LB 35 Fl G 2.5s	Cumberland Snd	30°	43'	29"N	081°	29'	04"W
RFL "A" Q W	Cumberland Snd	30°	43'	30"N	081°	29'	41"W
RRL "A" Iso W 6s	Cumberland Snd	30°	43'	40"N	081°	30'	05"W
RFL "A-1" Q R	Cumberland Snd	30°	43'	36"N	081°	29'	32"W
RRL "A-1" Iso R 6s	Cumberland Snd	30°	43'	41"N	081°	29'	41"W
LB 36 Fl R 2.5s	Cumberland Snd	30°	43'	41"N	081°	29'	41"W
LT 2 Fl R 4s	St Marys Riv	30°	43'	42"N	081°	29'	25"W
LT 3 Fl G 4s	St Marys Riv	30°	43'	23"N	081°	31'	51"W
DBN 5 G	St Marys Riv	30°	43'	16"N	081°	31'	57"W
DBN 6 R	St Marys Riv	30°	42'	58"N	081°	32'	05"W
DBN 8 R	St Marys Riv	30°	42'	37"N	081°	32'	02"W
LT 10 Fl R 4s	St Marys Riv	30°	42'	32"N	081°	32'	07"W
DBN 12 R	St Marys Riv	30°	42'	44"N	081°	32'	30"W
LT 13 Fl G 4s	St Marys Riv	30°	42'	58"N	081°	32'	42"W
East mooring buoy Fl W 2.5 s unreliable	St Marys Riv	30°	43'	06"N	081°	32'	54"W
West mooring buoy Fl W 2.5 s unreliable	St Marys Riv						

GEORGIA RECREATIONAL SALTWATER FISHING REGULATIONS

Resident and nonresident anglers (age 16 and older) who fish in fresh or saltwaters of Georgia must possess a Georgia fishing license. This license is required for hook and line fishing, cast-netting, seining, crabbing, gigging, sportbait trawling and harvesting shellfish. A Georgia fishing license is required for anglers returning to Georgia ports or transiting Georgia waters with recreational catches from federal waters beyond the state's 3-mile territorial sea. Reciprocal agreements with Alabama, South Carolina and Florida currently do not apply to saltwaters.

Charter captains may or may not choose to purchase an annual license that covers all of their clients. For this reason, anglers booking a charter should inquire whether they will need a Georgia fishing license or if they will be covered under the charter fishing license.

OBTAINING A FISHING LICENSE

There are four ways to buy a fishing license:
* There are 1,350 license dealers statewide; wildlife resource division offices, major retailers, sporting goods, bait & tackle shops, marinas and hardware stores.
  * Phone: 888-748-6887
  * Internet: www.permit.com
  * All licenses may be purchased by mail from the:

Department of Natural Resources
License Unit
2189 Northlake Parkway
Suite 108, Bldg. 10
Tucker, GA 30084

SALTWATER FISHING INFORMATION

Information and updates on licenses, regulation and fishing in Georgia's inshore and offshore saltwaters may be obtained by contacting:

Georgia DNR Coastal Law Enforcement
One Conservation Way, Suite 201
Brunswick, GA 31520-8687
Phone: 912-264-7237
Fax: 912-262-3166

Coastal Resources Division
Marine Fisheries Section
One Conservation Way, Suite 300
Brunswick, GA 31520-8687
Phone: 912-264-7218 or fax: 912-262-2318
www.ganet.org/dnr/crd

Federal Saltwater Fishing Regulations
3 to 200 miles offshore
South Atlantic Fishery Management Council
One Southpark Circle, Suite 306
Charleston, SC 29407
Phone: 843-571-4366

For information and updates on federal regulations and required permits for tunas, billfish and sharks contact:

National Marine Fisheries Service
HMS Management Division
1315 East-West Highway
Silver Spring, MD 20910
Phone: 301-713-2347
www.nmfs.gov

For information on the Gray's Reef National Marine Sanctuary contact:

Gray's Reef Sanctuary Program
10 Ocean Science Circle
Savannah, GA 31411
Phone: 912-598-2345
www.skio.peachnet.edu/noaa/grnms
Offshore Artificial Reefs

Georgia has 19 artificial reefs located from 6 to 80 miles offshore. Many are designated as Special Management Zones (SMZ) by the federal government. Within these zones only handheld hook-and-line and spearfishing gear may be used. For further information, coordinates and updates on Georgia's offshore artificial reefs, contact the Coastal Resources Division and ask for the Georgia Offshore Fishing Guide. See below for the coordinates of the Artificial Reef Buoys.

ARTIFICIAL REEF BUOYS

The following are the coordinates of the artificial reef buoys. Material descriptions and coordinates of all the reef components are needed to successfully fish these areas. Each reef is made up of several piles of debris ranging from concrete rubble, battle tanks, landing craft to barges and sailboats spread out near the buoys.

To get this information contact:

Georgia Coastal Resource Division
Department of Natural Resources
One Conservation Way
Suite 300
Brunswick, GA 31520-8687
Phone: 912-264-7218
Fax: 912-262-3143
Ask for information on Georgia's artificial reefs.

A Buoy

7.0 nautical miles east of Little Cumberland Island.
Loran C – 45447.0/61862.6
GPS - 30°55.918'N, 081°16.175'W

ALT Buoy

6.0 nautical miles east of Little St. Simons Island.
Loran C – 45536.0/61696.5
GPS - 31°18.649'N, 081°09.385'W

C Buoy

13.5 nautical miles east of Cumberland Island.
Loran C – 45372.5/61829.7
GPS - 30°50.747'N, 081°09.385'W

CAT Buoy

7.0 nautical miles east of St. Catherines Island.
Loran C – 45582.3/61489.8
GPS - 31°40.080'N, 080°58.555'W

CCA Buoy

22.0 nautical miles east of St. Catherines Island.
Loran C – 45496.7/61315.6
GPS - 31°43.505'N, 080°41.144'W

DRH Buoy

15.0 nautical miles east of Little St. Simons Island.
Loran C – 45465.6/61606.7
GPS - 31°17.896'N, 080°58.889'W

DUA Buoy

8.0 nautical miles east of Ossabaw Island.
Loran C – 45589.6/61414.8
GPS - 31°46.769'N, 080°54.188'W

F Buoy

9.0 nautical miles east of St. Simons Island.
Loran C – 45485.4/61787.7
GPS - 31°05.937'N, 081°12.808'W

G Buoy

23.0 nautical miles east of Cumberland Island.
Loran C – 45348.4/61700.1
GPS - 30°58.247'N, 080°58.804'W

J Buoy

17.4 nautical miles east of St. Catherines Island.
Loran C – 45495.5/61411.7
GPS - 31°36.110'N, 080°47.470'W

KBY Buoy

8.0 nautical miles east of Cumberland Island.
Loran C – 45395.7/61912.8
GPS - 30°46.590'N, 081°17.309'W

KC Buoy

9.0 nautical miles east of Wassaw Island.
Loran C – 45564.3/61324.2
GPS - 31°50.810'N, 080°46.550'W

KTK Buoy

7.0 nautical miles east of Blackbeard Island.
Loran C – 45555.5/61563.6
GPS - 31°31.255'N, 081°01.596'W

L Buoy

23.0 nautical miles east of Ossabaw Island.
Loran C – 45480.0/61263.6
GPS - 31°45.498'N, 080°36.475'W

SAV Buoy

6.0 nautical miles east of Tybee Island.
Loran C – 45589.7/61305.6
GPS - 31°55.261'N, 080°47.209'W

SFC Buoy

6.0 nautical miles east-southeast of R2 "B".
Loran C – 45384.5/61721.7
GPS - 31°00.386'N, 081°02.405'W

BOATING SAFETY ZONES

Boating safety zones have been established off Jekyll Island, Tybee Island, St. Simons Island and Sea Island. These zones extend from the northernmost point to the southernmost point of each of these islands and from the highwater mark to a distance of 1,000 feet seaward. From May 1 through September 30 powerboats, jet skis and other motorized craft are prohibited in these zones.

WANTON WASTE

Sort or cull your catch on the water. Return undersized or unwanted wildlife to the water alive. When you throw away wildlife you are not only wasting valuable resources, but you are also breaking the law!

SALTWATER FINFISH

SPECIES	OPEN SEASON	DAILY CREEL LIMIT	POSSESSION LIMIT	MINIMUM SIZE (INCHES)
Blue marlin*	All year	1	1	90LJFL
White marlin*	All year	1	1	66LJFL
Sailfish*	All year	1	1	63LJFL
Tarpon*	3/16 to 11/30	1	1	40FL
Amberjack	3/16 to 12/31	1	1	28FL
	No sale 4/1 to 4/30			
Cobia	3/16 to 11/30	2	2	33FL
Dolphin	All year	15	15	18FL
King mackerel	All year	3	3	24FL
Spanish mackerel	3/16 to 11/30	15	15	12FL
Sheepshead	All year	25	25	8FL
Atlantic sturgeon	No harvest allowed	0	0	0
Bluefish	3/16 to 11/30	15	15	12FL
Black sea bass	All year	20	20	10TL
Gag grouper	All year	2	2	24TL
	No sale 3/1 to 4/30			
Red drum	All year	5	5	14TL
			No red drum longer than 27in.	
Black drum	All year	15	15	10TL
Weakfish	All year	6	6	13TL
Flounder	All year	15	15	12TL
Whiting	All year	35	35	10TL
Spot	All year	25	25	8TL
Atlantic croaker	All year	25	25	8TL
Tripletail	All year	5	5	18TL
Red snapper	All year	2	2	20TL
Spotted seatrout	All year	15	15	13TL
Striped bass	All year	2	2	22TL

The season for striped bass downstream of the Savannah Lock and Dam is closed

SPECIES	OPEN SEASON	DAILY CREEL LIMIT	POSSESSION LIMIT	MINIMUM SIZE (INCHES)
Sand tiger shark	No harvest allowed	0	0	0
Small shark composite**	All year	2	2	30TL
Sharks***	All year	2****	2****	48TL
			Limit may include only one over 84 in.	
Red porgy	No harvest allowed	0	0	0

*	Gamefish or no sale status
**	Consists of Atlantic sharpnose, bonnethead & spiny dogfish
***	Consists of all sharks other than sand tiger shark & small shark composite
****	Two per person or boat, whichever is less

FL = fork length, TL = total length, for billfishes, LJFL = lower jaw fork length. See below for definitions.

SALTWATER FINFISH

Landing Requirements/Transfer Prohibition

All saltwater finfish (including sharks) under state or federal regulation must be landed with head and fins intact. Anglers must make catches available for inspection by government officials. Saltwater finfish subject to size and bag limits cannot be transferred to another person or vessel on the water. Commercial licenses are required to sell recreationally caught finfish.

Gear

A seine may not be used as a gill net (a net constructed of single webbing attached to a float line and lead line and fished in a stationary manner to ensnare or entangle fish in the meshes). A modified castnet or castnet with greater than 8 feet radius is allowed for taking fish for bait. Only flounder may be taken with a gig (any handheld shaft with single or multiple points, barbed or barbless). All seasons, hours, creel limits, minimum size limits and other regulation applicable to saltwater finfish apply regardless of the gear used.

Definitions

Minimum size: the specific size in length below which it is unlawful to take that finfish species. Minimum sizes for saltwater finfish are measured in three ways:

Total Length (TL) is the overall length of the fish and is measured from the tip of the snout to the extreme tip of the tail fin.

Fork Length (FL) is used to measure fish with deeply forked tails and is the distance from the tip of the snout to the fork of the tail.

Lower-Jaw Fork Length (LJFL) applies to billfish, such as marlins, and is the distance form the tip of the lower jaw to the fork of the tail.

Open Season: that specified period of time during which one may take certain finfish species from any water of the state.

Daily Creel Limit: the lawful amount of a species of finfish that a person may take in one day.

Possession Limit: the lawful amount of a species of finfish that a person can legally have at any one time.

SHRIMP

Baiting Shrimp

It is unlawful to place, deposit, distribute or scatter any bait of any kind in, on or over any waters so as to lure, attract or entice shrimp toward the bait or area where bait is placed. It is illegal to knowingly fish for shrimp in baited waters.

Disposition and Sale of Shrimp

It is unlawful for any person to sell or otherwise dispose of, for human consumption, any shrimp taken as bait. Shrimp recreationally harvested for personal consumption may not be sold.

Sport Bait Shrimping with Power Drawn Nets

A Georgia fishing license is required for taking shrimp for live bait with power-drawn nets 10 feet or smaller. Information on the specific net dimensions is available form DNR offices in Brunswick and Demeries Creek.

Areas, Seasons and Hours

A 10-foot sport bait trawl may be used to take shrimp only in rivers and creeks or portions thereof which have been opened to bait shrimping by the DNR. Charts of established "Bait Zones" are available at DNR offices in Brunswick and Demeries Creek (Richmond Hill). Unless otherwise designated, bait zones are open year-round for sport bait shrimping. Sport bait shrimping is legal only between the hours of ½ hour before official sunrise and ½ hour after official sunset.

Catch Limits – Sport Bait Trawls

A sport bait shrimper may not possess at any time more than two quarts of shrimp, no more than ½ pint of which may be dead and may not take more than four quarts of shrimp within a 24-hour period. When two or more persons occupy the same boat there may be no more than one pint of which may be dead and no more than eight quarts of shrimp may be taken within a 24-hour period.

Seines

A Georgia fishing license is required to use a seine for non-commercial purposes in the state's saltwaters. The shrimping season for seines is the same as that established for the food shrimping season. The Commissioner of the DNR can open the food shrimping season from May 15 through the end of February. During the open season seines may be used at any time of day in authorized areas.

Seine Sizes and Areas

Seines equal to or smaller than 12 feet long, with a maximum depth of four feet and a maximum stretch mesh of 1 inch may be used throughout the year and throughout Georgia's saltwaters. Seines up to 100 feet long and with a minimum stretch mesh of 1-¼ inches may be used on sand beaches of any barrier island in Georgia. Seines from 100 to 300 feet long and with a minimum mesh size of 2-½ inches may be used only on the ocean front sides of beaches. The use of seines over 12 feet long in any inlets or tidal sloughs is prohibited. Seines over 300 feet long are also prohibited. It is unlawful to use any seine in saltwaters such that it blocks more than half of the entrance of any tidal river, creek, slough or inlet to the ocean.

Seine Catch Limits

No one person taking shrimp solely by means of a seine, whether such person is acting alone or in a group of persons, may possess more than 24 quarts of shrimp with heads on or 15 quarts of tails taken by such seine in any 24-hour period. If any person or group of persons occupying the same boat is in possession of a castnet and a seine, such person or persons shall be subject to the limits imposed for shrimp taken by castnet.

Castnetting for Food Shrimp

A Georgia Fishing license is required to use castnets non-commercially to take shrimp for personal consumption. The season for castnetting for food shrimp is the same as that established for other commercial shrimping seasons. The Commissioner of the DNR can open the season from May 15 through the end of February. During the open season castnetting for personal consumption may be conducted at any time of day in all the state's saltwaters.

Castnet Construction

Castnets used recreationally to take food shrimp are restricted to a maximum net size of eight feet in radius with a minimum ½ inch bar mesh webbing and shall be constructed by uniform material from horn (thimble) to the lead line. All modifications, including duct tape, lawnchair webbing and bubble wrap are prohibited. The lead line must have a minimum of ¾ pound of weight per radius foot attached.

Food Shrimp Catch Limits

No person taking shrimp for personal consumption with a castnet may possess more than 48 quarts of heads-on shrimp or 30 quarts of shrimp tails in any day. When one or more persons occupy the same boat there may be no more than 48 quarts of heads-on shrimp or 30 quarts of shrimp tails on board at any time. No vessel owner shall allow the vessel to be used to take more than the allowable catch limits in any day.

Castnetting for Bait Shrimp

A Georgia fishing license is required to use castnets non-commercially to take shrimp for bait. There is no closed season for castnetting for bait. Castnetting for bait may be conducted at any time of day in all of Georgia's saltwaters.

Bait Castnet Construction

Bait shrimp castnets must be constructed of a minimum of 3/8-inch mesh webbing with a radius not greater than eight feet. Modifications are prohibited in castnets intended for taking bait shrimp. Bait shrimp castnets cannot be used to take shrimp for personal consumption. Castnets constructed to take shrimp for personal consumption may be used to take bait. However, at no time shall there be both a bait shrimp castnet and a food shrimp castnet aboard the same vessel.

Bait Shrimp Castnet Limits

Recreational castnetters collecting bait shrimp are limited to two quarts per person at any time, provided that person may take a maximum of four quarts of bait shrimp per day. When two or more persons occupy the same boat there may be no more than four quarts of bait on board the boat at any time and the persons occupying the boat may take no more than eight quarts of bait shrimp per day. Bait shrimp taken with a castnet may be alive or dead.

CRABS

A Georgia fishing license is required to harvest crabs for non-commercial purposes. Unless otherwise designated, saltwaters are open year round for recreational crabbing. Recreationally caught crabs may not be sold.

Gear

Up to six standard size crab traps (2 x 2 feet or smaller) may be used recreationally. Two unobstructed escapement rings (2 3/8 inch inside diameter) must be installed on an outside vertical wall. Each trap must be marked with a float bearing the owner's name and address. Traps should be sufficiently weighted to prevent loss in strong tidal currents. It is unlawful to place or set crab traps in the channel of any stream with a lawfully established system of waterway markers. Disposal of crab traps in public waters is a violation of State and Federal laws.

Subject to specific gear design criteria, sizes, time of day and area restriction outlined in these regulations, legal crabs may be taken recreationally year round in seines and castnets.

Crab Catch Limits

It is unlawful to take or possess any crab less than 5 inches from spike to spike across the back (other than a "peeler" or a "mature adult female" crab). Peelers must measure at least 3 inches from spike to spike across the back.

Other than licensed commercial crabbers, no person may take or possess more than one bushel of crabs during any 24-hour period on a boat with more than one person aboard.

SHELLFISH

A Georgia fishing license is required to take shellfish (oysters, clams) for non-commercial purposes. Saltwaters may be opened for taking oysters or clams between January 1 and December 31. Shellfish must be harvested between the hours of ½ hour before official sunrise and ½ hour after official sunset. Shellfish may only be taken with handheld implements. Recreationally harvested shellfish may not be sold.

Areas

Updated charts of approved public picking areas for shellfish should be obtained from the Coastal Resources Division's Ecological Services Section. See chartlets #004, #042, #043, #062, #067, and #081. Consult the DNR to make sure these areas are still approved. It is illegal to recreationally harvest shellfish except in designated public picking areas, unless authorized in writing by a private property owner with legal harvest rights to an area.

Private property owners wishing to harvest recreational quantities of shellfish or to issue permission to others must notify and provide the DNR with specific information. It is unlawful to give permission to take shellfish from a closed area. Harvesters taking shellfish from private property must have on their person proof of ownership or permission.

Shellfish Limits

Oysters must measure no less than three inches from hinge to mouth, unless the oyster cannot be removed from a legal-sized oyster without destroying it. For clams, the maximum depth from one shell half to the other must be at least one inch thick. Recreational quantity limits are up to two bushels of oysters and one bushel of clams per person per day, with a maximum limit of six bushels of oysters and one bushel of clams per boat per day.

Crabbers working from small open boats set traps for blue crabs in most tidal rivers of Georgia.

BAIT MINNOW TRAPPING

A Georgia fishing license is required to harvest bait minnows for non-commercial purposes. Bait minnows may be harvested year round. Recreationally harvested bait minnows may not be sold. Bait minnows may not be trapped in freshwater.

Gear

No more than two traps may be used recreationally, except that a United States Coast Guard licensed captain may use a maximum of four traps. Maximum dimensions for rectangular traps may not exceed 24 inches x 18 inches x 9 inches. Cylindrical traps may not exceed 24 inches in length and 30 inches in circumference. Recreational bait minnow traps shall have a mesh size of no smaller than ¼ inch bar mesh. The throat opening of the funnel shall not exceed ¾ inch in diameter. Each trap must have attached a tag or float bearing the name and address of the person using the trap. Subject to specific gear design criteria, sizes, time of day and area restrictions outlined in these regulations, bait minnows may also be taken recreationally year round in seines and castnets.

Possession Limits

No individual recreationally harvesting bait minnows may possess more than two quarts of bait minnows at any given time. A United States Coast Guard Licensed captain may possess not more than 10 quarts at any given time.

Reporting Violations

To report violations, contact the DNR Law Enforcement offices in Brunswick, 912-264-7237 or call the 24-hour hotline, 800-241-4113. To report violations in federal waters contact United States Coast Guard stations in Brunswick, 912-267-7999, and Tybee Island, 912-786-5440, or NOAA's 24-hour Fisheries Enforcement hotline 800-853-1964.

THE COLONIAL COAST BIRDING TRAIL

The coast of Georgia provides a wide array of habitats for both resident and migrant birds including ocean front beaches, salt marshes, maritime forests, abandoned rice fields, woodlands, tidal rivers, freshwater wetlands, riverine forests and others. The Colonial Coast Birding Trail offers birding opportunities in all of these diverse environments. Often located in fascinating historically or geographically important locations, the sites provide beautiful and interesting birding experiences. The time of year, the time of day, the weather, even the tides affect the numbers and variety of birds you will see making this trail one to enjoy over and over again. More than 300 species of birds have been sighted on the coast, a number comprising some 75 per cent of Georgia's bird species. Look for the excellent Colonial Coast Birding Trail brochure at all Georgia welcome centers.

The following birding trail site descriptions were gleaned from information compiled by the Colonial Coast Birding Trail project at the Georgia Department of Natural Resources, Wildlife Resources Division, Nongame Wildlife-Natural Heritage Section. About a dozen new sites have been proposed and the trail will grow in the coming years. For more information contact:

The Colonial Coast Birding Trail
Department of Natural Resources
116 Rum Creek Drive
Forsyth, Georgia 31029-6518.
Phone: 912-994-1438.

The eighteen Colonial Coast Birding Trail sites are as follows:

ANSLEY HODGES M.A.R.S.H PROJECT

Phone: 912-262-3173

Altamaha Wildlife Management Area. Ducks Unlimited's M.A.R.S.H (Matching Aid to Restore States' Habitat) program located on the remains of an old rice plantation. Many of the rice fields are managed to benefit waterfowl and other wildlife species.

Expect to see birds of prey in the fall and winter, shorebirds year round, songbirds year round, wading birds year round and waterfowl in the fall and winter. Wood storks, swallow-tail kites, bald eagles, king rails, painted buntings, mottled ducks, wood ducks, white ibis and glossy ibis all frequent this site. Look for common snipe feeding in exposed muddy areas. In summer look for wood ducks. In fall and winter black ducks, pintails, green-winged teal, northern shovelers and other waterfowl can be seen in the impoundment. Look for rails darting through the vegetation and in winter and spring bald eagles can be seen.

DIRECTIONS: Use exit 49 from I 95 and turn east onto SR 251. Travel to the junction of SR 251 and US 17. Turn right (south) on US 17 and continue through Darien. The entrance will be approximately 3.5 miles on the right.

CROOKED RIVER STATE PARK

Phone: 912-882-5256

This 500-acre state park is located on the banks of the Crooked River. The area produces several habitats including pine flatwoods, salt marsh and maritime forest.

Expect to see birds of prey in fall and winter, shorebirds year round, songbirds year round, wading birds year round and waterfowl in winter. Ospreys, bald eagles, wood storks and painted buntings frequent this site. Look for warblers during spring and fall migration. Look for nesting ospreys in spring and summer. Migrating shorebirds appear in early to mid-summer. Look for mergansers and other ducks in Crooked River. Listen and watch for painted buntings in spring and summer.

DIRECTIONS: Use exit 3 from I 95 at SR 40. Turn east on SR 40 and drive to the junction with SR 40 Spur. Turn left on SR 40 Spur and travel north approximately two miles. The park will be on the right side of the road.

CUMBERLAND ISLAND NATIONAL SEASHORE

Phone: 912-882-4336 for information
Phone: 912-882-4335 for reservations

Cumberland Island National Seashore is a largely undeveloped 36,000-acre barrier island. Access is by ferry or private boat. Extensive salt marshes border the island to the west and 16 miles of undisturbed beaches make up the east coast. A total of 322 species of birds have been seen on the island.

Expect to see songbirds in spring and fall, shorebirds year round, wading birds year round, waterfowl in winter and gull-like birds year round. Peregrine falcons, painted buntings, red knots, black skimmers and warblers frequent this large site. Look for peregrine falcons during fall migration. Painted buntings are common in summer. In spring, summer and winter look for shorebirds. Warblers visit during fall and spring migrations. Piping plovers may be spotted on the beach in winter.

DIRECTIONS: Use exit 3 from I 95 onto SR 40. Travel east on SR 40 for 10 miles to St. Marys. The Cumberland

Island National Seashore Headquarters is at the end of the road slightly to the right. It is necessary to use the ferry to travel to Cumberland Island. See the Services Section under *Parks and Wildlife Refuges*.

FORT MCALLISTER STATE HISTORIC PARK

Phone: 912-727-2339

Ft. McAllister saw considerable action during the Civil War resisting Gen. Sherman's March to the Sea. Located on the banks of the Ogeechee River the site contains a mix of saltmarsh and forested habitats accessed by good trails.

Expect to see songbirds year round, wading birds year round, and waterfowl in winter. Painted buntings, wood ducks, northern harriers, bald eagles, and ospreys frequent this site. Painted buntings are most often seen in late spring through summer along the causeway. Look for warblers during spring and fall migrations. Bald eagles are most often seen during winter and ospreys in spring and summer. Look for northern harriers winging low over the marsh in winter.

DIRECTIONS: Use exit 90 from I 95 and travel east through Richmond Hill on SR 144. Turn left on SR 144 Spur, drive to the end of the road to the park.

FORT MORRIS STATE HISTORIC SITE

Phone: 912-884-5999

Originally a Guale Indian village and later an active fort during both the Revolutionary War and the War of 1812. The fort protected the bustling seaport of Sunbury, now a "dead town". The site is approximately 70 acres in size and is composed primarily of salt marsh and forested upland.

Expect to see songbirds year round and wading birds year round. Yellow throated warblers, marsh wrens, clapper rails and painted buntings frequent this site. Painted buntings are best viewed in spring and summer. The woodlands on the site are havens for warblers during spring and fall migrations. Although most vocal in spring and summer, look and listen for marsh wrens and especially clapper rails (marsh hens) in the salt marshes throughout the year.

DIRECTIONS: Use exit 76 from I 95 at SR 38. Travel east on the Islands Highway about 3.7 miles to Trade Hill Road. Turn left onto Trade Hill Road and travel .7 mile to Fort Morris Road. Drive two miles to the entrance on the right.

FORT PULASKI NATIONAL MONUMENT

Phone: 912-786-5787

Located at the mouth of the Savannah River, this 5,600-acre national monument consists of McQueen's Island, Cockspur Island and the adjacent salt marshes. These diverse habitats are home to 200 species of birds.

Expect to see songbirds year round, shorebirds year round, wading birds year round and waterfowl in winter. Painted buntings frequent the edges of woodlands on Cockspur Island in spring and summer. This is also an excellent place to spot songbirds migrating in spring and late summer through fall. Throughout the year clapper rails (marsh hens), marsh wrens and seaside sparrows can be seen and especially heard in the marshes around the fort. Low tide is the best time for viewing shorebirds along the shoreline.

DIRECTIONS: Travel east from Savannah on Georgia Highway 80 (Victory Drive) for approximately 10 miles. The entrance to Fort Pulaski is on the left. Be careful of the oncoming traffic.

GOULD'S INLET AND EAST BEACH

Phone: 912-638-1422

East Beach, which includes Gould's Inlet, is a residential area of St. Simons Island. The site includes some county-owned areas.

Expect to see birds of prey year round, shorebirds year round, wading birds year round and waterfowl in winter. American oystercatchers, black skimmers, painted buntings, bald eagles, least terns and northern gannets can be seen at this site. Late afternoon around high tide is the best time for viewing birds in this area. Painted buntings use the upland habitats in spring and summer. Look for laughing gulls, black skimmers, royal and caspian terns on the beach. Common and red-throated loons, scoters, scaup and other waterbirds can be seen on the ocean in winter. Also in winter northern gannets can be seen dive bombing offshore in the ocean. During spring and fall migration warblers travel through this area.

DIRECTIONS: Use exit 38 from I 95 at the Golden Isles Parkway. Turn east onto SR 25 Spur and drive to US 17. Turn right (south) on US 17 and travel to the Torras Causeway. Turn left onto the causeway and proceed to St. Simons Island. The name of the highway will change to Demere Road. Proceed on Demere Road through two stoplights, past Bloody Marsh National Monument. Continue on East Beach Causeway until the Coast Guard parking lot. Turn left onto Bruce Drive just before the parking lot. The best place to park is in the Coast Guard parking lot.

HARRIS NECK NATIONAL WILDLIFE MONUMENT

Phone: 912-652-4415

This refuge is located on an abandoned World War 11 Army airfield. There are more than 2,700 acres of saltwater marsh, freshwater impoundments, mixed deciduous forests and open fields. These habitats support an amazing array of birds.

Expect to see songbirds in winter, birds of prey year round, wading birds year round, and waterfowl year round. Wood storks, white ibis and painted buntings frequent this site. May and June are the best months to view nesting wood storks, great egrets, snowy egrets, black-crowned night herons, anhingas and other waders. One of the best places in Georgia for viewing nesting wading birds, Harris Neck provides the only manmade nesting structures for wood storks. The nesting wading birds are best viewed with a spotting scope. Look for painted buntings in late spring and summer.

DIRECTIONS: Use exit 67 from I 95 and travel south on US 17 approximately one mile to Harris Neck Road (CR 246), just past the smallest church in America. Turn left onto Harris Neck Road and travel 6.5 miles to the entrance on the left.

HOFWYL BROADFIELD PLANTATION STATE HISTORIC SITE

Phone: 912-264-7333

This 1,268-acre site was a thriving rice plantation from 1800 to 1915. The habitats are saltmarsh, pasture and flatwoods.

Expect to see birds of prey in winter, songbirds year round, wading birds year round and waterfowl in winter. Wood storks, bald eagles, ospreys, glossy ibis, painted buntings, yellow-throated warblers, sharp-tailed sparrows and northern parulas frequent this site. Ospreys are most common in spring and summer. During fall and spring migrations look for warblers. Northern parulas and yellow-throated warblers can be seen in spring and summer. Throughout the year listen and look for clapper rails (marsh hens) and marsh wrens.

DIRECTIONS: From I 95 use exit 49, SR 251 (Briardam Road). Travel east on SR 251 to the junction with US 17. Turn right (south) onto US 17 and continue through Darien. The entrance is on the left approximately six miles south of Darien.

JEKYLL ISLAND CAUSEWAY

Phone: 912-877-4JEKYLL

The Jekyll Island Causeway cuts across the marshes to the island. These rich salt marshes are home to an amazing array of birds and other wildlife.

Expect to see shorebirds year round, wading birds year round, birds of prey year round and waterfowl in winter. Ospreys, bald eagles, clapper rails, northern harriers, roseate spoonbills, red knots, black-necked stilts, white ibis and wood storks may be seen from the causeway. Shorebirds are best seen at low tide from mid-summer through spring. In spring and summer look for nesting ospreys. Listen for clapper rails (marsh hens) and marsh wrens in the salt marshes. Watch for northern harriers flying low over the marsh in winter. Roseate spoonbills come in the summer.

DIRECTIONS: From I 95 use exit 29 at US 17. Drive north on US 17 (SR 520) to the SR 520 split. Turn right onto SR 520 and begin looking for the Colonial Coast Birding signs that mark the two bird sites along the causeway.

JEKYLL ISLAND—NORTH END BEACH

Phone: 912-877-4JEKYLL

This site is situated at the northern end of Jekyll Island at the mouth of St. Simons Sound. Although the beach is eroded more than the south end, the mix of beach, forest and saltwater habitats provides excellent birding.

Expect to see songbirds year round, shorebirds year round, wading birds year round, waterfowl in winter and gull-like birds year round. Least terns, red-throated loons, scoters, American oystercatchers and black skimmers frequent this site. Warblers are best seen during spring and fall migrations. In winter thousands of scaup and scoters raft just offshore. Common and red-throated loons fish off the beach in winter. Walking southwards along the beach is sometimes difficult at high tide.

DIRECTIONS: Use exit 29 from I 95 at the junction of US 17. Take US 17 (SR 520) north to the SR 520 split. Turn right onto SR 520 and continue to the tollbooth at

the east end of the Jekyll Island Causeway. Pay the fee and drive to the intersection with Beachview Drive. Turn left onto Beachview Drive and continue 4.5 miles to the north end of the island. The parking lot will be on the right.

JEKYLL ISLAND—SOUTH END BEACH

Phone: 912-877-4JEKYLL

This birding site is located on the accreting beach at the southern tip of Jekyll Island overlooking St. Andrew Sound.

Expect to see shorebirds year round, wading birds year round, waterfowl in winter and gull-like birds year round. Black skimmers, American oystercatchers, marbled godwits, jaegers, south polar skuas, northern gannets, piping plovers and glaucous gulls may be seen on or from the beach. Look for shorebirds around high tide from mid-summer through spring. Carefully examine gulls, rare species are sometimes found here. Do not disturb or come near any nesting bird, walk close to the water as far from the birds as possible. This is especially important during the hot months when an unprotected egg can fry in the sun. Look for scoters, loons, mergansers, buffleheads and other waterfowl swimming offshore in winter.

DIRECTIONS: Use exit 29 from I 95 at the junction of US 17. Take US 17 (SR 520) north to the SR 520 split. Turn right onto SR 520 and continue to the tollbooth at the east end of the Jekyll Island Causeway. Pay the fee and drive to the intersection with Beachview Drive. Turn right onto Beachview Drive, traveling south. Look for the soccer field and "Glory" boardwalk on the left. Turn left into the parking lot at the complex and walk the boardwalk to the beach, turn right and continue to the southern tip of the island.

MELON BLUFF NATURE PRESERVE

Phone: 912-884-5779

This 3,000-acre privately owned nature preserve is located on lands that were once part of an old rice plantation. The area offers opportunities to view birds in saltmarsh, woodland and creek swamp habitats.

Expect to see songbirds year round, wading birds year round, waterfowl in winter, shorebirds year round, birds of prey in winter and marsh birds year round. Wild turkeys, wood storks, clapper rails (marsh hens), roseate spoonbills and painted buntings may be seen in this area. During spring and fall migrations warblers visit. Listen for marsh wrens and clapper rails (marsh hens) in the vast marshlands.

DIRECTIONS: Use exit 76 from I 95 and travel east on Islands Highway approximately 3.2 miles. The nature center is on the right.

OKEFENOKEE NATIONAL WILDLIFE REFUGE

Phone: 912-496-3331 or 912-496-7836

This 396,000-acre area is the largest national wildlife refuge in the eastern United States. The refuge is a vast peat bog containing 70 islands. The swamps, forests, "prairie wetlands" and waterways provide habitat for more than 234 species of birds.

Expect to see songbirds year round, waterfowl in winter, birds of prey year round, and wading birds year round. Sandhill cranes, red-cockaded woodpeckers, prothonotary warblers, northern parulas and Bachman's sparrows may be seen at this site. Take the Swamp Walk, a ¾ mile boardwalk that leads to a 30-foot tall observation tower overlooking a wetland prairie. Wading birds, waterfowl and alligators may be viewed from this high position. Sandhill cranes are best viewed in winter. Spring is an ideal time to spot endangered red-cockaded woodpeckers along Swamp Island Drive. Look for these birds bringing food to their young housed in cavities dug in live pine trees.

DIRECTIONS: The Suwannee Canal Recreation Area is the eastern entrance to the refuge, located 11 miles southwest of Folkston off SR 121/23. Take SR 121/23 south from Folkston eight miles to the Okefenokee NWR entrance sign. Turn right and proceed three miles to the Visitor Center and Recreation Area.

RICHMOND HILL J. F. GREGORY PARK

Phone: 912-756-3345

The City of Richmond Hill operates this unique park. The 300-acre rice field predates the Civil War. A three mile walking trail runs along the top of a dike that encompasses the field, which today is a wooded wetland.

Expect to see songbirds year round, wading birds year round and waterfowl in winter. Prothonotary warblers, wood ducks and barred owls may be seen at this site. Look for warblers during spring and summer migrations. Prothonotary warblers are best seen from April to June.

DIRECTIONS: Use exit 90 from I 95 and travel east approximately three miles to the junction of SR 144 and US 17. Stay on 144 and continue east to the junction of SR 144 and Cedar Street. Turn left on Cedar Street and go less than .25 of a mile on Cedar.

SAVANNAH-OGEECHEE CANAL MUSEUM AND NATURE CENTER

Phone: 912-748-8068

This site contains the remnants of an extensive canal system that linked the Ogeechee River with the Savannah River during the 1800s. Today the area is a recreational facility that highlights the natural history of this rich floodplain forest while preserving the historic relics associated with a once-thriving artery of commerce. Excellent trails wind through flooded forests and lowlands.

Expect to see birds of prey year round, songbirds year round and wading birds year round. Prothonotary warblers, northern parulas, Swainson's warblers, wood ducks, Mississippi kites and swallow-tailed kites may be seen at this site. Look for the beautiful yellow prothonotary warblers and uncommon secretive Swainson's warbler in spring and summer. Look for warblers during spring and fall migrations. Watch the skies during spring and summer for Mississippi and swallow-tailed kites.

DIRECTIONS: Use exit 94 from I 95 and turn west onto SR 204 (Arglyle Road). Travel west approximately two miles. The entrance to the site is on the left.

SKIDAWAY ISLAND STATE PARK

Phone: 912-598-2300

This site is located on one of the inside barrier islands and is protected from the Atlantic by salt marshes and Wassaw Island. A tidal estuary, salt marshes, salt flats, tidal rivers and mature maritime forests characterize Skidaway Island State Park.

Expect to see songbirds year round, shorebirds year round, wading birds year round and waterfowl in winter. Ospreys, painted buntings, pileated woodpeckers and bald eagles frequent this site. Warbler watching can be spectacular during spring and fall migrations. Ospreys nest in spring and summer. Listen and look for marsh wrens and clapper rails (marsh hens) in the salt marshes. Look for painted buntings during spring and summer.

DIRECTIONS: From I 95 use exit 94 and go east on GA HWY 204 for 10.4 miles to Montgomery Crossroads. Turn right and drive 1.2 miles to Waters Avenue. Turn right (south) and continue until the road becomes the Diamond Causeway. The sign for Skidaway Island State Park is on the right and the entrance is on the left.

TYBEE ISLAND NORTH BEACH

Phone: 912-786-5917

Tybee Island is the northern most barrier island on the Georgia coast. This traditional and popular beach resort offers great birding opportunities. One of the best areas is located on the beach at the north end of the island.

Expect to see shorebirds in fall, winter and spring and gull-like birds year round. Purple sandpipers, piping plover and northern gannets may be seen from this site. This is the best place in Georgia to see purple sandpipers. Look for these birds in winter along the rocks and near the beach at high tide. Do not disturb or come near nesting birds, look carefully and stay out of their areas.

DIRECTIONS: From Savannah use US 80, Victory Drive, and travel east approximately 12 miles. At the first traffic light on Tybee Island turn left onto North Campbell Avenue then left again on Van Horn, which is at the dead end. Once on Van Horn take an immediate right onto Meddin Drive. The historic Tybee lighthouse is on the left and the North Beach parking lot is on the right, behind the museum and just past the corner of Meddin and Gulick Streets.

COASTAL GEORGIA BIRDS

Summer is March to September
Winter is September to March

LOONS

Common loon
Fairly common winter resident, fairly common transient

Red-throated loon
Uncommon winter resident

GREBES

Horned grebe
Fairly common winter resident

Pied-billed grebe
Nests, uncommon in summer, common in winter, common transient

PELICANS & THEIR ALLIES

American white pelican
Rare winter resident, rare transient

Anhinga
Nests, fairly common summer resident, uncommon winter resident

Brown pelican
Common permanent resident, fairly common winter resident

Double-crested cormorant
Uncommon summer, common winter resident

Northern gannnet
Fairly common winter resident

HERONS & THEIR ALLIES

American bittern
Uncommon winter resident, fairly common transient

Black-crowned night heron
Fairly common permanent resident, uncommon winter resident

Cattle egret
Common summer resident, rare winter resident

Glossy ibis
Uncommon summer resident, rare winter resident

Great blue heron
Common permanent resident

Great egret
Common permanent resident

Green-backed heron
Fairly common permanent resident

Least bittern
Fairly common summer resident

Little blue heron
Fairly common permanent resident

Snowy egret
Common permanent resident

Tricolored heron
Common summer resident, fairly common winter resident

White ibis
Common summer resident, uncommon winter resident

Wood stork
Fairly common summer resident, rare winter resident

Yellow-crowned night heron
Fairly common summer resident, rare winter resident

WATERFOWL

American black duck
Fairly common winter resident, fairly common transient

American wigeon
Fairly common winter resident

Black Scoter
Common winter resident, uncommon transient

Blue-winged teal
Uncommon winter resident, common transient

Bufflehead
Common winter resident, common transient

Canvasback
Fairly common winter resident, fairly common transient

Common goldeneye
Uncommon winter resident

Common merganser
Rare winter resident

Gadwell
Fairly common winter resident

Greater scaup
Rare winter resident

Green-winged teal
Common winter resident, fairly common transient

Hooded merganser
Rare summer resident, common winter resident, common transient

Lesser scaup
Common winter resident, common transient

Mallard
Fairly common winter resident, fairly common transient

Northern pintail
Fairly common winter resident, fairly common transient

Northern shoveler
Fairly common winter resident, fairly common transient

Oldsquaw
Uncommon winter resident, uncommon transient

Redbreasted merganser
Common winter resident, common transient

Redhead
Uncommon winter resident, uncommon transient

Ring-necked duck
Common winter resident, fairly common transient

Ruddy duck
Frequent winter resident

Snow goose
Rare winter resident

Surf scoter
Uncommon winter resident

White-winged scoter
Uncommon winter resident

Wood duck
Nests, common permanent resident

VULTURES, HAWKS & FALCONS

American kestrel
Nests, uncommon summer resident, common winter resident, common transient

American swallow-tailed kite
Rare summer resident

Bald eagle
When nesting a permanent resident, otherwise, uncommon transient

Black vulture
Nests, common permanent resident

Broad-winged hawk
Rare winter resident, fairly common transient

Cooper's hawk
Nests, uncommon permanent resident

Merlin
Uncommon winter resident, uncommon transient

Northern harrier
Common winter resident, common transient

Osprey
Nests, common summer resident, uncommon winter resident

Peregrine falcon
Uncommon winter resident, fairly common transient

Red-shouldered hawk
Nests, fairly common permanent resident

Red-tailed hawk
Nests, fairly common permanent resident

Sharp-tailed hawk
Uncommon winter resident, fairly common transient

Turkey vulture
Nests, common permanent resident

TURKEYS

Wild turkey
Nests, common permanent resident

RAILS, GALLINULES & COOTS

American coot
Nests, rare summer resident, common winter resident, common transient

Black rail
Rare winter resident, rare transient

Clapper rail
(locally called a marsh hen)
Nests, common permanent resident

Common moorhen
Nests, fairly common permanent resident

King rail
Nests, fairly common summer resident, uncommon winter resident

Purple gallinule
Nests, fairly common summer resident

Sora
Uncommon winter resident, fairly common transient

Virginia rail
Fairly common winter resident, fairly common transient

Yellow rail
Rare winter resident, rare transient

SHOREBIRDS

American avocet
Rare winter resident, rare transient

American oyster catcher
Nests, fairly common permanent resident

American avocet

Sanderling

American woodcock

Uncommon permanent resident, fairly common winter resident

Black-bellied plover

Uncommon summer resident, common winter resident, common transient

Black-necked stilt

Summer resident when nesting, rare transient

Buff-breasted sandpiper

Rare transient

Common snipe

Fairly common winter resident, common transient

Dunlin

Common winter resident, common transient

Greater yellowlegs

Rare summer resident, fairly common winter resident, common transient

Killdeer

Uncommon summer resident, common winter resident

Least sandpiper

Rare summer resident, common winter resident, common transient

Lesser golden plover

Rare transient

Lesser yellowlegs

Rare summer resident, uncommon winter resident, common transient

Long-billed curlew

Rare winter resident, rare transient

Marbled godwit

Uncommon winter resident, uncommon transient

Pectoral sandpiper

Fairly common transient

Piping plover

Uncommon winter resident, uncommon transient

Purple sandpiper

Rare winter resident

Red knot

Rare summer resident, uncommon winter resident, common transient

Red-necked phalarope

Rare transient

Red phalarope

Common winter resident, uncommon transient

Ruddy turnstone

Common permanent resident, uncommon summer resident

Sanderling

Common permanent resident, uncommon summer resident

Semipalmated plover

Uncommon summer resident, common winter resident, common transient

Semipalmated sandpiper

Rare summer resident, uncommon winter resident, common transient

Short-billed dowitcher

Rare summer resident, fairly common winter resident, common transient

Solitary sandpiper

Fairly common transient

Spotted sandpiper

Fairly common winter resident, common transient

Stilt sandpiper

Uncommon transient

Upland sandpiper

Rare transient

Western sandpiper

Uncommon summer resident, common winter resident, common transient

Whimbrel

Rare summer resident, rare winter resident, fairly common transient

White-rumped sandpiper

Uncommon transient

Willet

Nests, common permanent resident

Wilson's phalarope

Rare transient

Wilson's plover

Nests, common summer resident

GULLS, TERNS & SKIMMERS

Black skimmer

Common permanent resident

Black skimmer

Royal tern

Black tern
Fairly common summer resident, fairly common transient

Bonaparte's gull
Fairly common winter resident, common transient

Caspian tern
Uncommon permanent resident, fairly common transient

Common tern
Rare summer resident, rare winter resident, fairly common transient

Forster's tern
Rare summer resident, common winter resident, common transient

Great black-backed gull
Fairly common winter resident

Gull-billed tern
Nests, uncommon summer resident

Herring gull
Uncommon summer resident, common winter resident, common transient

Laughing gull
Common summer resident, common winter resident, common transient

Least tern
Nests, common summer resident

Lesser black-backed gull
Rare transient

Parasitic jaeger
Uncommon winter resident, uncommon transient

Pomerine jaeger
rare winter resident, uncommon transient

Ring-billed gull
Uncommon summer resident, common winter resident, common transient

Royal tern
Nests, common permanent resident

Sandwich tern
Uncommon summer resident, uncommon transient

DOVES

Common ground dove
Nests, common permanent resident

Mourning dove
Nests, common permanent resident

Rock dove
Common permanent resident

CUCKOOS

Black-billed cuckoo
Uncommon transient

Yellow-billed cuckoo
Nests, common summer resident, common transient

OWLS

Barred owl
Nests, fairly common permanent resident

Common barn owl
Nests, uncommon permanent resident

Eastern screech owl
Nests, fairly common permanent resident

Great horned owl
Nests, fairly common permanent resident

Long-eared owl
Rare winter resident

Short-eared owl
Uncommon winter resident

GOATSUCKERS

Chuck-will's-widow
Nests, common summer resident

Common nighthawk
Nests, fairly common summer resident

Whip-poor-will
Uncommon winter resident, uncommon transient

SWIFTS & HUMMINGBIRDS

Chimney swifts
Nests, common summer resident

Ruby-throated hummingbird
Nests, fairly common summer resident

KINGFISHERS

Belted kingfisher
Fairly common permanent resident, common winter resident

WOODPECKERS

Downy woodpecker
Nests, common permanent resident

Hairy woodpecker
Nests, uncommon permanent resident

Pileated woodpecker

Northern flicker
Nests, fairly common permanent resident, common winter resident, common transient
Pileated woodpecker
Nests, common permanent resident
Red-bellied woodpecker
Nests, common permanent resident
Red-headed woodpecker
Nests, uncommon summer resident
Yellow-bellied sapsucker
Common winter resident, common transient

FLYCATCHERS

Acadian flycatcher
Nests, fairly common summer resident
Eastern kingbird
Nests, common summer resident, common transient
Eastern phoebe
Common winter resident, common transient
Eastern wood-pewee
Nests, common summer resident
Gray kingbird
Rare summer resident, rare transient
Great crested flycatcher
Nests, common summer resident
Least flycatcher
Rare transient

SWALLOWS

Bank swallow
Uncommon transient
Barn swallow
Common transient
Cliff swallow
Rare transient

Northern rough-winged swallow
Fairly common summer resident, fairly common transient
Purple martin
Nests, common summer resident, common transient
Tree swallow
Common winter resident, common transient

JAYS & CROWS

American crow
Nests, fairly common permanent resident
Blue jay
Nests, fairly common permanent resident
Fish crow
Nests, common permanent resident

CHICKADEES & TITMICE

Carolina chickadee
Nests, common permanent resident
Tufted titmouse
Rare permanent resident

NUTHATCHES & CREEPERS

Brown creeper
Uncommon winter resident, uncommon transient
Brown-headed nuthatch
Nests, common permanent resident
Red-breasted nuthatch
Uncommon winter resident, uncommon transient
White-breasted nuthatch
Uncommon winter resident, uncommon transient

WRENS

Bewick's wren
Rare winter resident
Carolina wren
Nests, common permanent resident
House wren
Uncommon winter resident, uncommon transient
Marsh wren
Nests, common permanent resident
Sedge wren
Uncommon winter resident, uncommon transient
Winter wren
Uncommon winter resident

KINGLETS & GNATCATCHERS

Blue-gray gnatcatcher
Nests, common summer resident, uncommon winter resident
Golden-crowned kinglet
Uncommon winter resident

Ruby-crowned kinglet
Common winter resident

THRUSHES

American robin
Common winter resident, common transient
Eastern bluebird
Nests, common permanent resident
Gray-cheeked thrush
Uncommon transient
Hermit thrush
Common winter resident
Swainson's thrush
Common transient
Veery
Uncommon transient
Wood thrush
Nests, fairly common summer resident

THRASHERS

Brown thrasher
Nests, common permanent resident
Gray catbird
Nests, uncommon summer resident, common winter resident
Northern mockingbird
Nests, common permanent resident

PIPITS & WAXWINGS

Cedar waxwing
Fairly common winter resident
Water pipit
Fairly common winter resident

SHRIKES & STARLINGS

European starling
Nests, common permanent resident
Loggerhead shrike
Nests, fairly common permanent resident

VIREOS

Red-eyed vireo
Nests, common summer resident, common transient
Solitary vireo
Uncommon winter resident, common transient
White-eyed vireo
Nests, common summer resident uncommon winter resident
Yellow-throated vireo
Nests, fairly common summer resident, fairly common transient

WOOD-WARBLERS

American redstart
Common transient
Backburnian warbler
Rare transient
Bay-breasted warbler
Uncommon transient
Black-and-white warbler
Fairly common winter resident, common transient
Blackpoll warbler
Common transient
Black-throated blue warbler
Fairly common transient
Black-throated green warbler
Uncommon transient
Blue-winged warbler
Uncommon transient
Cape May warbler
Fairly common transient
Chestnut-sided warbler
Uncommon transient
Common yellowthroat
Nests, common permanent resident
Connecticut warbler
Rare transient
Hooded warbler
Nests, uncommon summer resident, fairly common transient
Kentucky warbler
Fairly common transient
Louisiana waterthrush
Fairly common transient
Magnolia warbler
Uncommon transient
Northern parula
Nests, common summer resident, common transient
Northern waterthrush
Uncommon transient
Orange-crowned warbler
Fairly common winter resident, fairly common transient
Ovenbird
Rare winter resident, fairly common transient
Palm warbler
Fairly common winter resident, common transient
Pine warbler
Nests, common permanent resident
Prairie warbler
Nests, fairly common summer resident, rare winter resident, fairly common transient
Prothonotary warbler
Nests, fairly common summer resident, fairly common transient
Swainson's warbler
Rare summer resident

Tennessee warbler
  Uncommon transient
Worm-eating warbler
  Uncommon transient
Yellow-breasted chat
  Uncommon summer resident, rare winter resident, uncommon transient
Yellow-rumped warbler
  Common winter resident, common transient
Yellow-throated warbler
  Nests, common summer resident, uncommon winter resident, common transient
Yellow warbler
  Common transient

TANAGERS

Scarlet tanager
  Uncommon transient
Summer tanager
  Nests, common summer resident

CARDINALS, GROSBEAKS, BUNTINGS & SPARROWS

Bachman's sparrow
  Nests, uncommon permanent resident
Blue grosbeak
  Nests, uncommon summer resident
Chipping sparrow
  Common winter resident
Dark-eyed junco
  Common winter resident
Field sparrow
  Nests, uncommon summer resident, common winter resident
Fox sparrow
  Uncommon winter resident
Indigo bunting
  Nests, uncommon summer resident
Northern cardinal
  Nests, common permanent resident
Painted bunting
  Nests, common summer resident
Rufous-sided towhee
  Nests, common permanent resident
Savannah sparrow
  Common winter resident
Seaside sparrow
  Nests, common permanent resident
Sharp-tailed sparrow
  Fairly common winter resident
Song sparrow
  Common winter resident
Swamp sparrow
  Common winter resident

Vesper sparrow
  Uncommon winter resident
White-throated sparrow
  Common winter resident

MEADOWLARKS, BLACKBIRDS & ORIOLES

Boat-tailed grackles
  Nests, common permanent residents
Bobolink
  Nests, fairly common transient
Brown-headed cowbird
  Rare summer resident, fairly common winter resident, common transient
Common grackle
  Nests, common permanent residents
Eastern meadowlark
  Nests, fairly common permanent resident, common winter resident
Northern oriole
  Rare winter resident, uncommon transient
Orchard oriole
  Nests, common summer resident
Red-winged blackbird
  Nests, common permanent resident
Rusty blackbird
  Uncommon winter resident

FINCHES

Purple finch
  Uncommon winter resident
Pine siskin
  Rare winter resident
American goldfinch
  Common winter resident
Evening grosbeak
  Rare winter resident

OLD WORLD SPARROWS

House sparrow
  Nests, fairly common permanent resident

ACCIDENTALS

Few records of sightings, found only occasionally:

Audubon's shearwater
Baird's sandpiper
Black-legged kittiwake
Brant
Bridled tern
Brown noddy
Burrowing owl

Canada warbler
Cory's shearwater
Dovekie
Eurasion wigeon
Fulvous whistling-duck
Glaucous gull
Golden eagle
Golden-winged warbler
Grasshopper sparrow
Great cormorant
Greater shearwater
Henslow's sparrow
Iceland gull
King eider
Kirtland's warbler
Lapland longspur
Lark bunting
Lark sparrow
Long-billed dowitcher
Magnificent frigatebird
Mississippi kite
Mottled duck
Mountain plover
Northern saw-whet owl

Philadelphia vireo
Razorbill
Red crossbill
Red-cockaded woodpecker
Reddish egret
Roseate spoonbill
Rough-legged hawk
Sabine's gull
Sandhill crane
Snow bunting
Snowy owl
Sooty shearwater
Sooty tern
Sprague's pipit
Tundra swan
Western kingbird
Western meadowlark
White-winged dove
Willow flycatcher
Wilson's storm-petrel
Wilson's warbler
Yellow-bellied flycatcher
Yellow-headed blackbird

ANNUAL EVENTS ON THE COAST

JANUARY

Jekyll Island—*Annual Bluegrass Festival*—January 1–3
Phone: 912-635-3636

FEBRUARY

Brunswick/Darien, Hofwyl-Broadfield Plantation—*February Black History*
Phone: 912-264-7333
St. Marys—*Mardi Gras*—Saturday before Ash Wednesday
Phone: 912-882-6200
Savannah—*Annual Heritage Celebration*—February 1–12
Phone: 912-897-3773
Savannah—*Savannah Irish Festival*—second weekend
Phone: 912-234-8444
Savannah—*Savannah on Stage International Arts Festival*—last weekend, first week in March
Phone: 912-236-5745
Sunbury, Fort Morris Historic Site—*Revolutionary War Re-enactment Battle*—first weekend
Phone: 912-884-5999

MARCH

Darien—*Blessing of the Fleet*—last weekend
Phone: 912-437-4192
Darien—*Spring Encampment at Ft. St. George*—March 3rd weekend
Phone: 912-437-4770
Jekyll Island—*Annual Jekyll Island Art Association Art Festival*—second weekend
Phone: 912-635-3920
Midway, Melon Bluff—*Great Azalea Kayak Races*
Phone: 912-884-5779
St. Simons Island—*Annual Tour of Homes and Gardens*—third Saturday
Phone: 912-638-3166
Savannah—*Annual Savannah Tour of Homes and Gardens*—late March or early April
Phone: 912-234-8054
Savannah—*St. Patrick's Day Parade*—March 17
Phone: 912-233-4804
Savannah—*Savannah on Stage International Arts Festival*—last weekend in February, first weekend in March
Phone: 912-236-5745

APRIL

Darien—*Darien Annual Tour of Homes*—third weekend
Phone: 912-832-6282
Jekyll Island—*Great Golden Easter Egg Hunt*—Saturday before Easter
Phone: 800-433-0225
Midway, Melon Bluff—*"Sink the Standard"*—last weekend
Phone: 912-884-5779
St. Simons Island—*Earth Day Festival*—third Saturday
Phone: 912-638-0221
Savannah—*Annual NOGS Tour of the Gardens*—third weekend
Phone: 912-238-0248
Savannah—*Annual Savannah Tour of Homes and Gardens*—late March or early April
Phone: 912-234-8054
Savannah—*Annual Sidewalk Arts Festival*
Phone: 912-239-1447

Savannah—*April Fools Road Run*—first weekend
Phone: 912-285-9235
Savannah—*Night in Old Savannah*—third weekend
Phone: 912-650-7846
Woodbine—*Annual Crayfish Festival*—last weekend
Phone: 912-576-3211

MAY

Brunswick—*Harborfest and Blessing of the Fleet*—second weekend
Phone: 912-265-4032
St. Simons Island—*Annual Seaside Fine Arts Festival and Georgia-Sea Island Heritage Festival*—
third weekend
Phone: 912-638-8770
Savannah—*Hargray Wireless Savannah Bridge Run*—first weekend
Phone: 843-689-3440
Savannah—*Savannah Seafood Festival*—first weekend
Phone: 912-234-0295
Savannah—*Scottish Games and Highland Gathering*—second weekend
Phone: 912-369-5203
Savannah—*Spring Tour of Historic Gardens*—second weekend
Phone: 912-234-1810

JUNE

Darien—*Tunis Campbell Festival*—fourth Saturday
Phone: 912-437-3900
Jekyll Island—*Country by the Sea Music Festival*—first weekend
Phone: 800-841-6586
Savannah—*Savannah Blues Festival at City Market*—first weekend
Phone: 912-232-4903

JULY

Darien, Ft. King George—*Cannons Across the Marsh*—July 4th
Phone: 912-437-4770
Richmond Hill, Ft. McAllister—*4th of July Barbecue, Picnic and Crafts Show*—July 4th
Phone: 912-756-2676 or 912-727-2339
St. Simons Island—*Sunshine Festival*—July 4th and 5th
Phone: 912-638-8771
Savannah—*Reds, Whites and Blues*—July 2–5
Phone: 912-232-4903
Tybee Island—*Fireworks on the Beach*—July 4th
Phone: 912-786-5444

AUGUST

Jekyll Island—*Annual Beach Music Festival*—last Saturday.
Phone: 800-841-6586
St. Simons Island, Neptune Park—*Georgia Sea Island Festival*.
Phone: 912-262-6934

SEPTEMBER

Kingsland—*Labor Day Catfish Festival*—first weekend
Phone: 800-433-0225
Richmond Hill, Ft. McAllister—*The Confederate Civil War Soldier*—first Saturday
Phone: 912-756-2676 or 912-727-2339

SEPTEMBER
(*continued*)

Savannah, Old Ft. Jackson—*Annual Crab Boil, Fish Fry & Auction*—Labor Day
Phone: 912-232-3945
Savannah, Ft. Pulaski—*Labor Day Special Events*—Labor Day
Phone: 912-786-5787

OCTOBER

Brunswick—*Coastfest*—first weekend
Phone: 912-264-7218
St. Marys—*Rock Shrimp Festival*—first Saturday
Phone: 800-868-8687
St. Marys—*St. Marys Fine Arts Festival*—first weekend
Phone: 912-882-6200
St. Simons Island—*Golden Isles Annual Arts Festival*—second weekend
Phone: 912-638-8770
Savannah—*Halloween on the River*—Halloween
Phone: 912-234-0295
Savannah—*Oktoberfest on the River*—first weekend
Phone: 912-234-0295
Savannah—*Savannah Greek Festival*—second weekend
Phone: 912-236-8256
Sunbury, Ft. Morris State Historic Site—*Revolutionary War Re-enactment*—first weekend
Phone: 912-884-5999

NOVEMBER

Brunswick and the Golden Isles—*Holiday Lights—A Celebration of Community*—
Thanksgiving Friday until January 1st
Phone: 912-265-0620
Darien, Ft. King George—*Drums Along the Altamaha*—second weekend
Phone: 912-437-4770
Midway, Melon Bluff—*Thanksgiving Weekend Wild Turkey Day*—Thanksgiving weekend
Phone: 912-884-5779
Savannah, Oatland Island Education Center—*Annual Crafts Festival and Cane Grinding*
Phone: 912-897-3773

DECEMBER

Brunswick—*First Night*—December 31st
Phone: 912-265-0620
Brunswick—*The Guyton Tour of Homes*—second Saturday
Phone: 912-754-3301
Brunswick/Darien, Hofwyl-Broadfield Plantation—*Plantation Christmas*
Phone: 912-264-7333
Richmond Hill, Ft. McAllister—*The Annual Winter Muster*—second weekend
Phone: 912-756-2676 or 912-727-2339
St. Marys—*St. Marys Candlelight Tour of Homes*—second weekend
Phone: 912-882-6200
Savannah—*Annual Christmas Tour of Homes*—first weekend
Phone: 912-234-1810
Savannah, Old Ft. Jackson—*Annual Civil War Re-enactment*
Phone: 912-232-3945

MANAGED HUNTS

The Georgia Department of Natural Resources website with hunt dates and downloadable maps is www.ganet.org/dnr/wild/game_mgmt. The hunt dates change annually.

The Altamaha Wildlife Management Area is open for hunts on specified days from August until May.
Phone: 912-262-3171 for exact dates.

Blackbeard Island is open for 2 and 3 day managed hunts in the fall and winter months,
the island will be closed to the general public during the hunts.
Phone: 912-652-4415 for exact dates.

Cumberland Island is open for 2 and 3 day managed hunts in the fall and winter months.
The north end of the island will be closed to the general public during the hunts.
Phone: 912-882-4335 for the exact dates.

Harris Neck Wildlife Refuge is open for 2 and 3 day managed hunts in the fall and winter months.
The refuge will be closed to the general public during the hunts.
Phone: 912-652-4415 for the exact dates.

Ossabaw Island is open for 2 and 3 day managed hunts in the fall and winter months.
Phone: 912-262-3173 for the exact dates.

Sapelo Island is open for 2 and 3 day managed hunts in the fall, winter and spring months.
Phone: 912-262-3173

Wassaw Island is open for 2 and 3 day managed hunts in the fall and winter months.
The island will be closed to the general public during the hunts.
Phone: 912-652-4415 for the exact dates.

SERVICES SECTION

ACCOMMODATIONS

BRUNSWICK

Brunswick Manor
825 Egmont St.
Old Town Brunswick
Brunswick, GA 31520
Bed & Breakfast
$75-$100
Phone: 912-265-6889

Days Inn
2307 Gloucester St.
Brunswick, GA 31520
$35-$70
Phone: 912-265-8830
800-272-6232
Fax: 912-264-3766

McKinnon House
Bed & Breakfast
1001 Egmont St.
Old Town Brunswick
Brunswick, GA 31520
$85-$125
Phone: 912-261-9100

Oak Park Inn
3104 Glynn Ave. (US Hwy 17)
Brunswick, GA 31520
Phone: 912-265-9301

Palms Motel
2715 Glynn Ave. (Hwy 17)
Brunswick, GA 31520
$35 and up
Phone: 912-265-8825

Quality Inn & Suites
3302 Glynn Ave. (US Hwy 17)
Brunswick, GA 31520
$40-$100
Phone: 912-264-9111
800-228-5151
Fax: 912-267-6474

Ramada Limited
3241 Glynn Ave. (US Hwy 17)
Brunswick, GA 31520
$41-$62
Phone: 912-264-8611
880-272-6232
Fax: 912-264-3766

Rose Manor Guest House
1108 Richmond St.
Hanover Square, Old Town
Brunswick, GA 31520
Bed & Breakfast
$65-$125
Phone: 912-267-6369

Sands Motel
2915 Glynn Ave. (US Hwy 17)
Brunswick, GA 31520
$28-$42
Phone: 912-265-1310

Seabreeze Motel
2697 Glynn Ave. (US Hwy 17)
Brunswick, GA 31520
$30-$45
Phone: 912-265-2282

CUMBERLAND ISLAND

Greyfield Inn
Cumberland Island
8 North Second St.
PO Box 900
Fernandina Beach, FL 32035-0900
Phone: 800-717-0821
904-261-6408

DARIEN

Fort King George Motel
Highway 17 South
Darien, GA 31305
Phone: 912-437-4780

Hampton Inn
610 Highway 251
Darien, GA 31305
Phone: 912-437-5558

Super 8
Highway 251 at I-95
Darien, GA 31305
Phone: 912-437-6660
800-800-8000
Fax: 912-437-3676

Open Gates
On Vernon Square
PO Box 1526
Darien, GA 31305
Phone: 912-437-6985

JEKYLL ISLAND

The Beachview Club
721 North Beachview Dr.
Jekyll Island, GA 31527
$99-$299
Phone: 912-635-2256
800-299-2228
Fax: 912-635-3770

Clarion Resort Buccaneer
85 South Beachview Dr.
Jekyll Island, GA 31527
$85-$175
Phone: 912-635-2261
888-412-7770
Fax: 912-635-3230

Comfort Inn Island Suites
711 North Beachview Dr.
Jekyll Island, GA 31527
$75-$175
Phone: 912-635-2211
888-412-7770
Fax: 912-635-2381

Days Inn Oceanfront
60 South Beachview Dr.
Jekyll Island, GA 31527
$79-$125
Phone: 912-635-3319
888-635-3003
Fax: 912-635-3348

Holiday Inn Beach Resort
200 South Beachview Dr.
Jekyll Island, GA 31527
$39-$139
Phone: 912-635-3311
800-753-5955
Fax: 912-635-2901

Jekyll Inn
975 North Beachview Dr.
Jekyll Island, GA 31527
$59-$129
Phone: 912-635-2531
800-736-1046
Fax: 912-635-2332

Jekyll Island Club Hotel
371 Riverview Dr.
Jekyll Island, GA 31527

$95-$189
Phone: 912-635-2600
800-535-9547
Fax: 912-635-2818
Ramada Inn Oceanfront
150 South Beachview Dr.
Jekyll Island, GA 31527
$54-$182
Phone: 912-635-2111
800-835-2110
Fax: 912-635-2758
Seafarer Inn & Suites
700 North Beachview Dr.
Jekyll Island, Ga 31527
Phone: 912-635-2202
800-281-4446
Fax: 912-635-2927
Villas by the Sea Hotel & Conference Center
1175 North Beachview Dr.
Jekyll Island, GA 31527
Phone: 912-635-2521
800-841-6262
Fax: 912-635-2569

LITTLE ST. SIMONS

The Lodge on Little St. Simons Island
PO Box 21078
St. Simons Island, GA 31522
$375-$600, cottages $700-$2,200, island $5,000-$7,100
Phone: 912-638-7472
888-733-5774
Fax: 912-634-1811
www.littlest.simonsisland.com

MIDWAY

Palmyra Plantation Barn
5836 Islands Highway
Midway, GA 31320
B&B, kayaking, 25 miles of trails
$120–$245
Phone: 912-884-5779
888-246-8188
Fax: 912-884-3046
Email: melonbluff@clds.net
www.melonbluff.com
Palmyra Plantation Cottage
5836 Islands Highway
Midway, GA 31320
B&B, kayaking, 25 miles of trails
$275
Phone: 912-884-5779
888-246-8188

Fax: 912-884-3046
Email: melonbluff@clds.net
www.melonbluff.com
Closed Christmas

OGEECHEE RIVER

Ft. McAllister Marina
3203 Ft. McAllister Rd.
Richmond Hill, GA 31324
Guest rooms with kitchenettes available
Phone: 912-727-2632
Fax: 912-727-2632
Email: FtMcAllister@CLDS.NET

ST MARYS

Cumberland Kings Bay Lodges
603 Sand Bar Dr.
St. Marys, GA 31558
From $30
Phone: 800-831-6664
Goodbread House
209 Osborne St.
St. Marys, GA 31558
Victorian Bed and Breakfast
$75 Sunday through Thursday
$85 Friday through Saturday
Phone: 912-882-7490
Guest House Inn and Suites
2710 Osborne Rd.
St. Marys, GA 31558
From $35
Phone: 912-882-6250
800-768-6250
Riverview Hotel
105 Osborne St.
St. Marys, GA 31558
Phone: 912-882-3242
Spencer House Inn
200 Osborne St.
St. Marys, GA 31558
Mary and Mike Neff, Innkeepers
Victorian Bed and Breakfast
Phone: 912-882-1872
888-840-1872
Fax: 912-882-9427
www.spencerhouseinn.com

ST SIMONS

Beach Club at St. Simons
1440 Ocean Blvd.
St. Simons Island, GA 31522

$105-$273 condos
Phone: 912-638-5450
800-627-6850, ext.772
888-STSIMONs
Fax: 912-638-2983
Days Inn, St. Simons Island
1701 Frederica Rd.
St. Simons Island, GA 31522
$65-$89
Phone: 912-634-0660
800-870-3736
Fax: 912-638-7115
Epworth by the Sea
100 Arthur Moore Dr.
St. Simons Island, GA 31522
$39-$79
Phone: 912-638-8688
Fax: 912-634-0642
Hampton Inn
2204 Demere Rd.
St. Simons Island, GA 31522
$69-$129
Phone: 912-634-2204
800-426-7866
Fax: 912-634-2885
Holiday Inn Express
299 Main St.
Plantation Village
St. Simons Island, GA 31522
$72-$86
Phone: 912-634-2175
800-HOLIDAY
Fax: 912-634-2174
The Island Inn and Coastal Conference Center
301 Main St.
Plantation Village
St. Simons Island, GA 31522
$62-$106
Phone: 912-638-7805
800-673-6323
888-STAYSSI
Fax: 912-638-7805
The King and Prince Beach & Golf Resort
201 Arnold Rd.
St. Simons Island, GA 31522
$70-$375
Phone: 912-638-3631
800-342-0212
Fax: 912-638-7699
North Breakers Condominiums
1470 Wood Ave.
St. Simons Island, GA 31522
$117-$359 condos
Phone: 912-638-5450
800-627-6850, ext.772

888-STSIMONs
Fax: 912-638-2983

Queen's Court
437 Kings Way
St. Simons Island, GA 31522
$50-$82
Phone: 912-638-8459
Fax: 912-638-0054

St. Simons Grand
1400 Ocean Blvd.
St. Simons Island, GA 31522
$235-$795 villas
Phone: 912-638-5450
 912-638-5855
 800-627-6850
Fax: 912-638-2983

St. Simons Inn by the Lighthouse
609 Beachview Dr.
St. Simons Island, GA 31522
$55-$89
Phone: 912-638-1101

Sea Gate Inn
1014 Ocean Blvd.
St. Simons Island, GA 31522
$55-$89
Phone: 912-638-1101

Sea Palms Golf & Tennis Resort
5445 Frederica Rd.
St. Simons Island, GA 31522
$99-$268
Phone: 912-638-3351
 800-841-6268
Fax: 912-634-8029

Shipwatch Condominiums
1524 Wood Ave.
St. Simons Island, GA 31522
$99-$174
Phone: 912-638-5450
 800-627-6850, ext. 772
 888-STSIMONs
Fax: 912-638-2983

SAPELO

Cornelia Bailey, author, storyteller
General Delivery
Sapelo Island, GA 31327
Helps with lodgings at Hog
Hammock
Phone: 912-485-2206

Eulonia Lodge Motel
Sapelo Island
Phone: 912-832-5175

Sapelo Island Reynolds Mansion
PO Box 15
Sapelo Island, GA 31327
Phone: 912-485-2299

Fax: 912-485-2140
$125 per person
Minimum two nights and
 minimum of 14 guests

The Weekender
General Delivery
Hog Hammock Community
Sapelo Island, GA 31327
Phone: 912-485-2277
Email: weekend@darientel.net
www.gacoast.com/navigator/
 weekender.html

SATILLA RIVER

Bailey's Mill Rentals
Charlie & Tricia Smith
PO Drawer 766
St Marys, GA 31558
Rates for one week to one
 month $550-$1600
Phone: 912-882-4152
Email: iwrk4u@eagnet.com
http://www.eagnet.com/
 baileyml/

SAVANNAH

NOTE: The following places of
accommodations were chosen
because of their convenience to the
waterfront, there are many more
places to stay in Savannah, see
www.yp.bellsouth.com or call the
free reservation service at 800-791-
9393 or 912-233-7666. The number
for the B & B reservation service is
912-232-7787 or 800-729-7787.

Ballastone Inn
14 East Oglethorpe Ave.
Savannah, GA 31401
Jean Claire Hagens, Innkeeper
Historic District B & B
$195-$375
Phone: 912-236-1484
 800-822-4553
Fax: 912-236-2646

Best Western Savannah Historic District
412 West Bay St.
Savannah, GA 31401
Historic District
Prices begin at $99.95
Phone: 912-233-1011
 800-528-1234
wwww.bestwestern.com

Broughton Street Bed & Breakfast
511 East Broughton St.
Savannah, GA 31401
Historic District B & B
Phone: 912-232-6633
Fax: 912-231-1111
Email: SavBnB@aol.com
http://broughtonst.com

Colonial Park Inn
220 East Liberty St.
Savannah, GA 31401
Historic District B & B
Phone: 912-232-3622
 800-799-3622

Days Inn-Days Suites
201 West Bay St.
Savannah, GA 31401
Historic District
$130-$150, $3 a day for parking
Phone: 912-236-4440
 800-325-2525

Desoto Hilton
15 East Liberty St.
Savannah, GA 31401
Historic District
$99-$219
Phone: 912-232-9000
 800-426-8483
 800-445-8667
www.savannah-online.com/
 hilton
www.hilton.com

East Bay Inn
225 East Bay St.
Savannah, GA 31401
Glenn Anderson, Innkeeper
Historic District B & B
$99- $179
Phone: 912-238-1225
 800-500-1225
Fax: 912-232-2709
www.eastbayinn.com

Eliza Thompson House
5 West Jones St.
Savannah, GA 31401
Carol L. Day, Innkeeper
Historic District B & B
$99-$210
Phone: 912-236-3620
 800-348-9378
Fax: 912-238-1920

Foley House Inn
14 West Hull St.
Savannah, GA 31401
Inge Svensson Moore, Inn-
 keeper
Historic Dsitrict B & B

$150-275
Phone: 912-232-6622
   800-647-3708
Fax: 912-231-1218
Email: foleyinn@aol.com
wwww.bbonline.com

The Gastonian
220 East Gaston St.
Savannah, GA 31401
Anne Landers, Innkeeper
Historic District B & B
$185-$350
Phone: 912-232-2869
   800-322-6603
Fax: 912-232-0710
Email: gastonian@aol.com
www.gastonian.com

Gaston Gallery Bed & Breakfast
211 East Gaston St.
Savannah, GA 31401
Two night minimum
Historic District B & B
Phone: 912-238-3294
   800-671-0716

The Grande Toots Inn
212 West Hall St. at Tattnall
Savannah, GA 31401
Delores Ellis, Innkeeper
Victorian District B & B
Phone: 912-236-2911
   800-835-6831

The Granite Steps
126 East Gaston St.
Savannah, GA 31401
Historic District B & B
Phone: 912-233-5380

Hamilton-Turner Inn
330 Abercorn St.
Savannah, GA 31401
Charlie & Sue Strickland,
   Innkeepers
Historic District B & B
$160-$260
Phone: 912-233-1833
   888-448-8849
Fax: 912-233-0291
Email:
   homemade@worldnet.att.net
www.hamilton-turnerinn.com

Hampton Inn Historic District
201 East Bay St.
Savannah, GA 31401
Historic District
Phone: 912-231-9700
   800-HAMPTON

Howard Johnson Inn
224 W. Boundary St.

Savannah, GA 31401
Historic District
Phone: 912-232-4371
   800-673-6316

Hyatt Regency Savannah
2 West Bay St.
Savannah, GA 31401
$219-$244
Phone: 912-238-1234
   800-233-1234
www.hyatt.com

Jesse Mount House
209 West Jones St.
Savannah, GA 31401
Rob & Judy Cunningham,
   Innkeepers
Historic District B & B
$160-$240
Phone: 912-236-1774
   800-347-1774
Fax: 912-236-2103
Email:
   rob@jessemounthouse.com
www.jessemounthouse.com

The Kehoe House
123 Habersham St.
Savannah, GA 31401
Melissa Exley, Innkeeper
Historic District B & B
$195-$250
Phone: 912-232-458
   800-820-1020
Fax: 912-231-1587

Lion's Head Inn
120 East Gaston St.
Savannah, GA 31401
Christie Dell'Orco, Innkeeper
Historic District B & B
$105-$220
Phone: 912-232-4580
   800-355-LION
Fax: 912-232-7422
Email: lionshead@sysconn.com
www.The-lions-head-inn.com

Magnolia Place Inn
503 Whitaker St.
Savannah, GA 31401
Kathy Medlock, Rob & Jane
   Sales, Innkeepers
Victorian District B & B
$135-$250
Phone: 912-236-7674
   800-238-7674
Fax: 912-236-1145
Email:
   B.B.magnolia@mci2000.com
www.magnoliaplaceinn.com

The Marshall House
123 East River St.
Savannah, GA 31401
Historic District
Phone: 912-644-7896
   800-589-6304

The Mulberry
601 East Bay St.
Savannah, GA 31401
Historic District
$179-$249
Phone: 912-238-1200
   800-HOLIDAY
Fax: 912-236-2184

Olde Harbour Inn
508 E. Factors Walk
Savannah, GA 31401
Glenn Anderson,
   Innkeeper
Historic District B & B
$109-$195
Phone: 912-234-4100
   800-553-6533
Fax: 912-233-5979
www.oldeharbourinn.com

Oglethorpe Lodge
201 East Bay St.
Savannah, GA 31401
Phone: 912-234-8888

Planters Inn
29 Abercorn St.
Savannah, GA 31401
Natalie Almon, Innkeeper
Historic District B & B
$110-$160
Phone: 912-232-5678
   800-554-1187
Fax: 912-232-8893
Email: Plantinn@aol.com

The President's Quarters
225 East President St.
Savannah, GA 31401
Historic District B & B
Phone: 912-233-1600
   800-233-1776

Quality Inn Heart of Savannah
300 West Bay St.
Savannah, GA 31401
Historic District
$99-$109
Phone: 912-236-6321
   800-228-5151
www.hotelchoice.com

River Street Inn
115 East River St.
Savannah, GA 31401
Historic District B & B

Phone: 912-234-6400
    800-253-4229

Savannah International Youth Hostel
    304 East Hall St.
    Savannah, GA 31401
    Historic District
    Phone: 912-236-7744

Savannah Marriott Riverfront
    100 General McIntosh Blvd.
    Savannah, GA 31401
    Historic District
    Phone: 912-233-7722
        800-228-9290
    www.marriott.com

Catherine Ward House
    118 East Walburg St.
    Savannah, GA 31401
    Historic District B & B
    Phone: 912-234-8564
    Fax: 912-231-8007

The Westin Savannah Harbor Resort
    Located on Hutchinson Island
    1 Resort Drive
    Savannah, GA 31421
    Phone: 912-201-2000
        800-937-8461

Whitaker-Huntingdon Inn
    601 Whitaker St.
    Savannah, GA 31401
    Victorian District B & B
    Phone: 912-232-8911

SEA ISLAND

The Cabin Bluff Lodge
    Cabin Bluff
    Woodbine, GA
    Corporate groups preferred, 3 night minimum. Owned by the Sea Island Company.
    Phone: 912-729-5960
        800-732-4752

The Cloister
    Sea Island, GA 31561
    $260-$334
    Phone: 912-638-3611
        800-SEA-ISLAND

SHELLMAN BLUFF

Shellman Bluff Motel & Campground
    Eulonia, GA 31331
    Phone: 912-832-5426

TYBEE ISLAND

(SAVANNAH BEACH)
Note: For more information on Tybee Island call 800-868-2322 or 912-786-5444

Beachcomber Inn
    20 Silver Ave.
    Tybee Island, GA 31328
    Phone: 912-786-6044

Best Western Dunes Inn
    1409 Butler Ave.
    Tybee Island, GA 31328
    Phone: 912-786-4591
        888-678-0764
    www.bestwestern.com

Days Inn
    1402 Butler Ave.
    Tybee Island, GA 31328
    Phone: 912-786-4591
        800-DAYS INN

Desoto Beach Hotel
    212 Butler Ave.
    Tybee Island, GA 31328
    Nov. to Feb. $59-$79
    Summer $95-$195
    Phone: 912-786-4542
        877-786-4542
    Email: desotohotl@aol.com
    www.desotobeachhotel.com

Econo Lodge Beachside Colony
    404 Butler Ave.
    Tybee Island, GA 31328
    Phone: 912-786-4535
        800-424-4777

Fort Screven Inn
    24 Van Horne St.
    Tybee Island, GA 31328
    Phone: 912-786-9255
    Fax: 912-786-5772
    Email: FSINN@aol.com
    www.tybeeisland.com/lodging/fsi

Howard Johnson
    Admiral Inn Beach Resort
    1501 Butler Ave.
    Tybee Island, GA 31328
    Phone: 912-786-0700
        800-793-7716

Hunter House
    1701 Butler Ave.
    Tybee Island, GA 31328
    Phone: 912-786-7515

Marsh Hen
    702 Butler Ave.
    Tybee Island, GA 31328
    Phone: 912-786-0378
        888-786-0378

www.TybeeIsland.com/
MarshHen.htm

Ocean Plaza Beach Resort
    15th Street & Oceanfront
    Tybee Island, GA 31328
    Phone: 912-786-7777
        800-215-6370

Rodeway Inn
    905 Butler Ave.
    Tybee Island, GA 31328
    Phone: 912-786-4470

Royal Palm Motel
    909 Butler Ave.
    Tybee Island, GA 31328
    Phone: 912-786-4763

17th Street Inn
    PO Box 2747
    Tybee Island, GA 31328
    Phone: 912-786-0607

Sundowner Oceanfront Inn
    1609 Strand Ave. & Oceanfront
    Tybee Island, GA 31328
    Phone: 912-786-4532

Tybee Retreat
    16 Van Horne St.
    Tybee Island, GA 31328
    Phone: 912-786-5555

WOODBINE

The Cabin Bluff Lodge
    Cabin Bluff
    Woodbine, GA
    Corporate groups preferred, 3 night minimum
    Phone: 912-729-5960
        800-732-4752

Stardust Motel
    Highway 17
    Woodbine, GA
    Phone: 912-576-3207

AIRPORTS

BRUNSWICK

Atlantic Southeast Airlines
    Phone: 912-267-1325
        800-282-3424

Glynco Jet Port
    500 Connole St.
    Brunswick, GA
    Phone: 912-265-2070

Jacksonville Airport
Phone: 904-741-3044

JEKYLL ISLAND

Jacksonville Airport
Phone: 904-741-3044
Jekyll Island Airport
Phone: 912-635-3636

ST MARYS

Jacksonville Airport
Phone: 904-741-3044
St. Marys Airport
400 A N Dandy
St. Marys, GA 31558
Phone: 912-882-4359

ST SIMONS/SEA ISLAND

Golden Isles Aviation
McKinnon Airport
St. Simons Island, GA
Phone: 912-638-8617
Jacksonville Airport
Phone: 904-741-3044

SAVANNAH

Airborne Express
Phone: 800-247-2676
Airtran
Phone: 800-247-8726
Continental Express
Phone: 800-525-0280
Daufuskie/Hilton Head Express
Phone: 800-480-0024
Delta Airlines
Phone: 800-221-1212
Delta's baggage phone:
912-966-3410
Delta's cargo phone:
912-966-3400
Savannah International Airport
Phone: 912-964-0514
US Airways
Phone: 800-428-4322
Baggage phone: 912-966-2800
Cargo phone: 912-964-7131

BATTERIES

BRUNSWICK

Advance Auto Parts
1931 Glynn Ave.
Brunswick, GA 31520
Phone: 912-261-2208
Auto Zone
2000 Norwich St.
Brunswick, GA 31520
Phone: 912-264-5400
**Brunswick Battery
& Electric Co.**
4183 Norwich St. Ext.
Brunswick, GA 31520
Phone: 912-265-6947

SAVANNAH

Auto Zone
30 West DeRenne Ave.
Savannah, GA
Phone: 912-352-7171
Auto Zone
1615 East Victory Dr.
Savannah, GA
Phone: 2-352-8825
Batteries Plus
7170 Hodgson Memorial Dr.
Savannah, GA
Phone: 912-352-0650
Fax: 352-9792
Email: bpsavannah@juno.com
www.batteriesplus.com
Bob's Battery Service
3936 Waters Ave.
Savannah, GA
Phone: 912-355-6017
**Interstate Battery Systems
of Savannah**
Highway 21
Rincon, GA
Phone: 912-826-2830

BOAT CHARTERS & CRUISES

ALTAMAHA RIVER

Also see *Darien, Brunswick*

Altamaha Fish Camp
1605 Altamaha Park Rd.
Brunswick, GA 31525
Bill and Rhonda Minder
Phone: 912-264-2342
Two Way Fish Camp
1400 Darien Highway
Brunswick, GA
Altamaha River fishing and
offshore fishing
Phone: 912-265-0410

BELLE BLUFF

**Belle Bluff Island Marina
& Campground**
Rt. 3, Box 3246-B25
Townsend, GA 31331
Charters, live bait
Phone: 912-832-5323
Bill Parker
Fishing out of Belle Bluff
Inshore fishing
Phone: 912-832-3030
Donnie Sikes
Fishing out of Belle Bluff
Inshore and offshore
fishing
Phone: 912-832-5737
Mark Smith
Fishing out of Belle Bluff
Offshore fishing
Phone: 912-832-5037
Wendell Wells
Fishing out of Belle Bluff
Offshore fishing
Phone: 912-832-6556
912-653-3872

BRUNSWICK

Also see *St. Simons*

B & D Marine
2429C Newcastle St.
Brunswick, GA
Phone: 912-264-1819
Backlash Charters
133 Highland Park Dr.
Brunswick, GA
Phone: 912-264-8274
Coastal Expeditions
3202 Third St.
Brunswick, GA
Phone: 912-265-0392
Captain Bill Cozine
Full day, bottom, Gulf Stream

trips, prize winning crew,
Brunswick area
Phone: 912-264-1819
Email: billfish@darientel.net

Captain Mike Evans
728 Pine Haven Circle
Brunswick, GA
Inshore charter service
Phone: 912-264-3807

Free Spooling Fishing Charters
107 Boyd Dr.
Brunswick, GA
Deep sea, inshore
Phone: 912-264-4459

Golden Isles Angling
706 Oak Lane
Brunswick, GA
Inshore fishing, guides
Phone: 912-264-1733

Golden Isles Cruise Lines, Inc
Emerald Princess
1 St. Andrews Court
Brunswick, GA 31520
Casino & dinner cruise ship
Located at Brunswick Landing
   Marina
Phone: 912-265-3558
   800-842-0115
   888-267-0177 (groups)
www.emeraldprincesscasino.com

Hammerhead Dive Center
1200 Glynn Ave.
Brunswick, GA
Offshore fishing & diving
Phone: 912-262-1778
Fax: 912-262-1774
   800-545-1778
Email:
   georgiascuba@technonet.com

Happy Hooker Charters
408 Howard Dr.
Brunswick, GA
Serious inshore, bottom fishing,
   trolling
Phone: 912-265-3298

Hildreth Charters
Greg Hildreth
Offshore bottom, offshore
   trolling, blue water trolling,
   diving, sightseeing
Phone: 912-261-1763

Hobo Enterprises
211 Choctaw Rd.
Brunswick, GA
Inshore, offshore, Gulfstream,
   light tackle & live bait
Phone: 912-265-3298

Inshore Fishing
107 Boyd Dr.
Brunswick, GA
Phone: 912-264-4459

Reel McCoy
PO Box 239
Brunswick, GA 31521
Captain Brian Jarriel
Specializes in slow trolling
   livebait, 8 to 25 miles
   offshore, also Snapper Banks,
   40 miles off
Fish guaranteed
Phone: 912-264-5111
   912-223-7790

Sequesters Charters
825 Egmont St.
Brunswick, GA
3 hour cruises
Phone: 912-265-6889

Troupe Creek Marina
375 Yacht Rd.
Brunswick, GA
Phone: 912-264-3862

Two Way Fish Camp
1400 Darien Highway
Brunswick, GA
Altamaha River fishing and
   offshore fishing
Phone: 912-265-0410

Wild Turkey II
Rick Smith
Inshore, offshore bottom &
   trolling, sightseeing
Phone: 912-264-3027

DARIEN

**Blackbeard School of Sailing &
Navigation**
GA SR 99 & Blue-n-Hall Rd.
Darien, GA 31305-1635
Nature & historical tours
Phone: 912-437-4878
Fax: 912-437-3073

Dan Drummond
706 Oak Lane
Brunswick, GA 31523
Inshore fishing
Phone: 912-264-1733

David Edwards
7 Jessica Dr.
Darien, GA 31305
Inshore specialist
Phone: 912-437-6908

Philip Kempton
1310 Wayne Street

Darien, GA 31305
Private excursions, island
   charters, sunset cruises,
   nature and historic tours.
Phone: 912-437-5708
pk@darientel.net

JEKYLL ISLAND

Coastal Expeditions
1 Harbor Rd.
Jekyll Island, GA 31527
Captain Vernon Reynolds
Inshore, offshore & deep-sea
   fishing. Sightseeing
Phone: 912-0265-0392

Captain Larry Crews
Jekyll Island, GA 31527
Offshore & inshore, full, half &
   three-fourths days. Family
   beach trips
Phone: 912-265-7529
   912-222-0697
Email: fishtrip@eagnet.com/
   edipage/bizness/offshore/

Golden Isles Water Sports
Jekyll Harbor Marina
Jekyll Island, GA 31527
Kayak & recreational boat rentals
Phone: 912-635-2938

Offshore Charters
Jekyll Harbor Marina
3405 Pelican Circle
Woodbine, GA 31569
Deep sea, offshore, inshore, fly
   fishing. Sightseeing and right
   whale watching in season
Phone: 912-222-0697
www.eagnet.com/edipage/
   bizness/offshore

Tradewinds One
Jekyll Harbor Marina
Jekyll Island, GA 31527
Head boat, half day fishing trips,
   Offshore, bottom fishing,
   diving, sunset cruises. Group
   or private charter
Phone: 912-635-3399

Weadore Sailing
Jekyll Harbor Marina
Office: Rt. 2, Box 2597
Townsend, GA 31331
Sailing charters plus Sunfish &
   Hobie rentals. Lessons
Phone: 912-223-4419
www.charternet.com/sailboat/
   weadore

MIDWAY

Kokomo Charters
Out of Yellow Bluff
Midway, GA
Offshore & inshore fishing
Phone: 912-764-6567

Sea Crews Charters
Out of Yellow Bluff
Midway, GA
Captain Jimmy Hill
Offshore sport fishing &
   bottom fishing
Phone: 912-884-7154
   770-787-5964

OGEECHEE RIVER

Dances With Fish Guide Service
Near Pooler
Fishing, camping, photography.
   Bass, redbreast, flyfishing for
   stripers.
Robert Conley
Phone: 912-748-5980

RICHMOND HILL

Diamond Cutter Charters
Captain Robert Anderson
Richmond Hill, GA 31324
Phone: 912-727-7922

ST MARYS

Canoe & Kayak Guided Tours
V.J. "Jack" Bryant
104 W Alexander
St Marys, GA 31588
History specialist
Phone: 912-882-5524

Fish Express Charters
St Marys, GA 31558
Offshore, full & half days
Phone: 912-882-6248

Fish Master Charters
St Marys, GA 31558
Phone: 912-729-5214

St Marys Charter Service
702 Conyers
St. Marys, GA 31558
Phone: 912-673-1066

ST SIMONS

Also see *BRUNSWICK*

Barry's Beach Service
420 Arnold Rd.
St Simons Island, GA 31522
Boat rentals
Phone: 912-638-8053

David Beard Charters
David Beard
Inshore, offshore trolling, surf
   fishing, sightseeing
Phone: 912-638-3473

The Boat Lot
106 Airport Rd.
St Simons Island, GA 31522
Boat rentals, crews available
Phone: 912-638-5678

Cap Fendig's Charters
106 Airport Rd.
St.Simons Island, GA 31522
Sunset & dinner trips, deep sea,
   offshore, inshore fishing
Phone: 912-638-5678

Captain C's Charters
Captain Carl Wynn
Golden Isles Marina
St Simons Island, GA 31522
Deep sea, Gulf Stream, inshore,
   guaranteed to catch fish,
   diving, nature and birding
   trips, right whale watching,
   overnight to Cumberland,
   sightseeing
Phone: 912-638-7646

Captain Hook, Inc.
217 West Point Dr.
St Simons Island, GA 31522
Inshore, offshore, customized
   trips
Phone: 912-638-9387

Captain Rudolph Beggs Charters
510 Longview Rd.
St Simons Island, GA 31522
Phone: 912-638-2874

Charter Fish, Inc.
PO Box 20694
St Simons Island, GA 31522
Offshore, inshore, bottom
   fishing, trolling
Phone: 912-638-7468
www.charternet.com/charters/
   charterfish

Coastal Charter Fishing
110 Bracewell Court
St Simon Island, GA 31522
Captain Jim Purciarele
Tarpon & shark fishing specialist, inshore, offshore, scenic,
   dolphin & alligator watching,

birding, moonlight cruises.
   Half & full days
Phone: 912-638-8228

Coastal Charters
113 Grand Oaks Lane
St Simons Island, GA 31522
Offshore, inshore, deep sea
   fishing. Sightseeing, barrier
   island trips, full & half day
   and hourly rates
Phone: 912-638-0492
   800-537-4178

Ducky II Charter Boat Service
402 Kelsall Ave.
St Simons Island, GA 31522
Captain Greg Smith
Deep sea, offshore, inshore, live
   bait fishing. Half & full days
Phone: 912-634-0312
www.coastalgeorgia.com/ducky

Dunbar Sales, Inc.
Golden Isles Marina
St Simons Island, GA 31522
Half day captained sailing
   charters
Phone: 912-638-8573
   800-282-1411

**Golden Isles Charter Fishing
Association**
Offshore, sounds & estuary
   fishing. Full & half days
Individuals or large groups
St Simons Island, GA 31522
Phone: 912-638-7673

Golden Isles Water Sports
104 Marina Dr.
Golden Isles Marina Village
St Simons Island, GA 31522
Airboat rides, fishing charters,
   para-sailing
Phone: 912-638-7245
   912-634-0052

Golden Isles Yachts
105 Marina Dr.
St Simons Island, GA 31522
Yacht charters
Phone: 912-638-5678
Fax: 912-638-5655

Great Adventures
202 C Sylvan Dr.
St.Simons Island, GA 31522
Inshore, offshore, deep-sea,
   Gulfstream fishing
Sightseeing.
Half & full days
Phone: 912-634-0503

Island Dive Center
101 Marina Dr.
Golden Isles Marina
Vacation and local dive trips
St. Simons Island, GA 31522
Phone: 912-638-6590
   800-940-3483
Fax: 912-638-4956

Kennedy Charters
511 Marsh Villa Rd.
St Simons Island, GA 31522
Fly and light tackle release
   fishing. Captain Larry
   Kennedy, Captain Mike
   Kennedy
Half & full days
Phone: 912-638-5454

Miss Bit Charter
813 ½ Oceanview Ave.
St Simons Island, GA 31522
Offshore, inshore, bottom and
   trolling fishing
Phone: 912-638-3474
   912-230-3474

Captain Mark D. Noble
Lawrence Rd.
St Simons, GA 31522
Phone: 912-634-1219

Pay Day Charters
Andy Hicks
Onshore, offshore bottom &
   trolling, bluewater trolling,
   fly fishing, sightseeing, diving
Phone: 912-634-0940

Salt Marsh Nature Tour
St. Simons Island, GA 31522
Marsh tours, birding, dolphin,
   sunset and full moon cruises
Phone: 912-638-9354
www.marshtours.com

Sea Island Yacht Club
Frederica River Dock
St. Simons, GA 31522
Vintage yachts available
   seasonally
Phone: 912-638-5145
   800-732-4752, ext. 5423

Spirit Cruises
Golden Isles Marina
St. Simons Island, GA 31522
Phone: 912-634-9026

Spot-n-Tails
Light Tackle Fishing
Captain Ed Stelle
St. Simons, GA 31522
Aphone: 912-778-3973
   912-638-5420

Capt.Ed@spot-n-tails.com

St. Simons Transit Co.
Water Taxi
105 Marina Dr.
St. Simons Island, GA 31522
Group trips, history, dinner,
   sunset cruises
Phone: 912-638-5678
   912-635-3152

Take Time Out
Captain Sam Wilson
Phone: 912-634-0503

Taylor's Fish Camp
North Lawrence Rd.
St. Simons Island, GA 31522
Inshore and bottom fishing
   charters, guides available
Phone: 912-638-7690

Vicki Ann Charters
Golden Isles Marina
St. Simons Island, GA 31522
Phone: 912-638-0001

SAVANNAH

Al Klein's Bottom Line Charters
Wilmington Island
Savannah, GA
Phone: 912-897-6503

Amick's Deep Sea Fishing
6902 Sand Nettles Dr.
Savannah, GA
Individuals and groups
Offshore fishing
Phone: 912-897-6759

Aquatic Charters
Whitmarsh Island
Savannah, GA
Phone: 912-897-4050

Backlash Charters
Captain Roger Straight
Savannah, GA
Inshore fishing, sightseeing
Phone: 912-238-4731

Bona Bella Fish Camp & Lodge
2740 Livingston Ave.
Savannah, GA
Inshore guide service,
   up to 150 people
Phone: 912-355-9601

Bonehead Charters
1317 Abercorn St.
Savannah, GA
Corporate & individual, to the
   Gulfstream
Phone: 912-234-0589

Bull River Eco Tours
Adventure Cruises
Bull River Yacht Club Marina
8005 Old Tybee Rd. (HWY 80
   East)
Savannah, GA 31410
Adventure & eco tours, fishing,
   dolphin tours, water taxis
Phone: 912-897-7300
Fax: 912-897-0668
Email: brmarina@aol.com

Captain Joe Dobbs
10 Pennystone Ret.
Skidaway Island
Savannah, GA 31411
Phone: 912-598-0090

Captain Ed
212 Battery Circle
Savannah, GA 31410
Boats located at Tybee, from
   4 to 15 hours, inshore,
   offshore, or to the Gulfstream
Phone: 912-897-1380

Fogle's Freshwater Guide Service
163 Stockbridge Dr.
Savannah, GA 31419
Savannah River, rods, tackle,
   bait, lunch, drinks included
Phone: 912-920-7021

Georgia Island Excursions
Atlantic Marine Services
534 Jackson Blvd.
Savannah, GA 31405
Serious fishing trips, excursions
Phone: 912-355-7058
http://www.georgiacoast.com

Isle of Hope Marina
50 Bluff Dr.
Savannah, GA 31406
Boat rentals
Phone: 912-354-8187

Low Country River Excursions
Bull River Marina
8005 Old Tybee Rd. (HWY 80
   East)
Savannah, GA 31410
Daily scheduled narrated nature
   cruises
Phone: 912-898-9222

Miss Judy
The Charter Boat
124 Palmetto Dr.
Savannah, GA
Deep sea fishing, sightseeing,
   specializing in corporate
   charters
Phone: 912-897-4921

Neva-Miss Charter Boat
Savannah, GA
Phone: 912-897-2706

Captain David Newlin
Deep Sea Fishing Charters
Savannah, GA
Phone: 912-756-4573

Oak Bluff Outfitters
4501 Habersham St.
Savannah, GA 31405
Fly and light tackle fishing trips
Phone: 912-691-1115
Fax: 912-691-1117
www.oakbluff.com

Salt Water Charters
111 Wickersham Dr.
Savannah, GA
Phone: 912-598-1814

Savannah Light Tackle Fishing Company
PO Box 3666
Savannah, GA 31414
Inshore & offshore fishing, full & half days, island tours, sunset & dolphin cruises
Phone: 912-355-3271

Savannah Riverboat Cruises
River Street Riverboat Company
9 East River St.
PO Box 10086
Savannah, GA 31412
Sightseeing, brunch, luncheon & dinner cruises, moonlight entertainment
Phone: 912-232-6404
800-786-6404
www.savannah-riverboat.com

Ski Unlimited
107 Jenkins Dr.
Savannah, GA 31405
Water skiing instructions, guaranteed
Phone: 912-691-0539
912-660-0501

SEA ISLAND

The Cloister Dock
Sea Island, GA 31561
Nature tours, private parties, luncheon & dinner cruises, overnight excursions along the coast
Phone: 912-638-5145
800-732-4752, ext. 5423

Inland Charter Boat Service
North First St.
Sea Island, GA 31561
Inshore, tarpon and shark fishing, crabbing, birding, marsh trips
Phone: 912-638-3611, ext. 5202
912-638-4261
800-732-4752, ext. 5202

SHELLMAN BLUFF

Lockwood Marine, Inc.
Rte. 2, Box 2277
Shellman Bluff, GA 31331
Boat rentals
Phone: 912-832-6250
800-365-1504
Fax: 832-6400
www.lockwoodmarine.com

Reefrunner Charters
Captain David Wallace
Rt. 2, Box 1575
Gray, GA 31302
Trolling, bottom fishing, sightseeing, island trips
Phone: 912-986-6162
912-832-3737
pager: 800-412-3119

Reel Easy Charters
Captain Fred Guy
Shellman Bluff, GA
Phone: 912-832-6209
Phone: 912-258-3282

Reel Escape
Captain Bud Thomas
Inshore, offshore, light tackle
Phone: 912-832-6333
912-270-5666

TYBEE ISLAND

Chimney Creek Fish Camp
Estill Hammock Rd.
Tybee Island, GA 31328
Phone: 912-786-9857

Dolphin Adventure & Deep Sea Fishing
Lazaretto Creek Marina
PO Box 787
Tybee Island, GA 31328
Sightseeing, sunset cruises, fishing—four to fifteen hours
Phone: 912-786-5848
800-242-0166

Marshland Adventures
Tybee Island, GA 31328

Inshore fishing, backwater excursions
Phone: 912-786-5943
912-308-7878

Palmetto Coast Charters
Captain Edwin Longwater
Tybee Island, GA 31328
Phone: 912-786-5403

Salt Creek Charter
114 Binnacle Court
Savannah, GA
Inshore fishing, sightseeing
Phone: 912-897-6307

Salty Dawgs Charters and Tours
PO Box 1366
Tybee Island, GA 31328
Sightseeing tours, fishing, full and half days
Phone: 912-786-5435

Sea Lark
Palmetto Coast Charters, Inc.
PO Box 536
Tybee Island, GA 31328
One to five days of cruising, gourmet cuisine, day and overnight trips
Phone: 912-786-5403

Sundial Charter Services
142 Pelican Dr.
Tybee Island, GA 31328
Coast Guard licensed
Phone: 912-786-9470
Email: Sundial@tybee.com

Tybee Island Charters
PO Box 1762
Tybee Island, GA 31328
Inshore & offshore fishing, full, half day and hourly rates
Focused sightseeing trips
Phone: 912-786-4801

BOAT CLEANING

ST SIMONS

Akers, Alan
Phone: 912-638-3163

L Mac's
Home or marina, boat detailing
Golden Isles area
Linda McNeal
Phone: 912-230-2893
Pager: 912-262-7782
800-755-3036

SAVANNAH

Yacht Management
Tim Quante
Phone: 912-354-3233
912-667-7691

BOAT DEALERS

BRUNSWICK

Atlantic Marine
3663 Community Rd.
Brunswick, GA
Sea Doo, Pro Sports, Lake
Sport Bass Boats, Carolina
Skiffs, Mariner, Tohatsu,
Yamaha.
Phone: 912-264-0150

Beasley Motor Sports
100 Marsh Rd.
Brunswick, GA
Kawasaki and Polaris jet ski
watercraft
Phone: 912-264-2610

Ellis Marine Inc
3687 Community Rd.
Brunswick, GA
Honda, Johnson, Yamaha, all
major brands
Phone: 912-264-4124
888-235-4003

Satilla Marine Inc
1807 Reynolds St.
Waycross, GA
Yamaha, Evinrude, boats
Phone: 912-285-8115

Shoreline Marine
3517 Darien HWY
Brunswick, GA
Pro Line, Mako Marine,
Sailfish, Yamaha, Evinrude

**Southeast Adventure
Outfitters**
US HWY 17 S
(Next to Spanky's)
Brunswick, GA
Kayaks, canoes
Phone: 912-265-5292

Suncoast Inflatables
Achilles, Alliance, Apex, Avon,
Caribe, Novurana,
inflatables & liferafts
Phone: 888-572-4317

www.suncoastinflatables.com

DARIEN

Also see *Shellman Buff*

Shoreline Marine of Darien
Phone: 912-437-4146

JEKYLL ISLAND

Jekyll Harbor Marina
1 Harbor Rd.
Jekyll Island, GA 31527
Phone: 912-635-3137

MIDWAY

Buck's Outboard Service
Isle of Wight
Midway, GA 31320
Evinrude, Johnson, OMC
parts, closed Sunday and
Monday
Phone: 912-884-5955

RICHMOND HILL

Shoreline Marine
I 95 and HWY 144, Exit 90
Richmond Hill, GA 31324
Mako, Proline, Sailfish,
Duracraft, Donzi, Key Largo
Phone: 912-756-2546
Fax: 912-756-2518

ST MARYS

C & C Marine & Auto
209 Spur 40
St. Marys, GA 31558
Carolina Skiff, Suzuki,
Mercury, Marine Force,
Mariner.
Phone: 912-882-0744

ST SIMONS ISLAND

Coastal Outdoor & Marine
117 Marina Dr.
St. Simons Island, GA 31522
Century Boats, Contender
Boats, Yamaha.
Phone: 912-634-2848

Dunbar Sales, Inc

Golden Isles Marina
St. Simons Island, GA 31522
Catalina, Morgan sailing boats
Phone: 912-638-8573

Golden Isles Yachts
105 Marina Dr.
St. Simons Island, GA 31522
Phone: 912-638-5678

Hampton River Club Marina
1000 Hampton River Club Dr.
St. Simons Island, GA 31522
Phone: 912-638-1210

Ocean Motion Surf Co.
1300 Ocean Blvd.
St. Simons Island, GA 31522
Sea kayaks, Hobie Cats,
sailboards
Phone: 912-638-5225
800-669-5215

Southeast Adventure Outfitters
313 Mallory St.
St. Simons Island, GA 31522
Kayaks, canoes
Phone: 912-638-6732

Suncoast Inflatables
Achilles, Alliance, Apex, Avon,
Caribe, Novurana,
inflatables & liferafts
Phone: 888-572-4317
www.suncoastinflatables.com

SAVANNAH

A Boater's Paradise
3005 East Victory Dr.
Thunderbolt, GA 31404
Bayliner, Johnson, Mercury,
Monterey, Mercruiser,
Volvo, OMC
Phone: 912-354-7759
912-351-0268 (parts)

**B & B Thunderbolt Marine
Services**
2704 Whatley Ave.
Thunderbolt, GA 31404
Phone: 912-354-5884

Beasley Motor Co, Inc
4317 Ogeechee Rd.
Savannah, GA
Polaris watercraft
Phone: 912-234-6446

Boat Center
Sam Smith's
49 Douglas St.
Savannah, GA
2 blocks north of Oglethorpe
Mall

Evinrude, Johnson, Yamaha, Mercury, Mariner, Force, Nissan, Chrysler
Phone: 912-355-0025

Coastmarine Inc.
2215 Dean Forest Rd.
Savannah, Ga
Sales and service, Cobia, Yamaha
Phone: 912-966-2550

Honda/Yamaha of Savannah
11512 Abercorn St.
Savannah, GA
Waverunner, Yamaha, Honda
Phone: 912-927-7070

Isle of Hope Marina
50 Bluff Dr.
Savannah, GA 31406
Honda, Suzuki, Campion, Angler, Carolina Skiffs, Hobie kayaks
Phone: 912-354-8187

Sail Harbor Marina
618 Wilmington Island Rd.
Savannah, GA 31410
Phone: 912-897-2896
Fax: 912-897-7252

Savannah Kawasaki Sea Doo
7210 Skidaway Rd.
Savannah, GA
Kawasaki, Suzuki, Sea Doo watercraft & jet boats.
Phone: 912 352-7710

Sea Island Yacht Sales Inc
109 East 66th St.
Savannah, GA
Luhrs, full brokerage
Phone: 912-356-3355

Sea Ray of Savannah
3518 Old Tybee Rd.
Thunderbolt, GA 31404
Sea Ray, Edgewater
Phone: 912-897-9881

SouthEast Boat Works
3227 Russell St.
Thunderbolt, GA 31404
Phone: 912-354-1607

Sports Center
21 Stephenson Ave.
Savannah, GA
Phone: 912-351-9288

SHELLMAN BLUFF

Lockwood Marine
Rte. 2, Box 2277
Shellman Bluff, GA 31331

Grady White Boats, Boston Whaler, Wellcraft, Carolina Skiff, Honda, Mercury, Evinrude, Yamaha, Force, Mercruiser, Volvo.
Phone: 912-832-6250
800-365-1504
www.lockwoodmarine.com

BOAT RAMPS

ALTAMAHA RIVER

Also see *Darien*

Altamaha Fish Camp
Chartlet #052
North Glynn County
Everett, GA
One double lane paved ramp. Floating dock.
From I 95 use exit 36 and go northwest on US HWY 341 for approximately 14 miles to Everett. Turn right (north) onto Altamaha Park Road and drive 1.25 miles to the end of the road.

BRUNSWICK

Blythe Island Beach Drive Park Boat Ramp
Chartlet #063
Brunswick, GA
Two single lane concrete ramps.
From I 95 use exit 29, go south on US HWY 17 for 0.6 mile to GA HWY 303. Turn right (north) 3.8 miles to Blythe Island Drive. Turn left 1.1 miles to Park Street. Turn right 0.1 mile.

Blythe Island Regional Park
Chartlet #063
Route 6, Box 224
Brunswick, GA 31525
6616 Blythe Island Highway
One single lane concrete ramp. Floating dock.
From I 95 use exit 29, go south on US HWY 17 for .6 mile to GA HWY 303. Turn

right (north) 3.6 miles to park entrance, drive 1.4 miles to ramp.
Phone: 800-343-7855

Mackay River Boat Ramp
Chartlet #059
Torras Causeway, .3 miles past Mackay River Bridge
Brunswick, GA
One double lane concrete ramp.
From I 95 use exit 38, go south on Spur 25 (North Golden Isles Expressway) 4.3 miles to US HWY 17. Turn right (south) and go 1.7 miles to Torras Causeway. Turn left (east) and go 3.7 miles, drive over the Mackay River Bridge preparing to turn right. After the bridge the boat ramp is .3 mile on the right (south) side of the causeway. Turn right making a U turn onto the side road and drive back to the river.

South Brunswick River Bridge
Chartlet #063
HWY 303 at the South Brunswick River Bridge
Brunswick, GA
One single lane concrete ramp.
From I 95 use exit 29 and go south on US HWY 17 .6 mile to GA HWY 303. Turn right (north) and go 1.5 miles to the South Brunswick River Bridge. The ramp is on the left before crossing the bridge.

Turtle River Boat Ramp
Chartlet #063
HWY 303 at the Turtle River Bridge
Brunswick, GA
One single lane concrete ramp.
From I 95 use exit 29 and go south on US HWY 17 for .6 mile to GA HWY 303. Turn right (north) and go 5.2 miles to the Turtle River Bridge. The boat ramp is on the left after crossing the bridge.

BRYAN COUNTY

See *Richmond Hill*

CAMDEN COUNTY

Also see *Little Satilla River,
St. Marys, Woodbine*

Harriett's Bluff Boat Ramp

Chartlet #082

East central Camden County on Crooked River.

One wide single lane paved ramp. Floating dock.

From I 95 use exit 7, go east on Harriett's Bluff Road for 5 miles to the Harriett's Bluff sign. Turn right and go .4 mile to Crooked River Road. Turn right; drive .3 mile to the ramp located on the left.

White Oak Creek Boat Ramp

Chartlet #071

Central Camden County

One wide single lane paved ramp. Floating dock.

From I 95 use exit 14, go north (westward) on GA Spur 25 2.3 miles to US HWY 17. Turn right (north) and travel 5.4 miles to White Oak Creek Bridge. The ramp is located on the north side of the bridge on the right side.

DARIEN

Also see *Sapelo River*

Blue n' Hall Boat Dock

Chartlet #046

Eastern Darien, located at The Ridge

Darien, GA

One single lane paved ramp. Floating dock.

From I 95 use exit 49, go south on GA HWY 251 for 1.2 miles to US HWY 17. Turn right (south) and drive .9 mile to GA HWY 99. Turn left (north) and go 4.4 miles to the Blue n' Hall Park sign on the right. Turn right and drive to the end of the road. The public facilities are slightly to the left.

Champney River Boat Ramp

Chartlets #048 and #050

McIntosh County, south of Darien.

Darien, GA

One double lane paved ramp. Floating dock.

From I 95 use exit 49, go south on GA HWY 251 for 1.2 miles to US HWY 17. Turn right (south) and go 3.3 miles, crossing the Champney River Bridge. South of the bridge turn left into the parking area.

Darien City Boat Ramp

Chartlets #048 and #050

Downtown Darien

Darien, GA

One single lane paved ramp. Floating dock.

From I 95 use exit 49, go south on GA HWY 251 1.2 miles to US HWY 17. Turn right (south) and drive 1.2 miles to Broad Street. Do not cross the bridge. Turn right onto Broad Street and go .1 mile, take the first left down to the river. The boat ramp is at the bottom of the road.

HARRIS NECK

Barbour River Landing

Chartlet #035

Eastern McIntosh County, east shore of Harris Neck.

One wide single lane paved ramp.

This boat ramp is closed from March 1 to August 1 during Wood Stork nesting and feeding season.

From I 95 use exit 67, go south on US HWY 17 for 1 mile to GA HWY 131. Turn left (south) and travel 7.1 miles to the end of Harris Neck Road (HWY 131). Turn left on Barbour Landing Road into Harris Neck Wildlife Refuge and drive .5 mile to the ramp. This last half-mile is sand and can be slippery driving. The boat ramp is on the right.

Harris Neck Wildlife Refuge Boat Ramp

Not shown on a chartlet

Eastern McIntosh County, northwest shore of Harris Neck.

One single lane paved ramp. This ramp is recommended for small boats only, it is slippery.

From I 95 use exit 67, go south on US HWY 17 for 1 mile to GA HWY 131. Turn left (south) and travel 6.2 miles to Harris Neck Creek Bridge located at Harris Neck Wildlife Refuge. Cross the bridge and turn left into the refuge. Ramp located on the left.

JEKYLL ISLAND

Jekyll Island Boat Ramp

Chartlet #066

South Riverview Dr.

Jekyll Island, GA 31527

One single lane concrete ramp.

From I 95 use exit 29 and go north on HWY 17 for 5 miles to the Jekyll Island Causeway (GA HWY 50). Turn right (east) and go 6.5 miles to Riverview Drive. Turn right (south) and drive .6 mile to Water Ski Park sign. Turn right and go .5 mile on a dirt road to the ramp.

LIBERTY COUNTY

Also see *Sunbury*

Liberty County Regional Park Boat Ramp

Chartlet #028

North central Liberty County, south of the Isle of Wight.

Midway, GA

One single paved lane, very narrow, recommended for small boats only.

From I 95 use exit 76 and drive west on GA HWY 38 for 1.5 miles to Isle of Wight Road. Turn right and go 1.9 miles to the park located on the right (west) before crossing Jones Creek Bridge.

South Newport River Boat Ramp

Chartlet #027

South central Liberty County on the South Newport River.

One wide single lane paved ramp. Floating dock.

From I 95 use exit 67, go south on US HWY 17 .75 mile to the South Newport River Bridge. Turn left (east) before crossing the bridge into the ramp area.

LITTLE SATILLA RIVER

Little Satilla Boat Ramp

Chartlet #063

North central Camden County on the Little Satilla River

One single lane ramp.

From I 95 use exit 26, go west on Dover Bluff Road for 1.8 miles to US HWY 17. Turn right (north) and go .7 mile. The ramp is on the right before crossing the Little Satilla River.

MCINTOSH COUNTY

Also see *Darien, Harris Neck, Sapelo River*

White Chimney Creek Boat Ramp

Chartlet #038, top of creek

North central McIntosh County, west of Shellman Bluff.

One narrow single lane paved ramp. Floating dock.

From I 95 use exit 58, go south on GA HWY 57 for 1 mile to US HWY 17. Turn left (north) and drive 2.2 miles to Pine Harbor Road. Turn right (east), go .1 mile to Shellman Bluff Road (at this point this road may be called Young Man Road on some maps). Turn left (north) onto this road and travel 4.5 miles to the White Chimney Creek Bridge. The ramp is across the bridge on the right (south) side of the road.

MIDWAY

See *Liberty County*

OGEECHEE RIVER

Also see *Richmond Hill*

Kings Ferry Community Park

Boat Ramp

Chartlet #022

South central Chatham County on the Ogeechee River

One double lane paved ramp. Floating dock.

From I 95 use exit 94 and go east on GA HWY 204 for 2.1 miles to US HWY 17. Turn right and go south on HWY 17 for 2.7 miles. The community park is located on the left before crossing the Ogeechee River.

RICHMOND HILL

Demeries Creek Boat Ramp

Chartlet #026

Southeastern Bryan County, south of Richmond Hill and south of Keller. North of Medway River.

One single lane concrete ramp. Floating dock.

From I 95 use exit 90 and drive east on GA HWY 144 for 14.1 miles. The ramp is located on the right, next to the Georgia Department of Natural Resources Law Enforcement Office.

Fort McAllister Ogeechee River

Boat Ramp

Chartlet #021

Eastern Bryan County. On the north side of the park on the Ogeechee River.

Richmond Hill, GA

One single lane paved ramp. Floating dock.

From I 95 use exit 90 and drive east on GA HWY 144 for 6.6 miles to GA HWY Spur 144. Turn left and go 3.7 miles to Fort McAllister State Park Entrance. The ramp is located on the left just before the park entrance.

Fort McAllister Red Bird Creek Boat Ramp—for camp users only.

Chartlet #021

Richmond Hill, GA

Eastern Bryan County. On the south side of the park, on Savage Island on Red Bird Creek.

One short single lane concrete ramp. Floating dock.

From I 95 use exit 90 and drive east on GA HWY 144 for 6.6 miles to GA HWY Spur 144. Turn left and go 3.7 miles to Fort McAllister State Park. Visitors must check in with the park office .1 mile beyond the entrance. The boat ramp and camp grounds are 1.5 miles past the park office. Use of the ramp is limited to campers and kayak rentals

Jerico River Public Boat Ramp

Chartlet #027

West of Keller on the Jerico River

Richmond Hill, GA

One single ramp, narrow.

From I 95 use exit 87 and go south on US HWY 17 approximately 2.9 miles. Turn left (south) at Belfast Siding Road. Continue on Belfast Siding passing under I 95 for about 4.4 miles to a boat ramp sign on the right. Make a tight turn to the right. Continue about .75 miles to the dead end, turn left. The boat ramp is at the end of the road.

ST MARYS

Crooked River State Park Boat Ramp

Chartlet #082

Central eastern Camden County, north of St. Marys.

St. Marys, GA

One double lane paved ramp. Floating dock.

From I 95 use exit 3, go east on GA HWY 40 for 3.6 miles to King's Bay Road. Turn left and drive 2.1 miles to GA Spur 40. Turn left (north) and travel 4.2 miles to the boat ramp located at the end of the road.

Dark Entry Creek Boat Ramp
Chartlet #086

South Camden County on the western side of St. Marys.

One unpaved single lane ramp.

From I 95 use exit 3, go east on GA HWY 40 for 5.5 miles to Dark Entry Creek Bridge. The ramp is located on the right (south side) before the bridge.

St. Marys City Boat Ramp
Chartlet #086

Downtown St. Marys

St. Marys, GA

Two wide single lane paved ramps. Floating dock.

From I 95 use exit 3 and go east on GA HWY 40 for 9.3 miles to St. Marys Street. Turn right and drive .1 mile to the boat ramp located on the left.

St. Marys River Boat Ramp
Chartlet #087

On US HWY 17

South central Camden County

One single lane ramp.

From I 95 use exit 3, go west on GA HWY40 1.8 miles to US HWY 17. Turn left (south) and drive 3.9 miles to the St. Marys River Bridge. The ramp is located on the left side of the road before crossing the bridge.

ST SIMONS

Village Creek Boat Ramp
Chartlet #058

Harrington

St. Simons Island, GA 31522

One single lane ramp.

From I 95 use exit 38 and go south on Spur 25 (North Golden Isles Expressway) 4.3 miles to US HWY 17. Turn right (south) and go 1.7 miles to Torras Causeway. Turn left (east) onto the causeway and drive 4.4 miles to Sea Island Road. Turn left

(north) and go 3.1 miles to Frederica Road. Turn left and drive 1.7 miles to Harrington Drive (at the Red Barn Restaurant). Turn right and go .9 mile to the end of the road. The ramp is located on the right. Creek may dry at low tide.

SAPELO RIVER

Belleville Boat Ramp
Chartlet #038

McIntosh County on the Satilla River

Darien, GA

One single lane paved ramp.

Ramp in need of repair, parking area is inadequate.

From I 95 use exit 58, go south on GA HWY 57 5.1 miles to Belleville Road. Turn left, drive 1.6 miles to the ramp. (Close to the end of the docks)

SATILLA RIVER

See *Woodbine*

SAVANNAH

Also see *Savannah River Boat Ramps in Chapter II*

Bell's Landing Boat Ramp
Chartlet #014

South Chatham County

Savannah, GA

One double lane paved ramp. Floating dock

From I 95 use exit 94 and go east on GA HWY 204 for 7.1 miles to Apache Avenue. Turn right (south) and drive .6 mile to the end of the avenue. The boat ramp and parking are on the left.

Houlihan Boat Ramp Park
Chartlet Savannah River #17

On the Savannah River at Port Wentworth

Savannah, GA

Two single lane concrete ramps. Floating dock.

From I 95 use exit 109 and go

south on GA HWY 30 for 2.7 miles. Turn left and continue south on GA HWY 30 for .9 mile to GA HWY 25. Turn left (north) for .8 mile. The park is located on the right before crossing the Houlihan Bridge.

Montgomery Boat Ramp
Chartlet #013

South Chatham County, on the Vernon River

Savannah, GA

One single lane paved ramp.

From I 95 use exit 94 and go east on GA HWY 204 for 10.4 miles to Montgomery Crossroads. Turn right and drive 1.2 miles to Waters Avenue. Turn right (south) and go about 2 miles. Turn right onto Whitfield Avenue; continue about 2.5 miles to the end of the road where the ramp is located.

Skidaway Narrows Park Boat Ramp
Chartlet #012

Southeast Chatham County on the Diamond Causeway leading to Skidaway Island.

Savannah, GA

Two triple lane paved ramps. Floating dock.

From I 95 use exit 94 and go east on GA HWY 204 for 10.4 miles to Montgomery Crossroads. Turn right and drive 1.2 miles to Waters Avenue. Turn right (south) and go 3.9 miles. The boat ramp park is on the right (south) side of the causeway before the bridge.

FW Spencer Community Park Boat Ramp
Chartlet #005

On Oatland Island, east of Wilmington River

Savannah, GA

One double lane paved ramp.

From I 95 use exit 99 and go east on I 16 for 7.8 miles to exit 35. Take the 37th Street Connector exit for .6 mile to 37th Street. Turn left (west) on GA HWY 204 for .8 to

Abercorn Street. Turn right and continue on GA HWY 204 for .3 mile to US HWY 80. Turn left (east) and drive 6 miles to the Islands Expressway. Turn left (west) on the Islands Expressway and drive 1.5 miles. The ramp is located on the right (north) side of the road.

Thunderbolt Boat Ramp
Chartlet #007
North side of HWY 80 Bridge (Wilmington River)
Savannah, GA
One single lane paved ramp.
From I 95 use exit 99 and drive east on I 16 for 7.8 miles to exit 35. Take the 37th Street Connector exit for .6 mile to 37th Street. Turn left (west) on GA HWY 204 for .8 mile to Abercorn Street. Turn right and continue on HWY 204 for .3 mile to US HWY 80. Turn left (east) and drive 4 miles to Macceo Drive located past the Wilmington River Bridge. Turn left and go .4 mile to the end of Macceo Drive.

SUNBURY

Sunbury Boat Ramp
Chartlet #026
Eastern Liberty County
Sunbury, GA
One wide single lane paved ramp. Floating dock.
From I 95 use exit 76 and drive east on GA HWY 38 for 4.4 miles to Fort Morris Road. Turn left and go 3.1 miles to Stevens Road. Turn right and go .3 mile to the ramp.

TYBEE ISLAND

Lazaretto Creek Boat Ramp
Chartlets #004 and #009
Tybee Island, GA
One double lane paved ramp. Floating dock
From I 95 use exit 99 and go east on I 16 for 7.8 miles to exit 35. Take the 37th Street Connector exit for .6 mile to 37th Street. Turn left (west) on GA HWY 204 for .8 mile to Abercorn Street. Turn right and go west on HWY 204 for .3 mile to US HWY 80. Turn left (east) and drive 13.6 miles to the Lazaretto Creek Boat Ramp on the right (south) side of the highway.

Tybee Island Boat Ramp
Chartlets #004 and #009
South end of Tybee
Tybee Island, GA
Beach launching.
From I 95 use exit 99 and drive east on I 16 for 7.8 miles to exit 35. Take the 37th Street Connector exit for .6 miles to 37th Street. Turn left (west) on GA HWY 204 for .8 to Abercorn Street. Turn right and continue on HWY 204 for .3 mile to US HWY 80. Turn left (east) and drive 16.6 miles to Jones Avenue located on Tybee Island. Turn right and go 1.6 miles to Chatham Avenue. Turn right and go .2 mile to Alley Way 3. The ramp is located at the end of the alley and crosses the beach. Recommended for small or light boats only.

WOODBINE

Satilla River Water Front Boat Ramp
Chartlet #072
Central Camden County in downtown Woodbine
One paved double lane ramp. Floating dock.
From I 95 use exit 14, go north (westward) on GA Spur 25 2.3 miles to US HWY 17. Turn right (north) and go .7 mile to the fishing dock located on the right before crossing the bridge. The ramp is to the right (east) of the dock.

BOAT STORAGE

BRUNSWICK

Brunswick Boat Marina
S Highway 17
Brunswick, GA 31520
Phone: 912-265-2290

Two Way Fish Camp
Ricefield Way
Brunswick, GA 31525
Phone: 912-265-0410

DARIEN

See *Brunswick*

MIDWAY

Halfmoon Marina
171 Azalea Rd.
Midway, GA 31320
Phone: 912-884-5819

Yellow Bluff Fishing Camp
118 Yellow Bluff Rd.
Midway, GA 31320
Phone: 912-884-5448

OGEECHEE RIVER

Fort McAllister Marina & Inn Inc.
3203 Fort McAllister Rd.
Richmond Hill, GA 31324
Phone: 912-727-2732
Email: FtMcAllister@CLDS.NET

ST SIMONS

The Boat Lot
106 Airport Rd.
St Simons Island, GA 31522
Phone: 912-634-1933

Golden Isles Marina
206 Marina Dr.
St. Simons Island, GA 31522
Dry stack storage
Phone: 912-634-1128

St Simons Storage
90 Skyline Dr.
St Simons Island, GA 31522
Phone: 912-638-6533

St Simons Surf Sailors
St Simons Island, GA 31522
Phone: 912-634-9533

Village Creek Landing
526 S. Harrington Rd.
St Simons Island, GA 31522

SAVANNAH

A Stor and Lock, Inc.
2311 East Victory Dr.
Savannah, GA 31404
Outside storage
Phone: 912-355-5860

Bahia Bleu
2812 River Dr.
Thunderbolt, GA 31404
Phone: 912-354-2283

Crab Shack at Chimney Creek
Tybee Island, GA 31328
Phone: 912-786-9857

Hogan's Marina
PO Box 31410
Savannah, GA 30505
36 Wilmington Island Rd.
Dry stack storage
Phone: 912-897-FISH
jhogan@hogansmarina.com

Isle of Hope Marina
50 Bluff Dr.
Savannah, GA 31406
Phone: 912-354-8187
Fax: 912-354-2684

Sail Harbor Marina and Boat Yard
606 Wilmington Island Rd.
Savannah, GA 31505
Phone: 912-897-1914

Savannah Bend Marina
Rte. 14 Box 188
Old Tybee Rd.
Thunderbolt, GA 31404
Dry stack storage
Phone: 912-897-3625

BOAT TRANSPORTING

BRUNSWICK

Aggressive Transport
Marine Division
Phone: 352-307-1106

Bob Glodek Boat Transporter
Phone: 904-823-9571
888-958-4741

Cobra Marine Transport
Phone: 800-779-4020

Out & In Boat Transit, Inc.
Phone: 843-884-1843

DARIEN

Krush Brothers
Darien, GA 31305
Phone: 912-437-2108

ST MARYS

Aggressive Transport
Marine Division
Phone: 352-307-1106

Bob Glodek Boat Transporter
Phone: 904-823-9571
888-958-4741

Cobra Marine Transport
Phone: 800-779-4020

SAVANNAH

Elite Marine
Phone: 800-813-1465

Out & In Boat Transit, Inc.
Phone: 843-884-1843

Hinckley Yacht Services
Thunderbolt, GA 31404
Phone: 912-352-1335

Sail Harbor Marina and Boat Yard
606 Wilmington Island Dr.
Savannah, GA 31410
Phone: 912-897-4214
912-786-4801

BOAT YARDS

BRUNSWICK

Brunswick Landing Marina
2429 Newcastle St.
Brunswick, GA 31520
50-ton travel lift, full-service yard, do-it-yourself allowed.
Phone: 912-262-9264
Pager: 912-262-8879

Credle's Complete Marine
South Highway 17
Brunswick, GA 31523
Haul out, full-service yard
Phone: 912-262-6003

Two Way Boat Yard & Reitz Marine
243 Marina Rd.
Brunswick, GA 31525
40-ton travel lift, mechanic on duty, full-service yard. No do-it-yourself.
Phone: 912-265-6944
912-267-6052
912-264-9492
912-223-4299
Pager: 912-262-8637

DARIEN

Colson Marine Railway
Eulonia, GA 31331
Phone: 912-832-5389

George's Boatworks
Darien, GA 31305
Railway
Phone: 912-437-4496

ST MARYS

North River Boat Yard
443 New Pt. Peter Rd.
St. Marys, GA 31558
Railway, Troy Smith
Phone: 912-882-3932

SAVANNAH

Hinckley Yacht Services
PO Box 5250
2400 Mechanics Ave.
Savannah, GA 31404
35-ton travel lift, full-service yard, mechanical repairs, shaft repairs and painting
Phone: 912-629-2400
Fax: 912-629-2404

Palmer Johnson Savannah, Inc.
301 North Lathrop Ave.
Savannah, GA 31415
Located on the Savannah River, full-service yard, yacht building
Phone: 912-234-6579
Fax: 912-239-1168
Email: info@pjsavannah.com

Sail Harbor Marina and Boat Yard
606 Wilmington Island Rd.
Savannah, GA 31410
30-ton travel lift, full-service yard, do-it-yourself allowed above the water line. $8 per foot for haul, pressure wash & launch. Do-it-yourself is $20 per day
Phone: 912-897-1914
www.sailharbormarina.com
(good website)

Thunderbolt Marine, Inc.
3124 River Dr.
Thunderbolt, GA 31404
Mail: PO Box 5860
Savannah, GA 31414
Full-service yard, haul & launch up to 1200 tons.
Phone: 912-352-4931
Fax: 912-352-4958

BOOK STORES (COASTAL)

BRUNSWICK

Book Exchange
4521 Altama Ave
Brunswick, GA 31520
Phone: 912-265-4087

The Book Mine
Brunswick Mall
Brunswick, GA 31525
Phone: 912-265-5317

Books-A-Million
163 Golden Isles Plaza
Brunswick, GA 31520
Phone: 912-264-3233

Waldenbooks
Glynn Place Mall
Brunswick, GA 31525
Phone: 912-267-7170

DARIEN

Fiddlers
PO Box 2417
155 HWY 17 Downtown Darien
Darien, GA 31305
Phone: 912-437-3161

EULONIA

Books On the Bluff
bookshop@darientel.net
www.gacoast.com/
bookshopinc.html
Harold & Virginia Hobson Hicks
Townsend/Eulonia, GA 31331
Phone: 912-832-6352
Fax: 912-832-2322

JEKYLL ISLAND

Jekyll Books & Antiques, Inc.
101 Old Plantation Rd.
Jekyll Island, GA 31527
Phone: 912-635-3077

ST MARYS

Once Upon a Bookseller
107 Osborne St.
St. Marys, GA 31558
Nautical charts
Phone: 912-882-7350

Up The Creek Xpeditions
111 Osborne St.
St. Marys, GA 31558
Phone: 912-882-0911

ST SIMONS

Beachview Books
215 Mallory St.
St. Simons Island, GA 31522
Phone: 912-638-7282

Blythe Island Antiques
1610 Frederica Rd.
St. Simons Island, GA 31522
Phone: 912-634-1610

The Bookmark
1607 Frederica Rd.
Tabby Plaza
St. Simons Island, GA 31522
Phone: 912-634-2132
Email: bookmark@darientel.net

G.J. Ford Bookshop
600 Sea Island Rd.
Shops At Sea Island
St. Simons Island, GA 31522
next to Harris Teeter
Phone: 912-634-6168
www.gjfordbookshop.com

Island Book Shelf
3603 Frederica Rd.
St. Simons Island, GA 31522
Phone: 912-638-9963

SAVANNAH

B Dalton Bookseller
Oglethorpe Mall
Savannah, GA 31406
Phone: 912-356-1440

Barnes & Noble Bookseller
7804 Abercorn St., Ext. 72
Savannah, GA 31406
Phone: 912-353-7757

The Book Lady
17 West York St.
Savannah, GA 31401
Phone: 912-233-3628

Books-A-Million
8108 Abercorn St.
Savannah, GA 31406
Phone: 912-925-8112

ExLibris Bookstore
228 Martin Luther King, Jr Blvd.
Savannah, GA 31401
Phone: 912-525-7550

E. Shaver Booksellers
326 Bull St.
Savannah, GA 31401
Phone: 912-234-7257

Waldenbooks
Savannah Mall
Savannah, GA 31419
Phone: 912- 927-1408

BRIDGES

SAVANNAH

Causton Bluff Bridge
Also called
Islands Expressway Bridge
Bascule bridge at marker G "27"
Monitors VHF channel 13
Phone: 912-897-2511

Skidaway Narrows Bridge
Also called Diamond Causeway Bridge
Bascule bridge near marker R "64"
Monitors VHF channel 13
Phone: 912-352-2733

BUSES

BRUNSWICK

Greyhound Bus Lines
1101 Gloucester St.
Brunswick, GA 31520
Phone: 800-231-2222
912-265-2800

SAVANNAH

CAT—Chatham Area Transit
Schedule information
Phone: 912-233-5767
Business office
Phone: 912-236-2111
Greyhound Bus Lines
610 W Oglethorpe Ave.
Savannah, GA 31401
Phone: 800-231-2222
912-232-2135
Southeastern Stages
610 W Oglethorpe Ave.
Savannah, GA 31401
Phone: 912-232-0062

CANOES & KAYAKS

BRUNSWICK

Southeast Adventure Outfitters
1200 Glynn Ave.
Hwy 17 South
Brunswick, GA 31520
Maps, gear, rentals, tours &
sales
Phone: 912-265-5292

DARIEN

Altamaha Canoe Excursions
Presented by Fort King
George
Fort King George Historic
Site
PO Box 711
Darien, GA 31305
Scheduled outings for begin-
ners to advanced.

Honeygall Creek, Altamaha
River, Lewis Island
Phone: 912-437-4770
Altamaha Wilderness Outpost
Altamaha River Bioreserve
229 Ft. King George Rd.
Darien, GA 31305
Canoe & kayak rental & sales
Phone: 912-437-6010
912-654-3632
www.broadriver.com

LIBERTY COUNTY

Melon Bluff
2999 Islands Highway
Midway, GA 31320
Rentals, scheduled events &
festivals, kayak races
Phone: 912-884-5779
888-246-8188
Fax: 912-884-3046
Email: melonbluff@clds.net
www.melonbluff.com

RICHMOND HILL

**Ft. McAllister State Historic
Park**
3894 Fort McAllister Rd.
Richmond Hill, GA 31324
Rentals on Red Bird Creek
Phone: 912-727-2330
912-727-3614

ST MARYS

Canoe & Kayak Guided Tours
V.J. "Jack" Bryant
104 W Alexander
St. Marys, GA 31588
History specialist
Phone: 912-882-5524
Up the Creek Xpeditions
111 Osborne St.
St. Marys, GA 31558
Phone: 912-882-0911

ST SIMONS

Barry's Beach Service Inc.
420 Arnold Rd.
St. Simons Island, GA 31522
Phone: 912-638-8053

Bedford Sportsman South
3405 Frederica Rd.
St. Simons Island, GA 31522
Phone: 912-638-5454
Ocean Motion Surf Co.
1300 Ocean Blvd.
St. Simons Island, GA 31522
Lessons, rentals, sales
Phone: 912-638-5225
Southeast Adventure Outfitters
313 Mallory St.
St. Simons Island, GA 31522
Maps, gear, rentals, tours &
sales
Phone: 912-638-6732

SAVANNAH

Isle of Hope Marina
50 Bluff Dr.
Savannah, GA 31406
Kayak rentals & sales
Phone: 912-354-8187
Ogeechee Outpost
Pine Barren Rd.
HWY 204
Bryan County, GA 31308
Phone: 912-748-6716
Rec Arts
15 East Broughton St.
Savannah, GA 31401
Canoes, kayaks, total outfitter
Phone: 912-201-9393
Fax: 912-201-9313
www.rec.arts.com
**Savannah Light Tackle Fishing
Co.**
PO Box 3666
Savannah, GA 31414
Ogeechee River canoe trip
Also see listing under Boat
Charters
Phone: 912-355-3271
Sea Kayak Georgia
PO Box 2747
1102 HWY 80 East
Tybee Island, GA 31328
Instruction, scheduled
outings, custom trips, sales
Phone: 912-786-8732
888-529-2542
Email: Seakayakga@aol.com
www.seakayakgeorgia.com
White's Canoes & Rentals
Bush Rd.
Savannah, GA

TYBEE ISLAND

Sea Kayak Georgia
PO Box 2747
1102 HWY 80 East
Tybee Island, GA 31328
Instruction, scheduled
    outings, custom trips, sales
Phone: 912-786-8732
    888-529-2542
Email: Seakayakga@aol.com
www.seakayakgeorgia.com

CANVAS WORK

BRUNSWICK

A-1 Uphostery
1928 Norwich
Brunswick, GA 31520
Phone: 912-264-8858

**Brunswick Bedding &
Upholstery**
405 G St.
Brunswick, GA 31420
Phone: 912-265-9285

**Modern Upholstery and Trim
Shop**
2108 Norwich St.
Brunswick, GA 31520
Phone: 912-265-3941

**Stitches By Ruth Custom
Marine**
3421-3 Cypress Mill Rd.
Brunswick, GA 31520
Phone: 912-262-9438

SAVANNAH

Big B Specialty Fabrication
Bloomingdale, GA 31322
Canvas enclosures, covers,
    metal work, T tops
Phone: 912-748-0840

Coastal Canvas Products
73 Ross Rd.
Savannah, GA 31405
Bimini tops, enclosures,
    metal work, interior &
    exterior upholstery
Phone: 912-236-2416

Ennis Auto Top Company
608 Montgomery St.
Savannah, GA 31401
Phone: 912-236-1400

Islands Marine, Inc.
9234 Ferguson Ave.
Savannah, GA 31406
Phone: 912-354-4778

Presley's Auto Trim Shop
3901 Bull St.
Savannah, GA 31401
Phone: 912-233-3163

Sea Stitch Canvas Products
2823 River Dr.
Thunderbolt, GA 31404
T tops, Bimini tops, enclo-
    sures, interior & exterior
    upholstery
Phone: 912-354-0304

Top Interiors
Phone: 912-354-1066

TYBEE ISLAND

Gotcha Covered
1303 Lovell Ave.
Tybee Island, GA 31328
Phone: 912-786-4032

CHAIN

BRUNSWICK

Adler Ling-Certex
618 Bay St.
Brunswick, GA 31520
Phone: 912-264-0301

Certified Slings & Cable, Inc.
154 Key Circle Dr.
Brunswick, GA
Phone: 912-264-0418

SAVANNAH

**Southeast Chain & Specialty
Co.**
49 Wahlstrom Rd.
Savannah, GA 31404
Phone: 912-232-0253

COURIER SERVICES

BRUNSWICK

FedEx
Phone: 800-463-3339
United Parcel Service
Phone: 800-742-5877
US Postal Service
Phone: 800-222-1811

ST MARYS

FedEx
Phone: 800-463-3339
UPS—United Parcel Service
Phone: 800-742-5877
US Postal Service
Phone: 800-222-1811

ST SIMONS

FedEx
Phone: 800-463-3339
United Parcel Service
Phone: 800-742-5877
US Postal Service
Phone: 800-222-1811

SAVANNAH

Airborne Express
Phone: 800-247-2676
DHL Worldwide Express
Phone: 800-225-5345
FedEx
Phone: 800-463-3339
Roadway Package System
Phone: 800-762-3725
United Parcel Service
Phone: 800-742-5877
US Postal Service
Phone: 800-222-1811

DIVING

BRUNSWICK

Hammerhead Dive Center
1200 Glynn Ave.

Brunswick, GA 31520
Sales, service, rentals
Phone: 912-262-1778
Email:
georgiascuba@technonet.com

JEKYLL ISLAND

Judy's Island Dive Center
107 Marina Dr.
Jekyll Island, GA 31527
Phone: 912-638-6590

KINGSLAND

Diver's Den
2475 Village Dr., Suite 109
Mariner's Village
Kingsland, GA 31548
Rentals, sales, service, trips
Phone: 912-882-7078

ST MARYS

Diver's Den
2475 Village Dr. Suite 109
Kingsland, GA 31548
Sales, rental, service, trips
Phone: 912-882-7078

Fish Masters Charters
St. Marys, GA 31558
Phone: 912-729-5214

ST SIMONS

Baker, George
Phone: 912-638-3333

Emerson's Underwater Yacht Service
St. Simons Island, GA 31522
Wm. Robert Emerson
Underwater maintenance,
repairs
Phone: 912-638-0924

Island Dive Center
Golden Isles Marina
101 Marina Dr.
St. Simons Island, GA 31522
Classes, rentals, trips, air fills
Phone: 912-638-6590
800-940-3483
Fax: 912-638-4956

Parks, Clay
Phone: 912-264-0511

SAVANNAH

Atlantic Marine Services Inc.
534 Jackson Blvd.
Savannah, GA 31405
Joel Formby
Underwater maintenance &
Marine recovery
Phone: 912-355-7058
Fax: 912-355-7050
Email: GaCoast@Juno.com

Diving Locker & Ski Chalet
74 W Montgomery Crossroads
Savannah, GA
Sales, service, rentals, trips
Phone: 912-927-6603
912-927-6604

Fantasia Scuba
5912 Ogeechee Rd.
Savannah, GA 31405
Rentals, sales, classes, trips
Phone: 912-961-9711
Email: scuba1017@aol.com

Hammerhead Scuba
Savannah, GA
Classes, local & distant trips
Phone: 912-961-7966

ELECTRONIC EQUIPMENT

BRUNSWICK

Circuit City Stores
137 Golden Isles Plaza
Brunswick, GA
Phone: 912-261-1766

H&H Furniture Appliances & Electronics
4990 Altama Ave.
Brunswick, GA
Phone: 912-265-8100

Pro Circuit Electronics
4755 New Jesup HWY
Brunswick, GA
Phone: 912-280-0003

Tackle Shack
3737 Community Rd.
Brunswick, GA
Phone: 912-264-4665

Radio Shack
Glynn Place Mall
Brunswick, GA
Phone: 912-267-1750

ST MARYS

Camden Electronics Inc
115 City Smitty Dr.
St. Marys GA 31588
Phone: 912-882-5025

Radio Shack
125 City Smitty Dr. 44
St. Marys, GA 31558
Phone: 912-882-5024
912-882-5025

ST SIMONS ISLAND

Coastal Electronics & Tools
307 Reynoso Ave.
St. Simons Island, GA 31522
Phone: 912-634-0930

Forbes Electronic Repairs
105 A Airport Rd.
St. Simons Island, GA 31522
Phone: 912-638-6536

Radio Shack Dealer
1600 Frederica Rd.
St. Simons Island, GA 31522
Phone: 912-638-4455

SAVANNAH

Boat US
11607 Abercorn St.
Savannah, GA
Phone: 912-925-2363

Boaters World Discount Marine Center
Savannah Crossings
Savannah, GA
Phone: 912-0216

Coastal Electronic Maintenance
8 Mall Court
Savannah, GA
Marine sales & service
Phone: 912-352-1444

Maricom Electronics
2911 River Dr.
Savannah, GA
Sales, service, installation of
marine electronics
Phone: 912-354-4542

Radio Shack
31 Chatham Plaza
Phone: 912-355-7162
2110 E Victory Dr
Phone: 912-232-1756
Oglethorpe Mall
Phone: 912-354-8487
Savannah Mall

Phone: 912-925-8812
Westside Shopping Center
Phone: 912-964-8375
West Discount Marine
7700 Abercorn St.
Savannah, GA 31406
Phone: 912-352-2660

EMERGENCY

Also see: *Police*
Boating Emergency
Phone: 800-241-4113

BRUNSWICK

Emergency: 911
Crisis Line
Phone: 912-264-7311
CSX Transportation Police Dept.
Railroad Emergencies
Phone: 800-232-0144
Emergency Management Volunteer Rescue Squad
Phone: 912-267-5678
Federal Bureau of Investigation
912-265-2560
404-679-9000
Georgia Bureau of Investigation
Phone: 912-921-5500
800-673-9213
Georgia Natural Resources
Communications Center
Phone: 800-241-4113
Glynn County Police
Phone: 912-638-1548
National Response Center
Toxic chemical & oil spills
Phone: 800-424-8802
Poison Control
Phone: 800-282-5846
912-264-7237
Southeast Georgia Regional Medical Center
Phone: 912-264-7000
US Coast Guard
Marine & Air Emergencies
Phone: 912-267-7999
US Customs
Phone: 912-267-2801
US Marshall
Phone: 912-264-8429
912-652-4212

BRYAN COUNTY

Emergency: 911
Ambulance:
912-756-2181
Police:
912-756-2181 (Keller)
912-756-2626 (Richmond Hill)
Sheriff:
912-653-3800
912-756-2282 (Richmond Hill)

DARIEN

Ambulance:
912-437-4150
Firephone:
912-437-4150
Forest Fire:
912-832-5103
912-832-4238
Georgia Bureau of Investigation
912-729-6198
800-282-8746
Georgia Department of Natural Resources
Phone: 800-241-4113
Georgia Poison Center
Phone: 800-282-5846
Medical:
912-437-4150
Police:
912-437-6644
Sheriff:
912-437-6622
US Marshalls Service
Phone: 912-264-8429
912-652-4212

ST MARYS

Emergency: 911
Camden Medical Center
Phone: 912-576-4200
Department of Natural Resources
Phone: 912-685-2145
Emergency Medical Health
Phone: 800-342-7843
Federal Bureau of Investigation
Phone: 912-232-3716
Georgia Bureau of Investigation
Phone: 912-729-6198
800-282-8746

Georgia Highway Patrol
Phone: 912-262-2380
Oil and Toxic Chemical Spills
Phone: 800-424-8802
Poison Control Georgia Hotline
Phone: 800-282-5846
US Coast Guard Brunswick
Phone: 912-267-7999
US Coast Guard National Response
Phone: 800-424-8802
US Marshall
Phone: 912-264-8429

ST SIMONS

Emergency: 911
Charter Hospital
Phone: 912-638-1999
Crisis Line:
912-264-7311
912-262-3088
800-254-3380
Georgia Game & Fish
Phone: 912-264-7237
Glynn County Police
Phone: 912-638-1548
Police:
912-638-1546
912-638-2111
Sea Island sub station
Phone: 912-638-3188
Main office: 912-267-5700
Southeast Georgia Regional Hospital
Phone: 912-466-7000
US Coast Guard
Phone: 912-267-7999
US Customs
Phone: 912-267-2801

SAPELO

Forest Fire:
912-832-5103
912-832-4238
Medical:
912-437-4150
Police:
912-437-6644
Sheriff:
912-437-6622

SAVANNAH

Emergency: 911
Chatham County Water-Way mishaps
Phone: 912-652-6500
Chatham-Savannah Drug Coast Guard Search & Rescue
Phone: 912-786-5106
912-786-5440
Crimes Hotline
Phone: 912-232-0402
CSX Transportation Police
Railroad emergencies
Phone: 800-232-0144
Drug Enforcement Administration
Phone: 912-652-4286
Federal Bureau of Investigation
Phone: 912-232-3716
Forest Fire
Phone: 912-748-4924
Georgia Bureau of Investigation
Phone: 912-871-1121
800-673-9213
Georgia Natural Resources
Phone: 800-241-4113
Marine & Air Emergencies
Phone: 912-786-5106
803-723-9378
National Response Center
Toxic chemical & oil spills
Phone: 800-424-8802
Poison Control Center Throughout Georgia
Phone: 800-282-5846
404-616-9000
404-616-9287
US Marshall
Phone: 912-652-4212
US Secret Service
Phone: 912-652-4401

FISHERMEN'S SUPPLIES & FISHING BAIT

ALTAMAHA RIVER

Altamaha Park & Country Store
1605 Altamaha Park Rd.
Brunswick, GA 31525
Live crickets, worms, minnows & shiners, fishing
supplies
912-264-2342
800-281-9322
Two Way Fish Camp
250 Ricefield Way
Brunswick, GA 31525
Live crickets, worms, minnows, shiners, live & dead
shrimp and minnows
Phone: 912-265-0410

BELLE BLUFF

Belle Bluff Marina
Rt. 3, Box 3246-B25
Townsend, GA 31331
Live shrimp. Dead—shrimp,
squid, ballyhoo, cigar
minnows, ribbon eels and
mullet
Phone: 912-832-5323

BRUNSWICK

Ace Hardware
205 Monck St.
Brunswick, GA 31520
Phone: 912-265-1321
Altamaha Fish Camp
Hwy 341
North Brunswick, GA
See Altamaha River
Phone: 912-264-2342
Branch's Bait & Tackle
7363 New Jesup Hwy
Brunswick, GA 31523
Bait
Phone: 912-264-4912
Brunswick Boat Marina
South Highway 17
Brunswick, GA 31520
Live shrimp, minnows, eels.
Dead shrimp, squid
Phone: 912-265-2290
Central Hardware
1730 Norwich St.
Brunswick, GA 31520
Fishing supplies
Phone: 912-265-3510

George's Bait
Torras Causeway
Brunswick, GA 31520
Open 7 days, 6 A.M. - 4 P.M.

McCall's Trawls
1001 Bay St.
Brunswick, GA 31520
Fishing supplies
Phone: 912-261-2244
Tackle Shack
3737 Community Rd.
Brunswick, GA 31520
Phone: 912-264-4665
Tommy's Bait
1455 S. Hwy 17
Brunswick, GA 31520
Troupe Creek Marina
375 Yacht Rd.
Brunswick, GA 31525
Live shrimp in season, live
eels and bull minnows.
Dead shrimp, squid,
ballyhoo, mullet, ribbon
fish and chum.
Phone: 912-264-3862

DARIEN

McIntosh Enterprises
Georgia HWY 251
Darien, GA 31305
Crab traps & supplies
Phone: 912-437-6679
McIntosh Rod and Gun Club
Rte. 1, Box 1414
Blue n Hall
Darien, GA 31305
Live shrimp. Dead—shrimp
Phone: 912-437-4677

HINESVILLE

Joe's Service Center
412 Gen Screven Way
Hinesville, GA 31313
Live shiners, minnows,
crickets & worms. Tackle,
cast nets
Phone: 912-368-6215

JEKYLL ISLAND

Jekyll Harbor Marina
1 Harbor Rd.
Jekyll Island, GA 31527
Live shrimp. Dead shrimp,
cigar minnows, finger
mullet, ballyhoo & squid
Phone: 912-635-3137

KILKENNY CREEK

Kilkenny Marina
HWY 144 East—Mile marker 21
3083 Kilkenny Rd.
Richmond Hill, GA 31324
Live shrimp. Dead—shrimp, squid, ballyhoo, cigar minnows, Boston mackerel, finger mullet
Phone: 912-727-2215

LITTLE SATILLA RIVER

Hickory Bluff Marina
307 Hickory Bluff Dr.
Waverly, GA 31565
Fishing tackle
Live shrimp, mud minnows. Dead bait—offshore
Phone: 912-262-0453

Ocean Breeze Marina & Campground
14 Ocean Breeze Dr.
Waverly, GA 31565
Live and dead bait, on Maiden Creek
Phone: 912-262-0058

MIDWAY

Halfmoon Marina
171 Azalea Rd.
Midway, GA 31320
Live shrimp, dead baits
Phone: 912-884-5819

Jeff's Bait & Crab House
Isle of Wight
Midway, GA 31320
Bait
Phone: 912-884-2707

Yellow Bluff Fishing Camp
118 Yellow Bluff Rd.
Midway, GA 31320
Live shrimp, mud minnows, eel, sometimes fiddler crabs. Live mullet for tournaments. Dead—shrimp, mud minnows, eel, mullet, ribbon fish, Spanish sardines, ballyhoo, squid
Phone: 912-884-5448

OGEECHEE RIVER

Ft. McAllister Marina
3203 Ft. McAllister Rd.
Richmond Hill, GA 31324
Seasonally live shrimp, mullet, bogies. Dead—shrimp, squid, mullet, ballyhoo, chum, chicken necks, ribbon fish
Phone: 912-727-2632

RICHMOND HILL

Also *see Kilkenny River and Ogeechee River*

Richmond Hill Marine & Sporting Goods
Ford Plaza Suite C
Richmond Hill, GA 31324
Fishing supplies
Phone: 912-756-2470

ST MARYS

Bait in St. Marys
By the public fish ramp downtown at the Fishing Outpost.

Jack Barwick's Marina & Cabins
Crooked River GA 31558
Phone: 912-882-3227

Riverhouse Fish Camp
US HWY 17 where it crosses the St. Marys River
St. Marys, GA
Bait & tackle

ST SIMONS ISLAND

Gisco Fresh Seafood Market
2020 Demere Rd.
St. Simons Island, GA 31522
Bait
Phone: 912-638-7546

Golden Isles Marina
206 Marina Dr.
St. Simons Island, GA 31522
Live and dead shrimp
Phone: 912-634-1128
Fax: 912-634-1786
www.gimarina.com

Hampton River Club Marina
1000 Hampton River Club Dr.
St. Simons Island, GA 31522
Live shrimp and squid. Dead—shrimp, squid
Phone: 912-638-1210

Orvis—the Bedford Sportsman South
3405 Frederica Rd.
St. Simons Island, GA 31522
Fishing supplies
Phone: 912-638-5454

St. Simons Island Bait & Tackle
121 Mallory St.
St. Simons Island, GA 31522
Bait & tackle, crabbing supplies
Phone: 912-634-1495

St. Simons Boating & Fishing Club
1000 Arthur Moore Dr.
St. Simons Island, GA 31522
Live and dead shrimp
Phone: 912-638-9146

SAPELO RIVER

Pine Harbor Marina
Rte. 3 Box 3196
Townsend, GA 31331
Live shrimp
Phone: 912-832-5999

SAVANNAH

Adams Bait House
2812 River Dr.
Thunderbolt, GA 31404
Bait
Phone: 912-352-7878

Bona Bella Marina
2740 Livingston Ave.
Savannah, GA 31406
Live crabs, shrimp, minnows
Phone: 912-355-9601

Bull River Yacht Club Marina
HWY 80 East at Bull River
8005 Old Tybee Rd.
Savannah, GA 31420
Frozen shrimp, squid, ballyhoo
Phone: 912-897-7300
Fax: Phone: 912-897-0668

Coffee Bluff Marina
14915 Coffee Bluff Rd.
Savannah, GA 31409
Live shrimp, sometimes eel.
Dead bait—squid, ballyhoo,
Spanish sardines, cigar
minnows, crabbing bait.
Call for bait info.
Phone: 912-925-9030

Cranman's Sporting World
401 East Montgomery Cross-
roads
Savannah, GA 31406
Bait and supplies
Phone: 912-921-1488

Hogans Marina
PO Box 30505
Savannah, GA 31401
Live shrimp, dead shrimp,
ballyhoo, squid
Phone: 912-897-FISH
Fax: 912-898-8929
Email:
jhogan@hogansmarina.com
www.hogansmarina.com

Jim's Quick Stop
922 Pennsylvania Ave.
Savannah, GA 31404
Tackle
Phone: 912-239-9700

The Landings Yacht Club
1 Harbor Circle
Skidaway Island
Savannah, GA 31411
Live & dead shrimp, offshore
ballyhoo, squid, mullet
Phone: 912-598-1901
Fax: 912-598-8316

Oak Bluff Outfitters
4501 Habersham St.
Savannah, GA 31405
Huge fly selection, fly tying
supplies
Phone: 912-691-1115
Fax: 912-691-1117
www.oakbluff.com

Pit Stop
400 NW Broad St.
Savannah, GA 31401
Bait
Phone: 912-526-7100

Port City Industrial & Marine Supply
1250 West Bay St.
Savannah, GA
Fishing supplies
Phone: 912-232-0722

Pro Bass Outfitters
6608 White Bluff Rd.
Savannah, GA
Tackle
Phone: 912-354-3377

River Supply, Inc.
2827 River Dr.
Thunderbolt, GA 31404
Tackle, rod & reel repair
Phone: 912-354-7777
800-673-9391
Fax: 912-354-3326

Skidaway Narrows Boat Ramp
Diamond Causeway
Savannah, GA 31406
Frozen bait, crabs

Wentworth Sales Co.
312 Cantyre St.
Pt. Wentworth, GA 31407
Fishing supplies
Phone: 912-964-5146

Woo's Hardware Store
Wilmington Island
Savannah, GA 31410
Tackle
Phone: 912-897-1366

SHELLMAN BLUFF

Fisherman's Lodge
Rte. 2 00 Fisherman's Lodge
Townsend, GA 31331
Live shrimp, fiddler crabs on
order. Dead—squid, shrimp,
ribbon eels, mackerel, cigar
minnows, fish oil, ballyhoo

Shellman Fish Camp
Rt. 2, Box 2439
Townsend, GA 31331
Live shrimp. Dead—shrimp,
squid, ballyhoo, Boston
mackerel, mullet.

TOWNSEND

See *Belle Bluff, Sapelo River,
Shellman Bluff*

TYBEE ISLAND

Arnie'S Beach Store
725 First St.
Tybee Island, GA 31328
Fishing supplies
Phone: 912-786-5904

Lazaretto Creek Marina
1 Old US HWY 80
Tybee Island, GA 31328
Live shrimp next door, frozen
squid
Phone: 912-786-5848

WAVERLY

See *Little Satilla River*

FUEL

ALTAMAHA RIVER

Two Way Fish Camp
250 Ricefield Way
Brunswick, GA 31525
Diesel, gasoline, lube oils
South shore of South Altamaha
River near Wood Cut. 4 n.
miles west of ICW R "216"
Phone: 912-265-0410

BELLE BLUFF

Belle Bluff Marina
Rt. 3, Box 3246-B25
Townsend, GA 31331
Gasoline, outboard oils
West shore of White Chimney
Creek, north of Sapelo River
Phone: 912-832-5323

BRUNSWICK

Also see *Altamaha River*

Brunswick Landing Marina, Inc.
2429 Newcastle St.
Brunswick, GA 31520
Diesel and gasoline, oils
East shore of East River, 2½ n.
miles north of Sidney Lanier
Bridge
Phone: 912-262-9264
912-638-1274

Gulf Dock
Osan Petroleum
1025 Bay St.
Brunswick, GA 31520
Sells Fina, Texaco, Citgo, not Gulf
Along the Brunswick harbor next to Cumberland Gas and Ice, east shore of East River
Office: 912-265-2275
Home: 912-638-1274

DARIEN

McIntosh Rod and Gun Club
Rte. 1, Box 1414
Darien, GA 31305
Gasoline
At Blue n' Hall on the west shore of May Hall Creek near Union Island
Phone: 912-437-4677

JEKYLL ISLAND

Jekyll Harbor Marina
1 Harbor Rd.
Jekyll Island, GA 31527
Diesel, gasoline, lube oils
East shore of Jekyll Creek at G "23"
Phone: 912-635-3137
Fax: 912-635-2633

Jekyll Wharf Marina
1 Pier Rd.
Jekyll Island, GA 31527
Diesel, gasoline, lube oils
East shore of Jekyll Creek at R "20"
Phone: 912-635-3152

KILKENNY CREEK

Kilkenny Marina
HWY 144 East, Mile marker 21
3083 Kilkenny Rd.
Richmond Hill, GA 31324
Diesel, gasoline
West shore of Kilkenny Creek, west of G "107"
Phone: 912-727-2215

LITTLE SATILLA RIVER

Hickory Bluff Marina
307 Hickory Bluff Dr.
Waverly, GA 31565
Gasoline, outboard oils
South shore of Little Satilla, west of Colonel's Island
Phone: 912-262-0453

MIDWAY

Halfmoon Marina
171 Azalea Rd.
Midway, GA 31320
Diesel, gasoline, outboard oils
Southwest shore of Colonel's Island, north shore of North Newport River
Phone: 912-884-5819

Yellow Bluff
118 Yellow Bluff Rd.
Midway, GA 31320
Gasoline, outboard oils
East shore of Colonel's Island, Ashley Creek west of Cedar Creek
Phone: 912-884-5448

OGEECHEE RIVER

Ft. McAllister Marina
3203 Ft. McAllister Rd.
Richmond Hill, GA 31324
Diesel, gasoline, lube oils
South shore of Ogeechee River, inland of Shad Island
Phone: 912-727-2632

RICHMOND HILL

See *Kilkenny River, Ogeechee River*

ST MARYS

Lang's Marina East
St. Marys St.
St. Marys, GA 31558
Diesel, gasoline, lube oils at the east dock
North shore of St. Marys River, north G "13"
Phone: 912-882-4452

ST SIMONS

Golden Isles Marina
206 Marina Dr.
St. Simons Island, GA 31522
www.gimarina.com
High speed gas and diesel fuel pumps, discounts on volume sales
West shore of south Frederica River, 1¾ n. miles north of ICW light G "249"
Phone: 912-634-1128
Fax: 912-634-1786

Hampton River Club Marina
1000 Hampton River Club Dr.
St. Simons Island, GA 31522
Diesel, gasoline, lube oils
South shore of Hampton River at Butler Point, 1¾ n. miles east of ICW
Phone: 912-638-1210

St. Simons Boating & Fishing Club
1000 Arthur Moore Dr.
St. Simons Island, GA 31522
Gasoline, outboard oils
East shore of south Frederica River, north of Torras Causeway bridge
Phone: 912-638-9146

SAPELO RIVER

Phillips Seafood
Belleville Point
Darien, GA 31305
Diesel located at a commercial dock that sells to yachtsmen.
South shore of Roscoe's Canal off the west shore of Sapelo River at Belleville Point. Call Charlie Phillips
Phone: 912-832-4423
Fax: 912-832-6228

Pine Harbor Marina
Rte. 3, Box 3196
Townsend, GA 31331
Gasoline
West shore of Sapelo River, beyond Belleville
Phone: 912-832-5999

SAVANNAH

Bull River Yacht Club Marina
HWY 80 East at Bull River
8005 Old Tybee Rd.
Savannah, GA 31410
Diesel, gasoline, outboard oils
South shore of Bull River south
of HWY 80 bridge
Phone: 912-897-7300
Fax: 912-897-0668

Chimney Creek Fish Camp
40 Estill Hammock Rd.
Tybee Island, GA 31328
Gasoline
West shore of Chimney Creek
Phone: 912-786-9857

Coffee Bluff Marina
14915 Coffee Bluff Rd.
Savannah, GA 31409
Gasoline, outboard oils
North shore of Forest River
Phone: 912-925-9030

Delegal Creek Marina
1 Marina Dr.
Savannah, GA 31411
Diesel, gasoline, lube oils
East shore of Delegal Creek, 2
n. miles northeast of R "86"
and the ICW
Phone: 912-598-0023

Hogans Marina
PO Box 30505
Savannah, GA 31410
Gasoline, oils
Turner Creek south of Johnny
Mercer Drive bridge
Phone: 912-897-FISH
Fax: 912-898-8929
Email:
jhogan@hogansmarina.com
www.hogansmarina.com

Isle of Hope Marina
50 Bluff Dr.
Savannah, GA 31406
Diesel, gasoline, outboard oils
West shore of Skidaway River
north of R "46A" On the
ICW
Phone: 912-354-8187
Fax: 912-354-2684

The Landings Yacht Club
1 Harbor Circle
Savannah, GA 31411
Diesel, gasoline, & lube oils
West shore of Wilmington River
south of G "23"
Phone: 912-598-1901
Fax: 912-598-8316

Lazaretto Creek Marina
1 Old US HWY 80
Tybee Island, GA 31328
Gasoline
East shore of Lazaretto Creek
south of HWY 80 bridge
Phone: 912-786-5848

Savannah Bend Marina
Rt. 14 Box 188, Old Tybee Rd.
Savannah, GA 31410
Diesel, gasoline, lube oils
East shore of Wilmington River
south of R "34" on the ICW
Phone: 912-897-3625
Email: Savbendmar@aol.com

Thunderbolt Marine, Inc.
3124 River Dr.
Savannah, GA 31404
Diesel, gasoline, lube oils
West shore of Wilmington River,
south of G "35" on the ICW
Phone: 912-356-3875
Fax: 912-352-0593

SHELLMAN BLUFF

Fisherman's Lodge
Rt. 2 00 Fisherman's Lodge Rd.
Townsend, GA 31331
Gasoline, outboard oils
West shore of Broro River at
Shellman Bluff
Phone: 912-832-4671

Shellman Fish Camp
Rt. 2, Box 2439
Townsend, GA 31331
Gasoline, outboard oils
West shore of Broro River at
Shellman Bluff
Phone: 912-832-4331

TOWNSEND

See Belle Bluff, Sapelo River,
Shellman Bluff

GOLF COURSES

BRUNSWICK

Brunswick Country Club
Highway 17 North
4041 Darien Highway
Brunswick, GA 31520
18 hole private course designed
by Donald Ross
Phone: 912-264-4377

Glynco Golf Course
Glynco Parkway, Vogel Rd.
Brunswick, GA 31520
9 hole public course designed by
NAS Glynco
Phone: 912-264-9521

Golden Isles Golf Center
4984 Altama Ave.
Brunswick, GA 31520
9 hole public course
Phone: 912-264-1666

Oak Grove Island Golf Club
100 Clipper Bay
Brunswick, GA 31525
18 hole public course
Phone: 912-280-9525
Fax: 912-280-0609

JEKYLL ISLAND

Jekyll Island Golf Courses
322 Captain Wylly Rd.
Jekyll Island, GA 31527
63 holes, public courses
designed by Joe Lee
Phone: 912-635-2368
912-635-3464
912-635-2170

RICHMOND HILL

Waterford Landing Golf Course
731 Waterford Landing Rd.
Richmond Hill, GA 31324
18 hole public course
Phone: 912-727-4848

ST MARYS

Laurel Island Links
233 Marsh Harbour Parkway
Kingsland, GA 31548
18 hole semi-private course
designed by Davis Love III

Phone: 912-729-7277
888-480-7277

Osprey Cove Golf and Residential Community
123 Osprey Dr.
St. Marys, GA 31558
18 hole semi-private course
designed by Mark
McCumber
Phone: 912-882-5575
800-352-5575

Pro 3's
1000 Pro 3's Parkway
St. Marys, GA 31588
Phone: 912-882-3837
877-444-7763

ST SIMONS

Hampton Club
100 Tabbystone
St. Simons Island, GA 31522
18 holes designed by Joe Lee
Phone: 912-634-0255
Email:
hampton@hamptonclub.com
www.hamptonclub.com

Sea Island Golf Club
Frederica Road at Kings Way
St. Simons Island, GA 31522
36 hole semi-private course
designed by Walter Travis
Phone: 912-638-5118

Sea Island Golf Club
100 Retreat Ave.
St. Simons Island, GA 31522
Phone: 912-638-5110

Sea Palms Golf and Tennis Resort
5445 Frederica Rd.
St. Simons, GA 31522
27 hole semi-private course
designed by George Cobb
Phone: 912-638-3351
800-841-6268
www.seapalms.com

St. Simons Island Club
100 Kings Way
St. Simons Island, GA 31522
18 hole semi-private course
designed by Joe Lee
Phone: 912-638-5130
912-638-5131

SAVANNAH

Bacon Park Golf Course
6161 Skidaway Rd.
Savannah, GA 31406
27 hole public course designed
by Donald Ross
Phone: 912-354-2625

Mary Calder Golf Club
West Lathrop Ave.
Savannah, GA
9 hole semi-private
Phone: 912-238-7100

Henderson Golf Club
1A Henderson Dr.
Savannah, GA 31419
18 hole public course designed
by Mike Young
Phone: 912-920-4653

The Landings—Deercreek
1 Landings Way
Skidaway Island
Savannah, GA 31411
18 hole private course designed
by Tom Fazio
Phone: 912-598-2551

The Landings—Marshwood
1 Landings Way
Skidaway Island
Savannah, GA 31411
18 hole private course designed
by Arnold Palmer
Phone: 912-598-2596

The Landings—Oakridge
1 Landings Way
Skidaway Island
Savannah, GA 31411
18 hole private course designed
by Arthur Hill

The Landings—Palmetto
1 Landings Way
Skidaway Island
Savannah, GA 31411
18 hole private course designed
by Arthur Hill
Phone: 912-598-2535

The Landings—Plantation
1 Landings Way
Skidaway Island
Savannah, GA 31411
18 hole private course designed
by William Byrd

LaVida Country Club
525 Windsor Rd.
Savannah, GA
Phone: 912-925-2440

Southbridge Golf Club
415 Southbridge Blvd.
Savannah, GA 31405
18 hole semi-private course
designed by Rees Jones
Phone: 912-651-5455

Savannah Golf Club
1661 E President St.
Savannah, GA 31404
18 hole private course
Phone: 912-236-4305

Savannah Inn & Country Club
Wilmington Island Golf Course
612 Wilmington Island Rd.
Savannah, GA 31410
18 hole semi-private course
designed by Donald Ross
Phone: 912-897-1615

SEA ISLAND

Sea Island Ocean Forest Golf Club
200 Ocean Rd.
Sea Island, GA 31561
Phone: 912-638-3611
912-638-5835
912-638-8820

SHELLMAN BLUFF

Sapelo Hammock
500 Marshview Dr.
Shellman Bluff, GA 31331
18 hole semi-private course
designed by Rusty Simmons
Phone: 912-832-4653
Fax: 912-832-5656

HISTORIC SITES AND MUSEUMS

BRUNSWICK

Brunswick History Museum
1319 Union St. (Lissner House)
Brunswick, GA 31520
Phone: 912-264-0442

Hofwyl-Broadfield Plantation
5556 US HWY 17 N
Brunswick, GA 31525
Phone: 912-264-7333

Liberty Ship Model
Mary Ross Park
Brunswick, GA 31520

Old Town National Historic District
Historic Downtown Brunswick
Offices: Old City Hall
1229 Newcastle St.
Brunswick, GA 31520
Ritz Theater
Golden Isles Arts & Humanities Assoc.
1530 Newcastle St.
Brunswick, GA 31520
Phone: 912-262-6934

DARIEN

Fort King George Historic Site
PO Box 711
Darien, GA 31305
Phone: 912-437-4770
www.gastateparks.org
9 A.M. to 5 P.M. Tue to Sat, 2 P.M. to 5:30 P.M. Sun, closed Mon, Thanksgiving, Christmas, New Year's Day
Hofwyl-Broadfield Plantation
See *BRUNSWICK* above
Tabby Ruins on the waterfront
South of Broad St.
Darien, GA 31305

GEORGIA

Georgia State Parks and Historic Sites
Phone: 770-389-7275
800-864-7275
8 A.M. to 5 P.M. Mon to Fri
www.gastateparks.org

JEKYLL ISLAND

Coastal Encounters Nature Center Aquariums
100 South Riverview Dr.
Jekyll Island, GA 31527
Phone: 912-635-9102
Email:
coastalkids@www.technonet.com
Jekyll Island Historic District
Museum Visitors Center
Stable Rd.
Jekyll Island, Ga 31527
Phone: 912-635-2762
Jekyll Island Museum
Visitors Center, Stable Rd.
Jekyll Island, GA 31527
Phone: 912-635-2762

MIDWAY

Fort Morris State Historic Site
2559 Fort Morris Rd.
Midway, GA 31320
Phone: 912-884-5999
9 A.M. to 5 P.M. Tues to Sat
9:30 A.M. to 5:30 P.M. Sun
Midway Museum
PO Box 195
Midway, GA 31320
Phone: 912-884-5837
10 A.M. to 4 P.M. Tues to Sat
2 P.M. to 4 P.M. Sun
closed Mon and all holidays
Seabrook Village
660 Trade Hill Rd.
Midway, GA 31320
Phone: 912-884-7008
10 A.M. to 4 P.M. Tues to Sat

RICHMOND HILL

Ft. McAllister State Historic Park
3894 Ft. McAllister Rd.
Richmond Hill, GA 31324
Phone: 912-727-2339
Park: 7 A.M. to 10 P.M.
Office: 8 A.M. to 5 P.M.
Historic site: 9 A.M. to 5 P.M. Tues to Sat, 2 P.M. to 5:30 P.M. Sun, closed Mon, Thanksgiving, Christmas & New Years Day
Richmond Hill Historical Society
Richmond Hill, GA
Phone: 912-756-3697

SAPELO ISLAND

Sapelo Island Visitors Center
Rte. 1, Box 1500
Darien, GA 31305
Interpretive center geared toward the barrier islands
Meridian Ferry Dock
Phone: 912-437-3224

ST MARYS

Orange Hall Museum
414 Osborne St.
St. Marys, GA 31558
Phone: 912-882-4000
800-868-8687

St. Marys Submarine Museum
102 St. Marys St. West
St. Marys, GA 31558
Phone: 912-882-2782
Email: submus@eagnet.com
www.eag.com/edipage/areaserv/submus/sunmus.htm
10 A.M. to 4 P.M. Tue to Sat, 1 P.M. to 5 P.M. Sun

ST SIMONS

Bloody Marsh Battle Site
Demere Rd.
St. Simons Island, GA 31522
8 A.M. to 4 P.M. daily
Coastal Encounters Nature Center Aquariums
PO Box 21243
St. Simons Island, GA 31522
Historic Coast Guard Station
East Beach Causeway
Phone: 912-638-0221
Fax: 912-638-0598
Email:
coastalkids@www.technonet.com
Ft. Frederica National Monument
Frederica Rd. North
St. Simons Island, GA 31522
Phone: 912-638-3639
Superintendent's address:
Rte. 9, Box 286-C
St. Simons Island, GA 31522
St. Simons Lighthouse and Museum of Coastal History
PO Box 1136
St. Simons Island, GA 31522
101 12ᵗʰ St., in the Village
Phone: 912-638-4666
www.novagate.com/~schoonerman/stsim.htm

SAVANNAH

Fort Jackson
1 Ft. Jackson Rd.
Savannah, GA 31404
Phone: 912-232-3945
Fort Pulaski National Monument
PO Box 30757
Savannah, GA 31410-0757
HWY 80 East
Cockspur Island
Tybee Island, GA 31328
Phone: 912-786-5787

Georgia Historical Society
501 Whitaker St.
Savannah, GA 31499
Phone: 912-651-2125
Fax: 912-651-2831

Ralph Mark Gilbert Civil Rights Museum
460 Martin Luther King, Jr. Blvd.
Savannah, GA 31401
Phone: 912-231-8900
Fax: 912-234-2577

Historic Savannah
The Savannah Area Convention and Visitors Bureau
PO Box 1628
Savannah, GA 31402-1628
Phone: 912-944-0456
877-SAVANNAH
Fax: 912-944-0468
Email: info@savannahvisit.com
www.savannahvisit.com

Savannah History Museum
303 Martin Luther King, Jr. Blvd.
Savannah, GA 31401
Phone: 912-238-1779
Fax: 912-651-6827
Email: shm@g-net.net

Savannah and Ogeechee Canal, Museum & Nature Center
681 Fort Argyle Rd.
(HWY 204)
Savannah, GA 31419-9239
Phone: 912-748-8068

Savannah's Riverfront
Phone: 912-232-1511

Ships of the Sea Museum
41 ML King, Jr. Blvd.
Savannah, GA
Phone: 912-232-1511

Telfair Museum of Art
121 Barnard St.
Savannah, GA 31401
Phone: 912-232-1177

The University of Georgia
Marine Extension Service
The Aquarium
30 Ocean Science Circle
Savannah, GA 31411
Located on Skidaway Island
Phone: 912-598-2496

Wormsloe State Historic Site
7601 Skidaway Rd.
Savannah, GA 31406
Phone: 912-353-3023

TYBEE ISLAND

Fort Screven
Tybee Island, GA 31328
Winter—1 P.M. to 5 P.M., except Tues
Summer—10 A.M. to 6 P.M. daily

Tybee Island Museum and Light Station
Tybee Island Historical Society
PO Box 366
30 Meddin Dr.
Tybee Island, GA 31328
Phone: 912-786-5801

Tybee Island Marine Science Center
PO Box 1879
Tybee Island, GA 31328

WOODBINE

Bryan Lang Historical Library
PO Box 725
Woodbine, GA 31569
Camden Ave. and 4th St.
Phone: 912-576-5841
8 A.M. to 5 P.M. Mon to Fri

HOSPITALS

BRUNSWICK

Glynn Immediate Care, P.C.
3400 Parkwood Dr. at Glynn Ave. (US 17)
Brunswick, GA 31520
Open Mon.-Fri. 8 A.M.–8 P.M., Sat., Sun., & Holidays noon-6 P.M. (closed Christmas Day)
Phone: 912-267-7600

Southeast Georgia Regional Medical Center
3100 Kemble Ave.
Brunswick, GA
24 Hour Emergency Room
Phone: 912-264-7000

DARIEN

Southeast Georgia Regional Medical Center
3100 Kemble Ave.
Brunswick, GA
24 Hour Emergency Room
Phone: 912-264-7000

ST MARYS

Camden Medical Center
2000 Dan Proctor Dr.
St. Marys, GA 31558
24 Hour Emergency Service
Phone: 912-576-4200

ST SIMONS

Island Convenient Care
2469 Demere Rd., Suite 112
St. Simons Island, GA 31522
Open Mon.–Fri. 9 A.M.-6 P.M.
Sat. 10 A.M.–2 P.M.
Phone: 912-638-1957

Southeast Georgia Regional Medical Center
3100 Kemble Ave.
Brunswick, GA 31520
24 Hour Emergency Room
Phone: 912-264-7000

SAVANNAH

Candler Hospital
5353 Reynolds St.
Savannah, GA
24 hour emergency service
Phone: 912-692-6000

Memorial Medical Center
4700 Waters Ave.
Savannah, GA
24 hour emergency service
Phone: 912-350-8000

St. Joseph's Hospital
11705 Mercy Blvd.
Savannah, GA
24 hour emergency service
Phone: 912-925-4100

HOTLINES

BIRDS

Colonial Coast Birding Trail
Phone: 912-994-1438

Rare Bird Alert
Phone: 770-493-8862 (state wide)
Phone: 912-244-9190 (South GA)

Report new species to:
Nongame-Endangered Wildlife Program

116 Rum Creek Dr.
Forsyth, GA 31029
Phone: 912-994-1438

BOATING

Boating Safety Hot Line
Phone: 800-368-5647

COAST

Protect the coast:
Coastal Georgia Center for
Sustainable Development
PO Box 598
Darien, GA 31305
Phone: 912-437-8160

DOLPHINS

Protect Dolphins
Office of Protected Resources
National Marine Fisheries
1335 East West Highway
Silver Spring, MD 20910
Phone: 301-713-2289
The Dolphin Project
PO Box 10323
Savannah, GA 31412
www.thedolphinproject.org

FISH

FISH Health Hotline
If you see ulcerated fish call:
Phone: 800-448-0012

FISHERIES

NOAA Fisheries Enforcement
Hot Line—800-853-1964

MARINE MAMMALS

Report sightings of dead or injured
marine mammals, including bottle-
nose & spotted dolphins, manatees
and any species of whales to:
800-241-4113

OIL & CHEMICAL SPILLS

Report oil and chemical spills to
the National Response Center
Phone: 800-424-8802

POACHERS

T.I.P. (Turn In Poachers)
To report game and fish law
violations, fish kills or
hazardous spills call:
800-241-4113

SOS

Sanctuary on the Sapelo
Help for injured or orphaned
birds
Phone: 912-832-5571

TURTLES

If you see an injured, dead or
harassed sea turtle call:
800-2-SAVE-ME

WASTE PUMP OUT

For station locations call:
800-ASK-FISH

WHALES

If you see a Right Whale, in
Georgia call: 800-272-8363, in
Florida call: 800-342-5367

WILDLIFE

You can help save wildlife,
Call:
Sanctuary on the Sapelo
Rte.3, Box 3261
Pine Harbor, GA 31331
Phone: 912-832-5571
fax: 912-832-6788
Email: emmy@sos4birds.org
Web site: www.SOS4birds.org

MACHINE SHOPS

BRUNSWICK

Barlow Welding & Machine Shop
6019 New Jesup Hwy
Brunswick, GA 31523
Phone: 912-265-5951

Carlin, C R
2309 Norwich St.
Brunswick, GA 31520
Phone: 912-265-6461
Dominey Machine & Propeller Service, Inc.
6005 Habersham St.
Brunswick, GA 31520
Phone: 912-264-2942
912-267-7084
www.dominey.com
Glynco Machine & Tool Co.
2590 Sidney Lanier Dr.
Brunswick, GA 31525
Phone: 912-264-1988

ST MARYS

Camden Machine & Welding
87 8th St.
St. Marys, GA 31558
Phone: 912-882-2558
Riverside Machine Shop
304 St. Marys St.
St. Marys, GA 31558
P.B. Alley, proprietor
Phone: 912-673-7942

SAVANNAH

A & B Fabrication and Repair
4250 Ogeechee Rd.
Savannah, GA 31405
Phone: 912-232-1343
Dixie Machine & Fabrication Co
512 Indian St.
Savannah, GA 31401
Phone: 912-233-4743
P & O Machine Shop
2400 Krenson St.
Savannah, GA 31415
Phone: 912-234-5394
Palmer Johnson Savannah
301 North Lathrop Ave.
Savannah, GA 31415
Phone: 912-234-6579
Fax: 912-239-1168
Email: info@pjsavannah.com
Thunderbolt Marine, Inc.
3124 River Dr.
Thunderbolt, GA 31404
Phone: 912-352-4931
Fax: 912-352-4958

MARINAS

ALTAMAHA RIVER

TWO WAY FISH CAMP
250 Ricefield Way
Brunswick, GA 31525
South shore of South Altamaha River, near Wood Cut. 4 n. miles west of ICW R "216"
Phone: 912-265-0410
Monitors VHF 16
Transients welcome
Floating docks
DEPTHS of approach: 6-20 feet
DEPTHS at docks: 20 feet
FUELS: diesel & gasoline, lube oils
SHORE POWER: 220 and 110, 50 and 30 amps
MECHANIC: on site
PROPANE: on site
HAUL OUT: electric hoist for boats up to 25 feet
(40-ton travel lift at the yard next door, see *BOAT YARDS*)
LAUNCH RATES: $6 for 16 feet, add $1 for each additional foot
LAUNDRY: on site
SHOWERS are available
RESTAURANT: Mudcat Charlie's is on site serving fresh seafood
STORE: useful fishing supplies and tackle, snacks and cold drinks, cold beer. CHARTS are for sale, ICE is available
BAIT: live—shrimp, shiners, minnows, crickets and worms, dead—shrimp, shiners, minnows, crickets, squid and ballyhoo
MODEM CONNECTION: available
Use above address for MAIL HOLDING, mark For Transient Yacht
CHARGES: $.75 per foot a day, $6.50 per foot a month.
CREDIT CARDS: Visa, Chevron, MasterCard, Discover, American Express, Novas
HOURS: 6 A.M. to 7 P.M.

BELLE BLUFF

BELLE BLUFF MARINA
Rte. 3 Box 3246-B25
Townsend, GA 31331
West shore of White Chimney Creek, north of Sapelo River
Phone: 912-832-5323
Monitors VHF 16
Transients welcome
Floating docks
DEPTHS of approach: 3 feet
DEPTHS at dock: 6 to 9 feet
FUELS: diesel, gasoline and outboard motor oils
SHORE POWER: NONE
MECHANIC: will call an independent mechanic
PROPANE: refills on site
HAUL OUT: electric hoist, up to 7,000 pounds for vessels up to 25 feet
LAUNCH RATES: varies by length, from $6 to $18
SHOWERS: available
STORE: snacks, cold drinks, beer, batteries, fishing tackle. Pool table! CHARTS are for sale and ICE is available.
BAIT: live shrimp, dead shrimp, squid, ballyhoo, cigar minnows, ribbon eels and mullet
MODEM CONNECTION: available
Use above address for MAIL HOLDING, mark For Transient Yacht
CHARGES: $.20 per foot per day, $3.00 per foot per month
CREDIT CARDS: not accepted
HOURS: summer—7 A.M. to 7 P.M., winter—7 A.M. to dark
CONTACT: Cathy Brown

BRUNSWICK

Also see *Altamaha River*

BRUNSWICK BOAT MARINA
South Highway 17
PO Box 802
Brunswick, GA 31520
Western end of Clubbs Creek on eastern shore of Brunswick
Phone: 912-265-2290
Floating docks
DEPTHS at dock: 3 feet
FUEL: Gasoline and outboard oils available
MECHANIC: will call an independent mechanic
HAUL OUT: electric hoist for boats up to 23 feet
RESTAURANT: Spankys next door
STORE: ICE, cold drinks & beer
BAIT: Live shrimp, minnows, eels. Dead shrimp, squid
No CREDIT CARDS
HOURS: 6 A.M.–6 P.M., closed Mondays

BRUNSWICK LANDING MARINA, INC.
2429 Newcastle St.
Brunswick, GA 31520
East shore of East River, 2½ n. miles north of Sidney Lanier bridge, downtown Brunswick.
Phone: 912-262-9264
Monitors VHF 16
Transients are welcome. This is a full-service marina with a full-service and do-it-yourself boat yard a little further up the river.
Floating docks
DEPTHS of approach: 24 feet
DEPTHS at docks: 12 to 6 feet
FUELS: diesel, gasoline and lube oils
SHORE POWER: 220 and 110, 100, 50 and 30 amps
CABLE TV and PHONE hook-up available
WASTE PUMP OUT: available
MECHANIC: diesel and gas mechanic on site
PROPANE: gas company will pick up and deliver to marina
HAUL OUT: 50-ton travel lift
LAUNDRY: on site and is free! Crew's lounge adjacent with TV and VCR. Weather is on channel 31.
SHOWERS: available
RESTAURANTS: in town are generally open only for lunch, see *RESTAURANTS* for more ideas
MARINE STORE: there is an ACE Hardware nearby, 3 blocks to the south
ICE: is available at Cumberland

Ice near the shrimp boats or across the street at the convenience store
CHARTS: for sale at ACE Hardware
MODEM CONNECTION: available
ATM: several within a few blocks, at the convenience store and at the banks on Gloucester Street
Use the address above for MAIL HOLDING or courier delivery, this is the boat yard address
CHARGES: $1.00 a foot per day
ELECTRICAL CHARGES: up to 44 feet-$4 per night, 45 to 54 feet-$6 per night, 55 feet and up-$10 per night. Monthly power is metered. Cable TV is $3 per night, monthly $25.
CREDIT CARDS: Visa, MasterCard and Discover
HOURS: 8 A.M. to 6 P.M. except Tuesdays when the hours are 8 A.M. to 5 P.M. If unable to find anyone on the docks, try the boat yard.
NOTE: This is the home of the Emerald Princess gambling casino boat

CREDLE'S COMPLETE MARINA

1455 South Highway 17
Brunswick, GA 31523
Mail: 1014 Richmond St.
Brunswick, GA 31520
West shore of the western end of Jointer's Creek, located on Colonel's Island
Phone: 912-261-1935
Fax: 912-262-6003
Monitors VHF 16
This is a boat yard
Floating docks
DEPTHS of approach: high tide only
DEPTHS at the dock: 6 feet LW
FUELS: can order diesel and lube oils
SHORE POWER: 110
MECHANIC: on site
PROPANE: can order
HAUL OUT: $7 per foot in and out plus blocking. $6 per foot a month for storage in the work area

STORE: marine supplies and parts. CHARTS may be ordered and ICE is available.
MODEM CONNECTION: possible
Use the HWY 17 address for MAIL HOLDING, mark For Transient Yacht
No CREDIT CARDS
HOURS: 8 A.M. to 5 P.M.
CONTACT: H. L. Credle

TROUPE CREEK MARINA

375 Yacht Rd.
Brunswick, GA 31525
West shore of Troup Creek, 1½ n. miles northwest of ICW R "238"
Phone: 912-264-3862
Monitors VHF 16, goes to 68
One spot is available for transients
Floating docks
DEPTHS of approach: 10 feet
DEPTHS at dock: 12 feet
FUEL: gasoline, lube oils
No SHORE POWER
MECHANIC: will call an independent mechanic
HAUL OUT: electric hoist, two 2-ton hoists for boats up to 24 feet
LAUNCH RATES: by length, varies from $6 to $16
RESTAURANT: snack bar on site
STORE: handy items, fishing tackle, cold drinks, snacks. DNR fishing maps and ICE are available
BAIT: Live shrimp, in season live eels and bull minnows. Dead shrimp, squid, bally-hoo, mullet, menhaden, ribbon fish, chum
Use above address for MAIL HOLDING, mark For Transient Yacht
CHARGES: $.70 a foot per day
CREDIT CARDS: for gas only, Visa and Master Card
HOURS: 7 A.M. to 6 P.M.

DARIEN

BLACKBEARD SCHOOL OF SAILING & NAVIGATION

GA SR 99 and Blue n' Hall Rd.
Darien, GA 31305-1635

Phone: 912-437-4878
Fax: 912-437-3073
Email: joesails@gate.net
This is a sailing school with dockage available
DEPTHS of approach: 14 feet
DEPTHS at docks: 12 plus feet
MECHANIC—outboard mechanic available, will call independent mechanic
LAUNDRY: on site
SHORE POWER: as well as compressed air available
MODEM CONNECTION: available
Use above address for MAIL HOLDING, mark For Transient Yacht
CHARGES: first night free, $8 per foot a month
No CREDIT CARDS
HOURS are variable, call in advance of arriving

DARIEN WELCOME CENTER MARINA

105 Ft. King George Dr.
Darien, GA 31305
Shown as city dock on chartlet #048
Phone: 912-437-5251
Fax: 912-437-5251
Email: chamber@darientel.net
Transients are welcome
They do not monitor the VHF
Floating docks
DEPTHS of approach: 6 feet at LW in Darien River
DEPTHS at docks: 12 feet plus
FUEL: not at dock, gasoline across the street
SHORE POWER: available
MECHANIC: ask in Welcome Center
RESTAURANTS: within easy walking distance
STORE: a convenience store is across the street
BAIT: one block away on Broad Street
MODEM CONNECTION: not available at the Welcome Center, computers are available at the library, 1/4 m. north
LAUNDRY: ½ m. north
MAIL HOLDING: is not available, the post office is 3

blocks north
CHARGES: $.75 per foot per night, 2 week maximum visit
CREDIT CARDS: no credit cards- cash or checks only
HOURS: Monday through Saturday 9 A.M. to 5 P.M.

MCINTOSH ROD AND GUN CLUB

Rte. 1 Box 1414
Darien, GA 31305
At Blue n' Hall on the west shore of May Hall Creek near Union Island
Phone: 912-437-4677
Monitors VHF 16
Transients are welcome
Floating docks
DEPTHS of approach: 14 feet
DEPTHS at docks: 11 feet
FUEL: gasoline, outboard motor oil
HAUL OUT: two 2-ton electric hoists for boats up to 33 feet
LAUNCH RATES: boats under 20 feet—$7, boats 20 feet and up—$2 per foot more. Boats over 23 feet need a high tide to be launched. Members pay $5, membership costs $25 a year and includes an annual party.
RAMP: the McIntosh County boat ramp is next door
STORE: useful fishing supplies, cold drinks and snacks. CHARTS of the area are for sale and ICE is available
BAIT: Live and dead shrimp, in season frozen squid and finger mullet
HOURS: dawn to dusk

JEKYLL ISLAND

JEKYLL HARBOR MARINA

1 Harbor Rd.
Jekyll Island, GA 31527
East shore of Jekyll Creek at G "23" on the ICW, south of Jekyll Causeway bridge
Phone: 912-635-3137
Fax: 912-635-2633
www.jekyllharbor.com
dockmaster@jekyllharbor.com
Monitors VHF 16
Transients are welcome

Floating docks
DEPTHS of approach: 8 feet
DEPTHS at docks: 12 feet
FUELS: diesel & gasoline, lube oils, Texaco high speed pumps
SHORE POWER: 110, 50 and 30 amps, $6 for 50 amps, $4 for 30 amps for the first 5 nights, weekly and monthly rates then take effect.
CABLE TV hook-up available
WASTE PUMP OUT is available
MECHANIC: will call an independent mechanic except on Sundays
HAUL OUT: fork lift with 18,000 pound capacity for boats up to 30 feet
LAUNCH RATE: $25 for in and out, wash and motor flush
LAUNDRY: on site
SHOWERS: New showers are available
COURTESY BICYCLES/CAR: are provided
PICNIC AREA: with gas grills
RESTAURANT: Sea Jays Café and Bar on site, low country boil prepared every night in season!
STORE: sells snacks, cold drinks, sun blocks and waterway guides
BAIT: live shrimp, dead shrimp, cigar minnows, finger mullet, ballyhoo, squid
ICE: block and crushed available
CHARTS are for sale
MODEM CONNECTION: available during and after hours
Use above address for MAIL HOLDING, mark For Transient Yacht
CHARGES: $1.30 a foot per day, $7.00 a foot per week, includes water and cable TV
CREDIT CARDS: Visa, Master Card, Discover, American Express, Diners Club and Texaco
HOURS: 7 A.M. to 6 P.M.

JEKYLL WHARF MARINA

#1 Pier Rd.
Jekyll Island, GA 31527
East shore of Jekyll Creek at R

"20" on the ICW, north of the Jekyll causeway bridge
Phone: 912-635-3152
Monitors VHF 16
Transients are welcome
Floating docks
DEPTHS of approach: 8 feet
DEPTHS at dock: 6 feet
FUELS: diesel & gasoline, lube oils
SHORE POWER: 220 and 110, 50 and 30 amps, the charge for electricity is $.25 per foot
MECHANIC: diesel mechanic available
RESTAURANTS: Latitude 31 and The Rah Bar are located on the dock and the Jekyll Island Club is across the street
STORE: useful supplies plus gifts, parts orders are welcome. Cold drinks are for sale and ICE is available
Use the above address for MAIL HOLDING, mark For Transient Yacht
CHARGES: $1.00 a foot per day
CREDIT CARDS: Visa and Master Card
HOURS: 10 A.M. to 5 P.M., will stay later if necessary

KILKENNY CREEK

KILKENNY MARINA

3083 Kilkenny Rd.
Richmond Hill, GA 31324
HWY 144 East—Mile marker 21
West shore of Kilkenny Creek, west of "G" 107
Phone: 912- 727-2215
Monitors VHF 16
Transients are welcome
Floating docks
DEPTHS of approach: 10 feet
DEPTHS at dock: 13 feet
FUELS: diesel & gasoline, oils for outboards
SHORE POWER: 220 and 110, 50 and 30 amps, $5 for 50 amps, $2.50 for 30 amps
HAUL OUT: electric hoist for boats up to 24 feet. Phone for rates.
LAUNDRY: is on site
SHOWERS: are available
RESTAURANT: the one next

door is open

STORE: useful fishing and picnic items, cold drinks, snacks.

ICE: is available.

BAIT: live shrimp, dead shrimp, ballyhoo, squid, cigar minnows, Boston mackerel, finger mullet

MODEM CONNECTION: available when the staff is not busy

Use the above address for MAIL HOLDING, mark For Transient Yacht

CHARGES: $1.00 a foot per day

CREDIT CARDS: All, Master Card, Visa, Texaco

HOURS: 7 A.M. to dark

CONTACT: Bob, Robert or Danny Bacot

LITTLE SATILLA RIVER

HICKORY BLUFF MARINA

307 Hickory Bluff Dr.

Waverly, GA

South shore of Little Satilla, west of Colonel's Island

Phone: 912-262-0453

Transients are welcome

Floating docks

DEPTHS of approach: 30 feet

DEPTHS at dock: 13 to 30 feet

FUEL: gasoline, lubricants for outboards

No SHORE POWER

MECHANIC: will call an independent mechanic

HAUL OUT: Electric hoist, 6,000 lbs. for vessels up to 28 feet

LAUNCH RATES: prices begin at $6 for boats 17 to 18 feet, and goes to $25

STORE: useful fishing supplies and tackle, snacks, cold drinks. DNR fishing charts for this area for sale and ICE is available

Use above address for MAIL HOLDING, mark For Transient Yacht

CHARGES: $4 a day at the dock

CREDIT CARDS: Visa and MasterCard

HOURS: 6 A.M. to 6 P.M.

CONTACT: Ben Slade

OCEAN BREEZE MARINA AND CAMPGROUND

14 Ocean Breeze Dr.

Waverly, GA 31565

West shore of Maiden Creek, to the west of Little Satilla River

Phone: 912-262-0058

Floating docks

DEPTHS of approach: 17 feet

DEPTHS at docks: 15 feet

No SHORE POWER

MECHANIC: will call an independent mechanic

HAUL OUT: two 5-ton electric hoists for boats up to 23 feet

LAUNCH RATES:
boats up to 16 feet—$6
17 to 19 feet—$9
20 to 21 feet—$10
larger vessels pay $12

STORE: fishing tackle, cold drinks, snacks

ICE: is available

BAIT: Live and dead shrimp

No CREDIT CARDS

HOURS: 6 A.M. to 6 P.M., 7 days a week

MIDWAY

HALFMOON MARINA

171 Azalea Rd.

Midway, GA 31320

Southwest shore of Colonel's Island, north shore of North Newport River

Phone: 912-884-5819

Monitors VHF 16, goes to 68

Transients are welcome

Floating docks (new!)

DEPTHS of approach: 14 feet

DEPTHS at docks: 35 feet at LW

FUELS: diesel & gasoline, oils for outboards

SHORE POWER: 220 and 110, 50 and 30 amps

MECHANIC: will call an independent mechanic

HAUL OUT: electric hoists, two three-ton hoists for vessels up to 28 feet, depending on width larger vessels may be launched

LAUNCH RATES:
$10 for under 17 feet
18 to 20 feet—$12
21 to 23 feet—$14

24 to 26 feet—$20
27 to 29 feet—$25
over 29 feet—$30

SHOWERS are available

STORE: useful supplies, fishing gear, cold drinks, beer, snacks, football on TV, country store atmosphere. CHARTS are for sale and ICE is available

MODEM CONNECTION: ask when the staff is not busy

CHARGES: $1.00 a foot per day, $.40 a foot per day if launched with the hoist. $5.00 a foot per month for wet storage. $2 a day for dinghy tie-up

CREDIT CARDS: Visa and Master Card

HOURS: summertime—6:30 A.M. to 8:00 P.M., Fri & Sat a little later, winter—7 A.M. to 7 P.M.

YELLOW BLUFF FISHING CAMP

118 Yellow Bluff Rd.

Midway, GA 31320

East shore of Colonel's Island, Ashley Creek east of Cedar Creek

Phone: 912-884-5448

Monitors VHF 16, goes to 68

This is a fish camp, transients are welcome

Floating docks

DEPTHS of approach: 3 feet

DEPTHS at docks: 3 feet

FUELS: gasoline, lube oils

MECHANIC: on site and independent mechanics

HAUL OUT: electric hoist for boats up to 35 feet

LAUNCH RATES:
$10 for under 19 feet
$12 for 20 feet
$15 for 21 feet
$18 for 22 feet
$21 for 23 feet
$1 a foot for over 24 feet

SHOWERS: available

STORE: useful fishing equipment, snacks, cold drinks

ICE is available

BAIT: live shrimp, mud minnows, sometimes live fiddler crabs and live mullet. Dead shrimp, mud minnows, eel, mullet, ribbon fish, Spanish sardines, ballyhoo, squid, sometimes other baits

MODEM CONNECTION: available

Use above address for MAIL HOLDING, mark For Transient Yacht

CHARGES: see *LAUNCH RATES* above

CREDIT CARDS: are not accepted

HOURS: 6 A.M. to 7 P.M.

CONTACT: Arthur Goodman or Rayburn Goodman

NORTH NEWPORT RIVER

See *Midway*

OGEECHEE RIVER

FT. MCALLISTER MARINA

3203 Ft. McAllister Rd.
Richmond Hill, GA 31324
South shore of Ogeechee River, inland of Shad Island
Phone: 912-727-2632
Fax: 912-727-2632
Email: FtMcAllister@CLDS.NET
Monitors VHF 16, goes to 68
Transients welcome
Floating docks
DEPTHS OF APPROACH: 6 feet
DEPTHS AT DOCKS: 23 feet
FUELS: Diesel & gasoline, lube oils
SHORE POWER: 220 and 110, 50, 30 and 20 amps
WASTE PUMP OUT: available
MECHANIC: lives on site
HAUL OUT: two electric hoists available for boats up to 42 feet. There is a public ramp nearby, the marina staff will help launch larger vessels. The ramp is for mid to high tide use.
LAUNCH RATES: boats up to 19 feet are charged $8
19 to 23 feet - $12
23 to 27 feet - $16

above 27 feet call for rate.

LAUNDRY: is available for dock customers

SHOWERS: are available

RESTAURANT: The marina cooks fresh food for take out, grilled sandwiches for lunch, seafood in the evenings. Call in advance.

GUEST ROOMS: with kitchenettes are available for overnight visits

STORE: has useful supplies, snacks and cold drinks. Parts are ordered quickly. CHARTS are for sale and ICE is available.

MODEM CONNECTION: available

Use above address for MAIL HOLDING, mark For Transient Yacht

CHARGES: $.95 a foot per day, discounts for Boat US members

CREDIT CARDS: Visa and Master Card

HOURS: 7 A.M. to 7 P.M. seven days a week, closed Christmas

CONTACT: Thomas Sander

RICHMOND HILL

See *Kilkenny Creek, Ogeechee River*

ST MARYS

JACK BARWICK'S MARINA & CABINS

Crooked River,
St. Marys, GA 31558
West of Crooked River State Park
Phone: 912-882-3227
Floating docks
Electric hoist

LANG'S MARINA, EAST & WEST

100 St. Marys St.
St. Marys, GA 31558
North shore of St. Marys River, north of G "13", 4 ½ n. miles west of ICW G "35"
Phone: 912-882-4452
Monitors VHF 16
Transients are welcome

Floating docks
DEPTHS of approach: 20 feet
DEPTHS at docks: 12 feet
FUELS: diesel & gasoline, lube oils, all at the East dock
SHORE POWER: 110, 30 amps 50 amps at East dock
WASTE PUMP OUT: available
MECHANIC: will call an independent mechanic
RAMP: public launching ramp next door
SHOWERS: are available
RESTAURANT: Lang's Marina Restaurant on site serving fresh seafood. Other restaurants within easy walking distance
ICE: is available
BAIT: is sold next door at The Fishing Outpost, see *FISHING BAIT & SUPPLIES*
ATM: within walking distance
Use above address for MAIL HOLDING, mark For Transient Yacht
CHARGES: $.75 a foot per day

ST SIMONS

GOLDEN ISLES MARINA

206 Marina Dr.
St. Simons Island, GA 31522
West shore of south Frederica River, 1 ¾ n. miles north of ICW
Phone: 912-634-1128
912-634-1786
www.gimarina.com
rose@gimarina.com
Monitors VHF 16, goes to 68
Transients are welcome
Floating docks
DEPTHS of approach: 6 feet LW
DEPTHS at docks: 15 feet
FUELS: diesel & gasoline, lube oils. High speed pump, discounts on volume.
SHORE POWER: 220 and 110, 50 and 30 amps. $4 for boats up to 44 feet, $6 for boats from 45 to 54 feet. $10 for boats 55 feet and over
CABLE TV: hook-up free with fuel purchase
WASTE PUMP OUT is available
MECHANIC: will call an

independent mechanic

Dry stack storage for boats up to 35 feet in length and 20,000 pounds weight

DRY STACK RATES: $8.50 a foot per month on annual contracts

LAUNDRY: on site

SHOWERS: are available

RESTAURANTS: one on site

MARINE STORE: a full-service marine store, Dunbar Sales, is on site as well as Coastal Outdoor & Marine, a boat dealer with a mechanic. The Island Dive Center is located here. CHARTS are for sale and ICE is available.

BAIT: Live and dead shrimp

MODEM CONNECTION is available as well as a fax machine and a copier.

CHARGES: $1.50 a foot per night, plus electricity. See *SHORE POWER* above. $7.00 a foot per week, $9.50 a foot per month, $8.50 a foot per year. Electricity metered separately.

SMALL BOAT CHARGES: for boats under 30 feet, $6 a foot per month near shore (tide restricted), $7 a foot per month not tide restricted

DINGY TIE UP: $5 per day

CREDIT CARDS: Visa, Master Card, Choice, American Express & Discover

COURTESY CAR: available for one hour at no charge, transportation to the local airport provided

HOURS: 7:00 A.M. to 7:30 P.M.

HAMPTON RIVER CLUB MARINA

1000 Hampton River Club Dr.

St. Simons Island, GA 31522

South shore of Hampton River on Butler Point, 1 ¾ n. miles east of ICW

Phone: 912-638-1210

Monitors VHF 16

Transients welcome

Floating docks

DEPTHS of approach: 6-8 feet

DEPTHS at docks: 8—10 feet

FUELS: diesel, gasoline and

lube oils

SHORE POWER: 110, 50 and 30 amps. 50 amps - $6 30 amps - $3

MECHANIC: on site and independent

HAUL OUT: fork lift for boats up to 35 feet, no sail boats

LAUNCH RATES: $2 a foot

A new LAUNDRY is on site

SHOWERS are available

STORE: a few marine items, cold drinks. CHARTS are for sale and ICE is available

Use above address for MAIL HOLDING, mark For Transient Yacht

CHARGES: $1.00 a foot per day, weekly rates available. Dinghy and small fishing boat tie-ups costs $7 a day. If launched here the rate is $7 per night.

CREDIT CARDS: Visa, Master Card and American Express

HOURS: 7 A.M. to 6 P.M. launched here the rate is $7 per night, someone on premises 24 hours a day

ST. SIMONS BOATING AND FISHING CLUB

1000 Arthur Moore Dr.

St. Simons Island, GA 31522

East shore of south Frederica River, north of Torras Causeway bridge

Phone: 912-638-9146

Transients are welcome

Floating docks

DEPTHS of approach: 20 feet

DEPTHS at dock: 20 feet

FUEL: gasoline, lubricants for outboards

SHORE POWER: 110

MECHANIC: will call independent mechanic

HAUL OUT: 4-ton hoist

LAUNCH RATES: boats under 18 feet–$8 18 to 22 feet–$10 22 to 26 feet–$14 over 26–$18

ICE: is available

BAIT: live and dead shrimp, call for bait information

CHARGES: if arriving by water the charge is $.50 a foot per

day, use the north docks only. If using the hoist the dockage rate is $6 a day for boats under 26 feet. Boats over 26 feet pay $10. Members of the fishing club pay half price.

CREDIT CARDS: not accepted

HOURS: 6:30 A.M. to 5:30 P.M. Tues–Fri, 6 A.M. to 6 P.M. Sat–Sun, closed Monday

TAYLOR'S FISH CAMP

Rt. 9 Box 280 N

Lawrence Rd.

St Simons Island, GA 31522

Western end of Lawrence Creek off the western side of Hampton River. East shore of St. Simons.

Phone: 912-638-7690 912-638-5731

Floating docks

DEPTHS of approach: 2 feet

DEPTHS at dock: 3 feet

HAUL OUT: 1-ton hoist

SAPELO RIVER

Also see *Belle Bluff, Shellman Bluff*

PINE HARBOR MARINA

Rte. 3 Box 3196

Townsend, GA 31331

West shore of Sapelo River, beyond Belleville

Phone: 912-832-5999

Transients welcome

DEPTHS of approach: 3 feet

DEPTHS at dock: 20 feet

FUEL: gasoline

HAUL OUT: electric hoist, 2 tons, for vessels up to 25 feet

LAUNCH RATES:
boats less than 15 feet - $6,
15 to 16 feet - $7,
16 to 17 feet pay $8
17 to 18 pay $9
18 to 19 pay $10
19 to 20 pay $11
21 to 23 pay $14
23 to 25 pay $15
over 25 feet pay $18

ICE is available

BAIT: live shrimp

CHARGES: $2 a day for small boats, others pay $.25 a foot per day

CREDIT CARDS not accepted

HOURS: 6 A.M. to 6 P.M.
CONTACT: Otis Temple

SAVANNAH

BAHIA BLEU MARINA

38112 River Dr.
Thunderbolt, GA 31401
West shore of Wilmington River
at G "35" on the ICW
Phone: 912-354-2283
Fax: 912-352-4629
Monitors VHF 16, goes to 68
Transients welcome, space
limited
Floating docks
DEPTHS of approach: 12 feet
DEPTHS at dock: 12 feet at LW
FUELS: diesel, gasoline at top of
dock, outboard oils
SHORE POWER: (2) 220 outlets
with 50 amps, plus 110 with
30 amps
MECHANIC: will call an
independent mechanic
LAUNCH RATES: Boat launch-
ing is available for storage
customers only.
SHOWERS: available
RESTAURANTS: within walking
distance
MARINE STORE: parts on hand,
useful cleaning supplies and
oils. The large River Services
marine store is across the
street.
ICE: available
Use above address for MAIL
HOLDING, mark For
Transient Yacht
CHARGES: from $1.25 to $2.50
a foot per day, plus $5.00 for
30 amps and $10.00 for 50
amps
CREDIT CARDS: MasterCard,
Visa, Discover, American
Express and Shell
HOURS: summer-
8 A.M. to 6 P.M Mon-Fri
8 A.M. to 7 P.M Sat & Sun
winter – 8 A.M. to 5 P.M, 7 days

BONA BELLA MARINA

2740 Livingston Ave.
Savannah, GA 31406
Country Club Creek off Herb
River
Phone: 912-355-9601

912-356-9151
Monitors VHF 16
Generally for vessels up to 30
feet, call if larger
Floating docks
DEPTHS of approach: 4 feet LW
DEPTHS at dock: 4 feet LW
SHORE POWER: 110
HAUL OUT: electric hoist for up
to 20 feet.
LAUNCH RATES: $10 in and
out, 20 feet maximum
SHOWERS: available
STORE with snacks, cold drinks,
ice, tackle and charts
BAIT: Live shrimp & minnows
CHARGES: $6.50 a foot per
month
CREDIT CARDS: not accepted
HOURS: 6:30 A.M. to 6:00 P.M.

BULL RIVER YACHT CLUB MARINA

8005 Old Tybee Rd.
Savannah, GA 31410
HWY 80 East at Bull River
West shore of Bull River south of
HWY 80 bridge
Phone: 912-897-7300
Fax: 912-897-0668
www.bullriver.com
Monitors VHF 16, goes to 07
Transients are welcome
Floating docks
DEPTHS of approach: 14 feet
DEPTHS at dock: 20 feet
FUELS: ValvTect marine fuel,
diesel, gasoline and outboard
motor oils
SHORE POWER: 220 and 110,
50 and 30 amps
WASTE PUMP OUT: portable
MECHANIC: will call indepen-
dent mechanic
SHOWERS are available
RESTAURANT: Williams
Seafood Restaurant is across
the street
MARINE STORE: basic, useful
items, CHARTS are for sale
and ICE is available
BAIT: frozen shrimp, squid and
ballyhoo
MODEM CONNECTION:
available
Use above address for MAIL
HOLDING, mark For
Transient Yacht

CHARGES: $1.00 a foot per day,
$4.00 a foot per week
$9.00 a foot per month
CREDIT CARDS: accepted
HOURS: 9 A.M. to 6 P.M. every day,
shorter hours in winter, will
stay longer when necessary
CONTACT: Michael J. Neal

COFFEE BLUFF FISH CAMP & MARINA

14915 Coffee Bluff Rd.
Savannah, GA 31409
North shore of Forest River
Phone: 912-925-9030
Monitors VHF 16 on weekends
Transients are welcome, space is
limited, inquire before arriving
Floating docks
Depths of approach: 15 feet
Depth at docks: 20 feet
FUEL: gasoline, lube oils
SHORE POWER: 220 and 110,
50 and 30 amps
WASTE PUMP OUT available
HAUL OUT: Electric hoists, two
two-ton hoists for boats up
to 26 feet
LAUNCH RATES: $1.00 a foot,
$10.00 minimum
STORE: snacks, cold drinks, ice
cream, fishing supplies and
other useful commodities.
CHARTS are for sale and ICE
is available
BAIT: live shrimp, dead squid,
ballyhoo, spanish sardine and
cigar minnows, call to ask
what bait is available
CHARGES: $.50 a foot per day
but hard to find space
CREDIT CARDS: Visa and
MasterCard
HOURS: 7 A.M. to 6 P.M.
closed Tuesdays
CONTACT: Freddie Love or
Darren Harris

DELEGAL CREEK MARINA

1 Marina Dr.
Savannah, GA 31411
Skidaway Island
East shore of Delegal Creek, 2
n. miles northeast of R "86"
and the ICW
Phone: 912-598-0023
Monitors VHF 16, goes to 68
Transients welcome
Floating docks

DEPTHS of approach: 4 feet LW
DEPTHS at dock: 30 feet
FUELS: diesel & gasoline, lube oils
SHORE POWER: 220 and 110, 50 and 30 amps
WASTE PUMP OUT is available
MECHANIC: will call an independent mechanic
LAUNDRY: on site
SHOWERS: available
CHARTS: ICE is available and there is a courtesy car
MAIL HOLDING only for monthly visitors, not transients
CHARGES: $1.10 a foot per day
CREDIT CARDS: Visa, Master Card and Chevron
HOURS: 8 A.M. to 6 P.M. in summer, 8 A.M. to 5 P.M. in winter. Staff will be available for boats with reservations.

HINCKLEY YACHT SERVICES
2400 Mechanic Ave.
PO Box 5250
Savannah, GA 31404
West shore of Wilmington River, south of R "34" on the ICW
Phone: 912-629-2400
Fax: 912-629-2404
Monitors VHF 16, goes to 68
This is a full-service boat yard
Transients are welcome
Floating docks
DEPTHS of approach: 17 feet
DEPTHS at dock: 12 feet
FUELS: none
SHORE POWER: 220 and 110, 50 amp – $8, 30 amps – $5
MECHANIC: on site
PROPANE: available off-site
HAUL OUT: 35-ton travel lift
TRAVEL LIFT RATES: $7.50 a foot, in and out, $3.00 a foot for bottom wash, $5.00 a foot for blocking. $150 minimum on 3 month stay.
SHOWER: available
MARINE PARTS: available
ATM: within walking distance
Use the above address for MAIL HOLDING, mark For Transient Yacht
CHARGES: $1.05 a foot per day, other rates upon request
CREDIT CARDS: Master Card

and Visa
HOURS: 8 A.M. to 6 P.M. Mon-Fri, 9 A.M. to 1 P.M. Sat

HOGANS MARINA
PO Box 30505
Savannah, GA 31410
East shore of Turners Creek, south of Johnny Mercer Drive bridge
Phone: 912-897-FISH
Fax: 912-898-8929
Monitors VHF 16
Transients welcome
Floating docks
DEPTHS of approach: 6 feet LW
DEPTHS at dock: 20 feet
FUELS: gasoline & lube oils
SHORE POWER: 110 & 30 amps
MECHANIC: will call an independent mechanic
HAUL OUT: fork lift and overhead monorail for vessels up to 35 feet, larger if boat is light
LAUNCH RATES: $1.00 a foot, includes recovery
SHOWER: available
RESTAURANTS: within walking distance
MARINE STORE: has useful supplies, charts and ice
BAIT: live shrimp seasonally, dead shrimp, squid, ballyhoo
MODEM CONNECTION: at nearby library
ATMs: within walking distance
CHARGES: $1.00 a foot per night, $.75 for BoatUS members, discount rates available for longer stays except in summer
CREDIT CARDS: MasterCard and Visa
CONTACT: Bubba Strickland

HYATT REGENCY SAVANNAH
2 West Bay St.
Savannah, GA 31401
South shore of the Savannah River in the City of Savannah's Historic District
Phone: 912-238-1234
Floating docks
SHORE POWER: included in dockage fee
TV: cable included in dockage fee
TELEPHONE: lines available at

additional charge
RESTAURANTS: within walking distance, with a hotel that offers room service as well as catering services to the dock
SERVICES: Trash and laundry pick up, security cameras aimed at the dock, security guards and assistance with docking 24 hours a day. Dockage includes use of an indoor pool, fitness center and showers.
CHARGES: $3.00 a foot a day, $5.00 a foot a day during special events
CREDIT CARDS: Visa, Master Card, American Express and Diners Club
HOURS: 8 A.M. to 5 P.M.
CONTACT: Jennifer Rochester
NOTE: the current may be very swift, docking with the bow heading up river, to the west, is recommended

ISLE OF HOPE MARINA
50 Bluff Dr.
Savannah, GA 31406
Isle of Hope
West shore of Skidaway River, north of R "46A"
Phone: 912-354-8187
Fax: 912-354-2684
Monitors VHF 16, goes to 68
Transients are welcome
Floating docks - new concrete floating docks
DEPTHS of approach: 10 feet
DEPTHS at dock: 8 feet
FUELS: diesel, gasoline and lube oils
SHORE POWER: 110, 50 and 30 amps, $8 for 50 and $5 for 30
MECHANIC: two on site and will call independents if requested
PROPANE: bottles are taken out
HAUL OUT: Electric hoist and a railway. The electric hoist will launch boats up to 26 feet. The railway can haul motor boats up to 55 feet, no sailboats, no do-it-yourself
LAUNCH RATES: electric hoist fees - $24 round trip
A new LAUNDRY has been built

New, tiled SHOWERS are available

RESTAURANTS: the marina will provide a ride to several nearby selected restaurants

STORE: Useful marine items, snacks, cold drinks and beer. Boat sales, kayak sales and rental.

Someone from the marina will drive you to a supermarket which will deliver you back to the marina.

CHARTS are for sale and ICE is available.

MODEM CONNECTION: This marina has a high speed modem at a designated table for computer users.

ATM: 1 ¼ miles

Use the above address for MAIL HOLDING, mark For Transient Yacht

CHARGES: $1.15 a foot per day, $.95 a foot per week. For the hoist users the daily rate drops to $.90 a foot. There is a public anchorage nearby, the marina charges $10.00 a day for dinghy tie up which includes access to the laundry and showers

CREDIT CARDS: Master Card, Visa, Discover

HOURS: 8 A.M. to 5 P.M. 7 days a week, summer hours are 8 A.M. to 6 P.M.

Closed Thanksgiving Day and for 2 weeks at Christmas

CONTACT: Charles C. Waller, Patti or Rick Gillis

THE LANDINGS YACHT CLUB

1 Harbor Circle
Skidaway Island
Savannah, GA 31411
West shore of Wilmington River, south of G "23"
Phone: 912-598-1901
Fax: 912-598-8316
Monitors VHF 16, goes to 68
Transients are welcome
Floating docks
DEPTHS of approach: 20 feet
DEPTHS at dock: 5 feet LW
FUELS: diesel, gasoline and lube oils
SHORE POWER: 220 and 110.

50 amps cost $8 a day, 30 amps cost $6 a day

WASTE PUMP OUT available

MECHANIC: will call an independent mechanic

HAUL OUT: 9600 pound travel lift for vessels up to 25 feet

STORE: cold drinks, beer, cleaning and fishing supplies, CHARTS are for sale and ICE is available.

BAIT: Live shrimp, dead shrimp, squid, ballyhoo, mullet

Use above address for MAIL HOLDING, mark For Transient Yacht

CHARGES: $1.10 a foot per day

CREDIT CARDS: Visa, MasterCard and Chevron

HOURS: 24 hours for gas, bait and ice. The store is open 8 A.M. to 5 P.M. in the winter, and in summers 8 A.M. to 7 P.M. on week days and 7 A.M. to 7 P.M. on weekends

CONTACT: Louis Ambos

SAIL HARBOR MARINA & BOAT YARD

606 Wilmington Island Rd.
Savannah, GA 31410
South shore of Turners Creek, marina closest to Wilmington River
Phone: 912-897-2896
Fax: 912-897-7252
Monitors VHF 16
Transients welcome
Floating docks
DEPTHS of approach: 6 feet
DEPTHS at dock: 7 feet
SHORE POWER: 220 and 110. 50 amps cost $3 a day, $15 a week, $40 a month. 30 amps cost $2 a day, $10 a week, $25 a month
MECHANIC: on site
HAUL OUT: 30-ton travel lift
LAUNDRY: on site
SHOWERS: available
RESTAURANT: nearest is ¼ mile and several are within 1 mile
MARINE STORE: useful marine items and gift shop with a large selection of Laser and Sunfish sailboat fittings
CHARTS for sale. ICE is

available.

MODEM CONNECTION: available

ATMs: about a mile walk away

Use above address for MAIL HOLDING, mark For Transient Yacht

CHARGES: $1.00 a foot per day, $5 a foot per week, $10 a foot per month. Storage charge is $9 a foot per month, electricity fee for storage ranges between $20 and $30. *see SHORE POWER* above for electricity charges

CREDIT CARDS: Visa, Discover MasterCard, American Express and debit cards

HOURS: 8 A.M. to 6 P.M. Mon to Sat, closed Sunday, dockmaster on call

CONTACT: Richard Long or Randy Weibel

SAVANNAH BEND MARINA

Rt. 4 Box 188
Macceo Dr.
Savannah, GA 31404
Old Tybee Rd., Thunderbolt
East shore of Wilmington River south of R "34" on the ICW
Phone: 912-897-3625
Fax: 912-898-9671
Email: Savbendmar@aol.com
Monitors VHF 16, goes to 68
Transients are welcome
Floating docks
DEPTHS of approach: 17 feet
DEPTHS at dock: 6 to 17 feet
FUELS: diesel, gasoline and lube oils
SHORE POWER: 220 and 110, 50 ($10) and 30 amps ($5)
MECHANIC: on property
PROPANE: disposable cannisters available
HAUL OUT: elevator, fork lift, 8,000 lbs, up to 30 feet .
LAUNCH RATES: $50. Next door to public boat ramp
LAUNDRY: on site
SHOWERS: available
RESTAURANT: on site
STORE: snacks, cold drinks, CHARTS and ICE
Ask for MODEM connection
ATM: within 5 minutes
Use above address for MAIL

HOLDING, mark For
Transient Yacht
CHARGES: $1.00 a foot per day,
$5.25 a foot weekly
CREDIT CARDS: Visa,
MasterCard, American
Express, Discover and Citgo
HOURS: Oct to Apr -
Mon to Fri, 8 A.M. to 5 P.M.
weekends, 8 A.M. to 6 P.M.
Apr to Oct - open 1 hour later

THUNDERBOLT MARINA

3124 River Dr.
Thunderbolt, GA 31404
Mail: PO Box 5860
Savannah, GA 41414
West shore of Wilmington River,
south of G "35" on the ICW
Phone: 912-352-4931
Fax: 912-352-4958
Monitors VHF 16
Transients are welcome
Floating docks
DEPTHS of approach: 20 feet
DEPTHS at dock: 18 feet
FUELS: diesel, gasoline and lube
oils
SHORE POWER: 220 and 110,
30, 50 & 100 amps
MECHANICS: on site, this is a
full-service boat yard
PROPANE 2.3 miles distant
HAUL OUT: up to 185 feet,
1,200 tons at the yard
LAUNDRY: on site
SHOWERS: available
RESTAURANTS: within walking
distance
MARINE STORE: some marine
supplies, ICE is available
MODEM CONNECTION:
available, data jacks
ATM: within walking distance
Use above address for MAIL
HOLDING, only with
reservation, mark For
Transient Yacht
CHARGES: $1.05 a foot per day
CREDIT CARDS: All major
cards
HOURS: 7:30 A.M. to 6:30 P.M.,
closed on Christmas

TUTEN'S FISH CAMP

7460 LaRoche Ave.
Savannah, GA 31406
South end of Herb River, west of
Isle of Hope

Floating dock
HAUL OUT: electric hoist for
boats up to 19 feet. Rates are
from $10 to $15
Owners live on site

THE WESTIN SAVANNAH HARBOR RESORT

Hutchinson Island
Savannah, GA 31402
On the north shore of the
Savannah River across from
the City of Savannah's
Historic District
Phone: 912-201-2000
Floating docks
SHORE POWER: 110 and 220,
50, 30 and 100 amps,
included in dockage fee
TV CABLE: included in dockage
fee
RESTAURANTS: in hotel and
across the river
WATER TAXI fees included in
dockage fee
CHARGES: Minimum of 25
feet, $4.00 a foot a day, rate
increases during special
events
RESERVATIONS required but
will accept unannounced
arrivals if there is room at the
dock
CREDIT CARDS: all major
cards accepted
SERVICES: the usual hotel
services, dockmaster available 24 hours a day
NOTE: the current may be very
swift, docking with the bow
heading up river, to the west,
is recommended

YOUNGS MARINA

Wilmington Island Rd.
Wilmington Island
Savannah, GA 31410
East shore of Turners Creek
Phone: 912-897-3836
912-897-2608
Mainly the dockage is for
shallow draft vessels
Floating docks
DEPTHS of approach: 4 to 6
feet extreme LW
DEPTHS at dock: dry at inner
docks on extreme LW, cannot
launch at extreme LW
SHORE POWER: 110

MECHANIC: will call independent mechanic
HAUL OUT: electric hoist, 2
motors for up to 4,000 lbs or
24 feet, some height restrictions
LAUNCH RATES: $12.00 for 16
feet, add $1.00 for each
additional foot
ICE is available
MAIL HOLDING is available
with prior arrangements
CHARGES: $5.50 a foot per
month, $10.00 a night
CREDIT CARDS: are not
accepted, will take local
checks, cash
HOURS: summertime
8 A.M. to 6 P.M. Mon to Fri
7 A.M. to 7 P.M. Sat
9 A.M. to 6 P.M. Sun
By appointment only during off
season

SHELLMAN BLUFF

DALLAS BLUFF MARINA

Rte. 2 Box 2606
Townsend, GA 31331
Two miles north of Shellman
Bluff
West shore of Julienton River,
north of Contentment Bluff,
south of Eagle Neck
Phone: 912-832-5116
This is a family serviced marina
operating at full capacity,
there is no room for tran-
sients at this time
Floating docks
DEPTHS of approach: 6 feet
DEPTHS at docks: 20 feet
SHORE POWER: 110, 30 amps
MECHANIC: will call an
independent mechanic
HAUL OUT: electric hoist, two
1-ton for boats up to 24 feet
LAUNCH RATES: $5 to $10
SHOWERS: available
STORE: T shirts are for sale and
ICE is available
CHARGES: $3 a foot per month,
usually there is a waiting list
HOURS: reasonable, owners live
on site
CONTACT: Catherine and Del
Turner

FISHERMAN'S LODGE

Rte. 2 00 Fisherman's Lodge Rd.
Townsend, GA 31331
West shore of Broro River at
Shellman Bluff
Phone: 912-832-4671
Monitors VHF 16
Transients welcome, this is a
popular fishing camp marina
Floating docks
DEPTHS of approach: shallow,
but there is always water
DEPTHS at docks: 6 feet
FUEL: gasoline and outboard
motor oils
MECHANIC: will call an
independent mechanic
HAUL OUT: 10,000 pounds,
boats to 34 feet. Vessel needs
to have lifting eyes, Lockwood
Marine will fit eyes.
LAUNCH RATES: prices based
on size
up to 18 feet - $10
from 18'1" to 22 feet - $15
from 22'1" to 24 feet - $24
over 24'1" - $1.25 per foot
RESTAURANTS: Hunter's Café is
within walking distance,
Speed's Restaurant is nearby.
STORE: useful marine items,
snacks, cold drinks, beer and
ice cream. DNR maps are for
sale and ICE is available.
Original driftwood and shell
arrangements are for sale.
BAIT: Year round live shrimp,
seasonal fiddler crabs, dead
shrimp, ribbon eels, mackerel, cigar minnows, fish oil
and ballyhoo.
CHARGES: No charge if the
vessel is launched at
Fisherman's Lodge. $3 to $5
if the boat stays more than 2
nights
CREDIT CARDS: Visa and
MasterCard
HOURS: daylight until dark
Benny and Teena Ammonds

SHELLMAN FISH CAMP

Rte. 2, Box 2439
Townsend, GA 31331
West shore of Broro River on
Shellman Bluff
Phone: 912-832-4331
Monitors VHF 16
Transients welcome, this is a
popular fishing camp marina
Floating docks
DEPTHS of approach: shallow,
but there is always water
DEPTHS at dock: 24 feet
FUEL: gasoline and outboard
motor oils
SHORE POWER: set up for
jump starts
MECHANIC: will call an
independent mechanic
HAUL OUT: electric hoist for
boats up to 26 feet. Vessel
needs to have lifting eyes.
Lockwood Marine will fit
eyes.
LAUNCH RATES: fees by length,
up to 18 feet - $10
from 18 to 20 feet - $15
from 21 to 26 feet - $20
over 26 - $25, pontoon boats
with lifting rings are $20,
jet skis are $15
RESTAURANT: Hunter's Café is
within walking distance and
Speed's Restaurant is nearby.
STORE: useful fishing supplies
and tackle, also snacks, cold
drinks and beer
ICE: available
BAIT: Live shrimp. Dead
shrimp, squid, ballyhoo,
Boston mackerel, mullet
MODEM CONNECTION: ask
when the staff is not busy
ATM: 20 miles away in Darien
CREDIT CARDS: Visa,
MasterCard and American
Express
HOURS: 6 A.M. to 6 P.M. - winter,
7 days a week,
later in summer
CONTACT: Gary and Ron Iler

TOWNSEND

See *Belle Bluff, Sapelo River,*
Shellman Bluff.
Dallas Bluff is listed with *Shellman*
Bluff.

TYBEE ISLAND

AJ's Dockside Rest. & Marina

PO Box 1411
Tybee Island, GA 31328
1315 Chatham Ave.
East shore of Tybee Creek, north
of Tybee Inlet
Phone: 912-786-9533
Fax: 912-786-4969
Transients welcome
Monitors VHF 16
Floating docks
DEPTHS of approach: 6 feet
from Wassaw Sound
DEPTHS at dock: 20 feet plus
MECHANIC: will call indepen-
dent mechanic
HAUL OUT: electric hoists for
8,000 pounds, up to 27 feet
LAUNCH RATES: $1.00 a foot
for 13 feet to 20 feet
21 to 23 - $25
24 to 26 - $35
27 to 30 - $50
jet skis are $15
jet boats are $20
RESTAURANT: and bar on site
MODEM CONNECTION: ask
when they are not busy
ATM: within walking distance
Use above PO address for MAIL
HOLDING, mark For
Transient Yacht
CHARGES: $1.00 a foot per day,
$9.00 a foot per month
CREDIT CARDS: Visa,
MasterCard, American
Express and Discover
HOIST HOURS: 8 A.M. to 6 P.M.

CHIMNEY CREEK FISH CAMP

40 Estill Hammock Rd.
Tybee, GA 31328
West shore of Chimney Creek
Phone: 912-786-9857
Floating docks
DEPTHS of approach: 3 feet
DEPTHS at dock: 12 feet
FUELS: gasoline
SHORE POWER: 110, 30 amps
HAUL OUT: 2-ton electric hoist
for boats up to 24 feet
LAUNCH RATES: fees are for in
and out,
for 18 feet and under - $9
for over 18 feet - $11
T tops - $16
pontoon boats $13
RESTAURANT: Crab Shack
ICE: available
CHARGES: see *LAUNCH RATES*
above

CREDIT CARDS: Visa and
MasterCard
HOURS: 7 A.M. to 6 P.M., every
day, closed Thanksgiving and
Christmas day
LAZARETTO CREEK MARINA
1 Old US HWY 80
Tybee Island, GA 31328
East shore of Lazaretto Creek,
south of HWY 80 bridge
Phone: 912-786-5848
Transients welcome but space is
very limited, verify before
going. Sightseeing and charter
fishing boats use this marina.
Floating docks
DEPTHS of approach: 8 feet
DEPTHS at dock: 12 feet
FUELS: gasoline
SHORE POWER: 110, 30 amps
MECHANIC: will call indepen-
dent mechanic
RESTAURANTS: Café Loco and
Loggerhead
GIFT SHOP: with convenience
items next door
CHARTS: ICE is available
CHARGES: $1.10 a foot per day
CREDIT CARDS: Visa and
MasterCard
HOURS: 8 A.M. to 5 P.M.

WAVERLY

See *Little Satilla River*

MARINE A/C & REFRIGERATION

BRUNSWICK

**Weatherite Air Conditioning,
Heating & Refrigeration**
3127 Johnston Cir.
Brunswick, GA
Phone: 912-264-9260

RICHMOND HILL

Howard Marine Service
Richmond Hill, GA
Phone: 912-352-0620

SAVANNAH

**Arledge Refrigeration, Heating &
Air Conditioning**
324 L'Arbre Rd.
Savannah, GA
Phone: 912-897-3175
Beard Marine Savannah
3101 River Dr.
Thunderbolt, GA
Phone: 912-356-5222
**Kesler Brothers Heating & Air
Conditioning**
2605 Whitaker St.
Savannah, GA

MARINE ENGINES

BRUNSWICK

Adams Marine Diesel Shop
1213 Newcastle St.
Brunswick, GA 31520
Phone: 912-265-9388
Caterpillar Marine Power
Systems
Carlton Company
124 Perry Lane Rd.
Brunswick, GA 31525
Phone: 912-265-5010
Cummins Southeastern Power
2060 W 21st St.
Jacksonville, FL
904-355-3437
Glynn Diesel Service
315 Crispen Blvd.
Brunswick, GA
Phone: 912-264-6466
Industrial Marine Diesel
209 Monck St.
Brunswick, GA 31520
Phone: 912-264-5566
Performance Power Systems Inc.
110 Central Junction Dr.
Savannah, GA
Phone: 912-232-0300
**Perkins Diesel Engines and
Twin Disc Marine, Inc.**
Kraft Power
675 A Progress Center Ave. NE
Lawrenceville, GA
Phone: 800-394-0078
Reitz Marine Service
225 Ricefield Way

Brunswick, GA 31525
Phone: 912-267-6052

SAVANNAH

Caterpillar Marine Engines
Carlton Co.
HWY 80 West
Savannah, GA
Phone: 912-964-7156
Cummins Diesel Engines
Cummins-Onan South Inc.
8 Interchange Court
Savannah, GA
Phone: 912-232-5565
Detroit Diesel Engines
Williams Detroit Diesel-Allison
14 Westgate Blvd.
Savannah, GA
Phone: 912-232-2602
Detroit Diesel Engines
Roberts Truck Center
Highway 21
Garden City, GA
Phone: 912-964-7507
Performance Power Systems, Inc.
110 Central Junction Dr.
Savannah, GA 31405
Phone: 912-232-0300
**Perkins Diesel Engines and Twin
Disc Marine, Inc.**
Kraft Power
675 A Progress Center Ave. NE
Lawrenceville, GA
Phone: 912-267-6052

MARINE SERVICES

BRUNSWICK

Atlantic Marine
3663 Community Rd.
Brunswick, GA 31520
Phone: 912-264-0150
Ellis Marine
3687 Community Rd.
Brunswick, GA 31520
Phone: 912-264-4024
Harris Boat Works
2814 Norwich St. Lane
Brunswick, GA 31520
Phone: 912-267-9653
Reitz Marine Service
225 Ricefield Way

Brunswick, GA
Phone: 912-267-6052

DARIEN

B & A Marine Concepts
Darien, GA 31305
Phone: 912-437-4590

Colson Marine Railway
Eulonia, GA 31305
Phone: 912-832-5389

George's Boatworks
Darien, GA 31305
Phone: 912-437-4496

ST SIMONS

Alan Akers
Golden Isles Marina
St. Simons Island, GA 31522
Yacht Maintenance
Phone: 912-638-3163

Dunbar Sales, Inc.
115 Marina Dr.
St. Simons Island, GA 31522
Marine services
Peggy Riley, Barney Riley
Phone: 912-638-8573
Fax: 912-638-6905
800-282-1411
Email:
dunbarsales@www.technonet.com

SAVANNAH

Adams Fiberglass
2823 River Dr.
Thunderbolt, GA 31404
Phone: 912-353-9696

Bath Repair
Aquatic Coatings
Jason Frazier
Fiberglass, gel-coat repairs
Phone: 843-683-2284
912-447-1957

Bull River Boat Works
PO Box 1885
Tybee Island, GA 31328
8005 Old Tybee Rd.

Joel Carter
Restoration, repair, fabrication,
painting
Phone: 912-898-8117

Butterfield Brothers Yacht Refinishing
320 Montgomery Cross Rd.
Savannah, GA 31406
Phone: 912-353-9497

Fine Yacht Finishes
3103 River Dr.
Thunderbolt, GA 31404
Phone: 912-692-8011

Gel-Pro
Authorized Sea Pro repair
Scott Floyd
Phone: 912-897-4919
Fax: 912-356-3391

Lovewater Marine Services
409 Edgewater Rd.
Savannah, GA 31406
Fiberglass work, painting
Del Love
Phone: 912-398-6496
Email: dlove@aol.com

Mobil Marine Services
1403 Kingsway
Savannah, GA 31406
Fiberglass repair & fabrication,
sand blasting, welding, towing
Chuck Manner
Phone: 912-355-9457
Pager: 912-239-4546

Mobil Services
Boat, engine & electrical repairs
Allen Hendrikson
Phone: 912-964-8654
Pager: 912-351-2854

Port City Fiberglass
3103 River Dr.
Thunderbolt, GA 31410
Charles P. Roy
Phone: 912-354-0068
912-655-1102

Robert's Glass & Plastics
Completely mobile
Rincon, GA
Phone: 912-826-7388

Sea Weaver Marine Services
1630 Wilmington Island Rd.
Savannah, GA 31410
Chris Weaver
Phone: 912-897-2317
seaweaver@usa.net

Yacht Interiors
Cabinets, woodwork, Corian
David Simmons
Phone: 912-897-5401

Yacht Management
Woodwork, fabrication,
finishwork
Tim Quante
Phone: 912-354-3233
912-667-7691

TYBEE ISLAND

Bull River Boat Works
PO Box 1885
Tybee Island, GA 31328
8005 Old Tybee Rd.
Joel Carter
Restoration, repair, fabrication,
painting
Phone: 912-898-8117

MARINE STORES

BRUNSWICK

Ace Industrial Commercial & Marine Supply
Corner Monck & Bay St.
Brunswick, GA 31520
Phone: 912-264-4024

Ellis Marine, Inc.
3687 Community Rd.
Brunswick, GA
Phone: 912-264-4024

DARIEN

First Georgia Hardware & Marine Supply
Broad St.
Darien, GA 31305
Phone: 912-437-4366

KINGSLAND

The Serious Sportsman
Behind Mariners Village
Kingsland, GA 31548
Phone: 912-882-2141

RICHMOND HILL

Richmond Hill Marine & Sporting Goods
Ford Plaza, Suite C
Richmond Hill, GA 31324
Phone: 912-756-2470

ST MARYS

St. Marys Parts & Supply, Inc.
1625 Osborne Rd.
St. Marys, GA 31558
Phone: 912-882-2442

Up the Creek Xpeditions
111 Osborne
St. Marys, GA 31558

ST SIMONS

Coastal Outdoor & Marine
Golden Isles Marina
206 Marina Dr.
St. Simons, GA 31522
Phone: 888-617-7589
912-634-2848

Dunbar Sales
Golden Isles Marina
#117, 206 Marina Dr.
St. Simons Island, GA 31522
Phone: 912-638-8573

Golden Isles Water Sports
Golden Isles Marina
#104, 206 Marina Dr.
St. Simons, GA 31522
Phone: 912-638-7245

SAVANNAH

A Boater's Paradise
3005 Victory Dr.
Thunderbolt, GA 31404
Phone: 912-354-7759

Air Sea Safety & Survival
120 Williman St.
Savannah, GA 31401
Phone: 912-238-3068

Boat Center
49 Douglas St.
Savannah, GA 31406
Phone: 912-355-0025

Boat US
11607 Abercorn St.
Savannah, GA
Phone: 912-925-2363

Boater's World Discount Marine Center
Savannah Crossings
13015 Abercorn St.
Savannah, GA 31519
Phone: 912-925-0216

Coastal Yacht Services
614 Suncrest Blvd.
Savannah, GA 31410
Phone: 912-897-7184

Maycrest Marine Supplies & Acces.
1609 Montgomery Cross Roads
Savannah, GA 31406
Phone: 912-354-2045

Release Marine
27 Magazine Ave.
Savannah, GA 31415
Phone: 912-236-5717

River Supply, Inc.
2827 River Dr.
Thunderbolt, GA 31404
Phone: 912-354-7777
Fax: 912-354-3326
800-673-9391

Warno-Cam Paint Co.
2310 Drayton St.
Savannah, GA 31401
Phone: 912-236-5741

West Marine (formerly E & B)
7700 Abercorn St.
Savannah, GA
Phone: 912-352-2660

SHELLMAN BLUFF

Lockwood Marine
Rte. 2, Box 2277
Shellman Bluff, GA 31331
Phone: 912-832-6250
800-365-1504
www.lockwoodmarine.com

MECHANICS

BRUNSWICK

Adam's Marine Diesel Shop
1213 Newcastle St.
Brunswick, GA 31520
Diesel repairs
Phone: 912-265-9388

Carlton Company
124 Perry Lane Rd.
Brunswick, GA
Diesel repairs
Phone: 912-265-5010

Ernies's Outboard Service
3944 Community Rd.
Brunswick, GA
Outboard repairs
Phone: 912-261-0170

Glynn Diesel Service, Inc.
315 Crispen Blvd.
Diesel repair
Brunswick, GA
Phone: 912-264-6466

Highway Equipment & Supply Co.
5366 Highway Ave.
Jacksonville, FL
Ford Marine Diesel repair
Phone: 800-827-3019

Industrial Marine Diesel
209 Monck St.
Brunswick, GA 31520
Diesel repair
Phone: 912-264-5566

Reitz Marine Service
225 Ricefield Way
Brunswick, GA
Outboard repairs
Phone: 912-267-6052

Shoreline Maine
3517 Darien Hwy.
Brunswick, GA
Outboard repairs
Phone: 912-261-0444

DARIEN

Outboard Rejuvenation
HWY 17 N
Darien, GA 31305
Certified in Mercury, Yamaha, OMC and most major brands
Phone: 912-437-5126

EULONIA

The Boat Place
Townsend, GA 31331
Phone: 912-832-5507

MIDWAY

Buck's Outboard Service
Isle of Wight
Midway, GA 31320
Phone: 912-884-5955

ST SIMONS ISLAND

Mai Kai Marine
315 Magnolia St.
St. Simons Island, GA 31522
Phone: 912-638-1136

SAVANNAH

B & B Thunderbolt Marine Services
2704 Whatley Ave.
Thunderbolt, GA 31404
Phone: 912-354-5884

Burns Outboard Service, Inc.
108 Busch Lane
Rincon, GA
Phone: 912-826-4512

Caterpillar Engines
Carlton Co.
HWY 80 West
Savannah, GA
Parts & service of marine engines
Phone: 912-964-7156

Cummins Diesel Engines
8 Interchange Court
Savannah, GA
Parts & service of marine engines
Phone: 912-232-5565

Hinckley Yacht Service
PO Box 3539
Savannah, GA 31404
Phone: 912-629-2400

Isle of Hope Marina
50 Bluff Dr.
Savannah, GA 31406
Mechanics on site
Phone: 912-354-8187
Fax: 912-354-2684

Landings Marine Services
1 Harbor Circle
Skidaway Island
Savannah, GA 31411
Phone: 912-598-8163

Mannion Marine Services
3120 Helen St.
Savannah, GA 31404
Johnson, Evinrude, Force, Mariner and Yamaha. OMC & Merc cruiser stern drives. Certified marine technicians.
Phone: 912-354-0760
Fax: 912-354-7669

Palmer Johnson
301 North Lathrop Ave.
Savannah, GA 31415
Full-service boat yard
Phone: 912-234-6579
Fax: 912-239-1168

Performance Power Systems, Inc.
110 Central Junction Blvd.
Savannah, GA 31405
Parts & service of marine engines
Phone: 912-232-0300

Savannah Bend Marina
Rte. 14 Box 188
Old Tybee Rd.
Thunderbolt, GA 31404
certified marine technicians
Phone: 912-897-3625

Williams Detroit Diesel-Allison
14 Westgate Blvd.
Savannah, GA 31405
Sales & service, 24 hour service
Phone: 912-232-2602

Yanmar Diesel Engines
Cummins-Onan South, Inc.
8 Interchange Court
Savannah, GA
Phone: 912-232-5565

OIL SPILL CLEAN-UP

BRUNSWICK

Environmental Recovery Group
251 Levy Rd.
Atlantic Beach, FL
Phone: 904-241-2200

SAVANNAH

Sea Tow Sea Spill
212 Falligant Ave.
Savannah, GA 31410
Phone: 912-897-4304

SWS Environmental First Response
16 Foundation Dr.
Savannah, GA 31408
Phone: 912-966-0686

OUTBOARD MOTORS

BRUNSWICK

Ellis Marine, Inc.
3687 Community Rd.
Brunswick, GA 31520
Phone: 912-264-4024

Shoreline Marine
3517 Darien Hwy
Brunswick, GA 31525
Phone: 912-261-0444

EULONIA

The Boat Place
Townsend, GA 31331
Phone: 912-832-5507

KINGSLAND

State Line Marine
HWY 17
Kingsland, GA 31548
Phone: 912-729-5565

RICHMOND HILL

Shoreline Marine
I 95 and HWY 15
Richmond Hill, GA 31324
Phone: 912-756-2546

ST MARYS

Castaway Marine
293 Pt. Peter Rd.
St. Marys, GA 31558
Phone: 912-882-3133

ST SIMONS ISLAND

Coastal Outdoor & Marine
117 Marina Dr.
St. Simons Island, GA 31522
Phone: 912-634-2848

Hampton River Club Marina
1000 Hampton River Club
St. Simons Island, GA 31522
Phone: 912-638-1210

SAVANNAH

Burns Outboard Service Inc.
108 Busch Lane Rd.
Rincon, GA 31326
Evinrude, Johnson, Mercury
and Mariner
Phone: 912-826-4512
Fax: 912-826-1831

Isle of Hope Marina
50 Bluff Dr.
Savannah, GA 31406
Honda Four Strokes and Suzuki
Phone: 912-354-8187

Sea Ray of Savannah
3518 Old Tybee Rd.
Thunderbolt, GA 31404
Mercruiser stern drives
Phone: 912-897-9881

PARKS & WILDLIFE REFUGES

ALTAMAHA RIVER

Altamaha River Bioreserve
The Nature Conservancy of Georgia
PO Box 484
Darien, GA 31305
Phone: 912-437-2162
For fishing information:
Wildlife Resources Division
108 Darling Ave.
Waycross, GA 31501
Phone: 912-285-6094

Altamaha Waterfowl Management Area
Georgia Department of Natural
Resources
Phone: 912-262-
3173BLACKBEARD ISLAND

Blackbeard Island National Wildlife Refuge
1000 Business Center Dr.
Suite 10
Savannah, GA 31405
Phone: 912-652-4415
Fax: 912-652-4385
http://www.fws.gov/~r4eao
US Fish & Wildlife
ServicePhone: 800-344-WILD

BRUNSWICK

Blythe Island Regional Park
6616 Blythe Island Highway
Rte. 6, Box 224
Brunswick, GA 31525
Phone: 912-261-3805
800-343-7855

Earth Day Nature Trail
Georgia Department of Natural
Resources
1 Conservation Way
Brunswick, GA 31520
Off US 17 at Sidney Lanier
Bridge
Phone: 912-264-7218
Open during daylight

CUMBERLAND ISLAND

Cumberland Island National Seashore
107 W St. Marys
St. Marys, GA 31558
Reservations phone:
912-882-4335
Fax: 912-673-7747
Administration phone:
912-882-4336
For Information write:
Superintendent

Cumberland Island National Seashore
PO Box 806
St. Marys, GA 31558
Fax: 912-882-5688
Ferry Reservations at
912-882-4335
10 A.M. to 4 P.M. Mon to Fri.
The ferry departs the mainland:
9:00 A.M. and 11:45 A.M.,
The ferry departs the island:
10:15 A.M. and 4:45 P.M..

Cumberland Museum
Downtown St Marys
St Marys, GA 31558
Open
10 A.M. to 4 P.M. weekdays,
1 P.M. to 3 P.M.
weekends & holidays
Collections from the mansions
Phone: 912-882-4336

DARIEN

Altamaha River Bioreserve
The Nature Conservancy of
Georgia
PO Box 484
Darien, GA 31305
Phone: 912-437-2162

GEORGIA

Georgia State Parks and Historic Sites
Phone: 770-389-7275
800-864-7275
8 A.M. to 5 P.M. Mon to Fri
www.gastateparks.org

GRAY'S REEF

Gray's Reef National Marine Sanctuary
10 Ocean Science Circle
Savannah, GA
17.5 miles east of Sapelo Island
Phone: 912-598-2345
Email:
GRNMS@ocean.nos.noaa.gov
www.skio.peachnet.edu/noaa/
grnms.html

HARRIS NECK

Harris Neck National Wildlife Refuge
1000 Business Center Dr.
Suite 10
Savannah, GA 31405
Phone: 912-652-4415
Fax: 912-652-4385
www.fws.gov/~r4eao
Sunrise to sunset

JEKYLL ISLAND

Jekyll Island Nature Walks
University of Georgia Marine
Extension Service
Jekyll Island, GA 31527
Phone: 912-635-2119

MIDWAY

Melon Bluff Heritage & Nature Ctr.
2999 Islands HWY
Midway, GA 31320

25 miles of trails
Phone: 912-884-5779
888-246-8188
9 A.M. to 4 P.M. Tue to Sun
Email: melonbluff@CLDS.net
www.melonbluff.com

OSSABAW ISLAND

Ossabaw Island Heritage Preserve
Wildlife Resource Division
Georgia Department of Natural Resources
Brunswick, GA 31520
Phone: 912-262-3173
Ossabaw Island Foundation
Public Use and Education
Ossabaw Island
PO Box 13397
Savannah, GA 31416
Phone: 912-233-5104

RICHMOND HILL

Ft. McAllister Historic Park
3894 Ft. McAllister Rd.
Richmond Hill, GA 31324
Savage Island Nature Trail, 1.3 miles
Phone: 912-727-2339
Park: 7 A.M. to 10 P.M.
Office: 8 A.M. to 5 P.M.
Historic site: 9 A.M. to 5 P.M. Tue to Sat, 2:00 P.M. to 5:30 P.M. Sun, closed Mon, Thanksgiving, Christmas & New Years Day

ST CATHERINES

St Catherines Island Foundation, Inc.
Superintendents office:
Phone: 912-884-5002
Archeological Lab: 912-884-5004
Wildlife Survival Center:
Phone: 912-884-5005
Maintenance Shop: 912-884-5009
New York Zoological Society:
Phone: 912-884-5006
912-884-5007

ST MARYS

Crooked River State Park
3092 Spur 40
St. Marys, GA 31558
Phone: 912-882-5256
800-864-7275
7 A.M. to 10 P.M.
Cumberland Island National Seahore Reservations
107 W St. Marys
St. Marys, GA 31558
Phone: 912-882-4335
Administraton phone: 912-882-4336

ST SIMONS

Ft. Frederica National Monument
Frederica Road North
St. Simons Island, GA 31522
Phone: 912-638-3639
Superintendent's address:
Rte. 9, Box 286-C
St. Simons Island, GA 31522
Neptune Park
St. Simons Village
St. Simons Island, GA 31522

SAPELO ISLAND

Sapelo Island National Estaurine Reserve
PO Box 15
Sapelo Island, GA 31327
Phone: 912-485-2251
Fax: 912-485-2141
Email: buddy.sullivan@noaa.gov
Reynolds Mansion:
Phone: 912-485-2299
Fax: 912-485-2140
Nature trail, 2 miles
Sapelo Island Visitors Center
Rte. 1, Box 1500
Darien, GA 31305
Ferry info: Phone: 912-437-3224
Group tours & field trips:
Phone: 912-485-2300
Wednesdays the ferry leaves the Visitor Center at 8:30 A.M. and returns at 12:30 P.M.
Fridays (June 1 to Labor Day only) the ferry leaves the Visitor Center at 8:30 A.M. and returns at 12:30 P.M.

Saturdays the hours are 9 A.M. and 1 P.M.
The last Tuesday of each month from March to October an extended tour is offered. The ferry leaves at 8:30 and returns at 3:00
Sapelo Island's Cabretta Campground
Contact the Reynold's mansion:
Sapelo Island Reynolds Mansion
PO Box 15
Sapelo Island, GA 31327
Phone: 912-485-2299
Fax: 912-485-2140

SAVANNAH

Oatland Island Education Center
711 Sandtown Rd.
Savannah, GA 31410
Nature trail, 1.75 miles
Phone: 912-897-3773
Savannah National Wildlife Refuge
1000 Business Center Dr.
Suite 10
Savannah, GA 31405
Phone: 912-652-4415
Fax: 912-652-4385
Savannah and Ogeechee Canal, Museum & Nature Center
681 Fort Argyle Rd.
(HWY 204)
Savannah, GA 31419-9239
Phone: 912-748-8068
Skidaway Island Park
52 Diamond Causeway
Savannah, GA 31411-1102
Big Ferry Nature Trail, 1.5 miles
Phone: 912-598-2300
912-598-2301
800-864-7275
Park: 7 A.M. to 10 P.M.
Office: 8 A.M. to 5 P.M.
University of Georgia Aquarium
Skidaway Island
30 Ocean Science Circle
Savannah, GA 31411
Phone: 912-598-3474
912-598-2496
Wassaw National Wildlife Refuge
1000 Business Center Dr.
Suite 10
Savannah, GA 31405
Phone: 912-652-4415
Fax: 912-652-4385

POLICE

BRUNSWICK

Brunswick Police
Chief of Police
206 Mansfield St.
Brunswick, GA 31520
Phone: 912-267-5560

Deputy Marshall
1229 Newcastle St.
Brunswick, GA 31520
Phone: 912-267-5583

Glynn County Police
Main Office
2747 4th St.
Brunswick, GA 31520
Phone: 912-267-5700

Precinct-North
80 Glynn Marsh Dr.
Brunswick, GA 31525
Phone: 912-267-5785

Precinct-South
7108 New Jesup Hwy.
Brunswick, GA 31523
Coastal Organized Drug
Enforcement
Phone: 800-593-2861

BRYAN COUNTY

Keller Police:
Phone: 912-756-2282
Phone: 912-756-2181
Richmond Hill Police
Phone: 912-756-2626

CHATHAM COUNTY

Emergency 911
Police Department
Non-emergency
Phone: 912-652-6500

Sheriff's Department
Phone: 912-652-7600

DARIEN

Police phone:
912-437-6644

Sheriff phone:
912-437-6622

EFFINGHAM COUNTY

Non-emergency
Phone: 912-754-3449

GLYNN COUNTY

Glynn County Sheriff
Phone: 912-554-7600

JEKYLL ISLAND

Jekyll State Patrol
Phone: 912-635-2303

ST MARYS

Emergency 911
Camden County Sheriff's Office
209 East 4th
Woodbine, GA 31569
Phone: 912-576-5335

St. Marys Police
418 Osborne
St. Marys, GA 31558
Phone: 912-882-4488

ST SIMONS ISLAND

Emergency 911
Police phone:
912-638-1546
Or 912-638-2111
Main office phone: 912-267-5700

SAVANNAH

Emergency 911
Non-emergency
Phone: 912-232-4141

TDD machine:
Phone: 912-651-6751

Desk sergeant:
Phone: 912-651-6675

Chief's office:
Phone: 912-651-6664

SEA ISLAND

Police sub-station:
Phone: 912-638-3188

WOODBINE

Emergency 911
Police phone: 912-576-3211

PROPANE

ALTAMAHA RIVER

Two Way Fish Camp
250 Ricefield Way
Brunswick, GA 31525
Phone: 912-265-0410

BELLE BLUFF

Belle Bluff Marina
Rte. 3, Box 3246-B25
Townsend, GA 31331
Phone: 912-832-5323

BRUNSWICK

National Propane
4182 Norwich St.
Brunswick, GA
Will pick up and deliver to
Brunswick Landing Marina
Phone: 912-265-8440

Two Way Fish Camp
250 Ricefield Way
Brunswick, GA 31525

ST MARYS

St. Marys Parts & Supply, Inc.
1625 Osborne Rd.
St. Marys, GA 31558
Phone: 912-882-2442

ST SIMONS ISLAND

Ace Hardware
Frederica Rd.
St. Simons Island, GA 31522
Longview Shopping Center
Phone: 912-638-3800

SAVANNAH

Propane Tanks Filled
UHAUL
8810 Abercorn Expressway
Savannah, GA
South of Oglethorpe Mall
Phone: 912-927-6550

UHAUL
3802 Ogeechee Rd.
Savannah, GA

West of Lynes Parkway
Phone: 912-233-9912

TOWNSEND

See Belle Bluff

TYBEE ISLAND

Rivers End Campground
Tybee Island, GA 31328
Phone: 912-786-5518

PROPELLERS

BRUNSWICK

Byrd's All-Purpose Welding & Propeller
148 New Jesup Hwy.
Brunswick, GA
Phone: 912-261-2767
Dominey Machine & Propeller Service, Inc.
6005 Habersham St.
Brunswick, GA
Phone: 912-264-2942
www.dominey.com

SAVANNAH

Advanced Portable Welding & Propeller
Savannah, GA
Phone: 912-354-3107
Champion Machine and Manufacturing Co., Inc
512 Indian St.
Savannah, GA
Phone: 912-232-4333
Dixie Machine & Fabrication Co
512 Indian St.
Savannah, GA
Phone: 912-233-4743

RENTAL CARS

BRUNSWICK

Affordable Auto Rental
5701 Altama Ave.
Brunswick, GA
Phone: 912-267-9703
Auto Rentals of Brunswick
3576 Darien Hwy.
Brunswick, GA
No credit cards required
Free pick-up and drop-off
Phone: 912-264-0530
Avis
Brunswick Phone: 912-267-7368
Glynco Jetport
Phone: 912-267-0326
800-331-1212
Coastal Auto Rental
1128 Chapel Crossing Rd.
Brunswick, GA
Phone: 912-267-7368
Enterprise Rent-A-Car
3421 Cypress Mill Rd., Suite 4
Brunswick, GA
Free pick-up
Phone: 912-262-1436
800-736-8222
Hertz
500 Connole St.
Brunswick, GA
Brunswick Glynco Jetport
Phone: 912-265-3645
800-654-3131

ST MARYS

Auto Rentals of Kings Bay
1928 Highway 40 East
Kingsland, GA 31548

ST SIMONS

Avis
Phone: 912-638-2232
800-331-1212
Hertz
Phone: 912-638-2522
800-654-3131
Island Rental Car
130 Airport Rd.
St. Simons Island, GA 31522
Phone: 912-638-0888

SAVANNAH

Alamo
Phone: 912-964-7364
800-327-9633
Avis
Phone: 912-964-1781
800-831-2847
Budget
Phone: 912-966-1771
800-527-0700
Cartemps
Phone: 912-920-4500
Cash Car Rental
5405 Montgomery St.
Savannah, GA
Phone: 912-354-1777
Discount Auto Rental
7010 Skidaway Rd.
Savannah, GA
Phone: 912-355-6661
Economy Rent a Car
Corner of White Bluff & Posey St.
Savannah, GA
Phone: 912-352-3444
Enterprise
Phone: 912-920-1093
912-355-6622
800-325-8007
Federal Rental Car
2310 Montgomery St.
Savannah, GA
Phone: 912-238-0034
Hertz
Phone: 912-964-9595
800-654-3131
Joe Thomson Auto Rentals
9602 White Bluff Rd.
Savannah, GA
Phone: 912-927-6611
National Car Rental
Phone: 912-964-1771
800-CAR-RENT
Savannah Car and Van Rental
236 Drayton St.
Savannah, GA
Phone: 912-233-6554
Sears
Phone: 912-966-1676
Thrifty Car Rental
Phone: 912-966-2277
Toyota Rent a Car
Phone: 912-927-1234
U Save Auto Rental
3006 Gibbons St.
Savannah, GA
Phone: 912-691-2009

RESTAURANTS

ALTAMAHA RIVER

Mudcat Charlie's
Darien Highway
Ricefield Way
Brunswick, GA 31525
Located at Two Way Marina, 2
miles south of Darien.
Fresh local seafood, steaks,
overlooking the Altamaha.
Open 7 days.
Phone: 912-261-0055

BRUNSWICK

Captain Joe's Seafood Restaurant
3303 Glynn Ave.
Brunswick, GA 31520
Seafood, steak, full menu, salad
bar.
Phone: 912-262-9878

Grapevine Café
1519 Newcastle St.
Brunswick, GA 31520
Seafood, chicken, vegetarian
dishes, homemade soups,
salad bar, sandwiches, great
desserts. Beer and wine.
Phone: 912-265-0115

Hooked on Barbie-Q
1510 Newcastle St.
Brunswick, GA 31520
Chopped pork barbecue,
smoked ribs. Lunch.
Carryout only.
Phone: 912-265-8108

Hungry Hannah's
606 Gloucester St.
Brunswick, GA 31520
Breakfast pitas, soups, salads,
burgers, sandwiches, daily
specials. Breakfast & lunch.
Phone: 912-265-8108
Fax: 912-265-9003

Jinrights's Seafood House
2815 Glynn Ave. (Hwy. 17)
Brunswick, GA 31520
Fresh seafood, N.Y. strip, grilled
chicken, cholesterol free
preparation.
Phone: 912-267-1590

Mack's Bar-B-Que Place
2809 Glynn Ave.
Brunswick, GA 31520
Phone: 912-264-0605

New China Restaurant
3202 Glynn Ave. (Hwy. 17)
Brunswick, GA 31520
Chinese cuisine
Phone: 912-265-6722

O'Henry's Saloon Sports Bar & Eatery
211 Monck St.

Spanky's
1200 Glynn Ave. (Hwy 17)
Brunswick, GA 31520
Fresh seafood daily, chicken
fingers.
Phone: 912-267-6100

Twin Oaks Drive-In
2618 Norwich St.
Brunswick, GA 31520
Barbecue, ribs, special battered
fries, Brunswick stew.
Phone: 912-265-3131

CUMBERLAND ISLAND

Greyfield Inn
Box 900
Fernandina Beach, FL 32035-0900
Located on Cumberland Island.
Regional specialties, gourmet
cuisine. Normally for guests
of the Inn only, however, call
in advance to possibly make
arrangements for dinner if
you plan to visit the island.
Phone: 904-261-6408
800-717-0821

DARIEN

See *Altamaha River, Sapelo River*
Archie's
US HWY 17
Darien, GA 31305
60 years of fried shrimp
Phone: 912-437-4363

B & J's Pizza Place
901 Northway
Darien, GA 31305
Buffet lunch, pizzas
Phone: 912-437-2122

Darien Restaurant
US HWY 17
Darien, GA 31305
Home cooking, specials.
Phone: 912-437-6574

JEKYLL ISLAND

**Bennigan's Irish American Grill
& Tavern (Clarion Resort
Buccaneer)**
85 Beachview Dr.
Jekyll Island, GA 31527
Burgers, drinks.
Phone: 912-635-2261

Blackbeard's Restaurant
200 North Beachview Dr.
Jekyll Island, GA 31527
Fresh local seafood.
Phone: 912-635-3522

Blue Marlin Grill (Days Inn)
60 South Beachview Dr.
Jekyll Island, GA 31527
Phone: 912-635-3319

**Café Solterra (Jekyll Island Club
Hotel)**
371 Riverview Dr.
Jekyll Island, GA 31527
Sandwiches, salads, pizza,
bakery items.
Phone: 912-635-2600, ext. 1003

**Crackers Country Fare & Deli
(Villas by the Sea)**
1175 North Beachview Dr.
Jekyll Island, GA 31527
Seafood, steaks, deli & hot
sandwiches.

**Denny's (Comfort Inn Island
Suites)**
711 North Beachview Dr.
Jekyll Island, GA 31527
Family style dining.
Phone: 912-635-2285

**The Grand Dining Room (Jekyll
Island Club Hotel)**
371 Riverview Dr.
Jekyll Island, GA 31327
Fresh seafood, steaks, pasta.
Sunday brunch.
Phone: 912-635-2600

**The Italian Fisherman (Jekyll
Inn)**
975 North Beachview Dr.
Jekyll Island, GA 31327
Italian cuisine, seafood, beef.
Phone: 912-635-2531

The Java Shop (Ramada Inn)
150 South Beachview Dr.
Jekyll Island, GA 31327

Breakfast buffet served daily.
Phone: 912-635-2111

The Rah Bar
1 Pier Rd.
Jekyll Island, GA 31327
Fresh fish, shellfish, steak, pasta.
Phone: 912-635-3800

Morgan's Grill (Golf Clubhouse)
Capt. Wylly Rd.
Jekyll Island, GA 31327
Burgers, hot dogs, sandwiches.
Phone: 912-635-4103

Pizza Inn (Comfort Inn Island Suites)
711 North Beachview Dr.
Jekyll Island, GA 31327
Pizza, Italian favorites. Free
Island delivery.
Phone: 912-635-3733

Remington's Bar & Grill
(Holiday Inn Beach Resort)
200 South Beachview Dr.
Jekyll Island, GA 31327
Phone: 912-635-3311

SeaJay's Waterfront Café
Jekyll Harbor Marina
1 Harbor Rd.
Jekyll Island, GA 31327
Low country boil buffet,
Brunswick stew, fine foods.
Phone: 912-635-3200

Zachery's Restaurant
44 Beachview Dr.
Jekyll Island, GA 31327
Seafood, steaks, chicken,
sandwiches. Beer, wine.
Phone: 912-635-3128

Zach's Eats & Treats
22 North Beachview Dr.
Jekyll Island, GA 31327
Sandwiches, pizzas, ice cream,
milk shakes.
Phone: 912-635-2040

KILKENNY RIVER

Kilkenny Riverhouse Restaurant
2943 Kilkenny Rd.
Richmond Hill, GA 31324
Overlooking Kilkenny River,
call in advance if possible.
Phone: 912-727-2522

OGEECHEE RIVER

Love's Seafood Restaurant
Highway South

Savannah, GA
Fresh local catfish, seafood,
steaks. On the Ogeechee
River.
Phone: 912-925-3616

ST MARYS

NOTE: All addresses on Osborne
above 800 require transportation
from the harbor.

Angelo's of Point Peter
944 Point Peter Rd.
St. Marys, GA 31588
Pizza, Italian dishes, delivers to
marina and downtown.
Phone: 912-882-3636

Bonzai Japanese Steak House
2714 C Osborne Rd.
St. Marys, Ga 31558
Phone: 912-882-8600

Borrell Creek Landing
1101 Hwy 40 East
St. Marys, GA 31558
Phone: 912-673-6300

Breaux's Cajun Café
2710 Osborne Rd.
St. Marys, GA 31558
Phone: 912-882-6250

Calico's Eatery & Catering
2603 Osborne Suite O
St. Marys, Ga 31558
Phone: 912-882-7977

Dairy Queen
2105 Osborne Rd.
St. Marys, GA 31558
Phone: 912-882-3778

Domino's Pizza
2506 Osborne Rd.
St. Marys, Ga 31558
Phone: 912-673-6100

El Potro Mexican Restaurant
1923 Osborne Rd.
St. Marys, GA 31558
Phone: 912-882-0900

Family Restaurant
2710 Osborne Rd.
St. Marys, GA 31558
Phone: 912-882-6250

Fat Boy Foods
1593 E Hwy 40
St. Marys, GA 31558
Phone: 912-729-2306

Hardee's of St. Marys
2605 Osborne Rd.

St. Marys, GA 31558
Phone: 912-882-1027

Greek and Mediterranean Grill
112 Osborne St.
St. Marys, GA 31558
Soups, salads, Greek specialties,
mousaka, spanakopita,
baklava.
Downtown.
Phone: 912-576-2000

Lang's Marina Restaurant
St. Marys St.
St. Marys, GA 31558
Fresh seafood, all you can eat
shrimp. Downtown.
Phone: 912-882-4432

McGauley Bar-Be-Cue
206 Finley
St. Marys, GA 31558
Phone: 912-882-5518

PaPa Luigis Italian Restaurant
143 City Smittys Dr.
St. Marys, GA 31558
Phone: 912-673-1557

Panorama
123 Osprey Dr.
St. Marys, GA 31558
Phone: 912-882-6575

Pauly's
102 Osborne St.
St. Marys, Ga 31558
Phone: 912-882-3944
Soups, sandwiches, steaks,
seafood, daily specials.
Downtown.

Pizza Hut
2511 Osborne Rd.
St. Marys, Ga 31558
Phone: 912-882-7504

St. Marys Seafood & Steak House
1837 Osborne Rd.
St. Marys, Ga 31558
Phone: 912-882-4187

Seagle's Waterfront Café
105 Osborne St.
St. Marys, Ga 31558
Fresh seafood, steaks, Seagle's
Saloon, live entertainment.
Downtown.
Phone: 912-882-4187

Sin Far Chinese Restaurant
133 City Smitty Dr.
St. Marys, GA 31558
Phone: 912-882-1800

Snack Bar at the Cove
123 Osprey Dr.

St. Marys, GA 31558
Phone: 912-882-6575

Subway
2603 U Osborne Rd.
St. Marys, GA 31558
Phone: 912-882-6050

Taco Bell
2514 Osborne Rd.
St. Marys, GA 31558
Phone: 912-882-7028

Tonua's
715 Osborne
St. Marys, GA 31558
All you can eat home cooked
buffet. Downtown.
Phone: 912-882-1555

Trolley's
104 West St. Marys St.
St. Marys, GA 31558
Burgers, wings, daily specials.
Downtown
Phone: 912-882-1525

Whispers Coffee House & Café
302 Osborne St.
St. Marys, GA 31558
Coffee shop, desserts, lunch
specials, book exchange.
Downtown.
Phone: 912-882-9424

**Woods River City Restaurant &
Spirits**
2200 Osborne Rd.
St. Marys, GA 31558
Phone: 912-882-1056

ST SIMONS ISLAND

The following lists of restaurants
are grouped by geographic location.

ST. SIMONS—SOUTH

The pier and Village
Blanche's Courtyard
440 Ocean Boulevard
St. Simons Island, GA 31522
Fresh seafood, hand cut steaks.
Phone: 912-638-3030

Brogen's
200 Pier Alley (in the Village)
St. Simons Island, GA 31522
Burgers, prime rib sandwich,
wings, sandwiches, salads,
pasta, specials.
Phone: 912-638-1660

CJ's Italian Restaurant
405 Mallery St.

St. Simons Island, GA 31522
Homemade pizza, pasta, salads,
subs, nightly dinner specials
Phone: 912-634-1022

Coconut Willie's
121 Mallery St.
St. Simons Island, GA 31522
Seafood, chicken, burgers,
steaks, pasta.
Phone: 912-634-6134

Dressner's Village Café
223 Mallery St.
St. Simons Island, GA 31522
Breakfast all day, scratch
biscuits, homemade soups,
pita sandwiches, best
hamburger
Phone: 912-634-1217

Fourth of May Café & Deli
444 Ocean Blvd.
St. Simons Island, GA 31522
Down home southern cuisine
featuring 8-9 vegetables
daily.
Phone: 912-638-5444

Frannie's Place Restaurant
318 Mallery St.
St. Simons Island, GA 31522
The best Brunswick Stew
Phone: 912-638-1001

Georgia Sea Grill
310 B Mallery St.
St. Simons Island, GA 31522
Fresh local seafood, pasta,
steaks, chicken, grilled
sandwiches, crabcakes, pasta.
Phone: 912-638-1197

Island Rock Café
303 Mallery St.
St. Simons Island, GA 31522
Salads, sandwiches, steaks,
pasta, seafood.
Phone: 912-638-0245

**J Mac's Island Restaurant & Jazz
Bar**
407 Mallery St.
St. Simons Island, GA 31522
Snapper with lobster, rack of
lamb, Angus beef, tuna,
salmon.
Phone: 912-634-0403

Mullet Bay
512 Ocean Boulevard
St. Simons Island, GA 31522
Seafood, steaks, sandwiches,
pasta. Casual.
Phone: 912-634-9977

The Sandcastle Café & Grille
117 Mallery St.
St. Simons Island, GA 31522
Breakfast buffet, fresh
crabcakes, burgers, pasta,
salads, shrimp.
Phone: 912-638-8883

The Vienna Bake Shop
507 Beachview Dr.
St. Simons Island, GA 31522
European pastries, sandwiches,
soups, bread and rolls.
Phone: 912-638-4354

ST. SIMONS—
SOUTHEAST

Ocean Boulevard

Chelsea
1226 Ocean Blvd.
St. Simons Island, GA 31522
Fresh seafood, pasta, veal, lamb,
steaks.
Phone: 912-638-2047

Crab Daddy's Seafood Grill
1217 Ocean Boulevard
St. Simons Island, GA 31522
Phone: 912-634-1120

Crab Trap
1209 Ocean Blvd.
St. Simons Island, GA 31522
Fresh seafood, fried, broiled,
blackened, grilled. Oysters
on the half shell. Steaks.
Phone: 912-638-3552

The King & Prince
201 Arnold Rd.
St. Simons Island, GA 31522
Fresh seafood, steaks, extensive
Sunday brunch.
Phone: 912-638-3631, ext. 316

Sweet Mama's
1201 Ocean Blvd.
St. Simons Island, GA 31522
Soups, sandwiches, salads.
Lunch only. Evening deserts.
Phone: 912-634-6022

ST. SIMONS—
SOUTHWEST

Demere Village, Retreat Village
Allegro Garden Room
2465 Demere Rd.
St. Simons Island, GA 31522

Continental, seafood, lamb,
beef, veal, pasta.
Phone: 912-638-7097

Allegro Café
2465 Demere Rd.
St. Simons Island, GA 31522
Fresh fish, pastas.
Phone: 912-638-6097

Burger King
Demere Rd.
St. Simons Island, GA 31522
Phone: 912-638-2207

El Potro Mexican Restaurant
2205 Demere Rd.
St. Simons Island, GA 31522
Authentic Mexican cuisine.
Fajitas, quesadillas,
chimichangas, enchiladas,
burritos, tamales.
Phone: 912-634-0703

McDonalds
Demere Rd.
St. Simons Island, GA 31522
Phone: 912-638-3139

Miyabi Japanese Seafood and Steak House
202 Retreat Village
St. Simons Island, GA 31522
Phone: 912-638-0885

Subway
Retreat Village
St. Simons Island, GA 31522
Phone: 912-638-5312

ST. SIMONS—SOUTH CENTRAL

Longview and Redfern Villages

Domino's Pizza
Deliveries
Phone: 912-638-1166

Ginos's Italian Restaurant
228 Redfern Village
St. Simons Island, GA 31522
Pasta, veal, chicken, seafood.
Phone: 912-634-9633

Huddle House
Phone: 912-638-7902

Kentucky Fried Chicken
Pizza Inn
Deliveries
Phone: 912-638-1778

Redfern Café
200 Redfern Village

St. Simons Island, GA 31522
Rack of lamb, seafood, veal,
pasta, Friday night bouillabaisse.
Phone: 912-634-1344

Sweet Mama's
1627 Frederica Rd.
(Longview Shopping Center)
St. Simons Island, GA 31522
Breakfast, lunch, desserts.
Phone: 912-634-6022

Wine & Cheese Cellar
211 Redfern Village
St. Simons Island, GA 31522
Grilled teriyaki sandwiches,
bacon-bleu cheeseburgers,
exotic broccoli salad, soups,
deli sandwiches, European
breads.
Phone: 912-638-2465

SAPELO RIVER

Buccaneer Club
Belleville, Sapelo River
Eulonia, GA
Specializing in seafood &
steaks. Docking available.
Phone: 912-832-5171

Pelican Point Restaurant & Lounge
Belleville, Sapelo River
Eulonia, GA
Huge seafood buffet, steaks.
Located on the shrimp docks.
Phone: 912-832-4295

SAVANNAH

Kevin Barry's Irish Pub
117 West River St.
Savannah, GA 31401
Food served until 2 A.M.
Traditional Irish music Wednes-
day through Sunday
Phone: 912-233-9626

Boar's Head
1 N. Lincoln St. Ramp & River
St.
Savannah, GA 31401
Live Maine lobster, local
seafood, steaks & chops.
Great desserts Phone: 912-
232-3196

Casbah
118 East Broughton St.
Savannah, GA 31401

Morrocan cuisine, belly dancing
Phone: 912-234-6168
www.CasbahRestaurant.com

Churchill's Pub
9 Drayton St.
Savannah, GA 31401
British cuisine, fish & chips,
bubble & squeak, bangers &
mash, shepherd's pie,
Yorkshire pudding. Imported
beer, stouts.
Phone: 912-232-8501

City Market Café
224 West Julian St.
Savannah, GA 31401
Fresh seafood, homemade
pizzas, salads, sandwiches,
pasta, steaks, fresh French
bread.
Phone: 912-236-7133

The Cotton Exchange
Seafood Grill & Tavern
201 East River St.
Savannah, GA 31401
Hearty sandwiches, seafood,
steaks, chicken, pasta,
homemade soups, salads.
Phone: 912-232-7088

The Express Café & Bakery
39 Barnard St.
Savannah, GA 31401
Gourmet coffees, espresso, fresh
breads, sandwiches, soups,
salads, great desserts.
Phone: 912-233-4683

Gryphon Tea Room
Corner of Bull & Charlton
Streets
Savannah, GA 31401
Serving lunch, dinner and
afternoon tea
Phone: 912-238-2481

Il Pasticcio
2 East Broughton
Savannah, GA 31401
Contemporary Italian Cuisine
Phone: 912-644-5199
912-231-8888
Fax: 912-231-8813

The Lady & Sons
311 West Congress St.
Savannah, GA 31401
Lunch buffet, fine Southern
cuisine.
Phone: 912-233-2600

Moon River Brewing Company
West Bay St.

Savannah, GA 31401
Full eclectic menu for lunch and
dinner with six fresh brewed
house beers.
Phone: 912-447-0943

Oglethorpe Brewing Co.
21 West Bay St.
Savannah, GA 31401
Fresh brews including chocolate
flavored stout. Steaks,
seafood and pasta.
Phone: 912-232-0933

The Olde Pink House
Reynolds Square
23 Abercorn St.
Savannah, GA 31401
Elegant seafood, beef tender-
loin, pork, lamb, chicken
and duck.
Phone: 912-232-4286

**The Oyster Bar Seafood
Restaurant & Raw Bar**
411 East River St.
Savannah, GA 31401
Fresh fish caught daily and
early bird specials.
Phone: 912-232-1565

The Pirate's House
45 South
East Broad & Bay St.
Savannah, GA 31401
A real, historic pirate's house.
Lunch and dinner, afternoon
desserts, coffee and cocktails.
Phone: 912-233-5757
912-233-1881

The Rail Pub
405 West Congress St.
Savannah, GA 31401
Food and spirits, full menu, late
night menu, special mixed
drinks and cigars.
Phone: 912-238-1311

River House Seafood
125 West River St.
Savannah, GA 31401
Eight to twelve varieties of fish
daily, steaks & chops, all
sauces homemade, salads,
sandwiches, pecan pie and
cheesecakes.
Phone: 912-234-1900

River Street Riverboat Company
9 East River St.
Savannah, GA 31401
2 hour dinner/entertainment, 1
½ hour Saturday lunch or

Sunday brunch while
cruising the Savannah River.
Reservations required.
Phone: 912-232-6404
800-786-6404

Sapphire Grill
110 West Congress St.
Savannah, GA 31401
Seafood, steak and lamb. Wine
bar open late, reservations
recommended.
Phone: 912-443-9962

Seasons
At City Market
315 West St. Julian St.
Savannah, GA 31401
Unique cuisine, serving lunch,
dinner and Sunday brunch
Phone: 912-233-2626

W.G. Shuckers
225 West River St.
Savannah, GA 31401
Specializing in steamed, broiled
and fried seafood
Phone: 912-443-0054

Six Pence Pub
245 Bull St.
Savannah, GA 31401
Lunch and dinner menus, live
entertainment, monthly cigar
and martini seminars

606 East Café
319 West Congress
Savannah, GA 31401
Eclectic dining in a bovine
setting with fresh seafood
daily
Phone: 912-233-2887

Soho South Café
12 West Liberty St.
Savannah, GA 31401
Unique lunches, salads, quiches
and homemade soups. Fresh
lump crab and shrimp cake,
all the freshest.
Phone: 912-233-1633

Telfair Square Café
114 Barnard St.
Savannah, GA 31401
Lunch, dinner and weekend
brunch.
Phone: 912-232-9095

Trattoria Rivazza NYCP
116 West Congress St.
Savannah, GA 31401
Great Italian cuisine
Phone: 912-234-7300

Tucson Grill
113 West Broughton
Savannah, GA 31401
Southwestern cuisine
Phone: 912-233-9669

Wet Willie's
River St.
Savannah, GA 31401
Great frozen daiquiris,
burgers, chicken, pizza and
quesadillas
Phone: 912-233-5650

SHELLMAN BLUFF

Hunter's Café & The Mud Bar
Shellman Bluff, GA
Wood grilled specials, seafood
and steaks.
Closed Monday.
Phone: 912-832-5771

Speed's Kitchen Restaurant
Eulonia, GA 31331
Fresh seafood, oyster stew.
Phone: 912-832-4763

THUNDERBOLT

Tubby's Tank House
2909 River Dr.
Thunderbolt, GA 31404
Seafood, steaks & chicken
Phone: 912-354-9040

TYBEE ISLAND

**AJ's Dockside Restaurant &
Marina**
1315 Chatham Ave.
Tybee Island, GA 31328
Fresh seafood, crab cakes and
waterfront dining
Phone: 912-786-9533

The Beachside Grill
404 Butler Ave.
Tybee Island, GA 31328
Grilled seafood, lamb and steaks
Phone: 912-786-4745

The Crab Shack
Chimney Creek
Tybee Island, GA 31328
Fresh local seafood, on the
water's edge.
Phone: 912-786-9857

The Oar House on Tybee
1311 Butler Ave.
Tybee Island, GA 31328
Seafood, steaks, lunch & dinner.
Phone: 912-786-5055

TAXIS

BRUNSWICK

Advantage Limo Service, Inc.
Phone: 912-261-9434
City Cab Service
24 Hour Service
Phone: 912-264-3760
Happy Hour Taxi
Phone: 912-267-9112
Yellow Cab Company
24 Hour Service
Phone: 912-265-0000

ST MARYS

Georgia Cab Co.
Phone: 912-673-6900

ST SIMONS

City Cab Service
24 Hour Service
Phone: 912-264-3760
St. Simons Cab Co.
24 Hour Service
Phone: 912-638-3790
St. Simons Transit, Water Taxi
Golden Isles Marina
#105, 206 Marina Dr.
St. Simons Island, GA 31522
Between St. Simons and Jekyll
   (plus custom service)
Phone: 912-638-5678
Yellow Cab Company
24 Hour Service
Phone: 912-265-0000

SAVANNAH

AAA Adam Cab, Inc
Airport Taxi
2101 Price St.
Savannah, GA
Phone: 912-927-7466

Airport Express
Phone: 912-964-0060
Dial A Cab
24 Hours
Phone: 912-239-9900
McCall's Shuttle Services
GA, FL & SC
Phone: 912-966-5364
Yellow Cab
Phone: 912-236-1133

TOURIST INFORMATION

Also see *the Annual Events on the Coast Section* in the Appendix

BRUNSWICK

EVENTS in Brunswick & The Golden Isles
Phone: 800-933-COAST (2627)
www.bgislesvisitorsb.com
Visitor's Bureau
4 Glynn Ave.
Brunswick, GA 31520
Phone: 912-265-0620
Fax: 912-265-0629
800-933-COAST (2627)
www.bgislesvisitorsb.com

DARIEN

Darien Welcome Center
McIntosh County Chamber of
   Commerce
105 Ft. George Dr.
PO Box 1497
Darien, GA 31305
Phone: 912-437-6684
Fax: 912-437-5251
chamber@darientel.net

JEKYLL ISLAND

Jekyll Island Museum and Historic District
381 Riverview Dr.
Phone: 912-635-2119
Stable Road: 912-635-2762
Stable Road: 912-635-2119

Jekyll Island Welcome Center
Jekyll Causeway
Phone: 912-635-3636

ST MARYS

EVENTS in St. Marys
Phone: 800-868-8687
   912-882-4000
www.gacoast.com/navigator/
   stmarys.html
St. Marys Tourism & Orange Hall
311 Osborne Rd.
St. Marys, GA 31558
Phone: 912-882-4000
   800-868-8687

ST SIMONS ISLAND

St. Simons Island Visitor/Tourist Info
US HWY 17:
Phone: 912-264-5337
   800-933-2627
St. Simons Visitors Center
Located in The Village
Phone: 912-638-9014

SAVANNAH

EVENTS in Savannah
Phone: 912-236-7284
Reservations in Savannah
Phone: 800-444-CHARM
   (2427)
www.savcvb.com
Email: info@savcvb.com
Savannah Area Convention & Visitors Bureau
101 East Bay St.
Savannah, GA 31401
Phone: 912-944-0456
Savannah Visitors Center
301 Martin Luther King, Jr.
   Blvd.
Savannah, GA 41401
Phone: 912-944-0455
   800-444-2427

TYBEE ISLAND

Tybee Island Chamber of Commerce/Visitors Center
East HWY 80
Tybee Island, GA 31328
Phone: 912-786-5444

TOWING SERVICES

BRUNSWICK

American Towing
102 General Robert E Lee Dr.
Brunswick, GA
Phone: 912-261-1163
VHF 16 and 12
Phone: 912-634-1777
Fax: 912-638-4503

Seatow Services Brunswick
411 Arnold Rd.
St. Simons Island, GA 31522
VHF 16 and 12
Phone: 912-634-1777
Fax: 912-638-4503

Turecamo of Savannah, Inc.
1027 Bay St.
Brunswick, GA 31520
Phone: 912-265-7519
Tug boats for ships

DARIEN

McIntosh Rod and Gun Club
Rte. 1 Box 1414
Darien, GA 31305
Located at Blue n' Hall
VHF 16
Phone: 912-437-4677

MIDWAY

Sea Tow St. Catherines
285 Timmons View Dr.
Colonel's Island, GA 31320
Operates out of Yellow Bluff
Fish Camp
VHF 16
Phone: 912-884-3435
912-258-2644
Pager: 912-235-9033

SAVANNAH

Atlantic Marine Services Inc
534 Jackson Blvd
Savannah, GA 31405
VHF 16
Phone: 912-355-7058
912-355-7050
Fax: 912-355-7058
Email: GaCoast@Juno.com
www.georgiacoast.com

SeaTow/Sea Spill
212 Falligant Ave.
Savannah, GA
24 hour service
Phone: 912-897-4304

Thunderbolt Marine
3121 River Dr.
Thunderbolt, GA 31404
Phone: 912-352-4931

Tow BOAT/US Savannah
Savannah & St. Catherines
Savannah Marine Tow, Inc.
PO Box 30244
Savannah, GA 31410
24 hour service
VHF 16
Phone: 912-898-9659
912-658-4912
800-391-4869

Turecamo of Savannah, Inc.
1027 Bay St.
Brunswick, GA 31520
Phone: 912-265-7519
Tug boats for ships

US COAST GUARD

BRUNSWICK

US Coast Guard
Brunswick Station
2 Conservation Way
Brunswick, GA 31520
Phone: 912-267-7999

CGC Smilax
Troup Creek
Brunswick, GA
Phone: 912-265-5645

ST MARYS

US Coast Guard Brunswick
Phone: 912-267-7999

SAVANNAH

US Coast Guard Search & Rescue
Emergency only, 24 hours
Phone: 912-786-5106

US Coast Guard Search & Rescue
Emergency only, 24 hours
Phone: 912-652-4648

US Coast Guard Search & Rescue
Phone: 912-786-5440

Boating Safety Hot Line
Phone: 800-368-5647

Coast Guard Station Tybee
Phone: 912-786-5440

Aids to Navigation
Phone: 912-786-5791
904-241-8401

Vessel Documentation
Phone: 800-799-8362

US POST OFFICES

BRUNSWICK

Brunswick Main Office
805 Gloucester St.
Brunswick, GA 31520
Phone: 912-280-1300

DARIEN

US Post Office
Darien, GA 31305
Phone: 912-437-4111

JEKYLL ISLAND

Jekyll Island Office
18 South Beachview Dr.
Jekyll Island, GA 31527
Phone: 912-635-2625

ST MARYS

US Post Office
St. Marys Downtown
206 Osborne St.
St. Marys, GA 31558
Phone: 912-882-2700

St. Marys Main Office
724 Charlie Smith Sr. Hwy
(Spur 40)
St. Marys, GA 31558
Phone: 912-576-5500

ST SIMONS

St. Simons Office
620 Beachview Dr.
St. Simons Island, GA 31522
Phone: 912-638-3041

Sea Island Office
Sea Island, GA 31527
Phone: 912-638-5172

SAPELO

US Post Office
Sapelo Island, GA 31327

SAVANNAH

Except for the office listed below, the post office stations in Savannah are not located near the water. Many marinas will hold and send mail, see *MARINAS*.

Wilmington Island Office
479 Johnny Mercer Blvd.
Savannah, GA 31410
Near Turners Creek

WELDING

BRUNSWICK

Bacon Welding Service
4101-1/2 Community Rd.
Brunswick, GA
Phone: 912-264-0483

Barlow Welding & Machine Shop
6019 New Jesup Hwy.
Brunswick, GA 31523
Phone: 912-265-5951

Byrd's All-Purpose Welding & Propeller
148 New Jesup Hwy.
Brunswick, GA
Phone: 912-261-2767

Carlin, C R
2309 Norwich St.
Brunswick, GA
Phone: 912-265-6461

Dominey Welding & Machine Shop
6005 Habersham St.
Brunswick, GA 31520
Phone: 912-264-2942

Glynco Machine & Tool Co. Inc.
2590 Sidney Lanier Dr.
Brunswick, GA 31525
Phone: 912-264-1988

Owens Welding & Steel Fabrication
7302 New Jesup Hwy.
Brunswick, GA
Phone: 912-265-2101

Rainey's Welding
809 Bay St.
Brunswick, GA 31520
Phone: 912-264-3675

Stokes Welding & Machine Shop
3484 S Highway 17
Brunswick, GA
Phone: 912-264-0478

DARIEN

American Welding & Fabrication
Darien, GA 31305
Phone: 912-437-5309

Jackson's Welding & Repair
Darien, GA 31305
Phone: 912-437-6579

ST MARYS

Camden Machine & Welding
87 8th St.
St. Marys, GA 31558
Phone: 912-882-2558

SAVANNAH

Advanced Portable Welding & Propeller
Savannah, GA
"I'll come to you"
Phone: 912-354-3107
Pager: 912-650-6413

Brichris Welding & Fabrication
123 Van Nuys Blvd.
Savannah, GA
Mobile service, all types of welding
Phone: 912-657-9530

DJ's Portable Welding
2525 E Gwinnett St.
Savannah, GA
Phone: 912-233-5570

P & O Machine Shop
2400 Krenson St.
Savannah, GA
On site service, all types of welding
Phone: 912-234-5394

YACHT BROKERS

BRUNSWICK

Dunbar Sales
Golden Isles Marina
St. Simons Island, GA 31522
Phone: 912-638-8573

SAVANNAH

DYB
14 New Orleans Rd.
Hilton Head Island, SC 29928
Phone: 843-785-4740

Fath Yacht Sales
618 Wilmington Island Rd.
Savannah, GA 31410
Jerry Fath
Phone: 912-897-0009
912-443-0782
912-667-5486
Fax: 912-898-0088
Email: FATHYACHTS@ aol.com
www.FATHYACHTS.COM

Palmer Johnson Yacht Sales
301 North Lathrop Ave.
Savannah, GA 31415
Phone: 912-234-6579

Sea Island Yacht Sales
109 East 66th St.
Savannah, GA
Phone: 912-356-3355

BIBLIOGRAPHY

Amos, William H. and Stephen H. Amos, *Atlantic & Gulf Coasts,* National Audubon Society Nature Guides, A Chanticleer Press Edition, Alfred A. Knoph, New York, 1985, 1998

Arnett, Jr., Dr. Ross H. and Dr. Richard I. Jacques, Jr., *Simon & Schuster's Guide to Insects,* A Fireside Book, Simon & Schuster, Inc., New York, New York, 1981

Ballentine, Todd, *Tideland Treasure,* University of South Carolina Press, 1991

Bartram, William, *Travels of William Bartram,* Edited by Mark Van Doren, Dover Publications, Inc., New York, New York, 1955

Beaton, Giff, *Birding Georgia,* Falcon Publishing, Inc., Helena, Montana, 2000

Bell, Jr., Malcolm, *Major Butler's Legacy, Five Generations of a Slaveholding Family,* The University of Georgia Press, Athens, Georgia 30602, 1987

Camden County Historical Commission, *Camden County, Georgia,* 1978

Clayton, Tonya D., Lewis A. Taylor, Jr., William J. Cleary, Paul E. Hosier, Peter H.F. Graber, William J. Neal, and Orrin H. Pilkey, Sr., *Living with the Georgia Shore,* Sponsored by the National Audubon Society, Duke Univeristy Press, Durham and London, 1992

Coleman, Kenneth, editor, *History of Georgia,* University of Georgia Press, Athens, 1977

Department of Natural Resources, Coastal Resources Division, *Angler's Guide to Georgia Saltwater Fishing Access Sites,* Brunswick, Georgia, 1996

Duncan, Marion B. and Wilbur H. Duncan, *Trees of the Southeastern United States,* The Universtiy of Georgia Press, Athens and London, 1988

Farrant, Don W., *The Lure and Lore of the Golden Isles, the Magical Heritage of Georgia's Outerbanks,* Rutledge Hill Press, Nashville, Tennesee, 1993

Fleetwood, William C. "Rusty", *Tidecraft,* WBG Maritime Press, PO Box 178, Tybee Island, Georgia, 1995

Georgia Conservancy, *A Guide to the Georgia Coast,* The Georgia Conservancy, Savannah, 1988

Gibbons, Whit and Patricia J. West, *Snakes of Georgia and South Carolina,* Savannah River Ecology Laboratory HerpOutreach Publication #1, University of Georgia, Second Printing, Aiken, SC

Hatchell, Robert, *St. Simons,* Sojourn Press, 1999, St. Simons Island, Georgia

Hudson, Charles, *The Southeastern Indians,* The University of Tennessee Press, Knoxville, 1976, reprinted 1992

Larson, Ron, *Swamp Song, A Natural History of Florida's Swamps,* University of Florida Press, Gainesville, Florida, 1995

Lenz, Richard J., *Longstreet Highroad Guide to the Georgia Coast & Okefenokee,* Longstreet Press, Inc., Marietta, Georgia 30067, 1999

Lombardo, Bruce, *Chew Toy of the Gnat Gods: Reflections on the Wildlife of the Southeast Coast,* Cherokee Publishing Company, Atlanta, Georgia, 1998

Ludlum, David M., *Early American Hurricanes 1492-1870,* American Meteorological Society, Boston, Massachusetts, 1963

McCash, June Hall, *The Jekyll Island Cottage Colony,* University of Georgia Press, 1998

McCash, June Hall and William Barton, *The Jekyll Island Club,* The Univeristy of Georgia Press, 1989

Milanich, Jerald T., and Samuel Proctor, editors, *Tacachale, Essays on the Indians of Florida and Southeastern Georgia during the Historic Period,* Larson, Jr., Lewis H., *Historic Guale Indians of the Georgia Coast and the Impact of the Spanish Mission Effort,* essay, University Press of Florida, Gainesville, 1978, reprinted 1994

Milanich, Jerald T., *The Timucua,* Blackwell Publishers, Cambridge, Massachusetts, 1996

Millus, Donald, *Fishing the Southeast Coast,* Sandlapper Publishing, Inc., Orangeburg, South Carolina, 1989

Milne, Lorus and Margery, *The Audubon Society Field Guide to North American Insects,* a Borzoi Book, Alfred A. Knopf, Inc., New York, New York, 1980

Nature Conservancy, The, *Georgia Wildlands, A Guide to Lands Protected by the Nature Conservancy of Georgia,* The Nature Conservancy of Georgia, 1996

National Oceanic and Atmospheric Administration Office of Ocean and Coastal Resource Management and the Georgia Department of Natural Resources Coastal Resources Division, *State of Georgia Coastal Management Program and Final Environmental Impact Statement,* December, 1997

Niering, William A. and Nancy C. Olmstead, *The Audubon Society Field Guide to North American Wildflowers,* Alfred A.Knoph, Inc.

Porcher, Richard D., *Wildflowers of the Carolina Lowcountry and Lower Pee Dee,* University of South Carolina Press, 1995

Reddick, Marguerite, Eloise Bailey and Virginia Proctor, editors, updated and revised by Peggy Aronson, *Camden's Challenge, A History of Camden County, Geor-*

gia, Camden County Historical Commission, 1976, revised 1994

Sehlinger, Bob and Don Otey, *Southern Georgia Canoeing,* Menasha Ridge Press, Birmingham, Alabama, 1980

Schoettle, Taylor, *A Guide to a Georgia Barrier Island,* Watermarks Publishing, St. Simons Island, Georgia, 1997

Scott, Thomas A. and Truman A. Hartshorn, *Georgia,* Microsoft Encarta 98 Encyclopedia

Stokes, Donald and Lillian, *Stokes Field Guide To Birds, Eastern Region,* Little, Brown & Company, Boston, New York, Toronto, London, 1996

Sullivan, Buddy, *Early Days on the Georgia Tidewater: The Story of McIntosh County and Sapelo,* McIntosh County Board of Commissioners, Darien, Georgia 1997

Teal, John and Mildred Teal, *Portrait of an Island,* Brown Thrasher Books, The University of Georgia Press, 1997

Tinkler, William P., *The US Army Corps of Engineers Atlantic Intracoastal Waterway Project in Georgia: A Study of Its History, Maintenance and Present Use,* Marshland Protection Section, Game & Fish Division, Georgia Department of Natural Resources, Brunswick, Georgia 31520, August, 1976

US Environmental Protection Agency and Fish and Wildlife Service, Office of Research and Development, US Department of the Interior, *Ecological Characterization of the Sea Island Coastal Region of South Carolina and Georgia, Volumes I and II,* December 1980

Vanstory, Burnette, *Georgia's Land of the Golden Isles,* The University of Georgia Press, 1970

Vocelle, James T., *History of Camden County Georgia,* Camden Printing Company, St. Marys, Georgia, 1914, reprinted 1989

Worth, John, *Georgia Before Oglethorpe, A Resource Guide to Georgia's Early Colonial Period 1521-1733,* http://members.aol.com/jeworth/gboindex.htm

INDEX

Index entries in all-capital letters designate a chart page by that name.